DEPRESSION CURED AT LAST!

Sherry A. Rogers, M.D.

1996

SK Publishing
Box 40101
Sarasota, FL 34242
1-800-846-6687

I

DEDICATION

One day I was struck by how everything is paired: two yellow butterflies danced by me, then two sanderlings played in the air nearby. Then I saw two salamanders in a mouth-to-mouth embrace on a branch of an orange tree. And by the water, two pelicans swooped and dove together, oblivious of the rest of the world, while two dolphins bobbed in the distance. Then I saw two turtles sunning themselves, and two deer grazing. The idea of pairs permeated my thoughts:

TWO BY TWO

When God commanded Noah,
He built his mighty ark.
He sweated, toiled, and built his craft
with trees and tar and bark.

Then as the Planner instructed,
animals boarded two by two.
And I thank our God, each and every day,
for pairing me with you.

As always, this book is dedicated to Luscious. Many have asked me who he is; you can get a glimpse of him on the cover of "WELLNESS AGAINST ALL ODDS".

ACKNOWLEDGMENTS

Special thanks to these kind gentlemen, each of whom supplied me with many references:

Mr. Trail Benedict, of Bio-Tech, Fayetteville Arkansas; Dr. Corey Resnick of Tyler Encapsulations, Gresham Oregon; and Dr. Martie Lee of Great Smokies Laboratories, Asheville North Carolina, and Mr. Mark Occhipint and Mr. John Casey of Nutritional Therapeutics, Smithville NY; Mr. Mark Watkins and Mr. Randy Ziegmont of American Lecithin Company, Oxford Connecticut, and Mr. Joseph Hattersley of Olympia Washington.

And thanks to my sister, Dr. Jan Hammond, Ph.D, for her constructive critique of chapter 9.

TABLE OF CONTENTS

VOLUME 1
ENVIRONMENTAL FACTORS

CHAPTER 1

CHAPTER 2

CHAPTER 3

VOLUME II
NUTRITIONAL FACTORS

VOLUME IV
TREATMENTS

TOO GOOD TO BE TRUE?

- How would you like to get **rid of depression** once and for all?

- How would you like to be **drug-free,** regardless of your diagnosis?

- How would you like to show your doctor that **depression is not a Prozac deficiency?**

- How would you like to be able to **turn on your brain's happy hormones** anytime you like?

- How would you like to get **rid of** all your other **medical problems?**

- It only sounds too good to be true if you are not well-versed in the **blueprint for 21st Century medicine.** For it **looks for causes and cures,** not drugs and surgery to merely put a Band-Aid on symptoms.

- If you would like to be healthier and happier than you have ever been before, come join the **21st Century medical evolution.**

- This is your chance to take **control.**

- This is your gift of **hope,** where there was none.

- We invite you to learn what even your **doctor does not yet know.**

- Just when you thought you were at the **end of your medical rope,** along comes the blueprint for health, happiness and perennial hope.

VOLUME I

(CHAPTERS 1-4)

ENVIRONMENTAL FACTORS

THE DEPRESSION EPIDEMIC AND IT'S HIDDEN FOOD, CHEMICAL, HEAVY METAL, AND MOLD CAUSES.

CHAPTER 1

THE UNDIAGNOSED EPIDEMIC

INTRODUCTION

There is a disease that constitutes the biggest epidemic in the history of mankind. For more than **one in two people** is or will be affected by it in their lifetimes. And if you do not have it yet, your chances of escaping are slim. The worst part is that even if you never get it, the factors that cause it also are the cause of nearly every other disease. Whether it be heart disease, arthritis or high cholesterol, chronic fatigue, fibromyalgia, lupus, interstitial cystitis, undiagnosable symptoms, allergies, chemical sensitivity, prostatitis or cancer, the causes of depression are common to all diseases.

For as you will learn, the label or name of your malady is inconsequential. The only thing that counts is what causes it. For only when you find the cause are you able to get rid of it forever, as opposed to being sentenced to a lifetime of drugs. We are going to focus, for ease of learning, on one disease, the cause of the biggest, yet unrecognized, and under-diagnosed epidemic in history, depression. And as you will learn, all that you learn about it can be applied to any of your other symptoms, for this book introduces you to the blueprint of modern **cause-oriented medicine.**

Depression is the worst illness or disease there is. Just imagine if you have a broken leg. You know the cause, and you know the amount of time during which healing should occur. There is hope. Or take as an example the most dreaded of diseases, cancer. As you will learn in here, there are many people who have totally healed their cancers after everything that medicine had to offer failed. There are those who have healed when medicine has frankly told them that there is nothing more that can be done; healed after surgery, radiation, chemotherapy, and bone marrow transplants have failed, and metastases dominated. So even the most dreaded cancer is not without hope.

So what makes depression so awful? What separates it from all other diseases which are much more physiologically painful and certainly potentially more fatal? The lack of **hope.** For without hope, these people would not have had the tools with which to venture outside of the medical model and heal the impossible. But by definition, **depression is the one disease devoid of hope,** at least in the eyes of the victim. Fortunately, nothing could be further from the truth. For depression has as many cures as it does causes. The trick lies in finding the one that relates to each individual. And that is what this landmark four volume book is all about.

The goals of this book are multiple. First is to show you that in the majority of cases, depression has identifiable and correctable hidden causes. In other words, there are environmental triggers, such as hidden food, chemical and mold sensitivities as well as vitamin, mineral, essential fatty acids and amino acid deficiencies that can cause depression. And hormone deficiencies, the leaky gut syndrome, intestinal dysbiosis, heavy metal toxicity, toxic encephalopathy or brain fog and many more causes are legion. For **no two people with depression have the exact same set of causes.**

The good news is, there are some pretty basic, inexpensive techniques to identify many of these causes and correct them once and for all. No longer does depression have to be treated as though it were a Prozac deficiency. A lifetime of

medications in fact, by not uncovering the real causes can not only **lead to an escalation of symptoms** , but to the creation of new and seemingly unrelated symptoms. And the most dreaded worsening of depression, culminates in suicide. For by not uncovering the real deficiencies that are the causes of depression, these can go on to cause other seemingly unrelated medical problems which can eventually also lead to death. The good news is that there are so many correctable causes of depression, it should no longer be shrouded in despair and hopelessness. And you can most likely learn to **heal the impossible** as many others have.

DISCLAIMER

By no means should you discontinue any medications until you have devoured this book and then discussed it with your physician. He will show you how to safely discontinue medications once you have found and corrected some of the triggers of your disease. Any medications can have serious withdrawal effects and need tender loving supervision. In fact this book is not to be a treatment for use by a depressed person. Instead it is a source of ideas for you to share with your physician so that together you two can explore the many potential causes and cures of your depression. And be ever mindful of the fact that even though you may uncover some interesting causes, it may not yet be advisable or safe to discontinue any medication until you are certain that all of the causes (the total load) have been identified.

The goal here is not only to find the causes of depression, but to get rid of it without drugs. As a side effect, it usually allows you also to get rid of all your other symptoms and brings you to a level of health that far exceeds anything you

3

have ever experienced before. For you will find, that you can make the body truly healthy as opposed to masking, or covering up symptoms with drugs. Only then can you reach a level of vitality, health, happiness and love that you never before thought was possible.

Remember, **this book is not intended as a treatment**, but as a guideline for you to work with your physician in helping you heal depression. And your physician must be the pivotal person in helping you wean yourself from medications. His knowledge, experience, and care are indispensable, and you cannot duplicate or substitute for it with any one book. Granted he may be unfamiliar with many things that are in here, but by sharing and working with him, you will most likely more than magnify your healing potential, many fold.

Note: Trademark names for medications are mentioned throughout this book. For the chemical name, description of beneficial effects and unwanted side effects, dose and manufacturer, the reader if referred to the **PDR (PHYSICIAN'S DESK REFERENCE)**. This book that describes all FDA approved prescription drugs (and there is a companion book for non-prescription drugs) is found in most physicians' offices and public libraries. Your local pharmacist can tell you whether generic equivalents exist.

AN EPIDEMIC IN DISGUISE

According to Dun & Bradstreet (IMS America division that tracks drug sales) the number of people treated with antidepressants between 1993 and 1994 increased 19%. That's 19% in one year, folks! Meanwhile the National Institutes of Mental Health disagrees and says 17.4 million or 10% of the population is treated for depression. But studies show that doctors miss diagnosing over 66% of the people who are depressed. So no matter how you cut it, even the most conservative estimate says we have an **enormous epidemic of depression** in this country (Newman J. Prozac and her sister, MIRABELLE,76-78,Aug 1995).

As an example, Prozac passed the FDA in 1988. By 1994 it was the fastest growing prescription drug. And it is the second biggest money-making drug in the U.S. with sales in the U.S. alone of over $1.2 billion. #1 is Zantac, which cuts stomach acid secretion so you become vulnerable for developing mineral deficiencies that can mimic or cause depression, not to mention causing you to succumb to a magnesium deficiency-induced heart attack. And Zoloft (a cousin to Prozac), which was passed in 1992 jumped from #21 to #10 on the drug hit parade .

Every day over 15 million people take a pill to feel better. Other studies show that more than 12 million Americans suffer from depression and that the number is rising. And remember there are other studies that show that over half (66%) of those who are depressed are not even diagnosed. So you can probably at least double that number. Depression's annual cost is estimated between $30 to $44 million dollars a year. And that ignores the drug addicts, alcoholics, learning

5

disorders, bulimia, hyperactivity, schizophrenia, manic-depression, bipolar abnormalities, anorexia, PMS, chronic fatigue, panic attacks, low achievers, undiagnosable syndromes, and scores of other diagnoses that cost much more money, yet are related to the same chemistry.

In 1988 Prozac was introduced. By 1993, sales reached $1.2 billion and they keep rising. And this ignores the other anti-depressants, doctor visits, time lost from work, etc. (Pine E, The Prozac Dilemma, WOMAN'S DAY, 74-81,3/14/95).

And what you may not know is there are scores of other labels that directly relate to the label of depression. And there is a constant search for more uses of Prozac to increase its market share even more. You will read how PMS has become a Prozac deficiency (Volume III). And over a third (36.6%) of people recovering from surgery get what is labeled as **post-operative delirium**. What this means is that after surgery, they get confused, crazy, disoriented, depressed, or a host of other cognitive dysfunctions showing that the brain is not functioning on all cylinders. And why shouldn't they since both surgery and the IVs and medications deplete nutrients that run the happy hormones.

In 26 studies, the incidence of post -surgery mental problems ranged from 0-78%. This is a huge number of people each day who suffer brain symptoms from the cumulative effect of toxic anesthesia, the flushing out of minerals with IVs, the loss of nutrients used to detoxify medications, etc. All it says is the total load of surgery, meds, anesthesia, IVs, the stress of being sick and in the hospital, the effects of the disease itself, etc. finally lowered the nutrient base to a level where the brain was temporarily out of commission. This little set-back can easily double and triple hospital stay, complications and expenses.

The unbelievable part is that current articles from major medical centers still fail to look for biochemical causes other than psychiatric (Dyer CB, Ashton CM, Teesdale TA, Postoperative delirium. ARCH INTERN MED, 155:461-465, 1995). And this complication of post-operative depression alone, not only prolongs the hospital stay and greatly increases the hospital costs, but increases the patient's vulnerability for future depression, heart attacks, and other diseases, including cancer.

And the longer he stays in the hospital, the greater his chances of going downhill faster. This includes the increased possibility of creating new symptoms, as he is attempting to survive on green jello. The costs to the American public are enormous. Clearly our **current form of medicine will bankrupt us** and simultaneously keep the chemical industry the number one money-maker as **physicians nurture a nation of drugged zombies.** The rules that govern HMOs (health maintenance organizations) are really guaranteeing disease and drug-maintenance.

You will learn of hundreds of correctable causes for depression of all types. Many of them are very inexpensive, many cost nothing. Many can be done at home. Now that you know the odds are in your favor to become happy, I hope this will give you enough hope to get rid of the cause of your depression once and for all. And you will learn that **this is a blueprint** for not only depression, but **all diseases.** It is the medicine of the future and the future is now. For to begin most treatments with drugs and surgery only, is to assure the sick get sicker, quicker, and the rich get richer. And you will lose your empowerment in every aspect of life.

This in no way has been an exhaustive book on all the causes of depression, but some of the most common and correctable. You could be depressed because of a subdural hematoma (blood clot) in the brain from a fall and bump of your head months ago. Or it could be because of the battered female syndrome. The causes are limitless, as are the treatments.

But if you use the 80-20 rule, 80% of the people will be better with 20% of the diagnostic and treatment armamentarium. And I believe after 26 years of medical practice that for the vast majority, that 20% lies within the scope of what we are presenting. Why even government studies show that the vast majority of all diseases, including cancer, have major influences from patients' diets and environments. So I'm merely trying to **take the mystery out of medicine** for you, to enable you to immensely magnify your chances of getting well, once and for all.

You need a physician who will help you find the **causes** of your depression. I suggest you do not choose one who won't read things you bring to him. And do not fall for the line that he is too busy to read. This is his business. Your health is his bread and butter. If he is too busy to grow and learn in his chosen field, you can do a lot better elsewhere.

He chose the business of keeping you alive. So he owes it to you to know as much as possible about it. It is part of the job he chose: to keep learning. It is his job to read everything you bring him that you feel relates to your health. Or he should refer you to someone who is interested enough in your health and who can help. For refusing to assess things that you bring to him that you feel are relevant to your health means, what you see is what you get. It means he is as smart as he ever will be. He is not interested. He is never going to grow any further. He is closed for learning. It means it is time for you to move on. But with HMOs, this is not often possible. This is where people power comes in.

Do not let anyone intimidate you so that it stops you from finding the causes for your depression, or any of your other symptoms. Life is passing you by, and is far too precious. For every moment of happiness that eludes you is gone forever. So let's get cracking. You have a lot of living to do. And a whole lot of happiness to experience, share and give. And never hesitate to remind those whom you have left in your wake, that **depression is not a Prozac deficiency.**

There is no question that **illness is epidemic** . People have a bag of pills, a laundry list of symptoms. And health is the topic of conversation everywhere. And now you know why. But what is even better, is that you know how to get rid of your symptoms. For we have used depression as merely a prototype or blueprint of the formula for every symptom.

At the top of the list of human maladies for the U.S., the land of plenty, is a disease that affects more than one in ten. It affects more people than all who have cumulatively died for our country in modern wars. Each year it affects more than 20 times the number of people who die of all cancers put together.

There is no question that **depression amounts to an epidemic** that is so silent that it may never be recorded in the annals of history. And you will learn why. Fortunately, you are about

to learn the answers. You do not have to be a part of this
EPIDEMIC IN DISGUISE.

THE MANY GUISES OF DEPRESSION

Depression, like many illnesses, has a whole spectrum of symptoms; no two people are exactly the same. Sure, when we think of depression we think of someone who feels hopeless and no longer cares about anything and nothing matters. Depression can accompany many diseases and actually be a side effect of diseases, such as chronic fatigue or a low thyroid as simple examples. Or it can manifest itself as a prolonged grieving period, or a psychotic state where there are extreme highs and schizophrenic-like mania interspersed with the extreme lows of depression. Or as is most commonly the case, it can just be that overwhelming feeling of being overwhelmed or trapped or feeling like a tremendous failure, or feeling unproductive or purposeless in life as though it were passing you by.

Depression can also be a life-threatening or debilitating physical illness, and a devastating cause of disability. The worst result of depression is suicide. Depression can begin gradually and sneak up on an unsuspecting victim, or occur precipitously as from loss of a job, failure in love, passing a landmark in age or the loss of someone irreplaceable. It is the nadir or depth of human despair with seemingly no end in sight. It appears to the beholder that it is incurable, without hope, and there is no way out.

Psychiatrists, in the institution of the American Psychiatric Association, have long been at work categorizing all types of mental disorders including depression and it's many phases. These are outlined in the DIAGNOSTIC AND STATISTICAL MANUAL OF MENTAL DISORDERS, REVISED (DSM-III-R, 1987). In this, they have determined that severe or major depression occurs in up to 26% of woman and 12% of men in their lifetimes. That is 1 in 4 women and 1 in 8 men. This is severe or major depression: this doesn't say anything about the moderate or more "minor" types which can be just as debilitating and for which no diagnosis is rendered, because it either goes unreported to a physician or unrecognized.

But I don't have to waste time telling you what depression is, because you obviously are all too familiar with it if you have picked up this book. What you are not familiar with are the tools you are about to learn to use. For with these tools, you have the potential to not only identify the causes and cures of your depression, but the causes and cures of every other ailment you have. Sounds preposterous? You bet! And what makes me such a hot authority? And if these techniques are so bloody great, then why haven't you and your psychiatrist heard of them before? Sounds more like some crazy scheme to merely sell another worthless "How to" book.

First of all, I am not naive enough to ever call myself an author. It is obvious I have no journalistic training. But as you will learn, the techniques in here apply to every illness. And the amount of money that could ever accrue from a book such as this (or any book for that matter) could never repay me for the hours that it took away from my life, and more importantly the hours it took me away from Luscious. And I am not even a psychiatrist, but a medical doctor whose specialty is environmental and nutritional medicine.

So why do it? Because I feel I must give back. I feel so lucky to have been rescued from the depths of despair by the techniques in this book that I must share them with the people that I know are out there suffering just as I was. I remember at several points my husband would ask, "Bunny, what is it that you want to do? What would make you happy? We can do anything your heart desires....anything that would make you happy. Do you want to move, travel? Do you want to practice, cut down, or quit?" And all I could do in response to a totally loving proposition from my Prince Charming was cry. For I had no idea that there was anything that could ever make my happy again. And that is when you know it is **biochemical**. That is when the warning bells should go off and announce, there is a diagnosable and treatable cause for this abnormal state of the brain.

As a physician, I read and studied everything I could get my hands on, tried every drug, enrolled in all sorts of psychiatric courses for physicians and lay alike, all to no avail. The ironic thing was that I had a very happy life. As the oldest of 8 children, from a poor family, I had, through scholarships and constant hard work, been not only the first person in my family to ever go to college, but to medical school as well. I put myself through and in addition, I was a female in the 1960's! I had (and still do 26 years later) the most perfect husband in the world, wonderful friends, a successful practice, and all the things that should have made me happy.

But the longer I was unsuccessful at curing my depression, the more other seemingly unrelated ailments I developed. It was like belonging to the disease-of-the-month club. Because I did not understand the true pathology of disease and depression (and it is still not taught to this day in medical schools), I did not know that if at first you fail to find the cause of a symptom and fail to fix what is broken, that you will inevitably go on to develop multiple other symptoms as the system continues to deteriorate.

No, I am surely not any smarter than other doctors. And I was never at the head of my medical school class. In fact, due to my brain fog from undiagnosed chemical sensitivity, it is amazing that I even finished. But I did have one major thing going for me that enabled me to get to the cause of depression for myself and thousands of others. I was so bloody sick, I had no choice. I was so colossally stuck that I had to find a way out. And I was fortunate enough to be given the resources to study night and day after office hours, travel around the world learning, and work at the problem until the answers appeared. And as readers of our other books know, my most precious gift has been the constant loving support and guidance from Luscious.

Years later when we had identified the causes, I asked my husband (God's greatest gift to me on earth), "Luscious, what did you think all those years when I was so crazy and so depressed? How did you ever have the love and strength to stand by me?"

"First of all, I knew there must be a cause. Like the nursery rhyme, when you were good, you were very, very good. But when you were bad, you were horrid. There had to be an explanation for such wide swings within the same person." And the many causes are what we are about to share with you. For not only did they solve my depression and all other symptoms, but that of thousands of my patients. My quarter of a century medical practice has enabled me to fine-tune many of these techniques. Luscious says we physicians call it the "practice of medicine", because we never quite get it right. He is correct, as usual. But that is also the fun of medicine; the fact that there is an endless discovery of ways in which to help people attain wellness.

So although with depression you may have lost all hope, you haven't lost your marbles. And although you may have lost all hope, you haven't lost your logic, and your innate instinctive intelligence. The logic that tells you that **depression is not a Prozac** or other medication **deficiency.** The logic that tells you that all problems have a cause and a solution. The turning point is when we reach that point of having sufficient data to figure them out. This book is designed to give you that data. In fact, **these techniques are not limited to depression.** They have been successful in a variety of brain diseases, including manic depression, obsessive compulsive disorders, schizophrenia, anxiety, panic attacks, depersonalization, phobias, addictions, eating disorders such as anorexia and bulimia, hyperactivity, attention deficit disorder, learning disabilities, dyslexia, autism, seizures, early Alzheimer's disease, Parkinson's, Tourette's syndrome, tics, multiple sclerosis, memory loss, mood swings, PMS, chronic fatigue and many other brain and non-brain diseases.

In truth, **no disease is completely appropriately treated until these techniques have been applied** to it. It doesn't matter if you have arthritis or cancer, occluded arteries or simple high blood pressure and cholesterol. As you will see, there is a **biochemical and environmental trigger or cause for most all** problems of mal-health. Once you learn the formulas of how to identify the causes, many of which are inexpensive and can be done at home, you are on your way to real health. For real health is not reliant upon drugs and surgery. It is the ability to awaken symptom-free, vivacious, enthusiastic, and happy.

THE CURRENT DIAGNOSIS OF DEPRESSION

When you look at the scientific literature, it is pretty scary what is happening in the world of depression. First of all, family physicians, who are the gate keepers of medicine, now actually **miss over 2 out of 3 patients who are depressed.** In one study, family physicians detected only 40 out of 143 confirmed as suffering from a depressive disorder (Anonymous, Family doc's show depression prowess, SCIENCE NEWS, 147:148, March 11, 1995).

In another paper issued by the **U.S. Public Health Service,** they stated that **family docs miss over 50% of people who have major depression.** And this doesn't say a thing about the depressions of lesser severity, which do not even get counted, diagnosed, treated, or recognized, or that do not even go to a doctor. Other researchers suggest that 66% of generally depressed patients are missed or are not diagnosed as depressed by their doctors. But if the depression is severe, then only 25% are missed.

In many articles, the signs of depression are spelled out for physicians. They can include sadness, discouragement, hopelessness, feeling of being blue or low or being down in the dumps, lack of enthusiasm, or loss of interest in person or things or activities that had been important or pleasurable.

Depression rarely exists alone. When depressed patients are finally diagnosed, these patients often have lack of energy or fatigue as a major part of their depression, in addition to **anxiety** or phobias or **fears.** Common features accompanying depression in addition to fatigue or loss of energy include disturbance in sleep and eating. And depression is commonly accompanied by other body complaints, feelings of guilt and worthlessness, agitation, irritability, memory defects, inability to concentrate, difficulty in thinking and making decisions, or thoughts of death and suicide (Massarelli JJ, Recognizing and treating depression in the elderly, INTERNAL MEDICINE WORLD REPORT, 10:3;10, February 1-14th 1995).

This author goes on to explain that unexplained symptomatic complaints, as well as disturbed sleep patterns, weight loss and alcohol abuse may be **clues to the diagnosis** of depression. In other words, if we can't figure out what is wrong with you when you complain of stomach, chest, nerve, arm, and etc. problems, then we should consider depression as a diagnosis then also. As with other authors, he then jumps into psychotherapy and drug treatment, with no thought for finding the correctable causes.

In terms of the cause, when it is looked for, the authors mainly concern themselves with only medication side effects, drug abuse, or simple medical causes like hypothyroidism (Kathol RG, Diagnosis and management of depression by primary care physicians: New guidelines, INTERNAL MEDICINE WORLD REPORT, 9:7;33 April 1-14th 1994). Then again, the author jumps right into drugs as the main treatment.

Another specialist states that part of the problem is that many primary care physicians hold the belief that depression is a non-specific syndrome. In other words, it is a **diagnosis of exclusion.** This is a major problem that it is considered a diagnosis of exclusion. This means that once a physician is stuck and doesn't know what else to do for the patient, he often slaps the label of depression on him (Coulehan JL, Managing depression in primary care, INTERNAL

MEDICINE WORLD REPORT, p 34-49 December 1994). Again however, once it is diagnosed, a few rudimentary medical conditions are ruled out (diabetes, liver disorders, anemia, etc.) and then drugs are used for the main therapy. In essence, **depression seems to be a drug deficiency.** For it is treated as though it were a deficiency of anti-depressant drugs.

You can plow through medical journal articles, scientific papers and psychiatric text books and no where will you find the differential diagnoses included in this book. No where do they look for the total package of hormonal and nutritional deficiencies, environmental triggers and the total body burden of stressors. But once you find these, as you will learn, you will have the power to heal your own depression without drugs. And should it ever attempt to rear its ugly head again, you are prepared to zap it at the onset, never letting it get a foot-hold or out of control again. The AMERICAN PSYCHIATRIC ASSOCIATION DIAGNOSTIC AND STATISTICAL MANUAL OF MENTAL DISORDERS lists the **criteria for their diagnosis** of depression. It includes a depressed mood or loss of interest and at least 4 other symptoms (from the group that follows) for over 2 weeks: changes in appetite and weight, disturbed sleep, agitation or its reverse, lethargy, retarded motor activity, fatigue and loss of energy, feelings of worthlessness or excessive guilt, suicidal thinking or attempts, and difficulty concentrating.

As you will see, these symptoms occur more frequently as persons age. So sometimes they are erroneously attributed to nothing more than aging. And they are indistinguishable from the brain fog or toxic encephalopathy of 21st century chemical sensitivity. The result is that many chemically reactive individuals are erroneously diagnosed as being merely depressed.

CAUTION: SUICIDAL THOUGHTS

Let's stop right here on the suicide idea, though. If you feel suicidal, or have thoughts of suicide or have made plans, please remember the old adage that it is always darkest before the dawn. For just when things seem to be at their worst, when it couldn't get any worse, that's when some of the nicest turnarounds, the most amazing miracles, the pleasantest surprises, and more have happened. You certainly would not want to miss the happy ending to this story, would you?

If you entertain any suicidal thoughts, please confide them in your friends, relatives and doctors. Enlist their help to watch over you as you heal. Many towns have a suicide hot line you can call, or support groups. You can always dial 911 and get an ambulance to take you to a hospital where you can be observed and protected against yourself for as long as you need. Or go to your doctor or an emergency room for your depression. Whatever you do, don't be dumb and miss out on some wonderful surprises.

Fortunately, most of the people who are depressed are not suicidal, but have such a wide variance in symptoms, that definitions are almost useless. That is why I have given you many different groups' definitions. But suffice-to-say, if you do not feel perky and bouncy and do not have a zest for life, you could be depressed. And if you rationalize your lack of energy and enthusiasm by blaming it on some other medical condition that you have, read on, for it is all related. And don't use the old cop-outs that you just need more sleep, have too much stress, or any other excuse. If you don't feel great, then let's find out why and rectify it. For as Granny told us, and as you will see, a stitch in time saves nine. In other words, fix it now or pay a far greater price later.

DEPRESSION IS NOT A PROZAC DEFICIENCY

As you see from this quick survey on how depression is diagnosed, it is often missed. And when it is diagnosed, it can merely be a substitute diagnosis to compensate for not knowing what else to give as a diagnosis. The underlying causes that are outlined in this book are not considered. Instead, people are automatically plopped on a drug.

We are going to talk about Prozac, not because I have any malice toward the drug itself, or its manufacturers, but because it is the one most in the limelight and has even been toted as a miracle drug for depression. It is the number one, most commonly prescribed drug. So it will only serve as a prototype for other drugs used in psychiatry for the treatment of depression. For once you can understand a great deal about one drug, then you will have a pretty good idea about many of the aspects of other drugs, even if they have different mechanisms of action and different side effects.

Sales figures for August, September and October of 1990 showed that over 400,000 new prescriptions for Prozac were being written in the United States. This means that nearly half a million new people were on this anti-depressant drug alone in only 3 months' time, a quarter of one year. This does not count all the people that were already on it, the 66% who were not diagnosed, nor all those on other anti-depressant drugs. Depression it appears is epidemic. Yet in spite of so many anti-depressants to choose from, with vast advertising and PR work, Prozac has managed to become a common name for the man in the street who equates it with the treatment of depression.

So what is so wrong about helping someone who feels depressed by giving him a drug like this? Actually, many people are very content taking their Prozac. It has helped them continue on with their lives. But three major problems occur from taking a drug like Prozac to "fix the mind".

SIDE EFFECTS

First of all, there are many side effects, which we will go into, which include worsening depression and suicide. **Second** of all, it covers up the symptoms, so the real cause is not looked for. The real causes often can progress, as you will see, and lead to many other illnesses, including sudden cardiac death. And third, when a person is a Prozac zombie, or zonked out on a drug, he does not have all of his normal responses. You have seen people on Prozac; it's like talking to the wall. They just don't have the spontaneity, vivaciousness and emotion that a normal person has. Their responses are blunted, and when this happens, the person's psycho-spiritual responses are blunted as well. This is a dangerous thing to be out of touch with your own emotions and spirituality.

Antidepressant drugs have many nasty side effects. First of all, most all of the psychiatric drugs can cause depression themselves, to the point that people are suicidal. They can also cause a condition called **tardive dyskinesia** with uncontrollable jerky tics and spasms of the voluntary muscles.

21

It can also cause a **tardive dementia**, where the person appears senile.

These side effects often come about because the work of metabolizing an anti-depressant uses up nutrients (like vitamins and minerals). Then when you finally reach a specific low and deplete certain nutrients, you start having side effects from that nutrient deficiency. And because you need that nutrient to properly metabolize or detoxify the drug, the unmetabolized by-product of the drug can also go on to cause nasty side effects. It turns out that in the clinical trials of testing Prozac, that there were 27 deaths, but this did not hold the FDA back from approving the drug in what was one of the fastest drug approvals ever noted.

With the freedom of information act, consumer groups have collated the evidence. That there have been over 1,885 suicide attempts and 1,734 deaths from Prozac as of September 1993. There have also been over 28,000 reports of adverse reactions. In spite of this, Prozac remains in the armamentarium of physicians and it remains under the protective wing of the FDA.

There are well documented studies of how members of the FDA's advisory committee received large research donations from the very company that makes the drug (Whittle TG, Wieland R, The story behind Prozac, the killer drug, how the FDA approved, whitewashed and continues to protect the most deadly prescription drug in history, in FREEDOM, Nov/Dec 1993). The issue regarding the FDA hiring consultants was even addressed in THE WALL STREET JOURNAL (Gutfeld R, FDA is urged to take steps to ensure objectivity of advisors, THE WALL STREET JOURNAL, Wednesday December 9, 1992).

But my goal is not to pick on the FDA or dwell on the politics of medicine, but to show you hopefully how to get free of depression and free of drugs. So let's move on to the other side effects of antidepressant drugs. As with any drug, there is a long list of effects, but as you have seen, worsening depression, suicide and death are certainly the ultimate.

One side effect is a condition called the **serotonin syndrome,** which is caused by an adverse reaction to this entire class of psychiatric drugs. The symptoms are that the patient feels drunk or dizzy. He has spasms or jerkiness of the muscles involuntarily. He feels restless and sweaty. His blood pressure and heart rate can change dramatically. He can have uncontrollable facial and eye movements, his temperature can change dramatically, he can have cardiac arrhythmia, shivering, sweating, he can become manic and crazy, teeth chattering and a multitude of other symptoms, as well as insomnia, headaches, body pain, flushing and even convulsions (Sternbach H, The serotonin syndrome, AMERICAN JOURNAL OF PSYCHIATRY 148:6, 705-713, June 1991).

Even though the syndrome has been well defined, as is true to the nature of medicine and psychiatry, the cause is not looked for nor understood. People have died from the serotonin syndrome. But if you take them off the drug early enough, most people will recover with seemingly no after effects. But current psychiatric guidelines fail to suggest looking for environmental causes. Furthermore, they fail to see that it is a wonderful opportunity to fix the depression and perhaps even simultaneously find the cause of all other symptoms. For when you get adverse symptoms from a drug, like the serotonin syndrome, it means that the drug has finally used up specific nutrients crucial in the body for its metabolism. And once they are depleted, the drug is metabolized in a different fashion and therefore produces different effects. We will discuss more of this in the nutrition section (Kline SS, Mauro LS, Scala-Barnett DM, Zick D, Serotonin syndrome versus neuroleptic malignant syndrome as a cause of death. CLIN PHARM 8:510-514, 1989).

You will notice a great deal of the symptoms of the serotonin syndrome resembled **drug addicts** and patients in **withdrawal**. Likewise, there is an antidepressant **withdrawal syndrome** with hot flashes, flushing, agitation, nausea, muscle tremors and sweating (Breggin PR, TOXIC PSYCHIATRY St. Martins Press, NY 1994 P163). In this reference you can read all about the various side effects of Prozac and how the scientifically controlled testing lasted a mere 6 weeks, it says. But in defense of the company, their reports that they send to physicians claim much longer trials.

The scary thing is that you can be prescribed drugs related to Prozac and not even be aware of it. For example, the new diet pill Redux (released 1996) is a distant cousin of the Prozac molecule. The purpose of this work is not to go into the political battles of medicine, but to be more practical and positive and show you how to heal your depression. However, you should be aware that an off-shoot of these politics is that there are many children now for whom Prozac and related drugs are being prescribed. When you look at all of the data on Prozac and children's deaths, one cannot help but become concerned. Prozac is being pushed now for **obsessive compulsive disorder** of children as well as depression and attention deficit disorder. But as you will learn, to sentence a child to a drug like Prozac without first exploring the techniques in this book is criminal.

To begin with, 83 children between the ages of 4 and 18 have attempted suicide while on Prozac. In an advertisement in a medical magazine, the manufacturer, Eli Lilly and Co. states that "more than 32,000 patients have participated in the clinical trials and more than 3,000 scientific articles have addressed its safety and usefulness". However, it would be quite unusual to generate 3,000 articles on a drug tested on only 32,000 patients. And I have been unable to get a list of these 3000 articles from the company.

Still, having only been in clinical trial for 6 weeks is a bit scary, and only being tested on 32,000 patients is a bit scary. For when scientists tested 85,000 people with 100 I.U. of vitamin E, for which there has never been a side effect, much less a death, the conclusion of the study was that it could not be recommended. The reason given was it had not been studied enough. Mind you, this is in spite of the fact that there were NO adverse effects from vitamin E. And in spite of the fact that in this study of 85,000 people, this tiny dose of vitamin E cut the cardiovascular disease rate in half. This is no small matter since cardiovascular disease is the number one cause of death and illness in the U.S. (Stampfer, NEW ENGLAND JOURNAL OF MEDICINE, 1993).

So even though the paltry, harmless, 100 units of vitamin E cut the cardiovascular risk of 85,000 people in half, and even though cardiovascular problems are the number one cause of death and illness and a major cause of economic loss in the United States, and even though there have never been any reported side effects from 100 I.U. of vitamin E, that simple treatment could not be recommended. But Prozac, which was tested on less than half of those people and has already accumulated over 28,000 adverse reactions and over 1,700 deaths, is still heartily endorsed by the FDA. And bear in

25

mind, vitamin E has been known about for decades and has infinitely more than 3,000 scientific articles written about it. Whereas, Prozac was passed in 6 weeks.

Likewise, non-steroidal anti-inflammatory drugs like Aleve, Advil, and ibuprofen are allowed over the counter without a prescription, even though there are on record numerous cases of fatal gastrointestinal hemorrhage. And even worse, the very diseases that they are designed to help, arthritis and auto-immune pain disorders, are actually caused by the drugs themselves, as you will read in the gut section. Plus these non-steroidal anti-inflammatory drugs that require no prescription can go on to cause fatal liver disease and multiple other diseases as you will learn.

And another travesty in medicine has occurred which potentiates disease; Tagamet (cimetidine) and Pepcid are over-the-counter (WALL STREET JOURNAL May 22, 1995). This means that the layman can turn off the acid secretion in his stomach, without nary a care as to why it is happening. It could be a stomach cancer or Candida infection from too many antibiotics. The bottom line is that as with all drugs, **the sick will get sicker quicker.** For if you turn off this acid, you compromise the ability of the stomach to absorb the precious minerals that we need daily for health. The same minerals that have been artfully stripped from our foods over the last few generations, whose depletion can be the very cause of depression. Furthermore, non-prescription drugs like Tagamet have another serious consequence: they are immunosuppressive. More on this later.

Something is amiss in our system. It appears that only those medications that are guaranteed to have a profound impact on keeping medicine in business are allowed over the counter. But efforts are underway to remove products that promote health and can reverse disease, namely the vitamins and minerals. Certainly there is much about the politics of medicine that should concern you, for it has a profound impact on your ability to get the treatments you need.

PROGRESS MEANS A CHEMICAL LOBOTOMY

You might naively think as I did that the government would protect us from any damaging treatments. But did you know that therapies are still done (and paid for by insurance companies) that cause permanent destruction of the brain? Remember Jack Nicholson's unforgettable performance in Ken Kelsey's classic, ONE FLEW OVER THE CUCKOO'S NEST? The story chronicled psychiatry as I recall it in the 60's in medical school. We saw the horrors of electrocortical therapy (ECT) which amounts to no more than electrocuting the brain in attempts to stop the depression. In other words, when you can't find what's wrong with it and fix it (or don't look for what's wrong), cut it out or burn it out. And in the past before ECT, they indeed did lobotomies, where a part of the brain was removed.

The scary part is that ECT has only been shown to be of **benefit for a maximum of 4 weeks after** the procedure has been done. Then the depression resurfaces. So you have in essence permanently destroyed part of the brain for a mere 4 weeks of improvement. And in some studies the effect was no better than the sham or pretend ECT. But with strong lobbying, the American Psychiatric Association convinced the FDA to continue to condone it. And so it is still done and paid for by insurances. In fact, what type of insurance a person has influences what type of treatment is offered to him. For example, if ECT is covered but an alternative is not, then ECT is done. The problem is that ECT causes shrinkage and permanent loss of brain, and many more problems. And it does not cure depression.

Yet in spite of this I found a 1994 medical textbook, STEIN'S INTERNAL MEDICINE, in agreement with the barbaric technique of cooking part of the brain. In the section on neurological disorders it actually says, "Approximately 60% of patients with delusional depression do not improve with antidepressant drugs alone, then either antidepressant-neuroleptic combinations or **ECT are required** to attain remission". Folks, you read it correctly, ECT is "required" in this day. This is scary.

In the current era of drugs, what we are actually doing is a sort of **chemical lobotomy** so you might feel safer. But I wouldn't. Many of the currently popular drugs have side effects of suicide, withdrawal, addiction. They can cause depression themselves, panic disorder, and memory and brain function loss. But you would be better off reading all the details and seeing the voluminous references in Peter Breggin, M.D.'s excellent TOXIC PSYCHIATRY, St. Martin's Press, NY, 1991.

It is scary to me, for example, when I look in the leading pharmacology text to learn about the "Drugs that induce affective disorders" (depression and other mental changes). They say that even though **depression is frequently caused by drugs,** even **drugs used to treat depression,** that it is probably important to use them. They rationalize that when patients get worse on an anti-depressant, the patients are probably merely going through an "unmasking process or part of the natural resolution of the psychosis" (THE

PHARMACOLOGICAL BASIS OF THERAPEUTICS, LS Goodman and A Gilman, ed.s, p 196, Macmillan Publ., NY, 1970). Medicine is a master at masking anything!

The data concerning the current popular tranquilizers like Xanax, Valium, Librium, Tranxene, Centax, Klonepin, Serax, Ativan, Restoril, Halcion, and others is not that encouraging either, with side effects like abuse and addiction, potential memory destruction and more. Taking these drugs amounts to merely a chemical lobotomy of a milder form. So let's move on and find the causes for depression so we no longer have to pretend it's a Prozac deficiency.

RESOURCES:

Eastgate J, CHILD ABUSE FROM PROZAC. AN INTERIM REPORT Citizens Commission On Human Rights, Los Angeles, CA 1994.

Death and near death attributed to Prozac, Citizens Commission On Human Rights, ibid.

Breggin PR, TOXIC PSYCHIATRY, St. Martins Press, NY 1994.

Whittle TJ, Wiland Richard, The story behind Prozac the killer drug, FREEDOM MAGAZINE, 6331 Hollywood Blvd., Suite 1200 Los Angeles, CA 90028.

Ravindran AV, et al, Primary early onset dysthymia biochemical correlates of the therapeutic response to fluoxetine, J AFFECT DISORD, 31:119-123, 1994

MISLEADING MEDICAL ADVERTISEMENTS

As the publications demonstrated, most physicians have a vague concept of what depression is and once they make their decision that the patient is depressed, drugs are prescribed. The drugs they choose are often the ones that are most heavily advertised. In fact, public health officials are concerned about the misleading advertisements that abound in medical journals.

In an evaluation of 109 pharmaceutical advertisements appearing in 10 leading medical journals, the reviewers disagreed with the advertisers claims in 30% of the ads. The reviewers disagreed that the drug that was being promoted was the drug of choice for the condition. They felt that 40% of the ads were not balanced with efficacy versus side effects and contraindications. They also disagreed with the advertisements' drug claims in 32% of them and found 32% of the headlines to be misleading regarding the effectiveness of the medications. In 44% of the cases, the reviewers felt that the advertisements would lead to improper prescribing if physicians had no other information (which usually they do not). In 28% of the cases, the reviewers would not have recommended publication of the advertisements and would have required major revisions in 34%. This is serious, since it is a main source of education for physicians regarding prescription drugs.

RESOURCES:

Wilkes MS, et al, Pharmaceutical advertisements in leading medical journals: Experts' assessments, ANNALS OF INTERNAL MEDICINE, June 1, 1992;116 (11): 912-919.

Kessler DA, Addressing the problem of misleading advertising, ANNALS OF INTERNAL MEDICINE, Ibid 950-951.

ECONOMIC IMPACT

Let's look at what effect depression has on not the individual, but on society. It has been determined that the **length of disability is greater for depression** than for other medical problems. And the relapse rate is greater for depressive illnesses than for other medical problems. In other words, it recurs frequently. Lastly, depressive disorders have been found to have the **largest medical plan costs of all behavioral diagnoses** (Conti DJ, Burton WN, The economic impact of depression in a work place, J OCCUP ENVIR MED, 16:9,983-988 September 1994).

And this article goes on to explain that **the prevalence of depression in a life time is 17%.** In other words, about 1 in 6 people will be expected to suffer from this (but as you learned, that only counts the ones lucky enough to be diagnosed). The economic burden of depressive disorders in the American work place cost **43 billion dollars in 1990** with absenteeism alone contributing 12 billion dollars. Other factors in the total cost include losses arising from lowered productivity, safety risks, accidents, suicide and the cost of inadequate and inappropriate treatment for depression. This article went on further to show that for **short term disabilities** in 1989-1992, the **number one illness was depressive disorders.** This was followed by low back pain and then heart disease.

Furthermore, of the **mental health diagnoses, depression occupies 51% of that pie.** It has been further shown that, for example, the 1993 dollars of treatment of one depressed patient by a primary care physician was estimated to be $1,060, compared with $3,760 if treatment was done by a psychiatrist (Anonymous, Current trends in depression care questioned, INTERNAL MEDICINE WORLD REPORT 10:2, 1 and 33, January 15-31, 1995). So you have seen that taking Prozac, or any other mind altering drug is fraught with potential side effects. Not the least of which is death. A further problem is that by masking a symptom with drugs, you have lost a golden opportunity to find the cause and fix it before it goes on to cause other illnesses and other problems, as will be shown in the total load chapter. And not only is there suffering and loss of income for the victim of depression, but society pays a large price for this disease, also.

DEPRESSION IS A BRAIN DISEASE AND/OR BRAIN ALLERGY

You have heard of heart disease, you have heard of kidney disease, you have heard of liver disease. But when it comes to depression, you don't hear about brain disease. Instead, we hear about drugs and psychotherapy. But depression is a medical disease that has correctable causes.

Diabetes is a metabolic problem and the causes are many. Milk allergy has been known to be one of the incitants of juvenile diabetics. Like many diseases, diabetes is a combination of diet, environment and genetics. For example, airborne pesticides can damage the pancreas. As well, the pancreas can become an allergic target organ as you will see. When it is ailing what do you get, but pancreatic disease and its many symptoms, which can include diabetes, poor pancreatic digestion and much more. Many diabetics by changing their diets, by reducing their chemical exposures, and by correcting nutrient and hormonal deficiencies, require less insulin and improve their diabetes. Or like a runny nose from milk allergy, the pancreas can over secrete if it is the allergic target organ. And when it does you may have **hypoglycemia** with depression, headache, and violent mood swings.

The brain is infinitely more complex than the pancreas. And in fact the function of the pancreas can affect the brain and vice versa. Brain disease includes anything that is wrong with the brain. Certainly depression is a major brain malady. The brain can become the allergic target organ just as easily as the nose can for spring pollens and molds. The brain can be a target organ for a hidden food allergy just as easily as the skin can be to a strawberry. And the brain can be an allergic target organ to a chemical exposure just as easily as the lung can.

When the brain has symptoms it cannot wheeze and cough, it cannot break out in hives. But it can present a depressive mood. Other symptoms including seizures, migraines, rage, schizophrenia, autism, obsessive compulsion, panic attacks, flying off the handle for no reason, learning disorder, attention deficit disorders, and violent mood swings are just some of the many different types of symptoms that the brain is capable of.

In spite of this, a peek at a current catalogue of multiple psychiatric text books (American Psychiatric Press, 1400 K Street, NW, Washington DC, 20005) reveals that none of them deals with looking for environmental and nutritional triggers to disease. They are all concerned with drugging the patient and psychotherapy, as though nothing else could effect the mind.

Yet to take it one step further, due to may reasons you will read about, the average person has one or more nutrient deficiencies these days. And the brain is not an isolated entity. If we are low or deficient in nutrients, these deficiencies have dramatic effects on our moods and how we think. For these are the very things that run the chemistry of the brain.

As you will see, **what I am about to teach you, applies to actually every symptom,** because we are now entering the era **of environmental and molecular medicine,** where we can find the causes for symptoms rather than merely drugging them. And the cost effectiveness and the clinical effectiveness of this form of medicine, has benefits that reach far beyond the patient. For they benefit not only the patient, but society and the economy, as well. And one last comment on the effect on society is that a certain percent of people with brain disease account for the horrors that periodically show up in the news. The people who go berserk and blow away a dozen innocent citizens in a moment or blow up buildings are the ones I refer to. We cannot solve those atrocities with antidepressant drugs. But we could, as you will see, make a significant positive change by incorporating in our daily lives and in the practice of medicine, some of the techniques that are in here.

REFERENCES:

Faivelson S, Worldwide depression on the rise, MEDICAL TRIBUNE, 14, Jan. 7, 1994

Anda R, et al, Depressed affect, hopelessness, and the risk of ischemic heart disease in a cohort of U.S. adults, EPIDEMIOLOGY,4L4;285-294, July 1993

Family Practice Recertification, Do emotions affect memory function in elderly person?, May 1993;150(5):44 J PSYCHIATRY, 150:3;1993

Newell GR, Stress and cancer: The interactions of mind and body, PRIMARY CARE IN CANCER, 29-30, 1991

DEPRESSION AND FATIGUE ARE LINKED

Depression is so tightly linked with fatigue, that in some cases they are indistinguishable. One is hard-pressed to figure out where one ends and the other begins. Also fatigue is one of the major criteria for making the diagnosis of depression. You can have depression without fatigue, but it is unlikely. Here are the government's **diagnostic criteria for diagnosing depression**. You must have 5 at the same time:

(1) depressed mood at least most of the day, daily for a minimum of 2 weeks. Children and adolescents can be irritable instead (I'm incensed at this and you will be too, once you finish the book. It shows blatant lack of knowledge of brain chemistry and biochemical individuality).

(2) markedly diminished interest or pleasure in almost all activities, most of the day, nearly every day

(3) weight change

(4) sleep pattern change (too little or too much)

(5) physical agitation or retardation

(6) fatigue

(7) feelings of worthlessness, guilt

(8) impaired concentration, indecisiveness

(9) recurrent thoughts of death or suicide

(From the U.S. Public Health Service, Wash., DC, Depression in adults, AMER FAM PHYS 51:7, 1701-1705, May 15, 1995.) The article goes on to say over half or **50% of people with major depression** (which excludes over half the depressed people who are depressed but do not meet the criteria) **are missed (not diagnosed) by their family doctors.** Furthermore, major depression accounts for up to 8% of patients seen by family doctors, and includes over 6 million people and costs $16 billion dollars a year.

And if medicine's track record for missing making the diagnosis of depression on over 50% of the people who are depressed were not bad enough, it turns out that older patients with significant depression often conceal or minimize their depression. The bottom line is that there is a lot of depression out there, that is being ignored. And people are needlessly suffering.

REFERENCES:

Anonymous, Geriatric patients found to under report symptoms of depression, INTER MED WORLD REP, 10:14, 33, Aug 1995 (reporting on Lyness, et al, J AMER GERIAT SOC, 43:216-211, 1995)

Hickie I, et al, Chronic fatigue syndrome and depression, LANCET, 337:922-923, Apr 13, 1991

Lane TJ, et al, Depression and somatization in the chronic fatigue syndrome, AMER J MED, 91:335-344, Oct 1991

Kendell RE, Chronic fatigue, viruses, and depression, LANCET, 337:160-162,Jan 19,1991

Landy AL, et al, Chronic fatigue syndrome: clinical condition associated with immune activation, LANCET 338L 8769,707-712, Sep 21, 1991

OVER-EATING: A FORM OF DEPRESSION

Because mental illness usually does not have positive x-ray findings and conventional blood tests to confirm and quantitate the suffering, it is difficult to define and quantitate it. Furthermore, it is difficult to accumulate enough people to constitute a study because medicine rigorously (and unrealistically) requires that all participants have very similar symptoms. What I'm getting at is that depression is merely a very common form of brain abnormality. It is like the common cold is to the body. And no two people are exactly the same.

But regardless of what symptoms you have, from hyperactivity, autism, seizures, insomnia or mood swings, to manic depression, LD, schizophrenia, chronic fatigue, panic disorder, obsessive compulsions, alcoholism or over-eating, **it matters not what your label is.** As you will see, there is a cause for everything. But because the chemistry of the brain is fairly similar, there are abnormalities common to many disorders that have completely opposite symptoms. This merely further supports the fact that even though we all have similar chemistry, when that chemistry goes awry, we need not all have the same symptoms or response or reaction. Appreciation of this explains why we should not rely on one's response to a particular class of drugs as part of the criteria for diagnosis. But unfortunately, this happens in medicine.

An example is that the basis for action of Prozac and other similar anti-depressants is to **decrease the degradation of serotonin** (one of the brain's happy hormones) so there is more in the brain to improve mood. But you do not need to manifest your abnormal serotonin metabolism by depression. It can be with over-eating. For research shows that this also is a condition of abnormal serotonin metabolism. And when you get to the sections on minerals and hormones, you will see that cravings (and abnormal serotonin metabolism) are there for a reason. They are a signal that something is wrong and we had better find the cause and get rid of the symptom once and for all. So the last thing we should do is ignore an opportunity to find the cause and mask the symptom with a drug for the rest of our lives. For a drug, in the work of detoxification of it, uses up even more vitamins and minerals. This can lead to further depression and a dozen other symptoms as well, some of which are lethal.

REFERENCES:

Jimerson DC, Lesem MD, Hegg AP, Brewerton TD, Serotonin in human eating disorders, ANN NY ACAD SCI, 600:532-544, 1990

Blundell JE, Serotonin and appetite, NEURO-PHARMACOLOGY, 23:1537-1551, 1984

Weltzin TE, Fernstrom M, Kaye WH, Serotonin and Bulimia Nervosa, NUTR REV, 52:12,399-405, 1994

LABELITIS, THE MOST LETHAL DISEASE

A major problem in medicine is that once you have a diagnosis like depression or fatigue, then everything else you have takes a **back seat**. In other words, once you have one of these labels, every other complaint is blamed on them and nothing else is taken seriously. The other complaints are often chalked up to **hypochondriasis**. Look at some of the titles of articles below and you get the feeling of what we see in consultation every day. Once you have one of these diagnoses, or another equally nebulous one like fibromyalgia or multiple chemical sensitivities, then you become a **second class medical citizen and are not taken seriously**. But as they reminded us in psychiatry in medical school, **all psychiatric cases die of legitimate medical illnesses.**

In medicine the word **somatization** means claiming physical symptoms where there are really none. In other words, it is a fancy word to mean a hypochondriac. The sad thing is that medicine has not yet figured out that **there is no such thing as a hypochondriac.** Just because the person may be complaining of the wrong thing, does not minimize the fact that something is wrong. Otherwise, why would he be complaining? The patient did not go to medical school so how should he know that his belly aches for example, are not so much what he ate, but what is eating at him? Just because he has the wrong diagnosis does not mean he is making up being out of balance. He still needs someone to determine why he came to the doctor's office and what can be done to fix it. In other words, there is no such thing as a hypochondriac. It is a cop-out used by medicine to save face; to keep us from looking so ignorant.

REFERENCES:

Manu P, et al, Panic disorder among patients with chronic fatigue, SOUTH MED J, 84:451-456, 1991

Manu P, et al, Somatization disorder in patients with chronic fatigue, PSYCHOSOMATICS, 30:388-395, 1989

Kreusi MJ, et al, Psychiatric diagnosis in patients who have chronic fatigue syndrome, J CLIN PSYCHIATRY, 50:53-56, 1994

Pawlikowska T, et al, Population based study of fatigue and psychological distress, BRIT MED J, 308:763-766, 1994

Walker EA, et al, Psychiatric disorders and medical care utilization among people in the general population who report fatigue, J GEN INTERN MED, 8:436-440, 1993

THE LABEL IS THE FOCUS

You see now that **in medicine, the label is the focus**. After that, it is drugs and surgery for the treatments. It is as though arthritis was a Motrin deficiency, and depression was a Prozac deficiency. There is no thrust to find the cause and get rid of it once and for all. **Cure is not the goal.** But addiction to symptom-relieving medications seems to be the focus. Is it a coincidence that the parent companies that own many insurance companies are pharmaceutical and chemical firms?

And now with cookbook medicine being ruled by **practice guidelines,** you are even more powerless and unlikely to have someone interested in finding the correctable causes. Once you have a label or diagnosis, you are restricted by your physician and insurance company to certain drugs. **A label becomes a dangerous thing,** for it can be a one-way street to getting worse. You could die from that label, for finding the correctable cause is not part of the **cookbook** practice guidelines that are directing how medicine is practiced. But with the techniques presented here, you, too, should be able to learn how to **heal the impossible.**

For we all know millionaires who are miserable, and poor people who are happy. We know people who have no problems, but are not happy, and those who have the burdens of the world on their shoulders, but it doesn't depress them. No, **there is more to depression than life circumstances.** The happy people have a resilience that in large part comes from the chemistry of the brain being in proper balance. Nothing depresses them. This is opposed to depressed persons where nothing can make them happy. The purpose of this book is to teach you how to have the happy chemistry in your brain all the time.

Meanwhile, let's begin what may turn out to be the most profitable adventure of your life. I invite you to join me as we explore what it will take to bring you maximum happiness.

POST SCRIPT:

Well-meaning people from all over the world have written in support of the ideas and with thanks for how much help the other books have given them. They are hesitant to express criticism, but they fear that the typos, grammatical errors, and lack of professional editing will detract from the message. So I had better explain so that these inconsistencies do not interfere with your health goals. I am a solo practitioner. I have no partner. Aside from my practice, I have a very unusual and demanding lifestyle. I lecture around the country, I teach advanced courses for physicians, I do frequent radio and television shows, I write for health magazines, medical journals, newsletters, and I have a special life outside of medicine.

I feel very beholding for having been able to learn enough to get so well. I have seen these techniques help so many others, even those kind enough to write, yet I have never met much less treated. I feel I must pay back and disseminate the information. I am without a doubt, driven. I have written 9 books in 9 years. And I'm not a writer , I'm a practitioner. These are referenced to the teeth, something that costs me tremendous time and money (much more than I could ever recover with any book sales).

Also, bear in mind that I write for an unusual combination audience: lay people and physicians, alike. So when you see too many references or get into a biochemical explanation that is beyond your needs, just plow right through. Skimming is O.K. There is no test afterwards. But you will amaze yourself at how much you do understand in the end. So don't lose the big picture by getting bogged down in minutia.

If that were not enough, I have never been able to use an editor, because I cannot find one who knows all the science and medicine. Sure they could check for typos, etc., but I need more than that. As a result, I must be my own editor. So bear with me. I'm peddling as fast as I can to help you get healthy as soon as possible.

CHAPTER 2

FOOD FOR THOUGHT

THE FOOD FACTOR: CAUSES AND CURES

Food allergy is one of the least diagnosed and most prevalent causes of symptoms, especially depression. Physicians get none to extremely little training during their 4 years of medical school in food allergy. In fact, most physicians know next to nothing about it and I was no exception. I knew absolutely nothing about food allergy---- until I developed multiple food allergies. Somehow that humbles the physician and turns him around a hundred and eighty degrees to learn all he can.

Food allergy can mimic nearly any symptom or disease you can think of. In fact, it is really unusual to find a patient who has resistant rhinitis, or nasal congestion, or chronic sinusitis, migraines, asthma, recurrent infections, epilepsy, hypertension, hypoglycemia, nephritis, lupus, schizophrenia, cystitis, prostatitis, fatigue, colitis, arthritis, or chemical sensitivity who does not have a food allergy. And of course, **depression is a leading symptom** of hidden food allergy.

To show you how far reaching food allergy can be, food allergy can cause hearing loss in children and adults. It can cause recurrent ear infections and the need to have PE or pressure equalizing polyethylene tubes in the ear drums. Food allergies can cause asthma, rheumatoid arthritis, bronchitis, nasal allergies, Meniere's disease, recurrent cystitis or bladder symptoms, prostatitis and urethritis, necrosis and other serious kidney disorders, migraines, seizures, chronic irritable bowel, ulcerative colitis, Crohn's disease, convulsions, numbness, tingling, inability to concentrate, and even diabetes and death (all references in Rogers SA, THE SCIENTIFIC BASIS FOR SELECTIVE ENVIRONMENTAL MEDICINE TECHNIQUE, this publisher).

Depression however, is a far more common symptom that can be produced by food allergy. But not only do hidden, unsuspected allergies to foods cause depression, but so does a change in the percentages of food categories ingested. For example, diet manipulation such as increasing the ratio of carbohydrates to proteins can change the content of brain **neurotransmitters or happy hormones like serotonin.** And serotonin is the very brain chemical (or neurotransmitter or happy hormone, whatever you prefer to call it) that Prozac and many anti-depressants increase in the brain to lessen depression. They work on that very principle of changing the concentration of brain serotonin (Fernstrom JD, Wurtman RJ, Brain serotonin content: Increase following ingestion of carbohydrate diet, SCIENCE, 1971; 174-1023-1025.

So if diet is that important in controlling brain function, that diet could even conceivably cause TIA's or transient ischemic attacks which are little strokes, and indeed it can (Ellis ME, Stevens DL, Transient cerebral ischemic attacks related to egg consumption, POST GRAD MED J, 1981; 57:642-644). Since each person is highly individual, we will look at the most common food problems and then show you how to diagnose your own specific ones.

SUGAR

After over 26 years in medicine, if I had to choose the **number one** food that has caused the most depression, it would be sugar. There are many mechanisms by which sugar can cause depression. First of all, someone can just plain be sensitive to it or you can even lack the enzyme sucrase or fructase to digest certain sugars properly. More importantly a diet high in sugars robs you of important nutrients.

For example, when you eat sugar you **lose chromium** in the urine. As you get low in chromium, this causes **sugar cravings** which then cause you to eat more sugar. Then you lose more chromium, step up your cravings, and eat more. This **vicious downward spiral** continues until you get a worse problem induced. It could be obesity, high cholesterol from too low a chromium, or hypoglycemia (low blood sugar) with mood swings or depression.

This scenario is very common so let's make sure you know it cold: As you eat more sugar, you lose more chromium. The more chromium you lose, the more you crave and so it becomes a vicious cycle until you get hypoglycemia from the chromium deficiency, complete with shaking, violent mood swings, headaches, and/or depression. As well, ingestion of much sugar also uses up manganese, magnesium, and many other minerals and vitamins as well (all references in Rogers SA, WELLNESS AGAINST ALL ODDS, this publisher).

Another method by which sugar can make someone depressed is if they have an overgrowth of a yeast called **Candida** in the intestine. When you have a great deal of antibiotics given to you or ingest a great deal of sugar, it can cause the overgrowth of **Candida albicans** in the intestine.

This yeast can then put out a toxin that makes people extremely depressed. Then when they eat sugar they feed this yeast and get even more depressed hours later. This is because the yeasts can double their numbers every 20 minutes if fed the proper diet. So in a few hours you can have a huge increase in not only yeasts but their depression-causing toxin. There is often much abdominal bloating that accompanies this yeast overgrowth as well, since the gas merely reflects the yeasts' increased turnover or growth.

As you will learn later, you can also be allergic to this yeast or mold and the brain can be the direct allergic target organ, with depression as the resultant symptom. Recall that ragweed inhalation can cause itchy eyes and runny nose. By the same token, inhaling or ingesting a yeast to which you are allergic, or worse yet, wearing it in your gut so that you effectively never get away from it, can be the cause of scores of symptoms. If the target organ is the brain, the symptom is depression.

To complicate things, evidence shows that Candida and other unwanted intestinal organisms have the ability to trans-locate or pass from the gut into the bloodstream. This is double jeopardy as these organisms can raise havoc taking up residence in unexpected places (more of how it actually gets into other tissues, including the brain in the Volume III).

But the major effect of sugar probably comes from its addictive potential. Because it tastes good, and because it can provide a fast fix for a falling afternoon blood sugar level, it is easy to become dependent upon its ability to pick you up. But the more it is used in this fashion, the more potential it has of depleting nutrients that eventually lead to hypoglycemia, or low blood sugar. In fact not only is depression commonly caused by hypoglycemia, but violent and criminal acts can be. But more about this in the hypoglycemia section (Volume III). Suffice to say for now, that a **trial off all sugar for 2 weeks** may produce remarkable relief from depression. The problem is you may find it impossible to do or go through wicked withdrawal symptoms (irritability, headache, weakness, overwhelming cravings, etc.) if you do not first correct hidden chromium and manganese deficiencies and Candida overgrowth or do the detox procedure. So read on.

REFERENCES:

Virkkunen M, Huttunen MO, Evidence for abnormal glucose tolerance test among violent offenders, NEURO-PSYCHOLOGY, 8:30-34, 1982.

Ferguson HB, Stoddard C, Simeon JG 1986. Double blind challenge studies of behavioral and cognitive effects of sucrose-aspartame ingestion of normal children. NUTR REV 44 (May,suppl.):144-50.

Christensen L, The role of caffeine and sugar in depression, THE NUTRITION REPORT, March 1991:9(3):17,24.

Duffy W, SUGAR BLUES, NY. Chilton, 1975.

Schoenthaler SJ, The effects of sugar on the treatment and control of antisocial behavior: a double-blind study of an incarcerated juvenile population, INT J BIOSOC RES, 3:1-19, 1982.

Schoenthaler SJ, et al, The impact of a low food additive and sucrose diet on academic performance in 803 New York City public schools, INT J BIOSOC RES, 2: 185-195, 1986.

Hunter BT, SUGAR AND SWEETENERS, Storey Com-munications, Inc. Gardenway Publ, Pownal VT 05261 (Bulletin A-30).

Yudkin J, SWEET AND DANGEROUS, Phantom Books, NY.

GLUTEN AND WHEAT

The **second most common food to cause depression** is wheat. And that likewise has several mechanisms. Some people are just plain sensitive to wheat and the brain happens to be the target organ. I recall the thrill of discovery that Dave had when he learned that wheat was the cause of his lifetime of depression and psychiatric treatments.

You see, instead of dust antigens causing histamine release in the lung with asthma, or ragweed antigens in the nose with nasal congestion, or strawberry in the skin with hives, these people develop depression when their total load of wheat gets to a certain level. I've known people who have seen a psychiatrist for 8 years and taken all sorts of anti-depressants only to find out that once they got off wheat they were happy people and needed no medications.

Another way that wheat sensitivity can cause depression is when you develop **celiac disease** or what is called **gluten enteropathy.** What happens is that these people make special antibodies to some of the proteins in wheat. When these antibodies attach to tissues in the intestine, they actually destroy the intestinal villi so that nutrients cannot be properly absorbed. Therefore, these people get malabsorption. They have a lot of gas, bloating, alternating diarrhea and constipation, and they have multiple nutrient deficiencies as a result. And most all of them have depression (references in Rogers SA, WELLNESS AGAINST ALL ODDS (this publisher).

A major problem with gluten sensitivity is that you have to be off wheat entirely for 6 months before the gut will properly heal. If you have the slightest trace of wheat during that time, then you have to start all over again. Unfortunately, wheat is not easy to avoid. People who are highly sensitive to wheat can even have someone stir a dish that they are cooking for them using a spoon that stirred (pasta) something with wheat in it. This tiny amount of wheat is enough to set them back and necessitate starting the healing process all over again for another 6 months. So if there is the slightest doubt that you have a gluten sensitivity you should read the above book and become extremely knowledgeable about it. THE E.I. SYNDROME, REVISED will give the hidden sources of wheat and directions for the diagnostic diet and how to avoid wheat withdrawal symptoms.

Because wheat is often associated in foods with sugar, be aware that when you are worse after a wheat-sugar combination that you may really be feeding an undiagnosed yeast problem, or have an undiagnosed sucrase deficiency or a sugar sensitivity as well as a wheat sensitivity.

REFERENCES:

Hallert CJ, Astrom J, Sedvall G, Psychic disturbances in adult coeliac disease III. Reduced central monoamine metabolism and signs of depression, SCAND J GASTROENTEROL, 17:1,25-28, 1982

Fukodome JS, Yoshikawa M, Opioid peptides derived from wheat gluten: Their isolation and characterization. FEBS Lett. 296:107-111, 1992. This paper shows the mechanism by which foods can also be addicting, and why the individual may go out of his way to eat the very foods he knows will eventually cause depression.

Dohan DC, Cereals and schizophrenia, ACTA PSYCHIAT SCAND 42, 1966, pp 125-52.

Dohan FC, Grasberger JC, Lowell FM, et al, Relapsed schizophrenics: more rapid improvement on a milk and cereal- free diet, BRIT J PSYCHIA, 115, May 1969, pp 596-6.

MOLD OR FERMENT FOODS

Because mold allergy in the air is so common a cause of depression, when people eat foods that have mold antigens in them, this can also cause depression. For the antigens merely get into the blood stream by an alternate route to affect the brain (see mold allergy chapter).

Foods that contain mold antigens are things that are several days old, even if they have been refrigerated. Likewise, obvious mold antigen containing foods are foods that contain yeasts or have risen, or have been aged, pickled, dried, or fermented. These include cheeses, all alcohol, bread, dried fruits, condiments and anything containing vinegar: and these include pickles, olives, catsup, mayonnaise, mustard, Worcestershire sauce, and salad dressings. As you can imagine, it is very difficult to avoid fermented foods. But once you learn what triggers your depression, there is incentive to avoid these and we will show you how later.

ADDITIVES, DYES, HORMONES

It is amazing what we add to our food supply. Most processed foods have a long list of chemicals that very few people are even familiar with. Just pick up anything in your pantry and read the ingredients or look at a loaf of bread. Bread should contain flour, yeast, salt and maybe a little sugar to help feed the yeast. So what are all those other chemical names doing in there? Also real bread should go bad in a day. But the bread with all these chemicals lasts infinitely longer.

Meanwhile, it has been known for a long time that additives, dyes, and hormones can cause allergic tension fatigue syndrome, hyperactivity, and learning disorders in children. Adults as well can have all these problems. But the main symptom that they show from additives of dyes, coloring, stabilizers, and hormones in foods is depression. It repulses me to put food additives in the section under food, for they really belong under chemicals. But since everyone thinks it is something they should be eating (or else why would they?), they shall remain here.

There are literally thousands of food additives, all of which, since they are ingested, must have an effect on the brain. Fortunately, most do not have a profound effect, except on those unlucky enough to have a hypersensitivity to them. But what we have learned from these individuals has helped us discover that many more people are affected than was previously thought. And the awful part of it is that no one has ever studied the cumulative effect of all these additives in one individual.

Let's look at one of the most commonly ingested additives that can cause depression, **aspartame.** You might recognize it as **Nutrasweet** or **Equal,** the artificial sugar substitute. If you want to skip pages of chemistry and politics, the bottom line is that it is metabolized into **methanol** and **formaldehyde.** It causes depression and other malfunctions of the brain in humans, to include mood changes, insomnia, mental retardation, and seizures. It has many other side effects (which you can read about with documentation, in TIRED OR TOXIC? this publisher).

Since aspartame is 40% aspartic acid, an excitatory amino acid, for some individuals it makes them hyper. Others get a paradoxical or reversed reaction and get depressed, while still others feel no reaction. It all depends on your individual biochemistry, genetics, nutrient status, and the rest of the total load, as you will learn. Aspartame is 180 times more potent than sucrose (table sugar) as a sweetener, and can cause marked blood increases in phenylalanine, a substance linked to addictive eating patterns.

There are numerous adverse effects of additives that are never mentioned. For example any foods that have a yellow color (and shades of orange, green, red) often contain the **yellow dye tartrazine**. The manufacturers are not obliged to put it on the label, either. All that has to go on the label is what the LAST person added. So if the baker bought flour that contained yellow dye (which makes the end product such as a cake or bread look like it contains eggs), he does not have to put tartrazine on the label, because he did not add it to the flour. The man he bought it from added it.

Anyway, tartrazine can lower zinc levels, and in turn worsen brain conditions that are dependent upon normal zinc status, like depression or hyperactivity. The examples are endless. But always remember that all additives and colorings are mere chemicals that eventually further deplete the detox nutrients that could have been used instead, to make the brain's happy hormones.

The bottom line on additives is that they are **designed to fool the public** into thinking the food is better than it is. As we mentioned, yellow dye is used to make you think the baked goods are enriched with eggs. MSG is a ubiquitous flavor enhancer to compensate for lack of freshness or removal of food constituents (so that the product won't go bad so quickly). The problem is that the removal of substances to slow food aging work because you have removed priceless vitamins, minerals, and amino acids that fungi and bacteria need in order to live. By having a resultant food that is nutritionally inferior, it is not as appealing or useful to these organisms or bugs. So they cannot use it for food; hence, it does not go bad as quickly. The problem is, **if the bugs don't want it, then why should you?** Are the bugs smarter?

And these chemicals used to disguise food deficits have deleterious effects on brain chemistry. They were not meant for the brain as fuel. In fact, they actually interfere with normal brain chemistry and the synthesis of our "happy hormones".

REFERENCES:

Boris M, Mandel FS, Food and additives are common causes of the attention deficit hyperactivity disorder in children, ANN ALLERGY, 1994; 72, 462-468.

Pardridge WM, Potential effects of the dipeptide sweetener aspartame on the brain, NUTRITION AND THE BRAIN, VOL.7, Wurtman RJ, Wurtman JJ, Raven Press, NY, 1986 Weiss B.

William's JH, Margen S, Abrans B, Caan B, FR, Behavior responses to artificial food colors, SCIENCE, 1980; 207:1487.

Anderson AFR, Migraine, an allergic phenomenon. AM J DIG DIS 5:1;14, 1934.

Kenney RA, 1980. Chinese restaurant syndrome. LANCET I(8163):311-12.

Hatten DG, Henry SH, Montgomery SB, Bleiberg MJ, Rulis AM, Bolger PM, 1983. Role of the Food and Drug Administration in regulation of neuro-effective food additives. IN NUTRITION AND THE BRAIN, VOL 6, ed Wurtman RJ and Wurtman JJ, 31-100, 1983, Raven NY.

Potts WJ, Bloss JL, Nutting EF, Biological properties of aspartame. I. Evaluation of central nervous system effects. J ENVIRON PATHOL & TOXICOL 3:341-53, 1980.

Wurtman RJ, 1985. Aspartame; possible effect on seizure susceptibility. LANCET ii:1059.

Hunter BT, FACT BOOK ON FOOD ADDITIVES AND YOUR HEALTH, Keats Publ, New Canaan CT, 1972.

Jacobson MF, EATER'S DIGEST: THE CONSUMER'S FACTBOOK OF FOOD ADDITIVES. Doubleday Anchor Books, Garden City NY, 1972.

Ferguson HB, Stoddard C, Simeon JG, Double-blond challenge studies of behavioral and cognitive effects of sucrose- aspartame ingestion of normal children, NUTR REV, 44 (May, suppl):144-50, 1986.

Reif-Lehrer L, Stemmermann MG, Monosodium glutamate intolerance in children, NEW ENG J MED: 1204-1205.

Creasey Wa, Malawista SE, Monosodium L-glutamate-inhibition of glucose uptake in brain as a basis for toxicity, BIOCHEM PHARM, 2917-2920.

Rowe K, Synthetic food coloring and hyperactivity: a double- blind crossover study, AUSTRALIAN PEDIATRICS, 24: 143-147, 1988.

Shaywitz B, et al. Effects of chronic administration of food coloring on activity levels and cognitive performance in normal and hyperactive developing rat pups, ANN NEUROL, 4:196, 1978.

Swanson J, Food dyes impair performance of hyperactive children on a laboratory learning test, SCIENCE, 207: 1485- 1487, 1980.

Coulombe RA, Sharma RP, Neurobiochemical alterations induced by the artificial sweetener aspartame (nutri-sweet). TOXIC APPL PHARM;79-85, 1986.

Olney JW, Brain damage in mice from voluntary ingestion of glutamate and aspartate. TOX; 125-129, 1980.

Hayashi T, Effects of sodium glutamate on the nervous system, KEIO J MED; 183-192, 1954.

Olney JW, Glutamate, a neurotoxic transmitter, J CHILD NEUROL; 218-226, 1989.

Walton RG, Seizure and mania after high intake of aspartame, PSYCHOSOMATICS' 218-220, 1986.

Johns DR, Migraine provoked by aspartame, NEW ENG J MED, Aug 14, 1986.

Schiffman, Aspartame and headache, NEW ENG J MED; 1201-1202, 1988.

Blaylock RL, EXCITOTOXINS, THE TASTE THAT KILLS, Health Press, Santa Fe NM, 1994. This entire book goes into how monosodium glutamate, aspartame, and MSG and other additives contribute to neurodegerative diseases.

Remington DW, THE BITTER TRUTH ABOUT ARTIFICIAL SWEETENERS, Vitality House International, 3707 N. Canyon Road #8C, Prov Utah 84604, 1986.

Levy F, et al, Hyperkinesis and diet: a double-blind crossover trial with a tartrazine challenge, MED J AUST, 1: 61-64, 1978.

Weiss B, Behavior responses to artificial food colors, SCIENCE, 207:1487-1489, 1980.

Ward NI, Soulsbury KA, Zettel VH, Colquhoun ID, Bunday S, Barnes B, The influence of the chemical additive tartrazine on the zinc status of hyperactive children -- a double-blind placebo-controlled study, J NUTR MED, 1:1, 51-58, 1990

Weiss B, Williams JH, Margen S, Abrans B, Caan B, FR, Behavior responses to artificial food colors, SCIENCE, 1980; 207:1487

Schwartz G, IN BAD TASTE: THE MSG SYNDROME, Santa Fe, NM, Health Press, 1988

Nemeroff CB, monosodium glutamate-induced neurotoxicity: Review of the literature and a call for further research, in: Miller SA, ed., NUTRITION AND BEHAVIOR, the Franklin Institute Press, 1981

Olney JW, Sharpe LG, Brain lesions in an infant monkey treated with monosodium glutamate, SCIENCE 166:386-388, 1969

Rosenbold L, CAN A GLUTEN FREE-DIET HELP? HOW? Keats Publishing, 27 Pine St., PO Box 876, New Canaan, CT 06840-0876

MILK

Milk allergy is probably one of the most common causes of nasal congestion. Many unsuspecting victims have had painful sinus surgery and nasal surgery only to find out that if they had stopped all milk products, they had no congestion and no reason to have any surgery. But don't be fooled. Just as milk can cause much histamine release resulting in nasal congestion or asthma, this histamine release can just as well cause depression in the brain. The only way you will know is to do a trial off all milk products for a while. The **E.I. SYNDROME, REVISED** will show you all the hidden sources of milk.

The well-known NEW ENGLAND JOURNAL OF MEDICINE article showed studies suggesting that milk allergy contributes to the pathology of the auto-immune disease, juvenile diabetes mellitus. There is no limit to the symptoms that you can get from milk ingestion if you are unknowingly allergic to it.

CAFFEINE

Caffeine is a major source of depression and that surprises people because they use caffeine in coffee, tea, chocolate, colas and other sodas to give them an "up" feeling. But just as with sugar, there can be a paradoxical down swing several hours later. Caffeine has long been a cause of not only bladder and prostate problems, but intestinal problems. More importantly it can cause severe depression. And a major problem with it is that as you try to go off it you may go through nasty withdrawal symptoms. Some people have horrible headaches, depression, irritability, exacerbation of fatigue, or even violent mood swings. It takes 4 days sometimes to get past withdrawal symptoms. And then should you have caffeine again, it may take another 4 days of withdrawal symptoms to get off again.

Note: A protocol to accelerate withdrawal is in WELLNESS AGAINST ALL ODDS.

Caffeine also potentiates hypoglycemia, which itself can be a major cause of depression. In one study they showed that caffeine resulted in a 23% decrease in the blood flow speed through the carotid arteries (to the brain). It also accentuates the sympathetic and adrenal system, making individuals more aware of hypoglycemia at blood levels that normally do not provoke hypoglycemia (Kerr D, et al, Effect of caffeine on the recognition and responses to hypoglycemia in humans, ANNALS OF INTERNAL MEDICINE, 1993; 119-799-804).

Sometimes people forget that as well as being in coffee and tea, caffeine is in cola drinks, chocolate, and over-the-counter tablets and capsules for pain, appetite control, colds and flu, and for staying awake.

REFERENCES:

Veleber DM, Templer DI, Effects of caffeine on anxiety and depression, J ABNORM PSYCHOL, 1984; 93:120-122

Greden JF, Fontaine P, Lubetsky M, Chamberlain K, Anxiety and depression associated with caffeinism among psychiatric in- patients, AM J PSYCHIATRY, 1978; 135:963-956

Hughes J, Clinical importance of caffeine withdrawal, NEW ENG J MED, October 15, 1992; 327(16):1160-1161.

Tondo L, Rudas N, et al, Course of seasonal bipolar disorder influenced by caffeine, J AFFECT DIS, 22:249-251, 1991.

Veleber DM, Templer DI, Effects of caffeine on anxiety and depression, J ABNORM PSYCHOL, 93:120-122, 1984.

Greden JF, Firestone P, Davey J, Goodman JT, Peters S, The effects of caffeine and methylphenidate on hyperactive children, J AMER ACAD PSYCH, 17(3):445-56, 1978.

Curatelo, PW, Robertson D, The health consequences of caffeine, ANN INTERN MED, 98(pt I):641-53, 1983

Elkins RN, Rapoport JL, Zahn TP, Buschbaum MS, Weingartner H, Kopin IJ, Langer D, Johnson C, Acute effects of caffeine in normal prepubertal boys, AMER J PSYCH 138(2):178-83, 1981

Fontaine P, Lubetsky M, Chamberlain K, Anxiety and depression associated with caffeinism among psychiatric in-patients, AM J PSYCH, 135:963-956, 1978.

Strain EC, et al, Caffeine dependence syndrome: Evidence from case histories and experimental evaluations, JAMA, 272(13):1043-1048, Oct 5, 1994.

Silverman K, Evans SM, Strain EC, Griffiths RR, Withdrawal syndrome after the double-blind cessation of caffeine consumption, NEW ENGLAND JOURNAL OF MEDICINE, 327(16): 110- 14, Oct 15, 1992.

Conclusions of the above paper: Persons who consume low or moderate amounts of caffeine may have a withdrawal syndrome after their daily consumption of caffeine ceases.

ALCOHOL

Alcoholism is a disease. It is an **abnormal chemistry** and an **allergy combined.** It also has a hereditary component. It is not a lack of moral fiber. For it is just as much a disease as diabetes or hypertension is.

Oddly enough some people who are alcoholics are not even aware of it. Some people become wonderful entertainers and frequently invite people to their homes so that they have an excuse for ingesting alcohol. Other surprises are that some people who are alcoholics don't even need alcohol everyday. They can go for weeks without it and then binge. Some people are so sensitive to alcohol that there is a dramatic change in their brain function and they can be depressed when they are on it or depressed afterwards without it during the withdrawal phase. Some lose total consciousness or have "black-outs" or lose memory for large chunks of time with minimal amounts that would be harmless to others.

Some of the chemistry of alcoholism has been worked out and we know how to supplement specific amino acids, vitamins, essential fatty acids, orphan nutrients, and minerals to help decrease the craving for it and foster the metabolism of "happy hormones". (See the section on nutrition in Volume II and WELLNESS AGAINST ALL ODDS.)

Just as with any hidden food sensitivity that can cause addiction as well as symptoms, there is a withdrawal period. Many alcoholics who have had excellent training through AA, know that the slightest amount of alcohol as in cough syrups or flavorings (like vanilla extract) in cooking, or even through skin absorption of after-shave products, for example, can reactivate strong cravings for alcohol. It is a deadly allergy for them.

Genetics is one of the mysteriously elusive parts of alcoholism that helps to make it difficult to comprehend. But one of the nasty facts is that the craving for alcohol can be genetically determined. It is not a matter of sheer will-power. But all is not lost. For as you will see, we know how to fool these happy hormone receptors in the brain without using alcohol or drugs.

If that were not enough, some individuals have sort of a mini still or fermentation vat in their guts. In other words, the types of bacteria in their guts and their type of diet, helps bacteria in their intestines, when digesting and fermenting their food, to actually make alcohol in the gut. This alcohol then goes on to be absorbed into their blood streams. These poor souls get drunk without ingesting alcohol. More on that in the gut section (Volume III).

REFERENCES:

Blum K, et al Alleic association of human dopamine D2 receptor gene in alcoholism, JAMA, 263:2055-2060, 1990.

Blum K, ALCOHOL AND THE ADDICTIVE BRAIN, Free Press, Macmillan NY, 1991.

Gill JS, Zezulka AV, Shipley MJ, Gill SK, Beevers DG, Stroke and alcohol consumption, NEW ENG J MED, 315:1041-46, 1986.

Hunnisett A, Howard J, Davies S, Gut fermentation (or the "auto-brewery") syndrome: a new clinical test with initial observations and discussion of clinical and biochemical implications, J NUTRIT MED, 1:1, 33-38, 1990

WATER

It seems impossible that anybody could be depressed from water. However, the average municipal city is so contaminated these days that even the front page of **U.S.A. TODAY** shows us that the average city water has over 500 chemicals in it. And you will see as you get through the section on chemical sensitivity, that many people have hidden chemical intolerance. And the brain again is the allergic target organ, triggering depression. (More on that in the chemical section, Volume II).

Chlorine is used in most city waters to kill bugs and that in itself can not only contribute to arteriosclerosis, nutrient deficiencies and cancers, but also depression in the vulnerable person. A simple water filter at the sink that you can switch on for drinking and cooking water can solve this problem.

REFERENCES:

Cantor, et al, Bladder cancer, drinking water source, and tap water consumption: A case control study, J NAT CANCER INSTIT, 79:1269-1279, 1987

Ziegler, et al, Bladder cancer mortality in Massachusetts related to chlorinated drinking water: a case-control study, ARCH ENVIRON HEALTH, 43:195-200, 1988

Morris, et al, Chlorination, chlorination by-products, and cancer, AMER J PUBLIC HEALTH, 82:955-963, 1992

IRRADIATED FOODS

One of the many travesties of this decade is the irradiation of foods. First it has been sneaked into our lives with very little scientific study of long-range effects. In addition, there is really no place to complain about it. You might think that you just won't buy any. But you probably already have, for labeling of irradiated components that have been put into food is not necessary. And even when irradiation has been done by the last man on the totem pole, still there is ambiguous ruling. And how does the grocer label a potato? And if another shipment of non-irradiated potatoes comes in, how does he separate them if he only has room for one type?

Some of the changes in food from irradiation include the formation of **trans fatty acids** that promote disease. We know enough to stay away from margarines that are high in trans-fatty acids (more in the section on essential fatty acids). But who would think of staying away from a chicken or peanut because trans-fatty acids have been induced by food irradiation? Food irradiation also **damages vitamin** E and many other vitamins. But worst of all, irradiated foods contain mutagens and carcinogens as well as radio-resistant fungi and carcinogenic mycotoxins (mold toxins).

Irradiation of foods can make them last longer and with less effort. For example, you can have milk or a chicken in your pantry, not in the refrigerator, and they may not go bad for a year. And the problem with irradiated foods does not end with the induction of cancer-promoting substances, and the reduction of nutrient quality (destruction of vitamins, for example). For the security of knowing a food will be irradiated allows sloppier handling by food processors in places where bacteria and mold can grow.

Because the food handlers know that most of the mold will be killed, they do not have to take as many precautions or worry that the food will go bad. But when mold grows in foods, it makes toxins that cause cancer, call mycotoxins. These are not destroyed by irradiation, often do not make the food go bad, and are not detectable. One mycotoxin, aflatoxin on peanuts, is a known promoter or cause of liver cancer. When you ingest irradiated food, you unknowingly consume more mycotoxins (cancer-causing chemicals) than ever before. And the work of detoxifying these mold toxins uses up nutrients. Add to this the fact that food irradiation lowers the nutrient density of food by destroying vitamins, and you readily appreciate the potential that it has to contribute to depression (more in the nutrient section, Volume II).

REFERENCES:

Bloomfield L, Webb T, Lang T, Food irradiation: a public health issue? J NUTIT MED 1:1, 75-80, 1990

Raica N, Scott J, Nielsen W, The nutitional quality of irradiated foods, RADIATION RES REV, 3:447, 1972

Nawar WW, Radiolysis of nonaqueous components of foods. In: Josephson ES, Peterson MS, eds. PRESERVATION OF FOOD BY IONIZING RADIATION. CRC Press, Boca Raton, 1983

Diehl JF, Radiolytic effects in foods, ibid

Florence TM, Cancer and aging -- the free radical connection. CHEMISTRY IN AUSTRALIA 1983, 50:166

Priyadarshini E, Tulpule PG, Aflatoxin production of irradiated foods, FOOD COSMET TOXICOL, 1976:14;293-295.

Piccioni R, Analysis of data on the impact of food processing by ionizing radiation on health and the environment, INT J BIOSOCIAL RES, 9(2):203-212, 1987.

DIAGNOSIS OF HIDDEN FOOD SENSITIVITY

We have looked at some of the most common foods that can cause mild to severe depression. A simple way of diagnosing whether you have food sensitivity is to go on what is called the **rare food diagnostic diet**. In other words, don't have any of the foods that you normally would have at least once every 2 weeks. Instead, have other foods as substitutes. In the **E.I. SYNDROME, REVISED** you will find the entire rare foods diagnostic diet spelled out. A simple example is given below, but there are many elaborations on this if you need further instructions.

Any food or food additives can be the culprit. And usually the rule is that there is more than one food for which the brain is the allergic target organ. In other words, it is rare to have merely one food allergy that affects the brain. If there is one, there are most likely others.

There are a couple of principles that you need to be aware of when dealing with food allergies. First is the **addiction-withdrawal.** Some people with severe food allergies actually are driven to ingest the very foods which are so bad for them. Sometimes the food that causes a depression is the person's favorite food. And when he is deprived of it, much like an alcoholic, he can go through withdrawal with shaking, heightened anxiety, or intensification of symptoms like depression.

If you think you might go through severe withdrawal in terms of a worsening of your depression, be sure to have someone with you at all times while on the diet. Let your family and friends know what you are doing.

At either end of the bell-shaped curve, either the initial withdrawing from commonly eaten foods or adding them back in later to identify the culprits, you could make your depression temporarily worse. Make sure someone is around to help you in case you react severely. There are ways to accelerate the withdrawal phase in WELLNESS AGAINST ALL ODDS. Plus if you get worse from withdrawal, merely eating the food which you are missing can reverse it. Likewise, when you add back foods to identify which ones made you depressed, eating only small test amounts can minimize your reaction, rather than pigging out on a large quantity.

FOOD AND MOOD

Without making this a ten-volume text book, I've tried to show you a sampling of an extensive amount of scientific material, psychiatric and biochemical literature that bears out what has been known for thousands of years: You are what you eat.

Furthermore, food allergies can select the brain as target organ with depression as the only or one of many symptoms. If that were not enough, you do not have to be allergic to a food for it to cause depression. Just the balance of food categories can change your mood. Some people are much happier when they eat a high carbohydrate diet of whole grains, greens, and beans. The reasons can be many, including the pH or alkalinity, the high nutrient density, etc. Others make more of the "happy hormones" in the brain with tryptophan or tyrosine, precursors found in a carnivore diet of meats at each meal.

There are many mechanisms by which what we ingest has a direct bearing on how the chemistry of the brain fares. For eons man has related certain foods to an increased libido, sleepiness, mental acuity, or tranquility. Even medicine uses diet commonly to regulate various disease states in the body like hypertension, diabetes, liver disease, heart disease, kidney disease, hypercholesterolemia, etc. And we know that food has a great bearing on not only physical metabolism, but mental metabolism as well. And mood is a mere extension of this. Since **food definitely controls mood,** you need now to learn how to manipulate food to your advantage.

MANIPULATING YOUR BRAIN'S
HAPPY HORMONES

No one meant for us to miserable. We actually make "happy hormones" in our brains. These are designed to make us feel good. But there are many things that can turn off these happy hormones, just as there are many things that can turn them on. And the amount of happy hormones you make in the brain, is directly related to the type of diet you ingest. The difficulty is that we are all different in our biochemistry, and hence, also unique in what foods make us the happiest.

In other words, many people feel really mellow and content on a high carbohydrate (**vegan** or alkaline) diet. Many use this to optimize their athletic performance. While others are **carnivores,** not vegans, and feel best with meat (acid diet) at every meal. They get weak and lose their zip if they lower their meat content. Then there is the **omnivore** who needs a balance of both vegan and carnivore to produce the optimum levels of happy hormones (serotonin being an example of just one of many). Your heredity can often have a bearing on diet type, as many feel best on the types of foods their ancestors ate. For certain we are all mentally healthier avoiding as many 21st century processed foods loaded with chemical additives. For the biochemical work that the body has to do in order to detoxify these chemicals can siphon nutrients away that could have been used to make more happy hormones. But more on this later.

The point is to have fun while you work through a few days of each diet type to determine which is best for your optimal brain function. The different diet types are described in WELLNESS AGAINST ALL ODDS.

REFERENCES:

Rogers SA, WELLNESS AGAINST ALL ODDS, Sand Key Publ, Box 40101, Sarasota FL, 34242 (has all the diet instructions for vegan to carnivore, acid to alkaline)

Fernstrom Jd, Wurtman RJ, Brain serotonin content: increase following ingestion of carbohydrates, SCI, 174:1023-1025, 1971

Fernstrom JD, Faller DV, Shabshelowitz H, Acute reduction of brain serotonin and 5-HIAA following food consumption: correlation with the ratio of serum tryptophan to the sum of competing amino acids, J NEURAL TRASM 36(2):113-121, 1975

Lieberman HR, Wurtman JJ, Chew B. 1986. Changes in mood after carbohydrate consumption among obese individuals. AMER J CLIN NUTR 44:772-78.

And in case you run across a physician who tries to intimidate you by telling you that you are crazy if you think food has a bearing on your depression, here a few more references (And there are many more. For the food and mood connection has been in the scientific literature for over 65 years!)

REFERENCES:

Brostoff J, Challacombe SJ, FOOD ALLERGY AND INTOLERANCE, Bailliere Tindall, West Washington Square, Philadelphia Pennsylvania 19105, 1989

Blum K, ALCOHOL AND THE ADDICTIVE BRAIN, Free Press, Macmillan, New York, 1991

Rinkel HJ, The technique and clinical application of individual food tests, ANN ALLERGY 2:504, 1944

Rinkel HJ, Randolph TG, Zeller M, FOOD ALLERGY, Charles C. Thomas Publ., Springfield, 58-102, 130, 1951

Randolph TG, Descriptive features of food addiction. Addictive eating and drinking, QUAT J STUD ALCOHOL, 17:198- 224, 1956

Rapp DJ, IS THIS YOUR CHILD, Wm Morrow & Co, NY, 1991, or Practical Allergy Research Foundation, P.O.B. 60, Buffalo, NY 14223 , 716 875-5578

Oski F, DON'T DRINK YOUR MILK

Rowe AH, Rowe A Jr, FOOD ALLERGY: IT'S MANIFESTATIONS AND CONTROL AND THE ELIMINATION DIET. A COMPENDIUM, CC Thomas, Springfield, 1972

Randolf TG, Specific adaptation, ANN ALLERGY, 1978; 40:333

Randolph T, Allergy as a cause of nuchal myalgia and associated headache. ARCH OTOLARYNGOL, 50:745, 1949

Shapiro RS, Eisenberg BC. Allergic headache. ANN ALLERGY 23:123, 1965

Rapp DJ, Double-blind case report of chronic headache due to foods and air pollution. ANN ALLERGY, 40:289, 1978

Monro J, Carini C, Brostoff J, Zilkha K. Food allergy in migraine: Study of dietary exclusion and RAST. LANCET, 2:1-4, 1980

Kailin EW, Hastings A. Electromyographic evidence of cerebral malfunction in migraine due to egg allergy. MEDICAL ANNALS OF THE DISTRICT OF COLUMBIA, 39:437, 1970

Campbell MB, Neurologic manifestations of allergic disease. ANN ALLERGY, 31;485, 1970

Hall K, Allergy of the nervous system: a review. ANN ALLERGY, 36-49, 1976

Staffierl D, Bentolila L, Levit L, Hemiplegia and allergic symptoms following ingestion of certain foods: a case report. ANN ALLERGY, 10:38, 1952

Blue JA, Syncope in allergy. ANN ALLERGY, 26:561, 1968

Miller JL, Evidence that idiopathic epilepsy is a sensitization disease. AM J MED SCI 1924;168:635.

Adamson WB, Sellers ED, Observations on the incidence of the hypersensitive state in one hundred cases of epilepsy. J ALLERGY 1931;3:39.

Fein BT, Kamin PB, Allergy, convulsive disorders and epilepsy. ANN ALLERGY 1968;26:241.

Stevens H, Allergy and epilepsy. EPILEPSIA 1965;6:205.

Blanton S, Mental and nervous changes in the children of the Volkschulen of Trier, Germany, caused by malnutrition. MENTAL HYGIENE 3:343-86, 1919

Dreyfus PM, Diet and nutrition in neurologic disorders. In MODERN NUTRITION IN HEALTH AND DISEASE, ed M.E. Shils and V.R. Young, pp 145-70, Lea & Febiger, Phila., 1988

Growdon JH, 1979a. Neurotransmitter precursors in the diet: their use in the treatment of brain diseases. In NUTRITION AND THE BRAIN, VOL. 3, ed R.J. Wurtman and J.J. Wurtman, 117-81, Raven, NY

Growdon JH, Gibson DJ, 1982. Dietary precursors of neurotransmitters: treatment strategies. In CURRENT NEUROLOGY, VOL 4, ed S.H. Appel, 117-44, Wiley, NY

Growdon JH, Wurtman RJ, 1982. Lecithin treatment of neuroleptic-induced tardive dyskinesia. In BIOLOGICAL ASPECTS OF SCHIZOPHRENIA AND ADDICTION, ed G. Hemmings, 129-38. London:Wiley.

Feingold BF, 1975. WHY YOUR CHILD IS HYPERACTIVE, New York: Random House.

Anonymous, 1979. Dietary management of juvenile delinquency. INTERNAT J OFFENDER THER COMPARATIVE CRIMINOLOGY 23:73-84

Gray GE, 1986. Diet, crime, and delinquency: a critique. NUTIT REV 44(May, suppl.):89-94.

Gray GE, Gray LK, 1986. Diet and juvenile delinquency. NUTRITION TODAY 18:14-22.

Green RG. 1976. Subclinical pellagra among penitentiary inmates. J ORTHOMOL PSYCH 5:68-73.

Kavale KA, Forness SR. 1983. Hyperactivity and diet treatment. J LEARN DISABIL 16:324-30.

Lieberman HR, Spring B, Garfield GS, 1986. The behavioral effects of food constituents: Strategies used in studies of amino acids, protein, carbohydrate and caffeine. NUTR REV 44(May, suppl.):61-70.

McEwen LM, Systemic manifestations of hypersensitivity to foods, ALLERG ET IMMUNOPATHOLGIA, Supp.1,91, 1937

Randolph, TG, Rinkle HJ, Zeller M, FOOD ALLERGY, Charles C. Thomas, Springfield II, 1951.

Rowe AH, FOOD ALLERGY, ITS MANIFESTATIONS, DIAGNOSIS, AND TREATMENT, Lee & Febiger, Phila, 1931.

Rowe AH, CLINICAL ALLERGY, Bailliere, Tindal & Cox, London, 1937

Rowe AH, ELIMINATION DIETS AND THE PATIENT'S ALLERGIES, Henry Kimpton, London, 1944

Shannon WR, Neuropathic manifestations in infants and children as a result of anaphylactic reaction to foods contained in their diet, AMER J DIS CHILD 24:89-94, 1922,

Speer F, ALLERGY OF THE NERVOUS SYSTEM, Charles C. Thomas, Springfield IL, 1970

Kolata G, Food affects human behavior. SCIENCE, Dec 17, 1982, 1209-1210

Wurtman RJ, Fernstrom JD. Effects of the diet on brain neurotransmitters. METAB, Feb 1977, 207-223.

Maltz G, Ketogenic diet can control seizures in epileptic children, FAMILY PRACTICE NEWS, Dec 15, 1994;23, 122-130 Wilkins Ave., Rockville, MD. 20852

Breneman JC. BASICS OF FOOD ALLERGY: ITS MANIFESTATIONS AND CONTROL AND THE ELIMINATION DIETS. A COMPENDIUM, Charles C. Thomas, Springfield, 1972

Finn R, Cohen HN. "Food Allergy". Fact or fiction. LANCET 1978: 1:426.

Cunningham-Rundles C, Brandeis WE, Good RA, Day NK. Bovine antigens and the formation of circulating immune complexes in selective immunoglobulin A deficiency. J CLIN INVEST 1979;64:272.

Zioudrou C, Streaty RA, Klee WA. Opioid peptides derived from food proteins: the exorphins. J Biol Chem 1979;254:2446.

Lonsdale E, et al, Crime and violence: A hypothetical explanation of its relationship with high caloric malnutrition, J ADVANCE MED, Fall 1994;7(3):171-180

Balyeat RM, Rinkel HJ. Further studies in allergic-migraine: Based on a series of two hundred and two consecutive cases. ANN INTERN MED 1931:,5:713

Andresen AFR. Migraine, an allergic phenomenon. AM J DIG DIS 1934, 5:1;14.

Randolph T. Allergy as a cause of nuchal myalgia and associated headache. ARCH OTOLARYNGOL 1949, 50:745.

Shapiro RS, Eisenberg BC. Allergic headache. ANN ALLERGY 1965, 23:123

******

Grant ECG. Food allergies and migraine. LANCET 1979, 1:966.

In the above study, 60 patients with frequent migraines were studied. Most of them had been using oral contraceptives, tobacco or ergotamine and had failed to improve by discontinuing these substances. Mean duration of migraines was 18 years for the women and 22 years for the men. Most patients had other symptoms, including lethargy, **depression,** anxiety, flushing dizziness, abdominal pain, constipation, diarrhea, or rashes. Each patient ate an exclusion diet for 5 days, consisting only of 2 low risk foods (usually lamb and pears) and drank only bottled spring water. Migraines disappeared by the 5th day in most cases. Each patient then tested 1 to 3 common foods per day, looking for reactions. **Mean number of foods causing symptoms was 10 per patient (range 1 to 30).** Foods most frequently causing symptoms and/or pulse changes were **wheat (78%),** orange (65%), egg (45%), tea and coffee (40% each), chocolate and milk (37%), beef (35%), corn and cane sugar and yeast (33% each), mushrooms (30%) and peas (28%). **When offending foods were** avoided, all patients improved. The number of headaches in the group fell from 402 to 6 per month, with **85% of the patients becoming headache free.** Exclusion only of amine-containing foods (e.g. cheese, chocolate, citrus, and alcohol) significantly reduced the number of headaches, but only 13% became headache free. **All 15 patients with hypertension at the start of the study became normotensive with the diet** plus avoidance of other precipitants.

******

Dees SC. Allergic epilepsy. ANN ALLERGY 1951;9:446

Adamson WB, Sellers ED. Observations on the incidence of the hypersensitive state in one hundred cases of epilepsy. J ALLERGY 1933;5:315

Fein BT, Kamin PB. Allergy, convulsive disorders and epilepsy. ANN ALLERGY, 1968;26:241

Campbell MB. Neurologic manifestations of allergic disease. ANN ALLERGY 1973;31:485

Rea, WJ. Environmentally Triggered Cardiac Disease. ANN ALLERGY, 40(4):243-51.Apr 1978

Crisp AM, Stonehill E, Aspects of the relationships between sleep and nutrition: a study of 375 psychiatric outpatients. BRIT J PSYCH, 122:379-94, 1973

Crook WG, Food allergy - the great masquerade. PED CLIN N AMER, 2:227, 1975

Withrow CD. 1980. The ketogenic diet: mechanism of anti- convulsant action. ADVANCES IN NEUROLOGY, 27(Review):635-42.

Connors CK, Blouin AG, 1983. Nutritional effects on behavior of children. J PSYCHIATRIC RES 17:193-201.

Peters JC, Harper AE, Adaptation of rats to diets containing different levels of protein: effects on food intake, plasma and brain amino acid uncertainties and brain neurotransmitter metabolism. J NUTR 115:382-98, 1985

Pollitt T, Thomson C. Protein-calorie malnutrition and behavior; a view from psychology. In NUTRITION AND THE BRAIN, VOL 2, ed. R.J. Wurtman and J.J. Wurtman, 261-306, Raven, NY, 1977

Spencer PS, Nunn PB, Hugon J, Ludolph AC, Ross SM, Roy DN, Robertson RC, 1987. Guam amyotrophic lateral sclerosis- parkinsonism-dementia linked to a plant excitant neurotoxin. SCIENCE 237:517-22.

Dreyfus PM, Diet and nutrition in neurologic disorders. In MODERN NUTRITION IN HEALTH AND DISEASE, eds. Shils ME, and Young VE, 1458-70, 1988. Lea & Febiger, Phila.

Goodwin JS, Goodwin JM, Garry PJ, 1983. Association between nutrition status and cognitive functioning in a healthy elderly population. JAMA 249:2917-21.

Goode JG, Curtis K, Theophano J, Group-shared food patterns as a unit of analysis. In NUTRITION AND BEHAVIOR, ed. Miller SA, pp.19-30, 1981, Franklin, Phila

Rowe AH Sr, ALLERGIC TOXEMIA. ITS MANIFEST-ATIONS, DIAGNOSIS, AND TREATMENT, Lea & Febiger, Phila, 1931

Randolph TG, Allergy as a causative factor of fatigue, irritability, and behavior problems in children, J PEDIATR 31:560, 1947

Grant E, Food allergies and migraine, J ALLERGY CLIN IMMUNOL, May 1980

Smith BL, Organic foods vs supermarket foods: Elemental levels, J APPL NUTR 45(1):35-39, 1993 (This study shows that organic foods have 2 1/2 times the nutrition of non-organic or conventional supermarket foods).

Kreitsch K, et al, Prevalence, presenting symptoms, and psychological characteristics of individuals experiencing a diet-related mood disturbance, BEHAV THER 19:593-604, 1988

King DS, Can allergic exposure provoke psychological symptoms? A double-blind test, BIOL PSYCHIATRY 16(1):3- 19,1981

Diamond H, Diamond M, FIT FOR LIFE, Warner Bks, NY, 1985

Mandell M, An experimentally induced acute psychotic episode following the intubation of an allergic food, 7th Ann Congr Amer Coll Allerg, Chicago, Ill Feb, 1951

Spring B, Effect of foods and nutrients on the behavior of normal individuals, NUTRITION AND THE BRAIN, VOL 7, cited

Rosenthal NE, Heffernan MM, Bulimia, carbohydrate craving, and depression: A central connection?, ibid

Sibbald B, Rink E, de Souza M. Is the prevalence of atrophy increasing? Br J Gen Pract 1990; 40: 338-40.

Rowe AH. Food allergy, its manifestations, diagnosis and treatment. JAMA 1928; 91: 162-31.

Egger J, Graham PJ, Carter CM et al. Controlled trial of oligoantigenic treatment in the hyperkinetic syndrome. LANCET 1985; 1: 540-545.

Littlewood J, et al, Platelet phenosulphotransferase deficiency in dietary migraine, LANCET 1982;i:983-986

Carter CM, Urbanowicz M, Hemsley R et al. Effects of few foods diet in attention deficit disorder. ARCH DIS CHILD 1993; 69: 654-8.

Egger J, Carter CM, Wilson J et al. Is migraine food allergy? A double-blind controlled trial of oligo-antigenic diet treatment. LANCET 1983; 2:865-9.

Egger J, Carter CM, Soothill JF et al. Oligoantigenic diet treatment of children with epilepsy and migraine. J PEDIATR 1989; 114: 51-8.

Rapp DJ. Weeping eyes in wheat allergy. TRANS AMER SOC OPHTHALMOL AND OTOLARYNGOL 1978; 18: 149.

Rapp DJ. Food allergy treatment for hyperkinesis. J LEARN DIS 1979; 12: 42-50.

Sandberg D. Food sensitivity: the kidney and bladder. In: Brostoff J, Challacombe SJ, eds. FOOD ALLERGY AND INTOLERANCE. London: Bailliere Tindall, 1987, 755-67.

Winkelman RK. Food sensitivity and urticaria or vasculitis. In: Brostoff J, Challacombe SJ, eds. FOOD ALLERGY AND INTOLERANCE. London: Bailliere Tindall, 1987, 602-17.

Hide D. Fatal anaphylaxis due to food. BRIT MED J 1993; 307: 1427.

Lagrue G, et al. Food sensitivity and idiopathic nephrotic syndrome, LANCET, 2: 277, 1987.

Jones V, Shorthouse M, McLoughlan P. Food intolerance, a major factor in the pathogenesis of the irritable bowel syndrome. LANCET 1982; 2: 1117-20.

Riordan AM, Hunter JO, Cowan RE. Treatment of active Crohn's disease by exclusion diet. LANCET 1993; 342: 1131-4.

Grant ECG. Oral contraceptives, smoking, migraine and food allergy. LANCET 1978; 2:581.

Mandell M, Conte A. The role of allergy in arthritis, rheumatism and associated polysymptomatic cerebral, visceral and somatic disorders: a double-blind study. PROC INT ACAD PREV MED 1982; 7: 5-16.

Werbach M, HEALING WITH FOOD, HarperCollins Publishing, Inc. New York 1993.

Hunter BT, YOUR FOOD AND WHAT'S BEEN DONE TO IT. Simon & Schuster, Inc. New York, 1971.

Wurtman RJ, Wurtman JJ, NUTRITION AND THE BRAIN VOL. 7, Raven Press NY, 1986.

Rogers SA, THE SCIENTIFIC BASIS OF SELECTED ENVIRONMENTAL MEDICINE TECHNIQUES, 1994, Sand Key Publ, Box 40101, Sarasota, FL, 34242 (for further food references and the in office technique for testing for food allergy)

DIET, CRIME, AND DELINQUENCY,
LD AND ADHD

There is no question that food has a monumental bearing on brain chemistry and can be a major cause of depression. There is a hefty burden that depression puts on its victims as well as on society that shares to tab for treatment. Yet other off-shoots of the reactions to foods by the brain are equally important. These include crime, delinquency, learning disability, hyperactivity, attention deficit hyperactivity disorder, and other undesirable brain functions.

As you already read, there are many references in the scientific literature for the fact that many times food sensitivity or intolerance is a major causative factor for these diagnoses. Unfortunately, in spite of all this data, children are not worked up for hidden food allergies (much less hidden vitamin, mineral, amino acid, and essential fatty acid deficiencies as you will learn). Instead, the diagnostic label is obtained. Then parents are given a choice of Ritalin (related to street speed or amphetamines, with unknown long- term consequences in the developing brain) or Prozac. In fact, I have seen parents who were told by the school system that unless their child was on a drug, they would not be re-admitted to school. Many of these children carry labels of hyperactivity, LD (learning disability) or ADHD (attention deficit hyperactivity disorder) with them indefinitely. Officials, teachers, and pediatricians rush to drug them, and special educational courses are created. The juvenile delinquent is punished or banished to a detention facility. And as with the juvenile criminal, there is nary a thought as to why his brain chemistry is amok. The foremost goal seems to be to punish and banish him to the same or worse eating habits in an institution. But all these victims, regardless of their useless diagnostic labels, have been grossly cheated by medicine and society if they have not been properly evaluated for undiagnosed food allergies. And as you will read later, there are a host of other entirely curable causes.

REFERENCES:

Garrison RH, Subclinical malnutrition and learning behavior among high school students, INT J BIOSOC RES 9(2): 153-159, 1987.

Schoenthaler SJ, Diet and criminal behavior: a criminological evaluation of the Arlington, Virginia proceedings, INT J BIOSOCIAL RES. Vol. 9(2); 161-181, 1987.

Schoenthaler SJ, Institutional nutritional policies and criminal behavior, NUT TODAY 1985: 20(3); 16-25.

Schoenthaler SJ, Diet and crime: an empirical examination of the value of nutrition in the control and treatment of incarcerated juvenile offenders, INT J BIOSOC RES , 1983: 4(1); 25-39.

Schoenthaler SJ, Doraz WE, Diet and delinquency: a milti- state replication, INT J BIOSOC RES, 1983: 4(2)74-84.

Schoenthaler SJ, The Los Angeles probation department diet- behavior program: an empirical analysis of six institutional settings, INT J BIOSOC RES, 1983 5(2); 88-98.

Schoenthaler SJ, The northern California diet-behavior program: an empirical examination of 3,000 incarcerated juveniles in Stanislaus County Juvenile Hall, INT J BIOSOC RES, 1983: 5(2); 99-106.

Schoenthaler SJ, The effects of citrus on the treatment and control of antisocial behavior: a double-blind study of an incarcerated juvenile population, INT J BIOSOC RES, 1983: 5(2); 107-117.

Schoenthaler SJ, Diet and delinquency: empirical testing of seven theories, INT J BIOSOC RES, 1985: 7(2); 108-131.

Schoenthaler SJ, Doraz WE, Wakefield JA, The impact of a low food additive and sucrose diet on academic performance in 803 New York City public schools, INT J BIOSOC RES, 1986: 8(2); 185-195.

Schoenthaler SJ, Diet and crime and delinquency: a review of the 1983 and 1984 studies, INT J BIOSOC RES, 1984: 6(2); 141- 153.

Schoenthaler SJ, Diet and behavior. NUTR TODAY, 1985: 20(6); 32-35.

Schauss A. DIET CRIME, AND DELINQUENCY. Parker House, Berkeley CA, 1980

Menzies IC, Disturbed children: the role of food and chemical sensitivities, NUTR HEALTH, 1984: 3(1/2); 39-54.

Thratcher RW, Fisbein DH, Computerized EEG, nutrition and behavior, J APPL NUTR, 1984: 36(2); 81-102.

King DS, Psychological and behavioral effects of food and chemical exposure in sensitive individuals, NUTR HEALTH, 1984: 3(3); 137-151.

Rippere V, Some varieties of food intolerance's in psychiatric patients: an overview. PEDIATRICS, 1985: 75; 182-186.

O'Banion DB, Armstrong B, et al, Disruptive behavior: a dietary approach, J AUTISM CHILD SCHIZOPH, 8(1978): 325-337.

Prinz R, et al, Dietary correlates of hyperactive behavior in children, J CONSULT CLIN PSYCHOL, 48: 760-769, 1980.

Radcliffe M, et al, Food allergy in polysymptomatic patients, THE PRACTITIONER, 225: 1651-1654, 1981.

Tryphonas H, et al.   Food allergies in children with hyperactivity, learning disabilities and/or minimal brain dysfunction, ANNALS OF ALLERGY, 42: 22-27, 1979.

Williams J, et al. Relative effects of drugs and diet on hyperactive behaviors: an experimental study, PEDIATRICS, 61: 811-817, 1978.

Crayton JW, Epilepsy precipitated by food sensitivity: report of a case with double-blind placebo-controlled assessment, CLIN ELECT, 12, 192, 1992.

Davidson H, Allergy and the nervous system, QUART REV ALLERGY APPL IMMUNOL, 6: 157, 1952.

Egger J, et al, Oligoantigenic diet treatment of children with epilepsy and migraine, J PED, 114: 51-58, 1989.

O'Shea J, et al. Double-blind study of children with hyperkinetic syndrome treated with multi-allergen extract sublingually, J LEARN DIS, 14: 189, 1981.

Satterfield J, Therapeutic interventions to prevent delinquency in hyperactive boys, J AMER ACAD CHILD ADULT PSYCHOL, 26: 56-64, 1987.

Scarnati R, An outline of hazardous side effects of ritalin (methylphenidate), INT J ADDIC, 21: 837-841, 1986.

Schmidt K, Weir W, Asch M, Clinical ecology treatment approach for juvenile offenders; for a copy of article write to Kenneth Schmidt, Box 693, Atascadero CA 93422.

For an excellent video on the effect of foods on children's brains and for Dr. Rapp's book on how to diagnose and treat food allergies in children, contact the Practical Allergy Research Found-ation, P.O. Box 60, Buffalo, NY 14223-0060, 1-800-787-8780

For an interesting book on balancing your nutrients (carbohydrates, proteins and fat) to optimally help depression, read THE ZONE, by Barry Sears (Harper Collins, NY, 1995). Just be aware that it may not be appropriate for your biochemical type and is loaded with processed foods.

CHAPTER 3

THE CHEMICAL CONNECTION: CAUSES AND CURES

INVISIBLE BRAIN POISONS

If you think you have trouble believing that everyday chemicals found in the average home and office can make people depressed, you can imagine how I felt. I had the most difficult time appreciating the depth of this, even when I was studying it and teaching it to other physicians. But it wasn't until I learned that it was a major cause of not only my depression, but that of hundreds of my patients that I was convinced. At the same time we began to understand where the depression-causing chemicals were found, how they caused depression, and then how to rectify it. These revelations were a major step for us all to become infinitely happier.

One of the big problems with chemical sensitivity is that it usually does not happen dramatically or quickly, but rather insidiously: it **sneaks up** on someone. Remember way back in the 1970's when people used urea foam formaldehyde insulation and the formaldehyde caused numerous symptoms? Well one of the main symptoms was depression. But as usual, medicine tends to ignore this symptom and place much higher emphasis on things that can be physically seen such as rashes, or heard such as asthma, or documented with x-rays such as pneumonia or arthritis.

The brain always seems to be treated as though it couldn't be a target organ and that any symptoms related to the brain must belong on the psychiatrist's couch. Furthermore, **most chemical sensitivities sneak up on a person over a period of weeks, months, or years, as the detoxification system is slowly damaged.** Occasionally, there will be a dramatic sudden onset of depression, for example, when new carpeting is installed or a building is renovated or freshly painted.

Usually depression caused by chemicals is also accompanied by many other chemically induced symptoms. These can include headache, inability to concentrate, mood swings out of proportion to life events, schizophrenia, and many other symptoms. In fact, it can be any symptom you can think of. Sometimes these symptoms over-shadow the depression and it takes a back seat. The depression is disregarded as a symptom and thought to be a "normal" result from having all the other medical problems.

We know now that many of these chemicals can cause depression by a variety of routes. For example, Evelyn was horribly depressed. When we worked her up we found that she had a zinc deficiency. Zinc runs the enzyme alcohol dehydrogenase and this is a major enzyme in detoxifying everyday home and office chemicals. One thing that Evelyn did not detoxify well because of her zinc deficiency was trichloroethylene. This chemical can be found out-gassing from carpets, home furnishings, copy machines, secretarial white-out, shampoos, commercial floor cleansers, polishes, plastics, waxes, glues and adhesives, and of course it is a common solvent in most industries or factories. It was a major part of her daily exposure in the plastics factory where she worked.

Another case was of an elderly woman who had just become a widow after 48 wonderful years. Because she no longer needed such a large home, her children set her up in a beautiful retirement condo. She became horribly depressed, but everyone assumed it was an extension of her grief reaction. But she continued to go down-hill rapidly over the first year. She became so senile, that her children had to take her out of the condo and find a facility with skilled nursing that could take care of her.

The neat thing was that in the month wait between checking out of the condo and entering the nursing home, she had to temporarily live with her daughter in her home. And much to their amazement, she became **"unsenile" and undepressed. Her depression and "senility" were her brain's reaction to the hydrocarbons that out-gassed from the new condo carpet** and construction materials. And getting her out of the condo was the cure she needed. We saw her and found nutrient deficiencies in her detox pathways that then helped her be less vulnerable to future exposures.

Also trichloroethylene out-gasses readily from freshly dry cleaned clothes. I remember one time I was sitting in the audience of an international symposium for physicians who were studying chemical sensitivity. One of the doctors who was very chemically sensitive was seated next to me and said, "Sherry, I don't want to hurt your feelings, but your jacket is making me very sick."

Suddenly I realized that I had just picked this jacket up from the dry cleaners and I had been feeling under par all morning since I had put it on. I took the jacket off and put it in the back of the room. I started to feel much improved. In fact, the next hour I gave my own lecture without a jacket and felt wonderful.

BRAIN FOG

So how does a simple chemical like dry cleaning fluid, or trichloroethylene (TCE), or perchloroethylene cause depression? There are many ways. For one, you can absorb it through the skin as in wearing dry cleaned clothes. Many medicines like estrogen patches, nitroglycerin patches, and motion sickness patches capitalize on the ability of the skin to transport substances in contact with it directly to the blood. Another way to get an environmental chemical into the body is by inhaling it. So the TCE or formaldehyde from a new carpet is in the blood stream just as easily as carbon monoxide can be inhaled to cause a fatal poisoning. It circulates through all the organs including the brain. If the brain cannot properly metabolize it and get rid of it or detoxify it, it backs up and accumulates in the brain.

When trichloroethylene is stored in the brain, sometimes it is converted to an alternative chemical, called chloral hydrate. Those of you my age and older will remember **chloral hydrate** as the old "Mickey Finn" or **knockout drops.** And that is exactly how a person feels who is sensitive to trichloroethylene. He feels spacey, dizzy, dopey, unable to concentrate, foggy or very depressed.

Other chemicals can do the very same thing as formaldehyde and trichloroethylene. Toluene out-gasses from paints, construction materials, plastics, home furnishings such as furniture, glues, over stuffed chairs, carpets and much more. And all of these chemicals (toluene, formaldehyde, trichloroethylene and more) are part of the ingredients of auto exhaust. Plus one of the heaviest places of chemical overload is, for the average person, a shopping mall. Because there you have a wide variety of new plastics and fabrics out-gassing.

In 1985, I was lecturing in China for three weeks with Dr. Theron Randolph (the physician who first discovered chemical sensitivity) and Dr. William Rea. My husband and I had just entered a store and could smell the glues for Formica countertops and hear the buzzing of saws and pounding of hammers. We agreed to split up for a few minutes while I picked up some items and Luscious looked over some near-by items. In a few minutes he came to retrieve me only to find his adult wife reduced to a waif huddled in the corner, crying uncontrollably, "Everybody else got all the good stuff, there is nothing left for us." Recognizing that I was helplessly out of my gourd, he gently picked me up by the scruff of my neck and said, "Well, that's enough glue-sniffing for you for one day." Twenty minutes into our walk outside on the streets of Hong Kong, I began to recover.

"Come on, I didn't say those things! You're kidding aren't you? Did I really embarrass you by sitting on the floor in a corner crying?"

Fortunately by that time in 1985, we knew too well how quickly the brain could be adversely affected by chemicals, and we knew how to get me out of it quickly. In earlier years, such was not the case and these reactions could persist for days. You can imagine the devastating effect this puzzling disease can have on relationships. It is frequently misdiagnosed as depression, manic depression, schizophrenia, hysteria, attention-seeking neurotic tendency, etc. Unfortunately, each of these labels implies that a drug is needed to control the symptoms. And cause becomes inconsequential.

Nowadays, I don't think I could get such a severe reaction, because I am infinitely healthier and more resistant to the effects of everyday chemicals Also, I am acutely aware of the most minor of warnings that I might be vulnerable, and try to take immediate measures to be sure to never get myself into such misery again.

Brain fog often accompanies the depression of chemical sensitivity, but it rarely is steady. In other words, it comes and goes. One day you are pretty clear or one part of the day. By contrast the next day or another part of the same day you can feel like an absolute **"space cadet";** it is very difficult to concentrate, and you feel spacey, dizzy, and dopey. Or your reaction may just be depression. This symptom in the medical literature is called **toxic encephalopathy,** but we who have had it and have experienced its agony firsthand call it the simpler term ---brain fog.

One researcher (Baker EL, A review of recent research on health effects of human occupational exposure to organic solvents. A critical review, JOURNAL OF OCCUPATIONAL AND ENVIRONMENTAL MEDICINE, October 1994, 36:10, 1079-1092) did a wonderful study. Dr. Edward L. Baker is director of the Public Health Practice Program office at the Centers of Disease Control and Prevention in Atlanta. He has carefully examined 16 scientific studies of chemically-triggered toxic encephalopathy (brain fog) from around the world involving more than 1,000 exposed workers in 6 countries and on 3 continents.

His results show that **toxic encephalopathy or brain fog** is a real phenomenon. He examined the results of researchers who have studied the effects of chemicals on twins and on people in the same occupation but in different locations. He studied brain fog in the literature from researchers using different diagnostic techniques and in studies that spanned over 15 years. In other words, he looked at brain fog studies inside out and upside down and from as many vantage points as he could to determine its nature.

The result is that no longer can anyone doubt that the 500 plus chemicals in the average city water and the average daily home environment are capable of crossing the blood brain barrier and creating brain fog and/or depression. It is fact, substantiated by many scientific publications. The major problem is that the majority of physicians who treat depression are unfamiliar with all this data. They have had no training in how to diagnose and treat depression caused by chemical sensitivity.

Everyday chemicals have the potential to interfere with the metabolism of brain neurotransmitters or happy hormones in a myriad of pathways. They interfere with synthesis and metabolism, they block receptor sites, poison enzymes, and much more. **Benzene** is common in gasoline, auto exhaust, room fresheners, adhesives for furnishings and construction materials. Styrene comes from plastics. Aluminum that can cause depression as well as Alzheimer's comes from drinking water, juice boxes, canned foods and drinks. And fluoride has many sources, one of which is Prozac. Meanwhile, all these chemicals can have damaging effects on brain neurotransmitters.

Chemical sensitivity can be tested in a variety of ways. We can measure the blood levels of chemicals before and after exposure to prove cause and effect (Accu-chem Labs, Richardson, TX). We can measure the efficiency of various parts of the detoxication pathways (phase I and phase II) before and after exposures, and we can measure whether the total chemical load in one environment versus another is too high and causing lipid peroxidation, glutathione depletion, accelerated aging, and further damage to the detox pathways (Great Smokies Laboratory, 1-800 522-4762). And we can test the effect of the chemical on the person in the office by the intradermal technique that we published in the U.S. government's N.I.H. medical journal, ENVIRONMENTAL HEALTH PERSPECTIVES (paper appears in toto in appendix of TIRED OR TOXIC?).

To give an idea of the usefulness of the technique, Joan had serious bouts of depression that left even her sweet and intelligent self doubting her own sanity. So double blind testing was done to salt water and other innocuous antigens. Then when we tested phenol (she did not know until all testing was complete what she was being tested to) she suddenly became overwhelmed with depression. She burst into uncontrollable tears, and behaved the way she did when she first became depressed. The same year they painted at work her depression surfaced. We could likewise turn her depression off with the proper neutralizing dose.

For Nancy, when we tested her to phenol, she became overtly schizophrenic. She started taking to the ceiling, just as she had the year she started working in a mall and had built a log cabin home. Likewise, the symptom could be terminated with the proper dose of phenol (provocation-neutralization technique).

REFERENCES:

Echeverria D, White RW, Sampaio C, A behavioral evaluation of PCE exposure in patients and dry cleaners: a possible relationship between clinical and preclinical effects, JOEM, 37:6, 667-680, June 1995.

Randolph, T.G.: Domiciliary chemical air pollution in the etiology of ecologic mental illness. INT J SOC PSYCHIATRY 16,243,1970.

Selye, H, The General Adaption. J ALLERGY 17:231-247; 289- 323;358,46.

Randolph, T.G.: The Specific Adaption Syndrome. J LAB CLIN MED 48: 934,56.

Meggs W, Neurogenic inflammation and sensitivity to environmental chemicals, ENVIRON HEALTH PERSPECT, 101:3. 234-238, 1993

Randolph, T.G.: The Ecologic Unit. HOSPITAL MANAGEMENT 97:45-47, March 1964 and 97:46, April, 1964.

Randolph, T.G.: PROC NATIONAL CONFERENCE ON AIR POLLUTION, U.S. Dept. of Health, Education and Welfare. Public Health Service Publication No.1022, U.S. Government Printing Office, Washington, D.C. , 1963 p.157.

Randolph, T.G.: Ecologic mental illness-levels of central nervous system reactions. PROC. THIRD WORLD CONGRESS OF PSYCHIATRY, Vol 1, Montreal, Canada, Univ. of Toronto Press, pp. 379-384, June 1961.

Randolph, T.G.: Allergic factors in the etiology of certain mental symptoms. J LAB CLIN MED, 36:977, Dec 1950

Randolph TG, Sensitivity to petroleum, including its derivatives and antecedents. J LAB CLIN MED, 40:931-932, Dec 1952.

Randolph TG, Depression caused by home exposures to gas and combustion products of gas, oil and coal, J LAB CLIN MED, 46:942, Dec 1955

Randolph TG, Ecologic mental illness-psychiatry exteriorized, J LAB CLIN MED, 54:936, Dec 1959

Randolph TG, Clinical Ecology as it Effects the Psychiatric Patient, INTERNAT J SOC PSYCHIATRY, 12:245-254, 1966

Randolph TG, Human Ecology and Susceptibility to the Chemical Environment, ANN ALLERGY 19:518-540, 1961

Randolph TG, HUMAN ECOLOGY AND SUSCEPTIBILITY TO THE CHEMICAL ENVIRONMENT, Charles C. Thomas Publ, Springfield, IL, 1962

Kailin E, Brooks C, Systemic toxic reaction to soft plastic food containers: a double-blind study, MED ANN DC, 32:1, 1-8, 1963

Randolph TG, A third dimension of the medical investigation, CLIN PHYSIOL, 2:1-5, winter 1960

Randolph TG, The provocative hydrocarbon test, Preliminary report, J LAB CLIN MED, 64:995, Dec 1964,

Simon GE, Allergic to life: psychological factors and environmental illness, et al, AMER J PSYCH, 147:7, 901-905, July 1990.

Randolph TG, Man-made seasonal sickness, J LAB CLIN MED, 62:1005-1006, 1963

Bland JS, A functional approach to mental illness. A new paradigm for managing brain biochemical disturbances, TOWNSEND LETTER FOR DOCTORS, 1335-1340, Dec 1994

U.S. Department of Health & Human Services, TOXICOLOGICAL PROFILE FOR STYRENE, Wash DC, Oct 1990

U.S. Department of Health & Human Services, TOXICOLOGICAL PROFILE FOR BENZENE, Wash DC, Oct 1992

Kahn MF, Bourgeois P, et al, Mixed connective tissue disease after exposure to polyvinyl chloride, J RHEUMATOL, 16:4, 533-535, 1989

Tanner CM, The role of environmental toxins in the etiology of Parkinson's disease, TINS, 12:, 49-53, 1989

Bigazzi PE, Mechanism of chemical-induced auto-immunity, IMMUNOTOXICOLOGY & IMMUNOPHARMACOLOGY, eds. J Dean, et al, Raven Press, NY, 1985,

Mc Kinnon RA, Nebert DW, Possible role of cytochromes P450 in Lupus erythematosis and related disorders, LUPUS 3:473-478, 1994

Zamora PO, Gregory RE, Brooks AL, In vitro evaluation of the tumor-promoting potential of diesel-exhaust-particle extracts, J TOXICOL ENVIRON HEALTRH, 11:187-197, 1983

Feldman RG, Ricks NL, Baker EL, Neuropsychological effects of industrial toxins: a review, AM J INDUST MED, 1:211-227, 1980

PESTICIDES

One of the worst chemicals to cause chemical sensitivity and depression is the family of pesticides. Pesticides were originally **designed as nerve gasses for chemical warfare**. When it was found that they were so good at killing humans, it was decided to use smaller doses to kill insects, worms, rodents, weeds, and much more.

Of course, one of the **chief target organs affected by pesticides is the brain.** And as you might now guess, depression is one of the primary symptoms that can result. The problem is that chronic pesticide poisoning is a cause for depression that is very insidious or sneaky. Sure it can happen all of a sudden after one particular exposure. But normally it happens very slowly over many unsuspected exposures, so that you barely realize it is happening and rarely suspect the cause.

Most schools, offices, and public buildings are pesticided in the evening, or on weekends, or after hours when no one sees it. So if you come in and start feeling lousy, cranky, or depressed throughout the day, it's unlikely that you are going to investigate the pesticide history of the building. More often you will leave the imprint of your mood on those unlucky enough to be around you. Fortunately, as you will learn, there are several ways to diagnose and treat pesticide-induced depression.

REFERENCES:

Kaloyanova FP, Batawi MA, HUMAN TOXICOLOGY OF PESTICIDES, CRC Press, Boca Raton FL, 1991.

Duffy FH, et al, Long-term effects of an organophosphate upon the human electroencephalogram, TOXICOL APPL PHARM 47, 161-176, 1979.

Hierons R, et al, Clinical and toxicological investigations of a case of delayed neuropathy in man after acute poisoning by an organophosphorus pesticide, ARCH TOXICOL 40, 279-284, 1978.

Tabershaw IR, et al, Sequelae of acute organic phosphate poisoning, J OCCUP MED 8:5-20, 1966.

Kurtz PJ, Dissociated behavioral and cholinesterase decrements following malathion exposure, TOXICOL APPL PHARMACOL 42:489-594, 1977. (This study shows that a low dose of malathion may disrupt behavior without significantly reducing cholinesterase activity, the blood test used to diagnose it. In other words, you can have a pesticide exposure that results in depression. But when a physician tells you that the blood test to show whether or not you are poisoned by the pesticide is negative, it does not rule out exposure as the cause).

Rea WJ, et al, Pesticides and brain function changes in a controlled environment, CLIN ECOL 2;3:145, 1984.

Callender T, Morrow L, Subramanian, Evaluation of chronic neurological sequelae after acute pesticide exposure using SPECT brain scans, J TOXICOL ENVIRON HEALTH, 41:275-284, 1993

Kailin E, Brooks C, Cerebral disturbances from small amounts of DDT; a controlled study, MED ANN DC, 32:1;1-8, 1966

ARE YOU A DEPRESSED DURSBAN DUMMY?
OR DO YOU JUST HAVE THE DURSBAN DEPRESSION?

Dursban (chlorpyrifos) is the most commonly used pesticide indoors and out (Aspelin). And it is a sneaky one and a nasty one. First there is no environment where you won't find it, as it is used on over 40 crops, on beef cattle and their feed, lawns, gardens, golf courses, and for foundation termites. It is found in plastics and textiles. Indoors it is used in **17% of households,** and is routinely sprayed in schools, offices, institutions, cafeterias, restaurants, on pets for fleas and ticks, and around the home for wasps. It is the most ubiquitous pesticide.

As an organophosphate, its action is to **inhibit the enzyme acetylcholinesterase.** This enzyme controls the metabolism or breakdown of the **number one neurotransmitter or happy hormone of the brain, acetylcholine.** This is the stuff that jumps across nerve junctions to make the nervous system conduct its electricity. It is the basic chemical that makes the brain and all the nerves and muscles work. And the action of pesticides is to poison this primary happy hormone!.

If that were not enough damage, pesticides also can inhibit or poison other enzymes like **ATPase** (necessary for the chemistry of energy), which results in **chronic fatigue.** And pesticides can inhibit the enzyme **cholesterol ester hydrolase,** resulting in **impaired cholesterol metabolism.** So to treat high cholesterol with a drug that inhibits cholesterol absorption will only make a person worse. And as you will learn, there is a higher rate of suicide in people on cholesterol-lowering drugs, because they failed to identify the real cause and fix it. And by taking cholesterol-lowering drugs you deprive the brain of the cholesterol it needs to make happy hormones. But more on that later. Pesticides also inhibit other enzymes that change how the body/mind handles stress (Civen), making a person less adaptable.

What is worse is that **chlorpyrifos (Dursban) is taken directly into the nervous system** (brain, spinal cord and long nerves) and is transformed to chlopyrifos-oxon. Yes, Dursban is actually metabolized into a compound that is **3000 times more potent** to the brain than the original or parent compound, chlorpyrifos (Chambers). If the body cannot metabolize all the pesticide you breathe in at once, it stores it in various tissues and organs and it slowly leaks out weeks, months, or years later (Chambers). **So new symptoms can begin long after the exposure has ended.**

The **danger** is that **pesticides cause delayed behavior changes, memory loss, and depression.** And these changes can come on very slowly, over a long time, so that they are barely perceptible (Bushnell, Pope). And when finally a problem is realized, rarely is pesticide poisoning looked for. Instead another chemical, like an anti-depressant, is added to a system that is already poisoned.

There are many other symptoms from pesticides besides depression, which is our focus. Delayed neuropathy with numbness, tingling, paralysis, poor coordination, weakness, cramps: and not all reversible (Fikes). And you can get any of these symptoms **from a single dose.** And Dursban exposure has lead to the development of **chemical sensitivity**, classic **brain fog** with inability to concentrate, degeneration of the retina, **auto-immunity**, and much more (Thrasher).

Dursban might be more familiar to you as **Raid Home Insect Killer, Ortho Flea-B Gon, D-Con Home Pest Control Killer,**

Spectracide Yard Flea and Tick Killer, or Spectracide Pet Flea and Tick Killer. But don't let the benign names fool you. Studies on various lengths and modes of exposures show a high rate of depression. The brain is a chief target organ, as pesticides are lipid seekers, and the brain is a highly lipid area. It also has a high density of acetylcholinesterase, the target enzyme of pesticides.

Besides depression, **organophosphate pesticides like Dursban** cause a loss of memory, problem solving ability, intellect, mental flexibility and abstraction capabilities, and cause paranoia, irritability, social withdrawal, anxiety, **brain fog, schizophrenia**, and sensitivity to criticism, to name a few. And this ignores the symptoms like **neuropathy** and paralysis, not to mention all the other target organs like kidney, heart, liver or lung disease, as examples. And do not forget its mutagenicity (ability to promote cancer cells) and teratogenecity (ability to cause birth defects), infertility, and a host of other permanent problems if it is not diagnosed and treated.

Pesticide poisoning, if it is **acute or sudden**, is easy to diagnose. Nausea, vomiting, cramps, dizziness, sweating, drooling, and convulsions are difficult to miss, but the chest pain can mimic a heart attack. Unfortunately, pesticide poisoning that causes depression is usually the delayed onset type, that may not begin to manifest symptoms until weeks or months after an exposure.

Many bizarre cases have given us a plethora of information. One unlucky group of professionals who get unexpectedly exposed are pilots. In fact it is a cause of **pilot error** and crashes. Yet it is not a requirement to measure levels of stored pesticide, much less the pilot's ability to detoxify these chemicals. In fact conventional medicine does not know how, relying on inferior tests. And it was learned from a few pilot cases that again, the symptoms can be much delayed after exposure, which further throws off suspicion from the real culprit.

Many cases in office workers and others have shown us that the blood test which conventional medicine relies on for diagnosis is worthless. Furthermore, the symptoms can persist for an inordinate amount of time, which is what you would expect. For any chemical that does not belong in the body puts a stress on the detox system and continuously depletes the detoxification nutrients as it persists as an uninvited guest. But the body uses up vitamins and minerals and other nutrients, as you will learn, in the work of trying to detoxify and get rid of pesticides. So when further silent exposures keeping adding to the total body burden of pesticide, and the detox nutrients keep getting lower, there is less ability for the body left with which to detoxify new chemicals. This process snowballs as it accelerates further deficiencies and produces more symptoms.

But worst of all, in regard to our interest in undiagnosed causes of depression, **Dursban inhibits the conversion of tryptophan into serotonin.** And serotonin is a temporary "happy hormone" in the brain, in fact the one that Prozac works on. And if not nasty enough by itself, Dursban is not infrequently combined with a pesticide from another class, like **Dieldrin** (which is an organochloride). Now you have the additional power to deplete brain happy hormones like **norepinephrine and dopamine,** as well as serotonin. What a disaster you can make of a person's brain! You can produce any mood disorder you can think of with this cocktail.

Furthermore, studies show the effects of Dursban and its class of pesticides can **persist or last months and years.** During this time they can decrease future tolerance to other chemical exposures. This in turn can foster the development of chemical sensitivity, which can then mimic any symptom.

So if you do not know the pesticide policy where you work, and if you allow pesticiding in your home or on your property, you may have the cause of your depression. For the diagnosis and treatment, see Volume IV. And for techniques which go way beyond the scope of this book, see TIRED OR TOXIC?, then WELLNESS AGAINST ALL ODDS.

REFERENCES:

Aspelin AL, 1994. PESTICIDE INDUSTRY SALES AND USAGE: 1992 AND 1993 MARKET ESTIMATES. Wash. DC; U.S.EPA. Office of Prevention, Pesticides and Toxic Substances. Office of Pesticide Programs. Biological and Economic Analysis Division (June).

Chambers JE, et al, 1993. Inhibition patterns of brain acetylcholinesterase and hepatic and plasma aliesterases following exposures to three phosphorothionate insecticides and their oxons in rat. FUND APPL TOXICOL 21:111-119.

Chambers JE, et al, 1989. Bioactivation and detoxification of organophosphorous insecticides in rat brains. in J Caldwell, DH Hutson, and GD Paulson, INTERMEDIARY XENOBIOTIC METABOLISM: METHODOLOGY, MECHANISMS, AND SIGNIFICANCE. Basingstoke, UK, Taylor & Francis, 99-115.

Civen MCB, et al, 1977. Effects of organophosphate insecticides on adrenal cholesteryl ester and steroid metabolism. BIOCHEM PHARMACOL 26:1901-1907.

Pope CN, 1992. Long-term neurochemical and behavioral effects induced by acute chlorpyrifos treatment. PHARMACOL BIOCHEM BEHAV 42:251-256.

Bushnell PJ, et al, 1993. Behavioral and neurochemical effects of acute chlorpyrifos in rats. Tolerance to prolonged inhibition of cholinesterase. J PHARMACOL EXPER THERA, 266(2):1007-1017.

Bushnell PJ, et al, 1994. Repeated inhibition of cholinesterase by chlorpyrifos in rats; Behavioral, neurochemical and pharmacological indices of tolerance, J PHARMACOL EXPER THERA 270(1):15-25.

Fikes JD, 1992. Clinical, biochemical, electrophysiologic, and histologic assessment of chlorpyrifos induced delayed neuropathy in the cat. NEUROTOXICOLOGY 134:663-678.

Thrasher JD, et al, 1993. Immunologic abnormalities in humans exposed to chlorpyrifos: Preliminary observations, ARCH ENVIRON HEALTH 48(2):89-93.

Jager KW, et al, Neuromuscular function in pesticide workers, BRIT J INDUSTR MED, 1970, 27, 273-278.

Dille JR, Central nervous system effects of chronic exposure to organophosphate insecticides, AEROSPACE MEDICINE, 35475- 478, May 1964.

Smith PW, et al, Cholinesterase inhibition in relation to fitness to fly, AEROSPACE MED, 39:754-758, July 1968.

Wood W, et al, Implication of organophosphate pesticide poisoning in the plane crash of a duster pilot, AEROSPACE MED, 10:1111-1113, 1971.

Senanayake N, et al, Neurotoxic effects of organophoshorus insecticides, N ENG J MED 1987;316:761-7631.

Rosenthal NE, et al, Exaggerated sensitivity to an organophosphate pesticide, AM J PSYCHIATRY, 148:2, 1991.

Hodgson MJ, et al, Organophosphate poisoning in office workers, J OCCUP MED, 28:434, 1986.

Organophosphate toxicity associated with flea-dip products: California, JAMA 260:22, 1988.

McKellar RL, et al, Residues of chlorpyrifos, its oxygen analogue, and 3,5,6-trichloro-2-pyridinol in milk and cream from cows fed chlorpyrifos. J AGR FOOD CHEM 24:283, 1976.

Joubert PH, et al, Chorea and psychiatric changes in organophosphate poisoning, S AFR MED J, 74;1:32-34, 1988.

Savage EP, et al, Chronic neurological sequelae of acute organophosphate pesticide poisoning, ARCH ENVIRON HEALTH, 43;1:38-45, 1988.

Gershon S, et al, Psychiatric sequelae of chronic exposure to organophosphorus insecticides, LANCET, 1371-1374, June 24, 1961.

Banks A, et al, Effects of chronic reactions in acetylcholinesterase activity on serial problem-solving behavior, J COMPARA PHYSIOLOG PSYCHOL, 64;2:262-267, 1967.

Anonymous, Pesticides may alter brain function, SCI NEWS, 129:88, Feb 8, 1986.

Sharma RP, Brain biogenic amines: Depletion by chronic dieldrin exposure, LIFE SCI 13:1245-1251, 1973.

Kohli KK, et al, Stimulation of serotonin metabolism by dieldrin, J NEUROCHEM 28:1397-1398, 1977.

Henderson M, et al, Do organophosphate insecticides inhibit the conversion of tryptophan to NAD+ in ovo?, TERATOLOGY, 26;2:173-181, Oct 1982.

Tabershaw IR, et al, Sequelae of acute organic phosphate poisoning, J OCCUP MED, 8;5:5-20, 1966.

Duffy FH, et al, Long-term effects of an organophosphate upon the human electroencephalogram, TOXICOL APPL PHARMACOL 47:161-176, 1979.

Nag M, Nandi N, Inhibition of monoamine oxidase activity by some organophosphate pesticides, IND J EXPER BIOL, 25, Aug 1987, 567-568.

Leiss JK, Savitz DA, Home pesticide use and childhood cancer: a case-control study, AM J PBLIC HALTH, 85:249-252, 1995

INERT INGREDIENTS

If that were not enough, envision a can of pesticide. On the label it gives you the long fancy chemical name of what the pesticide is and then it tells you that **99.9%** of the rest of the container is made of "inert ingredients". What this means is that this **vehicle** for the spray (also called the **carrier**) is supposed to be a harmless material and oftentimes it is a trade secret so that you cannot find out what it is anyway. If it is so harmless, why didn't they just use water? Or at least tell what is in it?

Unfortunately, the reason is simple. It is not inert. Many of the inert ingredient formulas contain a mixture of the very organic solvents that cause depression that we just talked about. These "inert ingredients" can include formaldehyde, toluene, benzene, trichloroethylene, as well as kerosene derivatives. And you already learned how these are far from harmless as they can cause severe depression by themselves. Plus the "inert ingredients" often contain other pesticides, and much more. So this can more than double or even triple the potential for the pesticide to be a sneaky, hidden cause of depression.

Koppell GO, THE SECRET HAZARDS OF PESTICIDES: INERT INGREDIENTS, New York State Dept of Law, Attorney General's Information Line, 1-800-771-7755, Albany NY, 1991.

NATURAL GAS

One of the primary home chemicals that is responsible for a significant amount of depression is natural gas. I have seen literally hundreds of people who have found that they were no longer depressed once they got rid of their gas: stove, water heater, clothes dryer, and heating system.

In the women's magazines there are frequently stories of entire families who became depressed and had many other symptoms when their heating system malfunctioned. One member of the family would have nausea, stomach or intestinal symptoms, another arthritis and body aches, and another headaches. And even the pets would have rashes, arthritis or lethargy. But depression is the major prominent symptom of natural gas sensitivity.

REFERENCES:

Randolph TG, Sensitivity to Petroleum: Including its derivatives and antecedents. J LAB CLIN MED, 40:931-932, Dec 1952.

Randolph TG, Depression caused by home exposures to gas and combustion products of gas, oil and coal, J LAB CLIN MED, 46:942, Dec 1955

Boris M, Boris G, Weindorf S, Association of otitis media with exposure to gas fuels, CLIN ECOL 3:195-198, 1986.

TOXIC ENCEPHALOPATHY:
AN EPIDEMIC IN DISGUISE

Toxic what? **Encephalopathy** means something wrong with the brain. And toxic encephalopathy means a brain that is toxic or poisoned and does not function properly because of some environmental toxin or chemical.

Toxic encephalopathy is just the medical word for under-diagnosed **brain fog**. The classic symptoms are often erroneously chalked up to normal aging, stress, poor memory, or a bad personality. Many people do not know that there is a cause and a cure for brain fog or toxic encephalopathy. In fact, many do not know that there is a silent epidemic of this.

What are the **symptoms of brain fog?** Dopey, dizzy, spacey, can't concentrate, poor memory, depressed for no reason, loss of interest, confusion, fatigue for no reason, or mood swings out of proportion to the trigger.

And the **causes of brain fog?** For many they are the everyday chemicals found in furnishings, building construction materials, cosmetics, toiletries, traffic exhaust, office supplies, pesticides, their "inert" carrier solutions for pesticides, as an example, and much more.

It might seem like a flight into fantasy to think that seemingly "harmless" everyday chemicals can affect the brain. But actually it is the number one target organ affected. For these chemicals can diffuse through the nose and lung membranes right into the blood stream and brain rather rapidly. And once there, if the person is low in any vitamins or minerals in the pathways to rapidly detoxify the chemical, then the

111

undetoxified amount backs up and starts to do its damage, producing these bizarre symptoms.

The danger lies in the fact that this erratic function of the brain can lead to accidents. As discussed, the inhalation of jet exhaust has been the cause of some **pilot error**. But there is no test of brain function in jet exhaust when in the flight simulator. Not knowing you have brain fog considerably jeopardizes personal relationships too, if it suddenly provokes mood swings. Or it can cause a child to be erroneously labeled as **learning disabled or attention deficit disorder or poor achiever**. It can lead to **poor work performance, depression** and the need for antidepressants, and is in part responsible for our current epidemic of Prozac use. And brain fog can lead to even criminal acts.

Fortunately, thanks to the studies of Dr. Edward L. Baker, Director of Public Health Practice Program at the Centers for Disease Control and Prevention in Atlanta Georgia, we understand that it is not a figment of our imaginations.

As shown earlier, he has carefully examined 16 studies of toxic encephalopathy from around the world involving more than 1000 exposed workers in 6 different countries on 3 different continents. And his results show that toxic encephalopathy is a real phenomenon. He has examined the studies of researchers who have studied the effects of chemicals on twins, and in people in the same occupations but in different plants, and using different diagnostic tests, and in studies spanning a period of 15 years. Yes, the evidence is now rolling in faster everyday and this doctor has done a superlative job of collating the studies.

No, you're not having "deja vu". I've repeated this again on purpose, after you have had a chance to digest the many new things you are learning. For **brain fog is such a common cause of depression and so frequently goes undiagnosed,** that I want to be sure you are not an unsuspecting victim of this tragedy.

No longer can anyone assume that the over 500 chemicals in the average U.S. municipal water supply are without effect on the body. Nor can they assume that the over 500 chemicals in the everyday home environment are benign. And neither are the hundreds of new chemicals that are invented each year harmless. We now know, for example, that when the brain is unable to detoxify some of these chemicals, it actually manufactures **chloral hydrate** in the brain, better known as the old "Mickey Finn" or knock-out drops. And these are exactly the symptoms of brain fog. Yes, we understand the chemistry and how to diagnose and treat this (for more, read TIRED OR TOXIC?).

But much good has come out of this. Because now that you have had your awareness piqued, you may be intrigued to discover how to diagnose and treat the symptoms. For example, often when chemically sensitive people are exposed to particular chemicals, such as perfumes, or formaldehyde or toluene in a shopping mall, they may suffer brain fog symptoms like depression, a headache or dizziness for days. Now there are inexpensive techniques that can be done at home (WELLNESS AGAINST ALL ODDS), where you can reverse the reaction within minutes.

And brain fog or toxic encephalopathy can be proven now radiologically (with x-ray techniques) with what is called a SPECT scan. But there are special techniques that the radiologist must know. But they are not known by conventionally trained radiologists who are not on the cutting edge of environmental medicine. However, the information is available in our journals, books, and courses for physicians.

So don't be surprised if through your reading you discover that you are not lazy, you're not stupid, you're not losing your mind. You're not tired, but toxic. You're not pooped, but poisoned. You're not dizzy or depressed or dopey. You are really suffering from an epidemic in disguise, brain fog or toxic encephalopathy.

REFERENCES:

Simon TR, Seastrunk JW, et al, Drug abuse: Diagnosis and therapy with SPECT. Radiological Society of N. Amer., 1991, RADIOLOGY 181 (P):129, 1991.

Simon TR, Hickey DC, Rea WJ, Johnson AR, Ross GM, et al, Breast implants and organic solvent exposure can be associated with abnormal cerebral SPECT studies in clinically impaired patients. Radiolog. Soc. of N.Amer., 1992, RADIOLOGY 185(P):234, 1992.

Baker EL, A review of recent research on health effects of human occupational exposure to organic solvents. A critical review, J OCCUP MED,36:10 1079-1092, Oct 1994

Callendae TL, Morrow K, et al, Three-dimensional brain metabolic imaging in patients with toxic encephalopathy, ENVIRON RES 60:295-319, 1993

THE TOXIC TEACHER SYNDROME

Each year we see scores of teachers who have the same story. It goes something like this: Because there was an increasing need for their special educational services, a new classroom had to be created for them. Sometimes the "new" room was actually a larger room that was partitioned off into smaller rooms. This partitioning often left the newly created room without windows and/or without the full use of the ventilation system. Sometimes, the room was a converted janitor's closet where cleaning supplies, pesticides, mops and buckets had been stored. Because it was originally designed as a storage closet, it also had no windows and was not part of the ventilation system.

As part of the renovation, the newly partitioned room or closet was emptied, painted and carpeted. Children who took classes in this room usually did so for a maximum of one period a day. But the teacher often spent her entire day, five days a week, in this renovated, under-ventilated small room.

Over a period of time, she developed a large array of symptoms, depending upon the individual; but the most common by far, were usually "brain fog" and depression. She gradually became spacey, dizzy, dopey, felt as though she couldn't concentrate well and was exhausted and depressed for no apparent reason. She usually had a host of other complaints that seemed unrelated, such as headaches, recurrent sinus infections, body aches and arthritis, nausea and irritable bowel, unexplained mood swings, painful or irregular menstrual periods and much more. But one of the predominating symptoms, solo or not was depression. It could come on quickly, almost overnight. But usually it sneaked up on the victim, waxing and waning as it slowly

115

built by imperceptible amounts over months. Then suddenly it became overwhelming and took center stage.

Also, she often had begun to react to (have symptoms associated with) exposures to chemicals that never before bothered her. Reactions were to such common articles as new carpeting, perfumes, cigarette smoke, paint, felt tip marking pens, and auto exhaust. The same thing happened with many foods where she could now precipitate symptoms by eating certain foods that had never bothered her before. For example, eating sugars or wheat would accentuate the brain fog or fatigue or depression.

Some of these toxic teachers were better on weekends, others were not. But they all passed their physical exams, blood tests and x-rays with flying colors, and no abnormalities could be found.

So what was the culprit of this mysterious depressive malady? It was CHEMICAL SENSITIVITY. It is caused by the inability to metabolize or detoxify the extra burden of chemicals from the renovation materials. The new rug, new paint, and new furnishings were all piled into this tiny room. Then the problem was further compounded by having inadequate ventilation. When the load to her system was too high, some of the chemicals were unable to be detoxified. This resulted in the slow accumulation of chemicals that backed up in the blood and began to create damage and symptoms.

Everything to a different degree is aging or oxidizing. Oxidation is a chemical reaction that is spontaneous. It is unavoidable, and part of the basis of life. As it happens, it disperses tiny amounts of the material being oxidized into the air. They are there regardless of whether or not we can smell it. This is called **off-gassing**. Some off-gassing is more noticeable than others. For example the off-gassing of a new car puts vinyl chloride, formaldehyde, toluene, and other chemicals in the air. These comprise part of the "new car smell".

Everything that is in the air reaches an equilibrium with the body. So some of the chemical also gets into the blood stream because we are breathing the air it is carried in. For example, carbon monoxide is odorless, but when it is in the air in sufficient concentration it can kill us. In lesser amounts, though, our body detoxification system metabolizes or neutralizes it, getting rid of it in the urine or bowel.

Some of the modern day chemicals are more difficult for the body to detoxify and they linger in the body undetoxified. When this happens, not only can they cause symptoms, but they back up and damage other parts of the body. This causes a domino effect of perplexing undiagnosable symptoms. We call this the **spreading phenomenon**.

You see, **we are the first generation of man ever exposed to so many new chemicals.** The average person in his home and work environment is exposed to over 500 chemicals a day. Normally, these do not cause any problem if he has a healthy detoxication system. Every chemical, whether we can smell it or not, quickly diffuses across the lung membranes into the bloodstream. Then if the detox system is healthy, the body gets rid of the chemical.

Most of us are healthy enough to detoxify these chemicals without even being aware of them. However, in some people, because the detox pathways are not as healthy, the chemicals back up. One sign of a person who may be becoming **chemically sensitive** is that he often **perceives odors that others cannot.** And many odors seem exaggerated and actually cause symptoms in him that they don't cause in other people. These include such symptoms as inability to concentrate, headache, depression or fatigue. And a more serious problem is that the symptoms and causes cannot usually be easily diagnosed with regular blood tests or x-rays. So often the victims are labeled malingerers or told the symptoms are all in their heads.

In a newly renovated room, there is a higher than average level of chemicals out-gassing, such as toluene from the paints and formaldehyde, 4-PC, and trichloroethylene from the carpets and construction materials. But as we saw, when the EPA installed new carpeting in one of their Washington mall offices in 1988, only 126 of the 2,000 workers developed the **sick building syndrome** or **tight building syndrome.** The rest of them were able to detoxify the 4-PC that the carpet emitted and had no symptoms. Whereas those unable to detoxify, had a variety of the typical indoor air sensitivity symptoms. Some recovered and some never have.

And when Anderson Laboratories tested mice in a jar with a piece of the carpeting, the mice were found dead in the morning. The results were aired on a special television documentary.

But back to our teacher. When she goes home at night, if her home is much less chemically contaminated, often she will clear out and feel rejuvenated for the next day. However, if at home she also has new carpeting or has recently painted, or someone smokes, her detox system continues to be over stressed and she does not clear out. A home with too much mold growth, a poorly vented gas stove or wood stove, vinyl wallpapers or drapes, or furniture coverings with stain-resistant coatings are some of the other items that could add to her home pollution.

Or if she is hooked on a lot of sweets and junk foods, her detoxification pathways are not as strong, because they are invariably low in certain vitamins or minerals necessary for optimal function of the detox enzymes.

When the body detoxifies chemicals, it does so at the expense of nutrients. In other words, **for every molecule of a pesticide or a chemical that we detoxify, we use up or lose a certain number of nutrients forever:** vitamins, minerals, amino acids, essential fatty acids, and accessory nutrients. Some of these are lost forever. So the **net effect of breathing a higher level of chemicals is to also become nutritionally depleted.**

In fact, pesticides are among the worst offenders in terms of being able to convert a previously healthy person into one who is now chemically sensitive. One problem is that many schools and offices pesticide by contract. In other words, they do not wait to see any bugs; they hire someone to spray poison regularly, regardless of activity.

If we have a strong healthful diet, high in nutrients, low in processed foods and sugars, we are usually able to keep up with the daily loss of nutrients from the work of daily detoxification. But people who have been on multiple antibiotics, birth control pills and other medications, have a high chemical exposure, eat a lot of sweets, have a high stress environment or have had years of off and on dieting are more vulnerable. They frequently have abnormally low vitamin or mineral levels to begin with that are crucial in the operation of the detoxification pathway.

When you add to this type of **compromised person** an additional load of renovation chemicals, some systems can no longer cope. Once these deficiencies are discovered, however, with blood and urine tests, they can be corrected and the integrity of the detoxication system can be restored.

As an example, Jane was a 34 year old Special Ed teacher who was moved into one of these renovated closets. Within the first three months, she started having headaches, depression, exhaustion, she couldn't think straight, she was getting recurrent sore throats, and was placed on multiple antibiotics. Her multiple exams always left the doctor shaking his head telling her he wished he were as healthy as she was. Perhaps she needed to see a psychiatrist.

When we saw her, her blood level of toluene, after a day at work, was twice as high as it was after a weekend at home. Measurements of her detox enzymes showed that parts of her detox pathways were deficient. Measuring some of the vitamins and minerals that are important in the body to detoxify toluene, showed that she was indeed low in zinc and several others. A **lipid peroxide** function showed her body was undergoing **accelerated deterioration or aging** due to too high a chemical load. This in turn left her ripe for future diseases. The good news is that all of this is correctable.

Zinc is in the enzyme, alcohol dehydrogenase, which as the name would imply, is important in **detoxifying alcohol** from the diet, as well. It made it easy for her to understand why, over the last few months, if she had a glass of wine with her husband and friends, one glass suddenly seemed like two or three. This is because when the enzyme to detoxify alcohol is deficient in zinc, alcohol cannot be degraded or metabolized as quickly as normal. It builds up in the system, and hence **one drink suddenly seems like two or three.** The body also uses this zinc-dependent enzyme to detoxify many common indoor air chemicals. The solution was to correct the zinc and other deficiencies, strengthen her detox pathways, and increase the ventilation in her classroom. Her symptoms diminished and she lost her concomitant sensitivity to alcohol.

Many cases are not this simple. After a while, many people instead develop sensitivities to indoor molds and chemicals. And they start to have reactions to commonly eaten foods, as well as have multiple nutrient deficiencies. The phenomenon is called the **spreading phenomenon** whereby people suddenly start developing sensitivities to many things that never bothered them before.

If the problem is diagnosed early enough, merely improving the ventilation in the room has solved the problem. Other times, a bake-out can be useful. In other words to accomplish this, the temperature is increased in the room, for example over weekends, to very high levels. The **heat accelerates the oxidizing or out-gassing of the chemicals** in the new paint and carpet. Of course, open windows and an aggressive increase in ventilation of the area is crucial to ensure that the chemicals get out of the building. It is no good if they are merely circulated throughout to the other rooms. Unfortunately, though, some materials will not finish out-gassing for years. Often the installation of air purifiers in the small classroom is necessary, too.

The quicker the situation is remedied, the easier it is to turn it off. For as it continues undiagnosed or untreated, the back up of unmetabolized chemicals can further damage other enzymes in the body, creating new symptoms and new medical problems. Unfortunately, physicians without special training in environmental medicine fail to see that all symptoms are connected. The **condition snowballs and is more difficult to correct the longer it goes unrecognized,** since more damage has occurred in the body.

A bake-out, air purifiers, increasing the ventilation and sometimes removing the culprit like a carpet or painting over an oil-based paint with a less toxic water-soluble one can often be all that is needed. But success is better the earlier the remedies are carried out. The symptoms and solutions vary tremendously with the individual circumstances. Good classroom ventilation, a less toxic home environment, and a healthy detoxification system in the teacher herself are crucial to her recovery. This includes good levels of all the vitamins and minerals, amino acids, essential fatty acids, and accessory nutrients.

Obviously, there are many documented cases of children, also, who have become chemically sensitive. And with their immature detoxification systems, sometimes they are hit harder. The problem is they do not possess the verbal sophistication to be able to say they can't concentrate. Instead they go on to be labeled **learning disabled.** Hopefully as information about the **toxic teacher syndrome** becomes more well-known, we will be able to nip it in the bud. This is our chance to prevent more teachers, as well as students, from becoming unsuspecting victims of this 21st century malady.

REFERENCES:

1. For further information on what tests should be done, and how to diagnose and treat, read **Tired or Toxic?** It also contains for physicians the scientific references and biochemical explanations of the disease, as well as what blood tests to order.

2. Call N.E.E.D.S., 1-800-634-1380 for information on air purification devices and glass tubes for measuring chemical contamination in the classroom air.

3. Morrow LA, Callender T, Lottenberg S, Buchsbaum MS, Hodgson MJ, Robin N, Pet and neurobehavioral evidence of tentrabromoethane encephalopathy, J NEUROPSYCHIATRY 2:4, 431- 5, Fall 1990.

4. Rogers SA, Zinc deficiency as a model for developing chemical sensitivity. INTERNAT CLIN NUTR REV, 10;1, 253, 1990.

5. Rogers SA, Magnesium deficiency masquerades as diverse symptoms, INTERNAT CLIN NUTR REV, 11;3, 117-125, July 1991.

6. Rogers SA, Chemical sensitivity, Parts I, II, III, Feb-Apr 1992, INTERNAL MEDICINE WORLD REPORT, 322-D Englishtown Rd, Old Bridge NJ 08857.

7. Ely EW, Moorehead B, et al, Warehouse workers' headache: Emergency evaluation and management of 30 patients with carbon monoxide poisoning, AMER J MED 98:145-154, Feb 1995.

8. Roger SA, Diagnosing the tight building syndrome, ENVIRONMENTAL HEALTH PERSPECTIVES, 76:195-198, 1987 (ENVIRON HEALTH PERSP is published by the United States government's National Institutes of Health).

TOLUENE

Toluene is an example of a VOH (volatile organic hydrocarbon), or everyday xenobiotic (foreign chemical), that most everyone comes into contact with. So let's look at this one to give you an idea of what the poor brain is up against each day. Then you can better appreciate how depression can be such a common symptom of chemical sensitivity.

First, **toluene (methyl benzene) is most likely the chemical that may give you a headache when the office is newly painted.** Another person may have the classic **brain fog** and **feel dopey, dizzy, spacey, and have irrational mood swings** out of proportion to any possible cause. Someone else can have asthma, another arthritis, or vasculitis, or myocarditis, and another depression. You see, the **biochemical individuality** of each person determines what area of the body becomes the target organ. Recall when the U.S. government's own EPA put 28,000 square feet of carpeting in one of its Washington mall offices in 1988, out of 2,000 workers, only 126 developed **E.I., or environmental illness.** And no two workers had the exact same symptoms. And for many, depression was the chief symptom.

Since toluene is **the most prevalent hydrocarbon in the atmosphere,** it is found in nearly every environment. It out-gasses from the glues for carpets, furniture, building materials, cosmetics, inks from printed books and pamphlets, cosmetics, nail polish, solvents, floor and furniture cutting oils, polishes, paints, varnishes, lacquers, resins, adhesives, cleansers, cigarette smoke, leather goods, auto and industrial exhaust, plastics and much, much more. As you see, it is difficult to avoid inhaling it in the course of a day.

And toluene **has caused every symptom from cardiac arrest to brain fog.** Its list of symptoms includes spoon-shaped nails, liver damage, learning disability, numbness, tingling, kidney stones, hyper-cholesterolemia, cancers, menstrual irregularities, infertility, aplastic anemia, muscular atrophy, addiction, confusion, mood swings, fatigue, insomnia, uncoordination, schizophrenia, and of course, depression.

Bear in mind I'm presenting a very minute sample to show you several things:

(1) That we are the first generation ever called upon to detoxify so many chemicals from every route (air, food and water) every day of our lives.

(2) The work of detoxification uses up nutrients and these resultant nutrient deficiencies can go on to cause any number of symptoms, including depression.

(3) These airborne chemicals that out-gas from our modern world can cause any symptom of their own, including depression.

(4) You'll notice from the publication dates that this information is not new. In fact, it is over a couple of decades old, and our own government has contributed to much of the data, yet

(5) Somehow the average physician is totally un-knowledgeable about looking for the cause of toluene-induced symptoms and how to treat them (if you doubt this, quiz him).

The bottom line is that you have not had a thorough work-up for the potential causes of your depression until you have been checked for chemical sensitivity.

REFERENCES:

United States Environmental Protection Agency, HEALTH ASSESSMENT DOCUMENT FOR TOLUENE, EPA-600/8-82-008F, Aug 1983, Office of Health and Environmental Assessment, Wash DC 20460.

Fischman CM, Oster JR, Toxic effects of toluene. A new cause of high anion gap metabolic acidosis, J AMER MED ASSOC, 241(16):1713-1715, 1979.

Tarsh MJ, Schizophreniform psychosis caused by sniffing toluene, J SOC OCCUP MED, 29(4):131-133, 1979.

Knox JW, Nelson JR, Permanent encephalopathy from toluene inhalation, N ENGL J MED , 275:1494-1496, 1966.

Gamberale F, Hultengren M, Toluene exposure. II. Psychophysiological functions. WORK ENVIRON HEALTH, 9(3):131- 139, 1972.

Hanninen H, Eskelinen L, Husman K, Nurminen M, Behavioral effects of long-term exposure to a mixture of organic solvents, SCAND J WORK ENVIRON HEALTH, 2(4):240-255, 1976.

Valciukas JA, et al, Neurobehavioral changes among shipyard painter exposed to solvents, ARCH ENVIRON HEALTH 40:47-52, 1985.

Larsen F, Leira HL, Organic brain syndrome and long-term exposure to toluene: a clinical, psychiatric study of vocationally active printing workers, J OCCUP MED 30:875-878, 1988.

Rea TM, et al, Effects of toluene inhalation on brain biogenic amines in the rat, TOXICOL 31 (1984)143-150.

Benignus V, Neurobehavioural effects of toluene: A review, NEUROBEHAV TOXICOL TERATOL, 3(1981) 407.

Tarsh MJ, Schizophreniform psychosis caused by sniffing toluene, J SOC OCCUP MED. 29(1979) 131.

Elji Y, Increased activity of monoamine oxidase by epoxy resin hardeners, TOXICOL LETT, 37 (1987) 27-32.

Gyntelberg F, et al, Acquired intolerance to organic solvents and results of vestibular testing, AM J IND MED 9:363-370, 198.

Lindstrom K, Changes in psychological performances of solvent-poisoned and solvent-exposed workers, AM MJ IND MED, 1:69-84, 1980.

Seppalainen AM, et al, Neurophysiological and psych-ological picture of solvent poisoning, AM J IND MED 1:31-42, 1980.

Bruhn P, et al, Prognosis in chronic toxic encephalopathy - a two-year follow-up study in 26 house painters with occupational encephalopathy, ACTA NEUROL SCAND 64:279-272, 1981.

Baker EL, Organic solvent neurotoxicity, ANNUAL REV HEALTH, 9:223-239, 1988.

Dager SR, et al Panic disorder precipitated by exposure to organic solvents in the work place, AM J PSYCHIATRY, 144:1056-1058, 1987.

Rea WJ, CHEMICAL SENSITIVITY, Vol I CRC Press, Boca Raton, 1992.

Foulks E, McClellan T, Psychologic sequelae of chronic toxic waste exposure, SOUTHERN MEDICAL JOURNAL, 85(2):122-126, Feb 1992.

Bower B, Sick buildings exert stressful impact, SCI NEWS, 260, April25, 1992.

Gerhard I, Prolonged exposure to wood preservatives induces endocrine and immunologic disorders in women, et al, AM J OBSTET GYN, 165(2):487-488, August 1991.

Lazar RB, et al, Multifocal nervous system damage caused by toluene abuse, NEUROL 33:1337, 1983

Rogers SA, CHEMICAL SENSITIVITY, 1995, Keats Publ, New Canaan, CT (also available from this publisher).

HEAVY METALS

Heavy metal poisoning is another cause of chemical sensitivity and depression. These metals come from a variety of places. **Lead** can come from auto exhaust, paint, and cooking utensils.

Aluminum can come from aluminum soda cans and aluminum-lined juice boxes that you see children carrying everywhere, cosmetics, and baking powder and salt (as an anti-caking agent). Aluminum also enters the body through use of deodorants (don't forget aluminum in these is absorbed across the skin), aluminum cooking pots (especially when you put something acid in them like tomato sauce). Further sources of toxic aluminum for the body is over-the-counter medications like antacids, unfiltered city water, aluminum-lined water reservoir for coffee makers, and much more. The coffee makers are particularly bad because the acidic coffee water sitting in them is heated as well. This helps pull more aluminum into the reservoir.

Mercury is in over-the-counter hemorrhoid preparations, dental fillings, and more. Some people can date the onset off their depression to a period following a certain root canal or "silver" amalgam (mercury) filling.

All these metals, even if they are merely applied to the skin as an anti-perspirant or hemorrhoid cream, are absorbed. Anything you put on your skin or in your mouth has the ability to transmigrate into the blood stream. Even over-the-counter hemorrhoidal creams contain mercury that can migrate into the bloodstream and brain. Many prescription medicines capitalize on the skin as a way of getting into the blood, such as with estrogen patches, motion sickness patches, and nitroglycerin patches. Anything you put on the skin you should want to be of the same quality as anything you would swallow. Because if it is on the skin, it does end up in the blood stream, just as though you ate or drank it.

Cadmium poisoning is another heavy metal usually picked up from cigarette smoke and auto exhaust, welding, plastics, paints, batteries, and tires. The list of heavy metal exposures is endless. The problem with these heavy metals is that they damage important enzymes by replacing the minerals in them, like zinc, that make them work. Furthermore, the body does not have a good way of getting rid of or detoxifying heavy metals. So once stuck in the body, they attach to enzymes that are missing some of their minerals such as zinc or magnesium. For example, a poor diet of junk foods eventually becomes deficient in many minerals. It is then those enzymes that are missing minerals that are the easiest targets for the heavy metals. For the heavy metals can sit right in those niches where the missing mineral belongs.

Once a heavy metal such as aluminum or lead or mercury is sitting in the enzyme instead of the mineral that nature intended, it damages the action of the enzyme so that it cannot work properly. In some cases, you do not even have to be deficient in a mineral. For heavy metals can even displace or boot out certain minerals, because they have a stronger affinity for the enzyme than the natural mineral does.

Tony was an intelligent young man but had never been as much of an achiever as his brother. He had consulted a psychiatrist regularly for over 8 years for severe depression. When he started reading more about the causes of depression he wanted to look for aluminum toxicity. He had decided to explore this possibility because he had used years of antacids for stomach problems and his wife had also cooked a great deal of spaghetti in aluminum pots over the years. Plus he drank coffee all day at work and the coffee pot water heater reservoir is aluminum.

His levels of aluminum in the urine and in the blood were much higher than normal. When we put him on an oral drug to pull the aluminum out, he became happy for the first time in 8 years and no longer needed his antidepressants nor his psychiatrist. And what made him even happier was he found that he was a much smarter person than he had ever dreamed of.

We could fill whole books just on the subject of everyday heavy metals and how they damage the brain preferentially. Depression is only one of the nasty symptoms, but many are reversible if diagnosed and treated (see WELLNESS AGAINST ALL ODDS for more details). For these metals are everywhere, in our food, air, toiletries, and water. For example, aluminum as you have learned is in every major municipal water supply, canned goods, cookware and coffee makers, cosmetics, antacids, salt and baking powders (as an anti-caking agent), and much more. And it has a bearing on depression and the senile brain known as Alzheimer's.

And even minerals that are essential in the body can be toxic and mimic heavy metals if taken in excess. This is one of the concerns with iron with which many foods are now fortified. It can mimic the brain degeneration of Alzheimer's.

And the effects of heavy metals on the brain are so very slow and subtle, that the majority of the time the diagnosis is never thought of. They can lead to learning disabilities, depression, senility, and much more brain impairment. And the problem is they can do so at surprisingly low levels.

REFERENCES:

Thatcher RW, et al, Effects of low levels of cadmium and lead on cognitive functioning in children, ARCH ENVIRONMENTAL HEALTH, 37:159-166, 198.

Needleman HL, The behavioral consequences of low-level exposure to lead, in: Sakar B, ED, BIOLOGICAL ASPECTS OF METALS AND METAL-RELATED DISEASES, Raven Press, NY, 219-224, 1983.

Sandstead HH, A brief history of the influence of trace elements on brain function, AMER J CLIN NUTR 43:293-298, Feb 1986.

Kaehny WD, et al, Gastrointestinal absorption of aluminum from aluminum-containing antacids, NEW ENG J MED, 296:1389-1390, 1977.

Davison AM, et al, Water supply aluminum concentration, dialysis dementia, and effect of reverse-osmosis water treatment, LANCET 9:785-787, 1982.

Banks WA, et al, Aluminum increases permeability of the blood-brain barrier to labeled DSIP and beta-endorphin: possible implications for senile and dialysis dementias, LANCET 26:1227-1229, 1983.

Martyn CN, Osmond C, et al, Geographical relation between Alzheimer's disease and aluminum in drinking water, LANCET, 59-60, Jan 14, 1989

Casdorph HR, Walker MW, TOXIC METAL SYNDROME, HOW METAL POISONINGS CAN AFFECT YOUR BRAIN, Avery Publ, Garden City Pk, NY, 1995.

Fulton B, Jeffrey EH, Absorption and retention of aluminum from drinking water. 1. Effect of citric and ascorbic acids on aluminum tissue levels in rabbits. FUNDAMENTAL AND APPLIED TOXICOLOGY, 14:788-796, 1990

Perl DP, Brody AR. Detection of aluminum by semi-x-ray spectrometry with neurofibrillary tangle-bearing neurons of Alzheimer's Disease. NEUROTOX; 1990: 133-137.

Perl DP, Broady AR. Alzheimer's Disease: x-ray spectro-metric evidence of aluminum accumulation in neurofibrillary bearing neurons. SCI; 1980: 297-299.

Aluminum, hot water tanks, and neurobiology, LANCET 1:781, 1989
U.S. Department of Health & Human Services, TOXICOLOGICAL PROFILE FOR ALUMINUM, Wash DC, Oct 1990

Richardson JS, Subbarao KV, Ang LC, On the possible role of iron-induced free radical peroxidation in neural degeneration
in Alzheimer's, ANN NY ACAD SCI, 648:326-327, May 11, 1992

LEAD

Lead is another heavy metal that can damage the brain by impairing brain enzymes. Lead has been known for decades to cause brain damage, for example, in children. And lead from paints and auto exhaust and industrial exhausts can contribute to hyperactivity.

Also, lead can cause depression and changes in "happy hormones" like GABA and dopamine. But blood levels are generally only useful for recent exposure, for heavy metals are stored. So the best test is a trial dose of an oral chelator with before and after urine tests. This will determine just what heavy metal and how much of it the body wants to get rid of (see WELLNESS AGAINST ALL ODDS for instructions). Remember, lead toxicity can accumulate very slowly, leading to depression where the cause is rarely sought.

REFERENCES:

Balestra DJ, et al, Adult chronic lead toxication: a clinical review, ARCH INT MED, 151:1718-1720, September 1991.

David OJ, et al, The relationship of hyperactivity to moderately elevated lead levels, ARCH ENVIRON HEALTH 38(6):341-346,1983.

Kishi R, Toshiko I, Hirotsugu M, Effects of low lead exposure on neuro-behavioral function in the rat, ARCH ENVIRON HEALTH, 38:25, 1983

Needleman HL, Gatsonis CA, Low level lead exposure and the IQ of children: a meta-analysis of modern studies, JAMA 263:673-678, 1990

Fine BP, Barth A, Sheffet A, Lavenhar MA, Influence of magnesium on the intestinal absorption of lead, ENVIRON RES 12:224-227, 1976

Singh NP, Thind IS, Vitale LF, Pawlow M, Intake of magnesium and toxicity of lead: an experimental model, ARCH ENVIRON HEALTH, 34:168-173, 1970

Burchfield JL, et al, The combined discriminating power of quantitative electroencephalography and neuropsychologic measures in evaluating central nervous system effects of lead at low levels, in Needleman JC (ed.): LOW LEVEL LEAD EXPOSURES, Raven Press, NY, 1980, 75-90

Ernhardt CB, et al, Subclinical levels of lead and developmental deficit — a multi-variate follow-up reassessment, PEDIATRICS, 67, 911-918, 1981

Needleman HL, et al, Deficits in psychologic and classroom performance of children with elevated lead levels, N ENGL J MED, 300:689-695,1979

Perlstein MA, Attala R, Neurologic sequelae of plumbism in children, CLIN PEDIATR, 5+292-298, 1966

Prull Be, Rompel K, EEG changes in acute poisoning with organic tin compounds, ELECTROENCEPH CLIN NEUROPHYSIOL, 29:215-122, 1970

Seppalainen AM, et al, Subclinical neuropathy at "safe" levels of lead exposure, ARCH ENVIRON HEALTH, 30:180-183, 1975

McMichael AJ, et al, Tooth lead levels and I.Q. in school age children: The Port Prairie cohort study, AMER J EPIDEM, Sep 15, 1994, 140(6):489-499

MERCURY

Did you ever wonder where the phrase **"Mad as a hatter"** came from? In previous centuries, the makers of hats used mercury in their work. Many became so notoriously crazy from mercury toxicity that the expression became common. It has long been known and documented (although denied by the keepers of the keys for the dental world), that mercury, a known toxic metal, can leach from **"silver" amalgam mercury** fillings and go directly to the brain.

But causing depression is probably the mildest thing mercury does. For it is avidly taken up in the pituitary (the master gland in the center of the brain) and can damage the function of every gland. It also initiates cancers.

A renowned man with double degrees, (P. Stortebecker, M.D., PhD.) who was the professor of neurology at the famed Karolinska Institute in Stockholm, Sweden did studies to advance this knowledge. Others have shown astounding results that confirm his work. For example, some leukemias will disappear, or multiple sclerosis might clear, once the amalgams are removed. For doing this can reduce a part of the total body burden of chemical stressors enough to allow the body to perform some extraordinary healing.

The **heavy metal poisoning** from mercury is likewise capable of **mimicking any disease**. And it can cause **auto-immunity** diseases, which can create any symptom. Recent studies have even shown that amalgams even increase our vulnerability to intestinal organisms by increasing antibiotic resistance to them.

REFERENCES:

Stortbecker P, DENTAL CARIES AS A CAUSE OF NERVOUS DISORDERS, Bio-Probe Inc., POB 58010, Orlando 32858-0160.

Pelletier L, et al, Autoreactive T cells in mercury-induced autoimmunity, J IMMUNOL, 140:750-754, 1988.

Reuter R, et al, Mercuric chloride induces auto-antibodies against U3 small nuclear ribonucleoprotein in susceptible mice, PROC NATL ACAD SCI USA 86:237-241, 1989.

McCabe MJ, Lawrence DA, Effects of metals on lymphocyte development and function, 193-216 In: Schook L, Laskin DL, XENOBIOTICS AND INFLAMMATION, Academic Press NY, 1994.

Summers AO, et al, Genetic linkage of mercury and antibiotic resistance in intestinal bacteria, ANTIMICROBIAL AGENTS CHEMOTHERAPY 37:825-834, 1993.

Smith PJ, Langolf GD, Goldberg J, Effects of occupational exposure to mercury on short-term memory, BR J IND MED, 40:413-419, 1983.

Lorscheider FL, Vimy MJ, et al, The dental amalgam mercury controversy--inorganic mercury and the CNS; genetic linkage of mercury and antibiotic resistance in intestinal bacteria, TOXICOL 97:19-22, 1995

Salonen JT, et al, Intake of mercury from fish, lipid peroxidation, and the risk of myocardial infraction and coronary, cardiovascular, and early death in eastern Finnish men, CIRCULATION, 91:645-655, 1995

FLUORIDE

The dangers of fluoride are often ignored. Fluoride can be very damaging to enzymes and can cause a host of symptoms, as it is an aging factor (Yiamouyiannis). And although a discussion of it is beyond the intended purpose of this book, please do not go on fluoride, for example, on the recommendation that it is good for osteoporosis, teeth, or any other reason until you have all the facts, comprehensive nutrient levels, and a consultation with a physician who is knowledgeable in biochemistry. And have a good filter system on your water.

P.S. And do not forget: **each molecule of Prozac** has not one, not two, but **three molecules of fluoride in it!** And it doesn't even prevent tooth decay!

REFERENCES:

Yiamouyiannis J, FLUORIDE THE AGING FACTOR, Health Action Press, 6439 Taggart Rd, Delaware OH 43015, 1986

U.S. Department of Health & Human Services, TOXICOLOGICAL PROFILE FOR FLUORIDE, Wash DC, July 1991

"MY DOCTOR PRESCRIBED MYLANTA"

How many times have we heard that commercial? What those patients don't know is that the Mylanta their doctor prescribed (and most of the over-the-counter antacids commonly prescribed by doctors), contains aluminum. Yes, the very aluminum that we are supposed to avoid if we want to stave off Alzheimer's pre-senile dementia is being prescribed.

Aluminum gets more difficult to avoid, since more people drink from aluminum cans and aluminum-lined juice boxes, and eat in restaurants where aluminum cookware is used. And most standard coffee pots have an aluminum chamber where the water is boiled, and some even store the acidic end product in aluminum-lined vessels and thermoses. Aluminum is an anti-caking ingredient added to baking powders and commercial table salt, deodorants, and is a common contaminant of ground water as well as many processed foods.

So if you truly have an irritated gastric mucosa (stomach lining), and need only temporary relief, doesn't it make more sense to use a non-aluminum antacid like ones containing aloe vera gel? Usually found in health food stores, they are aluminum-free and contain healing aloe vera extract.

For antacids rob your health in many ways. They bind with precious minerals, thereby inhibiting their absorption. This binding can lead to an eventual magnesium deficiency, for example. This in turn gives rise to fatigue, depression, irregular heart beat, high blood pressure, inability to metabolize cholesterol, chronic back muscle spasm and much more. Worse, by compromising your ability to absorb magnesium they can lead to the ultimate magnesium deficiency symptom, sudden cardiac death. Or antacids can slow the absorption of calcium, zinc, or iron. etc. You see, an antacid serves to sop up acid to decrease the irritation to the stomach lining so it can heal. The problem is that 50% of the people over 50 already have too little acid in the stomach for good absorption of minerals. So this only serves to compound the problem and add to nutrient deficiencies which then lead to the vulnerability for cancer, depression, and other diseases. But because they so abuse their stomachs with coffee, sodas, alcohol, spicy foods medications, and more, most people erroneously think that the burning is due to too much acid. So antacids calm the stomach by turning off your good stomach acid. But aloe vera heals without depleting acid.

The other problem with using an antacid is that it helps you put off finding the cause of your stomach distress. In fact, as people ignore finding the cause, worse symptoms appear where they eventually need stronger medications. The most common ones to be prescribed after the antacids are the H-2 blockers, known as Tagamet (cimetidine), or Zantac (ranitidine), or Pepcid. These do not neutralize or sop up the acid like Mylanta. They actually turn off the acid so well that some people develop actual B12 deficiencies, for example. And B12 deficiency can then cause serious depression. And now that these have non-prescription over-the-counter status, these problem side effects should flourish. And another problem that has been recently discovered makes the H-2 blockers even more dangerous. They are immuno-suppressive. In other words, they turn down the immune system. This in turn increases your vulnerability to many other diseases including cancer (Latimer case, WALL STREET JOURNAL, Oct 14,1991,A-1).

So what's the solution? Find the cause. Most likely you have had an x-ray to rule out a hiatus hernia, cancer, ulcer, gallstones, etc. When nothing is found, diagnoses such as gastritis, esophagitis, heartburn, irritable bowel, etc. are made. They simply mean the real cause has not been found. For the diagnoses merely mean there is inflammation and malfunction. But no one has found the cause.

What are some of the commonest causes of stomach distress that are not found?

(1) Hidden **food sensitivity** is at the top of the list. Coffee is the premier food to cause irritation of the stomach and esophagus, with cigarette smoking as a close second. But any food can cause the symptom. The sensitivities are highly individual. It could be chocolate for one, or tomato products, vinegars or alcohol. Follow the diagnostic diet instructions in THE E.I. SYNDROME, REVISED to find your cause.

(2) Another common cause of an irritated stomach is a gastric lining that has become inflamed not by food sensitivity, but by overgrowth of yeast, such as **Candida.** This commonly gets a head start when antibiotics have been taken and diets high in sugar are eaten. Candida is normally a harmless yeast (mold, fungus) that is everywhere. But in people who are weaker, due to hidden vitamin or mineral deficiencies, or other reasons, the yeast can establish a stronghold in tissues like the esophagus or stomach. Prednisone, antibiotics, birth control pills, high sugar diets and diabetes are the more common causes of intestinal dysbiosis (meaning abnormal organisms, like Candida, growing in the gut).

The treatment is to eat no sweets, no cross-reacting mold foods, and to use an anti-fungal medication that is safe and not absorbed. Nystatin is one such treatment and merely kills the yeasts on contact. Of course, you want to find out why you were vulnerable to the yeast in the first place, since only nutrient-deficient people can get it. (More on this in the Candida section, Volume III).

Other organisms can also inflame the gastric (stomach) and duodenal (small intestine) linings and even cause ulcerations. In some people the cause of their ulcer symptoms is actually a bacterial infection. Helicobacter pylori (Campylobacter pylori) is one such organism. There is an antigen blood test for this. And if undiagnosed, it can go on to cause stomach cancer also.

(3) An unsuspected **magnesium deficiency** can also cause gripping spasms of the epigastrium (just under the end of the breastbone or sternum). A 1990 study from the JOURNAL OF THE AMERICAN MEDICAL ASSOCIATION showed that doctors miss 90% of the people with magnesium deficiencies. Furthermore, U.S. government surveys showed that the average American diet provides only 40% of the daily requirement for magnesium (SCIENCE NEWS, 1988). Currently there is no blood test that will rule out magnesium deficiency. But there is a challenge test (described in TIRED OR TOXIC?).

(4) Also, one of the most common symptoms of **chemical hypersensitivity** is nausea. Some people think they have a stomach problem because inhaling toxic fumes from auto exhaust, paint, new carpet, a faulty gas heating system, renovations, etc. makes them nauseous or gives painful stomach spasms.

(5) Lastly, whenever you find yourself asking, "Was it something I ate?", don't forget to ask yourself, "Or is it **something that's eating me?"** For if you are harboring anger, fear, rage, jealousy, guilt or other harmful emotions, these too, can cause a tremendous outpouring of gastric acids.

Remember, regardless of how a symptom presents, **there is always a cause.** And to take a medication to cover it up or mask it is to only postpone the emergence of a worse symptom that will stem from ignoring the cause of the first one.

REFERENCES:

White DM, et al, Neurologic syndrome in 25 workers from an aluminum smelting plant, ARCH INTERN MED, July 1992;152:1443- 1448.

Crapper, DR, et al, Aluminum, neurofibrillary degeneration and Alzheimer's disease, BRAIN, 99:67-69, 1976.

Crapper-McLachlan DR, et al, Aluminum in human brain disease. In Sarkar C (ed.):BIOLOGICAL ASPECTS OF METALS AND METAL-RELATED DISEASES, Raven Press, NY, 209-218, 1983.

DeBoni U, et al, Neurofibrillary degeneration induced by system aluminum, ACTA NEUROPATHOL, 35:285-294, 1976.

Rogers SA, Magnesium deficiency masquerades as diverse symptoms: Evaluation of an oral magnesium challenge test, INTERN CLIN NUTR REV, 11:3, July 1991

Nagyvary J, Bradbury EL, Hypocholesterolemic effects of Al (3+) complexes, BIOCHEM RES COMMUN, 2:292-298, 1977.

PRESCRIPTION DRUGS

One of the least appreciated and most commonly involved chemicals that cause depression are prescription drugs. In fact, for most prescription drugs, depression is one of the leading side effects. **Beta blockers** for high blood pressure, angina, and stage fright can cause depression. Many **anti-depressants** themselves can cause depression as one of the side effects. The problem is that most anti-depressants do not accentuate depression until you have been on them for a while. It is only after they have had a chance to deplete nutrient levels that they start losing their effectiveness and make matters worse. But since it helped initially, you tend to disregard the worsening of your depression as caused by your anti-depressant. In fact, since it worked initially and then stopped, you tend to increase the dose or switch to another type of anti-depressant.

If you look in the PDR (PHYSICIAN'S DRUG REFERENCE, the book that describes the side effects of all prescription drugs) one **side effect of all antidepressants is depression.** For even if they don't cause depression right away, after months or years of use they deplete certain nutrients which then can secondarily go on to cause a slow, insidious and escalating depression. Eventually nobody can figure out what the cause is, except through a carefully physician-monitored trial of going off the drug. Even then you may suffer weeks of withdrawal symptoms (but the techniques in WELLNESS AGAINST ALL ODDS can minimize them drastically).

Drugs to lower **cholesterol** have been known to cause depression, in fact, so severely that many people die of suicide. And as stated, Tagamet, Zantac, Pepcid and other drugs to turn down acid secretion in the stomach can also cause a slow depression. Since they inhibit the stomach acid secretion, you no longer absorb your vitamins and minerals as well as you should, so you start to get a depression on that basis. We will talk more about that when we get to the nutrition section.

Recently, there have been hundreds of complaints by people who used Lariam. It is given for one month if you visit places, even for just a day, where you could get malaria. The side effect was hallucinations and often mental symptoms requiring hospitalization even **months after** the drug's use (Conde Nast's TRAVELER, Aug 1996, Pg 20, 1-800-WORLD-24).

Some of the **antibiotics** that are the most frequently used are toxic. A category called the **quinolones** includes such common brand names as **Cipro** and **Floxin**. These antibiotics can produce a wide variety of symptoms in the brain, not the least of which is depression. Other reactions include dizziness, confusion, insomnia, drowsiness, anxiety, tremors, headache and seizures. Since the most frequent effects on the brain is excitatory (they bind to and hence inhibit GABA sites), seizures can occur.

But the most disconcerting effect of this category of antibiotics is the large number of studies demonstrating mutagenicity and DNA breakage, aberrations and gene mutations. These are the mechanisms that can start cancer.

Of course, there are many non-central nervous system effects of antibiotics like arthritis, auto-immune, tendon rupture, gastrointestinal, dermatological, and many other adverse effects. There have also been cardiac toxicities, retinal degeneration, and more, like mitochondrial damage, which is a mechanism for initiating chronic fatigue, etc. And certainly we have all seen our share of chronic fatigue patients who were well until they had a certain antibiotic. Antibiotics are so frequently prescribed that aside from an obvious rash, other side effects like depression are often missed.

Up to 2 million patients are hospitalized each year and as many as 140,000 die of side effects or reactions related to various prescription drugs. Similar findings were revealed in a Harvard study in hospitals in New York in 1984. In that year, 98,000 had iatrogenic (physician-caused) problems, and 14% died. So never overlook the very drugs you take as a potential cause of your depression, regardless of how long you have taken them.

REFERENCES:

Takayama S, et al, Toxicity of quinolone antimicrobial agents, J TOXICOL ENVIRONM HEALTH, 45:1-45, 1995

Freedman DS, et al, Plasma lipid levels and psychologic characteristics in men, AM J EPIDEM, 141(6):507-517, 1995.

Morgan RE, et al, Plasma cholesterol and depressive symptoms in older men, LANCET, 341:75-79, January 9, 1993.

Duits N, Bos FM, Depressive symptoms and cholesterol lowering drugs, LANCET, 341:114, January 9, 1993.

Fanzini L, et al, Drug-induced depression in the aged: what can be done?, DRUGS AND AGING, 3(2):147-158, 1993.

U.S. News Investigative Report, What you--and maybe your doctor--don't know about your prescription's side effects could hurt you. Or even kill you., U.S.NEWS AND WORLD REPORT, 49-57, 56-57, Jan 9, 1995.

Leape LI, Error in medicine, JAMA 272:1851-1857, 1994.

Brennan TA, et al, Incidence of adverse events and negligence in hospitalized patients; Result of the Harvard Medical Practice Study I, N ENGL J MED, 324:370-376, 1991.

Leape LI, et al, The nature of the adverse events in hospitalized patients; Results of the Harvard medical practice study II, N ENG J MED, 324:377-384, 1991.

IMMUNIZATIONS

As with anything you put in the body, there is the potential of adverse reaction. And so it is with immunizations, especially the newer less time-tested ones, like hepatitis. And many injections contain mercury and other preservatives which can act upon the brain. Other newer immunizations, like chicken pox are particularly worrisome, as physicians do not even know how long it is good for, much less a host of other unanswered questions.

"Alleged link between hepatitis B vaccine and chronic fatigue syndrome", Bureau of Communicable Disease Epidemiology, CAN MED ASSOC J, Jan 1, 1992;146(1):37-38.

DIAGNOSING THE PROBLEM

So how would you ever go about discovering whether or not hidden chemical sensitivity, or pesticide poisoning, or heavy metal toxicity, or even your very own prescribed drugs might be causing your depression? Start with a good history, then create an oasis.

If you have gas utilities you can look at how long you have been in that house and how long you have been depressed. Sometimes it takes a few years to become sensitized, sometimes it happens right away within the first few months of moving in. Sometimes it is only in the winter months when the heat is turned up and the house is tightened. Sometimes the depression is in proportion to how much time has been spent in proximity to the gas stove or gas dryer. You can see if you feel happier in the summer when the heating system is turned off or happier away from home. The trouble is that some people are so tanked up with natural gas that it takes them 2 or 3 weeks to get rid of it. If they happen to be vacationing in a place that also has natural gas utilities, they will never really get cleared out. But certainly it is no mistake if they feel better when they are out camping or at the ocean on vacation.

Another way to see if chemical sensitivity might be causing your depression, is to remove the carpeting from the bedroom or chose a bedroom that is free of carpeting temporarily. Look at when the depression started in terms of new furnishings, especially a bed or bedroom carpet. A new bed is a **chemical catastrophe** for many people. The mattress contains pesticides, fire retardant, foam formaldehyde, and formaldehyde stain resistant chemicals on the covering. Likewise, some people bury their heads in a foam (formaldehyde) or down or feather (pesticided) **pillow** each night. The problem is that once you get sick or depressed from exposure to something as common as a new (formaldehyde-laden pressed board) **headboard** or **renovations** in the bedroom, as you become sicker, you tend to stay home more, and in bed. So you actually **spend more time in the place that is making you sick** in the first place. And you have little hope for recovery if the thought never crossed yours or your doctor's mind that you could be reacting to chemicals.

HAPPINESS CAN COME FROM SIMPLE CHANGES

So simple changes such as to cotton bedding and cotton pillows as well as several layers of cotton blankets over the mattress can be all that it takes for some people to awaken in the morning feeling less depressed. If your chemistry is not bogged down all night with the work of detoxifying, it can be shuttled for use in synthesizing happy hormones in the brain. Likewise, a good air cleaner can cover a host of sins in terms of pulling out chemicals. Even air cleaners that do not specifically have chemical filters can reduce some of the chemical overload because the chemicals, such as formaldehyde, will ride on the dust particles that the machine removes.

You can stop using pesticides in the home and even have your stored pesticide levels assayed. You can check the pesticide schedule at work and see what is used and how often, and specifically where it is used. And you can have a heavy metal screen done through a urine and blood test to see if you have an overload (described in WELLNESS AGAINST ALL ODDS). And you can directly measure your liver's detoxication capabilities as well as the overload of chemical stressors (lipid peroxides), not to mention the nutrients in the detox pathways. (More on these in Volume IV.)

Last but not least, discuss with your doctor the possibility of changing medications or having a supervised trial off of medications for a short time to determine whether or not the side effect of depression stems from that.

EVERYDAY CHEMICALS CAN
CHANGE BRAIN CHEMISTRY

The bottom-line is that everyday chemicals can dramatically change brain chemistry, creating brain fog, depression, or worse. For they use up nutrients and damage enzymes that should have been used to make happy hormones. By now it should not come as a surprise to you that the man responsible for the "McDonald's Massacre" left his welding job of 17 years a week before the slaughter of innocent victims. At his job exit interview he said the fumes were making him "sick and crazy". Of course, a brain full of cadmium and other heavy metals is the perfect set-up for such a meaningless act of violence (Walsh WJ, Biochemical profiles of violent behavior: Diagnosis and treatment, presented at the 30th Annual Meeting, American Academy of Environmental Medicine, 1995, syllabus available as well as full audio-cassettes).

If you want to learn more about chemical sensitivity it's diagnosis and treatment, then read TIRED OR TOXIC? followed by WELLNESS AGAINST ALL ODDS.

REFERENCES:

Rogers SA, TIRED OR TOXIC?, (1991), Sand Key Publishing, PO Box 40101, Sarasota FL, 34242 (this publisher)

Rogers SA, WELLNESS AGAINST ALL ODDS, (1994), Sand Key Publishing, PO Box 40101, Sarasota, FL, 34242

Rogers SA, CHEMICAL SENSITIVITY, (1995), Keats Publ, New Canaan CT (and this publisher)

Rea WJ, CHEMICAL SENSITIVITY VOL. I, Lewis Publishers, a division of CRC Press, Boca Raton FL, or 1-800-428-2343, 1992

Rogers SA, THE SCIENTIFIC BASIS OF SELECTED ENVIRONMENTAL MEDICINE TECHNIQUES, Prestige Publ, Box 3161, Syracuse NY 13220 (this publisher)

Rea WJ, CHEMICAL SENSITIVITY VOL. II, CRC Press, Boca Raton FL, or 1-800-428-2343, 1994

Rea WJ, CHEMICAL SENSITIVITY, VOL III & IV, ibid

Kaloyanova FP, Batawi MA, HUMAN TOXICOLOGY OF PESTICIDES, CRC Press, Boca Raton FL, 1991.

Arlien-Sovorg P, SOLVENT NEUROTOXICITY, CRC Press, Boca Raton FL, 1992.

Jakoby WB, ENZYMATIC BASIS OF DETOXICATION VOL. II, Academic Press, NY, 1980.

Klaassen CD, Amdur MO, Doull J, CASARETT AND DOULL'S TOXICOLOGY, THE BASIC SCIENCE OF POISONS. 3rd Ed, Macmillan Publishing Co, NY, 1986.

Randolph TG, Specific adaption, ANN ALLERGY 40:333, 1978.

Crook WG, Food and chemical allergies: relationship to behavior, J APPL NUTR, 35(1); 47-54, 1983.

Lieberman A, Hardman P, Preston P, Academic, behavioral, and perceptual reactions in dyslexic children when exposed to environmental factors-malathion and petrochemical ethanol, Dyslexia Research Institute, Inc, 4745 Centerville Road, Tallahassee FL 32308, 1981.

Rapp DJ, Double-blind case report of chronic headache due to foods and air pollution, Abstract 13, ANNALS OF ALLERGY, 40: 289, 1978.

Rea WJ, et al, Food and chemical susceptibility after environmental chemical overexposure: case histories, ANNALS OF ALLERGY, 41: 101-110, 1978.

Rea WJ, et al, Pesticides and brain function changes in a controlled environment, CLIN ECOL, 2: 145-149, 1984.

Rea WJ, et al, Toxic volatile organic hydrocarbons in chemically sensitive patients, CLIN ECOL, 2: 70, 1987.

White RF, Feldman RG, Proctor SP, Neurobehavioral effects of toxic exposures. In: White RF, ed, CLINICAL SYNDROMES IN ADULT NEUROPSYCHOLOGY: THE PRACTITIONER'S HANDBOOK. Amsterdam: Elsevier Science Publishers; 1992.

Echeverria D, Fine LF, Langolf G, Schork A, Sampaio C, Acute behavioral effects of toluene, BR J IND MED, 46:483-495, 1989.

White RF, Differential diagnosis of probable Alzheimer's disease and solvent encephalopathy in older workers, CLIN NEUROPHARMACOL, 1:153-160, 1987.

Hanninen H, Nurminen M, Tolonen M, Martelin T, Psychological tests and indicators of excessive exposure to carbon disulfide, SCAND J PSYCHOL, 1:163-174, 1978.

White RF, Feldman RG, Neuropsychological assessment of toxic encephalopathy, AM J IND MD, 1:395-398, 1987.

Baker EL, White RF, Chronic effects of solvents on the central nervous system and diagnostic criteria, Copenhagen: World Health Organization; Oslo: Nordic Council of Ministers; Washington DC: reprinted by U.S. Department of Health and Human Services, Public Health Service; 1985.

Baker EL, Feldman RG, White RF, Harley JP, Dinse GE, Berkey CS, Occupational lead neurotoxicity: a behavioral and electrophysiological evaluation, BR J IND MED, 41:352-361. 1984.

Stewart RD, Hake CL, Wu A, Kalbfleish J, Newton PE, Marlow SK, Vuciecevic-Salma M, Effects of perchloroethylene, DRUG INTERACTION AND BEHAVIOR AND NEUROLOGICAL FUNCTION, DHEW, 77- 191, 1977.

Anger WK, Neuro-behavioral tests used in NIOSH supported work-site studies, NEUROBEHAV TOXICOL TERATOL, 7:359-368, 1985.

Hanninen H, Eskelinen L, Husman K, Nuriminen M, Behavioral effects of long-term exposure to a mixture of organic solvents, SCAND J WORK ENVIRON HEALTH, 2:240-255, 1976.

Arlien-Soberg P, Bruhn P, Glydensted C, et al, Chronic painter's syndrome ACTA NEURO SCAND, 60:149-156, 1979.

Fidler AT, Baker EL, Lentz RE, Neurobehavioral effects of occupational exposure to organic solvents among construction painters, BR J IND MED, 44:292-308, 1987.

Anshelm-Olson B, Effects of organic solvents on behavioral performance of workers in the paint industry, NEUROBEHAV TOXICOL TERATOL, 4:703-708, 1982.

Hanninen H, Psychological picture of manifest and latent carbon disulfide poisoning, BR J IND MED, 28:374-381, 1971.

Anttila A, Pukkala E, Sallmen M, Hernberg S, Hemminki K, Cancer incidence among Finnish workers exposed to halogenated hydrocarbons, JOEM, 37:7, July 1995.

Kobayishi H, Hobara T, Kawamoto T, Higashihara E, Shimazu W, Sakai T, Effect of several organic solvents inhalation on systemic blood pressure, YAMAGUCHI MED J 32:211-216, 1983.

PRESCRIPTION MEDICATIONS ENHANCE CANCER

And do not forget that drugs, even if they are antihistamines or antidepressants, are still chemicals. They overload the system and have to be detoxified, too. And because of that, as well as being able to cause depression, they also enhance cancer by depleting nutrients that could have been used to protect against cancer. But more on this later.

REFERENCES:

Brandes LJ, Arron RJ, Bogdanovic RP, et al, Stimulation of malignant growth in rodents by antidepressant drugs at clinically relevant doses, CANCER RES, 52, 3796-3800, 1992

Brandes LT, Warrington RC, Arron RT, Enhanced cancer growth in mice administered daily human-equivalent doses of some H1-antihistamines: predictive in vitro correlates, J NATL CANCER INST, 86:770-775, 1994

Breitbart W, Bruera E, Chochinov T, et al, Neuropsychiatric syndromes and psychological symptoms in patients with advanced cancer, J PAIN SYMPTOM MANAGE 10:131-141, 1995

Newman TB, Hulley SB, Carcinogenicity of lipid lowering drugs, J AMER MED ASSOC, 275:55-60, Jan 3, 1996

THE SICK BUILDING BLUES

Ever since Bob got his longed for promotion to supervisor in Building C at the research center, he began getting progressively more depressed. Everything seemed black and bleak, negative and hopeless. Nothing perked him up except Sundays with his wife. Annie seemed to be able to snap him out of it. But by mid-week he was in the doldrums again. Perhaps the promotion was too much for him?

He rode it out several months, passing physicals with flying colors and trying the rounds of anti-depressants his doctor kept pushing. Then one day at coffee break he overheard conversations at several tables as he made his way to the machine. Everyone was discussing their health in one way or another. The idea struck him. What if it was the building? How would he ever find out? How would he go about investigating? Where could he begin?

He went to an environmental medicine specialist he had heard of and told his story. After a lengthy history she asked him to do six things:

1. To expose a petri dish or a mold plate in his bedroom and one in his office and see what the different types of molds were in each environment.

2. Skin test by provocation-neutralization testing to various airborne molds including those found on the plates and single-blind test to a couple of chemicals.

3. Do some blood tests that show the integrity of his detoxification liver enzymes and find out what minerals and vitamins are missing from his detoxification pathway.

4. Find out the type of heating system at work and at home, plus the pesticide history of each environment for the last year.

5. Begin a special diet to improve his detoxification function.

6. Begin reading to learn more about environmental medicine and how to get himself totally well.

As he was gathering information and reading, he began to learn to appreciate the clues that he had overlooked before. He was worse at work and as the week rolled on. Furthermore, he did clear at home. And there was a sweetish smell in the air at work.

His work-up revealed that steam heat was used at work and the steam was also disbursed into the air for humidification. It was the **anti-corrosive in the steam heat pipes** that created the faint, sweet odor. This anti-corrosive is a member of a chemical class called **amines** which looks similar to specific amines or neurotransmitters (the happy hormones) in the brain. They can sit in cell receptors designed to hold the neurotransmitter and displace them. In other words, they **stop the happy hormones from working properly.** The result is a relative deficiency of neurotransmitters sitting in the cell membrane receptors. And this leads to depression.

He also was sensitive on provocative testing to molds that were common to both environments, thus raising his total load threshold. Also, he was deficient in several nutrients in his detox pathway that would inhibit him from properly metabolizing the amines in the steam heating system.

He started a program to close off the heat in his office and use a temporary plug-in electric heater and an air purification machine in his bedroom and office. And he began weekly injections to build blocking antibody to mold to turn off his reactions to airborne molds and a nutrient program to correct his detox pathway nutrient deficiencies, plus a diet of whole foods with fewer food additives and processed foods. He became his old, happy self within weeks.

In fact, he began to thrive on solving problems and rallied when they came his way, just as in former times. He was back to the Bob who had earned that promotion. And he had learned to never doubt himself, but rather look for environmental triggers and the nutritional deficiencies that cause symptoms. Most important, he had learned to find the real solution whenever he has depression.

SO WHY HAVEN'T I HEARD ABOUT THIS?

As you will see later, this is more a battle of politics (money and control) rather than of science. I have not even presented 1/20th of the evidence. In fact, just a smattering is presented. There are, in spite of overwhelming evidence for chemical sensitivity, physicians who still think the patients are hypochondriacs and the doctors are quacks who claim treatment for chemical sensitivity. I feel intense embarrassment for a physician who staunchly maintains that there is still not enough evidence.

And misinformation is rampant concerning chemical sensitivity. It seems that I can turn to any current journal and find an "authority" writing on chemical sensitivity. Did you know that it also is a disease marked by a deficiency of anti-depressants? At least it appears so when you read the current journals: "Treatment is generally supportive and may include stress modification, biofeedback, antidepressants, and physical therapy." (Wald MS, Multiple chemical sensitivity syndrome, HOSPITAL PRACTICE, 28K-28O, Sep 15, 1995). I'd like to know how chewing up more detox nutrients in a person who already has an ailing or impaired detox system is supposed to cure him.

So do not become disillusioned if your doctor does not embrace your new-found knowledge. He is merely parroting what he has read. He does not have all the data that actually you, the patient, does. Either lend him this book, or maybe start him with THE SCIENTIFIC BASIS OF SELECTED ENVIRONMENTAL MEDICINE TECHNIQUES.   If after reading those two, or if he refuses to read, learn and grow, then move on. For your mental health is too precious. You cannot afford to wait until every physician catches up.

In Volume II, you will learn how voraciously our everyday home and office chemicals cause us to throw away precious nutrients that could have been used to make plenty of the brain's happy hormones.

REFERENCES:

Graber DR, Musham C, Bellack JP, Holmes D, Environmental health in medical school curricula: Views of academic deans, JOEM Vol 37:7, July 1995.

In the above study, academic deans at 126 US medical schools were surveyed in the Spring of 1994. Comparisons of means and frequencies, multiple regression, and factor analysis were used.   Study results showed only low to moderate expectations for graduate competence in seven environmental health competency areas.   Over two-thirds of deans (70%) indicated that there was "minimal" emphasis on environmental health at their schools; 61% thought that ideally there should be "moderate" emphasis. An "already crowded curriculum" and "too few qualified faculty" were frequently cited as barriers to greater emphasis on environmental health.   Students were identified most commonly as the group expressing the greatest support for environmental health education.   And most thought that the occupational medicine departments were the ones that should start teaching environmental medicine.   As history has shown, this was a grave mistake, still perpetuated.

Staudenmayer H, Selner JC, Failure to assess psychopathology in patients presenting with chemical sensitivities, JOEM, 37:6, 704-709, June 1993.

LABORATORIES:

Some of the laboratories that do specialized tests for various aspects of chemical sensitivity:

Doctors' Data Inc, POB 111, 170 W. Roosevelt Rd, West Chicago IL 60185, 1800-323-2784

Accu-Chem Labs, EHS, INC., 990 Bowser, Ste 800, Richardson TX 75081

Great Smokies Diagnostic Laboratory, 18A Regent Park Blvd Asheville NC 28806, 1-800-522-4762

Pacific Toxicolgogy Labs, 1-800-32-TOXIC

Meta-Metrix Medical Lab, 500 Peachtree Ind. Blvd, Norcross GA 30071, 404-446-5483

Antibody Assay Laboratories, 1715 E. Wilshire, #715, Santa Ana, CA 92705, 1-800-522-2611

Immunosciences Lab, Inc., 8730 Wilshire Blve, #305, Beverly Hills, CA 90211, 310-657-1077 or 1-800-950-4686

CHAPTER 4

MOLD MADNESS:

CAUSES AND CURES

Tom was hospitalized every spring and fall for his depression. The cause was found to be mold allergy and his brain was the target organ. For spring and fall are the peak seasons for mold, the time when showers of billions of spores permeate the air.

Molds are everywhere. They are **invisible**, microscopic organisms that you cannot see until they have grown into large colonies. You know if you left a piece of bread on your desk and came back in a few weeks you would have colonies of mold growth visible on it.

Mold allergy usually accompanies house dust, house dust mite, and pollen allergies as well. And these are known causes of the allergic tension fatigue syndrome, a frequent accompaniment of depression. But mold allergy by itself can be the primary cause of depression. Also, **the brain can be a target organ for mold allergy** resulting in headaches, migraines, inability to concentrate, burning eyes, Tourette's syndrome, obsessive compulsion, panic attacks, schizophrenia and many other symptoms. Most of the time when there is a chemical sensitivity, there is a mold allergy present as well.

Furthermore, mold itself does not even have to be present to cause depression. **Mycotoxins, or the toxins that molds make,** can do any of the damage that any chemical like formaldehyde, toluene, natural gas, or trichloroethyene can do. They can initiate cancers, they can cause chemical sensitivity, and just about any symptom that you can think of from high blood pressure to depression.

Unfortunately, there will be progressively more carcinogenic mycotoxins in our foods, as irradiated foods silently permeate our stores. You see, many fungi are radio-resistant, like Pullularia (Aureobasidium). This one is also particularly prevalent in the fall, but thrives all year. So although many other molds and bacteria may be killed by food irradiation, some forms will thrive. And alas, irradiation does nothing to mycotoxins that are already in food. Furthermore, when food is slated for irradiation, shippers can let down their guard, so to speak, with controls meant to lessen moldiness.

And mold , as important as it is in causing brain symptoms in certain individuals, is not the only inhalant allergen that can cause depression. House dust, house dust mites, animal danders, and pollens of grasses, trees and weeds, algae and much more can trigger the brain as the allergic target organ. Yes, just as easily as molds can trigger the nose, chest or skin with allergic rhinitis and sinusitis, asthma, or rashes like hives and eczema, they can choose the brain as the allergic target organ.

REFERENCES:

Speer F, ALLERGY OF THE NERVOUS SYSTEM, Charles C. Thomas, Springfield, IL, 1970

Crook WG, The allergic tension fatigue syndrome, in: ALLERGY OF THE NERVOUS SYSTEM, Ed. Speer FCC, Charles C. Thomas Publ., Springfield IL, 1970

Newbold HL, Philpott WH, Mandell M, Psychiatric syndromes produced by allergies: Ecologic mental illness. ORTHOMOLECULAR PSYCHIATRY. 2:84, 1973

Randolph TG, Ecologic mental illness. Levels of central nervous system reactions, THE THIRD WORLD CONGRESS OF PSYCHIATRY, 1:379, 1961

Crook WG, Harrison WW, Crawford SE, et al, Systemic manifestations due to allergy, PEDIATRICS, 27(pt1), 1961

Mandell M, Central nervous system hypersensitivity to house dust , molds, and foods, REV ALLER, 24, 1970

Randolph TG, Allergic factors in the etiology of certain mental symptoms, J LAB CLIN MED, 36:77, 1950

Schwartz HJ, Ward GW, Onychomycosis, Trichophyton allergy and asthma -- a causal relationship? ANN ALLERGY, ASTHMA, IMMUNOL, 74:6,523-5523, June 1995

Priyadarshini E, Tulpule PG, Aflatoxin production of irradiated foods, FOOD COSMET TOXICOL, 1976:14;293-295.

Piccioni R, Analysis of data on the impact of food processing by ionizing radiation on health and the environment, INT J BIOSOCIAL RES, 9(2):203-212, 1987.

CANDIDA CRAZINESS

To make matters worse, some people are **wearing mold**, or yeasts in their gut. So they never have a moment's relief; they never get away from the very mold they are reacting to. How do you get this mold or yeast? Very easily. For example, if you have a sore throat and take an antibiotic, the antibiotic does not make a bee-line for your throat. It goes through every part of the body. When it is in the intestine or the gut, it kills off many of the over 400 types of bacteria that are there to properly digest your foods. As well as bacteria, fungi (also called molds or yeasts) also grow in the intestines.

But fungi are resistant to these antibiotics, as they are killed by anti-fungals. So when the antibiotic for your strep throat has also killed off many of the bacteria that were living in happy balance with the yeast in your intestines, the yeast (which is resistant to antibiotics) now has a hay day. It grows rampantly unencumbered by competing bacteria.

One example of this type of yeast is called **Candida albicans**. This yeast can overgrow in the intestine after you have had even one dose of antibiotics. It can also grow when you have steroid hormones given to treat an illness or if you have a diet high in sweets. Once it grows, it can do numerous things. First you can just become allergic to it just as you are allergic to any mold or pollen in the air. The target organ for that allergy could be asthma, or eczema, or migraines. Or the brain can be the target organ with the resulting symptom of depression.

Likewise, the yeast can release toxins that produce headaches, fatigue or depression. **Acetaldehyde is one toxin that Candida releases** through its normal metabolism.

165

Unfortunately, acetaldehyde crosses the blood-brain barrier easily and is toxic to the brain and its neurotransmitters or happy hormones. Acetaldehyde from yeast is capable of **inhibiting the activity of monoamine oxidase** (responsible for the metabolism of other neurotransmitters or happy hormones in the brain) and serotonin, for example.

And not only can yeast's **acetaldehyde** cause severe depression, but it can **stimulate brain neurotransmitters that lead to addiction.** This can lead to repetition of self-defeating dietary habits (like craving and eating a lot of sugar). Then when you eat more sugar, you foster the growth of more yeast. This in turn makes more acetaldehyde. This is one of the often unrecognized **disease-perpetuating cycles** of medicine, that can, however, be stopped and reversed.

Acetaldehyde is the same chemical that **alcohol** is degraded to in the body. It is responsible for some of the same addictive eating (or drinking) patterns that people have when they have a gut over-grown with Candida. And acetaldehyde is the same chemical that many **airborne chemicals** that you have just read about are degraded to. It is an intermediate or stop-over step in the final metabolism of these everyday household and office chemicals. The problem exists when the acetaldehyde detox path is overloaded from both acetaldehyde from yeasts as well as from chemicals. This leads to serious symptoms, especially brain fog and depression.

Or the yeast by growing too viciously in the intestine, can inflame the intestinal lining and inhibit the proper absorption of minerals and result in depression in this way. Actually, there are over **12 different ways or mechanisms** by which any number of thousands of **yeasts** can overgrow in the intestine and **cause depression** (TIRED OT TOXIC? and WELLNESS AGAINST ALL ODDS). There is much more about this yeast problem in the chapter on the gut (Volume III).

One other nasty thing that an overgrowth of yeast in the gut can do is produce **thiaminase.** Thiaminase is a enzyme secreted by some species of Candida that breaks down **thiamine, or vitamin B1.** So just by producing thiaminase, Candida infections can be asymptomatic yet produce a silent B1 deficiency. Vitamin B1 is important in the energy pathway. This deficiency can be a sneaky cause of fatigue and depression. Studies have shown, for example, that mere supplementation of 50 mg a day of B1 in 72 epileptic patients improved their neuropsychological functions in verbal and non-verbal I.Q. testing (Botez MI, et al Thiamine and folate treatment of chronic epileptic patients: A controlled study with the Wechsler I.Q. scale, EPILEPSY RESEARCH, 1993; 16:157-163). But more on thiamine in the vitamin section.

Candida can likewise be so sneaky that it can cause other symptoms that will never make one think of Candida, such as fevers of unknown origin. We saw a young gal who came to the office from Amann, Jordan. She had fevers of unknown origin for years, resistant to all treatments. When we tested and gave injections to the molds to include Candida, the baffling symptoms of years all disappeared within weeks.

One of the most devastating problems with an overgrowth of yeasts in the gut like Candida, is the development of the **leaky gut syndrome.** For this can progress to auto-immune diseases, nutrient deficiencies, food and chemical allergies and more (see the leaky gut syndrome for much more on Candida, Volume III).

REFERENCES:

Barwick VS, et al, Fever of unknown origin: Due to Candida albicans or other fungi acting on the hypothalamus, BRAIN RESEARCH, 1994; 635:1-8.

Ridge JM, The metabolism of acetaldehyde by the brain in vivo, BIOCHEM J, 80;95-100, 1963.

Duritz G, Truitt EB, The role of acetaldehyde in the action of alcohol on brain norepinephrine and serotonin, FED PROC 22:272, 1963.

Eade NR, Mechanism of sympathomimetic action of aldehydes, J PHARMAC EXP THER 127:26-34, 1959.

Towne JC, Effect of ethanol and acetaldehyde on liver and brain monoamine oxidase, NATURE, London, 701:709-710, 1964.

Truss CO, Metabolic abnormalities in patients with chronic Candidiasis. The acetaldehyde hypothesis, J ORTHOMOL MED, 13:2, 1-28, 1983.

Shaw W, Kassen E, Chaves E, Increased excretion of analogs of Krebs cycle metabolites and arabinose in two brothers with autistic features, CLIN CHEM 41: 1094-1104, 1995.

Shaw W, Chaves E, Experience with organic acid testing to evaluate abnormal microbial metabolites in the urine of children with autism, PROC NAT MEET AUTISM SOC AMER, July 1996

AIRBORNE MOLD ALLERGY
STRIKES THE BRAIN

The most common mold allergies, however, are from airborne molds. There are literally thousands of types or species of molds in the air. They all have a certain predilection for specific times of day or night during which they produce billions of spores and make people's symptoms worse. They also have a seasonal predisposition. As an example, **Hormondendrum, also called Cladosporium, is the number one most common airborne mold in the world.** It classically produces showers of billions of spores around noon time.

But **Sporobolomyces, a Basidiomycete yeast,** puts out its showers of **spores at midnight.** So if you are suspicious of mold as one of the causes of depression, you would want to expose a mold plate at the time you are in that room. For example, if you awaken depressed, that is the time and place to expose a mold plate to determine what types and amounts of fungi or molds are present. Better yet would be to set your alarm early, say 3 a.m., and expose the plate a few hours before you normally awaken.

For airborne antigens, any organ can be the target organ. We know a food allergy can have as its target, tissues in the skin (hives), the lungs (asthma), the nose and sinuses (nasal congestion), the brain (migraine, brain fog, depression, schizophrenia, Tourette's syndrome, etc.), the bladder (interstitial cystitis and chronic cystitis), or the prostate (chronic prostatitis). So can molds, house dust, mites and pollens choose any target tissue. For example, ragweed sensitivity can induce baffling recurrent seasonal vaginitis or depression.

There are many problems that the mold allergic person is faced with. First of all, not only can **mold sensitivity effect any target organ** which includes the brain, but it can cause any symptom in the brain, including depression. It is not at all uncommon to see patients whose schizophrenia or manic-depression get so bad that they are hospitalized during the peak mold seasons each year, namely spring and fall.

One of the important things about mold allergy is that many of the **fungi cross react** with others. Since there are so many fungi, it is important to include as many of these cross reacting fungi as possible in the allergy extracts of someone who is adversely effected by molds.

Fortunately, there are many things the person with suspected mold allergy can do long before he consults his physician. It often depends on the type of mold involved. For example, many people with chronic Candidiasis in the vagina and elsewhere have dramatic reduction in the incidence and severity of their symptoms by decreasing sugar in the diet (Horowitz BJ, et al, Sugar chromatography studies in recurrent Candida vulvo vaginitis, J REPROD MED 29 (7):441-443, 1984). Likewise, people with Candida in the gut, toe-nails, fingernails and elsewhere have increased their Candida by eating sweets. Fortunately, many can reverse this process. They can begin to dramatically decrease it by stopping sweets, especially sugars, processed foods and fruits. Further details to come and in TIRED OR TOXIC?

REFERENCES:

Hoffman BR, Kozac PP, Shared and specific allergens in mold extracts, J ALLER CLIN IMMUNOL 63:213, 1979.

Galland L, Nutrition and Candidiasis, J ORTHO PSYCH, 14:50- 60, 1985.

Truss CO, The role of Candida albicans in human illness, J ORTHO PSYCH 10:2, 28-238, 1981.

CANDIDA IS A TOTAL LOAD PROBLEM

Candida is a yeast that can create horrendous depression in an individual by over a dozen different mechanisms. And there are as many ways of treating it as well. But foremost, you must realize that as with any "infection", it is the **vulnerability of the host** that determines how easy or difficult it is to eradicate. I will sometimes see people who have been treated with anti-fungals for years in attempt to get rid of it. This is foolish, for it can foster the development of a form of yeast (**Candida tropicalis**) that is **resistant to Nystatin**, one of the most useful prescribed drugs to eradicate yeast. In their uni-focused treatments, they have failed to recognize that there is more to the total load that must be addressed in that person. And by hammering away at a solo treatment puts the patient in danger of becoming sicker.

In other words, look at all the people with trashy diets, sucking down lots of sodas or alcohol and sweets, working in chemically over-loaded environments, and having frequent antibiotics who never get Candida. Don't ever fool yourself. Candida is not a lonesome yeast that merely needs an anti-fungal to kill it. In order to succumb to it, in order for it to grow in your body, you have to have a lot more wrong with you than you are unaware of. Most of the time the victims are just **not playing with a full deck of nutrients.** This is the factor that raises their vulnerability. But more on total load in that section (Volume IV).

A common mistake we'll see is someone who got better on a program to eradicate yeast. But they did not go far enough to discover **why they were vulnerable** enough to get it in the first place. So they never totally get rid of it. It begins to drive persistent cravings. But since they feel worse eating sugars (it causes the growth of further yeasts), they suck down more anti-fungals. This is a great way to foster the growth of Candida species that are highly resistant to anti-fungals. And taking anti-fungals while you are on antibiotics will foster resistant fungi even faster. So please learn more so that you can avoid these common mistakes and all the agony that goes with them. As you read further chapters, you will learn of what constitutes this increased vulnerability. Always be suspicious if you have "chronic yeast" or "chronic" anything. For what it really means is that the **total load** has not been addressed. More in the total load section.

The spectrum of how diligently yeast must be treated depends of the **host's health**. If yeast is simple to treat because the host is relatively healthy, something as simple as garlic can often eradicate it.

REFERENCES:

Tadi PP, et al, Anti-Candida and anti-carcinogenic potentials of garlic, INT CLIN NUTR REV 10(4):423-429, 1990.

Caporaso M, et al, Anti-fungal activity in human urine and serum after ingestion of garlic (Allium sativum), ANTIMICROB AGENTS CHEMOTHER 23(5):700-702:1983.

Sandhu DK, et al, Sensitivity of yeasts isolated from cases of vaginitis to aqueous extracts of garlic, MYKOS 23:691, 1980.

Moore GS, et al, The fungicidal and fungistatic effects of an aqueous garlic extract on medically important yeast-like fungi, MYCOLOGIA 69:341-348, 1977.

And, garlic doesn't just work in humans as an anti-Candidal substance, but in experimental animals as well (Prasad G, et al, Efficacy of garlic

(Allium sativum) treatment against experimental Candidiasis in chicks, BRITISH VETERINARY JOURNAL 136(5):448-451, 1980).

But remember, that every person with Candidiasis has to be vulnerable. In other words, there had to have been multiple factors that made them vulnerable to yeast. For not everyone who takes antibiotics and eats a lot of sugars gets Candida. They have to have nutrient deficiencies, allergies, gut problems or other problems in order to be so vulnerable or susceptible to this agent. (Montes LF, et al, Hypovitaminosis A in patients with mucocutaneous Candidiasis, JOURNAL OF INFECTIOUS DISEASES 128:227-230, 1973 and Cohen BE, et al, Enhanced resistance to certain infections in vitamin A treated mice, PLASTIC AND RECONSTRUCTIVE SURGERY, 55(2):192-194, 1974.

And as with any problem, there are multiple nutrients that are useful, like vitamin C (Brajtburg J, et al, Effects of ascorbic acid on the anti-fungal action of Amphotericin B, JOURNAL OF ANTI-MICROBIAL CHEMOTHERAPEUTICS 24(3):333-337, 1989). Likewise, many other nutrients have a bearing on one's vulnerability to foreign invaders. For example, animals given copper will have more resistance to yeast (Vaughn VJ, et al, Candida albicans dimorphism and virulence: role of copper, MYCOPATHOLOGICA 64(1):39-42, 1978).

And it is not just deficiency of nutrients that increases susceptibility. But the overload of certain nutrients such as iron, which is fortified in so many foods, can actually become a negative for many people, and increase vulnerability. (Abe F, et al, Experimental Candidiasis in iron overload, MYCO-PATHOLOGICA 89(1):59-63, 1985.

For every substance we put in the body has a **bell-shaped curve** of dose versus effect or activity. As an example, too little water, and we die of dehydration. Too much water and we die of drowning. But there is a huge area under the bell-shaped curve where many doses of water are beneficial to the body. Some substances have a very tine area under the curve. This implies that we need only a tad of this substance, but it is never-the-less, required. Cobalt is such a substance. We need it for B12 metabolism. But too much could produce heavy metal toxicity. Likewise, even minerals like iron that we may take for granted as being necessary and good for us can be a negative and actually toxic to us (and promote yeast over-growth) if we have too much (many foods are fortified with iron).

And patients low in magnesium, for example, are more prone to chronic Candida (Galland L, Normocalcemic tetany and Candidiasis, MAGNESIUM 4(5-6):339-344-1985). I think you get the picture, and you'll learn more in the nutrition section. You have to have something wrong with you in order to get sick, whether it be cancer, arteriosclerosis, high cholesterol, Candidiasis, or depression. Once you get one thing, like Candida, it then can snowball and create other symptoms such as depression and much more. The bottom line is that we must look for nutrient deficiencies with every symptom. Furthermore, we usually need to address the diet, environmental triggers, and much much more, as you will learn.

And again, don't forget that you need **sufficient stomach acid** here, too. Stomach acid is not only necessary to promote the absorption of minerals, but to inhibit the growth of Candida. And in this day and age where people can buy acid inhibitors and antacids without a prescription, and when they are given antibiotics for every unknown medical problem, it increases the chances of getting Candidiasis and then depression even more.

TREATMENT

To treat mold allergy you first need to diagnose it. The best thing to do is to send for a petri dish, also called a **mold plate.** Expose it according to the enclosed directions in your room for 1 hour. This could be your office, bedroom, family room, or any room (one plate per room). Then wrap it up and send it back in the mailer and our mycologist will report what types of molds and how much there is in that area.

Once you know the area that has too much mold, then you can use an air purifier to remove it, or take out the carpet, or both.

Or you could use petri dishes from your local hospital. But there are two major drawbacks; they use the wrong media (Sabouraud's), and they refuse to incubate the plate for six weeks to allow the slower growing fungi to mature and be identified.

You always want to **re-culture** to check on the effectiveness of your mold eradication procedures or environmental controls. If in spite of an air purifier you still have persistent mold in excess of a couple of colonies, consider removing the carpet, roof repairs, and check window casings, use lights in moldy closets, or see if trees surrounding the building need to be cut back. Sometimes gutters for the roof, or ditching to carry water away from the building foundation, or UV lights and dehumidifiers in the basement can cut down on the mold. In older buildings, covering a dirt basement floor with cement helps. These are termed **environmental controls** (there are many more in the E.I. SYNDROME, REVISED).

And **do not eat irradiated foods** (airlines, hotels, groceries, fast food places are all potential sources). As you have learned, some of their nutrient content has been destroyed by the process. But also recall that several types of fungi are radio-resistant, like Aureobasidium (Pullularia). And recall that because food handlers know that a food is slated for radiation, they may not take as much mold precautions as necessary, knowing that most of the organisms will be retarded by the irradiation process. But some molds and mycotoxins which are very potent causes of cancer, are not destroyed.

So if you are mold sensitive, you want to make sure that you eat fresh produce and grains that are properly dried and stored to reduce mycotoxins. (You will want to use a ferment free diet as a trial. Remember that a **ferment free diet** is one where you do not eat any foods that have been aged, pickled, dried, fermented, molded, yeasted, or otherwise have mold antigens in them.

This includes ketchup, vinegar, mayonnaise, salad dressing, alcohol (beer, wine, liquor), chocolate, tea, breads, biscuits, crackers, sausages, sauerkraut, soy sauce, miso, dried fruits, and much more. For many people who are allergic to airborne molds and get **depressed from breathing them, also get depressed from eating them.** (And crucial to anyone trying to eradicate a yeast problem is to eat no sugars in any form, including fruits while you are healing.) You can get plenty of vitamin C and fiber from many vegetables, so there is no danger. Many ethnic cultures do very well health-wise with no fruits. So certainly you could forego them for a few weeks or months.

One last thing should be remembered about pollen, dust, dust mite, and mold allergies. If they are not treated adequately with environmental controls, diet, and titrated allergy injections (free of the preservatives if the patient is allergic to these preservatives), then allergic symptoms will persist. When this happens, medications are used. And many allergy medicines have neuropyschiatric side effects which can also include depression (Bender B, et al, Neuropyschiatric effects of medications for allergic diseases, JOURNAL OF ALLERGY AND CLINICAL IMMUNOLOGY, 95:2, 523-528). So attention to **total load** is crucial.

And never forget that people can be depressed if they happen to be allergic to phenols used as a preservative in standard allergy injections. For the brain can be the target organ. Reading TIRED OR TOXIC? and WELLNESS AGAINST ALL ODDS will provide further information in detail about diagnosing and treating your own mold sensitivities.

The bottom line is look for common hidden allergy symptoms: have you ever had any allergies or currently have chronic nasal congestion, headaches, irritable bowel, arthritis, post nasal drip, chronic cough or clearing of your throat, recurrent infections, unwarranted fatigue, asthma, bronchitis, eczema? Be sure you do not miss a clue and a golden opportunity to see if part or all of the problem of your depression is caused by a sensitivity to pollens, animals, dusts, mites, molds, or other airborne antigens.

Even when some people think they are reacting to indoor chemicals, sometimes it is really the indoor mold to which they are reacting. And remember, you could also be wearing in your gut the very yeast or mold to which you are allergic. Therefore, you never get away from it, and consequently, you never get out of depression. Fortunately, we now have multiple tests available, as you will learn, to diagnose the presence and effects of yeast. And we have multiple ways of irradicating it.

But first, your next step will be to turn to Volume II of this 4-volume set to learn about the nutrition connection to depression. This background information is all setting the stage so that you will be better able to benefit from the diagnosis and treatment.

REFERENCES:

Rogers SA, Indoor fungi as part of the cause of recalcitrant symptoms of the tight building syndrome, ENVIRONMENT INTERNATIONAL, 17:4, 271-276, 1991

Mandell M, Mold allergy as a major cause of biologic mental illness. In CLINICAL ECOLOGY, L D Dickey, (ed). Springfield IL, Charles C. Thomas Co., ch. 22, p 259-61, 1976.

Rogers SA, A practical approach to the person with suspected indoor air quality problems, INTERN CLIN NUTR REV 11;3,126- 130, July 1991.

Al-Doory Y, Domson J, MOLD ALLERGY , Philadelphia, Lee & Febiger, 1984.

Rogers SA, Resistant cases: Response to mold immunotherapy and environmental and dietary controls, CLIN ECOL: ARCH HUMAN ECOL IN HEALTH & DIS, 5:3, 115-120, 1987/1988.

Rogers SA, A comparison of commercially available mold survey services, ANN ALLERGY, 50, 35-37, 1983.

Roger SA, In-home fungal studies: Methods to increase the yield, ANN ALLEGY 49:35-37, 1982.

Rogers SA, A thirteen month work, leisure, sleep environmental fungal survey, ANN ALLERGY, 52:338-341, May 1984

King DS, Can allergic exposure provoke psychological symptoms? A double-blind test, BIOL PSYCHIATRY, 16(1):3-19, 1981.

Malling HJ, Dreborg S, Weeke B. Diagnosis and immunotherapy of mold allergy. V. Clinical efficacy and side effects of immunotherapy with Cladosporium herbarum. ALLERGY 41: 507- 19, 1986.

Dales RE, Zwanenburg H, et al, Respiratory health effects of home dampness and molds among Canadian children, AM J EPIDEMIOL 134:196-203, 1991.

Martin CJ, Platt SD, Hunt SM, Housing conditions and ill health, BR MED J 294,1125-1127, 1987.

Targonski PV, et al, Effect of environmental molds on risk of death from asthma during the pollen season, J ALLERGY CLIN IMMUNOL, 95:955-961, 1995.

Kravchenko LV, et al, Biochemical changes in subacute mycotoxicosis induced by T-2 toxin in rats, TOXICOLOGY 42:77-83, 1986.

Beasley VR, TRICHOTHELENE MYCOTOXICOSIS: PATHOPHYSIOLOGIC EFFECTS, VOL II, CRC Press, Boca Raton, FL 1989.

Chi MS, El-Halawani ME, Waibel PE, Mirocha CJ, Effects of T-2 toxin in brain catecholamines and selected blood components in growing chickens. POULT SCI 60:137, 1981.

Crook W 6, Depression associated with Candida albicans infections, JAMA, 251:22, 2928-2929, June 8, 1984.

Crook WG, Candidiasis depression, HOSPITAL PRACTICE, 20:1A,12, Jan 30, 1985.

Randolph T, Allergic factors in the etiology of certain mental symptoms, J LAB & CLIN MED, 46:942, 1950.

Crook WG, Yeast can affect behavior and learning, ACAD THERAPY 19:517-526,1984.

Iwata K, A review of the literature on drunken symptoms due to yeast in the gastrointestinal tract, in Iwata K (ed):YEASTS AND YEAST-LIKE MICROORGANISMS IN MEDICAL SCIENCE, University of Tokyo Press, Tokyo, 260-268, 1976.

Iwata K, et al, Studies on the toxins produced by Candida albicans with special reference to their etiopathological role, pp 184-190, ibid.

Edwards DA, Depression and Candida, JAMA 253:3400, 1986.

Speer F, ALLERGY OF THE NERVOUS SYSTEM, Charles C. Thomas, Springfield IL, 1970.

Truss CO, Tissue injury induced by Candida albicans. Mental and neurological manifestations, J ORTHOMOL PSYCHIATR, 7(1):17-37, 1978.

Kaji H, et al, Intragastrointestinal alcohol fermentation syndrome: report of two cases and review of the literature, J FORENSIC SCI SOC, 24:461-471, 1984.

Truss CO, Metabolic abnormalities in patients with chronic Candidiasis. The acetaldehyde hypothesis, J ORTHOMOL MED, 13:2, 1-28, 1983.

Crayton J, Anti-Candida antibody levels in polysymptomatic patients; presented at the Candida Update Conference, Memphis TN, Sept. 16-18, 1988.

Kabe J, Aoki Y, Immediate and delayed responses caused by components of Candida albicans, JPN J ALLERGY 19:1999-206, 1970.

Kabe J, et al, Antigenicity of fractions from extracts of Candida albicans, J ALLERGY 47:59-75, 1971.

Odds FC, Pathogensis of Candida Infections, J AM ACAD DERMATOL, 1994;31;S2-S5 (Explains that Candida infections are the result of an interplay between fungal virulence and host defenses).

Bolivar R, et al, Candidiasis of the gastrointestinal tract, in GP Bodey, V. Fainstein (eds) CANDIDIASIS, New York, Raven Press, 1985.

Dhaliwal AK, Fink JN, Vaginal itching as a manifestation of seasonal allergic disease, J ALL CLIN IMMUNOL, 95:3, 780-782, 1995.

VOLUME II

(CHAPTERS 5-6)

NUTRITIONAL FACTORS

**THE NUTRITIONAL DEFICIENCY CAUSES;
HOW VITAMINS, MINERALS, AMINO ACIDS,
FATTY ACIDS AND ORPHAN NUTRIENTS
MAKE THE BRAIN'S HAPPY HORMONES**

CHAPTER 5

THE NUTRITION CONNECTION

In Volume I, you learned how foods, chemicals, pesticides, heavy metals, Candida, and ingested and airborne molds can cause depression. But the nutritional status is most likely the most important and simultaneously most ignored aspect of treatable causes of depression. It is no secret that nutrition as taught in medical schools has changed little in the last two decades (Barrocas A, Nutrition in medical education, PERSPECT IN APPL NUTR, 2:3, 17-20,1995).

Learning **environmental medicine breaks many of the rules** and models or paradigms **upon which drug-oriented medicine is based.** In fact it ushers in an exciting era of molecular medicine, where we can now usually find the causes of symptoms. We get rid of them rather than merely drugging them with endless years of expensive medications.

For one of the major problems for depressed individuals who are unknowingly chemically sensitive, as you now know, is that the **xenobiotic (foreign chemical) detoxication** system is not operating normally. And one of the reasons is that some of the nutrients (vitamins, minerals, amino acids and essential fatty acids) in the major detoxication pathways are deficient (too low). At first we had a tough time appreciating how this could happen in the land of plenty where foods are even fortified.

But as you will see, unsuspected **vitamin and mineral deficiencies are rampant in the U.S.** It is another **undiagnosed epidemic** and the cause of much **senseless suffering.** For these deficiencies not only explain why many people have depression, but are also the cause of many other symptoms and diseases.

HOW DO WE GET NUTRIENT DEFICIENT?

There are a number of ways. For starters, the processing of foods to alter taste and extend shelf life is a major cause. When you process **brown rice to form white** rice by grinding, bleaching, and other processes, **you lose roughly 80% of the many trace minerals,** like magnesium, manganese, copper, zinc, and more. (Schroeder 1969, 1971).

And an equivalent loss occurs when you go from whole wheat berries down to bleached white wheat flour, one of the mainstays of the standard American diet (SAD) in the form of white pasta and bread. So this last 50 years of processed foods is a vast experiment in what the human chemistry can adapt to. It is a huge experiment to see if by throwing out 80% of the nutrition from one of the major components of the diet, the health of mankind will suffer or not. It has.

Nutrients can be lost a number of other ways, as various cooking techniques reduce nutrient content, like microwaving. Likewise, nutrients are lost with storage (time) and heat, but also with other techniques of preservation, such as irradiation, which is done increasingly. Anything that disrupts the wholeness of a food accelerates its nutritional deterioration. For example, the current craze of buying salad already cut up is the height of stupidity. For not only does it cost much more than whole lettuce heads, but as soon as you cut lettuce, every 20 minutes it looses a major portion of its nutrient content. So by the time you eat it, there is scarcely any nutrient value remaining.

Nutrients are also lost from the soil with repeated growing of crops, or never completely develop with harvesting before natural ripening has occurred. Add to this the forced ripening with chemicals like ethylene of produce picked green, before it has matured, and you have one of the reasons a tomato in the winter can taste like cardboard. It is difficult to believe that it is in any way related to that succulent vegetable you grow in your garden. There are other factors that also reduce the nutrient value of foods. An example is EDTA used to preserve the green color of frozen broccoli, for it lowers the vitamin B6 in the vegetable.

But one more **cause of nutrient loss** is rarely mentioned or looked for in medicine: the loss from **overwork of the chemical detoxication pathways.** For as you learned, you are bombarded by over 500 home, office, and travel chemicals every day and you must detoxify them. Every time you walk into a grocery store and detoxify even one molecule of pesticide, you use up or throw away forever, one molecule of glutathione and other nutrients silently used by your body to detoxify this chemical. This loss occurs even if you cannot smell or perceive the chemical.

Surely, we are the first generation of man ever exposed to such an unprecedented number of chemicals. Detoxification is going on in most of us rather constantly. Most people are using up nutrients faster than ever by being in a constant state of accelerated detoxification. Since the average person is exposed to and must detoxify in excess of 500 xenobiotics (foreign chemicals) in a day, it comes as no surprise that a vast majority of people are nutrient deficient. And the scientific literature bears this out with astounding repetitiveness.

In essence, most people are losing or using up specific nutrients in the daily work of detoxifying our 21st century chemical environment. And the problem is that the loss of these nutrients then makes them sitting ducks for other medical problems. Yet, medicine is still not training doctors to look for curable causes of symptoms, much less training them to do thorough nutrient assessments. It is quicker and easier to write an Rx for a drug and get on to the next patient. Plus it is extremely lucrative for the drug industry. And it is lucrative for the insurance industry, as they are often spin-off companies of the chemical-pharmaceutical giants.

But this becomes extremely important to you when you learn from the scientific research that some "incurable" cancers, for example, have been literally cured by just giving vitamins. Take vitamin A, which is known not only to retard the development of malignancies (cancers) but to reverse some "incurable" types of cancers. But vitamin A is used up or depleted in the work of chemical detoxication. And it is depleted by chemotherapy.

Yes, you read that right. Scientists have discovered that vitamin A and its related compounds can actually reverse or cure some types of cancers, like some forms of otherwise incurable leukemia (many references in WELLNESS AGAINST ALL ODDS). And being exposed to daily chemicals can use up this precious vitamin A. But rather than do good environmental controls to reduce chemical exposure and prescribe inexpensive vitamins, many of the victims of this type of leukemia are not given this information nor given these options. Instead they are treated with expensive chemotherapy and bone marrow transplants, because their oncologists are in an experimental program or linked to a protocol that does not happen to be testing vitamin A.

Likewise, researchers have found that 4 vitamins a day will cut the recurrence rate for cancer in half. Yet it is not standard to do this. This represents a horrendous savings in lives and money and the vitamins cost pennies a day. But few physicians are even aware of these studies. Test your doctor. (Lamm D, J Urol, Jan 1994). We could go on with examples like this, but that is not our focus (more for folks interested in this subject in our other books and the newsletter).

Nutrient deficiencies are also common side effects of all drugs. Yet medicine rarely looks at the nutrient levels that have been driven down by drugs. For example, magnesium deficiency is a common side effect of diuretic (fluid pills, blood pressure pills) therapy. Yet an assay is rarely done, much less the more accurate test. And ironically, an undetected magnesium deficiency can be the very reason for the symptom for which the diuretic was prescribed in the first place (i.e., as in cases of magnesium deficiency-induced hypertension). And as you will learn, a magnesium deficiency is a common and inexpensively remedied cause of depression.

"IF YOU EAT A BALANCED DIET, YOU CAN'T GET DEFICIENT"

If you meet a physician who parrots this phrase, run as fast as you can. You cannot afford to wait for his medical knowledge to catch up to the 21st century.

This commonly offered medical advise overlooks the fact that the majority of the SAD (standard American diet) is processed, leaving only 25-75% of the original nutrients in food. We are the first generation to ever be continually detoxifying such an unprecedented number of daily chemicals (over 500, average). Add to the fact that the work of detoxication loses or uses up nutrients, and it is really a tribute to the design of our bodies that we do as well as we do. And even the diet itself is in trouble. In a Food and Drug Administration study to analyze 234 foods over 2 years, the government found the average American diet to have less than 80% of the RDA (recommended daily allowance) of one or more: calcium, magnesium, iron, zinc, copper, and manganese (Pennington, 1986).

Nutrient deficiencies are really so common that they are practically epidemic. In one study of patients admitted to a hospital, 23-50% had undiscovered deficiencies, and this was not a sophisticated analysis (Roubenoff, 1987). In other words, they did not do the nutrient tests that would catch even one-quarter of the deficiencies. And when other studies have demonstrated **magnesium deficiency in well over 50% of the population** (Rogers, 1991, Whang, 1990), it behooves any of us to condemn any symptom to a lifetime of medications without ruling out deficiencies. For as you can appreciate, even the most seemingly minor of symptoms, like anxiety or insomnia may be a sign of a magnesium or other nutrient deficit. And if undiagnosed, this magnesium deficiency can begin to insidiously disrupt arterial and cardiac integrity and consequently increase the vulnerability to life-threatening cardiac events (Seelig, 1989).

In other words, every symptom, regardless of how minor it is, brings you closer to a fatal one. But if warning symptoms of anxiety (from a magnesium deficiency) are unknowingly masked with a seemingly harmless tranquilizer, the opportunity to prevent more serious sequelae (like a heart attack from a worsening magnesium deficiency) is lost or at best delayed.

For in fact, it is fortunate that a magnesium deficiency can manifest as a plethora of symptoms. This provides many golden opportunities to diagnose it early. And there are many other nutrient deficiencies that contribute to arteriosclerosis, and often do so silently, like chromium (Boyle, 1977, Schroeder, 1970, Fuller, 1983, Press, 1990, Elwood, 1982). Unfortunately, when a chromium deficiency does cause one of its classic symptoms, like hypoglycemia with mood swings and depression (Anderson, 1984, 1986, Uusitupa, 1983, Offenbacker, 1980) that symptom is still not recognized by physicians as a reason to check for a chromium deficiency. Then when the person develops high cholesterol from the undiagnosed chromium deficiency, cholesterol lowering drugs are prescribed. But these can cause depression and suicide also, as you will learn.

THE INTER-CONNECTEDNESS
CAN NO LONGER BE IGNORED

So if nothing else, the **symptoms of anxiety and depression,** for example, **should never be medicated** to stomp them out. Rather, the **underlying cause or defect should be isolated** to prevent the person from an untimely death. Once the causes in this book have been exhausted, medications could be used as a last resort. Instead just the opposite occurs. Drugs are the **first** (and last, if you die) resort.

If this were not enough, look at how we compound some of these **biochemical blunders in medicine.** Magnesium and

190

vitamin E are both stripped from many processed foods. But magnesium deficiency plays a major role in the development of arteriosclerosis (Orimo, 1990, Seelig, 1980). And vitamin E deficiency is also important in the development of arteriosclerosis and cardiovascular disease (Gey, 1990). In fact, it can even protect against a magnesium deficiency-induced cardiac disease (Freedman, 1990) as well as reduce the size of a heart attack or myocardial infarct (Axford-Gatley, 1991) once you get one, and improve bypass success.

And vitamin E can speed your recovery from a heart attack (Ferrein, 1991, Reilly, 1991). As well, magnesium can reduce the severity, speed healing and often negate a fatal arrhythmia. And as you might guess, a magnesium deficiency can be induced by a vitamin E deficiency (Goldsmith, 1967, Haddy 1960). Hence another way for the **downward spiral.** For once symptoms are masked with drugs, and the environmental triggers and nutritional defects are not found and corrected, the **SICK GET SICKER.** There is a vast inter-connectedness of the body and its chemistry. We can no longer treat one organ system as though it is an isolated problem in an otherwise healthy body.

And it should come as no surprise that **both deficiencies, magnesium and vitamin E, also promote chemical sensitivities,** depression, arteriosclerosis, and cancer (Seelig, 1979). For the pathologies of many diseases are similar: it just depends upon the hereditary target organ predisposition and environmental vulnerability, the individual biochemistry, and the xenobiotic dose and time frame.

In other words, the causes are different for each individual. Each has his own unique total load. Somehow in medicine, because one drug type will ameliorate the symptoms in most people with similar symptoms, the thinking has erroneously led physicians to assume that when cause is found, it too, must be the same for all sufferers. But nothing could be further from the truth. This one fact has enormously slowed progress in conquering many diseases, especially arteriosclerosis, cancer, chemical sensitivities, and depression.

A similar error has occurred when researchers have attempted to study nutrients like they would study a drug: alone. They ignore the fact that **the total load is crucial.** For example, some studies on vitamin A were inconclusive for its cancer-sparing effect, in spite of its well-known anti-oxidant properties. This was in part because they tried to study it alone as though it were a drug. But high doses of vitamin A alone, or unbalanced, tend to suppress the level of vitamin E by as much as 40% (Meyskins, 1990). This creates a relative vitamin E deficiency. And that increases cancer. For remember, the relative balance of nutrients one to another, just like the pieces in an orchestra, is crucial to proper function. You rarely take a concerto and just use the oboe and none of the other instruments and expect the result to be a success. It would be like trying to show someone how a car worked by showing the carburetor only.

But there are scores of studies in the "scientific " literature that do just that. A major role of vitamin E is to be guardian of the cell membrane and not allow cancer-causing chemicals to penetrate into the genetic material. Since vitamin E is a necessary anti-oxidant that keeps carcinogens out of the cell, omitting it from a cancer study (ignoring its synergistic activity with vitamin A) negates the benefit of A. Likewise, when you do a study on vitamin E, for example, and do not include sufficient vitamin C, you cannot regenerate tocopheral from the tocopheroxyl radical to recycle and restore the usefulness of vitamin E (Bendich, 1986).

In other words, once you use vitamin E, it is shot and unusable again until you recycle it. This is done with vitamin C which restores the electron capacity to vitamin E so it can be used again. So you can begin to see why studies that make nutrients look worthless are merely the product of researchers who are not knowledgeable enough. The result is that vitamin E, in a study with poor design, does not manifest its full potential. It then, likewise, comes out looking less beneficial than it is, because of iatrogenic deficiencies.

To give another idea of how prevalent nutrient deficiencies are, in one study of elderly women in a nursing home, they found that 73% were low in vitamin D3, 57% were low in B6, 38% were low in vitamin C, 30% were low in selenium, and 28% were low in folic acid. These deficiencies would give anybody depression (Lowik M, et al, Marginal nutritional status among institutionalized elderly women as compared to those living more independently, JOURNAL OF THE AMERICAN COLLEGE OF NUTRITION, December 1992; 11(6):673-681.

Then remember every drug that is prescribed for these poor soles further lowers their nutrient status. The problem is that many of the drugs were probably prescribed for the symptoms brought about by the undetected deficiencies. In a nursing home, if the food doesn't kill them, the doctors will.

It is no small wonder that so many drugs stifle symptom manifestations when you see how similar the biochemical pathologies are. And yet see how individually unique the cause and treatments are if a search is made for the nutritional or biochemical defects and environmental triggers (Mago 1981, Rea 1977, 1978, 1981, Rogers 1992), or deficits and toxicities. Now you can readily appreciate that by **resorting to drugs, we set the patient up for the inevitable worsening,** like the ultimate premature failure in the form of **a fatal cardiac event** (Marino, 1991).

HOW THE SICK GET SICKER, QUICKER

You can begin to appreciate how clairvoyant you become as you read such articles as "Excess mortality associated with diuretic therapy in diabetes mellitus" (Warram, 1991). There was no mention of magnesium in this article. But yes, diabetes does foster the loss of magnesium (Lau 1985, Martin 1947) and vice versa, magnesium deficiency potentiates diabetes (Zonszein, 1991). And you know that diuretics cause magnesium loss. So it comes as no surprise. In fact, it is inevitable that a person with not one, but two mechanisms to potentiate magnesium loss (diabetes and diuretics) would succumb faster, probably of sudden death. They are so behind, they think they are first!

So a title like that, "Excess mortality associated with diuretic therapy in diabetes mellitus" merely means they are saying, "Golly, gee whiz! For some reason, when we give diuretics (fluid pills) to diabetics, they die even faster than other people do." No kidding! They should, fools. For the diuretic accelerates the magnesium deficiency. I would be utterly embarrassed to write such a ridiculous article, for it blatantly screams to the world that the authors do not know the chemistry of nutrition, disease, drugs, and the body. And they are dangerous to their patients.

The problem is that most of the authors of these papers a big-wigs at teaching hospitals and medical schools. And the journals are crammed full of these articles. On the average I find 1-3 of these atrocities in every major journal each month. That is a staggering loss of life. Now you are beginning to think like a specialist in environmental medicine when you see the **connectedness**. For environmental medicine forces the practitioner to relate all the events in the body to the total load. And when he fails to do so, he simply cannot help people heal. And **THE SICK GET SICKER, QUICKER.**

As one appreciates the complexity of this, it becomes easier as you learn how **interrelated** everything is. And this knowledge helps the physician to avoid **further blunders** that only serve to potentiate illness. The recommendation of **calcium for the prevention of osteoporosis** is one of a multitude of examples. Let's look at the problem.

Many people are deficient in calcium because the standard acidic processed diet is high in hidden **phosphates** (most processed foods, but soft drinks especially). And phosphates, which are in nearly all processed foods and sodas, **inhibit the absorption of calcium**. In addition, by eating large quantities of meats and sweets, this makes the body acidic. This acid requires a huge amount of buffering. When the plasma buffer reserves are exhausted, the body calls upon the calcium from the bone to buffer. Hence, eating phosphate-laden processed foods causes calcium loss from bones.

But to build bone, calcium is laid down in bone only when enough of the complementary minerals are present, such as zinc, copper, boron, and magnesium (Abraham, 1991). But when these are not present, taking extra calcium merely deposits the calcium in the toxic waste heap of the body, the

195

blood vessel wall (Tanimura, 1986). So instead of building bone, the calcium is used to accelerate arteriosclerosis, aging, and disease.

In other words, by haphazardly recommending calcium to a nation of people who are already consuming vast quantities of cheese, milk, ice cream and meats, and without measuring the erythrocyte (rbc) zinc, rbc copper, magnesium loading test, etc., we are potentiating the development of vascular calcifications instead of bone calcification. We are enhancing the deposition of extra calcium in the vessels of the heart and brain to hasten coronary artery disease, arteriosclerotic and nutrient-deficient depression, and senile brain disease; items already taking their toll on the economy.

And all because we fail, in an era of unprecedented high tech medicine with powerful prescription medicines, to analyze an individual's nutrient biochemistry and then prescribe a balanced correction. So it matters not whether we address a symptom, a disease, a metabolic process, or even an endocrine problem (Fatemi, 1990); **a complete work-up has not been done if a nutritional defect is not sought.**

In summary, we see (1) that by not reading the current biochemical and environmental literature, the physician is helping the SICK GET SICKER, QUICKER. Furthermore, (2) when drugs are used in the current medical system to mask symptoms, by ignoring the underlying cause, it is left to worsen and inevitably leave new symptoms in its wake. And (3) medications also have effects of their own that induce further nutrient deficiencies, thus potentiating the decline in health of the patient.

So, in the meantime, for starters, a good rule of thumb would be to use minimum processed foods, nothing that contains hydrogenated oils, and no margarines. Instead, have non-farmed ocean fish twice a week, and cut down on saturated fats from red meat. Eat butter on breads (and select breads that contain no hydrogenated oils), dress salads with flax oil, and cook with olive oil. And plan meals with a preponderance of fresh vegetables, whole grains, and beans, as well as nuts and seeds, fresh vegetable juices, and sea vegetables. Then start to assess the nutrient levels. More on this later.

REFERENCES:

(and there are more in WELLNESS AGAINST ALL ODDS

Abedin Z, et al, Cardiac toxicity of perchloroethylene, S MED J 73:1081-1083,1980

Abraham GE, The calcium controversy. J APPL NUTR 34:2,69-73, 1982

Abraham GE, The importance of magnesium in the management of primary postmenopausal osteoporosis. J NUTR MED 2,165-178, 1991

Altura BM, Altura BT, Gerrewold A, Ising H, Gunther T, Magnesium deficiency in hypertension: Correlation between magnesium deficient diets and microcirculatory changes in situ. SCIENCE 223,1315-1317, 1984

Altura BM, Altura BT, New perspectives on the role of magnesium in the pathophysiology of the cardiovascular system: I. Clinical aspects. MAGNESIUM 4:226-244, 1985

Anderson RA, Poansky MM, Bryden NA, Canary JJ, Chromium supplementation of humans with hypoglycemia. FED PROC 43:471,1984

Anderson RA, Chromium metabolism and its role in disease processes in man. CLIN PHYSIOL BIOCHEM 4:31041, 1986

Anonymous, New misgivings about magnesium. SCIENCE NEWS 133:32,356, 1988

Anonymous, Magnesium deficiency: A new risk factor for sudden cardiac death. INTERN MED WORLD REPORT 5:9,18,1990

ARCHIVES OF INTERNAL MEDICINE v.150: p519-522, p613-617, p496-500, 1990

Axford-Gatley RA, Wilson GJ, Reduction of experimental myocardial infarct size by oral administration of alpha- tocopherol. CARDIOVASCULAR RES 25:89-92,1991

Boyle E, et al, Chromium depletion in the pathogenesis of diabetes and arteriosclerosis. SOUTH MED J, 70:12,1449- 1453,1977

Cachs JR, Interaction of magnesium with the sodium pump of the human red cell. J PHYSIOL 400,575-591, 1988

Cannon LA, Heiselman DE, Dougherty JM, Jones J, Magnesium levels in cardiac arrest victims: Relationship between magnesium levels and successful resuscitation. ANN EMERG MED 16,1195-1198, 1987

Cox IM, Campbell MJ, Dowson D, Red blood cell magnesium and chronic fatigue syndrome. LANCET 337,757-760,1991

Delmi M, Rapin CH, Bengoa JM, Delmas PD, Vasey H, et al., Dietary supplementation in elderly patients with fractured neck of the femur. LANCET 335:1013-1016, 1990

Ebel H, Guenther T, Role of magnesium in cardiac disease. J CLIN CHEM CLIN BIOCHEM 21:249-265,1983

Elin RJ. The status of mononuclear blood cell magnesium assay, J AM COLL NUTR 6:2,105-107, 1987

Elwood JC, Nash DT, Streeten DHP, Effect of high-chromium brewer's yeast on serum lipids.J AM COLL NUTR 1:263, 1982

Fatemi S, Ryzen E, Flores J, Endres DB, Rude RK, Effect of experimental human magnesium depletion on parathyroid hormone secretion and 1,25-dihydroxyvitamin D metabolism. J CLIN ENDOCRIN METAB 73,1067-1072, 1991

Fehlinger R, Fauk D, Seidel K, Hypomagnesemia and transient ischemia cerebral attacks. MAGNESIUM BULL 6:100-104, 1984

Ferreira RF, Milei J, Llesuy S Flecha BG, et al, Antioxidant action of vitamins A and E in patients submitted to coronary artery bypass surgery, VASCULAR SURG 25:191-195,1991

Freedman AM, Atreakchi AH, Cassidy MM, Weglicki WB, Magnesium deficiency-induced cardiomyopathy: Protection by vitamin E. BIOCHEM BIOPHYS RES COMM 170:3,1102-1106,1990

Fuller JH, Shipley MJ, Rose Gm Harrwett RJ, Keen H, Mortality from coronary heart disease and stroke in relation to degree of glycaemia: the Whitehall Study. BR MED J 287:867-870,1983

Gallinger S, Rogers SA, MACRO MELLOW, Prestige Publ., Box 3191, Syracuse, NY, 13220, 1992.

Gey KF, Lipids, lipoproteins and antioxidants in cardiovascular dysfunction. BIOCHEM SOC TRANS 18:1041- 1045,1990

Goldsmith LA, Relative magnesium deficiency in the rat. J NUTR 93,87-102,1967

Haddy FJ, Local effects of sodium, calcium and magnesium upon small and large blood vessels of the dog forelimb. CIRCULATION RESEARCH 7,57-70, 1960

Hall RCW, Joffee JR, Hypomagnesaemia, physical and psychiatric symptoms. JAMA 224:13,1749-1751, 1973

199

Howard JMH, Magnesium deficiency in peripheral vascular disease. J NUTR MED 1:39-49, 1990

Iseri LT, French JH, Magnesium: Nature's physiologic calcium blocker. AM HEART J 108:1,188-192, 1984

Kaplan NM, Dietary aspects of the treatment of hypertension. ANN REV PUBLIC HEALTH 7,501-519,1986

Kline K, Cochran GS, Sanders EG, Growth-inhibitory effects of vitamin E succinate on retro virus-transformed tumor cells in vitro, NUTR CANCER 14:27-41, 1990.

Kremer JM, Michaler AV, et al Effects of manipulation of dietary fatty acids on clinical manifestation of rheumatoid arthritis. LANCET 189-197, Jan 26,1988

Lardinois CK, Neuman SL, The effects of antihypertensive agents on serum lipids and lipoproteins. ARCH INTERN MED 148. 1280-1288, 1988

Lazard EM, A preliminary report on the intravenous use of magnesium sulphate in puerperal eclampsia. AM J OBSTET GYNECOL 26,647-665, 1925

Leary WP, Reyes AJ, Magnesium and sudden death. SA MED J 64,697-698,1983

Mago L, The effects of industrial chemicals on the heart, 206-207 in Balazo T, ed., CARDIAC TOXICOLOGY, CRC Press, Boca Rayton, FL, 1981

Main AN, Morgan RJ, Russell RI, et al, Magnesium deficiency in chronic inflammatory bowel disease and requirements during intravenous nutrition. J PARENTERAL NUTR 5:15-19, 1985

Marier JR, Magnesium content of the food supply in the modern-day world. MAGNESIUM 5:1-8,1986

Marino PL, The hidden threat of magnesium deficiency. INTERN MED 12:6,32-46,1991

Martin HE, Wertman M, Serum potassium, magnesium and calcium levels in diabetic acidosis. J CLIN INVEST 26,217-228, 1947

Nicar MJ, Pak CYC, Oral magnesium deficiency, causes and effects. HOSPITAL PRACTICE 116A-116P, 1987

Offenbacher EG, Pi-sunyer FX, Beneficial effects of chromium-rich yeast on glucose tolerance and blood lipids in elderly subjects. DIABETES 29:919-925,1980

Orimo H, Ouchi Y, The role of calcium and magnesium in the development of arteriosclerosis. ANN NY ACAD SCI 598,444-457, 1990

Ornish D, et a;, Can life-style changes reverse coronary heart disease? LANCET 336:129-133

Pennington JA, Young BE, The selected minerals in foods surveyed from 1982 TO 1984, J AMER DIETETIC ASSOC 86:7,876, JULY 1986

Press RI, Geller J, Evans G, Effect of chromium picolinate on serum cholesterol and apolipoprotein fractions in human subjects. WEST J MED 152:41045,1990

Rasmussen HS, McNair P, Goransson L, Balslov S, Larson OG, Aurup P, Magnesium deficiency in patients with ischemic heart disease with and without acute, myocardial infarction uncovered by an intravenous loading test. ARCH INTERN MED 148, 329-332, 1988

Rayssiguier Y, Gueux E, Weiser D, The effect of magnesium deficiency on lipid metabolism in rats fed a high carbohydrate diet. J NUTR 111,1876-1883,1981

Rea WJ, Environmentally-triggered small vessel disease. ANN ALLERGY 38:245-251, 1977

Rea WJ, Environmentally-triggered cardiac disease. ANN ALLERGY 40:4, 243-251, 1978

Rea WJ, Recurrent environmentally triggered thrombophlebitis: A five-year follow-up. ANN ALLERGY 47:333-344, Part I, Nov 1981

Rea WJ, Johnson AR, Smiley RE, Maynard B, Dawkins-Brown O, Magnesium deficiency in patients with chemical sensitivity. CLIN ECOL 4:1,17-20, 1986

Rea WJ, Brown OD, Cardiovascular disease in response to chemicals and foods. In: Brostoff J, Challacombe R, eds FOOD ALLERGY AND INTOLERANCE. Balliere Tindall/Saunders, London/NY, 737-753, 1987

Resnick LM, Gupta RK, Laragh JH, Intracellular free magnesium in erythrocytes of essential hypertension: relation to blood pressure and serum divalent cations. PROC NATL ACAD SCI USA 81,6511-6515, 1984

Rhinehart RA, Magnesium metabolism: A review with special reference to the relationship between intercellular content and serum levels. ARCH INT MED 148,2415-2420,1988

Rogers SA, TIRED OR TOXIC?, Prestige Printing, Box 3161, Syracuse NY 13220, 1990

Rogers SA, THE CURE IS IN THE KITCHEN, ibid, 1991

Rogers SA, Chemical Sensitivity, Parts I, II, III INTERNAL MED WORLD REP, Feb 1992, Mar 1992, Apr 1992

Roubenoff R, et al, Malnutrition among hospitalized patients: problem of physician awareness. ARCH INTERN MED 147:1462- 1465.1987

Ryzen E, Elbaum N, Singer FR, Rude RK, Parenteral magnesium tolerance testing in the evaluation of magnesium deficiency. MAGNESIUM 4,137-147, 1985

Schroeder JA, Nason AP, Tipton IH, Essential metals in man, magnesium. J CHRON DIS 21,815-841, 1969

Schroeder HA, Mason AP, Tipton IH, Chromium deficiency as a factor in arteriosclerosis. J CHRON DIS, 23:123-142,1970

Seelig MS, Magnesium (and trace substance) deficiencies in the pathogenesis of cancer. BIOLOGICAL TRACE ELEMENT RESEARCH 1,273-197, 1979

Seelig MS, MAGNESIUM DEFICIENCY IN THE PATHOGENESIS OF DISEASE. EARLY ROOT OF CARDIOVASCULAR, SKELETAL, AND RENAL ABNORM-ALITIES. Plenum Med. Book Co., NY, 1980

Seelig MS, Magnesium requirements in human nutrition. MAGNESIUM BULL 3:suppl 1A:26-47, 1981

Seelig MS, Nutritional status and requirements of magnesium. MAG BULL 8,170-185, 1986

Seelig M, Cariovascular consequences of magnesium deficiency and loss: Pathogenesis, prevalence, and manifestations --- magnesium and chloride loss in refractory potassium repletion. AM J CARDIOL 53,4g-21g, 1989

Seelig CB, Magnesiuum deficiency in hypertension uncovered by magnesium load retention. J AM CLIN NUTR 8:5,455, abs.113, 1989

Shecter M, et al, Beneficial effect of magnesium sulfate in acute myocardial infarction. AM J CARDIOL 66:271-274, 1990

Singh RB, Cameron EA, Relation of myocardial magnesium deficiency to sudden death in ischemic heart disease. AM HEART J 103:3,399-450, 1982

Stendig-Lindberg G, Graff E, Wacker WE, Changes in serum magnesium concentration after strenuous exercise. J AM COLL NUTR 6:1,35-40, 1987

Tanimura A, McGregor DH, Anderson HC, Calcification in arteriosclerosis. I. Human studies. J EXP PATHOL 2:4, 261- 273,1986

UUsitupa MIJ, Kumpulainen JT, Voutilainen E, Hersio K, et al, Effect of inorganic chromium supplementation on glucose tolerance, insulin response and serum lipids in noninsulin- dependent diabetics. AM J CLIN NUTR 38:404-410,1983

Warram JH, Lori LMB, Valsania P, Christlieb AR, Krolewski AS, Excess mortality associated with diuretic therapy in diabetes mellitus. ARCH INTERN MED 151,1350-1356, 1991

Whang R. Qu TO, Aikowa JK, Watanabe A, Vannatta J, Fryer A, Markanich M, Predictors of clinical hypomagnesmia, hypokalemia, hypophosphatemia, hyponatremia and hypocalcemia. ARCH INTERN MED 144:1794-1796,1984

Whang R, Ryder KW, Frequency of hypomagnesemia and hypermagnesemia, requested versus routine. JAMA 263,3063- 3064, 1990

Whang R, Whang DD, Ryan MP, Refractory potassium repletion. ARCH INTERN MED 152,40-45, 1992

Zonszein J, Magnesium and diabetes. PRACT DIABETOL, 10:1-4, Mar/Apr 1991 THE NUTRIENT CONNECTION

THE NUTRIENT NEMESIS

When we look at **zinc,** another example, literature reports indicate that unsuspected zinc deficiency is also relatively common. In one study only 13% of randomly selected patients had normal zinc levels. That means that 87% were abnormal! In another study 68% of the population ingested less than 2/3 the RDA for zinc. Zinc deficiency has been shown to be prevalent throughout the world, in all age ranges, in pregnancy, chronic disease, after surgery, and in chemical sensitivity.

Magnesium deficiency is even more prevalent when you consider that government surveys show the average American diet provides only 40% or less than half of the recommended daily allowance (RDA) for magnesium. Others confirm its widespread deficiency in over 54% of 1033 patients. And again, its deficiency contributes to the total load of chemical sensitivity and depression in the patient. And of course, this deficiency is also important in a variety of other diseases from arteriosclerosis, arrhythmia, sudden death, and chemical sensitivity to osteoporosis, chronic low back pain and chronic fatigue.

Unfortunately, in U.S. medicine, there is currently a myth circulating, where it is not at all uncommon to hear a physician tell a patient that if he just eats a balanced diet, he need not concern himself about nutrient deficiencies. When in fact, nothing could be further from the truth. And it is dangerously far from the truth as the **JOURNAL OF THE AMERICAN MEDICAL ASSOCIATION** article, June 13, 1990, shows us. Among 1033 patients who were hospitalized for a variety of ailments, some of which they died from, over 54% of them were magnesium deficient.

The most alarming part was that **90% of the physicians never ordered a magnesium   assay.** And of those who did, the worst and least sensitive assay was done.   In other words, they used a test so old fashioned (serum magnesium, the same test that every doctor gets when he orders the chemical profile) that it looks normal even when a person is low. The test looks good even when the magnesium is low enough to be the cause of life-threatening angina, arrhythmia and even death.

Therefore, according to this study, it is **"reasonable and customary"** (a term insurance companies like to use to justify refusing to cover some items) for **90% of the physician population to fail to make the correct diagnosis** for lack of assessing nutrient levels. And the result is that patients died of cardiac arrhythmias or sudden cardiac death because of these undetected deficiencies.

Obviously, cases of solo deficiencies are rare, and multiple deficiencies are the rule.   In other words, if a person is deficient in one item, he is more likely to be deficient in some others as well. You can use any common disease as an example.   The literature is full of reports of, for example, **hypercholesterolemia** from copper deficiency, or chromium deficiency, or magnesium deficiency, vitamin C deficiency, etc.

The exciting part is that **once the individual's own unique biochemical defects have been identified and corrected, you may have a patient who needs no   medication.** It is so logical: if you suddenly cannot properly metabolize cholesterol, in spite of dietary modifications, you had better find our what is missing in the biochemistry of your cholesterol metabolism pathways. It does not mean you need a lifetime of a medicine costing $120.00 a month. More on **cholesterol-lowering drugs** later, and how they invariably **cause further symptoms, including depression and cancer.**

It is known now that some **blood pressure pills actually increase blood lipids (cholesterol and triglycerides). Additionally,** there is an **increase in suicide and accidental deaths with cholesterol-lowering drugs.** We will explain why later (Volume IV). And, of course, **all medications accelerate the loss of nutrients,** because each medication is merely another chemical that uses up or lowers nutrients in the process of the body trying to detoxify it.

This in no way detracts from the fact that our armamentarium of drugs is fantastic in the benefits it creates. But they do deny us the opportunity to identify the causes of many symptoms. As progressively more identifiable causes emerge for symptoms that we currently label as incurable, knowledge of the nutrient connection in medicine will grow. But not, regrettably, without many errors being made. Let's look at a current mistake.

THE MAGNESIUM MISTAKE

As of 1993, many clinical blood test laboratories have unfortunately added a serum magnesium to their routine general chemistry panels. But studies reveal that many docs do not know that the serum magnesium makes up only 1% of the total body magnesium. So a person can be dangerously low and the test will be perfectly normal.

There is a physiology in the body called **homeostasis**. It is the body's attempt to make serum or blood levels look good no matter how low the nutrient may be. For example, a person can be so low in calcium as to have severe osteoporosis. But the serum calcium will look normal. The reason the serum is protected (by **homeostasis**) is because it bathes all cells. If they are not bathed in enough calcium, you are probably in the emergency room with a seizure or heart attack. Better, the body says, to "rob Peter to pay Paul" and keep the majority of the body's cells bathed in the proper mineral, and let just one organ system suffer. So your teeth fall out or you get osteoporosis, but it beats sudden death from a seizure or heart attack. And **if you are smart enough**, the former symptoms give you enough time to figure out their causes.

So **do not have a serum magnesium test**. And if one is included in the chemical profile battery of tests, just ignore it. For this test will serve to give a false sense of security to those who do not yet know that the most accurate way to assess magnesium status is with a challenge test.

Meanwhile, assessing and correcting nutrient deficiencies has been a major tool in overcoming depression and chemical sensitivity. So when you hear someone saying, "There is no such thing as a nutrient deficiency in the United States if you just eat a balanced diet", I trust you can set them straight now. For without this knowledge, they have nary a hope of helping those heal who have severe chemical sensitivity and the seemingly endless array of symptoms that it can masquerade as. As for you, make sure that you at least have your daily anti-oxidants and multiple minerals (more on that later).

Clearly, **immune deficiency or immune dysfunction** can lead to depression. And it can result from any single nutrient deficiency or excess. This is why it is so important to have levels assessed and balanced (Beisel WR, Edelman R, Nauss K, Suskind RM, Single nutrient effects on immunologic functions; Report of a workshop sponsored by the Department of Food and Nutrition and its Nutrition Advisory Group of the American Medical Association. JOURNAL OF THE AMERICAN MEDICAL ASSOCIATION 245:1, 53-58, January 2, 1981).

It will come as no surprise to you to know that, for example, in the scientific literature there are studies demonstrating that if you look at some awful disease such as Alzheimer's, you find that if you compare these people with normal people, they have half the levels of protective vitamins A and E, for example. And yet this is not assessed (Zaman Z, Roche S, Fielden P, Frost PG, Niriella DC, Cayley ACD, Plasma concentrations of vitamins A and E and carotenoides in Alzheimer's disease, AGE AND AGING 21:91-94, 1992).

We can assess many other nutrients like amino acids and essential fatty acids. Yet these analyses are often unnecessary once the minerals are corrected. Usually the most important nutrients to correct are the minerals since these are what make so many critical enzymes work and take the longest to correct and incorporate into body enzymes. When vitamins are prescribed they can work immediately. But for minerals, the old enzymes must first be broken down, new enzymes must be synthesized and the minerals incorporated into them.

Most likely, magnesium is the most important all around mineral. It is in over 300 enzymes and even government publications show the average American diet provides less than half of what everyone needs in an average day. As you now know, the **serum magnesium test** which is part of a chemical profile (which is a test that most doctors do when you have a physical or any complaint) **is worthless.**

Since **less than 1% of the body's total magnesium is in the serum,** if that test is abnormal, you are in deep trouble because you can even be severely deficient and the test will look normal. Likewise, the rbc magnesium, which is a step better, is still an inferior test. The best test is the **magnesium loading test.** The directions are described in the back of **TIRED OR TOXIC?,** and the complete paper we published with results and references for doctors is in the back of **THE CURE IS IN THE KITCHEN.** An I.V. (intravenous) test is even better, for some.

The next most important, and commonly deficient minerals are copper, zinc and manganese which among other things, are in enzymes called **superoxide dismutase.** The function of these is to neutralize or gobble up free radicals so that they do not go on to destroy body tissues. Obviously, the family of S.O.D. enzymes is one of the most important enzymes in the body. For it is endlessly working to negate the constant chemistry that is silently working non-stop to bring on aging, chemical sensitivity, and in fact all diseases, including cancer and depression.

The best assay for minerals that run these crucial enzymes are blood tests for these specific minerals done on **rbc (red blood cells),** not serum, plasma, or whole blood. In other words, you must see your report. It must **specifically say rbc** zinc, **rbc** manganese, or **rbc** copper. If it merely says zinc, manganese and copper, then you know that the wrong test was done. You should **make sure to see your test results** for

210

this reason alone. For often even when the correct test was ordered, an incorrect test is done. But no one notices.

It is a fine point that has huge consequences. This is because the rbc test for minerals is rarely done, even though it is the most sensitive and the only one worth the money. Even when it is ordered, much of the time the less sensitive or inferior one is done. **So insist on seeing the results yourself.**

A third of the time when we mail prescriptions to our out of state patients to have their mineral levels checked, the labs do the inferior (and cheaper) serum assay instead; even though it is clearly typed to do the rbc assay. These serum or plasma assays are often normal even in the face of a serious deficiency. So **have no hesitancy about seeing your laboratory results.** It's your only safety mechanism. After all, who can you trust more than yourself to do a meticulous job in being sure the best was done?

Another important fact, is that the body can only assimilate so much for so long. So whenever you are on a program to take supplements, don't be afraid to listen to your body's innate wisdom. When you get to one of those days when you feel like "Ugh, I can't take another vitamin!", you know it is time to give the body a rest. It can only take in so much before it has to then assimilate it and put it to work.

So, whether your body needs 2 weeks on and one week off the supplements, or to take them every other day, or to spread out what has been written for one day over 2 or 3 days, so be it. We must listen to our own individual biochemistries.

NEVER FORGET THE BELL-SHAPED CURVE

When you think about it, the person with depression, cancer, arteriosclerosis, auto-immune disease, chemical sensitivity, or other serious disease has to be even more compromised in his nutrient status in order to have gotten sick in the first place. Plus, when one is sick, nutrients are used up and depleted even faster. So it is a downward spiral where the sick get sicker quicker.

As an example of vitamin potency, you learned, **vitamin A** has been found to reverse, turn off, turn around one of the most serious forms of leukemia for which there is no current medical treatment. This includes radiation, chemotherapy, bone marrow transplant or surgery. And scientists think they even know how it causes a redifferentiation of these cells. But it is not routinely used.

But as with any nutrient, prolonged, high doses of vitamin A can cause toxicity. As with everything, there is a **bell-shaped curve,** which changes with the person's condition. There is an optimal dose, on either side of which either an increase or a decrease in dose can lead to adverse effects that can culminate in death. So you must be very careful with it.

This toxicity is not a matter of just not feeling well. You see, in the brain there are some fluid filled cavities called **ventricles.** There are tiny canals through which this fluid flows into the spinal column and equilibrates, or equalizes pressure in the brain versus in the spinal column. If these tiny canals are plugged for any reason, the fluid builds up in the ventricles. They enlarge and they squash the brain against the immovable skull. This condition is called

hydrocephalus and can lead not only to depression, fatigue and headache, but severe brain damage, and death.

So caution and knowledge are necessary even with nutrient use. They are powerful substances.

HOW LONG CAN THIS BE IGNORED?

By now you see that medicine is forging ahead in the wrong direction, in spite of voluminous evidence. For example overt **malnutrition is seen in 40% of patients hospitalized for cancer** (Landel AM, Hammond WG, Meguid MM, Aspects of amino acid protein metabolism in cancer-bearing states, CANCER, 1:55 (1 Suppl): 230-237, 1985). And it is known that surgery, radiation and chemotherapy can result in further deterioration in nutritional status in patients (McAnena OJ, Daly JM, Impact of anti-tumor therapy on nutrition, SURG CLIN NORTH AMER, 66(6):1228, Dec 1986).

They also know that many foods contain nutrients that help induce detoxification enzymes and inhibit cancer (Steinmetz KA, Potter JD, Vegetables, fruit, and cancer. II. Mechanisms, CANCER CAUSES AND CONTROL 2(6):427-442, Nov 1991. Wattenberg LW, Inhibition of carcinogenesis by minor nutrients constituents of the diet, PROC NUTR SOC, 49:2, 173-183, Jul 1990). And they know that many vitamins and minerals and diet all play an important role in preventing and treating cancers. And we know there are diets that have reversed end-stage cancers when everything that medicine has to offer has failed.

And we know that the National Cancer Institute has grown from a budget of $2.5 million in 1974 to $55 million in 1988, without a proportionate improvement in cancer. Where are the oncologists who should be recommending diets and nutrients?

REFERENCES:

Greenwarld P, Light L, McDonald SS, Stern HR, Strategies for cancer prevention through diet modification, MED ONCOL & TUMOR PHARMACO THERAPY, 7(2-3): 199-208, 1990.

Wargovich MJ, Lointier PH, Calcium and vitamin D modulate mouse colon epithelial proliferation and growth characteristics of a human colon tumor cell line, CANAD J PHYSIOL & PHARMACOL, 65:3, 472-477, March 1987.

Lippman SM, Meyskens FL, Vitamin A derivatives in the prevention and treatment of human cancer, J AMER COLL NUTR 7:4, 269-284, Aug 1988.

Prasad KN, Mechanisms of action of vitamin E on mammalian tumor cells in culture, PROGR CLIN BIOLOG RES, 259:363-375, 1988.

Carter, et al, J AMER COLL NUTR, 12:3, 1993

Lamm D, J UROL, Jan 1994

Kallistratos GI, Fasskee EE, Karkabounas S, Charalambopoulos K. Prolongation of the survival time of tumor bearing Wistar rats through a simultaneous oral administration of vitamins C and E and selenium with glutathione, PROGR CLIN BIOL RES, 259:377-389, 1988).

McCully KS, Chemical pathology of homocysteine. II. Carcinogenesis and homocysteine thiolactone metabolism, ANN CLIN LAB SCI, 24:27-59. 1994

IS THERE A CONSPIRACY OF
IGNORANCE AND ARROGANCE?

When you try to discuss these exciting facts with someone in the field, there is a mixed reaction of (1) arrogance at the idea that someone should try to invade their field and (2) feigned ignorance of the facts. I say feigned, for I find it difficult to believe they are truly ignorant of scores of years of exciting work in their own field. So if the vast amount of data about nutrition is ignored for the cancer patient, you can partly understand why it really takes a back seat for the depressed patient.

I'm sorry to have bored you with so much detail, but most people are incredulous to find that deficiencies are so common and at the same time, the basis of correctable conditions. Besides that, this book is unique in that it is written for physicians as well as patients. So what if you know more about this aspect of medicine than any other physician you meet again? Hopefully you'll encounter one who wants to learn and grow with you in order to see you get well. We were all intimidated by this volume of information initially. But the desire to get well superseded it.

So a quick summary is:

(1) Nutrient deficiencies are so common, they are the rule.
(2) Processed foods contribute to nutrient deficiencies and
(3) The work of detoxifying this world depletes levels even further as this uses up more nutrients.
(4) Nutritional deficiencies are a part of nearly all symptoms.
(5) They must be properly assessed, for if the wrong types of levels are ordered, the results are worthless. (Soon we

215

will see what role each of the individual nutrients plays in depression.)

(6) You have to have some nutrient deficiencies in order to get sick.

(7) All drugs or medications further use up or deplete nutrients.

REFERENCES:

Schroeder HA, Losses of vitamins and trace minerals resulting from processing and preservation of foods, AM J CLIN NUTR 24:562-573, 1971.

Ebeling W, The relation of soil quality to the nutritional value of plant crops, J APPL NUTR 33(1):19-34, 1981.

Singh A, Day BA, DeBolt JE, Trostmann UH, Bernier LL, et al, Magnesium, zinc, and copper status of US Navy SEAL trainees, AM J CLIN NUTR 49:695-700, 1989.

Abrams SA. Stuff JE, Calcium metabolism in girls: current dietary intakes lead to low rates of calcium absorption and retention during puberty, AM J CLIN NUTR 60:139-743, 1994.

Morgan KJ, Stampley GL, Zabik ME, Fischer DR, Magnesium and calcium dietary intakes of the U.S. population, J AM COLL NUTR 4:195-206, 1985.

White HS, Inorganic elements in weighed diets of girls and young women, J AM DIET ASSOC, 55:38-43, 1969.

McWhirter JP, Pennington CR, Incidence and recognition of malnutrition in hospital, BRIT MED J, 945-948, 1994.

Calabrese EJ, Does exposure to environmental pollutants increase the need for vitamin C? J ENVIRON PATHOL TOXICOL ONCOL, 5:81-90, 1985.

Sandstead HH. A brief history of the influence of trace elements on brain function. AMER J CLIN NUTR, 293-298, Feb 1986.

Roubenoff R, et al, Malnutrition among hospitalized patients: a problem of physician awareness, ARCH INTERN MED 147:1462- 1465, 1987.

Watson G, Differences in intermediary metabolism in mental illness, PSYCH REP, 17;149-170, 1965.

Watson G, Currier WD, Intensive vitamin therapy in mental illness, J PSYCHOL, 49;67-81, 1960.

Watson G, Comfrey AL, Nutritional replacement for mental illness, J PSYCHOL, 38; 251-264, 1954.

Rosenberg IH, Miller JW, Nutritional factors and physical and cognitive functions of elderly people, AMER J CLIN NUTR, 55:1237-438, 1992.

Watson G, Vitamin deficiencies in mental illness, J PSYCHOL, 43; 47-63, 1957.

Lucksch F, Vitamin C and schizophrenia, WIENER KLINISCHER WOCHENSCRIFT, 53:1009-1011, 1940.

Caldwell WA, Hardwick SW, Vitamin deficiency and psychoses, J MENT SCI, Vol. 90, 95-108, 1944.

Jaffe R, Kruesi O, The biological-immunology window: a molecular view of psychiatric management, INT CLIN NUTR REV, 12(1):9-26, January

Sauberlich HE, Machlin LJ, ed. Beyond deficiency: New views on the function and health effects of vitamins, ANN NY ACAD SCIENCES 669:1-404, 1992.

Kato T, Brain Phosphorous Metabolism in Depressive Disorders Detected by Phosphorous-31 Magnetic Resonance Spectroscopy, J AFFECTIVE DISORDERS 26:223-230, 1992.

Benton D, Vitamin/mineral supplementation and intelligence, LANCET, 335:1158-1160, 1990.

Benton D, Roberts GM, The effects of vitamin and mineral supplementation on intelligence, the sample of school children, LANCET, 664: 140-143, 1988.

Haller J, Vitamins for the elderly: reducing disability and improving quality of life, AGING CLIN EXPER RES, 5 (suppl. 1):65-70, 1993.

Carney MP, Vitamins and mental health, BRIT J HOSP MED, 48(8), Oct. 21-Nov. 3, 1992.

SOLO NUTRIENT DEFICIENCIES ARE RARE

Often studies that fail to show improvement with one nutrient are merely examples of patients who have more than one deficiency. In fact, this was proven in studies where they found that the longer a person was depressed, the less often a single nutrient helped them when it was found to be low and corrected. This would make sense since the longer it is ignored, the greater the likelihood that other deficiencies have developed (Linder J, et al, Calcium and magnesium concentrations in affective disorder: difference between plasma and serum in relation to symptoms, ACTA PSYCHIATR SCAND 80:527-537, 1989).

In the study just mentioned, patients with recent depression had more correlation of improvement with correcting low levels than did patients with long standing depression. And that makes sense. Because as an illness continues, depression as one example, you will develop further deficiencies and damaged enzymes. So it becomes more difficult to cure. As another example, one study showed that 22% of patients with low serum calcium levels were magnesium deficient (Wang R, et al, Predictors of clinical hypomagnesemia: hypokalemia, hypophosphatemia, hyponatremia and hypocalcemia, ARCHIVES OF INTERNAL MEDICINE 144:1794-1796, 1984). This is understandable since undetected **deficiencies foster further development of other deficiencies.**

This bears out what I have always said and that is, it is **very difficult to get a solo deficiency.** Usually when there is one deficiency there are many more. And the longer a person has been symptomatic and the worse the symptoms are, the more likely you are going to find multiple deficiencies and environmental triggers.

We explained how **it is really criminal not to look for a magnesium deficiency in depressed patients.** Depression is a classic symptom of magnesium deficiency and it is very common. **Government studies show the average American diet provides only 40%, or less than half of the magnesium a person needs in a day.** And other researchers have found that patients with depression of unknown cause were found to have reduced total plasma magnesium levels. And recall that they used the least sensitive, worst test to assay magnesium. It misses a large percentage of patients who are indeed magnesium deficient. Now you can appreciate how common a magnesium deficiency is. And soon you'll see how commonly it is involved in depression (Hall RCW, et al, Hypomagnesemia: physical and psychiatric symptoms, JAMA 224(13):1749-1751, 1973).

And the beauty of it all is that once diagnosed, it is terribly easy and inexpensive to treat. And when you compare it to the cost of drugs and psychotherapy, the misery for the person, misery for the spouse, misery for the family, friends, and co-workers, lost time from work, and lost time from life, there is absolutely no contest. Last but not least, you never can be as happy on a drug as you can with all of your brain's happy hormones working naturally and optimally. For every drug works by turning off some part of your chemistry in order to stifle a symptoms. So with drugs on board, all of your chemistry cannot be functioning optimally.

DEFICIENCIES ARE NOT RARE

In spite of the data, patients consistently report that when they ask their physicians to check nutrient levels, they are met with a scowl and an exasperated proclamation that nutrient deficiencies are extremely rare in the United States. Yet in one study of 800 patients admitted to 2 American hospitals, over 55% of them had nutrient deficiencies (Nutritional therapy saves lives, and cost, MEDICAL WORLD NEWS, February 24, 1986, p.99). That's over half. Yet over half the patients in the hospital do not have nutrient assessments, at all. And when they do, inferior tests are usually done.

In another study of over **3,000 hospitalized American patients, 58% had one or more signs of malnutrition** (Kamath S, AMER MED NEWS, May 24-31st, 1985). There are many studies of nursing homes, hospitals, ICU's and much more confirming epidemic, multiple nutrient deficiencies. And the older the person gets, the more likely he is to be deficient (Werbach MR, NUTRITIONAL INFLUENCES ON MENTAL ILLNESS Third Line Press, Tarzana CA 91356, 1991).

Then if you look at individual nutrients, you find the same thing. For example, in one study 81% of people consumed less than 66% of the copper they needed in a day (Holden JM, et al, Zinc and copper in self-selected diets, J AMER DIET ASSOC 75:23-28, 1979). And, being in the hospital does not help them. In fact, it makes you get sicker quicker, as another study showed that the daily intake of copper in hospitalized patients in the United States was 0.76 mg. This is less than 1/4 of what you need in a day. It's even less than 1/2 of what the RDA is, which is notoriously low (Klevay LM, et al,

Evidence of dietary copper and zinc deficiencies JAMA 241:1916-1918, 1979).

Even the healthiest specimens that could be found had an inferior dietary intake. A study showed that 37% of 270 U.S. Navy sea, air and land trainees (SEALS) were below the RDA. So no wonder we all get as many diseases and as much depression as we do. Why even **one out of 3 of the healthiest specimens we can find in the U.S. is deficient in copper!** (Singh A, et al, Magnesium, zinc and copper status of U.S. Navy SEAL trainees, AMER J CLIN NUTR, 49:695-700, 1989).

And since copper is one example of a mineral whose deficiency can not only cause depression, but arteriosclerosis and hypercholesterolemia, it should be no surprise that young soldiers on autopsy were "suprisingly" found to have arteriosclerosis (Enos WF, et al, Coronary disease among United States soldiers killed in action in Korea, JAMA, 152:1090-1093, 1959).

I personally would be extremely embarrassed to have ever been quoted, as is still being quoted today, that the American diet provides all the nutrients necessary. For the **evidence is overwhelming** to the contrary. And it supports why we have so much illness including depression. It is common knowledge that the RDA of vitamin E, for example, is far below what it should be. For example, the NEW ENGLAND JOURNAL OF MEDICINE (1993) study showed that a mere 100 units cut the cardiovascular risk in half for 85,000 subjects. However, in spite of this, a study of over 11,000 people showed that the median intakes of vitamin E were considerably lower than the RDA (Murphy SP, et al Vitamin E intakes and sources in the United States, AMER J CLIN

NUTR 52:361-367, 1990). And still the U.S. Public Health service staunchly resists recommending that the populous take supplements. And they do not even recommend physicians to check levels.

Vitamin E has been stripped from most oils and grains. Yet its deficiency is a known factor in creating just about every illness you can think of from arteriosclerosis and depression to chemical sensitivity and cancer. And indeed, we have progressively more people with all these problems. And we are all paying for it in a multitude of ways.

And, as people get older, deficiencies and medical problems escalate. For example, in one study of over 400 people in a nursing home, 87% of them ingested less than the RDA for zinc (Elsborg L, et al, The intake of vitamins and minerals by the elderly at home, INT J VIT NUTRIT RES 53:321-329, 1983).

Even when you look at people who are not in a nursing home, but are supposedly normal American men and women, eating the diets that they want to eat, 68% have less than 2/3rds of the RDA for zinc (Holden JM, et al, Zinc and copper in self- selected diets, J AMER DIET ASSOC, 75:23, 1979). And we're merely giving a few examples of a few nutrients. The story is much worse. Therefore, it becomes imperative that **any physician claiming to do good, conscientious medicine cannot ever consider a patient undiagnosable or untreatable until environmental and nutritional assessments have been done.**

REFERENCES:

Williams RJ, BIOCHEMICAL INDIVIDUALITY, NY, John Wiley & Sons, 1957

Pauling L, Orthomolecular psychiatry, SCIENCE, 160:265-271, 1968

Pauling L, Vitamin therapy: Treatment for the mentally ill, SCIENCE, 160:1181, 1968

Williams R, NUTRITION AGAINST DISEASE, Pitman Publ, Corp, NY 1971

Pfeiffer C, Neurobiology of the trace metals zinc and copper, INTERNAT REV NEUROBIOL, (suppl 1), Academic Press, NY 1972

Cott A, Orthomolecular approach to the treatment of learning disabilities, SCHIZOPHRENIA, 3:2, 95-105, 1971

Pauling L, Orthomolecular psychiatry: Varying the concentrations of substances normally present in the human body may control mental disease, J NUTR MED 5:187-198, 1995

CHAPTER 6

VITAMIN AND MINERAL DEFICIENCIES CAUSE SERIOUS DEPRESSION

VITAMIN DEFICIENCIES

If you look at the symptoms from a deficiency of any vitamin, depression is usually among the top 5. This is because the chemistry of the brain depends on all the nutrients working in harmony. So rather than take a grueling in depth look at each nutrient, we'll surf among some highlights.

VITAMIN B1 OR THIAMINE

B1 deficiency is quite common, since more people prefer to select foods in Burger-King wrappers these days than prepare fresh vegetables at home. And because vitamin B1 or thiamine is essential in the energy pathway, it can affect any part of the body. Fatigue and depression are therefore very commonly correctable B1 deficiency symptoms.

If that were not enough, recall when we warned that many people have an overgrowth of yeasts like Candida albicans in their intestines? As you recall, it can be precipitated by antibiotics, diabetes, diets high in processed foods and sweets, and medications like prednisone, hormones, and more. The problem is that some species of yeast (Volume I) actually synthesize the enzyme, **thiaminase.** This breaks down and **destroys thiamine** before it ever gets a chance to be absorbed (references in WELLNESS AGAINST ALL

225

ODDS). And alcohol causes much B1 deficiency. More importantly, when the body is acidic (acid diet of meats and sweets, infection, faulty energy metabolism) it requires more B1 to right itself. When the brain is acidic, it is sad.

REFERENCES:

Schmidt LJ, Influence of thiamine supplementation on the health and general population with marginal thiamine deficiency, et al, J GERON, 46(1):M16-M22, 1991.

Carney MW, et al, Thiamine, riboflavin and pyridoxine deficiency in psychiatric in-patients. BR J PSYCHIATRY 141:271-272, 1982.

Williams RD, et al, Induced thiamin (B1) deficiency in man: relation of depletion of thiamine to development of biochemical defect and of polyneuropathy., ARCH INTERN MED 71:38-53, 1943.

Brozek J, Psychologic effects of thiamine restriction and deprivation in normal young men, AM J CLIN NUTR 5(2):109- 120, 1957.

Mamesh MS, Johnson BC, The effect of penicillin on the intestinal synthesis of thiamine in the rat, J NUTR 65:161- 167, 1958.

Bell IR, Edman JS, Morrow FD, Marby DW, Perrone G, Kayne HL, Greenwald M, Cole JO, Brief communication, vitamin B1, B12, and B6 augmentation of tricyclic antidepressant treatment in geriatric depression with cognitive dysfunction, AMER COLL NUTR, 11(2): 159-63, Apr 1992.

Bell IR, Edman JS, Morrow FD, Marby DW, Mirages S, Perrone G, Kayne HL, Cole JO, B complex vitamin patterns in geriatric and young adult inpatients with major depression, J AMER GERIATRICS SOC, 39(3): 252-7, March 1991.

VITAMIN B3

Much has been written about the wonderful use of vitamin B3 or niacin and many other nutrients by very progressive psychiatrists who have used these to clear mental cases including schizophrenia and depression for decades. Dr. Abram Hoffer of Victoria, British Columbia is undoubtedly one of the foremost leaders in this area, for many people with mental disease owe their sanity to him.

It is imperative that you be well-versed in the side effects of vitamin B3 or niacin before you use it. You must first understand that histamine is made daily and stored in granules inside of certain cells. When you take niacin, one of the things it does is cause an emptying of these histamine granules. When you pour a large amount of histamine into the blood stream, you get some of the symptoms of a severe allergic reaction, like flushing and itching.

Most commonly an overdose of niacin results in the skin first tingling and prickling, then becoming flaming red. At higher doses you feel like you were staked to a beach and left to die in the burning Caribbean sun. Not to worry, though, for with enough vitamin C, the histamine is soon metabolized and you return to normal. Indomethacin and aspirin can attenuate the reaction, as well as antihistamines like non-prescription Benadryl (diphenhydramine). Anyway, for people who need very high doses of niacin, they need to slowly deplete the histamine granules to avoid going through this nasty experience or **niacin reaction**.

So the first day you take the tiniest dose of B3 you can find, usually 25-50 mg (you may need to break up a 100 mg tablet). You take this dose methodically every 6 hours until you no longer feel any of the tingling or prickling. This means you have emptied out as much histamine from the cell granules as is possible at this dose. It may take just a few days or many, depending on the individual. When you no longer feel anything at this dose, advance up to the next dose (50 or 100mg, as you dare). Continue on this every 6 hours for as many days as needed until you no longer feel any histamine release. Then proceed to 150 or 200 mg every 6 hours, etc. Do not exceed 2000 mg per day, especially without medical supervision. Many need more but the higher the dose goes, the more likely that you will need intelligent intervention.

Obviously, when you have such high levels of one nutrient, you need a very well-balanced nutritional prescription, as this puts extra stress on your metabolic machinery. The doses that many schizophrenics and some depressives need can be as high as several thousand milligrams every 6 hours. But the results are worth it, if it provides the solution for that individual. An average dose can be anywhere from 100-500 mg every 6 hours or 4 times a day.

Because vitamin B3 is needed in so many pathways of the body, this protocol is used by some who need to reduce their cholesterol, and also by those doing a sauna detoxification program to mobilize and get rid of old pesticides, drugs, and other chemical residues in the body.

One last **caveat** is necessary. If you forget a dose, or abandon the program temporarily, never resume it at the dose you left off on. For as soon as you break the every 6 hour cycle (or an approximation, or perhaps you can get away with every 8 hours), those little granules fill up with more histamine. But when your dose is late or overdue, the granules are not emptied out on time. Therefore, the next dose may dump out a double or triple amount of histamine and provoke the nasty niacin reaction.

Imagine that you have worked up to 500 mg and stopped for a few days and then resumed 500mg. You will dump out all the histamine that dose can get rid of which has accumulated over the days of no doses. This can result in a **niacin flush** that you will never forget. So remember to go back to your initial dose if there is an interruption in your dosing. Don't start where you left off. For the whole idea of the build-up and consistency is to minimize histamine symptoms by keeping up with daily histamine production. And do **not use slow release or time-release niacin**. It has caused liver troubles. In fact, it would be prudent to check your liver enzymes even if you find plain niacin helpful. Once a month until you reach top dose, then every 3 months the first year and every 6 months the second year would suffice.

And the astute reader will recognize, by vitamin B3 having such a dramatic impact on not only histamine, but the mental health of some individuals, that this is just one more piece of evidence of how intimately **brain function is tied in with allergies.**

REFERENCES:

Hoffer A, ORTHOMOLECULAR MEDICINE FOR PHYSICIANS, Keats Publ., New Canaan CT, 1989.

Hoffer A, Mega vitamin B3 therapy for schizophrenia, CANA PSYCH ASSOC J 16:499-504, 1971.

Hoffer A, Treatment of schizophrenia with a therapeutic program based upon nicotinic acid as the main variable, MOLECULAR BASIS OF SOME

ASPECTS OF MENTAL ACTIVITY, VOLUME 3 (ed) O. Wallaas, Academic Press, New York 1967.

Hoffer A, The effect of nicotinic acid on the frequency and duration of rehospitalization of schizophrenic patients; a controlled comparison study, INT J NEURO PSYCH, 2:234-240, 1966.

Osmond H, Hoffer A, Massive niacin treatment in schizophrenia. Review of a nine year study. LANCET 1:316- 320, 1963.

Sydenstricker VP, CLeckley HM, The effect of nicotinic acid in stupor, lethargy and various other psychiatric disorders, AM J PSYCHIATRY, 98:83-92, 1941

Hoffer A, NIACIN THERAPY IN SCHIZOPHRENIA, Springfield IL, Charles C. Thomas, 1962

Hoffer A, Osmond H, Treatment of schizophrenia with nicotinic acid: a ten-year follow-up. ACTA PSYCHATR SCAND, 40:171-189, 1964

VITAMIN B6

Vitamin B6, or pyridoxine, is required to convert the dietary amino acid, **tryptophan into** the "happy hormone", **serotonin**. And it is needed to convert **phenylalanine** into **tyrosine** and then into **norepinephrine**, another "happy hormone". Also it is needed if the conversion of phenylalanine proceeds into **phenylethylamine**, another "happy hormone", the one that is produced in **"chocoholics"**. This produces the amphetamine-like feeling or "high" that people addicted to chocolate are controlled by, at least until they locate and correct their biochemical defect that makes them crave. But more about these happy hormones in the amino acid section. Suffice to say, a B6 deficiency, which is not rare, will disturb the **metabolism of amino acids, the building blocks of the brain's happy hormones.**

Like so many other vitamin deficiencies, B6 deficiency is very common. This is especially true for those who do not have at least **3-6 daily helpings of vegetables,** and 1-3 of fruits. Then if you are on any drugs, hormones (like birth control, estrogen-replacement), or are exposed to an excess of chemicals in your daily work or home environment that use up more B6, you get even more deficient.

B6 deficiency also makes the acetaldehyde released from Candida in the gut more damaging to the brain (Volume I). B6 deficiency is also a major cause of **arteriosclerosis** which in turn can cause depression by its own mechanism of compromising the circulation in the brain.

But **beware of physicians who only want to warn you of the dangers of vitamins.** For example, years ago a study of 5 psychiatric patients made national news because they had taken ridiculously dangerous doses of B6 for years, with no medical supervision and no balanced nutrients. Naturally they got nerve damage from such silliness. And the media blew it out of proportion as an excuse to warn people not to take vitamins. This showed total disregard for the importance of B6 in arteriosclerosis and in mental disease. A golden opportunity was once more missed to present nutrition in the proper light and save many lives. But medicine has sold a lot of Prozac since that time and a lot of angioplasties.

Another problem is that physicians unschooled in environmental medicine and nutritional biochemistry may see you have a B6 deficiency, but be unable to correct it. This is because it is not a robotic cookbook procedure like drug-medicine tends to be. Instead, for each step along the way you must know what other nutrients are called into play in order for this one to be properly utilized.

For example, if one is also deficient in **zinc**, the enzyme **pyridoxal kinase** suffers. Then you cannot convert the B6 (pyridoxine) that you take into the next step that allows it to be used in the body. So regardless of how much B6 you take, it will not correct your B6 deficiency. Likewise, magnesium is needed in many of those steps, and manganese must be present for the magnesium to work, etc. In other words, when you look for the actual treatable biochemical cause, gone are the days of **mindless medicine.**

REFERENCES:

Russ CS, et al, Vitamin B6 status of depressed and obsessive-compulsive patients, NUTR REP INT 27(4):867-873, 1983.

Carney M, et al, Thiamin and pyridoxine lack in newly-admitted psychiatric patients, BR J PSYCHIATRY 135:249-254, 1979.

Stewart JW, et al, Low B6 levels in depressed outpatients, BIOL PSYCHIATRY, 19(4):613-616, 1984.

Mattes JA, , Martin D, Pyridoxine in premenstrual depression, HUM NUTR: ALLP NUTR 36A, 131-135, 1982.

Adams PW, et al, Effect of pyridoxine hydrochloride (vitamin B6) upon depression associated with oral contraception, LANCET 1:897-904, 1973.

Baker H, et al, Inability of chronic alcoholics with liver disease, to use food as a source of folates, thiamin and vitamin B6, AM J CLIN NUTR 28, 1377-1380, 1975.

Bender DA, et al, Effects of estrogen administration on vitamin B6 and tryptophan metabolism in the rat, BRIT J NUTR 47, 609-614, 1982.

Bhagavan HN, Interaction between vitamin B6 and drugs. In VITAMIN B6: ITS ROLE IN HEALTH AND DISEASE, Reynolds RD, Leklem JE, Eds, 401-415, Liss NY, 1985.

Ebadi M, et al, Drug-pyridoxal phosphate interactions, Q REV DRUG METAB DRUG INTERACT 4:289-331, 1982.

Kakuma S, et al, Enhanced acetaldehyde hepatotoxicity in vitamin B6 deficiency, GASTROENTEROLOGY, 71:914, 1976.

Nobbs BT, Pyridoxal phosphate status in clinical depression, LANCET, 405-406, Mar 9, 1974

Bermond P, Therapy of side effects of oral contraceptive agents with vitamin B6. ACTA VITAMINOL ENZYMOL 4(1-2):45-54, 1982.

Hattersley JG, Vitamin B6: The overlooked key to preventing heart attacks, J APPL NUTR 47:1&2, 1995, in press

Schaumberg HH, et al, Sensory neuropathy from pyridoxine abuse: A new megavitamin syndrome, NEW ENGL J MED 309:445- 448, 1983

Azuma J, Kishi T, et al, Apparent deficiency of vitamin B6 in typical individuals who commonly serve as normal controls, RES COMMUN CHEM PATHOL PHARMACOL, 14:343-349, 1976

Kirsky A, Keaton K, et al, Vitamin B6 nutritional status of a group of female adolescents, AM J CLIN NUTR 31:946-954, 1978

Hampton DJ, Chrisley BM, Driskell JA, Vitamin B6 status of the elderly in Montgomery County, VA, NUTR REP INT 16:743- 750, 1977

VITAMIN B12

As you will see, it is extremely dangerous and the inappropriate practice of medicine to treat mental illness on a long term basis without checking for a B12 deficiency.

Every once in a while a paper is published in medicine that is called a **landmark paper**. This is because it verifies what we have believed all along, while others chose to ignore the benefits, waiting for additional proof. Such is the case with Lindenbaum's paper in 1988. In essence, he showed that it is practically malpractice to fail to assess the adequacy of vitamin B12 (cobalamin) when presented with any type of psychiatric disease., including depression.

Allow me to explain what erroneous thinking this paper corrected. Thirty years ago in medical school, we were all taught that the only time we should look for a B12 or folic acid deficiency is if there was a **macrocytosis**. Macrocytosis means big or large (macro) cells (cytosis). Cells are large if they hang around in the bone marrow too long waiting for a missing nutrient. Most cells mature in the bone marrow then are sent out into the blood stream where they serve their various functions. But if they are lacking in certain nutrients, they may come out too small (as in the "micro" - cytosis of iron deficiency) or in the case of B12 and folic acid deficiencies, too large. They actually wait to be "hatched" hoping they will finally get that missing B12. Hence it became the standard and condonable practice to only check for a B12 deficiency if a macrocytosis was seen.

But this study showed that people can have serious deficiencies and not have the telltale macrocytosis. As usual, it is a case in medicine of waiting too long for a sign that even your grandmother wouldn't miss. Showing docs that we must suspect deficiencies even when there is no macrocytosis was very important. And an additional lesson showed us that the deficiency could mimic any mental disease, especially depression. Alas, it is the proper practice of medicine to check for such deficiencies in any case of mental symptoms. **And it is not the practice of good medicine if one fails to check for B12 deficiency with any recalcitrant mental or neurological symptom.**

There are numerous other papers showing that B12 deficiency is a common cause of depression. But this one was particularly important because it once and for all annihilated the antiquated notion that had persisted for decades: that you had no business checking for a B12 deficiency unless there was a macrocytosis. For you see, this is a rather late sign, and need not rear its diagnostic head ever. Suffice to say, there are recorded cases of depression due to the deficiency of nearly every vitamin. But some like B12 deficiency are particularly well-researched for their role in depression.

Also bear in mind, the most common medical symptom in the world, **fatigue or tiredness or exhaustion** has been thoroughly researched and found to be the symptom of nearly every nutrient deficiency. And often **when there is fatigue, there is depression** as well. But it frequently goes unmentioned in a study because it is not easily quantifiable with a blood test, or it is not the symptom the researchers are studying. In order to study something as nebulous and subjective as depression, many feel they cannot mention it unless they do a vast amount of psychological testing to substantiate the diagnosis. So it is easier to ignore it. Furthermore, what person with depression is going to take the time or the interest to complete a lengthy questionnaire that takes hours to complete just to help out a study?

One out of 20 people admitted to a psychiatric hospital is low in B12. But not all are checked for it. The causes of B12 deficiency can be many, like lack of a stomach enzyme, called **intrinsic factor**, to allow its absorption. Other deficiencies can be traced to the use of medicines that can turn off stomach secretions, like Tagamet, Zantac, and Pepcid, and antacids like Mylanta and Maalox. B12 deficiency is also prevalent among vegetarians who do not eat meat. Avoiding meat can have great health benefits if you (1) are not genetically a carnivore, and (2) you know enough about sea vegetables to incorporate sufficient amounts in your diet to prevent a B12 deficiency (described in THE CURE IS IN THE KITCHEN). Because this book is designed to break the medical paradigm that depression is a Prozac deficiency, we are concentrating on how to find the treatable causes. Unfortunately, physicians who do not know how to find the causes, also are generally untrained in the optimum tests. For example, a serum B12 may be normal, but the urinary **methyl malonic acid** may be abnormal. For "neuropyschiatric disorders due to cobalamin deficiency occur commonly in the absence of anemia or an elevated mean cell volume and measurements of serum methylmalonic acid and total homocysteine both before and after treatment are useful in the diagnosis of these patients" (NEJM, 6/30/88).

Sometimes it may be more cost-effective to merely give a **trial injection of B12**. But this can bring shivers of horror to a physician who is not trained in environmental medicine and nutritional biochemistry. Authors of other papers below, even though they are from all disciplines of medicine, also recommend a therapeutic trial in depressed people, even those with normal levels. This is because of one reason: it works for some. And another person is rescued from **biochemical depression**. And I have never heard of a person who had a serious problem from a trial of B12.

It is unconscionable in light of all the scientific evidence to withhold a trial of a B12 injection (1cc SC or IM) from a person with depression. Of course, for maximum effectiveness it should be accompanied by at least 800 mg of folic acid and 50-100 mg of B6, as well as a balanced regimen (Volume IV).

Another fact that you should know at this point is how the "normal" values are obtained in the first place. They are actually obtained by averaging the levels found in blood that happens to be in the laboratory. In other words, **laboratories make the determination of normal ranges from the blood from sick people!** I found this hard to believe until I checked it out several times myself and with several labs. It all started to arouse my curiosity back in the late 1970's when one day the lab sent around a notice that the new range for B12 was no longer 200-900, but 160-900. I called up to ask how this could happen that suddenly people needed less B12 than they ever did before. They told me that periodically they have to take several samples and establish a new "norm".

Months later, the same happened for folic acid. Then a year later, the norm for folic acid dropped again. This is in spite of the fact that there are scores of papers showing that folic acid is a common deficiency. **And a deficiency of folic acid is a serious, yet correctable cause of neural tube defects of newborns, a common cause of depression, a nutrient that can reverse an abnormal PAP smear, and a contributing factor to arteriosclerosis.**

As an example, when women are folic acid deficient during pregnancy, they are at greater risk of giving birth to a baby with a severely malformed spinal cord that costs hundreds of thousands of dollars during the first years of life (not to mention the heartache and agony of the parents enduring all this in their precious baby). And it may result in permanent paralysis with a shortened lifetime, exorbitant illness and expense. But for pennies a day, simple folic acid supplements can prevent this. And scores of papers back this up. Yet the "norm" for folate has been lowered twice in the last 2 decades, a period of time when people are eating fewer vegetables, more processed foods, and fast foods low in folate!

I could make this a 12 volume book by covering all of this, but it would look so foreboding, that no one would attempt to read it, much less the depressed individual. So in order to give you the best shot at finding the correct physician who will help you isolate the actual causes of your depression, I will need to refer you then to the other books we've written. For they not only provide information for your physician to come to the courses we teach, but tests that you can do when you find a physician. These simple tests will enable you to test your physician to find out just how much chemistry he knows. We also provide phone consultations for people from around the world wanting to brain-storm and look at their healing options. Many use this as an opportunity to make a checklist of diagnostic tests and trials that they can then ask their doctor to do.

REFERENCES:

Lindenbaum J, Healton EB, Savage DG, Brust JCM, Garrett TJ, Podell ER, Marcell PD, Stabler SP, Allen RH, Neuropsychiatric disorders caused by cobalamin deficiency in the absence of anemia and macrocytosis, N ENGL J MED, 318:1720-1728, 1988.

Fine EJ, Neurologic signs of vitamin B12 deficiency, EMER MED, 198-201, July 15, 1992.

Joosten E, et al, Metabolic evidence that deficiency of vitamin B12 (cobalamin), folate, and vitamin B6 occur commonly in elderly people, AM J CLIN NUTR 58:468-476, 1993

Fine E, Myths about vitamin B12 deficiency, et al, SOUTHERN MED J, 1474-1481, December 1991.

Miller DR, Vitamin B12 status in a macrobiotic community, AMER J CLIN NUTR, 53: 524-529, 1991.

Narang RL, et al, Plasma cobalt and manganese in depression, 9(1):43-44, 1992.

Dowing, DMB, Cerebral manifestations of vitamin B12 deficiency, J NUTR MED, 2:89-90, 1991.

Carmel RMD, Subtle and atypical deficiency states, AMER J NUTR MED 34:108-114, 1990.

Fine, EMD, Neurologic signs of B12 deficiency, EMERG MED, 198-201, 1992.
Edwin E, Vitamin B12 hypovitaminosis in mental diseases, et al, ACTA MED SCAND, 177:689-99, 1965.

Bell I, Vitamin B12 and folate status in acute geropsychiatric inpatients: affective and cognitive characteristics of a vitamin nondeficient population, BIOL PSYCH 27(2):125-127, 1990.

Ellis FR, Nasser SM, A pilot study of vitamin B12 in the treatment of tiredness, BRIT J NUTR 30:277-283, 1973.

Bell I, B complex vitamin patterns in geriatric and young adult patients with major depression, et al, J AMER GER SOC, 33: 252-257, 1991.

Nilsson K, et al, Plasma homocysteine in relation to serum cobalamin and blood folate in a psychogeriatric population, EUROP J CLIN INVEST, 24: 600-606, 1985.

Downing D, Cerebral manifestations of vitamin B12 deficiency, J NUTR MED, 2: 89-90, 1991.

Holmes JM, Cerebral manifestations of vitamin B12 deficiency, BRIT MED J, 2:1394-1398, 1956.

Bell IR, Vitamin B12 and folate in acute geropsychiatric in patients, NUTR REP, 9(1): 1-8, January 1991.

Yulin Y, et al, Decline of serum cobalamin levels with increasing age among geriatric out-patients, ARCH FAM MED, 3:918-922, October 1994.

Edwin E, Holten K, Norum KR, et al, Vitamin B12 hypovitaminosis in mental diseases, ACTA MED SCAND 177:689-699, 1965

VITAMIN B12 IN SEA VEGETABLES

Note that much has been written about vegans being B12 deficient because they do not eat meat. However, smart vegans eat via macrobiotic principles (described in THE CURE IS IN THE KITCHEN). This is the diet that people with end-stage, "incurable" cancers have totally healed with. It incorporates specific amounts of sea vegetables, rich in minerals in the diet. These are an important source of B12.

REFERENCES:

Specker BL, et al, AMER J CLIN NUTR, 47:89-92, 1988.

van den Berg H, Brandsen L, Sinkeldam BJ, Vitamin B12 content and bioavailability of spirulina and nori in rats, J NUTRIT BIOCHEM 2(6);314-318.

FOLIC ACID

Every symptom that B12 deficiency can cause, a folic acid deficiency can cause as well, because they work in the same pathways. In fact whenever the B vitamins are added to a product, folic acid is usually there as well, and is often considered one of the B's, just because it works so **synergistically** with them. They are indispensable partners.

And you can appreciate that a folate deficiency is common, since the **average American consumes only 60% of the normal daily requirement.** Plus **using medications uses up or depletes** any that is available, thus further compromising the individual. A diet lacking in fresh raw green vegetables, the use of **drugs,** especially birth control, epilepsy drugs, recreational drugs, and **alcohol** can seriously lower folate to the point where depression is produced.

Folic acid is just one more example of the **vicious cycle in medicine.** Alcohol and chronic medications decrease folic acid levels. Anti-convulsants are particularly good at this. And when you have decreased folate levels you can have not only depression, but dementia (senility), memory loss, schizophrenia-like psychosis and other behavioral abnormalities. The worse you are, the more medication you are going to be put on. Yet the more medication you are on, the lower the folate levels can get (Nzengi G, Folate status and cognitive impairment, AGING CLINICAL EXPERI-MENTAL RESEARCH, 1994; 6: 69-72).

Clearly, when you look at the data, it's so overwhelming that it's actually criminal to put anyone on an anti-depressant without at least checking his serum folic acid level. And of course, you can extrapolate this, when you see the rest of the data, to just about every nutrient, as well as chemical, food and inhalant antigen there is.

In one series of 48 patients, serum folic acid levels were significantly lower in the depressed patient than in non-depressed patients (Ghadirian AM, et al, Folic acid deficiency and depression, PSYCHOSOMATICS 21(11):926-929, 1980). In other study, a quarter or **25% of 100 consecutive patients admitted with depression had low serum folic acid** levels (Reynolds EH, et al, Folate deficiency in depressive illness, BR J PSYCH 117:287-292, 1970.

REFERENCES:

Subar AF, et al, Folate intake and food sources in the US population, AM J CLIN NUTR 50:508-516, 1989.

Abou-Saleh MT, Coppen A, The biology of folate in depression: implications for nutritional hypothesis of the psychoses, J PSYCHIATRI RES 20(2):91-101, 1986.

Godfrey PSA, et al, Enhancement of recovery from psychiatric illness by methylfolate, LANCET 336:392-395, 1990.

Reynolds EH, et al, Methylation and mood, LANCET, 2:196-198, 1984.

Lietha R, Zimmermann M, Neuropsychiatric disorders associated with folate deficiency in the presence of elevated serum and erythrocyte folate: a preliminary report, J NUTR MED, 4:441-447, 1994.

Carney MWP, et al, Red cell folate concentrations in psychiatric patients, J AFFECT DIS, 9:207-213, 1990.

Crellin R, et al, Folate and psychiatric disorders: clinical potential, DRUGS, 45(5): 623-636, 1993.

Botez MI, et al, Neuropsychological correlates of folic acid deficiency: facts and hypotheses in: M.I. Botez and E.H. Reynolds, eds, FOLIC ACID IN NEUROLOGY, PSYCHIATRY, AND INTERNAL MEDICINE, Raven NY, 1979.

Levitt AJ, Joffe RT, Folate, B12 and thyroid function in depression, BIOL PSYCHIATRY , 33:522-553, 1993

Crellin R, Bottiglieri T, Reynolds EH, Folates and psychiatric disorders, DRUGS, 45:623-636, 1993

Wesson VA, Levitt AJ, Joffe RT, Change in folate status with antidepressant treatment, PSYCHIATRY RESEARCH, 53(3): 313-22, Sept 1994.

In the above study, 99 consecutive unmedicated outpatients with a major depressive illness had blood drawn for measurement of serum folate (SF), red cell folate (RCF), and vitamin B12 within 24 hours of completion of ratings of severity of depression at the beginning and ending of a 5-week trial of (the anti-depressant) desmethylimipramine (mean dose=149.2 mg/day, range=75-225 mg). It will come as no revelation to you that the worse cases of depression had the lower folate levels. And **the ones who did better on the drug had higher folate levels.** Wouldn't you be embarrassed to publish such a logical finding? I don't see why it is enough of a surprise to warrant publication.

Wilkinson AM, Anderson DN, Abou-Saleh MT, Wesson M, Blair JA, Farrar G, Leeming RJ, 5-Methlytetrahydrofolate level in the serum of depressed subjects and its relationship to the outcome of ECT, JOURNAL OF AFFECTIVE DISORDERS, 32(3): 163-8, Nov 1994.

Guaraldi GP, Fava M, Mazzi F, laGreca P, An open trial of methyltetrahydrofolate in elderly depressed patients, ANN CLIN PSYCHIATRY, 5(2): 101-5, Jan 1993.

Levitt AJ, Joffe RT, Folate B12 and thyroid function in depression, BIOLOGICAL PSYCHIATRY, 33(1): 52-3, Jan 1, 1993.

McLaughlin B, McMahon A, Folate and depression, BRIT J PSYCHIATRY, 162: N572, April 1993.

Bottiglieri T, Hyland K, Laundy M Godfrey P, Carney MW, Toone BK, Reynolds EH, Folate deficiency, biopterin and monoamine metabolism in depression, PSYCHOLOG MED, 22(4): 871-6, Nov 1992.

Wing YK, Lee S. Methylfolate and psychiatric illness, BRIT J PSYCHIATRY, 160: 714-5, May 1992.

Bell IR, Morrow FD, Read M, Berkes S, Perrone G, Low thyroxine levels in female psychiatric inpatients with riboflavin deficiency: implications for folate-dependent methylation, ACTA PSYCHIATRICA SCANDINAVICA, 85(5) 360-3, May 1992.

Anderson D, Wilkison A, Abou-Saleh M, Farrar G, Blair JA, Enhancement of recovery from psychiatric illness by methylfolate, BRIT J PSYCHIATRY, 160: 130, Jan 1992.

Rouillon F, Thalassinos M, Miller HD, Lemperiere T, Folates and post partum depression, J AFFECTIVE DISORDERS, 25(4): 235-41, Aug 1992.

Lee S, Chow CC Shek CC, Wing YK, Chen CN, Folate concentration in Chinese psychiatric outpatients on long-term lithium treatment, J AFFECTIVE DISORDERS, 24(4): 265-70, April 1992.

McKeon P, Shelley R, O'Regan S, O'Broin J, Serum and red cell folate and affective morbidity in lithium prophalaxis, ACTA PSYCHIATRICA SCANDINAVICA, 83(3): 199-201, March 1991.

Young SN, The 1989 Borden award lecture. Some effects of dietary components (amino acids, carbohydrate, folic acid) on brain serotonin synthesis, mood, and behavior, CANADIAN J PHYSIOLOGY & PHARMACOLOGY, 69(7): 893-903, July 1991.

Fine EJ, Soria ED, Myths about vitamin B12 deficiency, SOUTHERN MED J, 84(12): 1475-81, Dec 1991.

Procter A, Enhancement of recovery from psychiatric illness by methylfolate, BRIT J PSYCHIATRY, 159: 271-2, Aug 1991.

Cohen D, Dementia, depression, and nutritional status, PRIMARY CARE; CLINICS IN OFFICE PRACTICE, 21(1): 107-19, March 1994.

Ortega TM, Andres P, Lopez-Sobaler A, Ortega A, Redondo R, Jiminez A, Jimenez LM, The role of folates in the diverse biochemical processes that control mental function, NUTRICION HOSPITALARIA, 9(4): 251-6, Jul-Aug 1994.

VITAMIN C

Vitamin C deficiency is rarely considered in the U.S. This is in spite of the fact that it has been found to be a necessary part of the differential diagnosis for many conditions. For it has been the cause of such potentially fatal conditions like vasculitis which would have gone on to be treated with potentially carcinogenic or fatal chemotherapy and steroids (references in THE SCIENTIFIC BASIS OF SELECTED ENVIRONMENTAL MEDICINE TECHNIQUES). And, of course, **vasculitis** can cause serious brain pathology, not the least of which can be very severe depression. And vasculitis can be marked by one of the most frustrating symptoms in depression and mental illness: that of **fluctuation.** In other words, vasculitis can cause inflammation (and malfunction) in tissues one day, then they can be normal the next, and inflamed again the following week or month. Hence, the depression can **ebb and flow**, driving everyone nuts.

Yet to consider a vitamin C deficiency as part of the cause of depression is almost unthinkable. But if it is ignored, many will go on to drugs and as you know from there the sick get sicker. For one of the many roles of vitamin C is to **recycle** or reduce or put back into a useful form once again, the **minerals** after they have been used in a reaction. It also **recycles vitamin E** the same way. So without adequate levels of vitamin C (ascorbic acid), you can soon go on to exhibit all the symptoms of a myriad of mineral deficiencies as well as a vitamin E deficiency. And vitamin E alone has literally thousands of papers published regarding its role in nearly every disease you can think of from cancer to arteriosclerosis. One major role of vitamin E is to facilitate the detoxification of drugs and chemicals so they do not go on to trigger depression through unmetabolized remnants.

In one study, when they looked at the biochemical difference between patients who were suicidal and those who were not, the only difference was a **vitamin C deficiency in the suicidal** ones.

Vitamin C, or **ascorbic acid,** has numerous other functions that indirectly relate to the manifestation of depression. For example, it **detoxifies histamine,** thus attenuating allergic reactions to foods, dusts, pollens and molds that can cause depression. It is necessary for the proper **metabolism of drugs.** Thus a deficiency can make one who is on Prozac more vulnerable to the potential side effect, for example, of suicide. It is crucial for the metabolism of lipids, whereby a deficiency can cause arteriosclerosis that can then lead to depression (more about that later). And vitamin C is crucial in rheumatoid arthritis, cancer, diabetes, recurrent infection, folic acid metabolism, cataract formation, immunity, and many other factors that can potentiate depression.

But most importantly, vitamin C is necessary for the expression of the **acetylcholine receptor.** This is one of the exact sites on the surface of brain cells where the message to turn on the **happy hormones** is located. And if vitamin C is deficient, it just plain does not happen. And since Vitamin C has so many other beneficial functions, it makes a lot more sense to find and fix this deficiency than to be dependent on the drug industry for the rest of your life.

REFERENCES:

Hodges RE, et al, Clinical manifestations of ascorbic acid deficiency in man, AM J CLIN NUTR 24: 432-433, 1971.

Kitahara M, Insufficient ascorbic acid uptake from the diet and the tendency for suicide, J ORTHOMOL MED 2(4): 217-218, 1987.

Schorah CJ, et al, Plasma vitamin C concentration in patients in a psychiatric hospital, HUM NUTR CLIN NUTR 37C: 477-452, 1983.

Leitner ZA, Church IC, Nutritional studies in a mental hospital, LANCET, 1:565-567, 1957.

Milner G, Ascorbic acid in chronic psychiatric patients: A controlled trial, BRIT J PSYCHIATRY 109:294-299, 1963.

Chakraborty D, et al, Biochemical studies on polychlorinated biphenyl toxicity in rats: Manipulation by vitamin C, INTERNAT J VIT NUTR RES, 48, 22-31, 1977.

Low-Maus E, Vitamin C and the nervous system, MEDICINA CLINICA (Barcelona), 19: 299-303, 1952.

Berkenau P, Vitamin C in senile psychoses, J MENT SCI, 86: 675, 1940.

De Sauvage Nolting WJ, Vitamin C and schizophrenia, Geneeskundige Gids, 31: 424-425, 1953.

Padh H, Vitamin C: Newer insights into its biochemical function, NUTR REV, 49:3, 65-70, 1991

Knaack D. Podleski TR, Salpeter MM, Ascorbic acid and acetylcholine receptor expression. ANN NY ACAD SCI 498:77-89, 1987

Hoffer A, Osmond H, Scurvy and schizophrenia, DISEASES OF THE NERVOUS SYSTEM, 24: 273-285, 1963.

Milner G, Ascorbic acid in chronic psychiatric patients-a controlled trial, BRIT J PSYCH, 109: 294-299, 1963.

Griffiths AW, Ascorbic acid nutrition in mentally subnormal patients, J MENT DEF RES, 10: 94-104, 1966.

VanderKamp H, A biochemical abnormality in schizophrenia involving ascorbic acid, INT J NEURO, VOL 2: 204-206, 1966.

Pauling L, Evolution and the need for ascorbic acid. PROC NATL ACAD SCI USA, 67:1643-1648, 1970

Milner G, Ascorbic acid in chronic psychiatric patients: a controlled trial, BRIT J PSYCHIATRY 109:294-299, 1963

Pfeiffer CC, Lliev V, Goldstein L, Blood histamine, basophil counts, and trace elements in the schizophrenias, in ORTHOMOLECULAR PSYCHIATRY: TREATMENT OF SCHIZOPHENIA, Eds. Hawkins D, Pauling L, San Francisco, W.J. Freeman & Co, 1973, p. 463-510

Lucksch F, Vitamin C and schizophrenia, WIENER KLINISCHER WOCHENSCRIFT, 53:1009-1011, 1940.

Weykamp CW, et al, Vitamin C and glycohemoglobin , CLIN CHEM 41:713-716, 1995

Morgan AF, Gillum HL, Williams RI, Nutritional status of aging. III. Serum ascorbic acid and intake, J NUTR 55:431- 448, 1955

Dixit VM, Cause of depression in chronic scurvy, LANCET, 2(8151): 1077-8, Nov 17, 1979.

VITAMIN E

The deficiency of vitamin E has been studied profusely (VERIS, 5325 South Ninth Ave. LaGrange, IL 60525, 1-800-554-1708). One of the roles of vitamin E is to sit in the cell membrane and protect the membrane and its contents from chemical damage. Therefore, everything that a deficiency of phosphatidyl choline or glutamine or a number of other nutrients can do also applies to vitamin E. For the cell **membrane determines how the cell functions** under every circumstance.

So it should come as no surprise that the decrease in brain neurotransmitters caused by aging can be partially restored with vitamin E. Or that tardive dyskinesia, the uncontrollable jerky tics, grimaces and spastisities that come as a side effect from some drugs, can also be improved.

If that were not enough reason to check vitamin E **status** during depression, studies show that it **decreases the turnover of serotonin;** the very thing that many antidepressant medications attempt to do at a considerably higher price, and with far less eventual ancillary benefit. Vitamin E also **decreases the damage to the brain from alcohol,** another cause of depression. And it **decreases the drop in brain energy chemistry** (brain ATP, glucose, and glycogen) **that occurs in response to stress.** Hence, it will come as no surprise to you that Alzheimer's patients have significantly lower levels of vitamins than normals.

If that were not enough, vitamin E **retards amyloid** production, the very material **that causes Alzheimer's.** And don't kid yourself, **depression can be a precursor to Alzheimer's.** So the quicker you clear it up, the better. For you never know how far improperly treated symptoms can progress. As with most diseases, earlier treatment gives a lot better results and has a greater chance of total cure.

There are many more things that vitamin E accomplishes in the brain chemistry that relates to the biochemistry of depression. For example it is important in increasing the levels of the enzyme **delta-6-desaturase** enzyme. This enzyme, **D-6-D,** is necessary for the proper brain cell membranes and synapses where the **happy hormones** are released and work. In other words, you can take Prozac until the cows come home, but without enough vitamin E, it may not work. Delta-6-desaturase is necessary for the metabolism of essential fatty acids that control major parts of the brain and one's vulnerability to depression (as you will learn in that section). Vitamin E also restored and reversed the damaged functions of choline in aged rat brains used to study Alzheimer's disease.

Suffice to say, vitamin E is so important, and the chances of deficiency are so great, that it is preferred to merely supplement it rather than wasting money in checking a level. For do not forget, it is processed out of white flours and hydrogenated grocery store oils. So you very easily get deficient by eating the Standard American Diet (SAD!)

But be sure you only take **d-alpha tocopherol,** not dl- or d, l-alpha tocopherol. And if it does not specify, do not take it. The type with mixed tocotrienols is preferable (types, sources, doses in Volume IV). The dose does not require as precise a balancing act as the minerals do when they are low. For minerals, measuring blood levels is much more important.

One more word about Vitamin E (and this also applies to vitamins A, D and K) is that it is a **fat soluble vitamin**. This means that **you need pancreatic enzymes to help digest it**. But many people are deficient in them (we can measure your digestive enzyme ability) due to constant snacking and a high sugar diet, and therefore have a compromised absorption. Vitamin E can also be low because of an underlying intestinal malabsorption syndrome, but more on these in the gut section (Volume III).

THE HIDDEN SIDE EFFECT OF ALL DRUGS

All drugs have a hidden side effect that is rarely mentioned. **They use up and deplete nutrients.** Since they are a chemical, they use up vitamins, minerals, amino acids, essential fatty acids, and other nutrients in the works of metabolizing and detoxifying the drug. Therefore, **all drugs cause nutrient depletion.** And they rob us of nutrients that we could have used to make happy hormones!

REFERENCES:

Muller DPR, et al, Antioxidant deficiency and neurological disease in humans and experimental animals, FREE RADICALS AND THE BRAIN 1991;62-73. Edited by Packer L, et al, Berlin, 1991.

Castano A, et al, Effects of a short period of vitamin E deficient diet in the turnover of different neurotransmitters in substantia nigra and striatum of the rat, NEUROSCIENCE 53:179-185, 1993.

Westermarck T, et al, Vitamin E therapy in neurological diseases, in: VITAMIN E IN HEALTH AND DISEASE, 799-806, 1993, Ed. Packer L, et al, NY.

Marcus SR, et al, Interaction between vitamin E and glutathione in rat brain. Effect of acute alcohol administration, J NUTR BIOCHEM, 4:336-440, 1993.

Shaheen AA, et al, Effect of pretreatment with vitamin E or diazepam on brain metabolism of stressed rats, BIOCHEM PHARMACOL 46: 194-197, 1993.

Adler LA, et al, Vitamin E treatment of tardive dyskinesia, AM J PSYCHIATRY 150:1405-1407, 1993.

Weder B, Meienberg O, Wildi E, Meier C, Neurologic disorder of vitamin E deficiency in acquired intestinal malabsorption, NEUROLOGY 34(12): 1561-65, 1984.

Behl C, et al, Vitamin E protects nerve cells from amyloid B protein toxicity, BIOCHEM BCIOPHYS RES COMMUN 186: 944-950, 1992.

Despret S, Alteration of delta-6-desaturase by vitamin E in rat brain and liver, NEUROSCI LETT, 145:19-22, 1992.

Zaman A, et al, Plasma concentrations of vitamins A and E and carotenoids in Alzheimer's disease, AGE AGEING 21: 91-94, 1992.

Kartha VNR, Krishnamurthy S, Effect of vitamins, antioxidants and sulfhydryl compounds on in vitro rat brain lipid peroxidation, INTERNAT J VIT NUTR RES 48, 38-43: 1978.

Maneesub Y, Sanvarinda Y, et al, Partial restoration of choline acetyltransferase activities in aging and AF64A-lesioned rat brains by vitamin E, NEUROCHEM INT, 22:5, 487- 491, 1993.

255

THE MINERAL CONNECTION

Mineral deficiencies are very common. And they are a common cause of depression, yet rarely looked for. So to protect you, you had better become very knowledgeable about them. So let's begin.

Magnesium deficiency is one of the most prevalent mineral deficiencies. And you know why when you recall that government surveys show the average American diet provides only 40% or less than half of the recommended daily allowance (RDA) for magnesium. Others confirm its widespread deficiency in over 54% of 1033 patients. And that survey used the serum level to assay for magnesium adequacy. The problem is by measuring a serum magnesium, you miss more than a third of those who are low.

The important point is that in certain people, a magnesium deficiency contributes to nearly the total load for depression. In other words, there are many for whom once the magnesium is corrected, they are no longer depressed. And of course, this deficiency is also important in a variety of other diseases from arteriosclerosis, arrhythmia, sudden cardiac death, and chemical sensitivity to osteoporosis, insomnia, idiopathic jaw pain, muscle spasms requiring frequent chiropractic adjustments, hypertension, mood swings, irritability, chronic low back pain and chronic fatigue. **The bottom line is that a magnesium deficiency is the norm, and can mimic nearly every symptom. Yet the proper test is rarely done. It is unconscionable to ignore the possibility of a magnesium deficiency in a depressed individual.**

MAGNESIUM LEADS THE WAY AS AN EXAMPLE OF HOW THE SICK GET SICKER

Let's use magnesium as an example of the mineral deficiencies to show how common they are and how they cause many diseases including depression. We'll go into more depth with this one to serve as a good example or prototype for the other minerals.

But first, how does one get deficient in magnesium? As you've learned, with the **processing of foods** such as going from whole wheat or brown rice down to bleached white rice and bleached white flour, over **75% of the magnesium is lost** (Schroeder, 1969). U.S. government surveys confirm that the average American diet provides only 40% of the recommended daily amount of magnesium (SCIENCE NEWS, 1988). In another study 39% of the populous had less than 70% of the RDA for magnesium (Marier, 1986). Add to this the fact that sugar, phosphates (high in processed foods, soft drinks), alcohol, stress, and high fat diets further potentate magnesium deficiency (Seelig, 1989). Thus, it is not surprising that leading authorities in magnesium estimate that **80% of the populous is magnesium deficient.**

Because this fact is little known by physicians, and it very well could clear your depression, not to mention save your life, I'm going to reiterate. **There is no blood test to adequately rule out magnesium repleteness.** The serum level is the most commonly performed, but is far too insensitive to be of any value except in cases of severe deficiency. For only 1% of body magnesium is extra cellular or in the serum. The rest is inside the cells. (Rhinehart, 1988). A major disservice has been done since the serum magnesium has become a member of the chemical profile, so commonly done on patients. For this allows the doctor who does not know how insensitive the test is to assume magnesium repleteness when he sees it reported as normal. This is a serious assumption. Recall the JAMA study by Whang in 1990 showing that 90% of physicians never even think of ordering even the least sensitive test (a serum magnesium) in over 1000 patients who were so ill as to be hospitalized. And many of these died as a consequence of the magnesium deficiency not being diagnosed and corrected.

The **intracellular erythrocyte (red blood cell)** level is the best currently available blood test (Elin, 1987). But that, also, is too insensitive to be of reliable value. **The best test is a magnesium loading test** (Rasmussen, 1988, Seelig, 1989, Rea, 1986, Nicar, 1982, Ryzen, 1985, Rogers, 1991).

Next, let's see some of the many ways a magnesium deficiency causes symptoms. Magnesium causes muscle relaxation, while calcium (in general) causes muscle contraction or spasm. This spasm is proportionate to the severity of the magnesium deficiency.

And the seriousness of a magnesium deficiency is dependent upon the target organ. If the spasm from a magnesium deficiency is in the smooth muscle of the vascular tree, it can lead to hypertension (Altura, 1984, Seelig, 1989), peripheral vascular disease (Howard, 1990), or angina, arrhythmia, and **sudden death** (Singh, 1982, Leary, 1983). Magnesium deficiency also damages the sodium pump (Cach, 1988), providing a dual mechanism for edema, hypertension and other diseases including depression. For example, some women are depressed **premenstrually** merely because progesterone is at its peak then and is a strong anti-diuretic.

Hence, the edema or extra fluid retention in the brain causes a **witchy irritability** and depression.

Consider the magnesium deficiency that causes hypertension. If the cause is not sought, or just as bad, if a mere serum magnesium test is done and found to be normal, often the first drug to be prescribed is a diuretic. Now diuretics are known for the ability to induce hypokalemia (low potassium). But a magnesium deficiency is caused by diuretics as well. Hence, by taking a diuretic for PMS or magnesium-induced hypertension, you actually make worse the underlying cause of the symptom for which the drug was prescribed.

Hence, the hypertension or PMS can worsen, requiring other drugs, or progress and cause other symptoms such as refractory hypokalemia (Whang, 1992) or recalcitrant cardiac arrhythmia (Seelig, 1980, Marino, 1991). The latter spurs the use of calcium channel blockers, **but magnesium is nature's calcium channel blocker** (Iseri, 1984) and controls the calcium pump (Abraham, 1982). You can see what a mountain of symptoms can result by ignoring chemistry.

For even though the popularly prescribed calcium channel blocker improves the symptom of high blood pressure, the undiagnosed magnesium deficiency continues. Plus the calcium channel blocker can cause further magnesium deficiency by itself (Ebel, 1983). We get into the familiar downward spiral of disease where the SICK GET SICKER. And this is only the beginning. And not only does the diuretic accentuate hypomagnesemia, but it causes the loss of other nutrients used in the daily work of detoxifying the diuretic. If that were not enough, **diuretics raise lipids** (cholesterol and triglycerides) thereby accentuating arteriosclerosis (Lardinois, 1988). But magnesium deficiency itself also disturbs proper lipid metabolism. (Rayssiguier, 1981). So now **disordered lipid metabolism** is added to the initial problem of hypertension. Therefore, **by using drugs to mask symptoms, the path of illness is accelerated.** Multiple mechanisms intertwine and snowball and we get, just as in chemical sensitivity, the **spreading phenomenon** where the SICK GET SICKER.

With the exercise craze and his escalating medical problems, our unsuspecting patient may decide to jog. But **sweating accelerates the loss of magnesium** through the skin (Stendig-Lindberg, 1987). Sudden death from magnesium deficiency-induced cardiac arrhythmia may result (Anonymous, 1990), and may indeed have been the cause of sudden death among famous athletes. And before death, the magnesium deficiency can seriously compromise the metabolism of the brain's happy hormones and cause serious depression. But it is instead blamed on life events or the illness itself.

There are many examples in the literature that demonstrate medicine's serious neglect of the facts regarding nutrient biochemistry. For example, in one study of 22 cardiac arrest victims, over half or 59% had abnormal serum magnesium levels. **100% or all of those with abnormal serum magnesium died.** In the "normomagnesemic" group (many were not actually magnesium replete because the least sensitive indicator of magnesium status, a serum level, was used), 66% died (Cannon, 1987). So magnesium status (determined by the inadequate serum value) still made a significant difference between 0% versus 44% survival.

In another study of 103 patients with documented acute heart attack or myocardial infarction, patients were randomized into two groups.   One group received intravenous magnesium, the other group received placebo (a water injection). The in-hospital mortality of the placebo group was 17% compared to the 2% for the magnesium group. This left **the magnesium-treated group with a reduction in mortality of 88.2%** (Schectere, 1990).   If someone told you that you could **cut your chance of dying by 88%** with a $10 shot of magnesium that has barely any side effect, wouldn't you think that should be standard?   Yet with all this data, magnesium status is not routinely and optimally evaluated to this date.   At least many (but not all!) hospitals and emergency rooms are now giving an IV of magnesium stat to heart attack victims as soon as they enter.

More worrisome is the fact that it is not yet universally routine for physicians to check the magnesium status of patients currently under indefinite or lifelong treatment for chronic diseases of the vascular system. This is in spite of reports where hypokalemia (low potassium), hypocalcemia (low calcium), and/or hypophosphatemia could not be corrected until the hypomagnesemia was diagnosed and corrected (Whang, 1984, 1992). And, of course magnesium deficiency has a major bearing on the development of arteriosclerosis, the number one cause of morbidity and mortality (Orimo, 1990).   And **arteriosclerosis is a major cause of depression** in the elderly. Despite the fact that there are over 30 million hypertensive Americans (Kaplan, 1986), and despite the fact that magnesium deficiency is a part of the cause for many (Altura, 1981, 1984, 1985, Resnick, 1984), **90% of physicians do not check for a magnesium deficiency in the United States, even in patients so sick as to be hospitalized** (Whang, 1990). And this is in an era where such phrases as "reasonable and customary" dictate what the patient can have as his standard care. It becomes clear that the **standard is not in the best medical interest of the patient** or the society that picks up the medical tab. We tend to be overly drug-oriented and skip looking for the cause, jumping right to the drug.

As another example of how we tend to undervalue nutrient biochemistry in medicine, in an issue of a popular internal medicine journal there was an article on muscle cramps, one on Raynaud's phenomenon (cold, bluish- or reddish-white fingers with painful spasms), and one on the correction of resistant potassium deficiencies (hypokalemia). All three problems can be classic symptoms of magnesium deficiency. Yet magnesium deficiency was not even mentioned in the entire issue (ARCH INT MED, 1990). But lots of drugs were. Every month a perusal of the leading medical journals results in the same staggering findings. Drugs are the presumed answer to all symptoms.

Since diseases of the cardiovascular system are the number one cause of death and dying in the United States, and consequently a major part of the **12% of the GNP expenditures that go for medical care,** this is no small matter. And bear in mind that **magnesium is an example** of **but one of over 40 nutrients** that we are limiting this whole discussion to for simplicity. But bear in mind that if magnesium is so important in saving lives, as from a heart attack, and the news is not universally known in medicine, you can appreciate where the miserable status of the other over 40 nutrients is. And when **correcting magnesium can stop a heart attack from progressing to death** and yet is not used, you can appreciate why it will be even longer before its use in depression is acknowledged.

In one study that did not use sophisticated nutrient analyses, 59 patients with a mean age of 82 and a recent hip fracture were studied. One half of the group received a few nutrient tests and supplements, while the other half of the group did not. **The rate of medical complications for the group that had attention to nutrients was 44% compared with 87% for the other, or nearly double. And the mean duration of hospital stay for the nutrient group was 24 days versus 40, nearly half.** The death rate in this highly fragile, aged and injured group was 24% for the nutrients group versus 37%.

A few vitamins have cut the complications and hospital stay in half. Yet still in spite of the enormous health and financial benefits, this is not standard care (Delmi, 1990). Instead we are in an era where patients and their physicians are penalized for deviating from the "standard" of care. Yes, you heard right. Even when studies show that **giving vitamins cuts in half the hospital stay, the complications and the death rate,** it is not done. And any physician who does it, risks penalties for deviating from the norm. Just think of the Medicare savings alone, not to mention the agony of the victims who had a doubled hospital stay or death.

Chronic magnesium deficiency has been implicated in some cases of **TIA (transient ischemic attacks) or mini-strokes** (Fehlinger, 1984), organic brain syndrome (Hall, 1973), and contributes to the pathology of Alzheimer's disease. And we haven't begun to touch upon the over 40 other symptoms that this one deficiency, magnesium, can produce. Intestinal spasms mimicking colitis (Main 1985), cerebral spasm called **migraines,** bronchial spasms of asthma (Rollo, 1987), chronic fatigue (Cox, 1991), **unwarranted depression,** or the fallopian spasms of infertility are possible. And, of course, the symptoms of chemical sensitivity can be wholly or in part produced by magnesium deficiency (Rogers, 1991).

It is interesting that emergency injections of magnesium have been the time-honored treatment for often tragically fatal **toxemia of pregnancy** for over 60 years (Lazard, 1925). But the correct prophylactic determination of magnesium status, so easy to do with a urine loading test (Rogers, 1991), is not routine with pregnancy, before this sometimes fatal event. Instead the norm is to wait until it is a catastrophic emergency, and infinitely more difficult to treat.

Other **common magnesium deficiency symptoms** include a host of **psychiatric symptoms** like **irritability, anxiety, agitation, panic attacks,** and more (Hall, 1973). You can begin to appreciate how one almost feels clairvoyant when he/she sees an article on panic disorder in cardiology patients (Beitman, 1991). And again, with no mention of the one common deficiency that could be the cause of both symptoms, an undiscovered magnesium deficiency. But remember, magnesium deficiency isn't the only thing that can cause **panic disorder,** as chemical sensitivity (which is commonly accompanied by depression) can cause this.

Yet the recent National Institutes of Health Consensus Statement On Panic Disorder mentions neither environmental triggers nor nutrient deficiencies in the differential diagnosis (SCIENCE NEWS, 1992). Nor do they mention that stress and magnesium deficiency are mutually enhancing; in otherwords, each causes the other. (Seelig, 1981, Boullin, 1967).

For the perception of stress causes neurotransmitters called **catecholamines** to be made. This stress through catecholamine induction enhances magnesium deficiency. But magnesium deficiency causes irritability, agitation, and panic. This in turn pushes more on the **neurotransmitters or catecholamines**: another spiral mechanism of how the SICK GET SICKER when environmental and biochemical causes are not sought. For you see **stress causes magnesium loss, and magnesium loss causes more stress hormones to be made** in the brain. And the way to buck the cycle is not with a drug, but to find and correct the deficiency.

The most common clinical findings of magnesium deficiency in some studies were in the brain with personality changes and depression. If the serum magnesium level improved to 1.5 mg/dl, the psychological manifestations tended to improve (Hashizume N, Mori M, An Analysis of Hypermagnesemia and Hypomagnesemia, JAP J MED, Jul/Aug, 1990;29(4):368-472). But they neglected to stress that.

NOTE: You can take all the minerals in the world, but fail to correct deficiencies if you are deficient in stomach acid, **hydrochloric acid** (Kassarjuan Z, et al, Hypochlorhydria: A factor in nutrition, ANN REV NUTR 9:271-285,1989)

Since magnesium is in over 300 enzymatic reactions it shouldn't come as a surprise that magnesium deficiency can cause depression, schizophrenia, obsessive-compulsion, and every brain pathology you can name.

THE MAGNESIUM CYCLE OF DISEASE:

[1]

eating the American diet	→	causes magnesium deficiency
drinking alcohol	→	"
eating sweets, white sugar	→	"
eating bleached white flour	→	"
eating bleached white rice	→	"
medications like diuretics	→	"
stress, sweating, etc.	→	"

[2]

magnesium deficit → causes cardiac arrhythmia, chronic back spasms, bladder spasms, asthma, migraine, irritable bowel, PMS, **depression**, fatigue, insomnia, panic attacks, depression, sudden death, hypertension, etc.

[3]

magnesium deficiency can cause hypertension which is treated with a diuretic, which → causes magnesium deficiency. This can cause the hypertension to worsen and/or any of the above symptoms.

[4]

as more symptoms appear → more medications are used

[5]

the metabolism of medications uses up magnesium → worsens magnesium deficiency

[6]

meanwhile the mag deficit is not diagnosed and → continues to worsen, creating more symptoms, until a person has a severe debilitating depression or a heart attack and dies; and no one ever knows why.

So bare minimum, regardless of what your diseases or symptoms are, and in fact even if you are well, please do the magnesium loading test. Your life may depend on it. It is the most commonly deficient mineral and crucial in over 300 enzymes. It may be a major turning point for you, or silently protect you from getting whatever your body is currently working on. And remember, where there is one deficiency, there are others. Rarely do they occur alone, so check the other intracellular levels.

REFERENCES:

Dyckner T, Wester PO, Effect of magnesium on blood pressure, BRIT MED J, 286, 1847-1849 June 11, 1983.

Zawada ET, Ter Weeja, Mc Clung DE, Magnesium prevents acute hypercalcemic hypertension. NEPHRON 47:109-114, 1987.

Motoyama T, Sano H, Fukuzaki H, Oral magnesium supplementation in patients with essential hypertension. HYPERTENSION, 13:227-232, 1989.

Motoyama T, Sano H, Suzuki H, Kowaguchi K, Saito K, Furuta Y, Fukuzaki H, Oral magnesium treatment and the erythrocyte sodium pump in patients with essential hypertension. J HYPERTENSION, 4(Suppl 6): S682-S684, 1986.

Cade, JFJ, A significant elevation of plasma magnesium levels in schizophrenic and depressive states. MED J AUST i:195-196
1964.

Hoschl C, Do calcium antagonists have a place in the treatment of mood disorders?, DRUGS, 42(5):721-729, 1991.

Kanofsky JD, Magnesium deficiency in chronic schizophrenia, INTERNAT J NEUROSCI, 61:87-90, 1991.

Dunner DL, Meltzer HL, Schreiner HC, Fieglson J, Plasma and erythrocte magnesium levels in patients with primary affective disorders during chronic lithium treatment, ACTA PSYCHIAT SCAND. 51:104-109, 1975.

Frizel D, Coppen A, Marks V, Plasma magnesium and calcium in depression, BR J PSYCHIAT, 115:1375, 1969.

Herberg L, Bold AM, Sex differences in mean serum magnesium in depression, LANCET I:128-129, 1972.

Herzberg L, Herzberg B, Mood changes and magnesium. A possible interaction between magnesium and lithium, J NERVMENT DIS 165:423-426, 1977.

Durlach J, Magnesium depletion and pathogenesis of Alzheimer's Disease, MAG RES, 217-218, 1990.

Langley WF, Mann D, Central nervous system magnesium deficiency, ARCH INTERN MED, 593-596, 1991.

Ebel H, Gunther T, Magnesium metabolism: a review, J CLIN CHEM BIO-CHEM, 257-270, 1980.

Cohen PG, Hypomagnesmic encephalopathy, MAGNESIUM, 203, 1985.

Wessely S, Magnesium and chronic fatigue syndrome, LANCET 337:1094-1095, May 4, 1991.

Naylor GJ, Fleming LW, Stewart WK, McNamee HB, Poidevin D, Plasma magnesium and calcium in depressive psychosis, BR J PSYCHIAT, 120:683-684.

Shaw DM, Frizel D, Camps FE, White S, Brain electrolytes in depressive and alcoholic suicides, BR J PSYCHIAT, 115:69-79 1969.

Henrotte JG, Type A behavior and magnesium metabolism, MAGNESIUM, 5:201-210, 1986.

McGuire R, Type A stress a drain on magnesium, MED TRIBUNE, p.1, May 15, 1984.

Cox I, Campbell M, Dowson D, Red blood cell magnesium and chronic fatigue syndrome, LANCET, 227: 757-60, 1991.

Hall RCW, Joffe JR, Hypomagnesemia: Physical and psychiatric symptoms, JAMA 224(13):1749-1751, 1973.

Kanofsky JD, et al, Is iatrogenic hypomagnesemia common in schizophrenia?, J AMER COL NUTR, 10(5):537/14, October 1991.

Romano T, et al, Magnesium deficiency and fibromyalgia syndrome, J NUTR MED, 4:165-167, 1994.

Hall RCW, Joffe JR, Hypomagnesemia. Physical and psychiatric symptoms, J AMER MED ASSOC 224:1749-1751, 1973.

Alexander PE, Van Kammen DP, Bunney WE, Serum calcium and magnesium levels in schizophrenia: Relationship to clinical phenomena and neuroleptic treatment, BRIT J PSYCHIATRY, 133:143-149, 1978.

PREMENSTRUAL SYNDROME
AS ONE TYPE OF DEPRESSION

Because premenstrual depression is so pervasive, it deserves special mention. When I was in medical school in the 60's, there was no such thing as premenstrual syndrome (PMS). But there are enough of us still around who can vouch for the undefinable agony and the multitude of unpredictable symptoms. It may not have had a name, but for sure it was around. Anyway, the recognition of it decades later was a boon for women.

The depression that often accompanies PMS can reach truly psychotic proportions and mimic mental aberrations worse than depression. Putting its timing and limited duration aside, the best part is that there are many causes and triggers. A common participant to the pathology of **PMS depression,** for example, is as you now know, magnesium deficiency. And there is no lack of scientific documentation, although it is largely ignored. As with every malady, magnesium is not the only factor. **You must address the TOTAL LOAD** of factors to get rid of PMS depression. For some, testing and giving minuscule neutralizing doses of hormones can turn off the symptoms within minutes (this is covered in THE E.I. SYNDROME, REVISED).

Unfortunately, the drug industry has recognized another opportunity to hook millions of more unsuspecting women on Prozac by suggesting its use in PMS depression (Associated Press; Study backs Prozac for severe PMS, SARASOTA HERALD-TRIBUNE, 5A, June 8, 1995).

Clearly, premenstrual syndrome is a cyclic form of severe depression. And just as with depression, medicine seems to go out of its way to devise complex names or labels. PMS in the scientific literature is also known as **"late luteal phase dysphoric disorder"** and it's also called **"premenstrual dysphoric disorder".** Sure, PMS has abnormal serotonin chemistry. But there are also many papers showing that PMS is made worse by ingesting certain foods, inhaling certain chemicals, and being low in certain nutrients like vitamin B6 and magnesium. Yet, just as with general depression, **medicine is trying to treat PMS as though it were a Prozac deficiency and disregard all of the many causes.** Meanwhile, they cloak the disorder in mysterious labels.

The commonly prescribed drugs Prozac, diuretics, huge doses of hormones and more are a far cry from fixing the real problem. Don't fall into that trap (more in Volume III on hormones).

REFERENCES:

Facchinetti F, et al, Oral magnesium successfully relieves premenstrual mood changes, OBSTET GYNECOL 78(2):177-181, 1991.

Abraham GE, et al, Serum and red cell magnesium levels in patients with premenstrual tension, AM J CLIN NUTR 34(11):2364-2366, 1981.

Redmond DE, et al, Menstrual cycle and ovarian hormone effects on plasma and platelet monoamine oxidase (MAO) and plasma dopamine-hydroxylase activities in the Rhesus monkey, PSYCHOSOM MED 37:417, 1975.

Abraham GE, Management of the premenstrual tension syndromes: Rationale for a nutritional approach, in Bland ED, 1986: A YEAR IN NUTRITIONAL MEDICINE, Keats Publ, New Canaan CT, 1986.

Sherwood RA, et al, Magnesium and the premenstrual syndrome, ANN CLIN BIOCHEM, 23(6):667-670, 1986.

Mira M, et al, Vitamin and trace element status in premenstrual syndrome, AM J CLIN NUTR, 47:636-641, 1981.

Steiner M, et al, Fluoxetine in the treatment of premenstrual dysphoria, NEW ENGL J MED, 332:1529-1534, 1995.

Rapkin AJ. The role of serotonin in premenstrual syndrome. CLIN OBSTET GYNECOL, 35:629-636, 1992.

Winslow R, Study finds Prozac helpful in the treatment of PMS, WALL STREET JOURNAL, B1, B7, Thurs June 8, 1995

COPPER DEFICIENCY

A literature search on just about any nutrient reveals a wealth of information substantiating widespread and unrecognized deficiencies. For example, let's look at **copper, a mineral** whose adequacy is not routinely checked for. When we think of copper, we often think of toxic or high levels from copper tubing and water pipes. But actually the **majority of Americans are deficient in copper.** A National Institutes of Health study showed that 81% of people have less than two-thirds of the RDA (recommended daily allowance) of copper.

Another study revealed that hospital meals provide only 1/5th of the copper needed or 0.76 mg of copper per day. Yet people need 2-4 mg of copper for health, and even more for healing and chemical exposures. Another study by the FDA showed that when they analyzed 234 foods which are the core of the American diet, they provided less than 80% of the RDA of copper. And in another study of 270 **United States Navy SEAL trainees (highly selected "healthy" young men) 37% had low plasma copper levels.** And plasma copper is a very insensitive indicator of copper status.

Since they used an inferior test to assess copper adequacy, that means they missed some men who were low. So the facts are that over a third of young "cream of the crop" healthy men are copper deficient. And that **low copper can cause arteriosclerosis** and high cholesterol. So it should come as no surprise that they also found a high rate of arteriosclerosis in young soldiers at autopsy.

What this means is that **nutrient deficiencies contribute to chronic degenerative diseases of older age, but the process begins in teen-agers!** In other words, copper deficiency is an example of one of many very common mineral deficiencies that is rarely checked for, and begins in teen-agers. And when allowed to go undetected, can surface as the very diseases we treat adults for like high blood pressure and high cholesterol. And both high blood pressure and high cholesterol can contribute to depression by a variety of mechanisms. For not only is the senile brain ripe for depression, but medications used to treat them can cause depression. Yet medicines fail to correct the causes, and are merely used to cover up the symptoms. Is it any wonder that **arteriosclerosis** continues to be the **number one cause of illness and death** in the U.S.?

Another study showed that **80% of Americans get** 1 mg or less of copper per day, which is **1/4th of the copper they need for a day.** While another study which analyzed twenty different types of U.S. diets, showed only 25% of the people got 2 mg of copper a day (1/2 of what they need). But the majority of the diets provided only 0.78 mg of copper per day. So numerous copper studies seem to point to the fact that **the majority of people are deficient.** When we randomly studied 228 of our patients, 165 or 72% were deficient in copper.

So, no matter whose studies you look at over the last 20, years there is a wealth of data showing that **copper deficiency is rampant in the United States.** Among the symptoms that can stem from copper deficiency in its over 21 enzymes is hypercholesterolemia (**high cholesterol**). Another copper deficiency problem is arteriosclerosis or **hardening of the arteries,** which causes early heart attacks, high blood pressure, strokes, and Alzheimer's. And arteriosclerosis is the number one cause of death and disease in the western world. Many copper enzymes are responsible for keeping us from chronic fatigue, **depression**, premature aging and much more. (And furthermore, many of the enzymes of copper are needed to detoxify chemicals. And bear in mind copper is an example of but one of 40 essential nutrients.)

A number of minerals are crucial to the brain for protection against aging. For example, mineral deficiencies can impair myelin metabolism which is one of the defects of multiple sclerosis (Sandstead HH, A brief history or the influence of trace elements on brain function, AM J CLIN NUTR, 43:293-298,1986). And copper as well as manganese are two minerals that have been reported as better in vegans than those on the standard American fare, which may just be one more reason out of scores of reasons why many people with MS have improved on a macrobiotic diet.

Copper is not always easy to correct when it is deficient. Fortunately, there are several forms to chose from since one form is not perfect for everyone. And often copper is best absorbed when taken alone. That is, at a meal but with no other minerals. In this way, there is minimal competition for the **mineral transporters.** (These are specialized proteins that carry copper and other minerals across the gut wall and into the blood stream. Sometimes copper needs to be taken along with 10 grains of betaine HCl to facilitate its absorption. For betaine mimics stomach acid and helps ionize minerals for better absorption.)

So in essence, **copper** is another good example of a trace mineral that **is slowly diminishing in the American diet.** And because it is in 21 enzymes, many of which have to do with cholesterol metabolism, it has a role in why the number one cause of death and illness is on the rise. So why are so many people foolishly on expensive drugs that do nothing to

275

correct the underlying causal deficiencies? Instead of finding out why they have high cholesterol, they merely take a drug to turn off cholesterol absorption. But more importantly for the depressed individual, **cholesterol is crucial for the synthesis of the brain neurotransmitters.** That is in part why **cholesterol-lowering drugs lead to increased depression and suicide** (more on that in Volume IV).

So copper deficiency is very common, can lead to a variety of cardiovascular problems, not the least of which is abnormal carbohydrate and abnormal cholesterol metabolism. Both of these have a profound effect on the brain. And copper is directly involved in enzymes in the brain that direct synthesis of our happy hormones and brain energy.

And never forget that just as any mineral can be too low and cause deficiency symptoms which include depression, on the flip side levels can be too high. When copper is toxic (see Volume I for heavy metal poisoning) it damages crucial enzymes so that we cannot make sufficient happy hormones in the brain. High copper can come from copper water pipes with an acidic water (chlorine will help promote the leaching of copper into the water), and pesticides can leave copper residues, as examples.

REFERENCES:

Wolf WR, et al, Daily intake of zinc and copper from self- selected diets, FED PROC 36:1175, 1977.

Conlan D, et al, Serum copper levels in elderly patients with femoral-neck fractures, AGE AGING 19:212-214, 1990.

Hunt CE, Carlton WW, Cardiovascular lesions associated with experimental copper deficiency in the rabbit, J NUTR 87:385, 1965.

Klevay LM, Viestenz KE, Abnormal electrocardiograms in rats deficient in copper, AM J CLIN NUTR 32:856, 1979.

Allen KGD, Klevay LM, Hyperlipoproteinemia in rats due to copper deficiency, NUTR REP INT 221295-299, 1980.

Klevay LM, et al, Increased cholesterol in plasma in a young man during experimental copper depletion, METABOLISM, 33L1112-1118, 1984.

Cohen AM, et al, Effect of copper on carbohydrate metabolism in rats, ISR J MED SCI, 18:840-844, 1982.

Bawkin RM, Mosbach EH, Bawkin H, Concentration of copper in serum of children with schizophrenia, PED 27:642, 1961

Haffron D, Serum copper and oxidase activity in schizophrenic patients, ARCH NERUOL PSYCHIATRY 78:317, 1957

Munch-Peterson S, On serum copper in patients with schizophrenia, ACTA PSYCHIAT SCAND, Suppl 25:423, 1950

Scheinberg IH, Morell AG, Harris RS, Bergen A, Concentration of ceruloplasmin in plasma of schizophrenics, SCIENCE 126:925, 1957

INAPPROPRIATE IRON TREATMENT

Iron deficiency can lead to anemia and fatigue, but rarely depression. But **iron overload can lead to depression, and it is usually iatrogenic, or caused by a physician.** Because we see this blunder so frequently, here is how it happens. Iron deficiency classically causes red blood cells to look small and light colored, since they are deficient in iron. We call this **microcytosis** (small cells) and **hypochromia** (not enough color). Hence, whenever a doctor sees a microcytic, hypochromic anemia, he often assumes it is from iron deficiency and treats it, without further testing.

However, **copper also causes a microcytic hypochromic anemia.** And when you give iron instead, it not only can cause iron excess that can escalate to toxicity, but the iron causes a further lowering of the already low copper. So as the person gets more anemic, his doctor may push harder on the iron. Hence, the patient gets more **copper anemic and iron toxic.** I have witnessed this scenario more times than I would like to see. The moral of the story is, when you treat something, try to know what it is you are treating. And if it is resistant, then you know there is something else low that is inhibiting it from correcting. For example, **magnesium won't correct if you are manganese deficient, potassium won't correct if you are too low in magnesium, and iron won't correct if you are copper deficient.**

The thing to note in regard to iron toxicity (more in Volume I on heavy metal toxicity) is that much that has been learned about the dangers of **lead poisoning** and its effects on the brain, can be said also for the effects of too much iron in the brain. For lead, initial studies were done on very high levels of lead, something your grandmother could diagnose.

278

Unfortunately, it was overlooked that lower levels of lead toxicity could also cause brain disturbances with **lowered IQ and depression.** And lead overload or toxicity is not limited to children.

We have alerted people to the dangers of lead from paints, auto exhaust, etc., but we neglect to advise them that many foods are fortified with extra iron, which can in some individuals create such an **iron overload** as to slowly **mimic the effect lead toxicity in the brain** and heart.

So be careful when you are prescribed iron, for it is a perfect way of inducing (if not worsening a most likely already existing) copper deficiency. Often the story goes like this:

*****

CASE SCENARIO:

A young woman will complain of fatigue. A cbc (complete blood count) will show a low hematocrit (percentage of red blood cells). So the doctor assumes that the blood is low or anemic due to an iron deficiency. Hence, he prescribes iron, but never actually checks the iron level or the other frequent causes of microcytic anemia (small cells and low red blood cell count), which can include a copper deficiency.

If her anemia is in part due to a deficit of copper, not only will it fail to correct, but the more iron he gives, the worse he makes the copper deficiency, and the anemia. Unfortunately, the more resistant to correction she gets, the more iron he gives. So he drives the copper even lower!

*****

And this copper is necessary in brain enzymes to enable you to make sufficient "happy hormones". And if the patient has an uncorrected anemia and continues to complain of fatigue, often more iron is pushed. Yet copper is necessary in the enzyme cytochrome oxidase for energy production. So no wonder there is worsening fatigue. And it is necessary in converting thyroid hormone T4 to T3. I'll spare you the details of what the other copper enzymes do. But recall as one more example, copper's essential role in super oxide dismutase for the chemically sensitive individual and those with inflammatory conditions like arthritis.

So giving too much iron can do a lot more besides worsen the hypocupremia (low copper or copper deficiency). Iron overload can contribute to heart disease, Alzheimer's and deficiencies of other minerals, like manganese. And it can mimic lead toxicity. And to make matters worse, we fortify processed foods with this heavy metal. Also drinking water can have elevated iron from industrial run-off or naturally occurring ores. So read on, for iron overload, like any heavy metal poisoning, can be the cause of your depression.

REFERENCES:

Richardson JS, Subbarao KV, Ang LC, On the possible role of iron-induced free radical peroxidation in neural degeneration in Alzheimer's disease, ANN NY ACAD SCI, 648:326-327, 1992.

Do diets high in iron impair manganese status?, NUTR REV 51:3, 86-88, 1993.

Are we at risk for heart disease because of normal iron status?, NUTR REV, 51:4, 112-115,1993.

Cutler P, Iron overload in psychiatric illness, AMER J GERIAT, 148:147-148, January 1991.

Tucker DM, et al, Iron status and brain function, AM J CLIN NUTR 39:105-113, 1984

Youdin MBH, et al, Putative biological mechanism of the effect of iron deficiency on brain chemistry and behavior, AMER J CLIN NUTR, 50:607-617, 1989

ZINC

When we look at **zinc,** literature reports indicate that unsuspected zinc deficiency is also relatively common. In one study only 13% or less than one in six of randomly selected patients had normal zinc levels. But again these were serum levels, notoriously insensitive. To verify that many more are deficient, another study showed that 68% of the population ingested less than 2/3 the RDA for zinc. Zinc deficiency has been shown to be prevalent throughout the world, in all age ranges, in pregnancy, chronic disease, after surgery, and in chemical sensitivity.

Zinc deficiency can also cause depression. Fourteen patients with primary affective disorder were compared to 14 age and sex matched controls for plasma zinc levels upon admission. **Plasma zinc levels were lower in the depressed patients.** Upon discharge and recovery the patients' plasma zinc levels increased. Since zinc is important in over 90 metalloenzymes, deficiency can affect many brain enzymes, one of which is **dopamine beta-hydroxylase.** This is necessary for production of the neurotransmitter or happy hormone **noradrenaline** (from dopamine). Furthermore, zinc deficiency may result in impaired membrane transport and also impaired **transport of vitamin B12** leading to reduced cerebrospinal fluid and brain B12 availability (McLoughlin). These in turn can also lead to depression.

Or zinc deficiency can lead to **faulty hormone binding.** This means that you can have normal blood tests for circulating levels of a hormone like thyroid, estrogen, DHEA, or testosterone. But if **zinc deficiency is damaging the hormone receptors,** the hormone never binds properly to the cell to cause its action. This is a real nightmare for the patient. For he has the net effect or symptoms of a hormone deficiency since the hormone cannot work. But every time his doctors measure the levels of the hormone floating in the bloodstream, he gets a report that there is plenty of hormone and that there is no problem. The frustrating answer to the problem is a zinc deficiency **impairing the action of the hormone on the cell.** Zinc deficiency can cause many other symptoms besides depression, like chemical sensitivity, **inability to correct vitamins B6 and A deficiencies** (zinc dependent enzymes pyridoxal kinase and alcohol dehydrogenase), brain fog, poor digestion, diabetes, alcohol intolerance, fatigue, and much more (Rogers, 1990).

Over 20 years ago Dr. Carl Pfeiffer observed that when people were zinc deficient, they often **had white streaks on their fingernails.** And as they improved their zinc status, not only did the hair and nails strengthen, but the white spots disappeared. We have observed this scores of times as well. In fact, since fingernails grow about a millimeter a month, you can tell in which month the zinc deficiency started.

REFERENCES:

McLoughlin IJ, et al, Zinc in depressive disorders, ACTA PSYCHIATR SCAND, 82:451-453, 1990.

Reuven S, Zinc deficiency and cerebellar disease, INTERNAT J NEUROSCI, 60:21-26, 1991

Van Der Rijt C, et al, Overt hepatic encephalopathy precipitated by zinc deficiency, GASTRO, 100:1114-1118, 1991.

Rosenberg IH, Importance of zinc for hormone binding and signal transduction: Limiting mechanisms in zinc deficiency?, NUTR REV, 49:12, 369-370, 1991

Nichols J, Morgan J, Taylor A, Postnatal depression and zinc status--a preliminary report, J NUTRIT MED, 3:1, 35-42, 1992

Pfeiffer CC, Jenney EH, Fingernail white spots: Possible zinc deficiency, JAMA 228, 157, 1974

Mares-Perlman JA, Subar AF, Block G, Greger JL, Luby MH, Zinc intake and sources in the USA adult population:1976-1980, J AMER COLL NUTR 14:4, 349-357, 1995

THE CHROMIUM CATASTROPHE

Chromium is a mineral that is low in the standard (high in processed foods) American diet and is chiefly responsible for regulation of sugars. You can get **serious hypoglycemia (low blood sugar)** from chromium deficiency that creates violent mood swings and depression.

And chromium deficiency is important for much more than causing hypoglycemia with mood swings and depression. It is important in regulating cholesterol metabolism as well. But more importantly, when a person is deficient in chromium he tends to **crave foods** and cannot get enough satisfaction through the glucose pathway. Hence, there are studies showing that in the last decade there has been an 8% increase in overweight in the United States (Kuczmarski RJ, et al, Increasing prevalence of overweight among U.S. adults. The National Health and Nutrition Examination Survey 1960-1991, JAMA July 20, 1994; 272 (3): 205-211).

For when you are deficient in chromium, **you crave sweets unmercifully (a cause of overeating)** or have cravings which can lead to **bingeing and bulimia.** More on chromium in the hypoglycemia section. Suffice it to say, when you normalize sugar metabolism by making sure chromium is adequate, then headaches, depression, insomnia, and a host of other brain problems melt away. The problem is that 80% of the population is deficient in chromium, **a deficiency that we worsen every time we eat sugars.**

THE VICIOUS CHROMIUM CRAVING CYCLE:

eating sweets	→	lowers chromium (lost in urine)
low chromium	→	triggers sweet cravings
sweet cravings	→	cause one to eat more sugar
eating sugar	→	triggers the loss of further chromium
low chromium	→	triggers more sweet cravings, arteriosclerosis, hypoglycemia, high cholesterol, mood swings, **depression**, poor digestion (in trypsin), obesity, etc.

But unfortunately, chromium deficiency is only one example of how a hidden or unsuspected common nutrient deficiency can have devastating effects on the whole body and mind. Many other common mineral deficiencies, like manganese also can cause defective carbohydrate metabolism, complete with cravings and hypoglycemia (more on this in the hypoglycemia section, Volume III).

REFERENCES:

Mertz W, Chromium in human nutrition: A review, J NUTR 123:626-633, 1993.

Passwater RA, THE LONGEVITY FACTOR: CHROMIUM PICOLINATE, Keats Publ, New Canaan CT, 1993.

Schrauzer GN, Shrestha KP, Arce MF, Somatopsychological effects of chromium supplementation, J NUTRIT MED, 3:1, 43- 48, 1992.

Cook R, Benton D, Chromium supplementation improves chronic headaches: a case-study, J NUTRIT MED, 3:1, 61-64, 1992.

THE DIET DISASTER

Now you understand why people cannot lose weight. It is often because they have nutrient deficiencies. They are driven by natural instincts to find the food that will correct their deficiencies. But because of poor knowledge, they choose the wrong foods to eat. So it should not come as a surprise that there is also more depression among overweight people. Because as you see, a chromium deficiency can cause hypoglycemia, cravings, depression, poor digestion of other nutrients and a snowballing into many other illnesses.

But, as usual, when there is one disease that you can blame all the rest on, then it is often done. So depression is blamed on the obesity, or the over-eating or obesity is blamed on depression. And the more you diet, the more deficient you get. And heaven help you if you have surgery, chemical exposures, a root canal, a prescription drug, or an accident that further lowers your nutrient levels. You now understand that if you are a patient in the drug-oriented world, you cannot win, because no one is looking at the chemistry that is causing all of your symptoms. There is only one way to go: down that long spiral tube where **the sick get sicker, quicker.**

REFERENCES:

Wallace WJ, Sheslow D, Hassink S, Obesity in children: a risk for depression, ANN NY ACAD SCI, 699: 301-3, Oct 29, 1993.

Sheslow D, Hassink S, Wallace W, DeLancey E, The relationship between self-esteem and depression in obese children, AN NY ACAD SCI, 699: 289-91, Oct 29, 1993.
Abstract: In this study obese pediatric patients showed significant depression and lowered self-esteem.

Mendels J, Clinical management of the depressed geriatric patient: current therapeutic options, AMER J MED, 95(5A): 13S-18S, May 24, 1993.

DiPietro L, Anda RF, Williamson DF, Stunkard AJ, Depressive symptoms and body weight, INTER J OBESITY & RELATED METAB DISORDERS, 17(8): 485-6, Aug 1993.

Istvan J, Zavela K, Weidner G, Body weight and psychological distress in NHANES, INTER J OBESITY & RELATED METAB DISORDERS, 16(12): 999-1003, Dec 1992.
Abstract: These results indicate that relative body weight is weakly related to psychological distress among women but not men, and that cigarette smoking does not significantly modify this relationship.

Wing RR, Marcus MD, Blair EH, Epstein LH, Burton LR, Depressive symptomatology in obese adults with type II diabetes, DIABETES CARE , 13(2): 170-2, Feb 1990.

Fischer J, Johnson MA, Low body weight and weight loss in the aged, J AMER DIETET ASSOC, 90(12): 1697-706, Dec 1990.
Abstract: Low body weight and rapid unintentional weight loss are highly predictive of mortality and morbidity in the elderly population. Weight loss is frequently reported in elderly patients. Acute and chronic diseases are leading causes of involuntary weight loss. Whereas physical disease probably accounts for a majority of cases of involuntary weight loss, psychiatric disorders such as dementia and depression also may result in severe nutritional deficiencies. As 50% of Americans have lost all of their teeth by age 65, chewing problems are often present. Other factors that contribute to poor nutritional status include alterations in the gastrointestinal tract, functional disabilities, lowered socioeconomic status, and social isolation. Finally, because of the increase in both physical and psychiatric disease, the elderly are major users of prescription drugs. Drug/nutrient interactions can result in anorexia and weight loss. The findings indicate that factors causing unintentional weight loss are highly interrelated and difficult to separate. Health care professionals must monitor body weight in elderly persons and carefully evaluate any cases of rapid, unintentional weight loss to prevent further deterioration of health status.

Palmer TA, Anorexia nervosa, bulemia nervosa: causal theories and treatment, NURSE PRACTIONER, 15(4): 12-18, 21, April 1990.

Wurtman JJ, Brzezinski A, Wurtman RJ, Laferrere B, Effect of nutrient intake on premenstrual depression, AMER J OBSTET GYNEC, 161(5): 1228-34, Nov 1989.

Abstract: Consumption of a carbohydrate-rich, protein-poor evening test meal during the late luteal phase of the menstrual cycle (PMS) improved depression, tension, anger, confusion, sadness, fatigue, alertness, and calmness scores (p less than 0.01) among patients with premenstrual syndrome. No effect of the meal was observed during the follicular phase or among the control subjects during either phase. Because synthesis of the brain serotonin, which is known to be involved in mood and appetite, increases after carbohydrate intake, premenstrual syndrome subjects may over consume carbohydrates in an attempt to improve their dysphoric mood state.

Slaiman S, Restricted diets restrict antidepressant efficacy, PRACTITIONER, 233(1472): 972, 975, July 8, 1989.

Rothchild M, Peterson HR, Pfeifer MA, Depression in obese men, INTER J OBESITY, 13(4): 479-85, 1989.

Baucom DH, Aiken PA, Effect of depressed mood in eating among obese and non-obese dieting and non-dieting persons, JOURNAL OF PERSONALITY & PSYCHOLOGY, 41(3): 577-85, Sept 1981.

Bech P, Hey H, Depression or asthenia related to metabolic disturbances in obese patients after intestinal bypass surgery, ACTA PSYCHIA SCAND, 59(5): 462-70, May 1979.

Bowen RC, Shepel L, Physical and psychological complications after bypass for obesity, CANADIAN MED ASSOC J, 116(8): 771-5, April 23, 1977.

Backman L, Johansson C, Thor'en P, Allgen LG, Hallberg D, S-tryptophan concentrations after intestinal bypass in extreme obesity, ACTA MEDICA SCANDINAVICA, 201(4): 285-9, 1977.

Garetz FK, Breaking the dangerous cycle of depression and faulty nutrition, GERIATRICS, 31(6): 73-5, June 1976.

Kuehnel RH, Wadden TA, Binge eating disorder, weight cycling, and psychopathology, INTERN J OF EATING DISORDERS, 15(4): 321-9, May 1994.

Ross CE, Overweight and depression, J HEALTH SOC BEHAV, 35(1): 63-79, March 1994.

Cohen D, Dementia, depression, and nutritional status, PRIMARY CARE; CLINICS IN OFFICE PRACTICE, 21(1): 107-19, March 1994.

Glueck CJ, Tieger M, Kunkel R, Tracy T, Speirs J, Streicher P, Illig E, Improvement in symptoms of depression and in an index of life stressors accompany treatment of severe hypertriglyceridemia, BIOLOG PSYCHIA, 34(4): 240-52, Aug 15, 1993.

Weidner G, Connor SL, Hollis JF, Connor WE, Improvements in hostility and depression in relation to dietary change and cholesterol lowering. The family heart study, ANN INTERN MED, 117(10): 820-3, Nov 15, 1992.
Abstract: Those who consumed a low-fat, high complex- carbohydrate diet at the end of the study showed significantly greater improvements in depression (P=0.044; difference in improvement, 2.9 points) and aggressive hostility (P=0.024; difference in improvement, 2.7%) compared with those who ate a high fat "American diet". Improvements in diet appear to be associated with reductions in depression and aggressive hostility as well as with lowered plasma cholesterol levels.

Wing RR, Marcus MD, Blair EH, Burton LR, Psychological responses of obese type II diabetic subjects to very-low calorie diet, DIABETES CARE, 14(7): 596-9, July 1991.

MANGANESE

Manganese, not to be confused with magnesium, is a mineral that has several major roles in the brain, especially in curing depression. First it is nearly impossible to correct a magnesium deficiency if manganese is also deficient. Second, it is important in **blood sugar control and hypoglycemia**. And it is also important in the detox pathways in super oxide dismutase. It has been implicated in helping memory and Alzheimer's, and more. Yet bear in mind that it can also cause nasty symptoms if one is toxic in manganese. Manganese has been pivotal in turning off many people's depression, especially when there was also a magnesium and/or chromium deficiency accompanying it.

REFERENCES:

English WM, Report on the treatment with manganese chloride of 181 cases of schizophrenia, 33 of manic depression and 16 of other defects or psychoses at the Ontario Hospital, Brockville, Ontario, AMER J PSYCHIAT 9:569, 1964

Kimura M, Yagi N, Itokawa Y, Effect of subacute manganese feeding on serotonin metabolism in the rat, J TOX ENVIR HEALTH, 4:P 701-707, 1978.

Patterson KY, Holbrook JT, et al, Zinc, copper, and manganese intake and balance for adults consuming self-selected diets, AMER J CLIN NUTR, 40:1397, 1403, 1984

Baly DL, et al, Effects of manganese deficiency on pyruvate carboxylase and phosphoenolpyruvate carboxykinase activity and carbohydrate homeostasis in adult rats, BIOLOG TR ELEMENT RES, 11:201-212, 1986

Neff NH, et al, Selective depletion of caudate nucleus dopamine and serotonin during chronic manganese dioxide administration, EXPERIMENTIA, 25:1140-1141, 1969

Hoskin RG, The manganese treatment of schizophrenic disorders, J NERV MENT DIS, 79:59, 1934

I like to show some of the older references as above to show you how long a lot of this has been around. With all the computer searches available today, docs can easily find the current references. But a number of the pioneers might never get their rightful place in history once these older references are lost, for the computer searches tend to only go back so many years, conveniently leaving many wonderful pioneers in oblivion.

LITHIUM, VANADIUM, CESIUM

Lithium is a well-known prescription treatment for specific types of depression. However, lithium is an element or mineral, just as magnesium and copper are. It may well be that these people have a deficiency of lithium and other nutrients along these crucial brain pathways.

Non-prescription lithium is available from Bio-Tech, Fayetteville, Arkansas, who prefer that you get it from your physician or health food store. N.E.E.D.S. and Emerson's Ecologics carry it. Lithium comes as a 5 mg capsule that contains 167 mg of elemental lithium.

Closely related to lithium is another element or mineral that is rarely thought of in terms of therapeutic effect or possible deficiency. But **cesium** also has a bearing on fixing the chemistry of depression. Not only does cesium have anti-depressant effects, but it has shortened the recovery time of the brain to the effects of alcohol as well as prescription drugs that have a side effect of depression.

I have discovered only **one source for cesium:** Bio Tech, 1-800 345-1199. Cesium comes as 100mg or 500mg. Always start with the lowest dose, just one for a few days, then increase every few days by an extra capsule, to 5 a day. The reason for caution is that some people are more depressed, as it is not their missing mineral. Therefore it can drive even lower the minimal levels of other crucial minerals that are precariously low.

Proceed carefully. As there is no assay at this time, it is strictly trial and error. I would also add that it is low on the list of potential things that are missing in depression. For example, it is not nearly as common a cause of depression as a magnesium deficiency is. It is just that it is one of those items that for a particular set of people, has turned them around and was the final part of the total load that was missing. For that reason, because it has been important, it is included here.

Another trace mineral that is very important to diabetics is vanadium. Hence, you can understand at least one of the mechanisms that might explain why it has also helped depression, since the main fuel for the brain is sugar.

REFERENCES:

Messiha FS, Lithium, rubidium and cesium: Cerebral pharmacokinetics and alcohol interactions, PHARMACOL BIOCHEM & BEHAV, 21:1, 87-92, 1984.

Messiha FS, Antidepressant action of cesium chloride and its modification of chorpromazine toxicity in mice, BR J PHARMACOL, 64:9-12, 1977.

Messihia FS, Cesium: a bibliography update, PHARM BIOCHEM BEHAV, 21:113-129, 1984.

Messiha FS, Krantz J, Effect of cesium ion on cerebral activity of the mouse, AM J PHARMACOL, 145:17-21, 1973.

Messiha FS, Cesium ion: Antagonism to chlorpromazine and levodopa-induced behavioral depression in mice, J PHARM PHARMACOL 27:873-874, 1975.

Ali, SA, Peet M, Ward NJ, Blood levels of vanadium, caesium, and other elements in depressive patients, J AFFECT DIS, 9: 187-191, 1985.

Yung CY, A synopsis on metals in medicine and psychiatry, PHARM BIOCHEM BEHAV, 21: 41-47, 1984.

Naylor GH, Smith AHW, Vanadium: a possible etiologic factor in manic depressive illness, PSYCHOL MED 11:249-256, 1981.

Paragas MG, Lithium adverse reactions in psychiatric patients, PHARM BIOCHEM BEHAV, vol.21: 65-69, 1994.

Ghadirian AM, Lehmann HE, Neurological side effects of lithium: organic brain syndrome, seizures, extra pyramidal side effects, and EEG changes, COMP PSYCH 21: 327-335, 1980.

West AP, Meltzer HY, Paradoxical lithium neurotoxicity: a report of five cases and a hypothesis about risk for neurotoxicity, AM J PSYCH 136:963-966, 1979.

Yung CY, A review of clinical trials of lithium in medicine, PHARM BIOCHEM BEHAV, vol. 21: 51-55, 1984.

Copper A, A prophylactic use of lithium in unpopular depression, J R SOC MED 76: 293-301, 1983.

Turner JG, Brownlie BE, Lithium as an adjunct to the treatment of thyrotoxicosis, AUST NZ J MED 6: 249, 1976.

White MG, Fetner CD, Treatment of the syndrome of inappropriate secretion of anti-diuretic hormone with lithium carbonate, N ENG J MED 292: 390-392, 1975.

Nordenstrom J, Elvius M, Bagedahl-Strindlund M, Zhao B, Torring O, Biochemical hyperparathyroidism and bone mineral status in patients treated long-term with lithium, METABOLISM: CLINICAL & EXPERIMENTAL, 43(12): 1563-7, Dec 1994.
Abstract: Lithium is known to interfere with normal calcium homeostasis. (The reason this is included is that hyperparathyroidism as you will see, can also cause aggression, and lithium may be the key for some people).

SELENIUM

Selenium is crucial in the detox pathway, in protection of cell membranes, in **making thyroid hormone**, in the metabolism of the essential fatty acids, and much more as you will learn. So no wonder it has a bearing on depression, as does every mineral. You get the picture. **Get a physician with a bio-chemical, not a drug approach to all illnesses.**

Benton D, Cook R, The impact of selenium supplementation on mood, BIOLOGICAL PSYCHIATRY, 29(11): 1092-8, June 1, 1991.

Abstract: The lower the level of selenium in the diet the more reports of anxiety, depression, and tiredness, which decreased following 5 weeks of selenium therapy. The results are discussed in terms of the low level of selenium in the food chain in some parts of the world.

*****

We could go on for every mineral and show how it contributes to depression if there is a significant deficiency. The evidence is overwhelming. But by now anyone with depression should be convinced to look for mineral deficiencies if they want to get rid of their depression. The HOW TO section will detail what levels to get (Volume IV). In the meantime, let's proceed to the amino acids.

THE OSTEOPOROSIS OUTRAGE

Most people know that osteoporosis is a lack of calcium in the bones. But what most do not know is that calcium is inhibited from being absorbed when we eat processed foods and soda drinks containing **phosphates**. Also, even if you take enough calcium, it cannot get into the bone unless you have enough of the other minerals needed to incorporate it and hold it in bone. These include magnesium, manganese, selenium, molybdenum, zinc, copper, etc. And taking calcium without assessing and correcting for deficiencies of these minerals, forces the calcium into the arteries of the body in the brain and heart. For **when you are deficient in the minerals** that hold calcium in the bone, **calcium cannot be taken up into the bone.** So instead it gets taken up by the toxic waste site; the cholesterol patches of damaged arteries. Hence the term **hardening (calcification) of the arteries.** As well as the minerals, many vitamins play a role in preventing osteoporosis, like vitamins D and K, etc.

Now you see the idiocy of a study that in essence says, people who are depressed are also more prone to get osteoporosis. Of course they are! They had deficiencies that gave them depression. Then when the deficiencies remained undiagnosed and uncorrected, the deficiencies inevitably went on to cause other diseases, like osteoporosis. How embarrassing for the researchers and tragic for the patients who remained undiagnosed and improperly treated. They never did go on to treat the depression. (Schweiger U, Deuschle M, et al, Low lumbar bone mineral density in patients with major depression, AMER J PSYCHIA, 151(11):1691-1693, Nov 1994).

HYDROCHLORIC ACID

And remember, no minerals get proper absorption without adequate gastric hydrochloric acid. And as people age, they gradually make less of it for a variety of reasons. This is a very important, yet frequently overlooked deficiency.

REFERENCES:

Gledhill t, et al, Epidemic hypochlorhydria, BR MED J, 289:1383-6, 1985

Carter RE 2nd, The clinical importance of hypochlorhydria (a consequence of chronic Heliobacter infection): its possible etiological role in mineral and amino acid mal-absorption, depression and other syndromes, MEDICAL HYPOTHESES, 39(4): 375-83, Dec 1992.

Carter RE, Helicobacter (AKA Campylobacter) pylori as the major causal factor in chronic hypochlorhydria, MED HYPOTHESIS 39; 367-374, 1992.

Kasarjian Z, Russell RM, Hypochlorhydria: a factor in nutrition, ANNU REV NUTR 9:271-285, 1989.

Russell RM, Micronutrient absorption and hypochlorhydira, J AM COLL NUTR 13;5:530, 1994.

CASE EXAMPLE:

Sam had 2 years of depression, resistant to medications. His magnesium loading test, rbc copper and rbc manganese were low. Prescribed nutrients only partially helped. But when gut studies (Volume III) suggested digestive deficiencies, addition of betaine corrected the mineral deficiencies and ended his years of depression.

THE HAPPY HORMONES
ARE MADE FROM AMINO ACIDS

Man has been in search of the "happy hormones" in the brain for centuries. He has tried alcohol, hallucinogens in the forms of herbs and weeds, cacti (peyote), mushrooms, nuts and seeds (nutmeg), and certain foods like oysters, etc. He has also learned a great deal by manipulating moods with drugs and studying the blood, spinal fluid and urine during and afterward. He knows there are a host of what I call "happy hormones" or more properly **neurotransmitters** in the brain.

One problem is, people are too dog-gone biochemically unique. **One man's meat is another man's poison.** And in one person a particular neurotransmitter will be **excitatory,** while in another, the very same one acts in an **inhibitory** fashion. Regardless, they are all made in the body from the building blocks, amino acids. So let's look at how some of the more important amino acids influence depression.

TRYPTOPHAN

There is not one drug that helps all people with depression. And even when you find one that is beneficial, there is no promise that it will keep on acting that way. Its benefit may wane with time, until it can even become a negative and give worse depression and even create new symptoms. I suspect when these events happen, that you have depleted nutrients that were essential for the proper metabolism of the drug. And now that they have been used up, the drug is no longer metabolized via the same pathways. There are people who swear by Prozac, and those who swear at it. It has saved many from financial, social and medical ruin, while others

299

never felt worse in their lives than when they took it. And some died.

Regardless, there is a subset of people in whom slowing down how fast the body metabolizes or gets rid of one happy hormone, **serotonin**, is how the Prozac class of drugs works. Obviously, there are other biochemical ways to accomplish this same feat, as its chemistry has been studied for years. We know **that the body makes its own serotonin from the amino acid tryptophan.** It needs B6, magnesium, and a host of other nutrients to accomplish this task. And like Prozac, it works for some and not for others. I think it also depends on what their actual biochemical glitch is. For those in whom Prozac does not work, they may have enough serotonin, and need a different happy hormone, or need to fix a different biochemical pathway glitch.

All that aside, serotonin is the primary neurotransmitter that Prozac and other anti-depressants in that class are aimed at increasing. In order to make our own serotonin, you need **tryptophan** which is an **essential amino acid.** That means we cannot live without it, as it is necessary in other reactions in the body as well. In the 1980's a Japanese manufacturer of tryptophan for most of the nutritional supplement companies in the United States, was using genetic engineering and tried to short-cut one of the stages in the manufacturing. When they did so it created a toxic aldehyde. Some people developed the **eosinophilic myalgia syndrome,** and some people even died from it. Many of those who did not die are still very damaged. Rightly so, the United States stopped all tryptophan sales and recalled all that was available. But when they had finished the investigation, they failed to allow it back on the market as a non-prescription amino acid. Yet, when prescription and over-the-counter drugs have had

300

serious problems, many were returned to the market place, and some were never removed to begin with (Redux, 1996).

At the same time, Prozac was released. It certainly makes one wonder if there was some connection since Prozac made more money in the first two years than all the other anti-depressants together made in the preceding two years. Tryptophan, which is infinitely less expensive than Prozac, was not allowed back on the market. This is in spite of the fact that it is an essential amino acid. And it is in spite of large groups of scientists showing all the data that tryptophan was indeed safe to re-enter the market and that the one manufacturer was the sole cause of the problem.

Some people were in desperate trouble without their tryptophan and had to get it from other countries, and some people found that tryptophan was again available to veterinarians. **In the U.S., a medical doctor can now prescribe it for you.** Also, tryptophan is available in IV solutions. There is one more available source. In order to be converted to serotonin (**5 hydroxytryptamine**), tryptophan must first be converted to 5 hydroxytryptophan (5-HTP). In other words, serotonin's immediate precursor is 5-HTP and this can be obtained non-prescription from health food stores. The dosage to start with would be a 25 mg. tablet at mealtime and increase it using 1-3 tablets, 1-3 times a day with meals. (Available from Bio-Tech).

REFERENCES:

Young SN, The clinical psychopharmacology of tryptophan. In NUTRITION AND THE BRAIN, VOL 7, Wurtman RJ, Wurtman JJ (ed.) Raven Press, NY, 49-88, 1986.

vanPraag HM, Lemus C, Monoamine precursors in the treatment of psychiatric disorders, ibid 89-138.

Benkelfat C, et al, Mood-lowering effect of tryptophan depletion: Enhance susceptibility in young men at genetic risk for major affective disorders, ARCH GEN PSYCHI, 51:687-697, 1994.

Cleare AJ, MBBS, Effects of alterations in plasma tryptophan levels on aggressive feelings, ARCH GEN PSYCH, 51:1004-1005, Dec 1994.

Kitahara M, Dietary tryptophan ratio and suicide in the United Kingdom, Ireland, the United Stated, Canada Australia, and New Zealand, OMEGA J HEALTH DYING 18:71-76, 1987.

Coppen A, Wood K, Tryptophan and depressive illness, PSYCHOLOGICAL MED 8:49-57, 1978.

Delgado PD, et al, Serotonin function and the mechanism of antidepressant action, ARCH GEN PSYCHIA, 47:411-418, 1990.

Young SN, The clinical psycho-pharmacology of tryptophan in RJ Wurtman, JJ Wurtman, eds, NUTRITION AND THE BRAIN VOLUME 7, Raven Press, NY, 49-88, 1986.

van Praag HM, Studies in the mechanism of action of serotonin precursors in depression, PSYCHOPHARML BULL 20:599-602, 1984.

McGrath RE, et al, The effect of L-tryptophan on seasonal affective disorder, PSYCHIATRY, 51(4):162-163, April 1990.

Reuven S, L-Tryptophan in neuropsychiatric disorders: A review, INTER J NEUROSCI, 67:127-144, 1992.

Quadbeck H, Lehmann E, Tegeler J, Comparison of the antidepressant action of tryptophan, tryptophan/5- hydroxytryptophan combination and nomifensine, NEUROPSYCHO, 11(2): 111-115, 1984.

van Hiele LJ, 1-5 Hydroxytryptophan in depression: the first substitution therapy in psychiatry? NEUROPSYCHOL, 6: 230- 240, 1980.

Ferrier IN, et al, Relapse in chronic depressives on withdrawal of L-tryptophan, LANCET, 336:380-381, Aug 11, 1990.

Maes M, et al, The decreased availability of L-tryptophan in depressed females: clinical and biological correlates, NEURO PSYCHOPHARM BIOL PSYCHIAT, 14:903-913, 1990.

van Praag H, de Haan S, Depression vulnerability and 5-hydroxytryptophan prophylaxis, PSYCH RES, 3: 75-83, 1980.

Chouinard G, Young SN, Annabelle L, Siourkes TL, Kirakos RZ, Tryptophan-nicotinamide combination in the treatment of newly admitted depressed patients, COMMUN IN PSYCH, 2: 311-318, 1978.

Coppen A, Eccleston EG, Peet M, Plasma tryptophan binding and depression, ADV BIO PSYCHO, 11: 325-333, 1974.

Wood K, Total and non-bound plasma-tryptophan in depressive illness, LANCET, 1977.

Dam H, Mellerup ET, Rafaelsen OJ, Diurnal variation of total plasma tryptophan in depressive patients, ACTA PSYCH SCAN, 69: 190-196-1984.

Evans GW, Normal and abnormal zinc absorption in man and animals: the tryptophan connection, NUTR REV, 38: 137-141, 1980.

Farkas T, Dunner DL, Fieve RR, L-tryptophan in depression, BIOL PSYCH, 11(3), 1976.

Slutsker L, et al, Eosinophilia-myalgia syndrome associated with exposure to tryptophan from a single manufacturer, JAMA, 264: 213-217, 1990.

Lindberg D, et al, Symptom reduction in depression after treatment with L-tryptophan or imipramine, ACTA PSYCHIATRICA SCAND, 287-294, Sep 1979

Delgado PL, Price LH, Miller HL, Salomon RM, Aghajanian GK, Heninger GR, Charney DS, Serotonin and the neurobiology of depression.

Effects of tryptophan depletion in drug-free depressed patients, ARCH GEN PSYCHIA, 51(11): 865-74, Nov 1994.

Karege F, Widmer J, Bovier P, Galliard JM, Platelet serotonin and plasma tryptophan in depressed patients: effect of drug treatment and clinical outcome, NEUROPSYCHO-PHARMACOLOGY, 10(3): 207-14, May 1994.

Gronier B, Azorin JM, Dassa D, Jeanningros R, Evidence for a defective platelet L-tryptophan transport in depressed patients, INTER CLIN PSYCHOPHARMACO, 8(2): 87-93, Summer 1993.

Salomon RM, Miller HL, Delgado PL, Charney D, The use of tryptophan depletion to evaluate central serotonin function in depression and other neuropyschiatric disorders, INTER CLIN PSYCHOPHARMACOL, 8 SUPPL 2: 41-6, Nov 1993.
Abstract: Results suggest that alterations in serotonin, dopamine, and noradrenaline systems may not reflect the primary pathology causing depressive illness.

Heninger GR, Delgado PL, Charney DS, Price LH, Aghajanian GK, Tryptophan-deficient diet and amino acid drink deplete plasma tryptophan and induce a relapse of depression in susceptible patients, J CHEM NEUROANAT, 5(4): 347-8, July-Aug 1992.

Price LH, Charney DS, Delgado PL, Heninger GR, Serotonin function and depression: neuroendocrine and mood responses to intravenous L-tryptophan in depressed patients and healthy comparison subjects, AMER J PSYCHIA, 148(1): 1518-25, Nov 1991.

AMINO ACIDS ARE THE BUILDING BLOCKS
OF THE HAPPY HORMONES

You begin to get the picture. Just as there were many mineral and vitamin deficiencies that cause depression, there are many amino acid deficiencies that are the causes as well. We could go through every nutrient, and especially the amino acids, and show how and why each is deficient and where it fits into the chemistry to cause depression. This is truly the **era of molecular medicine.** But as you might also suspect, some nutrient deficiencies are far more common causes of depression than others.

And as you have already surmised, **every place a drug works there is probably a natural or God-given nutrient correction** that could be made that would more inexpensively and permanently fix what is broken. And this is done without sentencing you to a lifetime of a drug that is $200 a month, potentially addicting, and potentially able to stop working at any time. In addition, the drug can cause suicidal worsening, and invariably leads to other symptoms, since it failed to fix what was broken in the first place.

And do not be so naive as to think that even though the mechanism of action of tryptophan is to increase the availability of serotonin, that serotonin levels directly relate to the level of depression. Many of us have measured blood serotonin levels in people on and off antidepressant drugs. And researchers have confirmed what we observed: there is no direct correlation. **There is more to the chemistry of a happy brain than the mere serotonin level.** And even if it were directly related, sooner or later the mechanism has to become depleted of rate-limiting nutrients that drive the chemistry (Delgado P, et al, Serotonin and the neurobiology of depression: Effects of tryptophan depletion in drug-free depressed patients, ARCH GEN PSYCHIATRY, 51:864-875, Nov 1994).

So besides vitamins and minerals that you have already learned about, amino acids are other indispensable nutrients which the body must have in order to properly function. In depression, probably no category is more important nor been more thoroughly researched than the amino acids. We normally get them from dietary proteins found in meats, whole grains, fish and fowl, beans, nuts, seeds, and more.

The important thing about amino acids is that some of them work as well as, and in some cases better than, the anti-depressant drugs. You know anti-depressant drugs of the Prozac family, as an example, work by slowing down the detoxification in the brain of the happy hormone, serotonin. But the brain makes its own serotonin every day from the amino acid tryptophan. It also makes many other happy hormones and they are all in a very delicate balance. But by taking a drug, you fail to correct the underlying deficiency, and soon may create worsening deficiencies. That's why the drug "fix" rarely lasts forever. In addition, you have disrupted the normal delicate balance of the brain chemistry.

Numerous studies show that by increasing tryptophan, depression is often lifted. But bear in mind this depends upon what the initial cause of malfunction or deficiency was that triggered the depression in the first place. Still, all the vitamins and minerals that are needed to allow tryptophan to be metabolized also need to be replete. As well, this does not mean we can ignore the environmental factors that you have learned about, like sensitivities to foods, chemicals and molds.

Since amino acids are the very substances that happy hormones are built from, you can imagine the research that has gone on. The same misconception repeatedly occurs, though. Researchers seem to be looking for something that affects a vast percentage of the people who are depressed. So when they find something that helps a few depressed people, it does not receive much attention, for they want it to be a major factor for a large number, hence large drug profits. Consequently, only a drug that axes a malfunctioning pathway can fill the bill.

But **finding the causes is highly individual.** I have never seen two people with the exact same set of biochemical and ecological causes. Medicine does not seem to fully grasp the point yet of the **biochemical individuality** of us all, nor the importance of the **total load.** On second thought, I guess they have. That's why drugs back up to a common biochemical fork in the road and axe the whole pathway (calcium channel blockers, serotonin re-uptake inhibitors, anti-histamines, H-2 blockers, ACE inhibitors, etc., but more in Volume IV). Meanwhile, if you feel particularly good on aminos, be sure to try the carnivore diet in **WELLNESS AGAINST ALL ODDS.**

TYROSINE

Another amino acid beneficial as a precursor to other happy hormones and successful in many cases of depression is tyrosine. It is the **precursor to DOPA,** which in turn is the precursor to **nor-adrenaline and epinephrine.** Some individuals feel a boost in physical or mental energy when they take tyrosine. They are more clear-headed and less irritable, while others can have the opposite effect. You need to remember we are all biochemically unique.

But because tyrosine is the **precursor to adrenaline or epinephrine,** it can make manic-depressives become dangerously manic. Remember adrenalin or epinephrine is the **"fight or flight"** hormone, **the stress hormone,** the one that you feel pumping through your system when you are **scared to death.** Like everything in the body, there is a fine balance. You cannot live without that hormone, as one of its many functions is to maintain your blood pressure.

But like everything else, if it is too excessive, or is on the high end of the bell-shaped curve, it is just as dangerous as being on the low end. It could be so high as to cause a **hypertensive crisis** or stroke, for example. So there should be strict medical supervision if you plan a trial of this. And I would urge amino acid levels first to be sure the trial is even warranted, for the aminos are easily assayed. Hence, there is no need for a foolish trial that could lead to serious worsening. Every substance has a finite balance.

In regard to the prescription anti-depressants, Effexor helps raise norepinephrine as well as serotonin levels. So if you improved on this, it suggests that the amino acids that promote these two neurotransmitters, tryptophan and tyrosine (plus the vitamins, minerals, and accessory nutrients that make the chemical reactions work), might help you. Likewise, Wellbutrin increases norepinephrine and dopamine. So tyrosine supplementation (and other complementary nutrients) might be a good bet for people who markedly improved on this drug.

Tetrahydrobiopterin is a folic acid derivative. By itself and with tyrosine it has aided depression. A product that contains both is called Norival, and is available from Ecological Formulas Cardiovascular Research Ltd., 1061-B Shary Circle, Concord CA 94518, PH 1-800-888-4585.

REFERENCES:

Gibson CJ, Tyrosine for the treatment of depression, ADV BIOL PSYCH 10:148-159, 1983.

Banderet LE, et al, Treatment with tyrosine, a neurotransmitter precursor, reduces environmental stress in humans, BRAIN RES BULL 22;759-762, 1989.

Gelenberg AJ, et al, Tyrosine for depression, J PSYCHIATR RES, 17;2:175-180, 1983.

Benkert O, et al, Blood-brain movements of tryptophan and tyrosine in manic-depressive illness and schizophrenia, J NEURAL TRANSM, 15 suppl:189-196, 1979.

Gelenberg AJ, Wurtman RJ, L-tyrosine in depression, LANCET, Oct 1980.

Wojcik JD, Gibson CJ, Wurtman RJ, Tyrosine for depression, J PSYCHIAT RES, 17(2): 175-180, 1982-83.

Goldberg IK, L-tyrosine in depression, LANCET, Aug 1980.

Wurtman RJ, et al, Brain catechole synthesis: control by brain tyrosine concentration, SCI 185; 183-184, 1974.

Gibson CJ, et al, Tyrosine for the treatment of depression, ADV BIOL PSYCHIATR 10:148-159, 1983

Gelenberg AJ, et al, Tyrosine for the treatment of depression, AMER J PSYCHIATR 137:622-623, 1980.

Curtius H, et al, Successful treatment of depression with tetrahydrobiopterin, LANCET i:657-658, 1983.

Curtius H, etal, Tetrahydrobiopterin: efficacy in endogenous depression and Parkinson's disease, J NEURAL TRANS, 55:310- 318, 1982.

Levine R, et al, Tetrahyrobiopterin in patients with affective disorders, LANCET i:283, 1984.

Hashimoto R, et al, Total biopterin levels of plasma in patients with depression, NEUROPSYCHOLBIOL, 17:176-177, 1987.

Duch DS, et al, Urinary excretion of biopterin and neopterin in psychiatric disorders, PSYCHIAT RES 11:83-89, 1984.

Sved AF, Fernstrom JD, Wurtman RJ, Tyrosine administration reduces blood pressure and enhances brain norepinephrine release in spontaneously hyperactive rats, PROC NAT ADAC SCI, Wash DC, 76:7;3511-3514, 1979

MAO INHIBITORS

Another class of prescription anti-depressant drugs, and potentially much more dangerous, are the monoamine oxidase inhibitors, or MAO inhibitors. Monoamine oxidase, or MAO, is an enzyme that breaks down or metabolizes some neurotransmitters or happy hormones. By inhibiting the metabolism of the happy hormones, it helps raise the levels of **GABA (gamma amino butyric acid)**. But the MAO class of anti-depressants is usually used as a last resort. For it has a potentially lethal side effect of serious high blood pressure if while you take it, you ingest anti-histamines, certain aged cheeses, processed meats like sausages and other foods with additives. Fortunately, as you will learn, there are harmless non-prescription herbs and accessory nutrients that can inhibit MAO safely and without side effects.

GABA, which can come from glutamine, is actually part of a class of happy hormones called **inhibitory**. In other words, they have a **calming effect** on the brain. Interestingly, another inhibitory neurotransmitter closely related to GABA in function is **glycine.** But glycine is used heavily in the detox system to detoxify everyday chemicals, like toluene from new paint or carpet adhesive, as examples. Obviously, when it becomes "used up" in these functions, the net effect on the brain can be one of **agitated depression.** For the calming effect of glycine has been lost. (We measure the loss of glycine in the work of detoxification as the urinary conjugate, **hippuric acid.**)It is fascinating how the function of the happy hormones is so tightly allied with the daily detoxification system and how much control we actually have over our moods once we comprehend all of this.

One more note on the MAO inhibitors: please **do not take them** unless you absolutely have to. And then work with a professional to rule out the treatable causes in this book so you can get off them. They are potentially very dangerous drugs. A new one just was released, Serzone. When you read all the restrictions that accompany it, it is a wonder they can find anyone to treat with it. For you practically have to be well , on no meds, totally refrain from alcohol , over 18 years of age, not be elderly, not be chemically sensitive, etc. Gee, if you were that healthy, it doesn't seem that you would need it. Anyway, as you will learn, some non-prescription herbs, like hypericum, can inhibit MAO, safely.

REFERENCES:

VanPraag HM, Lemus C, Monoamine precursors in the treatment of psychiatric disorder, NUTRITION AND THE BRAIN, VOL.7, ed.s Wurtman RJ, Wurtman JJ, 89-138, 1986.

Pety F, Sherman AD, Plasma GABA levels in psychiatric illness J AFFECT DIS, 6(2):131-138, 1984.

Growdon JH, Neurotransmitter precursors in the diet: their use in the treatment of brain diseases, NUTRITION AND THE BRAIN, VOL 3, ed Wurtman RJ, Wurtman JJ, 117-81, Raven NY, 1979.

Goodman LS, Gilman A. THE PHARMACOLOGICAL BASIS OF THERAPEUTICS, 5th ED, 431-432, Macmillan Publ.,NY, 1975

Suzuki O, et al, Inhibition of monoamine oxidase by hypericin, PLANTA MEDICA, 50: 272-274, 1984.

PHENYLALANINE

Another important neurotransmitter is **nor-epinephrine or nor- adrenaline.** Its amino acid precursor is **L-phenylalanine.** Phenylalanine can also be converted into **phenylethylamine** which is an amphetamine like neurotransmitter abundant in chocolate and probably responsible for **chocoholics'** addiction to chocolate. Phenylalanine has also helped **pain,** and one of the uses for anti-depressants is also to help with intractable pain. Obviously, it is preferable to find the cause of the pain. And if the pain persists then proceed with an amino acid rather than an anti-depressant drug, which can be potentially addicting and that will create further deficiencies in the work of detoxifying it.

Some people have much better moods when they take phenylalanine with B6. The dose for this would be to start with 500 mg of L-phenylalanine in the morning and at noon and then increase the trial to 2-3 of them twice daily. Whenever you raise doses, raise them slowly after several days and evaluate the same dose for several days before going higher.

REFERENCES:

Sabelli HC, et al, Clinical studies on the phenylethylamine hypothesis of affective disorder: urine and blood phenylacetic acid and phenylalanine dietary supplements, J CLIN PSYCHIATRY 47(2): 66-70, 1986.

Beckmann H, et al, DL-phenyalanine vs imipramine: a double- blind controlled study, ARCH PHYCHIAT NERVENKR, 227:49-58, 1979.

Beckmann H, Phenyalanine in affective disorders, ABV BIOL PSYCHIATRY, 10:137-47, 1983.

Heller B, Pharmacological and clinical effects of D- phenylalanine in depression and Parkinson's disease, in Mosnaim, Wolf, Eds, NONCATECHOLIC PHENYLETHYL-AMINES, PART 1, Marcel Dekker NY, 397-417, 1978.

Beckmann H, Strauss MA, Ludolph E, DL-phenylalanine in depressed patients: an open study, J NEURAL TRANS, 41: 123- 24, 1977.

Budd K, Use of D-phenylalanine, an enkephalinase inhibitor, in the treatment of intractable pain, ADV PAIN RES AND THER, 5: 305-308, 1983.

Donzelle G, et al, Curing trial of complicated oncologic pain by D-phenylalanine, ANESTH ANALG, 38: 655-58, 1981.

Fox A, Fox B, DLPA TO END CHRONIC PAIN AND DEPRESSION, New York: Long Shadow Books, 1985.

Friedman M, Gumbmann MR, The nutritive value and safety of D-phenylalanine and D-tyrosine in mice, J NUTR, 114: 2089-2096, 1984.

Mann J, Peselow ED, Snyderman S, Gershon S, D-phenylalanine in endogenous depression, AM J PSYCHIATR, 137(12): 12, 1980.

Partoles M, Minaa MD, Jorda A, Grisolia S, Caffeine intake lowers the level of phenylalanine, tyrosine and thyroid hormones in rat plasma, IRCS MED SCI, 12: 1002-1003, 1984.

TAURINE

Taurine is a special amino acid-like compound. A deficiency of taurine can cause depression, but also can contribute to chemical sensitivity with compromised ability to detoxify everyday chemicals, seizures, congestive heart failure, cardiac arrhythmia's, visual problems, and much more. And we run out of taurine faster than other "amino acids" because it is a major constituent of bile. So it is thrown away quite regularly in digestion. Also, we hook glutathione (made from glutamic acid, glycine, and cysteine), onto chemicals in our blood in order to detoxify and dispose of them in the bile. But that cysteine could have been used to make taurine or bile. **So the more chemicals we detoxify, the more potential taurine we throw away in the stool.**

A major problem is that all these detoxifiers could have been used to make happy hormones instead! And not only that but once they are thrown away in the bile, they are passed into the gut and are lost forever. So we jeopardize more happy hormone synthesis as well as lose further nutrients that could have gone on to make additional happy hormones, when our environments are too chemically overloaded. In essence, **nutrients that should have been used to make happy hormones, are flushed down the toilet when we live in a chemically overloaded environment.**

Hence, as a major component of bile and glutathione, taurine is lost with chemicals that we have detoxified as they are dumped into the bile and then the colon. And if there is extra **infection or inflammation** going on in the body, it is shuttled there to work, as another role of taurine is that of controlling inflammation. And it is also the **most prevalent amino acid in the heart, retina, and brain.** So it is easy to understand why an important brain amino acid that is used so heavily elsewhere in the body, can become depleted by other events (like chemical toxicity, infection, inflammation). And this deficiency can then lead to depression, seizures, chemical sensitivity, arrhythmia, blindness, and more.

REFERENCES:

Bergamini L, Mutani R, Delsedime M, Durelli L, First clinical experience on the anti-epileptic action of taurine, EUROPEAN NEUR, 11: 261-269, 1974.

Bonhaus DW, The transport, biosynthesis and biochemical actions of taurine in a genetic epilepsy, NEUROCHEM INTER, 5: 413-419, 1983.

Bratty PJA, Hansen S, Kennedy J, Urquhart N, Dolman CL, Hereditary mental depression and Parkinsonism with taurine deficiency, ARCH NEUROL, 32(2): 108-113, 1975.

Tachiki KH, Hendrie HC, Kellams J, Aprison MH, A rapid column chromatographic procedure for the routine measurement of taurine in plasma of normals and depressed patients, CLIN CHIM ACT, 75: 455-465, 1977.

Usdin E, Hamburg DA, Barchas JD, Hereditary mental depression with taurine deficiency, Oxford University Press, 1978.

Barbeau A, Huxtable RJ, TAURINE AND NEUROLOGICAL DISORDERS, Raven Press, NY,1978

Perry TL, Bratty PJA, Hansen S, et al, Hereditary mental depression and Parkinsonism with taurine deficiency, ARCH NEUROL 32:108-113, 1975

Bradford RW, Allen HW, Taurine in health and disease, J ADVANCE MED, 9 (3): 179-201, Fall 1996

ASSESSING AND TREATING
AMINO ACID DEFICIENCIES

Never start out testing or supplementing amino acids first. The reasons are many:

1. Amino acid deficiency is statistically not the leading cause of depression.

2. It is rarely, if ever a solo deficiency.

3. When there are amino acid deficiencies, there are usually deficiencies of **minerals and vitamins** that are necessary in the metabolism of the amino acids. Once these are corrected, the amino acid abnormality can often correct itself. If amino acids are taken without correcting these vitamins and minerals that are essential for them to proceed to make happy hormones, they will not be effective.

4. Amino acids are not without toxic effects. Methionine can trigger already established cancers to grow at an accelerated rate. Cysteine can cause Candida to change into pleomorphic types that are more aggressive and difficult to eradicate. Amino acids can cause a severe worsening of depression and trigger other abnormalities in the brain function.

5. Amino acids can seriously overload the liver and kidneys, causing failure to function, which can be fatal, etc.

6. Amino acid deficiencies often will not correct if membrane deficiencies, like phosphatidyl choline and essential fatty acids deficiencies are not corrected first. More on that in their respective sections.

Food allergy and vitamin and mineral deficiencies have turned out to be statistically more relevant as a starting point for those suffering from depression. So it is not recommended to start with something like amino acid deficiencies that are far less frequently the cause.

Once the minerals have been assessed and corrected, along with other more important parts of the total load, then amino acid testing may be in order. There are several excellent labs that can assess individual quantitative plasma and 24 hour total urinary amino acids. Some of the better known or larger commercial laboratories have inferior assays. For example, they do not even have a norm for many of the aminos, whereas the labs recommended, specialize in this. They have made it their business to have the best assays available, complete with normal values for reference.

There is nothing wrong with a supervised trial of amino acids after mineral corrections have been made, if an amino acid assessment is too expensive. Again, you would do better to play the odds and look for the most commonly and easily correctable causes. Slagel's book is also a great guide. You could start with a general amino acid complex or a trial of the most likely aminos individually.

Most all of the amino acid trials when they start out are better done as solo aminos, especially if you forego measuring levels. Usually a 500 mg capsule is evaluated for a few days before advancing slowly every few days to a top dose of 2 twice a day. Aminos should have expert supervision as they have more of a potential for an unexpected worsening of depression than most nutrients.

And remember, when evaluating amino acids, titration of dose is more important than with other nutrients. Titration is merely a methodical or step-wise slow increase in dose, with effect evaluated at each step along the way. It is sort of what can be done with alcohol. You are **titrating** yourself if when you drink alcohol you first do not feel any effect. Then with a little more you feel slightly relaxed. Then a little more, slightly silly, then with more, manic (wild) or sleepy, depending on your individual chemistry. Then drunk. The object is to titrate (or fine tune) the dose to keep it equal to the metabolic rate that has you just slightly relaxed, not blotto and destroying brain neurons.

Because amino acids have such a bearing on the inhibitory and excitatory neurotransmitters (happy hormones), they need even greater care. Several days would be needed to evaluate, as an example, a 500mg dose . Then it could be 500mg twice a day for a few more days. Every few days you could increase the dose by 500 mg to a maximum of 1-2 500mg capsules 2-3 times a day. But many other nutrients would be necessarily prescribed to aid in the metabolism of this extra amount of amino acid to facilitate its proper action. And naturally the dose would be curtailed any point along the way if adverse symptoms occurred. For remember, what is a stimulatory amino acid to one person, may be inhibitory to another.

One last caveat. Beware of taking a nutrient where you start feeling better and then it begins to lose its effectiveness or even **backfires and makes you worse**. What has happened is you have corrected something that was low. But, the metabolic work shortly depleted some other marginal key nutrient, hence, your worsening. You must identify the missing nutrients.

LABORATORIES:

For special amino acid analyses plus interpretations for doctors who are unfamiliar with amino acid chemistry:

Doctors Data, PO Drawer 400, Lisle IL 60532
1-800-323-2784

Monroe Laboratories Rt 17, POB 1, Southfields NY, 10975
914-351-5134

Meta-Metrix Laboratory, 5000 Peachtree Ind. Blvd, Ste 110, Norcross GA 30071, 404-446-5483

REFERENCES:

Slagel P, THE WAY UP FROM DOWN, Random House NY, 1987.

Sahley BJ, THE NATURAL WAY TO CONTROL HYPERACTIVITY WITH AMINO ACIDS AND NUTRIENT THERAPY, The Watercress Press, 5282 Medical Drive, Suite 160, San Antonio Texas 78229-6043. 1989.

Sahley BJ, THE ANXIETY EPIDEMIC, 1994, ibid

Maas JW, Biogenic amines and depression-biochemical and pharmacological separation of two types of depression, ARCH GEN PSYCH 32:1357-1361, 1975.

Blomquist HK, Gustavson KH, Holmgren G, Severe mental retardation in five siblings due to maternal phenylketonuria, NEUROPED, 11(3): 256-262, 1980.

Borison RL, Maple PJ, Havdala S, Diamond BI, Metabolism of an amino acid with antidepressant properties, RES COMMUN CHEM PATHOL PHARM, 21: 363-66, 1978.

Juorio AV, A possible role for tyramines in brain function and some mental disorders, GEN PHARMA, 13: 181-183, 1982.

Anonymous, Eat your way to a headache, LANCET, 1-4, Dec. 1980.

Anderson GM, Gerner RH, Cohen DJ, Fairbanks L, Central tryptamine turnover in depression, schizophrenia, and anorexia: measurement of indoleacetic acid in cerebrospinal fluid, BIOL PSYCH, 19(10): 1427, 1984.

Krieger DT, Martin JB, Brain peptides, NEW ENG J MED, April, 876-885, 1981.

Portoles M, Minana MD, Jordan A, Grisolia S, Caffeine intake lowers the level of phenylalanine, tyrosine and thyroid hormones in rat plasma, IRCS MED SCI, 12: 1002-1003, 1984.

Niskamen P, Huttunen M, Tamminen T, Jaaskelainen J, The daily rhythm of plasma tryptophan and tyrosine in depression, BRIT J PSYCHIAT, 128: 67-73, 1976.

van Praag HM, Precursors of serotonin, dopamine, and norepinephrine in the treatment of depression, ADVAN BIOL PSYCH, 14: 54-68, 1984.

SAM

S-adenosyl methionine is such a mouthful, that you can call it SAM. It is a derivative of the amino acid methionine and has been important in depression. The important thing to recall is that methionine, makes **methyl groups to detoxify chemicals**. The body also uses these methyl groups to protect the genetic material, DNA, from fostering cancerous changes. But as you now see, when SAM is used up protecting us from the chemical environment, we don't have enough to go around for making happy hormones.

Methionine also makes **cysteine**, which by itself helps to detoxify chemicals, or as a component of **glutathione**, detoxifies other types of chemicals. And the body chemistry can proceed from methionine to cysteine to make **taurine**, which you just learned about. The bottom line is that these amino acid derivatives that have been so necessary to make happy hormones, and have been useful in the treatment of depression, **are used up in the work of detoxifying our chemical world.** It is really an astonishing wonder that only 1 in 5 persons suffers from a major depression in a lifetime, when you consider how the odds are against us. Fortunately, we know how to diagnose and treat the causes.

REFERENCES:

Agnoli A, Andreoli V, Casacchia M, Cerbo R, Effects of S- adenosyl-L-methionine upon depression symptoms, J PSYCH RES, 13: 43-54, 1976.

Muscettola G, Galzenati, M, Balbi A, SAM versus placebo: a double-blind comparison in major depressive disorders, LANCET, July 1984.

Kagan BL, et al, Oral S-adenosylmethionine in Depression: a randomized double-blind, placebo-controlled trial, AMER J PSYCH, 147:5:591-595, May 1990.

Rosenbaum JF, et al, Anti-depressant potential of oral S- adenosyl-L-methionine, ACTA PSYCH SCAND, 81: 432-436, 1990.

Carrier PB, et al, S-adenosylmethionine treatment of depression in patient's with Parkinson's disease, CURR THER RES, 48(1): 154-159, July 1990.

P.S. Remember that there are many factors associated with the amino acids in order for them to work. For example, the enzymes called peptidases are necessary for the proper metabolism of amino acids. But most peptidases require zinc for their activity, and zinc needs adequate gastric acid for its absorption. But read on and you'll see that we eventually pull it all together, between Volumes I and IV.

THE BIOCHEMICAL AND GENETIC
BASIS OF PERSONALITY

As you become progressively become more a student of environmental medicine and nutritional biochemistry, you begin to appreciate why we have so much control over symptoms, and that there are so many variables that play a role. For example, you have learned how food allergy (which has about a dozen different mechanisms) has a profound influence on brain function. It can cause just about any brain symptom you can think of from epilepsy, stroke, or learning disability to schizophrenia, Tourette's or depression.

You have learned that mold and other airborne allergens can cause the same depression as ingested molds. And you have learned that the chemicals that we breathe, drink and eat likewise have a profound effect on the brain. Next we went into the nutrient deficiencies of vitamins, minerals, and then amino acids. You learned how deficiencies of any one or more of these can also cause depression. And you saw how environmental chemicals overload and deplete many of these nutrients via the work of detoxifying them. Later, you will learn about the roles essential fatty acids, hormones, the leaky gut, and much more (Volume III).

A person's individual **total body burden of sensitivities and deficiencies** is highly individual. And not surprisingly, genetics also plays a role. For example, you are familiar with the type A personality: the high achiever, impatient, driven, easily angered, ambitious, volatile, aggressive, and more prone to heart attacks. Studies have shown that these types more often have elevations of epinephrine and norepinephrine, the stress hormones. It is surmised this may be so because they have decreased activity of the MAO (monoamine oxidase) set of enzymes that metabolize and modulate the level of these neurotransmitters. As you learned in WELLNESS AGAINST ALL ODDS, this chemistry goes beyond the brain. We know that these people are in **sympathetic overdrive** much of the time, and therefore shut down their digestive functions, as well as other functions that promote healing. They are in the fight or flight mode.

The great news is that by knowing this, we can moderate the diet and nutrients to favor a better chemistry, without drugs. Food and nutrients can be manipulated to tone down or rev up the sympathetic and autonomic nervous systems that govern physiology and behavior.

REFERENCES:

Smith DF, Type A personalities tend to have a low platelet monoamine oxidase activity, ACTA PSYCHIATR SCAND 89:88-91, 1994.

Fernstrom JD, et al, Neutral amino acids in the brain: changes in response to food ingestion, J NEUROCHEM, 30:1531- 1538, 1978.

Fernstrom JD, et al, Brain serotonin content: physiological dependence on plasma tryptophan levels, SCIENCE, 173:149-152, 1971.

Wurtman RJ, et al, Brain catechol synthesis: control of brain tyrosine concentration, SCIENCE, 185:183-184, 1974.

Spring B, et al, Effects of protein and carbohydrate meals on mood and performance: interactions with sex and age, J PSYCHIATR RES, 17:155-167, 1983.

Prin RJ, et al, Dietary correlates of hyperactive behavior in children, J CONSULT CLIN PSYCHOL, 48:760-769, 1980.

Wurtman RJ, Behavioral effects of nutrients, LANCET, 1:145- 147, 1983.

ESSENTIAL FATTY ACID DEFICIENCIES: IS YOUR DEPRESSION BECAUSE YOU ARE DUE FOR AN OIL CHANGE?

There are good oils and bad oils in your body. The good oils also called **essential fatty acids or EFA,** fall into 2 categories, **omega-3 and omega-6 oils.** Both categories are essential for life, health, and freedom from depression. For oils make up lipids for cell membranes and nerve coverings. There are actually layers of lipids in the cell membrane, much like the layers of a sandwich.

And there are **receptors** or control sites on these **membranes** where the happy hormones are screwed in, much like a light bulb. But the essential fatty acids are not only a major part of the cell's regulatory membranes, but also for the endoplasmic reticular **detox membranes,** the protective **nuclear** membranes, and energy-controlling **mitochondrial** membranes. Now you can appreciate why deficits in essential fatty acids have a major bearing on depression. For they control everything, and are especially crucial for the function of the nervous system, and above all, the brain. Without the right oils, the brain is not happy. And as you will see, the vast majority of people eating out of the grocery stores and restaurants have a high percentage of the wrong, destructive fatty acids or oils in their membranes. And this can lead not only to depression but all diseases.

The bad oils are called **trans-fatty** acids, and you don't want any of them, although you have plenty. They come from all those years of **polyunsaturated hydrogenated oils.** You know, the ones with the picture of the heart on them. French fries, commercial breads, cookies, donuts, candy bars, salad dressings, fried foods, egg-beaters, margarine's, and the regular grocery store cooking oils (but not virgin olive oil. That is O.K.) contain damaging trans-fatty acids.

Real oils originate from the pressing or squeezing of nuts and seeds like olives, corn, almonds, safflower, etc. But because they can go bad or rancid rather quickly, the food processing industry learned that if you chemically change oils by cooking them at over 400 degrees Fahrenheit, they will no longer go bad, or at least they take infinitely longer to do so. The problem is that this high abnormal heat does several things. It causes a twist in the molecule so that it goes from a natural cis-form to an unnatural and damaging trans-form. And these **man-made, damaging molecules sit right in the control seat for happiness, the cell membrane.** Once these molecules become inserted in the brain membranes where the happy hormone receptors are, they gum up the works. The receptors and other membrane functions simply do not function correctly, much like a broken key.

THE MARGARINE MISTAKE

Remember butter in the 1940's (before so many preservatives were used) would go bad if it sat out? Today's margarines, however last for ages, because they are **15-35% trans-fatty acids.** Studies show that these trans fatty acids (N ENG J MED, Mensink 323: 439, 1990) are potentially even more damaging than saturated fats, as in a juicy steak. In fact, Europe was smarter (or less controlled by food lobbyists and the chemical/pharmaceutical cartel) than we are, because in the past they would not allow U.S. margarine into the country. They knew it promoted disease (and we think the French paradox is all due to wine!). In addition, the hydrogenation of oils does a lot of other nasty things to these "foods" besides creating trans-fatty acids. It also destroys or lowers the levels of various vitamins (like E) and minerals, thus making it easier for these deficiencies to promote disease. But there are whole books on these subjects (Enig book is excellent for physicians).

Anyway, years of eating the wrong acids leads to malfunction in a variety of ways: cancer, diabetes, arteriosclerosis, chemical sensitivity, depression, you name it. And likewise, correction of EFA deficiencies covers a wide range of symptoms, because we are down to a fundamental biochemical level of body function. Clearly, since EFAs are needed to make the cell membranes which house the receptors for the happy hormones, as well as many other hormones and regulatory proteins, they affect all of our chemistry.

You see, you can have the best levels of serotonin or any other of the brain's happy hormones. But if cell membrane receptors are defective, they cannot carry out their duties. It does not matter how high the levels of happy hormones are. They just cannot turn on the happy hormone chemistry if the cell membrane receptors are damaged or malfunctioning due to EFA deficiencies.

Unfortunately, there is not one, but there are many ways that the trans-fatty acids of the food processing industry damage our chemistry. An omega-6 deficiency can occur as the trans-fatty acids not only hog the receptor sites of membranes (so the good oils cannot fit in). They also damage the enzyme (**delta-6-desaturase**) that converts the good oils like non-hydrogenated (cold-pressed) omega-6 oils (corn, safflower, etc.) to a form that can be properly used in membranes. So as usual, there are multiple mechanisms operating to potentiate further disease in the body once we start ingesting processed foods. Hence, the old sick get sicker landslide.

> If you want to calculate the percentage of bad trans-fatty acids in a food, the manufacturer must have provided 4 measurements: total fat, saturated fat, polyunsaturated fat, and monounsaturated fat. You simply add the grams of the last three, and subtract that total from the first value, total fat. The difference is the grams of trans-fatty acids.

You might wonder how we got into this mess of using hydrogenated oils. Cardiologists, hospital nutritionists, and most of medicine still recommend them. In fact, tonight the American Heart Association was on a T.V. commercial endorsing Promise margarine (August 1996). That's incredible in light of decades of scientific research! Cardiologists and hospital nutritionists still recommend all sorts of "plastic eggs", corn oils, oils with pictures of hearts on them, margarines, and many more foods loaded with trans-fatty acids. The grocery stores are full of them. Read the label of nearly any processed food. Hydrogenated oil (listed as soybean oil or vegetable oil) is usually a constituent.

Years ago after the war, food chemists looked for a cheap source of cooking oil and a way to make it last. Hydrogenation of soy and cottonseed oils seemed to be the answer. The processed and fast food industries really capitalized on them after massive advertising. Whether or not anyone knew then how they would damage the cell membrane and usher in an era of drugs to temporarily cover up the damage, I don't know. But for sure by 1956 (Sinclair, in Enig's book) the scientific question was posed and from that time on knowledgeable scientists have warned of the dangers, but could not fight big food industry lobbyists.

As a result, we now have people whose average intake per day of trans-fatty acids ranges from 35%-55%. It potentiates the changes of cancer, high cholesterol, and many aspects of lipid metabolism that have far-reaching effects for the person. This damage to the cell membranes can result in any disease or symptom you can think of. But when we get stuck in medicine, we diagnose depression and hope an anti-depressant will help the victim ignore his symptoms.

Of course, depression is one of the symptoms that can arise from these cellular glitches. Other common symptoms include arteriosclerosis, cardiac arrhythmia, hypertension, cancer, chemical sensitivity, fibromyalgia, chronic fatigue, lupus, etc., etc. But instead of fixing the cellular glitch, support groups are formed so that victims can commiserate with one another.

The cure? Simply never eat again any breads, cookies, French fries, margarines, grocery store hydrogenated vegetable and nut oils, "light" butter, meats and fishes that have been fed commercial livestock feed containing hydrogenated oils, and of course, no processed foods with hydrogenated oils. We even have a generation of animals with more disease, because they eat table scraps or commercial pet food with hydrogenated oils. (Caution the use of canola oil, as it is a genetically engineered rape seed oil to get rid of the erucic acid. And non-hydrogenated coconut oil is fine, but difficult to find fresh. Obviously, fresh cold-pressed oils are best.]

The other part of the cure is to replace your trans fatty acids with good clean organic omega-6 and omega-3 oils with a balanced nutritional program. And eat primarily whole fresh foods, including whole oils. Make **better butter** for table use, which is 1/3 flax oil. The commercial "light" butters are cut with hydrogenated oils, so forget those. (You can make your own ghee, which is merely clarified butter and add flax to that, also. Use virgin olive oil or cold-pressed organic safflower or corn oils for cooking at low heat. Use flax or virgin olive, or cold-pressed organic walnut, etc., on salads. Do not use canola which is a genetically engineered rape seed oil (to remove the fatal erucic oil).)

We are literally changing the cellular chemistry of man and beast, for the worse. By creating new molecules (trans-fatty acids) that damage the brain receptor chemistry, you might say **we have learned to manufacture molecules of madness.**

REFERENCES:

Enig MG, TRANS FATTY-ACIDS IN THE FOOD SUPPLY: A COMPREHENSIVE REPORT COVERING 60 YEARS OF RESEARCH, Enig Assoc., Ste 500, White Oak Center Bldg, 11120 New Hampshire Ave, Silver Spring MD, 20904-2633, ph 301-593-4471

Zock PL, Katan MB, Hydrogenation alternatives: effects of trans fatty-acid versus linoleic acid on serum lipids and lipoproteins in humans, J LIPID RES 33:399-410, 1992

Hill EG, et al, Intensification of essential fatty acid deficiency in the rat by dietary trans-fatty acids, J NUTR 109: 1759-1765, 1979.

Siguel EN, Essential and trans-fatty acid metabolism in health and disease, COMPREHENSIVE THERAPY 20:9, 500-510, 1994.

Mensink RP, Katan MB, Effect of dietary trans-fatty acids on high-density and low-density lipoprotien cholesterol levels in healthy subjects, N ENGL J MED, 323: 439-445, 1990.

OMEGA-6 OIL DEFICIENCY
CAN MIMIC DEPRESSION

As trans-fatty acids create blocks in the chemical pathway of cell lipids, and as further deficiencies arise from our poor selections of foods and careless lifestyles (for example, alcohol, sugars, stress, cigarettes, etc.), we need to find ways to repair this damage. Luckily, researchers found one oil that bypasses some enzyme steps that can correct an omega-6 deficiency. It comes from the seed of the evening primrose flower and is called **oil of evening primrose, or EPO** (Efamol being one reliable brand).

The dose for a trial would be 3-6 capsules a day. However, any time you are making a correction, you need other nutrients to complement it. For the correction of such a serious deficiency calls upon the body chemistry to do more. It needs more nutrient backup in order to incorporate the missing nutrient. Secondly, deficiencies are rarely solo.

EPO deficiency correction (it is cheaper to do a therapeutic trial than first diagnose it with blood tests) has improved many recalcitrant conditions. This includes schizophrenia, PMS, and tardive dyskinesia (the bizarre uncontrollable movements that are frequent side effects of drugs, especially those to control anxiety, depression and other mental symptoms). Also EPO replacement has helped hyperactivity (which is often the paradoxical childhood counterpart to adult depression), multiple sclerosis, Parkinson's, alcohol dependence, alcohol withdrawal, and much more, not to exclude other mental problems, including depression.

REFERENCES:

Ylikorkala O, et al, Prostaglandins and premenstrual syndrome, PROG LIPID RES, 25:433-435, 1986.

Gibson RA, The effect of dietary supplementation with evening primrose oil of hyperkinetic children, PROC NUTR SOC AUST, 10:196, 1985.

Wolkin A, et al, Essential fatty-acid supplementation in tardive dyskinesia, AM J PSYCHIATRY, 143:912-914, July 1986.

Horrobin DF, Essential fatty acids and prostaglandin's in schizophrenia and alcoholism. In: Shagass C, et al, BIOLOGICAL PSYCHIATRY 1985. PROC WORLD CONG BIOL PSYCH. Elsevier, 1163-1165, 1986.

Karpe F, et al, Ethanol dependence in rats on diets high and low in EFA, ACTA PHARMACOL TOXICOL SUPPL, 57(1):Abs 43, 1985.

Leonard BE, et al, Changes in alpha-aminobutyric acid and serotonin following the acute and chronic administration of alcohol -- interactions with carnitine and gamma-linolenic acid, ACTA PHARMACOL TOXICOL SUPPL, IBID Abs 7.

Glen AI, et al, EFA in the treatment of the alcohol dependency syndrome, In: Birch GG, Lindley MG, eds. ALCOHOLIC BEVERAGES, London: Elsevier, 203-221, 1985.

Century B, A role of the dietary lipid in the ability of Phenobarbital to stimulate drug detoxification, J PHARMACOL EXPERM THERA, 185;2:185-194, 1973.

Mitchell EA, et al, Hyperactivity: essential fatty acid profile and the effects of supplementation with evening primrose oil. 2nd International Congress on Essential Fatty Acids, Prostaglandin's and Leukotrienes, Abstracts, London UK, 1985 Mar 24-7: Abs 114.

Bouruignon A, et al, Onager oil in the treatment of schizophrenia in the hypothesis of a deficit in prostaglandin. L'ENCEPHALE, 10:241-244, 1984.

Holman CP, Bell AF, A trial of evening primrose oil in the treatment of chronic schizophrenia, J ORTHOMOLECULAR PSYCH, 12:302-304, 1983.

Horrobin DF, Prostaglandins, essential fatty acids and psychiatric disorders: a background review. In: Horrobin DF, ed. CLINICAL USES OF ESSENTIAL FATTY ACIDS, Montreal: Eden Press, 1982.

Parmigiani P, Evening primrose oil (Efamol) and captopril in schizophrenia: a preliminary report, ibid, 209-214.

Horrobin DF, CLINICAL USES OF ESSENTIAL FATTY ACIDS, Eden Press, Montreal, 1982

Horrobin DF, Schizophrenia: reconciliation of the dopamine, prostaglandin, and opioid concepts and the role of the pineal, LANCET, 1979 Mar 10:529-531.

Burgess JR, et al, Essential fatty acid metabolism in boys with attention-deficit hyperactivity disorder, AM J CLIN NUTR, 62: 761-768, 1995.

Williams LL, Kiecolt-Glaser JK, Horrocks LA, Hillhouse JT, Glaser R, Quantitative association between altered plasma esterified omega-6 fatty acid proportions and psychological stress, PROSTAGLANDINS LEUKOTRIENES & ESSENTIAL FATTY ACIDS, 47(2): 165-170, Oct 1992. Abstract: Omega-6 FA metabolism may be affected during stress. Since plasma FA proportions may affect immune cell membrane function(s), we suggest that altered values of plasma FA's may be an important component of the physiological effects of psychological stress.

McAdams C, Leonard BE, Changes in platelet aggregatory responses to collagen and 5-hydroxytryptamine in depressed, schizophrenic and manic patients, INTERN CLIN PSYCHOPHARMACOL, 7(2): 81-5, Nov. 1992.
Abstract: The results of this study suggest that changes in the polyunsaturated fatty acid composition of the platelet membrane (collagen effect) and the 5-hydroxytryptamine type 2 receptor (5-HT effect) may occur in these major psychiatric disorders.

Demisch L, Heinz K, Gerbaldo H, Kirsten R, Increased concentrations of phosphatidylinositol (PI) and decreased esterification of arachidonic acid into phospholipids in platelets from patients with schizoaffective disorders or atypic phasic psychoses. PROSTAGLANDINS LEUTOTRIENES & ESSENTIAL FATTY ACIDS, 46(1): 47-52, May 1992.

OMEGA-3 OIL DEFICIENCY
CAN MIMIC DEPRESSION

The other essential fatty acid deficiency, aside from omega-6, is omega-3. Good sources are **flax seed oil**, also known as (food grade) **linseed oil**. This has the same litany of beneficial effects on the brain, behavior, and mental illness. It just depends upon which one you are deficient in. In fact, I've been more impressed with the results of omega-3 oil than EPO as a more common deficiency. We have done no studies, however, because anyone that sick has multiple nutrient deficiencies. So correcting more than one thing at once, negates the value of a study on a solo item (as though it were a drug). Nevertheless, an omega-3 deficiency can be the reason for depression, chemical sensitivity, and just about any other illness you can think of, because its chemistry is so fundamental to the operation of the cell.

The dose of a trial of linseed or flax oil would be 1-3 tsp. a day. And never prolong such an unsupervised trial beyond a few months, as you can upset the biochemical balance of other nutrients, especially the essential fatty acids and vitamin E.

Another source of oil to correct an omega-3 oil deficiency is **fish oil (EPA or eicosapentaenoic acid)**. Omega-3 oil is commonly deficient in the diet because people eat less fish as well as less unhydrogenated seed oils. Even worse, they now eat predominantly farmed fish rather than real fish. **Real fish eat other fish and sea vegetables, both high in omega-3 oil.** Farmed fish eat hydrogenated soybean pellets from commercial feed stores. Hence, analysis of the fats of farmed fish shows you might as well eat a steak. For it is omega-6 trans fatty acid oils that you are getting from the soybean-based commercial fish food, not the desired natural n-3. The moral: Even for the fish, **you are what you eat.** Likewise, commercial feedlot beef has 2-17% poly-unsaturated fatty acids, compared with wild game that eat from nature's bounty and have 30-60% (NEW ENG J MED, 312, 383-389, 1985).

Omega-3 oil deficiency is so commonly deficient, that just about any condition you can think of has been slowly improved or prevented with it, from cancer to heart disease, from chemical sensitivity to depression. Again, the reason why so many conditions are affected is because we are down to a very basic cellular level. It is the same reason why a dangerous drug like prednisone works for a zillion serious medical problems. You are down to a rudimentary level where you shut off the immune system's inflammatory response.

REFERENCES:

Enig MG, TRANS-FATTY ACIDS IN THE FOOD SUPPLY: A COMPREHENSIVE REPORT COVERING 60 YEARS OF RESEARCH, Enig Assoc., Ste 500, White Oak Center Bldg, 11120 New Hampshire Ave, Silver Spring MD, 20904-2633, ph 301-593-4471

Neuringer M, Connor WE, n-3 fatty acids in the brain and retina: Evidence for the essentiality, NUTR REV, 44(9);285, 1986.

Rudin DO, The major psychoses and neuroses as omega-3 essential fatty acid deficiency syndrome: Substrate pellagra, BIOL PSYCHIAT, 16(9):837-850, 1981.

Gray JB, et al, Eicosanoids and essential fatty acid modulation in chronic disease and chronic fatigue syndrome, MED HYPOTHESIS, 43:31-42, 1994.

Dohan FC, Wartime changes in hospital admissions for schizophrenia, ACTA PSYCHIATR SCAND, 42:1-23, 1966.

Bates C, ESSENTIAL FATTY ACIDS AND IMMUNITY IN MENTAL HEALTH, Life Sciences Press, WA, 1987.

Erasmus U, FATS THAT HEAL, FATS THAT KILL, Alive Books, Burnaby, BC Canada, 1987.

Rudin DO, The major psychoses and neurosis as n-3 essential fatty acid deficiency syndrome: Substrate pellagra, BIOL PSYCHIATR, 16:837-850, 1981.

Rose DP, et al, Influence of diets containing eicosapentaenoic or docosahexaenoic acid on growth and metastasis of breast cancer cells in nude mice, J NATL CANCER INST 87:587-592, 1995

Hibbeln JR, Salem N, Dietary polyunsaturated fatty acids and depression: When cholesterol does not satisfy, AMER J CLIN NUTR, 62:1-9, 1995

WHAT COMES FIRST,
DEPRESSION OR DISEASE?

Congratulations! You now understand more about the operation of the body chemistry and some of the causes of disease than many physicians. Consequently, you can understand how ludicrous all the papers are that make the astounding discovery that depression is commonly associated with allergies like asthma, chemical sensitivity, diabetes, and yes, just about any disease. The reason is clear. The disturbed chemistry that creates the disease, can also eventually create depression, and vice versa.

The problem lies with the physician who is not aware of this chemistry. For he assumes that because the person also has depression, that probably the depression caused the other symptoms. Many "scientific" papers embarrassingly show the lack of understanding of the biochemistry of the whole big picture that you are now aware of. You comprehend that when one area gets so badly damaged by deficiencies, it is extremely likely that other areas will also eventually be affected. And since the brain is so vulnerable, it is a good bet that the brain will become one of the involved target organs.

Instead, **physicians unknowledgeable in all this chemistry try to blame symptoms on the mental aspect.** Or they are surprised that there are two or more target organs affected at the same time, since they told us in medical school that more than a couple of problems suggests a mental diagnosis! So when you find a doc who is knowledgeable or interested in this (and don't be afraid to test him. You would test your car mechanic, I hope), hang onto him.

REFERENCES: (The abstracts are included for interested physicians, whereas others may want to skip right to chapter 7.)

Allen GM, Hickie I, Gandevia SC, McKenzie DK, Impaired voluntary drive to breathe: a possible link between depression and unexplained ventilatory failure in asthmatic patients, THORAX, 49(9): 881-4, Sep 1994. ABSTRACT: These results suggest that depressed mood may predispose an asthmatic patient to impaired voluntary activation of the diaphragm. Such individuals would be at increased risk of rapidly developing ventilatory failure if faced with severe airway narrowing.

Hashiro M, Okumura M, Anxiety, depression, psychosomatic symptoms and autonomic nervous function in patients with chronic urticaria, JOURNAL OF DERMATOLOG SCIENCE 8(2): 129-35, Oct 1994.

Badoux A, Levy DA, Psychological symptoms in asthma and chronic urticaria, ANN ALLERG, 72(3): 229-34, March 1994.

Salvaggio JE, Psychological aspects of "environmental illness", "multiple chemical sensitivity", and building- related illness, J ALLERG CLIN IMMUNOL, 94(2 pT 2): 366-70, Aug. 1994.

Janson C, Bjornsson E, Hetta J, Boman G, Anxiety and depression in relation to respiratory symptoms and asthma, AMER J RESPIR CRIT CARE MED, 149(4 Pt 1): 930-4, Apr. 1994. ABSTRACT: We conclude that there is an association between reported respiratory symptoms and psychological status. However, there was no evidence that patients with diagnosed bronchial asthma had more anxiety and depression that those without asthma. This result indicates that it may be valuable to include psychological status indicators in respiratory symptom questionnaires.

Michel FB, Psychology of the allergic patient, ALLERGY, 49(18 Suppl): 28-30, 1994.

Gauci M, King MG, Saxarra H, Tulloch BJ, Husband AJ, A Minnesota multiphasic personality inventory profile of women with allergic rhinitis, PYCHOSOMAT MED, 55(6): 533-40, Nov-Dec 1993.

ABSTRACT: Skin reactivity to grass pollen and mold allergens was positively correlated with depression and psychothenia. Two possible mechanisms explaining the link between psychological factors and allergic rhinitis include (1) the effect of cortisol on IgE production or (2) the production of mediators during an allergic reaction which travel from the nose to the brain.

Simon GE, Daniell W, Stockbridge H, Claypoole K, Rosenstock L, Immunologic, psychological, and neuropsychological factors in multiple chemical sensitivity. A controlled study. ANN INTERN MED, 119(2): 97-103, July 15, 1993.
ABSTRACT: Psychological symptoms, although not necessarily etiologic, are a central component of chemical sensitivity.

Marshall PS, Allergy and depression: a neurochemical threshold model of the relation between the illness, PSYCHOLOG BULL, 113(1): 23-43, Jan 1993.
ABSTRACT: Empirical studies suggest a very high prevalence of atopic disorder in people with depression.

Rubin NJ, Severe asthma and depression, ARCH FAM MED, 2(4): 433-40, Apr 1993.
ABSTRACT: The comorbity of severe asthma and depression is frequent and complicates the patient's comprehensive medical management. Asthma and depression are thought to interact to worsen both conditions, especially at the severe end of the spectrum of disease. This article reviews the current thinking regarding the synergistic effect of the two disorders, highlighting the importance of considering both disorders in the comprehensive management of severe asthma. Outpatient management and treatment issues addressed include the use of screening/case-finding tools, medication management, physician counseling, and referral.

Bartoloni C, Guidi L, Pariante CM, Di Giovanni A, Pili R, Cursi F, Tricerra A, Tempesta E, Frasca D, Psychological status and immunological parameters of institutionalized aged, PANMINERVA MEDICA, 33(3): 164-9, Jul-Sep 1991.
ABSTRACT: Depression, which is the most common psychiatric problem in aged people, seems to be linked with alterations in immunological function. Depressed elderly showed impaired

immunological function as compared with non-depressed ones, either "in vitro" or "in vivo". Lymphocyte stimulation with phytohemagglutinin (PHA), T cell growth factor (TCGF) production (induced by stimulation with PHA) and cutaneous delayed hypersensitivity (CDH) were reduced in depressed aged subjects. As far as lymphocyte proliferation with PHA in the whole group were concerned, no differences were found comparing the present results with those obtained in a former study. Although it is difficult to understand the significance of the immune imbalance associated with depression in the elderly, our results suggest that psychological status could influence the immunological functions in old people.

Smith RS, The macrophage theory of depression (published erratum appears in Med Hypotheses 1991 Oct; 36(2): 1781). MEDICAL HYPOTHESES, 35(4): 298-306, Aug 1991.

ABSTRACT: Excessive secretion of macrophage monokines is proposed as the cause of depression. Monokines when given to volunteers can produce the symptoms necessary for the Diagnostic and Statistical Manual of Mental Disorders, Third Edition Revised (DSM-III-R) diagnosis of major depressive episode. Interleukin-1 (IL-1) can provoke the hormone abnormalities linked with depression. This theory provides an explanation for the significant association of depression with coronary heart disease, rheumatoid arthritis, stroke and other diseases where macrophage activation occurs. The 3:1 female/male incidence of depression ratio is accounted for by estrogen's ability to activate macrophages. The extraordinary low rate of depression in Japan is consistent with the suppressive effect of eicosapentanoic acid on macrophages. Fish oil is proposed as a prophylaxis against depression and omega-6 fat as a promoter. Infection, tissue damage, respiratory allergies and antigens found in food are some of the possible causes of macrophage activation triggering depression.

Patriarca G, Schiavino D, Nucera E, Colamonico P, Montesarchio G, Sarraceni C, Multiple drug intolerance: allergological and psychological findings, JOURNAL OF INVESTIGATIONAL ALLERGOLOGY & CLINICAL IMMUNOLOGY, 1(2): 138- 44, Apr 1991. Latter was also performed in 20 normal

ABSTRACT: In order to evaluate pseudoallergic reactions to drugs, we studied a particular group of patients intolerant towards many drugs, pharmacologically dissimilar and administered during different periods of time These patients consider themselves as "allergic" to "all" drugs. Twenty female patients, all with a history of intolerance to at least three drugs, chemically and antigenically dissimilar and not belonging to the same category of drugs, were studied. These patients underwent an allergological testing (negative in all cases) and a psychodiagnostic test (Rorschach's test); the control subjects. The psychodiagnostic findings demonstrated the negative psychological constitution of the experimental group in which the presence of a smaller quantity of energy leads to a minor capability of expressing emotions and to a major expression of depressive feelings. These patients suppress emotions to a greater extent, probably because of an expressive inhibition, while in the control group there is a possibility of mental elaboration. This implies that during the early period of emotional development with their parents, attempts to express affection received negative and frustrating replies. Therefore in later development, the expression of affection was suppressed. This last dynamic consideration, together with the former energetic and structural findings, demonstrates the pathogenic complexity of multiple drug intolerance, including, together with dysmetabolic, hormonal (clear prevalence of female subjects), autonomic and dysreactive factors, an important psychosomatic component.   The diagnosis therefore also includes a careful psychodiagnostic test.

Bell IR, Jasnoski ML, Kagan J, King DS, Depression and allergies: survey of a nonclinical population, PSYCHOTHERAPY & PSYCHOSOMATICS, 55(1): 24-31, 1991.

RESOURCES: Get a catalogue from these places for difficult to find high quality nutrients.

N.E.E.D.S.	1-800-634-1380
Emerson Ecologics	1-800-654-4432
Tyler Encapsulations	1-800-869-9705
Ecological Formulas	1-800-888-4585
Klaire Laboratories	1-800-533-7255
Allergy Research Group	1-800-545-9960
Thorne Research	1-800-228-1966

For physicians and lay who want more education in nutritional biochemistry (books, courses, seminars, tapes, slides for physician lectures, etc.):

American Academy of Environmental Medicine
4510 W. 89th St, Ste 110
Prairie Village KS 66207
913/642-6062 ---- moving shortly

Environmental Treatment Center   (Rea, WJ)
8345 Walnut Hill Ln, Ste 205
Dallas TX 75231
214/368-4132

HealthComm International, Inc.   (Bland, J)
5800 Soundview Dr.
Gig Harbor WA 98335
206/851-3943

Northeast Center for Environmental Medicine   (Rogers,SA)
2800 W. Genesee Street
PO Box 2716
Syracuse, NY 13220-2716
315/488-2856

CHAPTER 7

SOME OF THE BEST KEPT
SECRETS IN MEDICINE:

ORPHAN ACCESSORY NUTRIENTS

There are **over 40 known essential nutrients** in the body. These fall into the general categories of **vitamins, minerals, fatty acids, and amino acids.** But there are nutrients that are just as crucial for the function of the body, that do not fall into any of these 4 categories. I call these **orphans, or accessory** nutrients. For many of these, there are no blood tests to measure levels. Additionally, most are not considered essential by government committees that establish the pitifully low guidelines for dosages of the known nutrients that are required by the body (called the RDA's or recommended daily allowance).

As a quick example, the revered NEW ENGLAND JOURNAL OF MEDICINE (Stampfer, 1993) article showed that with a mere 100 I.U. of vitamin E, we can cut the cardiovascular risk in half. But many studies show that 400 I.U. is a much wiser dose. Anyway, the official U.S. Government RDA is less than 10 I.U. Yes, you read correctly, less than 1/10th of the lowest effective dose. Why? Partly because food lobbyists put pressure on the committees to keep RDA's low so they do not have to fortify the foods they have stripped in processing. There are many other reasons that we have gone into in other works.

We know how many of these orphan or accessory nutrients work in the body's chemistry. And many happen to be the missing magic ingredients that finally hone our chemistry into a finely-tuned, happily functioning wonderful piece of machinery. Unfortunately, orphan nutrients, in spite of voluminous evidence, are nearly totally ignored by medicine. This is because they are not patentable; so there are no exclusive rights over them, hence no huge profits. There are many more than I have included here, but let's look at the magic that some of them can do.

PHOSPHATIDYL CHOLINE

Phosphatidyl Choline or **PC** is a major nutrient that is never tested in medicine. In fact, we don't even have a test for it. But it is probably deficient in most people, and as you will see, **a major unsuspected cause of much illness**, especially depression.

First of all, you know that depression can be triggered by allergies to foods, chemicals, and molds. And you know that depression can be triggered by deficiencies of vitamins, minerals, essential fatty acids, amino acids, or any combination (as is more common) of all of the things above. And you know that the major way that medicine handles depression is with drugs and many of the most popular drugs for the treatment of depression work by changing the kinetics or metabolism of serotonin. They either inhibit its uptake or inhibit its metabolism at other sites. In other words, they alter the level of the neurotransmitter or happy hormone.

346

But recall that **there are other neurotransmitters or chemical messengers in the brain besides serotonin.** In fact there are many of them. **For all cells have to talk to one another or communicate with one another.** No cells exist in the body all alone without contact with others. This communication in the brain takes place via many types of neurotransmitters, but the major one is not serotonin. It is **acetylcholine.**

And **acetylcholine is made in the body from phosphatidyl choline. Acetylcholine is the chemical messenger** that jumps between nerves and muscles to make the muscles fire off and contract or work. It's also the chemical that jumps between nerve to nerve junctions to send important messages, in the form of thoughts and emotions. The message could be for example, to make us secrete from various glands or secrete other neurotransmitters or happy hormones.

SCENARIO:
Someone could come in and tell you that the person that you love the most in the world has just died in a tragic accident. They don't have to touch you. Yet, they have caused a tremendous biochemical reaction in your body. You suddenly become filled with anguish, depression, fear, sorrow, and much more. And how did you do it? You did it by releasing neurotransmitters which effected many different end organs, different nerves, different glands, different muscles, all contributing to give you those horrible feelings. **Acetyl choline is what turns a thought into physical body changes.**

Acetyl choline is responsible for most of the brain chemistry, and directly affects our moods and our memory, especially short term memory (and in fact, it is lower in people who have Alzheimer's senile dementia). It is also important in

347

guarding against the brain fog of chemical sensitivity and most importantly, depression.

And as you learned, some of the most common environmental chemicals to damage the neurotransmitter acetylcholine choline are pesticides. For pesticides turn off the enzyme that is part of the normal breakdown of acetyl choline. That's part of the reason why **pesticides** are such a hidden cause of depression. They actually inhibit the enzyme that properly metabolizes acetylcholine (acetylcholinesterase). Thus they **paralyze** or damage the very most basic and important driving force of the whole nervous system, including the brain. **Pesticides poison the main brain happy hormone or neurotransmitter, acetyl choline.**

Another major way that **cells communicate** one to another is **via receptors on the surface of the cell membrane.** And you guessed it, we use phosphatidyl choline (and EFA's) to make these receptors and to make the cell membrane itself. Recall, the **cell membrane is analogous to the computer keyboard.** And the receptors are the keys that transmit the directions to the cell interior.

For example, there are receptors that cause allergy. When an allergen such as a food or mold attaches to the antibody in the blood stream, this combo then attaches onto a cell and causes the release of a mediator, like **histamine.** The histamine then causes secretion from mucous glands or can cause dilatation or constriction of blood vessel walls, for example. If the cell is in the nose and the mediator released is histamine, then a runny nose results. That is why you take anti-histamines. If the cell is in the brain, then a headache, migraine, mood swing or depression can result.

The cell surface is also where hormones and other regulatory proteins attach. But receptors deficient in phosphatidyl choline(or EFA's) are defective and do not function properly, even when there are adequate levels of hormones. The integrity of the cell membrane, critical for normal function, must have the correct layers of phosphatidyl choline as well as the minerals, essential fatty acids, and other nutrients.

OUR CHEMICAL ENVIRONMENT
STEALS OUR HAPPY HORMONES

But **we lose or throw away phosphatidyl choline every day** from a variety of chemical processes that are going on in the body. For example, if we detoxify the new carpet at work when molecules of toluene reach our liver through the nose and blood, then we lose PC. Thus far for phosphatidyl choline, there are **3 crucial areas** where it is necessary: the nervous system's messenger **acetyl choline**, the computer keyboard or **cell membrane** where receptor sites are, and the **detox membranes**. For any of these 3 areas, if any is deficient in PC, the result can be depression. For the function of all 3 areas is dependent upon adequate phosphatidyl choline (PC).

And since **we use up or lose phosphatidyl choline every day in the work of detoxifying this world** (and in many other body reactions), it is important that it get replaced quickly if there is a deficiency of it in the computer keyboard (our cell membrane). The body, when it runs out of phosphatidyl choline in one place, will actually "eat" it off another place in your body. We call this **"autocannibalism"**. We actually cannibalize our own cells and rob Peter to pay Paul. So we put the stolen phosphatidyl choline wherever the body thinks it needs it most importantly. This, of course, leaves other areas deficient. It also can cause an **unexplained fluctuation of symptoms.**

Thus, **every time we detoxify chemicals we use up or deplete phosphatidyl choline from the detox membranes in the endoplasmic reticulum.** Since we are the first generation of man to ever have been exposed to so many chemicals and to ever be called upon to detoxify so many chemicals in a day, **we also use up phosphatidyl choline faster than any other generation.** To compound the problem, **we also eat progressively fewer of the foods that are rich in PC.** So it is a losing battle, and the hidden unexplainable biochemical basis for much disease. For as the endoplasmic reticulum (where chemicals are detoxified inside the cell), brain and cell membranes run out of PC, we can get any symptom imaginable, including depression.

So, let's get back to the important brain "happy hormone" or neurotransmitter, acetylcholine. A quick review will help you recall that it is damaged by pesticides, other foreign chemicals use up the phosphatidyl choline in the detox membranes, and we eat it off the membranes ourselves with our autocannibalism act.

But, other nasty things happen to make it so that we can't even synthesize or make as much as we need. One of the chemicals that the body can make phosphatidyl choline out of (and into) is **choline.** But choline is often low in the diet because people eat so much processed food and junk food. Choline is high in liver, but we hardly eat liver any more because it's the chemical factory of the animal and it concentrates all the pesticides and antibiotics and chemicals such as growth hormones that the animal was fed in the feedlot.

350

The next good food source for choline is peanuts and peanut butter. But these often have the undetectable mold toxins called aflatoxins on them which are capable of causing cancer. Other foods high in phosphatidyl choline are eggs. But foolishly, people rarely eat those any more because of the cholesterol. Cauliflower is quite high in choline (and in addition, also contains phyto-chemicals that actually fight off cancers). Suffice to say, many people are most likely low in choline and phosphatidyl choline just because of their diets. Yet choline is a chemical that the body must have in order to manufacture acetyl choline.

If that weren't enough, choline's entire role is not merely to make **acetylcholine (the chemical that makes the entire brain and nervous system work) and phosphatidyl choline (the chemical that makes all cell membranes work).** If that were the case we probably wouldn't see so much depression. But choline also goes on to make **glycine** which has many roles in the detox pathway, in the work of silently detoxifying our daily chemicals. And do not forget that you learned in the amino acid section that the amino acid glycine also modulates the brain's happy hormones.

As far as detoxification goes, in the **acylation reaction of glycine** plus a chemical like toluene (from carpet, paint, auto and industrial exhausts, plastics, etc.,) the body makes hippuric acid and it puts this conjugate out in the urine. So if they just painted at work or glued down a new carpet, your body uses up (and throws away in the urine) glycine in order to attach it to the toluene in your blood stream and drag it out into the urine as hippuric acid. This is the way the body detoxifies or gets rid of the toxic toluene that we breath in from a newly painted room or from carpet glue, to avoid brain fog. Toluene, as you will see later, is one of the common chemicals that we come into contact with every day.

The problem is that glycine is lost with the toluene, so we use it up once more, much faster in a chemically contaminated world. Hence, there is less to go around for glycine's role in the brain: hence one more mechanism where **chemical overload fosters abnormal brain chemistry and depression.** The body is using glycine, made from choline, that could have been used to further either the acetylcholine pathway or the phosphatidyl choline pathway. Alas, another mechanism that robs the brain of its nutrients for proper function.

If that were not enough, **glycine is necessary for making glutathione.** Glutathione is a tripeptide that the body hooks onto chemicals in the liver in order to drag them out into the bile and then into the gut. But by getting rid of or detoxifying chemicals in this way, **the body also throws away the glutathione.** And well as choline being necessary for glycine synthesis, it is also necessary for making methyl groups. And methyl groups are another entity that attach onto foreign chemicals in our body to detoxify them. But the body throws this conjugate away also in the work of detoxification. This process of attaching methyl groups to chemicals to drag them out into the bile is called "alkylation". So here are **3 products that are shunted away from choline to use for detox and they all eventually get thrown out!** Down the toilet go precious glycine, glutathione, and methyl groups, that could have been used to make happy hormones.

And we are by no means done. Another way that the body uses up choline is in **acetylation.** In this detoxification pathway, the body ties up another special chemical, an acetyl group, by hooking it onto foreign chemicals. It then gets rid of them also through the bile and gut.

This is wonderful for the body that's toxic because it gives it more than one choice of pathways with which to detoxify the over 500 chemicals that we inhale every day. The problem is **that glycination, sulfonation, methylation, and acetylation all use up choline derivatives.** So we keep using up the same chemical precursor that we really needed in order to make phosphatidyl choline for the cell membrane receptors and detox membranes and acetylcholine as the brain's neurotransmitter. Now you understand many more reasons that explain why there is so much depression.

So in essence, choline produces at least four chemicals for the conjugation and detoxification pathways of foreign chemicals in our system. And every time we detoxify a chemical, these four chemical constituents from the acylation of glycine to hippuric acid, to the conjugates of glutathione, methylation (alkylation), and acetylation, all use choline. **So the everyday environmental chemical overload steals from our health and from our happy hormones.** Let's look at how just a deficiency of phosphatidyl choline can snowball into a multitude of disease states. Everywhere it is potentially lost from the body in a detoxification reaction or by damage, you'll see the symbol (L).

Phosphatidyl choline:
> lost from detox membrane, endoplasmic reticulum (L)
> acetyl choline metabolism inhibited by pesticides
> cell membranes damaged by chemicals, drugs (L)
> cell receptors, regulatory proteins, damaged (L)
> mitochondria, damaged (L)
> nuclear membrane, damaged (L)

cell organelles (L)
low in diet
forms **choline:** which forms acetyl choline
 can reform phosphatidyl choline
 makes glycine for glutathione (L)
 glycine acylation to hippuric acid (L)
 acetylation to acetyl CoA for ATP
 methylation (alkylation) (L)
Forms **methionine:**
  methylates DNA for cancer prevention
  methylation depleted in phase II (L)
  with lysine forms carnitine
  homocysteine (with lack of nutrients)
  choline
  forms **cysteine** for:
   alkylation (L)
   glutathione (L)
   acetyl CoA to ATP
   metallotheinine
   endorphins
   forms **taurine:**
    bile (L)
    anti-inflammatory,
    etc.

Every time we detoxify chemicals we run the risk of using up more choline that could have helped foster the happy hormones in the brain instead. Now you can understand even more, why chemical contamination of home, office, person, diet, and water can lead to depression. In fact, **multiple pathways lead to depression.** If you follow all the chemistry of choline into phosphatidyl choline, and the reverse, which is the preferred reaction, phosphatidyl choline into choline, you will see how nearly every symptom and disease can be caused by a mere deficiency of choline and/or phosphatidyl choline. And depression can lead the way.

For without proper choline, you can follow the biochemistry of how we develop arteriosclerosis, the #1 cause of death and illness, as well as cancer, the #2 cause of death and illness. For choline is used to generate methyl groups, the lack of which on genetic DNA promotes cancer. And you just saw four mechanisms of chemical detoxification, which overlooked the loss of phosphatidyl choline from the endoplasmic reticular membranes during the work of detoxification as another mechanism contributing to both conditions. For **we actually rip PC off the detox membranes in the work of detoxication.** In essence, you can create any disease or any symptom with a mere deficiency of choline-derived acetylcholine or its sister products, phosphatidyl choline and choline. And certainly depression is no exception. And it often heads the list. (In just one week in the office, I talked with 3 people who were happier since taking Phos Chol, 7 who were no longer as chemically sensitive, 6 who had better memory, and 5 who had healed their leaky guts (Volume III).) (Phos Chol must be balanced with accessory nutrients and usually takes 1-9 months to correct. This is dependent on how badly damaged their membranes are, how many chemicals they still expose themselves to, how meticulously they avoid the membrane-damaging trans-fatty acids, etc. For obviously, it is easier to heal a membrane that has all the proper nutrients and is not continually being beaten up with a bad diet and environment.)

DIAGNOSING AND TREATING
PHOSPHATIDYL CHOLINE DEFICIENCY

So what can you do to improve the levels of choline and phosphatidyl choline in your body? First of all, make sure that you have cauliflower frequently, because it is a good source and it has many other health benefits as well, like anti-carcinogenic phytochemicals. Also, once you have normal nutrient levels, eggs are a wonderful source of phosphatidyl choline. The people who have to worry about high cholesterol when they eat eggs are people who are not playing with a full deck of nutrients. They are usually low in the nutrients that properly metabolize the egg cholesterol.

But if you suspect a severe PC membrane deficiency (a very common reason why many never get better from their symptoms), you'll need to diagnose it. Probably the simplest and most direct way would be to measure your rbc potassium and rbc calcium (National Medical Services, Willow Grove, PA).

In no way should this be construed to be the same as the serum, plasma, or a whole blood assays. It must be rbc source (a red blood cell assay). You'll know if you have the correct test because the norm for rbc potassium is 76-100 and it will say that on the laboratory report. The norm for the proper rbc calcium test is 2.8-4.3. For when the rbc potassium or rbc calcium are low, it more than not indicates that the potassium and calcium pumps in the rbc membrane are defective or damaged. And a likely source is a deficiency of PC. It is not an absolute test, as it may indicate other problems, including trans-fatty acid overloads (see EFA section), as well as an essential fatty acid deficiency.

356

Lecithin is a time-honored source of phosphatidyl choline. Unfortunately it is only 12% phosphatidyl choline and has other products in it that may not be necessary. The very best form of phosphatidyl choline is called Phos chol Concentrate (originally by Adv. Nutr. Tech., then sold to American Lecithin Company 1-800-364-4416). It is available in liquid form and 1 tsp. contains 3,000 mg of phosphatidyl choline. Accept no other form. This is the most concentrated form you can get and the daily dose would be 1 or 2 tsp. for starters. It is known that 1 tbs. a day is sufficient to double the plasma and brain levels. But there is lots more you need to do before you consider that. The same company makes a capsule called "Phos Chol 900" which if you are not glycerin sensitive, contains 900mg of phosphatidyl choline. For soy sensitive people we are investigating alternative sources.

There are other products that contain phosphatidyl choline, but when you read the label carefully none of them compare to this one product in strength, only in price. And some of them do not actually even measure the primary ingredient as phosphatidyl choline, but as phosphatides or a phosphatidyl complex. This means other things are involved as in lecithin and it is not an optimal product. You could use choline such as choline citrate which comes in capsules or liquid. But then you must rely on the body's ability to convert the choline to phosphatidyl choline and much of it gets lost in the detox pathways as explained, and it causes a nasty fishy body odor. However, there is benefit from using limited choline citrate in addition to PC, (plus accessory nutrients to balance it all).

For people who cannot tolerate Phos chol, they could possibly back up the pathway and see if the precursor phosphatidylserine is tolerated. This also benefits depression, providing you have the nutrients to convert it further to phosphatidyl choline However, for many reasons, it would be preferable for most to go directly to PC, since the body can store PC but not choline.

REFERENCES:

Maggioni M, Picotti GB, et al, Effects of phosphatidylserine therapy in geriatric patients with depressive disorders, ACTA PSYCHIATR SCAND 81(3):265-27, Mar 1990

Crook TH, Tinklenberg J, et al, Effects of phosphatidylserine in age-associated memory impairment, NEUROLOGY, 41:644-649, 1991

Kidd PM, Phosphatidyl serine; membrane nutrient for memory. A Clinical and mechanestic assessment, ALT MED REV 1;2: 70-84, 1996

P.S. Phosphatidyl choline is really all one word. But to fascilitate learning such difficult terms, we have split it into 2 words.

PHOSPHATIDYL CHOLINE:
WHY SOME PEOPLE NEVER GET WELL

A few pages ago you may have never given a thought to phosphatidyl choline or PC. But now and forever you know it as an extremely important nutrient. It is an integral part of every membrane. This includes the **mitochondrial membranes where energy is made,** the **endoplasmic reticulum where chemicals are detoxified,** the **nuclear membrane where the DNA or genetic structure is protected** so that chemicals cannot penetrate and cause the changes that bring about cancer, and most importantly **the cell membrane with its receptors and channels,** analogous to the computer keyboard. For our allergies and all diseases originate with dysfunction of cell membranes. And PC is integral for its function, and a key reason why some never heal.

As you know, there is less phosphatidyl choline in the diet these days because people rarely eat beans, peanuts, cauliflower, eggs and liver which have some of the highest contents of phosphatidyl choline. Not only do we not get enough phosphatidyl choline in the diet but unfortunately most people are low in one or more nutrients which are needed to metabolize the phosphatidyl choline and choline.

Other reasons why we need more phosphatidyl choline is that, as you saw, it is **used up and thrown away** as we detoxify chemicals. And since we're the first generation to be exposed to so many chemicals, **it is used up faster now than ever.** And when the body does not have enough of it, it will do its "autocannibalism" act. It will eat the phosphatidyl choline, for example, off brain membranes so that we can supply it to the liver cell membrane. Then, the brain that is deficient gets depressed, mood swings, poor memory, or

Alzheimer's. This **auto-cannibalism** is the very cause of many **senile brain changes,** in fact when you take PC, sometimes one of the first changes you notice is improved memory or loss of depression.

Last but not least, the most important reason that we have to correct phosphatidyl choline is that if you follow the pathways that it is in, it can be a **major explanation for why some people,** regardless of what they have, **never get totally well.** And **a** lack of phosphatidyl choline (as verified clinically) can keep you depressed indefinitely. It is one of the select nutrients that we should probably take forever. Even if you only take some once a week, it beats none at all.

REFERENCES:

Canty DJ, Zeisel SH, Lecithin And Choline In Human, Health and Disease, NUTRITION REVIEWS, 52:10, 327-339, October 1994.

Blusztajn JK, Lischovitch M, Richardson UI, Synthesis of acetylcholine from choline derived from phosphatidyl choline in a human neuronal cell line, PROC NATL ACAD SCI U.S.A., 84: 5474-5477, 1987.

Blusztajn JK, Wurtman RJ, Choline and cholinergic neurons, SCIENCE, 221, 614-619, Aug 1983

Growdon JH, Wurtman RJ, Lecithin treatment of neuroleptic- induced tardive dyskinesia, BIOLOGICAL ASPECTS OF SCHIZOPHRENIA AND ADDICTION, ed G. Hemmings, 129-38. London: Wiley, 1982.

Wurtman RJ, Effects of dietary amino acids, carbohydrates, and choline on neurotransmitter synthesis, THE MOUNT SINAI J MED 55;1:75-86, 1988.

Wurtman RJ, et al, Lecithin consumption raises serum-free choline levels, LANCET, 2:68-69, 1977.

Conlay L, et al, Marathon running decreases plasma choline concentrations, N ENG J MED, 315;892, 1986.

Cohen EL, Wurtman RJ, Brain acetylcholine. Control by dietary choline, SCIENCE, 191: 561-562, 1976.

Barabeau A, Growdon JH, Wurtman RJ, Eds, Choline and lecithin in brain disorders, NUTRITION AND THE BRAIN, VOL 5, Raven Press, 1979

Lopez GC, Berry IR, Plasma choline levels in humans after oral administration of highly purified phosphatidylcholine (PC) in capsules, in ALZHEIMER'S DISEASE: ADVANCES IN BASIC RESEARCH AND THERAPIES, RJ Wurtman. SH Corkin and JH Growdon, eds., PROCEEDINGS OF THE FOURTH MEETING OF THE INTERNATIONAL STUDY GROUP ON THE PHARMACOLOGY OF MEMORY DISORDERS ASSOCIATED WITH AGING, Zurich, Jan 16-18, 1987

Growdon JH, Use of phosphatidylcholine in brain diseases: An overview, in Hanin I, Ansell GB, LECITHIN, Plenum Publ, 1987

Cohen BM, Lipinski, JF, Altesman RI, Lecithin in the treatment of mania: double-blind, placebo-controlled trials, AM J PSYCHIA, 139:1162-1164, 1982

Davis JM, Critique of single amine theories: evidence of a cholinergic influence in the major mental illnesses, RES PUBL ASSOC RE MENT DIS 54:333-546, 1975

Food and Drug Administration Task Force, American College of Neuropsychopharmacology, Neurological syndromes associated with antipsychotic drug use: a special report, ARCH GEN PSYCHIA 28:463-467, 1973

Growdon JH, Cohen EL, Wurtman RJ, Treatment of brain diseases with dietary precursors of neurotransmitter, ANN INTERN MED, 86:337-339, 1977

Growdon JH, Wheeler S, Graham HN, Plasma choline responses to lecithin-enriched soup, PSYCHOPHARMACOL BULL, 20:603-606, 1984

Hirsch MJ, Wurtman RJ, Lecithin consumption elevates acetylcholine concentrations in rat brain and adrenal gland, SCIENCE, 207:223-225, 1978

Hitzemann R, Mark C, Hirschowitz J, Garver D, Characteristics of phospholipid methylation in human erythrocyte ghosts: relationship(s) to the psychoses and affective disorders, BIOL PSYCHIATRY, 20:397-407, 1985

Little A, Levy R, Chuaqui-Kidd P, Hand D, A double-blind, placebo controlled trial of high-dose lecithin in Alzheimer's disease, J NEUROL NEUROSURG, PSYCHIA, 48:736-742, 1985

Gundermann KJ, (ed.) THE "ESSENTIAL" PHOSPHOLIPIDS AS A MEMBRANE THERAPEUTIC, Polish Section of European Society of Biochemical Pharmacology, Inst. Pharm. & Toxicol, Medical Academy, Sz Czecin, Poland, 1993 (1-800-364-4416).

Wurtman RJ, Blusztajn JK, Maire JC, "Autocannibalism" of choline-containing membrane phospholipids in the pathogenesis of Alzheimer's disease - a hypothesis, NEUROCHEM INT, 7:369- 372, 1985

Cohen BM, et al, Lecithin in the treatment of mania: Double- blind placebo controlled trials, AMER J PSYCH, 139:1162-1164, 1982.

Cohen EL, et al, Brain acetyl choline, increase after system choline administration, LIFE SCIENCES, 16:1095-1102, 1975.

Davis KL, et al, Choline for tardive dyskinesia, NEW ENG J MED, 293; 152, 1976.

Growdon JH, et al, Lecithin can suppress tardive dyskinesia, NEW ENG J MED 298: 1029-1030, 1978.

Daldessariani RJ, et al, Dopamine and the pathophysiology of dyskinesias induced by anti-psychotic drugs, ANN REV OF NEURO SCI, 3:23-41, 1980.

Davies P, et al, Selective loss of central cholinergic neurons in Alzheimer's Disease, LANCET, 2:1403-1976.

MEMBRANE FLUIDITY DETERMINES DISEASE

Besides phosphatidyl choline being necessary for the synthesis of acetylcholine, the primary neurotransmitter in the brain, it has a fundamental role in membrane fluidity. You need to understand that as we age our cell membranes become stiffer and less fluid. Hence, they do not function as well, nor do they allow the passage of essential nutrients back and forth. We call this **"loss of fluidity"** or loss of elasticity or loss of flexibility, aging. And we also call loss of membrane fluidity by various disease names, like aging, hardening of the arteries or **arteriosclerosis** of the heart, kidney, brain, etc.

The concept of membrane fluidity explains also, why one nutrient such as phosphatidyl choline can have so many actions in the body. It can help depression by making sure the happy hormone membrane receptors are flexible enough to grab onto the hormones. Yet in another person, restoring membrane fluidity can cure chemical sensitivity, or heal a recalcitrant cardiac arrhythmia in another. For when you work on a molecular biochemistry level, you actually fix many things at once. This is opposed to drugs which merely mask a symptom by axing or turning off a defective pathway. They merely block the biochemistry that is no longer functioning well. Hence, names like anti-histamines, calcium channel blockers, beta-blockers, H-2 inhibitors, ACE inhibitors, serotonin re-uptake inhibitors (Prozac), etc.

Loss of fluidity has many causes, but crucial is insufficient dietary PC. And equally damaging are those nasty trans fatty acids you read about in the EFA section.

Loss of fluidity in the cell membranes can cause malfunction of the calcium channels which are tiny pores in the cell membrane. But instead, when the person exhibits cardiac arrhythmia, hypertension, or angina we use a medication (calcium channel blockers, that cost over $100 a month and help the sick get sicker quicker, and can even potentiate cancers as you will learn) to bypass rather than fix what is broken. And likewise, when we do that the drugs not only use up important nutrients in their metabolism, but they create other disturbances in other pathways (more on how prescription heart medicines potentiate cancers later).

REFERENCES:

Alarcon RD, et al, One carbon metabolism disturbances in affective disorders, a preliminary report, J AFFECT DIS, 9:297-301, 1985.

Hirata F, Enzymatic methylation of phosphatidyl ethanolamine increased erythrocyte **membrane fluidity**, NATURE, 275; 219- 220, 1978.

L-GLUTAMINE

L-Glutamine is the most abundant, free amino acid in the plasma and also in the cerebral spinal fluid that bathes the brain and spinal cord. It has been very useful in fighting depression (Cocchia, R, Anti-depressive properties of L-glutamine. ACTA PSYCHIATR BELG, 76: 658-666, 1976).

And this amino acid has helped improve mood and depression in active cancer patients (Young LS, et al, Patients receiving glutamine supplemented intravenous feedings report an improvement in mood, JPEN 17: 422-427, 1993; and Young LS, Schelting AM, Bye R, Wilmore DW, Can test of patient well-being be used to evaluate nutritional efficacy? An affirmative answer. JPEN, 16:20s, 1992).

Yet this should come as no surprise since **L-glutamine is metabolized into two brain neurotransmitters.** One is the excitatory neurotransmitter **glutamic acid (glutamate)** and the other is the inhibitory **gamma amino butyric acid or GABA.** As always, we need the yin and yang of happy hormones with opposing effects for the complete balance of mood (Shank RP, Kempbell GL, Metabolic precursors of glutamate and GABA, In HORTZ L, et al, GLUTAMINE, GLUTAMATE, AND GABA IN THE CENTRAL NERVOUS SYSTEM, Liss Publ, New York, 355-369, 1983).

Studies show that blood levels of GABA are lower in depressed men than in the controls (undepressed). (Petty F, et al, Low plasma gamma-aminobutyric acid levels in male patients with depression, BIOL PSYCHIATRY 32:354-363, 1992). As well, GABA has even helped **decrease alcohol addiction** (Rogers LL, Pelton RB, Glutamine in the treatment of alcoholism, QUART ST 18: 581-587, 1957 and Rogers LL,

365

Pelton RB, Williams RJ, Amino acid supplementation and voluntary alcohol consumption by rats, J BIOL CHEM 220: 321-323, 1956).

Furthermore, glutamine has even helped the depression that follows **strokes** and has helped improve **memory and IQ.** EEG or brain wave tests were used to prove this (Manna V, Martucci N, Effects of short-term administration of cytidine, uridine and L-glutamine, alone or in combination on the cerebral electrical activity of patients with chronic cerebral vascular disease. INT J CLIN PHARM RES 8:199-210, 1988).

Furthermore, even though the studies on alcoholism only used a dose of about 5 tsp. a day total, other treatments have required much larger doses. But studies have shown that doses up to 60 grams a day are safe (Ziegler TR, et al, Safety and metabolic effects of L-glutamine administration in humans, JPEN 14 (Suppl: 137S-146S), 1990).

More importantly they have found that L-glutamine decreases **post operative pain,** inflammation and **edema** or swelling (Jain P, Khanna NK, Evaluation of anti-inflammatory and analgesic properties of L-glutamine, AGEN ACT 11:243-249, 1981).

And glutamine has also **improved the IQ of mentally deficient children,** which it should if you are deficient in one of the neurotransmitters that depends on glutamine (Rogers LL, Pelton RB, Effects of glutamine on IQ scores of mentally deficient children, TEX REP BIOL MED 15: 84-90, 1957).

If this were not enough, there are many other useful effects of glutamine. For example, it not only helps decrease tumor growth, but it selectively **helps chemotherapy** to get to the tumor to kill it faster, thus sparing normal cells from being exposed to excessive chemotherapy.

REFERENCES:

Austgen TR, Dudrick PS, Sitren H, Bland KI, Copeland E, Souba WW, The effects of glutamine enriched total parenteral nutrition on tumor growth and host tissues, ANN SURG 215: 107-113, 1992.

Souba WW, Glutamine and cancer, ANN SURG 218: 715-728, 1993.

Rouse K, Nwokedi EC, Woodliff J, Epstein J, Klimberg VS, Glutamine enhances selectivity of chemotherapy through changes in glutathione metabolism, JPEN 17:28s, 1993.

Klimberg DS, et al, Glutamine facilitates chemotherapy while reducing toxicity, JPEN 16 (Suppl 1): 83s-87s, 1992.

Klimberg DS, et al, Effect of supplemental dietary glutamine on methotrexate concentration in tumors, ARCH SURG 127: 1317-1320, 1992.

As well, glutamine has many beneficial effects on **slowing aging** and in promoting healing the gut. In fact, it **keeps radiation from damaging the intestines** when radiation is used for controlling abdominal tumors. It has a host of beneficial effects in terms of healing the leaky gut, healing the liver, the immune system, preventing post operative and post surgical trauma, reducing the healing time for burns and the deterioration of muscle. What a **facilitator of healing!** But find a surgeon who uses it!

The dose has been raised as high as 20 and 40 grams twice a day with no adverse effect. The problem is that it is very expensive at that high a dose. It comes in a powder form of 1/4 tsp. = 500 mg., so 1 tsp. would be 2 grams. Another form has twice the amount or nearly 5 grams/tsp. In many studies 10-20 grams twice a day were used. However, I have seen remarkable changes in patients with as little as one tsp. a day. So that is a good starting dose. Furthermore, many studies successfully used 500 mg three times a day.

It is important that when L-glutamine is used as a therapy, that it is taken in water, but not in fruit juices since acidity destroys it. Therefore, it also must be taken between meals since again, acidity will damage it. So, in water, between meals, twice a day, with no food in the stomach 1-2 hours before and after would give optimum absorption for this expensive, but very important nutrient. Certainly everyone with depression should evaluate whether or not this is one their biochemical glitches.

But as with **any amine, it can make depression or mania worse,** depending on your chemistry. So always have medical supervision or guidance. Just as glutamine is also important in many conditions and in slowing down aging, it should not come as a surprise that it is also important for normal brain metabolism of happy hormones and for helping depression. In fact, many deficiencies that come with aging like B6 deficiency and elevated homocysteine levels (which are known to potentiate arteriosclerosis) can also cause depression (Bell IR, et al, Plasma homocysteine in vascular disease and in non-vascular dementia of depressed elderly people, ACTA PSYCH SCAN 85:386-390, 1992).

Glutamine is also important in **increasing alkali reserves** in the body. Whenever the body is in trouble it becomes acidic. Diabetics get diabetic acidosis. If we have a heart attack we're acidic; if we have a severe auto accident with much trauma we become acidic. And when **some people become**

depressed when they are too acid. And when people eat the wrong diet or are over exposed to too many chemicals (more than metabolize), they become acidic. Glutamine therefore, has another role in helping to normalize this chemistry. In addition, it even increases the plasma growth hormone levels (Welborne TC, Increased plasma bicarbonate and growth hormone after an oral glutamine load, AMER J CLIN NUTR 1995; 61:1058-1061).

You see, we've lost touch with the fact that the body is a large whole of multiply interacting entities. They all need to be in good balance to have wellness. And any one thing that is off can lead to any symptom including depression. Consequently, **every symptom including depression is a God-given opportunity to correct what is broken and fix** it rather than let it go on to cause other problems that could be fatal.

RESOURCES:

* Cambridge Nutraceuticals, One Liberty Sq., 10th Fl, Boston MA 02109, 1-800-265-2202.

REFERENCES:

Souba WW, Klimberg S, Schloerb P, Rombeau J, GLUTAMINE: PHYSIOLOGY, BIOCHEMISTRY AND NUTRITION IN CRITICAL ILLNESS, RG Landes Publ, Austin TX 1993.

Ravel JM, Et al, Reversal of alcohol toxicity by glutamine, J BIOLOG CHEM, Sep 1982.

Rogers LL, et al, Effect of glutamine on IQ scores of mentally deficient children, TEX REP BIOL MED, 15:1, 1957.

Salloum RM, Souba WW, Klimberg VS, Glutamine is superior to glutamate in supporting gut metabolism, stimulating intestinal glutaminase activity and preventing translocation, SURG FOURUM, 40:6-8, 1989.

Burke D, Alverdy JC, Aoys E et al, Glutamine supplemented TPN improves gut immune function, ARCH SURG, 124:1396-1399, 1989.

Fox AD, Kripke SA, DePaula J et al, Effect of a glutamine supplemented enteral diet on methotrexate-induced enterocolitis, J PEN, 12, 325-331, 1988.

Souba WW, Klimberg VS, Hautamaki RD et al, Oral glutamine reduces bacterial translocation following abdominal radiation, J SURG RES, 481:1-5, 1990.

Klimberg VS, Salloum RM, Kasper M et al, Oral glutamine accelerates healing of the small intestine and improves outcome following whole abdominal radiation, ARCH SURG, 125: 1040-1045, 1990.

Klimberg VS, Souba WW, Solson DJ et al, Prophylactic glutamine protects the intestinal mucosa from radiation injury, CANCER, 66: 62-68, 1990.

Helton S, Jacobs D, Bonner-Weir J, et al, Effects of glutamine-enriched parenteral nutrition on the exocrine pancreas, J PEN, 14: 344-352, 1990.

Mebane AH, L-glutamine and mania, AMER J PSYCH, 141(10): 1302-1303, 1984.

Lochs H, Hubl W, Metabolic basis for selecting glutamine-containing substrates for parenteral nutrition, J PEN, 14(4): 114S-117S, 1990.

CARNITINE

You recall that acetylcholine is the primary messenger or neurotransmitter in the brain. Well, acetyl carnitine has a **structural similarity to acetylcholine.** And in many studies it not only **protects the brain from the aging** of free radicals (oxidative damage from our chemical exposures, for example), but it was tested in 481 subjects at 500 mg three times per day for 90 days and found to improve not only depression, but **memory, emotion, and alertness.** And it had no side effects. And since acetylcholine is the main neurotransmitter, it can use all the help we can give it.

Just as phosphatidyl choline is crucial in the chemistry of making brain membranes as well as the chief neurotransmitter, acetyl choline, so is carnitine. And just as phosphatidyl choline synthesis can be impaired because the body uses up some of the prime ingredients in the work of detoxifying everyday chemicals, the same occurs for carnitine.

Most physicians have a very poor knowledge of carnitine (if you don't believe it, ask him to tell you about it). Biochemistry is down-played in our medical education and drugs are stressed instead. So we don't have to learn very much chemistry. **The emphasis is not on fixing what is broken, but merely masking the symptom.** And there is continued push once we are in practice by insurance companies and HMOs (health maintenance organizations or more accurately, disease, drug and doctor-visit maintenance organizations) to drug patients and not look for the causes. And don't forget. All these nutrients are non-prescription so there is no huge profit to be made by a pharmaceutical firm, nor can any firm have exclusive rights over them.

Anyway, carnitine is a common body constituent that can become deficient. An when it does, depression can be the symptom. **Carnitine is made in the body from two amino acids, lysine and methionine.** The problem that you will immediately recognize is that methionine is an amino acid that can be used up or pushed into other pathways and used for the detoxification of everyday chemicals. So then **there is not enough methionine left over to be used for making carnitine.**

Remember, the body does what it perceives as the most important thing to keep you alive first. And when it sees the over 500 chemicals that are in the average home environment each day, it makes this a priority to clean them out of the blood stream and tissues as efficiently as possible. Keeping you supplied with happy hormones is not considered by the body to be a life or death priority. So let's look at the multitude of ways we use up and throw away methionine (and methyl groups that come from it) in the work of daily detoxification of chemicals.

The ways that methionine is used up in the detox pathway are many. Recall that attaching methyl groups to a chemical (methylation or alkylation) is one of the ways the body has to detoxify many chemicals. But more importantly, **methyl groups are used for the methylation of amines, a crucial step in making our "happy hormones" in the brain.** So if we use up too many methyl groups in the work of detoxifying, there are not enough to methylate or make happy hormones.

Methylation (mere attaching of a methyl group) is also used to further metabolize and detoxify certain happy hormones in the catecholamine category. **Catecholamines** are a category of important brain neurotransmitters or "happy hormones" that determine our moods. Some moods like fear, panic, anxiety, rage, sadness or depression we want to "get over" with as quickly as possible. It takes methyl groups to accomplish this.

Isn't it not only logical but so exciting that we should have control over the very chemicals that the anti-depressant medications control? These catecholamines include adrenaline (the fight or flight hormone that makes you feel excited or panicky or fearful), norepinephrine, dopamine, and dopamine. We control all of our neurotransmitters, including others like histamine and serotonin.

As an example, I am a person that is unaffected by blood. As a former emergency room physician, I can eat a sandwich while performing an autopsy. The little scientist in me takes over and is so intensely excited by learning and doing, that I am not squeamish. But you could show me clips from a tasteless movie and I could vomit. You never had to touch my stomach. My neurotransmitters did all the work.

So what I am saying is that if, for example, you constantly stress yourself with **worry or anger** (or any bad thought), you produce the bad neurotransmitters in the brain that must be metabolized. The hooking of a methyl group onto the neurotransmitter is a common way for the body to polarize the molecule to make it easier to detoxify (called methyl conjugation). The attachment of a methyl group make the molecule heavier so that it can be dragged out into the bowel or urine and gotten rid of. That is why if tickled, you don't laugh forever.   Neurotransmitters have short lives and are metabolized just like any other chemical in the body.

So not only does the work of detoxifying everyday chemicals use up or deplete methyl groups and other nutrients that could have been used for proper metabolism of our happy hormones, but persistent **bad thoughts or worry can also deplete methyl groups** (that could have been used to foster carnitine or phosphatidyl choline).   More on this in the stress section (Volume III).

Whatever you do, remember this, for it is important for many reasons: **persistent bad thoughts (worry) can deplete the nutrients that would have otherwise gone on to be used to make happy hormones.**   Now you can begin appreciate that **a bad thought can be just as bad for you as inhaling a bad chemical.**   It also depletes nutrients and also has to be detoxified.   And a bad thought is as bad as eating an allergenic food that causes the release of histamine which also has to be detoxified by this route and depletes nutrients.

And when you do not have enough methionine to make carnitine, you may also not have enough methionine to make glutathione (via cysteine) to detoxify other daily chemicals, or to detox chlorine in water, or to detox the body's hypochlorite ion, leading to chronic inflammation, like an arthritis, tendonitis, chronic pain syndromes, or recurrent infections (more of that in TIRED OR TOXIC?).   And the ultimate methyl deficiency disease is cancer as the genetic DNA of cancer is hypo- or under-methylated.

So let's get back to the fact that you need methionine to make choline, which then goes on to make acetyl choline, the chemical messenger or happy hormone that makes the brain work. You also need methionine to make cysteine to make acetyl CoA, which then goes on to make ATP (cellular energy). You need methionine chemistry to regulate insulin, and make endorphins (the body's pain relievers or analgesia). For if we lack sufficient methionine when all this detox chemistry is finished, then we set ourselves up for developing arteriosclerosis, osteoporosis, chemical sensitivities, and cancer. For you recall, when our genetic material, DNA, does not receive enough methyl groups to protect it from daily harmful chemicals, it can turn on the message to form cancer cells (REA, vol. 1).

So now you see that recurring theme of **how the sick get sicker,** when you not only fail to fix what is broken, but overload yourself with negative and unhappy thoughts, commonly called **worry.** Each deficiency has multiple pathways where it should have been used. This produces ramifications in many other seemingly unrelated systems. The problem is that in medicine we divide physicians into artificial specialties. So the fellow who gives you a drug for your arthritis is not aware that he missed an opportunity to find the causes and repair it before it goes on to cause chemical sensitivity or a cancer in 1-10 years.

For if the arthritis was due to a simple nightshade allergy, the non-steroidal anti-inflammatory drug the doctor prescribes can go on to cause the leaky gut syndrome. This in turn can damage the carrier proteins, so you get nutrient deficiencies that compromise the protection of your genetic DNA against the toluene in the wall paint at work, and you get a cancer (much more on this in WELLNESS AGAINST ALL ODDS).

And the fellow who is treating your high cholesterol is not aware that too low a cholesterol can lead to suicidal depression.   Nor is he aware that the same deficiencies that may be causing your high cholesterol (copper, magnesium, manganese, chromium, etc.) may also be causing your depression.   And the fellow who is treating your back spasm does not know that he missed a golden opportunity to correct your undiagnosed magnesium deficiency that causes muscle spasm, depression or can progress to sudden cardiac arrest.

CONSIDER CARNITINE FOR
MEDICATION-RESISTANT SYMPTOMS

So back to carnitine, which all this is preparing you for. Lipids are just a classification of fats in the body.   And there are many types of lipids.   One class of lipids are the neutral fats like triglycerides, which become elevated if you have too much breads and sweets and do not have the minerals to properly metabolize them.   Triglycerides can go on to do the same damage that cholesterol does.

Other types of lipids are the phospholipids, like phosphatidyl choline, of which you just learned.   Last there are the sterols, which include many of your glandular hormones, which also have a profound effect on brain chemistry.

Anyway, fatty acids (as you learned in the essential fatty acid section) are the main building blocks of the brain (sorry, but we really are "fat heads").   And **fatty acids are the main source of energy for the brain's ATP.**   And the only way the body can turn fatty acids into **ATP or brain energy** is to get the fatty acids inside the mitochondria, a little bean-shaped factory inside of cells.   And the only way for the raw materials, fatty acids, to get into this energy factory (the mitochondria) is to be carried in on the backs of carnitine!   So carnitine determines how efficiently the energy is made that runs the body, including the brain. Now that you know more about the biochemistry of carnitine than 99% of the physicians you will meet (and probably more than you ever wanted to know for yourself). Let's look at what a carnitine deficiency can do, and especially how it can mysteriously contribute to depression.

As you are learning, when an entity has multiple uses in the body and profoundly affects basic biochemical pathways, it can produce a variety of symptoms. A deficiency in carnitine can cause high cholesterol, heart failure, senile brain with memory loss, fatigue which is especially worse after exercise, Alzheimer's, insomnia, and last but not least, depression.

And a search of the scientific literature confirms what we have witnessed in clinical practice. And that is that **carnitine has been successfully used to help all sorts of conditions that resisted treatment by medications.** These include normalizing high cholesterol; reversing heart failure; improving memory, thought process, Alzheimer's, and pineal melatonin release for better sleep; increasing nerve growth factor, as in stroke recovery; helping hypoglycemia, cravings and weight gain; and protecting against senile brain degeneration.

Most importantly, carnitine has cleared or markedly improved depression in those for whom it was a deficiency. And the beauty was, it caused **no side effects.** And that is the main reason you have probably never heard of it. It is relatively cheap and does no require a prescription. And it can correct basic biochemical defects when combined with the proper complementary nutrients after careful assay by a physician trained in nutritional biochemistry.

But as with any nutrient correction, you must bear three things in mind. (1) **A nutrient is not a drug.** In other words, **it does not work alone, but in concert or symphony with other nutrients.** For if taken alone as a drug, you set yourself up to get worse symptoms, even if you are in need of it. You might even feel better for a short while, but as soon as you deplete the needed accompanying nutrients, you will start downhill and get worse.

(2) **If you are low in one nutrient, more than likely you are low in others. It is very difficult to get a solo deficiency.** So better to fix it all at once so the parts can work in harmony. They have a far greater chance of helping you that way. And in fact, to ignore doing this is one major reason for failure, even when you are taking nutrients that are important for you. And if they do not produce the desired result, you might form the erroneous opinion that they are no good for you and will not help your depression.

(3) Carnitine, like any other nutrient, helps the most if you happen to be deficient in it. If you are not deficient, or if a relative increase in it does not improve symptoms, then you either do not need extra, or you are still missing another part of the total load which is necessary in order to heal.

Most importantly, **L-acetyl carnitine has a structural similarity to acetylcholine** and can produce cholinergic activity in the brain as well as provide neuronal (brain cell) protection from oxidative damage (aging) caused by free radicals, especially those generated from defective mitochondrial function (Salvioli G, et al, L-acetyl carnitine treatment of mental decline in the elderly, DRUGS EXPTL CLIN RES 1994; 20(4):169-176.

You owe yourself a trial of acetyl L-carnitine or N-acetyl carnitine, 500 mg. twice a day for a month balanced with other nutrients, especially phosphatidyl choline (details later).

REFERENCES:

Tempesta E, et al, L-acetylcarnitine in depressed elderly subjects, A cross-over study vs. placebo. DRUGS EXP CLIN RES 13:417-423, 1987.

Gecele M, Francesetti G, Meluzzi A, Acetyl-L-carnitine in aged subjects with major depression: clinical efficacy and effects on the circadian rhythm of cortisol, DEMENTIA, 2: 333-337, 1991.

Salvioli G, Neri M, L-acetylcarnitine treatment of mental decline in the elderly, DRUGS EXPTL CLIN RES, 20(4): 169-176, 1994.

Sinforiani E, et al, Neuropsychological changes in demented patients treated with acetyl-L-carnitine, INT J CLIN PARMACOL RES, 10:69-74, 1990.

Calvani M et al, Action of acetyl-L-carnitine in neurodegeneration and Alzheimer's disease, ANN NY ACAD SCI, 663: 483-486; 1992.

Bella R, Biondi R, Raffaele R, Pennisi G, Effect of acetyl-L- carnitine on geriatric patients suffering from dysthymic disorders, INT J CLIN PHARMACOL RES, 10:355-360, 1990.

Bowman B, Acetyl-carnitine and Alzheimer's disease, NUTR REV, 50: 5,142-143, 1992.

Bodis-Wollner I, Physiological effects of acetyl-levo-carnitine in the central nervous system, INT J CLIN PHARM RES, X(1/2)109-114, 1990.

Tommaso A, Micheli A, et al, Aging brain: effect of acetyl-L-carnitine treatment on rat brain energy and phospholipid metabolism, A study by 31H NMR, BRAIN RES, 526: 106-112, 1990.

Costell M, O'Connor JE, Grisolia S, Age-dependent decrease of carnitine content in muscle of mice and humans, BIOCHEM & BIOPHYS RES COMM, 161: 3, 1135-1143, 1989.

Paradies G, Ruggiero FM, et al, The effect of aging and acetyl-L-carnitine on the activity of the phosphate carrier and on the phospholipids composition in rat heart mitochondria, BIOCHIMICA ET BIOPHYSICA ACTA, 1103: 324-326, 1992.

Bodis-Wollner I, Chung E, et al, Acetyl-levo-carnitine protects against MPTP-induced parkinsonism in primates, J NEURAL TRANSM (P-D Sect) 3:63-72, 1991.

White HL, Scates PW, Acetyl-L-carnitine as a precursor of acetylcholine, NEUROCHEM RES, 15:6, 597-601, 1990.

Patacchioli FR, Amenta F, et al, Acetyl-L-carnitine reduces the age-dependent loss of glucocorticoid receptors in the rat hippocampus: an autoradiographic study, J NEUROSCI RES, 23:462-466, 1989.

Imperato A, Ramacci MY, Angelucci L, Acetyl-L-carnitine enhances acetylcholine release in the striatum and hippocampus of awake freely moving rats, NEUROSCI LETT, 107: 251-255, 1989.

Vecchi GP, et al, Acetyl-l-carnitine treatment of mental impairment in the elderly: evidence from a multicentre study, ARCH GERONTOL GERIATR, Suppl 2: 159-168, 1991.

Salvoli G, Neri M, L-acetylcarnitine treatment of mental decline in the elderly, DRUGS UNDER EXPERIMENTAL & CLINICAL RESEARCH, 20(4): 169-76, 1994.

Herrmann WM, Dietrich B, Hiersemenzel R, Pharmaco-electric and clinical effects of the cholinergic substance --acetyl-L-carnitine--in patients with organic brain syndrome, INT J CLIN PHARMACOL RES, 10:1-2;81-4, 1990

Di Giulo AM, Gorio A, Bertelli A, Mantegazza P, Ferraris L, Ramacci MT, Acetyl-L-carnitine prevents substance P loss in the sciatic nerve and lumbar spinal cord of diabetic animals, INT J CLIN PHARMACOL RES 12:5-6;243-246, 1992

Corbucci GG, Menichetti A, Cogliatti A, Nicoli P, Arduini A, et al, Metabolic aspects of acute cerebral hypoxia during extracorporeal circulation and their modification induced by acetyl-carnitine treatment, INT J CLIN PHARMACOL RES 12:2;89-98, 1992

Herrmann WM, Stephan K, Efficacy and clinical relevance of cognition enhancers, ALZHEIMER DIS ASSOC DISORD, 5 suppl 1:S7-12, 1991

Carta A, Calvani M, Bravi D, Bhuachalla SN, Acetyl-L-carnitine and Alzheimer's disease: pharmacological considerations beyond the cholinergic sphere, ANN NY ACAD SCI, 695:324-326, Sep 24, 1993

Matsulka M, et al, Comparison of the effects of L-carnitine, D-carnitine and acetyl-L-carnitine on the neurotoxicity of ammonia, BIOCHEMICAL PHARMACOLOGY, 46(1):159-164, Jul 6, 1993

Davis S, et al, Acetyl-L-carnitine: behavioral, electro-physiological, and neurochemical effects, NEUROBIOL AGING, 14(1):107-115, Jan-Feb 1993

Lino A, et al, Psycho-functional changes in attention and learning under the action of L-acetylcarnitine in 17 young subjects. A pilot study of its use in mental deterioration, CLINICA TERAPEUTICA, 140(6):569-573, Jun 1992

Hirata F, Axelrod J, Phospholipid methylation and biological signal transmission, SCIENCE 209:1082-1090, 1980

Furlong, JH, Acetyl-L-carnitine: metabolism and applications in clinical practice, ALT MED REV 1:2: 85-93, 1996

LIPOIC ACID

Lipoic acid is used in the body to facilitate reactions concerned with energy as well as detoxification. It is a fascinating non-prescription nutrient, made by the body. As an example of its potency, there is no known cure for certain types of poisoning by mushrooms of the Amanita family. Yet lipoic acid administration has been life-saving. It has also reversed serious hepatic failure and returned liver function tests to normal. However, because it is not patentable, it is not usually mentioned in standard toxicology texts.

Lipoic acid is an amazing anti-oxidant for 2 reasons. First, most anti-oxidants have limited specific functions. Like B-carotene quenches singlet oxygen radicals, vitamin E quenches peroxyl radicals, and glutathione quenches hydroxy radicals. But lipoic acid does all of these. If that were not great enough, it recycles vitamin E, vitamin C, glutathione and other anti-oxidants back to their useful form. It is the **only known universal anti-oxidant and anti-oxidant recycler.**

I have never seen it be the solo answer for depression, but it should be an important addition or adjunct to a treatment regimen. Lipoic acid is cheap, has no known side effects, and has a variety of uses, among which is improving memory, depression, chemical sensitivity, venom neurotoxicities, chemically-induced nerve damage, radiation damage, cancer gene protection, inhibiting HIV (AIDS virus) growth helping diabetes, heavy metal poisoning (including mercury), inhibiting cataracts, hypoglycemia, Parkinson's, aging, lactic acidosis, heart and liver disease and much more.

The starting dose is 1-2 capsules 100 mg each, two or three times a day, titrated. Another name for it is thioctic acid.

REFERENCES:

Stoll S, et al, The potent free radical scavenger alpha-lipoic acid improves memory in aged mice: putative relationship to NMDA receptor deficits, PHARMACOL, BIOCHEM, BEHAV, 16(1):799-805, Dec 1993

Packer L, Witt EH, Tritschler HJ, Alpha-lipoic acid as a biological antioxidant, FREE RAD BIOL MED, 19:2; 227-250, 1995

Lozano RM, et al, Thioredoxin-linked reductive inactivation of venom neurotoxins, ARCH BIOCHEM BIOPHYS, 309(2):356-3662, Mar 1994

Mizuno M, et al, Effects of alpha-lipoic acid and dihydrolipoic acid on expression of proto-oncogene c-fos, BIOCHEM BIOPHYS RES COMM 200(2):1136-1142, Apr 29, 1991

Fomichev VI, et al, The neurohumoral systems of patients with ischemic heart disease and under emotional-pain stress: the means for their pharmacological regulation, KARDIOLOGIIA, 33(10):15-18, 3, 1993

Ramakrishnan N, et al, Radioprotection of hematopoietic tissues in mice by lipoic acid, RAD RES 130(3):360-365, Jun 1992

Altenkirch H, et al, Effects of lipoic acid in hexacarbon-induced neuropathy, NEUROTOXICOLOGY & TERATOLOGY, 12(6):619- 622, Nov-Dec 1990

Suzuki YJ, Tsuchiya M, Packer L, Thioctic acid and dihydrolipoic acid are novel anti-oxidants which interact with reactive oxygen species, FREE RAD RES COMMS, 15(5): 255-263, 1991

Bland JB, PREVENTIVE MEDICINE UPDATE, POB 1729, Gig Harbour WA, 98335, Clinician of the Month Interview, June 1990, (206)-851-3943.

DEANOL

Some depressed people get relief from a compound called deanol, short for **dimethyl aminoethanol**. It increases the content of and **enhances the action of acetylcholine.** It perks up the brain, improves learning in some LD (learning disability) victims, and improves fatigue and memory. It also has been of benefit in drug-induced movement disorders, tics, Tourette's, and other unclassifiable neurological disorders. And it is much safer than the commonly prescribed Ritalin (methylphenidate) which is potentially addicting, can potentiate arteriosclerosis, and is related to street "speed".

Extra caution should be used with deanol, as someone with manic-depressive psychosis could be precipitated into an exacerbation. It is abundant in sardines and anchovies. As a brain stimulant, it takes several weeks to attain maximum effect.

The only source I know is Bio-Tech, 1-800-345-1199, through which your physician or pharmacy can order it as DNZ-2, as 100 or 250 mg. The dose is individually titrated and combined with complementary nutrients.

REFERENCES:

Lewis JA, Young R, Deanol in learning disorders, J CLIN PHARMACOL THERAP 15:210, 1974 Miller E, Deanol in the treatment of levodopa-induced dyskinesias, NEUROLOGY 24: 116- 119, 1974.

Anonymous, Dimethylaminoethanol in the treatment of blepharospasm, N ENGL J MED, 289: 697, 1973.
Pfeiffer CC, et al, Stimulant effect of 2- dimethyl-aminoethanol, possible precursor of brain acetylcholine, SCIENCE, 126: 616-611, 1957.

Pfeiffer CC, et al, Stimulant effect of 2- dimethyl-aminoethanol, possible precursor of brain acetylcholine, SCIENCE, 126: 616-611, 1957.

Finney JW, et al, Deanol and Tourette syndrome, LANCET, 989, Oct 31, 1981.

Casey DE, Deanol in the management of involuntary movement disorders: A review, DIS NERV SYST, 38: 7-15, 1977.

Branyon DW, Deanol treatment of tics in a 10 year old girl, AM J PSYCHIATRY, 140: 7 ,950, 1983.

Marsh GR, Linnoila M, The effects of Deanol on cognitive performance and electrophysiology in elderly humans, PSYCHOPHARM, 66: 99-104, 1979.

Ansell GB, Spanner S, The effects of 2-dimethylaminoethanol on brain phospholipid metabolism, J NEUROCHEM 9: 253-263, 1962.

Perry EK, Gibson PH, Blessed G, Perry RJ, Tomlinson BE, Neurotransmitter enzyme abnormalities in senile dementia, J NEUROL SCI, 34: 247-265, 1977.

Ferris SH, Sathananthan G, Gershon S, Clark C, Senile dementia: treatment with Deanol, J AMER GERIAT SOC, vol. 25, 1977.

Millington WR, McCall AL, Wurtman RJ, Deanol acetamidobenzoate inhibits the blood-brain barrier transport of choline, ANN NEUROL 4: 302-306, 1978.

Pfeiffer CC, Jenney EH, Gallagher W, Smith RP, Beran W, Killam KF, Killam EK, Blackmore W, Stimulant effect of 2- dimethylaminoethanol, possible precursor of brain acetylcholine, SCI, 126: 610-611, 1957.

Lewis JA, Young R, A double-blind comparison of deanol and methylphenidate in children with learning disorders, Unpublished data, Riker Laboratories, 1973.

Lewis JA, Young R, Deanol in learning disorders, CLIN PHARM THER 15: 210, 1974.

DiMascio A, Finnerty RJ, Deaner in the treatment of hyperkinetic children, unpublished data, Riker Laboratories, 1973.

Miller E, Deanol in the treatment of levodopa-induced dyskinesias, NEUROL 24:116-119, 1974.

Janowsky DS, El-Yousef MK, Hubbard B, Sekerke HJ, Cholinergic reversal of manic symptoms, LANCET 1:1236-1237, 1972.

Zahniser NR, Chou D, Hanin I, Is 2-dimethylaminoethanol (deanol) indeed a precursor of brain acetylcholine ? A gas chromatographic evaluation, J PHARM EXP THERAP.

Haudrich R, Wang FLP, Clody DE et al, Increase in rat acetylcholine induced by choline or deanol, LIFE SCI 17: 975, 1975.

Re O, 2-Dimethylaminoethanol (deanol): A brief review of its clinical efficacy and postulated mechanism of action, CURR THER RES 16: 1238, 1974.

PANTETHINE

Like carnitine, pantethine is needed to move fatty acids in and out of the cell's mitochondria where energy is made. But more importantly, it has successfully lowered cholesterol and other lipids, without the nasty side effects (which include suicide) of the cholesterol-lowering drugs. Since it is not stored, we require a steady supply. Cholesterol has been lowered 20% with as little as 300 mg four times a day, and without the side effects that come from the cholesterol-lowering drugs that also compromise the chemistry of your sex hormones and brain neurotransmitters.

Do not confuse it with pantothenic acid, a relative, as the pantethine form is the preferred form (it is what we call in biochemical terms, more biologically active). Not only does high cholesterol have the potential to cause depression, but the cholesterol-lowering drugs have depression as a potential side effect. And there is no readily available measurement of pantethine. So if you have high cholesterol and depression, for sure you would want to consider a trial of it with your health professional. (Sources include Nutritional Therapeutics and other sources).

REFERENCES:

Da Col PG, et al, Pantethine in the treatment of hyper-cholesterolemia: a randomized double-blind trial versus tadenol, CURR THER RES 36:314, 1984

Maggi GC, Donati C, Griscuoli G, Pantethine: a physiological lipid-modulating agent in the treatment of hyperlipidemias, CURR THER RES, 32:380, 1982

Shinomya M, et al, Effect of pantethine on cholesterol ester metabolism in rat arterial wall, ARTEROSCLEROSIS, 36:75, 1980

Farina R, et al, Effects of pantethine on different models of experimental hyperlipidemia in rodents: a comparison with clofibrate, PHARMACOL RES COMM 14:499, 1982

Miccoli R, et al, Effects of pantethine on lipids and apolipoproteins in hypercholesterolemic diabetic and non- diabetic patients, CURR THER RES 38:545, 1984

Angelico M, et al, Improvement in serum lipid profile in hyperlipoproteinaemic patients after treatment with pantethine: a cross-over, double-blind trial versus placebo, CURR THER RES 33:1091, 1983

HERBS:
THE WONDERFUL WORLD OF WEEDS

ST. JOHN'S WORT

There are herbs that have been written about for years which have a long history of having helped depression. Herbology is one area I have little experience in. But the references show me there is validity and that we should never stop learning. We'll look at just a few that I have seen be helpful.

The most commonly cited herb for depression is **St. John's Wort** (Hypericum perforatum). There is a caution of photosensitivity with this herb. In one study they had 66% of the patients improve their depression on the substance. This shows me that I have to open my closed mind to the wonderful world of weeds. And indeed, some people with depression have reported improvement with it.

St. John's Wort (hypericum perforatum) is an example of but one of many common herbs that have been known to help depression, and researchers even know how this one works. It irreversibly **inhibits monoamine oxidase (MAO).** In other words, it slows down the metabolism or destruction of your happy hormones. So they stay around longer, improving your mood. You will recall that there are prescription anti-depressant medicines that are monoamine oxidase inhibitors. However, these are extremely dangerous and you can die from the side effects of them if you just so much as take an antihistamine or eat the wrong food. But St. John's Wort does not have these side effects.

REFERENCES:

Schmidt U, Sommer H, St. John's wort extract in the ambulatory therapy of depression. Attention and reaction ability are preserved, FORTSCHR MED 111(19): 339-342, 1993.

Woelk H, Multicentric practice study analyzing the function the functional capacity in depressive patients, FOURTH INTERNATIONAL CONGRESS ON PHYTOTHERAPY, Munich Germany, abstract SL54. Sep 10-13, 1992.

Muldner H, Zoller M, Antidepressive effect of a hypericum extract standardized to the active hypericine complex, ARZNEIM FORSCH, 34: 918-920, 1984.

Suzuki O, et al, Inhibition of monoamine oxidase by hypericicin, PLANTA MEDICA, 50: 272-274, 1984.

Harrer G, Sommer H, Treatment of mild/moderate depressions with Hypericum, PHYTOMEDICINE , 1:3-8, 1994

Holzl J, Demisch L, Gollnik B, Investigations about antidepressive and mood changing effects of Hypericum perforatum, PLANTA MED 55:643, 1989

Thiede HM, Walper A, Inhibition of MAO and COMT by hypericum extracts and hypericin, J GERIATR PSYCHIATRY NEUROL, 7(Suppl 1): S 54-56, 1994

Schlich D, et al, Treatment of depressive conditions with hypericum, PSYCHOL, 13:440-444, 1987

Sommer H, Harrer G, Placebo-controlled double-blind study examining the effectiveness of an hypericum preparation in 105 mildly depressed patients, GERIAT PSYCHIA NEUROL, 7 Suppl 1:S9-11, Oct 1994.
Abstract: One hundred and five outpatients with mild depressions of short duration were treated in a double-blind study with either 3x300 mg hypricum extract or placebo. The therapy phase was 4 weeks. The effectiveness was judged according to the Hamilton Depression Scale after 2 and 4 weeks. The values of the mean basic score in these periods

fell from 15.8 t 9.6 or 7.2 in the active group, an in the placebo group, from 15.8 to 12.3 and 11.3. The difference between active and placebo groups were statistically significant with P<.05 and P <.01 achieved after 2 and 4 weeks, respectively. In the active group, 28 of 42 patients (67%) and, in the placebo group, 13 of 47 patients (2% responded to treatment). Notable side effects were not found.

Woelk H, Burkard G, Grunwald J, Benefits and risks of the hypericum extract L1 160: drug monitoring study with 3250 patients, J GERIAT PSYCHIAT NEUROL, 7 Suppl 1: S34-8, Oct 1994.
Abstract: Effectiveness and acceptance of a 4-week treatment with hypericum extract L1 160 were investigated by 663 private practitioners. The result of the 3250 patients (76% women and 24% men), were recorded using data sheets. The age of the patients ranged from 20 to 90 years (mean 51 years). Of the patients, 49% were mildly depressed, 46% intermediate, and 3% severely depressed. In about 30% of the patients, the situation normalized or improved during therapy. Undesired drug effects were reported in 79(2.4%) patients and 48 (1.5%) discontinued the therapy.   Most frequently noted side effects were gastrointestinal irritations (0.6%), allergic reactions (0.5%), tiredness (0.4%), and restlessness (0.3%).

GINKGO BILOBA

Likewise, there is considerable data on **Ginkgo biloba** which **has improved memory, thinking, and brain blood flow.** The interesting thing is that it is so unheard-of in the U.S., yet non-toxic and able to improve poor cerebral or brain blood flow in the aging, depression-prone brain. It also, like St. John's Wort, inhibits MAO. And it is relatively free of side effects.

REFERENCES:

Wesns K, et al, A double blind, placebo-controlled trial of Ginkgo biloba extract in the treatment of idiopathic cognitive impairment in the elderly, HUM PSYCHOPHARMACOL, 2: 159-169, 19870.

Kleijnen J, et al, Ginkgo biloba for cerebral insufficiency, BR J CLIN PHARMACOL, 34: 352-58, 1992.

Kleijnen J, Knipschild P, Ginkgo biloba, LANCET 340: 1136-1139, November 7, 1992.

Foster S, Ginkgo biloba, BOTANICAL SERIES #304-GINKGO, American Botanical Counsel, Box 201660, Austin TX 78720, p. 3-7, 1990.

Vorberg G, Ginkgo biloba extract (GBE): a long-term study of chronic cerebral insufficiency in geriatric patients, CLIN TRIALS J, 22:149-157, 1985

Taillandier J, et al, Ginkgo biloba extract in the treatment of cerebral disorders due to aging, PRESSE MED, 15:1583- 1587, 1986

Emerit I, et al, Radiation-induced clastogenic factors: anticlastogenic effect of Ginkgo biloba extract, FREE RAD BIOL MED, 18:985-991, 1995

White HL, Scates PW, Cooper BR, Extracts of Ginkgo biloba leaves inhibit monoamine oxidase, LIFE SCI 58: 1315-1321, 1996

VALERIAN

Insomnia is a frequent accompaniment and sometimes a contributing cause of depression. Insomnia is common in 29-33% of the U.S. population. But the non-prescription herb **valerian** is as effective in some individuals as prescription drugs that can go on to cause addiction, like Halcion. As usual, herbal preparations costs $1/5^{th}$ that of the prescription drugs, most of which are in the class of benzodiazepines. This class of drugs includes Valium, Librium, Dalmane, Serax, Restoril, Klonopin, Xanax, and others. They work by enhancing the neurotransmitter GABA, which usually causes a hangover effect and/or addiction, something you do not get with the herb.

If you use it, get the 0.8% valeric acid which is valerian extract. Take it 1/2 hour before bed, 150-300mg.

REFERENCES:

Mennini T, et al, In vitro study on the interaction of extracts and pure compounds from Valeriana officinalis roots with GABA, benzodiazepine and barbiturate receptors in the rat brain, FITOTERAPIA, 54: 291-300, 1993.

Leathwood P, et al, Aqueous extract of valerian root (Valeriana officinalis L.) improves sleep quality in man, PHARMACOL BIOCHEM BEHAVIOR, 17: 65-71, 1982.

Balderer G, Borbely AA, Effect of valerian on human sleep, PYSCHOPHARMACOL, 87: 406-409, 1989.

Dressing H, et al, Insomnia: Are Valerian/Melissa combination of equal value to benzodiazepine? THERAPIEWOCHE, 42: 426- 436, 1992.

FOR THOSE WHO WOULD LIKE TO LEARN MORE ABOUT HERBS:

Murray MT, NATURAL ALTERNATIVES TO OVER-THE-COUNTER AND PRESCRIPTION DRUGS, William Morrow & Co., NY, 1994

Mowrey DB, THE SCIENTIFIC VALIDATION OF HERBAL MEDICINE, Cormorant Books, 1986.

Heinerman J, SCIENCE OF HERBAL MEDICINE, Bi-World Publ, POB 1144, Orem, Utah, 84057

Murray MT, THE HEALING POWER OF HERBS, Prima Publ, Rocklin CA, 1991

DOES DEPRESSION LEAD TO ALZHEIMER'S?

"Why do you also include references to Alzheimer's? I thought this book was about depression", you might ask. Depression does not necessarily lead to Alzheimer's dreaded presenile dementia or senility. But one must always bear in mind that long before someone gets a senile brain syndrome of any type, they may have depression as the only sign that the brain is vulnerable for becoming a target organ for end-stage disease.

You recall that in medicine, we mainly deal with the end result or damaged organ. Like we deal with heart disease, or kidney disease or a pancreas damaged by auto-antibodies which then manifests as diabetes. Medicine generally shuns diseases when they are more preventable or at an early stage. Instead it concentrates on "saving the day" when we get to the end stage of destruction where there is something that a drug can work on.

In the early vague stages where symptoms are not well-defined, there is no drug, except maybe tranquilizers and anti-depressants. That is when you experience the old run-around of "Come back if it gets worse or in 6 months and we'll see how it has progressed". Or you are perhaps intimidated and made to feel like a hypochondriac for wanting help with a symptom, because it is not yet bad enough to justify a recognizable label and warrant a drug.

But symptoms inevitably progress. For example, you first get hypertension. Then in a few years they find you now have lupus (and that the hypertension was a mild precursor to it). Now you are ready for the life-threatening drugs: steroids and chemotherapy, which is about all there is available for the disease if you use the non-environmental or non-cause seeking approach to medical problems. And practice guidelines do not include looking for environmental or nutritional causes at any stage, early or late. But they do include plenty of drugs. And for the depression that accompanies lupus, they also use drugs. The sad thing is that a great deal is reversible in many individuals with the techniques in this and the previous books. For as even Granny knows, a stitch in time saves nine!

Meanwhile, because of the anti-hypertensives used for the initial presentation of your disease as high blood pressure, for example, you may have gone on to get arthritis, angina, arrhythmia, migraines, or depression. Obviously, you are better off finding the cause of every symptom as soon as it rears its warning head. It stands to reason that the earlier that symptoms are addressed, the more nebulous they will be. But also they are easier to heal. Often a simple diet change and nutrient correction are all that is required to get rid of early hypertension. And clearly when you can reverse atherosclerotic lesions in heart vessels with the macrobiotic diet, clogged brain vessels should be no different (Ornish, LANCET, 1990 and Rogers SA, THE CURE IS IN THE KITCHEN).

RESOURCES:

N.E.E.D.S., 1-800-648-1380 for all items mentioned in this book, especially hard to find items, like the Phos Chol, L-glutamine powder, etc.

Emerson Ecologics, 436 Great Rd., Acton MA 01720, 1-800-654-4432 for supplements, Phos Chol, etc.

Nutritional Therapies, POB 5963, Hauppauge NY 11788, 1- 800-982-9158 for pantethine, L-glutamine, etc.

Macro Pharmaceuticals Int., 15770 W. 6th Ave, Golden CO 80401, 1-800-277-9553 for liquid homeopathic dilutions of minerals without alcohol for those who tolerate nothing else.

American Lecithin Company, 115 Hurley Rd, Unit 2B, Oxford CT 06478, 1-800-364-4416, for Phos Chol.

Cardiovascular Research, LTD, Concord CA 94524, for thioctic (lipoic) acid, 1-800-888-4585.

Nature Works, a division of ABKIT, Inc., 207 E. 94th St., 2nd Fl., NY, NY 10128, ph 1-800-843-9535 for lipoic acid.

Cambridge Nutraceuticals, 1 Liberty Sq., 10th Fl., Boston MA 02109, ph 1-800-265-2202 for glutamine.

Metabolic Maintenance Products, Sister, OR 97759, for lipoic acid and more, (541) 549-7800.

There are lots of nutrients we did not touch, like vitamins D and K, bioflavenoids, CoQ10 and more. The reason? There is a limit to the size of a book that many will read. But many aspects of these will be covered in the ongoing subscription newsletter and subsequent books, for they relate to many other diseases as well, like cancer.

So in Volume I you learned about the environmental (food, chemical, mold and Candida) causes of depression. In this volume you learned about the nutrient deficiencies, especially the importance of many orphan nutrients. Now turn to Volume II for the hormone-gut-mind connection.

VOLUME III

(CHAPTERS 8-9)

METABOLIC FACTORS

THE HORMONE, GUT AND MIND CONNECTION

CHAPTER 8

THE HORMONE AND GUT CONNECTIONS:

CAUSES AND CURES

In Volume I, we saw the food, additives, chemical, pesticide, heavy metal, Candida and mold causes of depression. Then in Volume II, we learned of the deficiencies of vitamins, minerals, amino acids, essential fatty acids and orphan nutrients that play a role in depression. Now for the hormone-gut-mind connection.

GLANDULAR GLITCHES:

THYROID

Many hormone deficiencies and excesses have profound effects on brain function. We'll start with the simpler and more common tests. But bear in mind that there are more sophisticated assays and challenge tests with which to identify glandular glitches. This is not an endocrinology text, but a great guide applicable to the majority of depression causes.

There are many hormone deficiencies or excesses that can play havoc with the brain and cause depression. The most commonly checked hormone abnormality that can cause depression is thyroid. Usually depression occurs more readily when thyroid is deficient as opposed to over-productive, but either can occur. Beside depression, hypothyroidism can cause the person to gain weight easily, to become sluggish, and usually be constipated. A sensitive TSH plus a T3 and T4 are necessary to diagnose this.

If the thyroid is possibly hyperactive and causing depression, you also need to add a T3 by RIA test for thyrotoxicosis. And for suspicion of any type of thyroid problem, also get **thyroid auto-antibodies.** For many people make antibodies that attack their own thyroid. This causes the thyroid to be mal-functioning one day, yet on the day the doctor checks the T3 and T4 it may be O.K. But if there are antibodies to it, you know there is or will be abnormal, erratic function (more on that in the leaky gut section).

And if you find a thyroid deficiency, do not think that it means that you will be on synthetic thyroid the rest of your life. But instead, find the cause of the under-active thyroid. Everyone knows the thyroid is dependent upon iodine for function. But do not forget to look at the other nutrients. For example, selenium is crucial for proper thyroid function. Yet it is also depleted when extra detoxication work is required of the body. For selenium is used up in the selenium-dependent enzyme, glutathione peroxidase. Also, selenium is often stripped from processed foods or is lacking in foods grown on selenium deficient soils. And as you learned in Volume II, it may be a lack of phosphatidyl choline that keeps the thyroid receptors from functioning properly. Your thyroid may make enough hormone and the blood tests may be normal. But because of membrane receptor damage, you may not be able to use that thyroid hormone until the membrane has been repaired (Volume II and IV). And after 26 years I must admit there are people whose blood tests are normal but they improve half a dozen symptoms with a trial of natural thyroid. This means to me that we have done a real disservice (by denying a trial of thyroid) to many who had probably made adequate thyroid to be measured by a blood test, but whose hormone molecule was defective and did not do its job in the cell.

REFERENCES:

Berry MJ, banu l, Larsen PR, Type I iodothyronine deiodinase is a selenocysteine-containing enzyme. NATURE 4:A371, 1990.

Levitt AJ, Joffe RT, Folate, vitamin B12 and thyroid function in depression, BIOLOG PSYCH, 33: 52-53, 1993.

Haggerty JJ, et al, Subclinical hypothyroidism: a modifiable risk factor for depression, AMER J PSYCH, 150: 508-510, 1993.

Pop VJM, et al, Microsomal antibodies during gestation in relation to postpartum thyroid dysfunction and depression, ACTA ENDOCRIN, 129: 26-30, 1993.

Anonymous, Subclinical hypothyroidism suspected as factor in some antidepressant resistance, FAMILY PRACTICE NEWS, 20(9): 33, May 1-14, 1990.

Barsano CP, Garces J, Iqbal, Metabolic implications of low dose triiodothyronine administration in rats: relevance to the adjunctive use of triiodothyronine in the treatment of depression, BIOLOGICAL PSYCHIATRY, 35(10): 814-23, May 15, 1994.

Cole PA, Bostwidk JM, Fajtova VT, Thyrotoxicosis in a depressed patient on L-triiodothyronine, PSYCHOSO-MATICS, 34(6): 539-40, Nov-Dec 1993.

Joffe Rt, Triiodothyronine potentiation of fluoxetine in depressed patients, CANAD J PSYCHIAT, 37(1): 48-50, Feb 1992.

PARATHYROID HORMONE

Many glandular disturbances have psychiatric symptoms. For example, the parathyroid gland consists of 4 tiny, less than pea size glands surrounding the thyroid gland in the neck. In over 400 patients with hyperparathyroidism, a quarter of them supported the fact that endocrine disturbances cause psychiatric symptoms. For more information, see lithium section in Volume I.

REFERENCES:

Joborn C, et al, Psychiatric symptomatology in patients with primary hyperparathyroidism, UPS J MED SCI 91(1):77-87, 1986.

Alarcon RD, et al, Hyperparathyroidism and paranoid psychosis: Case report and review of the literature, BR J PSYCHIAT 145:477-1984.

SEX HORMONES

Many men are depressed because they have a testosterone deficiency and, likewise, women can have a depression based on a testosterone deficiency. A simple blood test can diagnose it. In fact, the addition of a little testosterone added to estrogen replacement therapy has lifted depression and loss of sex drive.

Equally, women can have depression because estrogen, testosterone, or progesterone levels are too low. Urine and blood tests can be used to diagnose this. Some women have menopausal depression along with hot flashes, but cannot tolerate taking estrogen drugs because of breast tenderness, or vaginal bleeding, or a strong family history of cancers of the breast and reproductive organs. In that case, creams like Yamcon or Progest can be rubbed into the skin. They are made from a natural wild yam which contains a plant-produced progesterone. Once absorbed across the skin into the body it can be metabolized into progesterone or estrogen as the body needs. Since this is more natural and has not been found to have any side effects (like cancer which can be a side effect of prescribed estrogen replacement therapy, like Premarin), it is the preferred form for many women. It does take 2 to 3 months to build an adequate level, however.

Because there is so much controversy, let's pause and take a look at the issues clouding ERT or HRT. These are medicine's terms for **"estrogen replacement therapy"** or **"hormone replacement therapy"**. Every post-menopausal woman knows how she is hounded by the gynecologist to take estrogen. The arguments are that:

1. It will keep the tissues like the vagina supple and younger, so that they do not painfully dry up, making intercourse impossible. Plus,
2. estrogens lower the rate of heart attack and other arteriosclerosis symptoms. And she is reminded,
3. estrogen will lower the rate of bone loss or osteoporosis. How can we argue with such logic? Easily.

First I did about 40 pap smears a day when I was in general medicine. As a woman, I was on the look-out for clues as to what might be that elusive fountain of youth. For sure, it is not estrogen. Comparing women who had used it for years with women who had never used it, there was no correlation. The integrity of the tissues reflects the integrity of the total body health. You make less vaginal lubricating secretions just like some people make less saliva because of deficiencies in the body.

If you do need estrogen because it most easily solves your problem, then get the levels measured. For it is astounding to see the level of estrogen in the blood on the various estrogen pills or patches. It is abnormally high. It is no wonder that there is a higher cancer rate, especially of the breast and uterus, in women who take extra hormones (NEW ENGLAND JOURNAL OF MEDICINE, 332:1589-1593, 1995). I cannot figure out why most gynecologists who prescribe it seldom look at the blood levels. They are surprisingly higher than anyone would dare to intentionally use, yet they are rarely looked at. I guess there is blind faith in drugs because of concerted advertising.

In terms of the risk of cardiovascular disease, it is clearly related to diet and lifestyle. Your choice of foods and nutrient status that remains after you have detoxified your environment all day determine in large degree your cardiac aging rate. And last, to prescribe calcium and hormones for osteoporosis prevention is to be totally ignorant of the causes of osteoporosis and arteriosclerosis.

For osteoporosis is caused by lack of calcium getting into the bone, because the minerals necessary to hold calcium in the bone are deficient. But medicine does not routinely look for these common and prevalent mineral deficiencies, as you have read. Nor does it recommend changing the diet by recommending getting off **processed foods,** that further **inhibit good calcium uptake** by being high in phosphates. The phosphates that processed foods are so full of, inhibit the absorption of calcium. Yet most hospital dietitians recommend a plethora of processed foods. And rarely does the doctor recommending calcium stress the importance of exchanging processed foods for whole foods.

Clearly the prescription of **extra estrogen is carcinogenic.** In addition, rarely are the levels measured and they happen to be extraordinarily distorted from the norm. **Premarin** derives its name from a condensation of the term **pregnant mare's urine.** For this is where it is taken from, pregnant horses' urine. Somehow I think if God wanted half the population over 50 dependent for the rest of their lives on the pharmaceutical world, He would have devised a different scheme.

As for the extra calcium, because most women lack the necessary complement of accessory minerals to put calcium in the bone, it goes on to cause accelerated arteriosclerosis and aging. For when you lack the minerals (which is so common) to put the calcium in the bone, it instead goes to the **body's toxic waste site, the arteries** of the heart, brain, and elsewhere. And since physicians recommending calcium rarely look at the other minerals, they have no idea of whether or not the patient has enough of the other minerals to hold the calcium in the bone versus storing it in the arterial wall. Bare minimum they should assess the magnesium loading test, and rbc values for zinc, copper, chromium, manganese, calcium, potassium, and selenium. **So by prescribing estrogen and calcium to a nation of women, we are making them age faster toward the ultimate degenerative changes we call arteriosclerosis and cancer.** There are many infinitely more healthful options (read TIRED or TOXIC?, then WELLNESS AGAINST ALL ODDS, and subscribe to the HEALTH LETTER if you need further data).

People do not actually have to be low in hormones either in order for the hormones to be responsible for depression. For many pesticides and other environmental chemicals look like hormones in their chemical structure. Because many environmental chemicals resemble hormone receptors, they can sit in hormone receptors and damage them. Or they turn them on or off, in ways that would result in abnormal function in spite of normal levels of hormone on blood tests.

For example, it is known that many **estrogenic pesticides** have been the cause of breast cancer. So have dioxins emitted from incinerators. Likewise, these **chemicals can derange hormone function without discernible, abnormal blood tests for hormone function.** Likewise, many phthalates (plasticizers) can mimic estrogen receptors and damage them or promote unwanted change. Phthalates are the stuff that make plastics flexible, are one of the most abundant industrial contaminants in the environment, and are found in vinyl floor tiles, adhesives, plastic food tubs, plastic wraps, plastic plumbing, pesticides, leather, paper, and etc.

In these people, sometimes neutralization of the hormone effect is more successful than actually giving hormones in allopathic doses. This technique is described in THE E.I. SYNDROME REVISED, where minuscule doses of a hormone are injected just under the first layer of skin. They can turn on or turn off various psychiatric symptoms that are hormonally induced within minutes, simplifying diagnosis and treatment (references for the technique are found in THE SCIENTIFIC BASIS OF SELECTED ENVIRONMENTAL MEDICINE TECHNIQUES).

For more on hormones, refer back to the PMS section in Volume II.

REFERENCES:

Hearing Explores Threats of Estrogenic Pesticides, THE NUTRITION WEEK, 2-3, November 12, 1993.

Gerhard I, Prolonged exposure to wood preservatives induces endocrine and immunologic disorders in women, et al, AM J OBSTET GYN, 165(2): 487-488, August 1991.

Anonymous, No harm in adding a little testosterone, SCI NEWS, 147:294, May 13, 1995.

Boschert S, Testosterone loss linked with memory dysfunction, FAM PRACT NEWS, p 5, Oct 1, 1994.

Raloff J, Beyond estrogens; Why unmasking hormone mimicking pollutants proves so challenging, SCIENCE NEWS, 148:44-45, July 15, 1995.

Anonymous, Newest estrogen mimics the commonest?, ibid p47.

DHEA

DHEA, or **dehydroepiandrosterone** (de hydro epi an drost' er one), is an adrenal hormone which becomes lower with age in many people. An unsuspected deficiency of it can cause depression. The best test is an unconjugated DHEA. Do not settle for a DHEA sulfate or serum DHEA, as it is not sensitive enough, although it is the test most commonly done. For the sulfated is the DHEA that has been conjugated for the body to throw away. Whereas the unconjugated is the actual hormone that is available to the body, hence a much more sensitive indication of adequacy. Point in fact, the serum value is often normal while the unconjugated is abnormally low.

It can be supplemented with prescription DHEA which is available in less than half a dozen pharmacies throughout the United States. DHEA is also important as an anti-aging and anti-cancer hormone. Recently it has become available on non-prescription status, but I would not recommend use without monitoring effects and blood levels of unconjugated DHEA. And never forget that even if it helps, you want to nourish the adrenal gland so it can eventually make its own DHEA again. For by merely taking exogenous DHEA, you inhibit or turn off your own gland's natural production. Furthermore, DHEA can cause panic attacks, insulin resistance and other more serious consequences.

DHEA SOURCES:

College Pharmacy 1-800-888-9358

Wellness Health & Pharmacy 1-800-227-2627

408

Apothecary Pharmacy 1-800-869-9160

Apothecure, Inc 1-800-969-6601

REFERENCES:

Regelson W, Kalimi M, Dehydroepiandrosterone (DHEA) - - The multifunctional steroid. II Effects on CNS, cell proliferation, metabolic and vascular, clinical and other effects. Mechanism of action? ANN NY ACAD SCI, 719:564-574, 1994

Shealy CN, DHEA: THE YOUTH AND HEALTH HORMONE, Keats Publishing, New Canaan CT, 1996

Sahelian R, DHEA: A PRACTICAL GUIDE, Avery Publ.

Kalimi M, Regelson W, THE BIOLOGICAL ROLE OF DEHYDROEPIANDROSTERONE, de Guyter, NY 1990

Mortola JF, Yen SS, The effects of oral DHEA on endocrine-metabolic parameters in post-menopasusal women, J CLIN ENDOCRINAOL METAB 71:696-704, 1990

Fava M, Rosenbaum JF, et al, DHEA-sulfate/cortisol ratio in panic disorder, PSYCHIATRY RES 28:345-350, 1989

Leblhuber F, et al, Dehydroepiandrosterone sulfate in Alzheimer's disease, LANCET 336:449, 1990

OTHER ADRENAL HORMONES

This is not designed to be a textbook on endocrinology, but it is important to know that many other adrenal hormones also play a role in depression. You might want to start with the cortrosyn stimulation test to determine whether you have a lazy adrenal, then progress to other adrenal parameters, like MHPG (3-methoxy-4-hydroxy-phenylethlyleneglycol), a metabolite of noradrenaline. A 24 hour urine for metanephrines and catecholes can identify **adrenal tumors,** etc.

Depression, chronic fatigue, fibromyalgia, PMS, chemical sensitivity and many other types of non-descript problems have been helped by finding the **lazy adrenal syndrome** first described by Dr. William Jeffreys. Dr. Jeffreys is a pioneer endocrinologist at the University of Virginia School of Medicine in Charlottesville. He described it in the NEW ENGLAND JOURNAL OF MEDICINE in 1995 and in 1981 wrote his medical textbook, SAFE USES OF CORTISONE. The directions for the lazy adrenal and the cortrosyn stimulation test are in TIRED OR TOXIC?

Depression has also been seen with too high a level of the adrenal hormone, cortisol. In one interesting study researchers used a drug, ketoconazole (Nizoral Rx). When they saw that it also improved depression in patients, they assumed that it was the cortisol-lowering properties of the drug that relieved the depression. However, those of you in the know, realize that ketoconazole (Nizoral) is a strong systemic anti-fungal used to eradicate Candida. And Candida intestinal overgrowth is a much more common cause of depression that we see compared with cortisol elevation.

410

Who knows? Maybe these patients had both mechanisms contributing to their depression.

REFERENCES:

Anand A, Malison R, et al, Antiglucocorticoid treatment of refractory depression with ketoconazole: A case report, BIOLOG PSYCHIATRY 37(5): 338-340, 1995.

Thakore J, Dinan TG, Cortisol synthesis inhibition: A new treatment strategy for the clinical and endocrine manifestations of depression, BIOLOG PSYCHIATRY 37:364-368, 1995.

Stalleicken D, et al, Observation of the course of cognitive deficits. Results of a multi-center study involving psychological test operations, NEUROLOGIE PSYCHIATRIE, Special Issue 1:64-69.

Stokes PE, et al, Pituitary-adrenal function in depressed patients, J PSYCHIATR RES 12:271-281, 1995.

Bloomingdale KL, et al, The dexamethasone suppression test and platelet monoamine oxidase activity as predictors of psychosis in depression, BIOL PSYCHIATRY, 21: 390-393, 1986.

AND DON'T OVERLOOK
INHALED NASAL STEROIDS

Allergy sufferers are often prescribed nasal steroids. They are administered by a little "puffer" called an inhaler, usually 2 squirts in each nostril 2-4 times a day. They are meant to decrease nasal congestion and allergic symptoms. Usually they are only needed by people who have not addressed their total load of stressors (see Total Load)

They are marketed as safe, but there are people who get serious depression from systemic absorption of these. So you may want a trial off from them. Besides it will force you to find all the causes of your allergies and get rid of drugs once and for all.

Also inhaled nasal steroids can give depression by another mechanism. They can cause overgrowth of Candida in the mouth and throat (Willey RT, Milner JR, et al, Bechomethasone diproprionate aerosol and oropharyngeal Candidiasis, BR J DIS CHEST 70: 32-38, 1976).

REFERENCES:

Goldstein ET, Preskom SH, Mania triggered by a steroid nasal spray in a patient with stable bipolar disorder, AM J PSYCHIAT 146:1076-1077, 1989.

Lewis LD, Cochrane GM, Psychosis in a child inhaling budesonide, LANCET 2: 634, 1983.

Meysboom RHB, Budesonide and psychic side effects, ANN INTERN MED 109: 683, 1988.

MELATONIN

Melatonin is a hormone produced by the pineal gland in the center of the brain. A deficiency of melatonin can cause depression. It is also the hormone necessary to stave off jet lag and correct insomnia in some (again, depending upon their biochemical deficiencies and needs). It can be purchased in the health food store and there are several reputable sources.

BUT CAUTION: I have seen a half dozen people who got wicked depression from taking melatonin. So always keep an open mind when evaluating something new.

Also, Prozac (fluoxetine) can react adversely with melatonin and neither has been studied that long, much less together. Therefore, I would not mix them.

REFERENCES:

Rimland B, Melatonin: Researchers say hormone markedly improves sleep, behavior of developmentally disabled children, AUTISM RESEARCH REVIEW, 4182 Adams Ave., San Diego CA 92116, 8(3):1-2, 1994.

Raloff J, Drug of darkness, SCI NEWS, 147:399-301, May 13, 1995.

Rao ML, et al, Blood serotonin, serum melatonin and light therapy in healthy subjects and in patients with non-seasonal depression, ACTA PSYCHIATR SCAND, 86: 127-132, 1992.

Anonymous, Chronic fatigue syndrome may be linked to hormonal deficiency, INFECT DIS NEW , 1,4, February 1992.

Studd J, Gender and Depression, LANCET, 340: 794, September 26, 1995.

Thompson C, et al, Seasonal affective disorder and season-dependent abnormalities of melatonin suppression by light, LANCET, 336: 703-706, September 22, 1990.

Demitrack MA, et al, Evidence for impaired activation of the hypothalamic pituitary-adrenal axis in patients with chronic fatigue syndrome, J CLIN ENDOCRIN METAB, 73:1224-1234, 1991.

Rozenwaig R, Grad BR, Ochoa J, The role of melatonin and serotonin in aging, MED HYPOTH, 23:337-352, 1987.

Souetre E, Rosenthal N, Ortonne JP, Affective disorders, light and melatonin, PHOTODERMATOLOGY, 5:107-109, 1988.

Waldhauser F, Ehrhart B, Forster E, Clinical aspects of the melatonin action: Impact of development, aging, and puberty, involvement of melatonin in psychiatric disease and importance of neuroimmunoendocrine interactions, NEURO-IMMUNOL REV, 671-681, 1993.

Pierpaoli W, Regelson W, Colman C, THE MELATONIN MIRACLE, Simon & Schuster, NY, 1995.

Childs PA, et al, Effect of fluoxetine on melatonin in patients with seasonal affective disorder and matched controls, BR J PSYCHIATRY 166: 196-198, 1995.

Huether G, et al, Effects of indirectly acting 5-HT receptor agonists on circulating melatonin levels in rats, EUR J PHARMACOL, 238: 249-254, 1993.

Birdsall TC, The biological effects and clinical uses of pineal hormone melatonin, ALT MED REV 1;2:94-102, 1996

GUT LEVEL MEDICINE:

PANCREAS

The pancreas can be under- or over- active. When it is under-active and does not secrete enough insulin, you have diabetes. Or you can have pancreatic insufficiency in terms of not secreting sufficient pancreatic enzymes like amylase, pancrease, and lipase to be able to properly digest foods, especially fats. Both affect the brain.

More importantly the pancreas can hyper-secrete especially when it is deficient in chromium, zinc, or manganese. When it over secretes or puts out too much insulin; it causes rapid drops in the blood sugar that can produce depression as the only symptom. This depression can be very severe, or can lead to mania. Or it can be accompanied by unexplainable mood swings, headaches, dizziness, weakness, intense cravings, and a host of other symptoms. A **6 hour glucose tolerance test** is necessary in order to determine if you have hypoglycemia.

Also it is important for you to know that the pancreas can become an allergic target organ just like the brain can, or the nose. For example, if the nose is allergic when you breathe pollen or drink milk, the nose hyper-secretes and you have increased mucous or phlegm. When the pancreas is the allergic target organ, it also hyper-secretes. But since its normal production is not of phlegm but insulin, it makes extra amounts of insulin. When this happens, the insulin bottoms out the sugar and a person can become clammy, have unexplained and sometimes violent mood swings, headaches and/or depression.

Some people have what we call a flat glucose tolerance curve on a 6 hour glucose tolerance test. In other words, the sugar never rises past 120 mg % even when they drink the sugar for the test. This means they never get an elevated sugar level from a meal. The consequence is that this may drive them to eat constantly, never being satiated or satisfied. Some people will put out an extra amount of insulin 3 or 4 hours after a meal. That is when they become extremely sleepy, or depressed, or headachey, or just plain exhausted. These people find that if they eat every few hours, it prevents this from happening. However, it is better to find out what the triggers and deficiencies for malfunction of the pancreas are (like chromium or manganese).

Sometimes it does not matter how low the sugar is, but **how fast it falls.** For a dramatic change in blood sugar can also create depression. For example, one study of patients in whom they could not find a rational explanation for their mental symptoms, showed that **rapid fall hypoglycemia** was the cause for depression, fatigue, sugar cravings, PMS and many other symptoms that they had (Budd ML, Hypoglycemia and personality, COMPLEMENTARY THERAPIES IN MEDICINE, 1994; 2:142-146).

Sometimes certain foods are eaten that the person is allergic to and that makes the pancreas hyper-secrete. For example, they could be allergic to wheat. So when they eat wheat the pancreas over-secretes insulin and they get a hypoglycemic depression. If they eat the same number of calories but from a different antigenic source, like rice, millet or buckwheat, they have no reaction. Or they are breathing molds that they are allergic to and the pancreas is the target organ rather than the nose. For this you can receive hypo-sensitization injections after testing has provoked the hypoglycemia.

Provocation-neutralization testing, as described in THE E.I. SYNDROME REVISED, will tell you if an ingested food, chemical, or mold triggers the hypoglycemia; for when testing it, it can duplicate the symptom. The actual medical paper describing the skin testing technique and published in the U.S. government's N.I.H. journal, is reprinted in the back of TIRED OR TOXIC?

Hypoglycemia is so common, and so commonly a cause of depression, that it is safe to say that probably **no one should be put on a life-time of anti-depressant drugs without a 6 hour glucose tolerance test.** Unfortunately, a 4 hour test is much too short to diagnose the problem, since hypoglycemia often does not occur until the 5th or 6th hour. Also you should see your results. For we have seen far too many that were abnormal, but patients were told they were normal. The proof of the pudding is that when it was corrected, they improved. The parameters of a **normal** 6 hour glucose tolerance test include:

1. You should not have induced your depression, mood swings or other symptoms during the test. So keep a diary of how you feel during the test. Unfortunately, medicine does not require a diary as part of the interpretation of the test, although it is an important component.
2. The starting value should be between 85-110 mg %.
3. ½ hour after drinking the corn sugar solution (and you corn-allergic people must remember that this is also a corn test for you), the sugar should be between 120-150 mg %.
4. At 1 and 2 hours, it should be in the range of 120-150. More importantly, the curve from start to 2 hours, should all be in an upward direction. In other words, each succeeding number should be higher.

417

5. At 3 hours the curve can start going down, but not more than 30 points in an hour. 80-130 mg % is the permissible range.
6. At hours 4, 5, and 6, the values should hover between 80-110 mg %.

What should raise your suspicion are (1) adverse symptoms during the test, (2) a flat curve that never goes about 120 mg %, (3) fast dives of more than 30 points in an hour, and (4) any dips below 75 mg %. If you have any of these abnormalities, you should next consult a physician to determine if you have diabetes or hypoglycemia, a problem of malabsorption, a pancreatic tumor, or a pancreas which is an allergic target organ.

REFERENCES:

Wilkerson CF, Recurrent migrainoid headaches associated with spontaneous hypoglycemia, AM J MED SCI, 218: 209, 1949.

Ford CV, Bray GA, Swedloff RS, A psychiatric study of patients referred with a diagnosis of hypoglycemia, AMER J PSYCHIATRY, 133: 290-94, 1976.

Anonymous, Cognitive function in diabetes affected by hypoglycemia, not hyperglycemia, INTERN MED WORLD REP, 10:13, 46, July 1995.

CHROMIUM IS CRUCIAL
FOR HYPOGLYCEMIA CONTROL

Logically we have put chromium in the mineral section. But it is so crucial to the control of glucose, insulin and the resultant hypoglycemia, that it deserves special mention here. There is much data concerning the ability of chromium to regulate not only sugars but lipid (cholesterol) metabolism. Yet it is commonly deficient. Thus it amazes me how medicine could escape testing every person for it, much less those with diabetes, obesity, high cholesterol, arteriosclerosis, hypoglycemia, and depression. For these are **late** symptoms of chromium deficiency. As physicians, we should be concerned with prevention or early symptoms at best.

For obviously, we have missed the boat once the patient progresses to a terminal symptom of disordered glucose and lipid metabolism. For that is when the labels emerge like diabetic gangrene, cataracts, blindness, neuropathy, kidney disease, or he has a heart attack or stroke, or gets senile or "organic brain disease" with depression.

REFERENCES:

Anderson RA, et al, Supplemental chromium effects on glucose, insulin, glucagon and urinary chromium losses in subjects consuming controlled low-chromium diets, AM J CLIN NUTR, 54: 909-916, 1991.

Anderson RA, et al, Supplemental chromium effects on glucose, insulin, glucagon and urinary chromium losses in subjects consuming controlled low-chromium diets, AM J CLIN NUTR, 54: 909-916, 1991.

Foster DW, Insulin resistance – a secret killer? N ENG J MED, 320: 733-734, 1989.

Jeejeebhoy KN, et al, Chromium deficiency, glucose intolerance, and neuropathy reversed by chromium supplementation, in a patient receiving long-term total parenteral nutrition, AM J CLIN NUTR, 30:531-538, 1977.

Martinez OB, et al, Dietary chromium and effect of chromium supplementation on glucose tolerance of elderly Canadian Women, NUTR RES, 5:609-620, 1985.

Mossop RT, Effects of chromium (III) on fasting blood glucose, cholesterol and cholesterol HDL levels, in diabetics, CENTR AFR J MED 29:80-82, 1983.

Mertz W, Chromium in human nutrition: A review, J NUTR 123: 626-633, 1993.

Glinsman WH, et al, Plasma chromium after glucose administration, SCIENCE (Washington DC) 152:1243-1245, 1966.

Haylock SJ, et al, The relationship of chromium to the glucose tolerance factor II, J INORG BIOCHEM 19:105-117, 1983.

Anderson RA, Polansky MM. Effect of chromium supplementation on insulin binding and C-peptide values of hypoglycemic human subjects, AM J CLIN NUTR, 41: 841-848, 1985.

Anderson RA. Chromium intake, absorption and excretion of subjects consuming self-selected diets, AM J CLIN NUTR, 41: 1177-83, 1985.

CRUSHING CRAVINGS

Do you want to lose that urge to kill when someone gets between you and your favorite food? Do you want to stop being obsessed with where your next food fix will come from? Would you like to have days free of preoccupation with food, so you could concentrate on more important things than when you'll get your next coke, coffee or goodie? Are you scared by your increase in girth? Then first you need to understand why you have cravings.

We rarely see animals in the wild who are over-weight, depressed, walking on crutches or sucking down Motrins or Darvons. That's because they live by instinct. If they are thirsty, they drink. If they are sick they fast or change their nests. But we have lost many of our protective instincts. If we are thirsty it is usually because we need to balance too much salt, or we drink to satiate a sweet craving, or we drink to wake up or drink to relax. We rarely live by instinct, because it has been submerged by our addictions. Then the addictions cause further symptoms that we suppress with drugs.

When you think about it, there are basically six categories of **causes for cravings:**

1. One, the individual craves because he is **eating out of balance.** For example, the person who eats too many processed high salt foods will crave sugars to balance it. Too high a fat diet will also cause a craving of either sugars or salts or both. These people frequently disgust themselves because they eat to the point of pain even when they are not hungry. They need to nip the cycle of too high a salt, fat, or sugar diet in the bud. One of the

quickest things to do is start a diet of whole foods and greatly reduce the processed foods. What are whole foods? Things like brown rice and fresh vegetables and beans (directions in MACRO MELLOW).

2. The second reason for cravings you could kill for is **hypoglycemia**, or low blood sugar. This can disguise itself as depression, headaches, horrid fatigue, or vicious mood swings, for example. And hypoglycemia can have many causes. But the commonest is a combination of too many sweets, coffee, alcohol, and other processed foods, food additives like MSG, large meals, late meals so that the pancreas never gets adequate rest time, and frequent snacking; again, literally **wearing out** the pancreas.

3. A third cause of insatiable cravings is an overgrowth of a yeast in the intestines call **Candida**. This yeast often gets a head start in the gut after you have had a bout of antibiotics. But other medications such as ulcer and stomach prescriptions to decrease the acid in the stomach, birth control pills, and prednisone can do it. Since the yeasts thrive on sugars, but also need them to survive, they can cause you to crave sweets. But at the same time these very sweets cause yeasts to grow even faster, thus causing you to crave even more. A vicious cycle.

You can padlock the refrigerator door, but it will be futile. For you are mercilessly driven to satisfy that craving. The treatment is to go on the yeast program that is outlined in THE E.I. SYNDROME, REVISED. Temporarily cut out all sweets (including fruits) and to replace processed foods with whole grains and vegetables, and eat beans or fish, fowl or meat. Other yeasts, bacteria, protozoa and parasites can also take over in the gut causing intestinal

422

dysbiosis and the leaky gut as you will discover in the next section.

4. The 4th common reason for wicked uncontrollable cravings is by far the sneakiest: unidentified **nutrient deficiencies**. At first you might think that could not apply to you, because you live in the land of plenty and eat a wide variety of foods. But we have the dubious distinction of being the first generation of man ever to eat so many processed foods.

    For example, to make bread nowadays, white flour is used. To make this highly processed food, nutritious whole wheat is ground into flour, then bleached to make it white. Unfortunately, this process reduces the minerals such as magnesium, chromium, and copper by as much as 80% . And what can a chromium deficiency cause? The very hypoglycemia that caused your cravings, for starters. And a deficiency of all three minerals (which is very common, since most people eat bread every day) can cause high cholesterol, and many other symptoms.

    In fact, the reason many people have high cholesterol is because they do not have all the minerals needed to properly metabolize their cholesterol. But instead of discovering the biochemical cause behind the high cholesterol, diets of more processed foods (margarines egg-beaters, etc.,) are actually prescribed by physicians. And to compound the error, expensive cholesterol-lowering medications then potentiate loss of further nutrients in the work of detoxication. For recall that every drug uses up nutrients via the body's detoxification of it. These nutrients could have been used to prevent cancer or metabolize cholesterol, as examples. And these medications, by interfering with the cholesterol metabolism, can go on to potentiate Alzheimer's (early senility), early heart attacks, depression, suicide, and degenerative disease.

So how do you correct this? Have your doctor draw your vitamin and mineral levels as described for him and you (Volume IV). And once the deficiencies are diagnosed and corrected, make sure you are on a diet of whole real foods that are rich in these nutrients so you never get that way again.

5. There are other causes for cravings as well. But the fifth category is one of hidden or unsuspected **food sensitivities.** For example, it is common for many people to be driven by cravings when they eat any food containing wheat. In other words, they can eat two different foods each with the same number of calories. But if they have the pancreas as an allergic target organ for one food and not the other, the allergenic food will cause a larger insulin secretion.

One woman, presented at the Annual Scientific Session of the American Academy of Environmental Medicine by Dr. William J. Rea, had such severe uncontrollable hypoglycemia, that a major medical center removed part of her pancreas in an attempt to correct this life-threatening condition. Her sugars would drop so precipitously that she would become comatose. When even this drastic maneuver failed to control her hypoglycemia, she was evaluated by Dr. Rea in Dallas. Her sugar could be precipitously dropped by specific foods and mold exposures. Once the causes were identified, she then had control of her sugars for the first time in her life. And as we have repetitiously stressed, control of symptoms by the patient is key in environmental medicine.

6. **Chemical exposures** are common triggers for the pancreas to over-react, too. Not only can pesticides cause acute pancreatitis, but severe hunger and or hypoglycemia. This chemical overload can come from such common sources as from auto exhaust fumes, new carpet, gas furnaces, paint, and other out-gassing constituents of the normal environment. Everyday products outgas formaldehyde, toluene, xylene and other hydrocarbons that abnormally stimulate the brain's appetite center or the pancreas in those affected. Some people are ravenous when they are in certain chemically-overloaded environments, like shopping malls, their own homes with the furnace on, recently renovated offices, pesticided areas, or hotels.

All of the above have been detailed in TIRED OR TOXIC? and WELLNESS AGAINST ALL ODDS and the SCIENTIFIC BASIS OF SELECTED ENVIRONMENTAL MEDICINE TECHNIQUES. And they contain the scientific references for statements in this article for interested physicians. Isn't it interesting that some of the same factors that can cause the pancreas to function abnormally are some of the very same triggers for abnormal brain function and depression?

So next time you have a **craving,** look at it as a **gift** or an **early warning.** For it is the only way your body has of alerting you that you are eating wrong, have hypoglycemia, intestinal dysbiosis, or have an undiscovered nutrient deficiency or food or chemical sensitivity. Luckily, by discovering and correcting the causes early, you may just be staving off that first heart attack from an undiagnosed magnesium deficiency or whatever other symptom would have been next. For by ignoring and improperly feeding your craving, you ignore the real cause of your craving, and allow the problems to progress. You are actually **lucky if you have depression** versus a heart attack! You have been given a gift. You have the opportunity of fixing what's broken. Some people are not given that option; they just die.

GUT LEVEL MEDICINE:

THE LEAKY GUT SYNDROME

It should be no surprise to anyone that if the colon or the gut is not healthy then the rest of the body cannot be. For this is where all food and nutrients are absorbed. Furthermore, if the gut becomes damaged or leaky, then it allows bacterial products of putrefaction and toxins to get into the bloodstream that not only make people tired and depressed, but overload the liver thus leaving it less able to detoxify everyday chemicals. In turn, these chemicals back up in the system and can also lead to depression. So by having a sick or leaky gut, you accentuate depression by many different pathways or routes.

HEALING FROM THE INSIDE OUT

The purpose of the gastrointestinal tract (gut) is multi-fold. (1) It digests foods, (2) absorbs small food particles to be converted into energy, (3) carries nutrients like vitamins and minerals attached to carrier proteins across the gut lining into the bloodstream, (4) contains a major part of the chemical detoxification system of the body, and (5) synthesizes immuno-globulins or antibodies that act as the first line of defense against infection.

The leaky gut syndrome is an extremely common problem, yet is seldom tested for. It represents a hyperpermeable intestinal lining. In other words, large spaces develop between the cells of the gut wall that then allow bacteria, toxins and foods to leak in. This might sound good, but it is actually a double-edged sword.

INFLAMMATION CAUSES LEAKY GUT

Once the gut lining becomes inflamed or damaged, its functions become impaired. The spaces open up and allow large food antigens, for example, to be absorbed into the body. Normally, the body "sees" only small, tiny food antigens. When it sees these new, large ones, they are foreign to the body's defense system. So an attack results in the production of antibodies against these once harmless foods.

Once antibodies against foods are produced, they often resemble antigen receptors in common body parts. If, for example, an antibody directed toward potato recognizes a knee receptor that resembles it, the antibody can do many things like attach to the joint. This then turns on an inflammatory reaction where a person may suddenly have arthritis that is induced by ingesting a food that used to be harmless. Or, if antibodies end up in the lungs, a person may have asthma and unsuspected food allergy may be one of the triggers. Food allergies can precipitate symptoms in any organ at any time, once the gut develops these large, leaky spaces.

Furthermore, these large spaces allow the absorption of toxins that normally would not penetrate the protective barrier of the gut. Then toxins may overload the liver so that chemicals cannot be detoxified. Now the person has food and chemical sensitivities. And as you will learn, a worse allergy mediated by auto-immune auto-antibodies can be initiated, as well.

It might sound like a good thing that the gut can become leaky. It might be assumed that it would enable the body to absorb more amino acids, essential fatty acids, minerals and vitamins. In fact, the opposite is true. Because in order for the body to absorb a mineral, a carrier protein must be attached. This protein hooks onto the mineral and actually carries it across the gut wall into the bloodstream. But when the bowel lining is damaged through inflammation, these **nutrient carrier proteins get damaged** as well. The result is **malabsorption.** So in addition to new food and chemical allergies and auto-immune diseases, the leaky gut victim may develop mineral and vitamin deficiencies, in spite of taking adequate levels of them. He would be lucky to get away with depression as his only symptom!

BUGS, DRUGS, FOOD AND MOOD
PRECIPITATE SYMPTOMS

What can cause the inflammation that leads to the leaky gut syndrome? Examples include (1) abnormal flora (e.g., bacteria, parasites, protozoa and yeasts), (2) chemicals that irritate the gut (e.g. ingested alcohol and food additives or inhaled xylene), and (3) food allergens, (4) emotions, and (5) genetic and acquired enzyme deficiencies (e.g. lactose deficiency and celiac disease), and more. (You might say the causes are **bugs, drugs, food, and mood!**)

For example, when people take antibiotics they are at risk of developing overgrowth of antibiotic-resistant yeast or fungi (e.g. Candida). Likewise, it is known in medicine that antibiotics can cause overgrowth of Clostridia difficile, an organism that can cause relentless colitis with diarrhea.

429

Or a diet high in sweets, alcohol and caffeine can irritate the gut lining. Or, if a person has a lactase deficiency and ingests dairy products in spite of symptoms, a leaky gut can be triggered. For a person with acquired celiac disease, eating barley, oats, rye or wheat can cause a chronic inflammation of the gut lining with serious **malabsorption.** Some people are sensitive to fermented foods (e.g., alcohol, bread, catsup, cheese, mayonnaise, salad dressings and vinegar), or anything that has been aged, fermented or pickled and contains mold allergens.

Others are irritated by processed foods and the chemicals in them. Some intestinal linings can be inflamed secondary to the use of prednisone and other steroids and from food or water poisoning with such organisms as Giardia lamblia, Klebsiella, Citrobacter or Helicobactor.

But one of the main causes of leaky gut syndrome is a classification of medications called **non-steroidal, anti-inflammatory drugs (NSAIDs).** This includes a large number of non-prescription and prescription medications that are used for various types of aches/pains and sprains, arthritis, fibromyalgia, and premenstrual syndrome.

There are many over-the-counter, non-prescription drugs in the NSAID classification. These include aspirin, ibuprofen (Motrin, Advil) and naproxen sodium (Aleve, formerly prescription Naprosyn). NSAIDs are a direct, major cause of the leaky gut syndrome, because they inflame the intestinal lining and cause a widening of the spaces between cells.

CONSEQUENCES ARE SERIOUS

* When the gut is inflamed it does **not absorb nutrients** and foods properly, so fatigue and bloating can occur.

* When large food particles are absorbed, **food allergies** and new symptoms are created (e.g., arthritis or fibromyalgia).

* When the gut is inflamed, **carrier proteins are damaged**, so malabsorption and nutrient deficiencies occur. These can cause any symptom (e.g., magnesium deficiency-induced angina, copper deficiency-induced high cholesterol).

* When the detoxification pathways that line the gut are compromised, **chemical sensitivity** can arise. Furthermore, the leakage of toxins overburdens the liver so that the body is less able to handle everyday chemicals.

* When the gut lining is inflamed, the protective coating of your own gut antibodies can be lost. With loss of the secretory immunoglobin A, the body becomes more vulnerable to **infections** in the intestines from bacteria, protozoa, viruses and yeasts (e.g. Candida).

* When the intestinal lining is inflamed, bacteria and yeast (there are hundreds of species in the intestine) can **translocate**. In other words, they can pass from the gut cavity into the bloodstream and set up infection anywhere else in the body, including the brain (Berg 1988, Deitch 1987).

* When there is the formation of **auto-antibodies**, sometimes the antigens that leak across the gut wall look similar to antigens on tissues. So when the protective antibody is made to attack, it also attacks the tissues. This is how auto-immune

431

diseases get started. Lupus, multiple sclerosis, rheumatoid arthritis, myocarditis, cardiomyopathy cause dermato-myositis, iritis, thyroiditis are some of the members of this ever-growing category of mysterious "incurable" diseases.

Now you can begin to appreciate another mechanism for how the **sick get sicker** when the real cause of symptoms is masked by drugs and not looked for. For if the leaky gut is chalked up to "irritable bowel disease" or "spastic colon" or "nervous colon", as it often is, the victim is on the fast road to illness.

CAUSES OF LEAKY GUT

Intestinal dysbiosis (Candida, etc.)
Medications (NSAIDs, etc.)
Food allergy
Chemical sensitivity
Celiac disease, malabsorption
Auto-immune disease
Digestive insufficiencies
Poor diet
Nutritional deficiencies
and more

BUT THE LEAKY GUT CAUSES

Food allergy
Chemical sensitivity
Brain fog/toxic encephalopathy
Auto-immune disease (RA*, etc.)
Nutritional deficiencies
Labelitis (CFS*, FM*, etc.)
IBS*

Depression
and more

* RA=rheumatoid arthritis, CFS=chronic fatigue syndrome,
  RM=fibromyalgia, IBS=irritable bowel syndrome

COMMON SCENARIO FOR LEAKY GUT

An otherwise healthy person might take an antibiotic for a sore throat. The antibiotic not only goes to the throat, but also through the entire system, killing off beneficial bacteria that normally inhabit the intestines. When these bacteria are killed, the normally antibiotic-resistant fungi that remain have no competition. They grow uninhibited in large numbers, inflame the intestinal lining, and cause leaky gut.

Then, when antigens leak across, the victim may develop new food allergies, for example, resulting in arthritis, headaches, asthma or any symptom. He may start having gas, bloating, pain, alternating diarrhea and constipation, which is often labeled "irritable bowel syndrome" or "spastic colon". In fact, it is actually a cover-up for the honest answer, "We don't know why you have gas, bloating, and indigestion, and we never look for environmental and nutritional causes".

Many medical specialties do this renaming or labeling of symptoms. **Chronic fatigue means the same: "We don't know why you are chronically tired, and we do not look for environmental and nutritional causes."** Migraine just means they don't know why you have blinding headaches, and they don't look for environmental and nutritional causes, etc. What does interstitial cystitis mean? Or chronic prostatitis, or sarcoidosis, fibromyalgia, lupus, or attention deficit disorder, or depression?

Anyway, with the leaky gut the carrier proteins get damaged so then there is poor absorption of minerals. This leads to fatigue, inability to concentrate, multiple chemical sensitivities, depression and other symptoms. Or, they can develop further infection with these fungi and other organisms as the gut lining becomes more debilitated. These toxins overload the liver-detoxification pathways and suddenly the person is reactive to chemicals that never bothered him before. If the brain is the chief target organ, depression may be the primary symptom.

So what do people do who have arthritis, asthma, brain fog, chronic fatigue, chemical sensitivities, headaches, depression, irritable bowel and more? They usually go to various doctors, few of whom will ever test for leaky or hyperpermeable gut.

LEAKY GUT SYNDROME AND FIBROMYALGIA
WHAT IS THE CONNECTION?

There are catch-all or cop-out terms in medicine now that are used as an easy way to label disease without having to identify the environmental triggers or biochemical defects as causes. Instead of discovering the real source of the problem, symptoms are collected and given a mysterious new name. Then drugs are prescribed to mask the symptoms. Chronic fatigue syndrome, premenstrual syndrome and many other disorders fit this description. They have no known cause, no curative treatments and no definitive diagnostic tests to prove them.

A similar disease term is fibromyalgia. It is diagnosed by a history of bizarre aches and pains that can move over the body or stay in certain places. No amount of medication seems to help. Usually there are trigger points that are sensitive and out of proportion to anything that has happened to the body. These can be found by palpating different areas. Obligatory diagnostic criteria for fibromyalgia are general aches, pains, stiffness in 3 or more sites for 3 or more months, tender points, and no other explanation for the symptoms.

Minor criteria include disturbed sleep, fatigue, paresthesias, pain, headaches, and irritable bowel (often the cause!) (Goldenberg DL, Fibromyalgia syndrome, J AMER MED ASSOC, 257:20, 2782-2787, May 22/29, 1987; and editorial, Fibromyalgia, JAMA, ibid 2802-2803).

The conventional medical treatment for fibromyalgia consists of non-steroidal, anti-inflammatory drugs (NSAIDs) from ibuprofen to naproxen sodium and countless others. These NSAIDs are heavily used in medicine when we have no idea how to cure a problem. They turn down the body's inflammatory healing response to diminish pain. This makes the person think that they are beneficial. But, for example, when NSAIDs are used for arthritis, they actually accelerate joint deterioration (references in HEALTH LETTER). And NSAID drugs do nothing to isolate the cause or get rid of disease. They are used as a **mainstay of masking,** not treatment. And they can actually cause or initiate fibromyalgia, and worsen fibromyalgia once it has started. **In essence, the very drugs most commonly prescribed actually cause the disease; hence they guarantee it will get worse.**

Now you know many facts which are common causes of resistant symptoms. NSAIDs cause widening between cells in the intestinal or gut lining. This is called **intestinal hyperpermeability or the leaky gut syndrome.** These large spaces allow toxins, bacterial products and foods to pass into the bloodstream. When the body "sees" these new or foreign particles, it mounts an attack and starts sending antibodies to fight them. Hence, new food allergies, for example, can surface. And food allergies can mimic any symptom.

When the body makes antibodies to fight against bacterial and food products, these happen to have antigenic sites that are similar to many of the body's proteins. So, when people eat certain foods, the antigens made, which subsequently cross into the bloodstream, find similar looking antigenic sites in the body, such as on muscles and bones. Then, these auto-antibodies start attacking those areas, causing inflammatory reactions. The resultant pain and body aches are classic fibromyalgia symptoms. But, since wheat, for example, never caused these people to ache before and they've eaten it every day of their lives, it is the last thing they are suspicious of.

Furthermore, bacterial toxins that leak through the gut can damage the liver and reduce its ability to handle other chemicals in the environment. So, now people suddenly have chemical sensitivities, complete with brain fog and depression, as well.

People vary tremendously in the causes of their fibromyalgia. However, when looking at cases of "untreatable", "incurable" fibromyalgia that improved, there is a common thread. Most people affected have hidden dust, mold, and pollen allergies, as well as headaches, sinusitis, asthma or post nasal drip as milder symptoms for which they normally would not have consulted a physician. In fact, all of them, without fail, have had vitamin or mineral deficiencies, as well as hidden mold, food and chemical sensitivities.

Most importantly, people need to remember that there are tools to diagnose and treat the causes of fibromyalgia. No longer do people have to be a diagnostic puzzle, forever living on drugs. Fibromyalgia is now curable in the era of molecular and environmental medicine.

There is more information about the diagnosis and treatment of the leaky gut syndrome as well as references in THE SCIENTIFIC BASIS OF SELECTED ENVIRONMENTAL MEDICINE TECHNIQUES and WELLNESS AGAINST ALL ODDS.

THE 8-R OUTLINE

HOW TO TEST AND TREAT

(First we'll give an overview, then more details)

The leaky gut syndrome treatment is done in 8 phases:

First you need to:
(1) **Recognize** or **diagnose** that it is there and its cause.

To diagnose leaky gut syndrome (or malabsorption), one merely needs to do the intestinal permeability test which is an easily performed urine test done at home. Your doctor merely writes a prescription for it and you call the 800# for the lab that will send you the kit and complete instructions.

437

In addition a (comprehensive digestive stool analysis) will tell you if it is caused by Candida, etc., or if the pattern suggests malabsorption (then you might consider celiac disease, treatment described in WELLNESS AGAINST ALL ODDS).

If the pattern suggests malabsorption, then consider celiac disease as described in WELLNESS AGAINST ALL ODDS. Next, get a comprehensive digestive stool analysis to find the correctable cause (Candida, etc.) of the leaky gut.

(2) **Remove** the cause.

(3) **Re-inoculate** the beneficial bacterial flora, and restore function by

(4) **Replacing** enzymes.

(5) **Recall** the total load and how chemical sensitivity can keep the gut damaged. So rectify the body as well as gut overload of xenobiotics (see chemicals, Volume I).

(6) **Repair** function with missing nutrients, FOS, L-glutamine, etc., and

(7) **Restore** good function with fiber, chewing and more.

(8) **Repent** or **rectify** the cause. You need to stay off NSAIDs, caffeine and alcohol. Then, you must change the diet so you are not eating foods that you are allergic to. The rare food diagnostic diet described in TIRED OR TOXIC? is a tool to help you identify foods you are sensitive to.

Sometimes the treatment will involve taking anti-fungals or anti-microbials to remove or kill organisms that have overgrown, infected and inflamed the gut. These can be diagnosed through the CDSA (comprehensive digestive and stool analysis; same lab, requires specific prescription for this also).

Invariably, you'll need to :
(5) **repair** or improve gut function. This is done by many means. As an example, fructo-oligosaccharides are a special class of sugars that do not usually foster yeast growth. They are a preferred source of fuel to facilitate healing of the intestinal lining. Likewise, the amino acid, L-glutamine is important in healing the gut wall in the small intestine, and butyrate is used to heal the large intestine. And don't forget nutrient deficiencies like phosphatidyl choline are crucial to gut healing.

As stated, you will need to:
(3) **reinoculate** the gut by putting the "good bugs" back by using probiotics like acidophilus and bifidus organisms. These have many beneficial properties in the gut.

Then you need to:
(7) **restore** function. This is done by increasing fiber, chewing thoroughly, and (4) **replacing** digestive enzymes, if they are indicated. This helps improve the breakdown of food into smaller, less antigenic particles, and promotes better utilization of food.

There are many other entities to promote healing: antioxidants, bioflavonoids, short-chain fatty acids, flax teas, phosphatidyl choline, EFAs, kudzu, correcting nutrient deficiencies, etc. (see HEALTH LETTER). Sometimes, the thing to do is allow the gut to rest by fasting. The CDSA results help to determine what is needed.

Last, you need to:

(8) **repent or rectify** the cause. By this I mean, you need to change your ways. For if you return to your fast food diet, gulping food, NSAIDs and other damaging medications, alcohol, sweets and sodas, you'll be right back where you started.

But as explained, the major step in recovery is to first properly diagnose the leaky gut syndrome. Without knowing it exists, there is little chance in healing, and without follow-up, you won't know when you have succeeded.

So you might say the "8-R's" recipe for healing the gut is to:

Recognize	(diagnose)
Remove	(kill bugs)
Re-inoculate	(add good bugs)
Replace	(enzymes, etc.)
Repair	(FOS, glutamine, nutrients)
Recall	(detox the body)
Restore (function)	(fiber, chewing) and
Repent or Rectify	(change your diet habits, stop NSAIDS , etc.)

The leaky gut syndrome is prevalent because of today's lifestyles and medical practices, including medicating every pain without finding the cause, using antibiotics too frequently instead of finding out why the person is so vulnerable, eating processed foods, not routinely testing for nutrient deficiencies, etc. And the leaky gut can lead to the development of nearly any number of symptoms and diseases, including depression. Unfortunately, it is rarely looked for in "modern medicine".

The exciting part is that **if you are at an impasse** with depression or any other symptom and cannot seem to rally, you may find that you now need to **heal from the inside out**. Because an undiagnosed leaky gut can be the reason why many are at an impasse with their diseases. Let's look at it in more detail.

THE BEST TEST FOR THE LEAKY GUT

The best test to diagnose the leaky gut is called the intestinal permeability test. It involves drinking a solution of two sugars. One is **lactulose,** to which the gut is quite impermeable. In other words, **lactulose requires a carrier protein** as it does not just simply diffuse across the gut wall. It takes energy and work to get it across.

The second sugar is **mannitol** which should easily absorb right across the gut without any problem. The protocol is to drink a mixture of the two sugars in between collecting before and after urine samples. The measurement of the amounts and ratios of the two sugars tells us whether or not the gut is leaky or whether there is **malabsorption** (suggestive of celiac disease, food allergies, parasites and many other problems). And some individuals have more than one problem, which explains why they have been so "undiagnosable" and chronically unwell. **The leaky gut has been the reason why some people have never completely healed.**

If the lactulose whizzes through the gut and is collected in a large amount in the urine then you know it's leaky or hyperpermeable. Whereas, if the mannitol does not diffuse across easily, then you know that there is quite a bit of damage and probable malabsorption.

In order to test the gut to see if there are abnormal parasites, a special "Purged parasites" test is available. This is usually done in conjunction with the "Comprehensive Digestive Stool Analysis" The CDSA, shows what abnormal yeasts, protozoa, and bacteria are present and tells if you have proper levels of digestive enzymes. For example, if on the leaky gut test you see in the stool elevated triglycerides, fats, fatty acids and undigested food, then you know that there is also low pancreatic function. Once you know you have the leaky gut, (a positive intestinal hyperpermeability test), then it is imperative to proceed to a CDSA to find out **why** it is leaky.

A good way to suspect that you have abnormal bacteria is if you have very **foul gas,** or a lot of gas, or **bloating,** or indigestion, or alternating diarrhea and constipation. Then you would definitely do a CDSA (comprehensive digestive and stool analysis) and 7-day Candida culture.

But don't forget that the gut can be a target organ for chemical sensitivity. Many times when we are testing people in the office for chemicals, we will put on a certain chemical test (single blind). They immediately have intestinal spasm and have to run to the bathroom with diarrhea. Sometimes just doing a simple coffee enema as described in WELLNESS AGAINST ALL ODDS will tell you that you feel much happier and healthier when the gut is detoxified. And that tells you that a **toxic colon may be a part of the cause of your depression.**

When the gut is damaged and leaky there is also damage to the carrier proteins and this leads to nutrient deficiencies, since you cannot absorb all of your minerals. So again, you can see that it's a disease that has multiple ramifications. And each damaged pathway can contribute its own part to making the patient sicker, and the depressed person more depressed.

You might wonder why gastroenterologists don't do these tests. I have asked myself the very same question. They are trained to look for lesions like cancer and ulcers. Consequently it is frequent for people to be told they have "irritable bowel syndrome". But this is just a garbage term for "We don't know why you have gas, bloating, indigestion, malabsorption, alternating diarrhea and constipation, and abdominal pain and depression." They do not seem very concerned with cause, which appears to be a recurring theme in "modern" drug-oriented medicine.

It would be wonderful if you could find a gastroenterologist who is interested in cause. In other words, one who tests for the leaky gut and the above parameters. If and when you do find one, stay with him. Because one who is interested in correcting the function rather than just finding lesions, is one that can lead you out of depression quicker.

There is another organism that can infect the upper area of the gastrointestinal system, the bacterium **Helicobactor pylori**. This was known in the past as Campylobacter pylori. H. Pylori is a gram negative bacterium that grows in the gastric mucosa, in other words, in the lining of the stomach. The interesting thing about it is that it is **the only bacterium known to man that can cause ulcers and cause stomach cancer.** And gut bugs have recently been found to be a culprit in coronary artery disease (but more on that in the subsequent publications). And depression can result as a side effect of any of this through multiple mechanisms.

443

And as usual, "modern" drug-oriented medicine has many ways to increase your chances of getting H. pylori. As an example, a prescription drug for stomach symptoms is Prilosec (omeprazole), used especially if the above recommended tests are bypassed. The problem is that it increases the likelihood of getting H. pylori (ten-fold) and thus the resultant possibility of cancer.

You can test for this by having a blood test to see if you make antibodies to H. pylori. That does not mean that you have it, now, however. But it certainly does mean that you had it in the past. And if you never had the treatment, repeat the antibody titer to see if the infection is still present (the antibody level will be rising if the bug is still growing). There are many antibiotics that treat it. It also in some people is sensitive to bismuth, commonly found in Pepto Bismal.

Once again, you have learned one more reason why depression is definitely not a drug deficiency. Rather, it's a problem of not looking for the environmental and biochemical causes and certainly **the gut connection** should not be overlooked. Now you can begin to see why there are papers in the scientific literature showing that when people got off certain foods that they were no longer schizophrenic. Because not only is food allergy one of the classic causes of depression, but it also can cause the leaky gut. And the wrong food can precipitate depression by more than two mechanisms; it is a double whammy, like so many other stressors or causes.

Likewise, **gluten enteropathy** or **celiac disease** is a condition that can start at any time. Some people are so highly allergic to wheat (and barley, rye, and oats) that even a trace amount of these will leave their guts in a condition of malabsorption for up to 6 months. Consequently, they don't get the good nutrients that they need in the brain for nurturing the happy hormones. But they do get lots of toxins and additives which overload the gut, the brain and other organs to create numerous adverse symptoms. Once again, it becomes a double whammy.

You can appreciate now even more that there are multiple mechanisms for how the things that go wrong can lead to depression. It matters little if depression or a "legitimate illness" appeared first. It should be clear why it is so hard to get out of depression unless you find the cause and "fix what's broken." Now you understand why there are many papers in the literature, for example, showing that people with schizophrenia or depression were simply healed once they got off gluten containing foods (more about that in WELLNESS AGAINST ALL ODDS).

One last word about celiac disease, a serious form of gluten intolerance that results in malabsorption. There are blood tests to diagnose it (anti-gluten antibodies and anti-gliadin antibodies). But there are people for whom the tests are normal, yet a 6-9 month trial of a gluten-free diet healed their malabsorption. No test is perfect, but **your body never lies.**

TREATING THE LEAKY GUT

Treating the leaky gut goes far beyond what I will present here. But if you are familiar with the old 80-20 rule, you'll recall that about 80% of the people will respond to using only 20% of the armamentarium. So that's what you'll see here; the first line treatment to which the majority respond. The others will need a more personalized program with their physician.

For it is much more involved to work through the remaining 80% of the program which the vast majority of people do not need.

To reiterate, first in treating the leaky gut is to find out why it is leaky. Hidden food allergy is a major cause, and by following the rare food diagnostic diet in THE E.I. SYNDROME, REVISED, you'll most likely figure out your hidden food allergies. Next most common is an unsuspected infection of the gut like Candida from years of sporadic antibiotics, lots of sweets, or bacterial and protozoa infections stemming from eating out, contaminated municipal waters and more. The drill is to have a test of the stool to determine if parasites, bacteria, protozoa, or fungi (yeasts or molds) are present. Then specific therapies can be prescribed to kill these organisms.

Or lucky ones with milder cases can bypass all that and use some well thought out combination products that contain herbs that are generally safe and inhibit the growth of many of these organisms, saving themselves much time, prescription drug side effects, and money. An example of such a product is Paragard (Tyler Encapsulations or N.E.E.D.S.), which contains popularly used herbs to eradicate the most commonly encountered abnormal organisms ("bugs") in the gut.

Fortunately, by using herbal preparations that kill these abnormal levels of bacteria, yeast, and protozoa, you avoid harmful antibiotics that can leave you with a yeast infection or overload an already toxic liver. Artemesia, citrus seed extract, berberine, gentian, and walnut extract are many of the useful ingredients all rolled into Paragard, taken as 1-2

446

capsules 3 times a day, between meals and preferably not when you take glutamine.

For example, one ingredient is an extract of black walnut (Juglans nigra), which has been used for years in folk medicine as a treatment for fungus (Tetsuro I, et al, Isolation and identification of the anti-fungal active substance in walnuts, CHEM PHARM BULL, 15(2):242-245, 1967).

Studies indeed show that it is as effective as prescription anti-fungals (Clark AM, Jurgens TM, Hufford CD, Antimicrobial activity of juglone, PHYTOTHER RES 4:1, 11, 1990). In other studies the naphthoquinones of the black walnut extract completely inhibited fungal growth (Tripathi RD, et al, Structure activity relationship amongst some fungitoxic a-naphthoquinones of angiosperm origin, AGRIC BIOL CHEM, 44(10):2483-2485, 1980).

We could continue in this fashion and dissect all of the ingredients to show why and how they are effective against a vast majority of intestinal pathogens that cause the leaky gut syndrome. For remember, the whole reason for treating the gut is that it not only adds to the total load, but it compromises nutrient absorption that can go on to cause depression. And the diseased gut can go on to cause depression of its own by many other mechanisms.

There are many other products to heal the gut that contain many of the needed items rolled into one capsule. Let's look in more detail at the rationale for some of the other treatment modalities. Fortunately, there are dozens of known entities that help repair the gut.

First of all, **glutamine** is so healthful to the gut that it actually **inhibits radiation-induced colitis.** In other words, when people have cancer in the abdomen they often have radiation to the abdomen. Sometimes even though the radiation kills the cancer, the patient dies because the radiation also kills the gut. But if glutamine is given, a mere 500 mg 3 times a day, the gut does not get damaged by radiation. This is pretty potent proof of the protective effect of glutamine, which in this application is mainly on the small bowel. Start with a teaspoon of the powdered L-glutamine (see the section on glutamine) 5 grams, twice a day in water, later reducing it. It must be taken with no food in the stomach for 2 hours before and after, as acid destroys its activity. Or it can be taken as part of the Permeability Factors which also includes other beneficial ingredients.

Enterogenic Factor (Tyler) is an example of another combination therapeutic which contains fructo-oligo saccharides or FOS. These are the preferred nutritive source for regenerating and healing intestinal cells. It also contains the beneficial **probiotics or gut flora.** For replacing the gut flora with the proper beneficial or good bugs or bacteria has many roles from promoting healing of the gut, to inhibition of the translocation or migration of nasty bugs directly into the bloodstream to other organs. These in turn can release toxins that promote depression, fatigue and much more.

Furthermore, the integrity of the gut flora (how many of the "good bugs" you have in the gut) also has a major bearing on how foreign chemicals are metabolized that we breathe in. For you now know that hypersensitivity or inability to metabolize and detoxify chemicals is a major cause of depression. And a large part of the detoxification system resides in the lining of the healthy intestines. But the function is greatly decreased if the gut is leaky or has the wrong organisms in it (Cole CB, et al, The influence of the host on expression of intestinal microbial enzyme activities involved in metabolism of foreign compounds, J APPL BACTERIOL 1985, 59, 549-553, also see WELLNESS AGAINST ALL ODDS and THE SCIENTIFIC BASIS OF SELECTED ENVIRONMENTAL MEDICINE TECHNIQUES). Enterogenic Factor contains probiotics (beneficial organisms) as well as the FOS, all in one.

So a logical step for a neophyte who has a documented leaky gut might be, Enterogenic concentrate (one tsp. in water three times a day between meals), Permeability factors (1-2 capsules three times a day between meals), as well as the Paragard (2 caps 2-3 times a day between meals). There are many other beneficial healing tools for the gut, but these are good basic starters, and perhaps all that is needed.

But remember, if you choose a shot-gun treatment and do not succeed right away, abandon it and do it the right way. Start with a proper diagnosis, then an individualized prescribed treatment. Likewise, when you have done any treatment for a month or more and there are no results, go back to square one. Determine precisely what is wrong with the bowel so that you can reformat your program. For example, say you did the leaky gut test and found it was leaky and decided to work on the many food allergies that you know you have. By doing the CDSA (comprehensive digestive stool analysis) you might have found that you had a gut full of yeast or Proteus that is causing the inflammation to continue in spite of your efforts. Or say you did a CDSA and found Klebsiella and started treating that. If you were not succeeding, do a leaky gut test. It may point out something worse than the leaky gut, like a malabsorption, which will continue to make your

449

life miserable until you treat that. In that case you might want to explore anti-gliadin and anti-gluten antibodies and a gluten-free diet, as an example.

And back to treatment, there are scores of other therapeutic modalities that are beneficial, but require a specialist to help you implement the program. For example, short chain fatty acids, like butyric acid, help the large bowel to heal. In fact butyric acid is such an important nutrient, that it, like vitamin A and some other nutrients, has caused **redifferentiation or return to normal of cancer cells.** Now you can understand why it must be beneficial in conditions like ulcerative colitis, Crohn's, and cancer, not to mention intestinal hyper-permeability or leaky gut. To cover the remaining 80% of the program, we would need a book devoted solely to the gut. But that is not our focus here.

Another example of a beneficial factor is epidermal growth factor which is high in certain glandulars, especially extracts of salivary gland, prostate, and duodenum. Oral extracts of these tissues have healed ulcers, infantile necrotizing ulcerative colitis, and other problems. Important also in the healing of the gut are enzymes, flavonoids and anti-oxidants, lipoic acid, phosphatidyl choline, etc., as well as local glutathione and N-acetyl cysteine.

Even though N-acetyl cysteine can become glutathione in the system, both forms are necessary to heal the gut because glutathione taken orally is not totally absorbed and so works locally on the gut. But N-acetyl cysteine is better absorbed, thus helping the toxic liver recover. For as you will recall, the leaky gut allows bacterial and other toxins easier access to the liver via the blood. When the liver is not healthy it retards

450

the healing of the gut. And the opposite is also true: if the gut is not healthy the liver cannot heal.

And as usual, **just as important as what we take in is what we don't take in.** When you have a leaky gut it may be damaged from alcohol, non-steroidal anti-inflammatory drugs, H2-blockers and other medications, chemotherapy, fasting, food allergies, gluten enteropathy or celiac disease, inhaled pesticides, non-organic pesticided and chemically laden food, parasites, or abnormal amounts of certain bacteria, fungi or yeast. There are so many other items here that it would take volumes to cover them all.

For example, it is well known that even when people are low in nutrients, if they do not have enough **hydrochloric acid,** they cannot absorb the nutrients that they need. And now, with H2-blocker medicines such as Tagamet (cimetadine), Axid, and Pepsid (famotidine) being available over the counter without needing a prescription, many more people can turn off their acid (Recker RR, Calcium absorption and achlorhydia, NEW ENG J MED, 313 (2):70-73, 1985.

And do not neglect common sense. If you spend time chewing your food (try to do fifty times a mouthful), you will promote better absorption. For you not only break it down, but you take some of the work away from the gut. Mixing food well with saliva spares the pancreas of increased work (and overwork). And when you really taste some of the food you eat, you may opt for more "real" food.

When you are using many nutrients and other products to heal the gut, it is probably a better idea to hold off on your nutrient corrections for a while. You'll get more for your money by correcting nutrient deficiencies once the gut is more efficient at absorbing and utilizing your nutrients. If they are just going to pass through unused, why take them until the gut is healed?

For actually, by trying to correct nutrient deficiencies at the same time you are healing the gut will just irritate the gut further, waste money and drive you crazy with the timing of taking everything. There is only so much work that the gut can do at one time. So it would be recommended to heal it first and then proceed to correcting nutrient deficiencies, or take the nutrients only 2 days a week while you are healing the gut.

You may recall how we are always talking about the "total load" and once more I must remind you that it is the most important concept in medicine. Because when the detox system (cytochrome P450) is overloaded in the body, we make **free radicals.** These free radicals are dumped into the bile and so are the chemicals that we detoxify dumped into the bile. This toxic bile then dumps into the gut, irritates and inflames it, perpetuating leakiness. So, if your chemical overload is low, the gut has a much better chance of healing and doing so quickly. This is where anti-oxidants and coffee enemas, as explained in WELLNESS AGAINST ALL ODDS, can help you heal faster.

REFERENCES:

Whitehead WE, The disturbed psyche and irritable gut, EUROP J GASTROENTER HEPAT, 6:483-488, 1994.

Wood NC, et al, **Abnormal intestinal permeability. An etiologic factor in chronic psychiatric disorders,** BR J PSYCHIATRY, 150:853-856, 1987.

Hunter JO, Food allergy—or enterometabolic disorder?, LANCET, 338:495-496, Aug 24, 1991.

Bentley SJ, et al, Food hypersensitivity in irritable bowel syndrome, LANCET, 1983;II:295-297, 1983.

Bayliss CE, et al, Some aspects of colonic microbial activity on irritable bowel syndrome associated with food intolerance, ANN 1st SUPER SANITA 2:959-964, 1986.

Burke DA, Axon ATR, Adhesive Escherichia coli in inflammatory bowel disease and infective diarrhea, BR MED J, 297:102-104, 1988.

Shive W, Glutamine in treatment of peptic ulcer, TEXAS STATE J MED, 53: 1957.

Okage S, et al, Inhibitory effect of L-glutamine on gastric irritation and back diffusion of gastric acid in response to aspirin in the rat, DIGEST DIS, 20:626, 1975.

Hwang TL, et al, Preservation of small bowel mucosa using glutamine-enriched parenteral nutrition, SURG FORUM, 38:56, 1987.

Barber AE, et al, Glutamine or fiber supplementation of a defined formula diet. Impact on bacterial translocation, tissue composition, and response to endotoxin, JPEN, 14:335-343, 1990.

Gilliland SE, et al, Antagonistic action of lactobacillus acidophilus toward intestinal and food-borne pathogens in associative cultures, J FOOD PROT 40:820-823, 1977.

Hosono A, et al, Anti-mutagenic properties of lactic acid cultured milk on chemical and fecal mutagens, J DAIRY SCI 69:2237-2242, 1986.

Reddy G, et al, Inhibitory effect of yogurt on Ehrlich ascites tumor cell proliferation, J NATL CANCER INST 52:815-817, 1973.

Fernandes CF, Therapeutic role of dietary lactobacilli and lactobacillic fermented dairy products, FEMS MICROBIOLOGY REVIEWS 46: 343-356, 1987.

Jackson P, et al, Intestinal permeability in patients with eczema and food allergy, LANCET i:1285-1286, 1981.

Cairns SA, London A, Mallick NP, Circulating immune complexes following food: delayed clearance in idiopathic glomerulonephritis, J CLIN LAB IMMUNOL, 6:121, 1981.

Walker W, Transmucosal passage of antigens, Schmidt E (Ed.), FOOD ALLERGY, Vevey; Raven Press NY, 1988.

Reinhardt M, Macromolecular absorption of food antigens in health and disease, ANN ALLERGY 53:597, 1984.

Editorial, Antigen absorption by the gut, LANCET ii:715-717, 1978.

Soderstrom T, Hansson G, Larson G, The Escherichia coli K1 capsule shares antigenic determinants with the human gangliosides GM3 and GD3, N ENGL J MED, 310:726-727, 1984.

Stephansson K, Dieperink M, Richman Dm et al, Sharing of antigenic determinants between the nicotinic acetylcholine receptor and proteins in Escherichia coli, Proteus vulgaris, and Klebsiella pneumoniae, N ENGL J MED 312:221-225, 1985.

Paganelli R, Levinsky R, Atherton D, Detection of specific antigen within circulating immune complexes: validation of the assay and its application to food antigen-antibody complexes formed in healthy and food-allergic subjects. CLIN EXP IMMUNOL 46:44-53, 1981.

Berg R, Wommack E, Deitch EA, Imunosuppression and intestinal bacterial overgrowth synergistically promote bacterial translocation from the GI tract, ARCH SURG 123:1359-1364, 1988.

Deitch EA, et al, Bacterial translocation from the gut impairs systemic immunity, SURGERY, 109:269-276, 1991.

Deitch EA, et al, The gut as portal of entry for bacteremia: the role of protein malnutrition. ANN SURG, 205,:681-692, 1987.

Jenkins A, Trew DR, Crump BJ et al, Do non-steroidal anti- inflammatory drugs increase colonic permeability? GUT, 32:66-69, 1991.

Bjarnason I, Williams P, Smethurst P et al, Effect of non- steroidal anti-inflammatory drugs and prostaglandin's on the permeability of the human small intestine, GUT, 27:1292-1297, 1986.

Bjarnasson I, Williams P, Smethurst P, et al, Intestinal permeability and inflammation in rheumatoid arthritis: effects of non-steroidal anti-inflammatory drugs, LANCET, 2:1171-1174, 1984.
SUMMARY: In patients with RA and osteoarthritis, EDTA absorption was increased; this was associated with evidence of ileocecal inflammation by Indium-111 leukocyte scans. The effect was not seen in patients not taking NSAID.

Busch J, Hammer M, Brunkhorst R, Wagener P, Determination of endotoxin in inflammatory rheumatic diseases--the effect of nonsteroidal anti-inflammatory drugs on intestinal permeability, J RHEUMATOL, 47: 156-160, 1988.
SUMMARY: Endotoxemia occurs in 31% to 50% of patients with ankylosing spondylitis, rheumatoid arthritis and Crohn's disease. NSAID exposed patients had the highest levels.

Berg RD, **The translocation of normal flora bacteria** from the gastrointestinal tract to the mesenteric lymph nodes and other organs, MICROECOLOGY AND THERAPY, 11:27-34, 1981. Review.
SUMMARY: Increase in translocation with cytotoxic drugs, aggravated by antibiotics.

Parrilli G, Iaffaili RV, Capuano G, et al, Changes in intestinal permeability to lactulose induced by cytotoxic chemotherapy, CANCER TREAT REP, 66: 1435-1436, 1982.
SUMMARY: Chemotherapy for lymphoma induced a transient rise in lactulose absorption.

Hyams JS, Sorbitol intolerance: an unappreciated cause of functional gastrointestinal complaints, GASTROENTEROLOGY, 84: 30-33, 1983.

Ravich WJ, et al, Fructose: incomplete intestinal absorption in humans, GASTROENTEROLOGY, 92:383-389, 1989.

Galland L, Leaky gut syndromes: breaking the vicious cycle, TOWNSEND LETTER FOR DOCTORS, 145/146: 62-68, 1995.

Tache Y, Wingate D, BRAIN-GUT INTERACTIONS, CRC Press, Boca Raton, 1990.

Fernandes CF, Shahani KM, Anti-carcinogenic and immunological properties of dietary lactobacilli, J FOOD PROTECTION, 53(8):714-710, 1990.

Hidaka H, et al, Effects of fructo-oligosaccharides on intestinal flora and human health. BIFIDOBACTERIA MICROFLORA, 5(1):37-50, 1986.

McKellar RC, et al, Metabolism of fructo-oligosaccharides by Bifidobacerium spp, APP MICROBIAL BIOTECHNOL, 31:537-541, 1989.

Fishbein L, et al, Fructo-oligosaccharides: A review. VET HUM TOXICOL, 30(2):104-107, 1988.

Breurer RI, et al, Rectal irrigation with short chain fatty acids for distal ulcerative colitis, DIG DIS SCI, 36(2):185- 187, 1991.

Sankaranarayanan K, et al, Effects of sodium butyrate on X- ray and bleomycin induced chromosome aberrations in human peripheral blood lymphocytes, GEN RES 56:267-276, 1990.

Nathan D, et al, Increased cell surface EGF receptor expression during butyrate-induced differentiation of human HCT-116 colon tumor cell clones, EXP CELL RES, 190:76-84, 1990.

Poillart P, et al, Butyric monosaccharide ester-induced cell differentiation and anti-tumor activity in mice: Importance of their prolonged biological effect for clinical application in cancer therapy, INT J CANCER, 49:89-95, 1991.

Jass J, Diet, Butyric acid and differentiation of gastrointestinal tumors, MED HYPOTH, 18:113-118, 1985.

Crayhon R, HEALTH BENEFITS OF FOS, Keats Publ, New Canaan Ct, 1995.

Planchon P, et al, New stable butyrate derivatives alter proliferation and differentiation in human mammary cells, INT J CANCER, 48:443-449, 1991

Stoddart J, etr al, Sodium butyrate suppresses the transforming activity of an activated N-ras oncogene in human colon carcinoma cells, EXP CELL RES, 184:16-27, 1989

NOTE: As you see from a smattering of references, the leaky gut can cause depression. And, **chemotherapy can cause depression.** Therefore, some of the depression in cancer patients could be ameliorated (and their chances of longer survival improved) by diagnosing and properly treating the leaky gut. Also, it would have many other benefits like promoting nutrient absorption and decreasing their risk of infection, as examples. Unfortunately, this is not standard in cancer programs. And as we showed earlier, radiation can cause leaky gut. This can be easily prevented, but likewise is not commonly done. More about cancer protection and treatment in books and newsletters already in progress. Suffice to say, these 4 volumes provide a necessary background for the person seriously interested in healing the impossible.

LEAKY GUT, LEAKY BRAIN MEMBRANES

The brain has always been considered remote and isolated from the rest of the body. Medicine calls it **immunologically privileged**: more or less separated from the effects of other things going on in the rest of the body. This was because of the presence of the membrane called the **blood brain barrier.** The blood brain barrier controls the flow of substances in and out of the brain and excludes normally large proteins and molecules.

However, **the blood brain barrier can become leaky** just as the gut can develop the leaky gut syndrome, and just as cancer cells have leaky cell membranes. In similar fashion, the blood brain barrier can be damaged and leak and allow larger molecules into the brain than normal. Leaky blood brain barrier membranes can result in inflammatory conditions of the brain which would include depression. This can be caused by immunologic reactions as in multiple sclerosis or mediated by inflammation from viral infections, allergic encephalomyelitis, Candida, damage from trans-fatty acids, chemical sensitivities, nutrient deficiencies like phosphatidyl choline, and a host of other pathologies are possible.

Auto-immunity can develop with cross-reactivity to foods, chemicals, and other environmental factors. **Molecular mimicry** occurs where antibodies to one substance share similar reactive sites with other substances. Suffice to say, anyone can develop a sensitivity to anything at any time that can attack any organ, including the brain. And depression may be the major symptom.

REFERENCES:

Kascsac RJ, Wisinewski HM, Pathogenesis of virus induced and auto-immune nervous system injuries, in: CHILD NEUROLOGY AND DEVELOPMENTAL DISABILITIES by JH French, S Harel, P Casaer, MI Gottlieb, I Rapin, DC DeVivo, eds. P89-98, Paul H. Brooks, Baltimore, 1989.

Lassmann H, Rossler K, Zimpirch F, Vass K, Expression of adhesion molecules and histo-compatibility antigens at the blood brain barrier, BRAIN PATHOL 1, 115-123, 1991.

Schook LB, Lanskin DL, XENOBIOTICS AND INFLAMMATION, Academic Press NY, 1994.

BEYOND THE LEAKY GUT

It might seem that the leaky gut is not a big deal, since it is so far removed from the brain. But the ramifications are tremendous and touch many facets of our developing world. For example, there are progressively more **irradiated** foods, often without labels. Most shrimp, herbs, potatoes, and other products are nearly routinely irradiated now. Many problems exist for this.

First the ionizing radiation turns some of the food chemicals into mutagens, substances capable of changing our genetics and producing cancer. Many of the products of this radiation are cytotoxic. Also the irradiation of foods, as you have learned, lowers the vitamin content by actually destroying some of the vitamins. Also it does not do a thing to inactivate carcinogenic mycotoxins (Volume I). Also some species of Salmonella are radio-resistant, as are some species of mold like Pullaria (Aureobasidium). And if you have a leaky gut, guess what? They can pass from the gut into the blood stream (called **translocation**) and into the brain.

For research shows that the **bacteria and yeasts in the gut** and even the **foods** can **translocate from the gut to the bloodstream to the brain.** This **makes the brain more vulnerable than ever to everything we eat,** and the cause progressively more difficult to diagnose, since none of this is standard in drug-oriented medicine. And there will be no end. For food allergies, anti-inflammatory drugs, chemotherapy, alcohol, and endotoxins and abnormal yeast growths after antibiotics can all foster a leaky gut. This makes entry of anything into the leaky brain membranes easier. The sick will get sicker, and the depressed may see no end until the causal approach is used.

GUT LEVEL MEDICINE

I know we've thrown a lot at you, so let me recap some essential facts that you have learned. We'll put them together in another way so that you can see another big part of the picture necessary for healing the brain. First, at bare minimum, **one out of four people has the irritable bowel syndrome,** in other words, the gut is not healthy (BRIT MED J Jan 11, 1992,304:87). Much of it can be due to the leaky gut.

Everything in the gut can make its way into the blood. And the **blood brain barrier is often leaky** as well, allowing anything to penetrate into the brain. These studies were done with radiographically labeled materials taken up directly into the brain. (Kare MR, Schechter PJ, et al, Direct pathway to the brain, SCIENCE 163:952-953, 1968).

Whenever the body sees substances that are foreign, it can make antibodies that can become the basis of an inflammatory **auto-immune** phenomenon. In other words, the basis of much disease. For example, even though Alzheimer's is known to partly be triggered by aluminum ingestion, you need many other factors. If you are low in anti-oxidant nutrients, you have a diminished protection against aluminum. But vitamin C normally displaces aluminum into the urine. Alzheimer's also has an "allergic" or antigenic component to it as well (Wolozin BL, et al. A neuronal antigen in the brains of Alzheimer's patients, SCIENCE, 232:648-650, May 2, 1986).

Unfortunately, some gut bacteria share antigenic similarities with the actual site in the brain where the happy hormone acetyl choline sits. And you now know that acetyl choline is the number one most important neurotransmitter or "happy hormone". In other words, some gut bacteria look like they belong in the acetylcholine receptor in the brain. So they sit there and block the action of the real hormone. This can lead to many brain symptoms, including depression. In essence, **the leaky gut can cause any brain malfunction you can think of.** And if it is not recognized and corrected, the brain may never have an opportunity to heal. **Clearly the reason some depression victims never heal is because no one did any "gut level medicine".**

REFERENCES:

Steffansson, et al, Sharing of antigenic determinants between the nicotinic acetylcholine receptor and proteins in Escherichia coli, Proteus vulgaris, and Klebsiella pneumoniae. Possible role in the pathogenesis of myasthenia gravis, N ENGL J MED, 321:4, 221-225, Jan 24, 1985.

Well CL, Maddaus MA, Simmons RL, Proposed mechanism for the translocation of intestinal bacteria, REV INFECT DIS, 10:958- 968 (1988).
SUMMARY: Translocation of bacteria is part of the normal process of antigen-sampling by gut phagocytes. Incomplete killing may allow pathological translocation.

Husby S, Jensenius JC, Svehag SE, Passage of undergraded antigen into the blood of healthy adults. Further characterization of the kinetics of uptake and the size distribution of antigen, SCAND J IMMUNOL, 24:447-455 (1986).
SUMMARY: In healthy adults minute quantities of dietary protein circulate after meals as intake protein and as circulating IgG immune complexes.

Hemmings WA, The entry into the brain of large molecules derived from dietary protein, PROC ROY SOC LOND, B 200:175- 192 (1978).
SUMMARY: Feeding iodine-labeled gliadin or bovine IgG to rats produces protein-bound labeled iodine in brain as part of high molecular weight material bearing antigenic characteristics of the fed protein.

CONCLUSIONS: The adult human small intestine shows some permeability to large molecules and bacterial under normal conditions; this increases in infancy and senescence.

Spaeth G, Berg RD, Specian RD, Deitch EA. Food without fiber promotes bacterial translocation from the gut, SURGERY, 108: 240-24, (1990).
SUMMARY: Both elemental feeding and TPN induced bacterial translocation in rats. Cellulose was protective.

Souba WW, Klimberg VS, Hautamaki RD, et al, Oral glutamine reduces bacterial translocation following abdominal radiation, J SURG RES, 48:1-5, 1990.

Hamilton IH, Cobden I, Rothwell J, Axon ATR, Intestinal permeability in celiac disease: The response to gluten withdrawal and single-dose gluten challenge, GUT, 23:202-210 1982.

Ukabam SO, Cooper BT, Small intestinal permeability as an indicator of jejunal mucosal recovery in patients with celiac sprue on a gluten-free diet, J CLIN GASTRO, 7:232-236, 1985.
SUMMARY: Lactulose/mannitol excretion is elevated in celiac disease and decreases toward normal with gluten-free diet. There is good correlation between the ratio and changes in intestinal histology.

Falth-Magnusson K, Kjellman N-Im, Odelram H, et al, Gastrointestinal permeability in children with cow's milk allergy: effect of milk challenge and sodium cromoglycate assessed with polyethyleneglycols (PEG 400 and PEG 1000). CLINICAL ALLERGY, 14:277-286, 1984.
SUMMARY: Oral cromolyn prevents the increased permeability induced by dietary challenge. (But more importantly, cow's milk allergy induces leaky gut).

Andre C, Objective diagnostic test of therapeutic efficacy by a measure of intestinal permeability, LA PRESSE MEDICALE (Paris) 15:105-108, 1986.
SUMMARY: Patients with food allergy showed normal mannitol and slightly increased lactulose absorption compared to controls. Ingesting a food allergen produced an immediate increase in lactulose and decrease in mannitol absorption which was prevented by oral cromolyn.
CONCLUSIONS: There is little difference in baseline permeability between atopics and controls. Feeding an offending food to a patient with **food allergy increases** permeability. It is mediator-driven.

Measuring elevated permeability after an antigen-laden meal provides objective evidence of food allergy, especially if cromolyn blocks increase.

Note: The neurotransmitter acetylcholine is one word. But because we are attempting to teach lay people medical facts that many physicians do not know, I've cut the word into 2 parts. I've done this just to make it a little easier to see, say, and remember. I felt it was not as foreboding as the long term, acetylcholine.

CANDIDA: A MAJOR CAUSE
OF INTESTINAL DYSBIOSIS

So as you have learned, there are many causes of the leaky gut. But foremost are the non-steroidal anti-inflammatory drugs used for arthritis, pain, PMS, headache, fibromyalgia, muscle and joint problems, inflammation, and in cases when it is not known what else to do. Food allergies are another common cause. And not insignificant are the **intestinal dysbioses.** This merely means bugs growing in the intestine that do not belong there, at least in the amounts in which these are present. They get there through food and other causes. But mostly the wrong bugs become plentiful in the gut through an imbalance in intestinal flora with antibiotics, prednisone, cortisol, birth control pills, estrogens, and a diet of sweets, breads, and alcohol. In essence, most of it is **iatrogenic** or caused by the treatments of medicine.

Chief among the "bad guys" or undesirable organisms, as you now know, is **Candida albicans.** But just as commonly we see Candida krusei and Candida parasilosis. Fortunately, we rarely see Candida tropicalis, which is resistant to Nystatin. The Candida yeast is not killed, but conversely is stimulated by the high-powered antibiotics we take. It inflames the gut wall, as any uncontrolled infection would do, leading at first to gas, bloating, alternating diarrhea and constipation, then fatigue, brain fog, body aches, and depression, to name a few. Eventually it can mimic anything from multiple sclerosis, fibromyalgia, and depression, to migraines, chemical sensitivity, or colitis. A good clue to whether you have Candida overgrowth is if you are worse after ingestion of sweets or ferments (review Volume I).

Surprisingly, medicine has staunchly resisted recognizing the importance of Candida. In the late 1970's a serendipitous treatment of Candida vaginitis resulted in a surprising cure for depression. Orion Truss, an internist, was covering for a physician friend one weekend. When called in to treat a lady who had a yeast vaginitis, he barely remembered her when she frantically called him the next day. What had he given her, she wanted to know. Because for the first time in years her depression had lifted.

He thought little of this until it happened again. Then he realized it might be something that should not be ignored in medicine. He went on to write papers and books about it, and lovingly Dr. William Crook popularized it. Since then thousands of people have been helped because of the efforts of these two men (more in TIRED OR TOXIC?, including details of the mechanisms of its pathophysiology, diagnosis and treatment).

The problem is that medicine has continued to downplay the magnitude of the problem. In fact, a recent medical publication goes on to ignore the entire possibility. Perhaps one reason is that when yeast starts taking over or growing in the body, it does not do so in everyone. Instead it only happens in those who are not playing with a full deck of nutrients; in other words, in those who are nutritionally deficient and therefore vulnerable to attack. For **attack** by any organism **depends more on the terrain or soil**, so to speak, of the victim, rather than the virulence of the bug. That's why everyone does not get the flu when it comes around; only **those who are vulnerable or who have a deficient terrain.**

One of the major clues to Candida, when a physical clue appears, is the growth of yeast on the tongue. It can be a white, yellow, brown, gray, or black growth, depending on which type of fungus it is. (But realize that all coated tongues do not mean Candida specifically, but merely a toxicity of some sort.) Of course, when the growth of Candida is on the tongue, it means that soon enough it can be up and down the entire esophagus. This results in an undiagnosed cause of esophagitis, for which H-2 blockers like Tagamet or Zantac or Pepcid are prescribed. The problem is that these make it worse. For they cut down the stomach acid that is intended to inhibit or kill the yeast, and that is also needed for absorption of nutrients. Then the yeast can progress to grow in the entire gastrointestinal (GI) tract until you finally get the full-blown scenario as described. Again, **ignoring cause and suppressing symptoms with drugs makes the sick get sicker, quicker.**

Anyway, I recently read a published article telling doctors that the black tongue is "self-limited" and quite "benign", and of no consequence for the physician to concern himself with (Olivero JJ, Case in point column, 24, May 15, 1994, HOSPITAL PRACTICE). It is difficult to believe there are so many areas of medicine that are still ignorant of the potential seriousness of undiagnosed yeast infections.

In another recent publication for doctors, a classic Candida tongue made the cover of the journal as an unexplained finding when 600 Gulf War victims were studied. These people, of course, have classic environmental illness with all the trimmings (Milner BI, Plezia RA, Toxic exposure sign: Desert shield/desert storm, CUTIS, 55:5, 289-305, May 1995). And remember a common factor contributing to the underlying nutrient deficiencies that can cause depression is hypochlorhydria, or low stomach acid. As people age, they tend to make less stomach acid. Thus they are more prone to Candida overgrowth as they no longer absorb their minerals well. This adds further to the vulnerability for yeast overgrowth.

For more on Candida, see volume I.

REFERENCES:

Gledhill T, et al, **Epidemic hypochlorhydria**, BR J MED, 289: 383-386, 1985.

Deitch, EA, Maejima K, Berg RD, Effect of oral antibiotics and bacterial overgrowth on the translocation of the gastrointestinal tract micro-flora in burned rats, J TRAUMA, 25: 385-392, 1985.

Deitch EA, Berg RD, Specian RD, Endotoxin promotes the translocation of bacteria from the gut, ARCH SURG, 22: 185- 190, 1987.

O'Dwyer ST, Michie HR, Ziegler TR., et al, A single dose of endotoxin increases intestinal permeability in healthy humans, ARCH SURG, 123: 1459-1464, 1988.

Sudduth WH, The role of bacteria and enterotoxemia in physical addiction to alcohol, MICROECOLOGY AND THERAPY, 18: 77-81, 1989. HYPOTHESIS: alcohol increases gut permeability to endotoxin, responsible for hepatic damage and symptoms of toxicity.

Gupta TP, Ehrenpreis MN, Candida-associated diarrhea in hospitalized patients, GASTROENT, 98: 780-785, 1990.

Caselli M, Trevisani L, Bighi S, et al, Dead fecal yeasts and chronic diarrhea, DIGESTION, 41: 142-148, 1988.

Kane JG, Chretien JH, Garagusi V, Diarrhea caused by Candida, LANCET, 335-336, 1976.

Alexander JG, **Thrush** bowel infection: existence, incidence, prevention and treatment, particularly by a lactobacillus acidophilus preparation, CUR MED DRUGS, 8:3-11, 1967.
COMMENTS: Most are retrospective uncontrolled multiple case reports. Caselli, et al, and Alexander stress the importance of fecal smears, noting that cultures may be falsely negative. Alexander stresses the importance of allergic mechanisms in production of diarrhea-induced Candida.

Galland L, et al, Giardia Lamblia infection as a cause of chronic fatigue, J NUTR MED, 1:27-31, 1990.

Brabander JO, Blank F, Butas CA, Intestinal moniliasis in adults, CAN MED ASSOC J, 77: 478-482, 1957.

A DIRECT ROUTE FROM GUT TO BRAIN

Not only is what is growing in the gut able to secondarily cause depression, but with translocation and a damaged or leaky blood brain barrier, you can get anything that is in the gut, into the blood stream and across the blood-brain barrier and into the brain. This is important in terms of food choices, as it appears that the government (due to the full-time job of powerful food lobbyists?) watches the needs of big business more diligently than it watches the scientific literature or pays attention to common sense.

As an example, the Department of Agriculture (USDA) wants to define fecal matter as an acceptable part of the American diet, even though it acknowledges the dangers of food poisoning and other illnesses. "USDA pleads that condemning poultry carcasses contaminated with fecal matter during processing would work an economic hardship on the poultry industry." In other words, because meat and fowl handlers lobbied in government halls, it is acceptable to offer us progressively more contaminated proteins.

This is dangerous when we recall that everything in the gut has the potential for getting into the brain. And recall earlier that some species of mold (Pullularia or Aureobasidium) and some species of bacteria (Salmonella) are resistant to food irradiation. So we have an increased chance of having these introduced into the diet as well (more in food irradiation, Volume I).

REFERENCES:

Leonard RE, Chicken feces fine to eat, says new USDA proposal, NUTRITION WEEK, 24;27:4-5, July 22, 1994.

Piccioni R, Analysis of data on the impact of food processing by ionizing radiation on health and the environment, INT J BIOSOCIAL RES, 9(2):203-212, 198.

Kuzin AM, Kryukova LM, Mutagenic action of metabolites formed in irradiated plants, DOLKLADY AKAD NAUK SSSR, 137, 205-206, 1961.

Makinen Y, et al, Cytotoxic effects of extracts from gamma- irradiated pineapples, NATURE, 214: 413, 1967.

ENZYMES HELP DEPRESSION

As a physician, I was taught very little about enzymes 30 years ago in medical school, aside from the use of a few to improve digestion and speed healing after surgery. Now the biggest news about enzymes concerns the "clot busters" like streptokinase and urokinase for breaking up clots in coronary arteries as an emergency intravenous procedure.

But my first awareness of enzymes being used for "dissolving" cancers came when I read of Dr. Wm. Donald Kelley, a Texas dentist who in 1969 had inoperable pancreatic cancer and was given 6 months to live. Having read 2 books detailing his program, I was impressed when I contacted him in 1993 to find he was still alive. Then the real test came when I watched a personal friend reduce a liver painfully swollen with cancer using enzymes. Subsequently, I began discovering autobiographical reports showing that other lay people knew about these techniques and had also cleared metastatic cancers, after they were given up on by medicine with only days and weeks to live. Anne Frahm chronicled the details of her cancer reversal and survival in A CANCER BATTLE PLAN (Pinon Press, Colorado Springs, 1993), as one example.

Scientists the world over know that **cancer is an antigen-antibody disease**. In fact, the body makes an antigen that attacks the cancer cell. That is why antigen tests like the CEA, PSA, CA-125, etc. are used to diagnose cancers of the colon, prostate, and ovary, as examples. The exciting fact is that the body has a better chance at killing the tumor once a protective fibrin-like coating has been removed. For this coating covers up or hides the antigenic sites so the body cannot recognize and destroy the cancer. We need a way to remove this protective shield.   And enzymes can do this (further references in the subsequent breast cancer book).

The relevant part here is that not only do enzymes dissolve the protective shield surrounding cancer cells, but they dissolve antigen-antibody complexes.   And since this is a major way that the leaky gut can cause symptoms throughout the body (via auto-immune antibodies), enzymes help some forms of depression (as from lupus, etc.), as well.

Of course, as in cancer and other diseases, enzymes are not effective as a solo treatment. They must be part of a specific program of organic whole foods and/or juices, nutrients, loving support, a strong spirituality, and special detoxification procedures like coffee enemas (all of the protocols, enemas, diet, enzyme doses, references, etc. are spelled out in WELLNESS AGAINST ALL ODDS). The coffee enemas, as weird or sordid as they may sound, are literally life-saving. You see, the toxicity of dead cancer cells is so high that if their by-products are not quickly detoxified, they can cause death of the person. And many a person has died free of cancer after successful cancer therapies have gotten rid of their cancer. The problem is that no one got rid of the toxicity from the dead tumor cells, and the patient died.

This toxicity occurs, for example, with people who cause special types of leukemic cells to revert to normal cells with special doses of vitamin A or retinoic acid. Physicians who are unaware of the importance of detoxifying the person who is killing cancer have called this "mysterious" death the **retinoic acid syndrome.** For high doses of retinoic acid are able to cure a special type of leukemia. But the researchers described how the patients went on to die anyway of this mysterious toxicity after the cancer was cured.

As a specialist in environmental medicine, we have used this knowledge about the power of enzymes to dissolve antigen-antibody complexes, in many diseases, like arthritis, food allergies, and celiac disease (Phelan JJ, et al, Celiac disease: the abolition of gliadin toxicity by enzymes from Aspergillus niger, CLIN SCI MOLEC MED 53:35-43, 1977).

We have also used them successfully in hundreds of chemically sensitive patients to reduce the toxic encephalopathy of brain fog from chemical sensitivity. In many cases when patients with chemical sensitivity have exposures that might result in days of brain fog, they can often clear within 20 minutes with the enzymes and enema procedure done at home. I was incredulous myself, until I did them and appreciated the results firsthand, as well as in hundreds of other patients and non-patients of mine.

You know that chemical sensitivity can cause depression. And obviously people with cancers can get very depressed, as do people with auto-immune diseases that secondarily affect the brain and cause depression. So if these are part of the cause of your depression, read WELLNESS AGAINST ALL ODDS for further details on dissolving the cancer-protectors and antigen-antibody complexes that may be behind your depression. I didn't intend to send you to medical school, but merely to demonstrate that in spite of the huge number of potential causes of depression, the vast majority have wonderful treatment options.

There are many lifestyle factors that can serve to weaken and deplete our natural pancreatic reserves. Just the escalating dietary choices containing sugars can stress the demands of the pancreas. Add to that the high amounts of dietary fats requiring pancreatic lipases and you can begin to appreciate factors that strain its productivity. Furthermore, such common deficiencies as zinc can jeopardize pancreatic enzyme output. And even everyday home and office chemicals and pesticides can act to damage pancreatic enzyme function. (Marsh, et al, Acute pancreatitis following cutaneous exposure to an organophosphate insecticides, AM J GASTROENTEROLOGY, 83:1158-1160, 1988).

Meanwhile, there are different protocols for the way in which enzymes are taken as well as the doses and the types. For example, since most healing occurs when the body is at rest, or at night, it is important for people with serious illnesses to take at least one dose at about 2 a.m. At this time the body should be finished with digestion, is not in motion, and so can concentrate more on the work of healing. In contrast, daytime doses taken with meals are used to facilitate the absorption of the much needed healing nutrients extracted from foods.

There are numerous forms of enzymes. For example, there are plant-derived enzymes for those who need to avoid animal products, and animal glandulars for those who, because of allergies, must avoid mold antigens (Aspergillus oryzae) that are in most plant-derived enzymes. For the reader who needs more, the details of the protocols, the explanation of their mechanisms and references are contained in WELLNESS AGAINST ALL ODDS.

But for now, the exciting part is that there is a non-toxic, relatively inexpensive, and natural therapy that can enhance the chances of healing cancers and other diseases that is not being utilized. Since it has been pretty much in hiding for nearly a century, the time is ripe to incorporate it into our treatment strategies. If that were not enough reason to use enzymes, consider the special needs of the depressed person. First of all, chances are he has other disease processes going on besides "pure" depression. And since a vast majority of diseases including cancers, Alzheimer's, arthritis, etc. are auto-immune in nature, it is likely that there is cerebral or brain involvement, since these diseases know no organ boundaries. Only man has created these artificial boundaries, hence sending you to one doctor for your gut, another for your cancer, and another for your depression. It's as though none of the conditions has anything to do with the others.

So since enzymes **"dissolve" antigen-antibody complexes**, it certainly would seem plausible for the depressed person with concomitant auto-immune disease (rheumatoid arthritis, multiple sclerosis, lupus, thyroiditis, fibromyalgia, etc.) to turn down or turn off the inflammatory process in a natural and unharmful way. This is in contrast to the diverse drugs that are used which then go on to further compromise the chemistry and ultimate proper brain function. And remember that the pathology of depression in some auto-immune diseases may actually be antibodies directed toward brain tissues, as in antigen-antibody complexes of lupus or Alzheimer's directed toward brain tissues.

It turns out that even Alzheimer's or presenile dementia is an auto-immune phenomenon (Fillit HM, et al, Antivascular antibodies in the sera of patients with senile dementia of the Alzheimer's type, J GERONTOL 42(2):180-184, 1987). Likewise, auto-antibodies have been identified for cancers, arthritis, Crohn's, ulcerative colitis, chronic pancreatitis, hepatitis, ankylosing spondylitis, multiple sclerosis, glomerulonephritis, etc. And oral enzymes have been used to successfully treat these as well as pelvic inflammatory disease, post-herpetic pain, prostatitis, chronic cystitis, to minimize the harmful effects of radiation, thrombophlebitis, and much more, as well as lower lipid levels. (So from multiple levels of causation, enzymes may be worth a month trial (in concert with a total program) in depressed persons with concomitant diseases.)

(Last, but not least, enzymes are crucial for decreasing the effect of food allergies, a common cause of leaky gut and of depression even without leaky gut. An enzyme program is a crucial part of healing the leaky gut.)

By now you can see that every time you take an antibiotic, you risk getting a Candida overgrowth and leaky gut. Every time you take a pain reliever like aspirin, ibuprofen, Advil, Aleve, or Motrin, or when you use the stomach acid inhibitors like Zantac, Pepcid, Axid, Tagamet, etc., you run the same risk. (From there on it may be depression from poor nutrient absorption, depression from intestinal dysbiosis, depression from auto-immune disease, depression from food allergy, or any of the other ways in which a leaky gut can cause or contribute to depression.)

REFERENCES:

Desser L, Rehberger A, Induction of tumor necrosis factor in human peripheral blood mononuclear cells by proteolytic enzymes. ONCOLOGY 47: 474, 1990.

Laffaioli RV, et al, Prognostic significance of circulating immune complexes in a long-term follow up of breast cancer patients, ONCOLOGY, 45:337-343, 1988.

Beaufort F, Reduction of side effects of radiation therapy with hydrolytic enzymes, THERAPEUTIKON 10:577-580, 1990.

477

Ransberer K, Enzyme therapy of cancer, THERAPEUTICS (DIS HEILKUNST) 102:22-34, 1989.

Schedler M, et al, Adjuvant therapy with hydrolytic enzymes in oncology –Hopeful effort to avoid Bleomycinum induced pneumotoxicity?, J CANCER RES CLIN ONCOL, 116:1, 1990.

Hall DA, et al, The effect of enzyme therapy on plasma lipid levels in the elderly, ARTHEROSCLEROSIS 43:209, 1982.

Lopez DA, Williams RM, Miehlke M, ENZYMES. THE FOUNTAIN OF LIFE, The Neville Press, 18 Broad ST, STE 601, Charleston SC 29401, 1994. SUMMARY: For as the voluminous references in this book show, enzymes have been used to improve the status of cancer patients remarkably. And along with this has been a marked relief from depression (p243).

Uffelmann K, Vogler W, Fruth C, The use of proteolytic enzymes in extra-articulator rheumatism, GENERAL MEDICINE (ALLGEMEINMEDIZIN), 19:4;151, 1990.

Werk W, Horger I, The immune profile of rheumatoid arthritis patients before and after enzyme therapy (including a discussion of the mechanism of effectiveness), LAB J RES LAB MED, 7:273, 1980.

Stauder G, et al, Randomized prospective trial of adjuvant use of hydrolytic enzymes in abdominal cancer patients given radiotherapy, GERMAN J ONCOL 23:7, 1991.

Seifert J, et al, Quantitative analysis about the absorption of trypsin, chymotrypsin, amylase, papain, and pancreatin in the G.I. tract after oral administration. GENERAL PHYSICIAN (ALLGEMEINARZT), 19:4, 132-137, 1990.

Dittmar FW, Luh W, Treatment of fibrocystic mastopathy with hydrolytic enzymes, INTERNAT J EXP CLIN CHEMOTHER, 6:1, 9-20, 1993.

Pastorino U, Hong WK, Eds, CHEMOIMMUNO PREVENTION OF CANCER, 1st INTERNATIONAL CONFERENCE, Vienna, Austria, 1990, Thieme Med Publ, 381 Park Ave S, NY NY 10016, 1991.

Benchimol S, Fuks A, Jothy S, Beauchemin N, Shirota K, Stanners CP, Carcino-embryonic antigen, a human tumor marker, functions as an intercellular adhesion molecule, CELL, 57:327-344, 1989.

Dittmar FW, Weissenbacher ER, Therapy of adnexitis -- enhancement of the basic antibiotic therapy with hydrolytic enzymes, INTERNAT J FETO-MATERNAL MED, 2:3, 15-24, 1993.
This paper shows how enzymes facilitate the penetration of costly antibiotics into difficult to treat areas, like the ovaries and uterus, thereby displacing the need for I.V. antibiotics.

Pecher O, (Beese EW, translation), ORAL ENZYMES, BASIC INFORMATION AND CLINICAL STUDIES, 1992, Muco Pharma GmbH & Co, Alpenstrafe 29, 82538 Geretsreid 1, Germany.

Wolf M, Ransberger K, ENZYME THERAPY, 1972, Vantage Press, NY.

Buch SP, et al, Human lung cancer--a comparative study of the levels of circulating immune complexes in pulmonary blood draining the tumor area and peripheral venous blood, INT J CANCER 42:837-840, 1989.

Buch SP, et al, A prospective study of circulating immune complexes in patients with breast cancer, INTERNAT J CA, 41:364-370, 1988.

Dasgupta MK, et al, Circulating immune complexes in multiple sclerosis: relation with disease activity, NEUROL 32: 1000- 1004, 1982.

Fillit HM,, et al, Antivascular antibodies in the sera of patients with senile dementia of the Alzheimer's type, J GERONTOL 42:2;180-184, 1987.

NOTE: Many more references can be found in WELLNESS AGAINST ALL ODDS and THE SCIENTIFIC BASIS OF SELECTED ENVIRONMENTAL MEDICINE TECHNIQUES.

LABORATORIES FOR STOOL STUDIES:

Great Smokies Diagnostic Laboratory, 18A Regent Park Blvd. Asheville NC 28806, 1-800-522-4762

Meridian Valley Clin Lab, 24030 132nd Ave., SE, Kent WA 98042, 1-800-234-6825

Lexington Professional Center, 133 E. 73rd ST, New York, NY, 10021, 212-988-4800

PRODUCTS TO TREAT THE GUT:

Tyler Encapsulations, 2204-8 NW Birdsdale, Gresham OR 97030, 1-800-869-9705

N.E.E.D.S., 1-800 634-1380

CHAPTER 9

THE FORGOTTEN FACTOR IN HEALING

What would you say if I told you there is yet another factor crucial to healing that has been over-looked by medicine? And what would you say if you found out this factor important in healing has been ignored even though it does not cost a cent? And this factor has been ignored, even though there are over **250 studies** in the **medical literature** proving its validity. That is in far excess of the number of studies it takes for a drug to pass FDA scrutiny and become standard treatment for a disease like depression. And contrary to drugs that pass FDA inspection with flying colors like Prozac as an example, that had over 28,000 reported side effects and 1,700 deaths, this factor has **no adverse side effects**.

And this forgotten factor has been proven to be of benefit in 83-92% of the studies. And no disease seems to be immune to the benefits of this factor. It helps all symptoms, all disease states, from hypertension to post surgery healing and depression, alcohol abuse, drug abuse, suicide, and more. The forgotten factor? **Faith.** A religious commitment, a relationship and communication with your chosen God. A belief in a power greater than man, that provides guidance and security.

Somehow, in spite of scientific data, medicine seems to be able to tune out the evidence when it comes to things that fall into two categories: (1) things that do not cost any money or do not make a lot of money, either as a procedure that a doctor does to you, or in the form of a drug, and (2) things that detract from the doctor being the central focus or hero and central controlling factor in your getting well. And you will notice that nutritional and molecular biochemistry, environmental medicine, and faith or a spirituality all fall into those two categories.

THE FAITH FACTOR
IS SCIENTIFICALLY PROVEN

You may be as shocked as I was when I learned that not only have physicians and scientists studied faith as a factor in healing, but it is **scientifically validated as a tool to improve medical outcome.** In one study, patients were 4 times less likely to commit suicide when they had a faith. And in a review of other studies, **90% of the studies showed that the faith factor was protective against suicide.** And if the patients so much as thought of suicide, they viewed it as a negative or inappropriate plan of attack for solving their depression and problems.

In another study of elderly women with hip fractures, those with the faith factor were less depressed, and could walk further by the time they were released from the hospital. And elsewhere we have cited Byrd's famous study that was done double blind on patients recovering from a heart attack. Not only did the patients not know which of them was being prayed for, but the people praying for them did not personally know the patients they were praying for. And none of the people had ever met. Yet those prayed for had a statistically superior record in many ways. They had fewer complications, fewer deaths, and needed less medication, for starters.

Recall that the macrobiotic diet is a diet explained in THE CURE IS IN THE KITCHEN. Many people have reversed and totally healed their cancers after they were given up on by medicine. They were failures with everything medicine has to offer. Although it is inexpensive, consists of God-given foods, and can be done by nearly anyone, it requires knowledge about it on the part of the person doing it. And just as the success in macrobiotics is proportional to the amount of study time invested in making sure it is done properly, spirituality likewise, has benefits in proportion to the amount of dedication and interest vested in it. In other words, there is no substitute for learning all you can about factors that cost no money yet have remarkable results, whether they relate to diet or spirituality.

REFERENCES:

Byrd RB, Positive therapeutic effects of intercessory prayer in a coronary care unit population, SOUTHERN MEDICAL J, 81: 826-829, 1988.

Gartner J, Larson DB, and Allen G, Religious commitment and mental health: A review of the empirical literature, J PSYCHOL THEOL, 19(1):6-25, 1991.

Pressman P, et al, Religious belief, depression, and ambulation status in elderly women with broken hips, AM J PSYCHIATRY, 147(6):758-760, 1990.

Larson DB, Faith: The forgotten factor in healthcare, AMER J NATURAL MED, 2:4, 10-15, May 1995 (Impact Communications, Inc., POB 12496, Green Bay WI 54307-249).

Larson DB, THE FAITH FACTOR: AN ANNOTATED BIBLIOGRAPHY OF CLINICAL RESEARCH ON SPIRITUAL STUDIES, Health care Research Inst, 6110 Executive Blvd, Ste 680, Rockville MD 20852, 1800-580-NIHR.

Larson DB, THE FAITH FACTOR , VOL II, ibid.

Larson DB, THE FORGOTTEN FACTOR IN HEALTH AND MENTAL HEALTH: WHAT DOES THE RESEARCH SHOW?, ibid.

Onarecker CD, Sterling BC, Addressing your patients' spiritual needs, FAM PRAC MANAG, 44-49, May 1995.

Kuhn C, A spiritual inventory of the medically ill patient, PSYCHIATRIC MED, 6:87-100, 1988.

Joyce CRB, Welldon RMC, The objective efficacy of prayer: a double-blind clinical trial, J CHRONIC DIS, 18:367-377, 1965.

STRESS PERCEPTION AND SPIRITUALITY

The majority of people who are on anti-depressants, are people who are functioning quite well in society. Not even their close friends know they are on a mind- and mood-altering drug. I loathe categorizing people, but there are many common patient-types who present with depression. So let's look at a few.

A typical patient-type is what I call the **"Super Woman Syndrome"**. Ever since women's lib in the 1970's, we have really screwed ourselves into an impossible to fulfill role. Most woman now are wives and mothers, some are even single parents, and work outside the home at another job as well. They are literally overwhelmed with obligations and have no time for enjoyment. If they do, they are just too exhausted to enjoy anything. They go to bed thinking about the schedule for the next day and awaken rehearsing their routine so they can jam it all into one day. When they do get to have a little relaxation, they are so exhausted, it usually is a passive, vicarious form of entertainment such as a movie or a theater production. And you know what a lifestyle like this does to your nutrient status. She ends up with fast foods, convenience packaged foods, and a low nutrient status. Add to this the nutrient depletion that stress performs, alcohol, sodas, cigarettes and you have **a disaster begging to happen.**

And the male counterpart to Superwoman is what I call the **3-M Man,** or the **Multi-Media Man.** Talk about bringing work home from the office, this man carries his office with him wherever he goes! At home, in the car, and at the office, he has linked himself with the rest of the world via portable fax machines, cell phones, computers, electronic mail, and every beeping electronic gadget he can get his hands on. He even has mini-modules that fit in his palm, fit in his brief case, fit in his golf bag, strap onto his wrist, or sit on his lap in the train, plane, boat, or toilet and keep his brain in perpetual high gear (McCartney S, The multi-tasking man: Type A meets technology, THE WALL STREET JOURNAL, B1, B2, Apr 19, 1995).

In fact, his level of irritability reaches its peak when at night he tries to relax and watch television with the family. The only problem, is that as an executive or manager, he is also a control freak; so he gets to man the remote channel changer. And as multi-media man who has been barraged with problems to solve all day, he gets bored with more than 30 seconds on any channel. So he drives the rest of the family crazy with his maniacal channel surfing. Plus from his PC, he has developed the habit of double-clicking! When he does land on a station, it is usually one of the "scream and shout" political commentary or debate programs. That further irritates everyone else who is in the mood for a relaxing mindless form of entertainment to soothe their rattled nerves after the day.

These fellows, likewise, are an accident waiting to happen, with either a stress-related depression or other brain malady ("nervous breakdown"), or heart attack, etc. For this constant surge of adrenaline is often additionally augmented by coffee, cigarettes, sodas, chocolate, decongestants, caffeine-containing pain pills, alertness pills, and other sympathetic nervous system stimulators.

Since he is such a workaholic, he is not a very good athlete. So he periodically ventures onto the tennis court with as much enthusiasm as he takes to a committee meeting. As a result his injuries leave him no alternative but to suck down

NSAIDs. But there inevitably comes a time of end-organ overload and exhaustion. If it happens in the brain in the form of depression, he is lucky. If the heart is the target organ, he is dead.

Another common type of depressed woman I have commonly observed in 26 years of practice is what I call the **"Repressed Lady"**. Let's see how the repressed child becomes the depressed adult. You know if a three year old falls off his bike and gets angry with himself for having failed in front of anxious spectators that he was showing off for, he can have one of two reactions. He can be **mad or sad**. If he gets mad, his anger is directed at the bike; he kicks it, maybe uttering some expletives that he has picked up at home or on T.V. In this case he will be rewarded by the mock shock and delight of his proud parents, reveling in his precociousness.

However, let a little girl dressed in gingham display this same aggressive behavior, and more than likely, she will be reprimanded for not being lady-like. In time she learns that she gets her rewards by being feminine, helpless, vulnerable, and you guessed it, sad. In fact, if she cries, it most likely will win her a seat on Daddy's lap. So she learns early to **repress any anger and turn it into sadness** in order to get the goodies in life.

And that is a message that is difficult for many women to unlearn. They go through **life experiencing anger as depression**. Then they spend fortunes in psychotherapy to learn that they **are not sad, but mad**. They may even go through Gestalt therapy and learn how to beat pillows as imaginary replicas of significant people in their past, in order to live out this anger and repressed aggression. For they have learned the lady-like message too well.

Then there is the **Doormat**. The **perpetual people pleaser**. She or he can be a co-dependent abused wife, or he can be the nice guy who never lets his feelings out, lest anyone would not like him. The Doormat is determined to keep peace at all costs. He keeps everything bottled up and lets it eat away at him.

One of the most pitiful is the **selfish, sarcastic love-starved** individual. They may appear on the outside to have everything. But inside they are suffering from a deficiency of nurturing. They have always felt the world owed them love, since they were cheated early on. Or they merely have a perception that they were cheated. As an example, they may have been the eldest child, hence "Mommy's little helper". While the younger ones had an excuse to be messy or receive cuddling because they were so small and cute, this one only got rewards or praise for work. Hence, they evolved into work-aholics, driven people still looking for love as their reward. Because the world doesn't work that way and they cannot communicate the problem, their anger turns to sarcasm and selfishness. Fortunately, love melts all of this away.

A variant of this person is one I call **"Just following the rules"**. Imagine the child growing up in a busy, hard-working family. There is not enough time for parents to spend with the children. And when they do, it is time shared with all the siblings vying for affection at once. But what happens when he is sick or injured? Everything comes to a screeching halt. Mom or Dad takes off time from work to care for him. He has their exclusive attention all to himself, lavishly nurturing him. Who could ask for anything more: **affection on demand**. And it's not bad for Mom or Dad either. They get an unexpected break from work, a mini vacation. So there are no guilt vibes sent to the kid.

And what is the take-home message? When you're down a quart or two in nurturing, get sick or injured. This is exactly how some sickness-prone or accident-prone children and adults operate. It is their only known way to get tanked up on the attention and love they are missing.

Needless-to-say there are many other character types that I have observed to be pertinent precursors to depression, as these are mere examples. Like any other disease, depression has a total load of multiple factors that contribute to its final manifestation. One of the contributing factors as well as symptoms of depression is when **life has lost its passion,** its excitement, its drive, its reason for being; it works both ways since that's one of the main driving forces of depression as well as one of the main symptoms.

Regardless of which comes first, when people become so **over-whelmed** they don't know how to cope any longer, that's when passion dies. For there is just no time for it. When **life's demands overwhelm our ability to cope and feel,** it saps every ounce of energy, mental and physical. At this point it is often impossible to separate depression from fatigue. The two are inextricably intertwined in one victim. Survival and meeting self-imposed deadlines and schedules become the main focus in life. But without the mental and physical time to devote to a passion, passion withers and dies out of neglect or disuse. And when passion dies, it fuels the destructive fires of depression.

Yet if we all pause a moment and take stock of our lives, for each one of us, no matter how important we seem to be, if we died tomorrow, the world would go right on. It wouldn't miss a beat. Think of important statesmen and presidents, people who had tremendous responsibility, who died suddenly. We shed our tears, but we all kept functioning. So how important then does that make those many things that you just have to do? Those things that overwhelm you and lead to depression.

Next, let's step back and look at people who have survived a serious illness or injury, or have lost someone close to them. Many of these people have changed their perception of stress because they have **changed their priorities**. No longer are the ways of the world going to dictate their daily schedules. They have seen beyond man's world and have realized how precious our time here is. The message: **Like beauty, stress is in the eye of the beholder**. You only have to look for the other perspective that you are ignoring. **Stress is an illusion**. It has always been amazing to me how two people can perceive stress in totally opposite ways. One person can perceive a situation as stressful, and develop ulcers or cancers or depression. In contrast, another person sees stress as a clue that he needs to take some courses in time management or re-think his priorities. Or he sees a potentially stressful situation as merely a challenge to his problem-solving abilities and actually something that he looks forward to.

STRESS IS A DOUBLE-EDGED SWORD

Never lose sight of the fact that stress can do much damage to the body. Not only can nutrient deficiencies lead to poor neurotransmitter chemistry in the brain resulting in poor ability to deal with stress, **but stress lowers nutrients and damages immune system cells**. As you learned, low nutrients and subsequent immune system compromise set the body up for further disease, not the least of which is cancer (LANCET 834-836, 1977).

In other words, nutrient deficiencies can lead to inappropriate metabolism of stress hormones and result in depression. And the opposite also happens. Stress can result in nutrient deficiencies, which can then lead to depression. Recall the nutrients used up in the work of detoxifying the brain's **worry hormones**. These nutrients could have been used to synthesize happy hormones.

Recall the study of men whose wives were dying of breast cancer. When the wives died, the T cells of the husbands reached an all-time low, making them vulnerable to any disease. Numerous studies show the effect of stress on various physiological systems of the body. So for sure an inordinate amount of **perceived stress** does no good. Whereas, we cannot live without it either, or we die of boredom. As in everything, **balance is key**.

There are many more studies showing that major depression can cause impaired immune function indicated by lower natural killer cell activity and many other parameters. In other words, **if you are sad enough, you can damage your immune system** and you are ripe enough for other diseases including cancer (Zisook S, et al, Bereavement, Depression and immune function, PSYCHIATRIC RESEARCH, 52:1-10, 1994).

And it should come as less of a surprise to you that in a study of people who had had a **heart attack, those who were depressed had a 6 1/2 times more chance of dying.** And you know why. Actual stress (the perception or interpretation of life events into stress) lowers crucial nutrients like magnesium and choline-derived methyl groups. But on the flip side, magnesium deficiency is one deficiency that predisposes you to a heart attack and predisposes you to further depression and even sudden cardiac death. And a magnesium deficiency makes it harder to resuscitate you and reduces your chance of survival. But the practice guidelines (the cookbook directives that all of medicine is molding itself into currently) do not include looking at the appropriate assay that would even diagnose a magnesium deficiency, much less look for the other causes of depression.

The medical evidence is overwhelming of how stress adversely affects your health. It can raise your blood pressure, raise your cholesterol, or make your blood more easy to clot so you are ripe for a heart attack or stroke. Or it can knock down your white blood count so you are more ripe for infection or cancer.

"For truly, **A merry heart doeth good like medicine**: but a broken spirit drieth the bones" (Pro 17).

REFERENCES:

Zoler ML, Psychosocial elements added to CAD risk: behavioral medicine may extend survival after myocardial infarction, FAM PRACT NEWS, 24(24): 1, 15, December 15, 1994.

Linkins R, Comstock GW, Depressed mood and development of cancer, AMER J EPID, 132 (5): 962-970, 1990.

Henrotte JG, Type A behavior and magnesium metabolism, MAGNESIUM, 5:201-210, 1986.

McGuire R, Type A stress a drain on magnesium, MED TRIBUNE, p1, May 15, 1984.

Barthrop RW, Depressed lymphocyte function after bereavement, LANCET. 2:834-836, 1977.

Kronfol Z, et al, Impaired lymphocyte function in depressive illness, LIFE SCI, 33:241-247, 1983.

Schliefer SJ, et al, Suppression of lymphocyte stimulation following bereavement, JAMA, 250:374-377, 1983.

Miller AH, ed, DEPRESSIVE DISORDERS AND IMMUNITY, APA Press, WA, 1989.

Editorial: Depression, stress and immunity, LANCET, 1:1467, 1987.

Glasser R, et al, Stress, loneliness, and changes in herpes virus latency, J BEHAV MED, 8:249, 1985.

Muldoon MF, Herbert TB, Patterson SM, Kameneva M, Raible R, Manuck SB, Effects of acute psychological stress on serum lipid levels, hemoconcentration, and blood viscosity, ARCH INT MED, 155:615-620, 1995.

Winslow R, Warning: Managed care may be hazardous to your blood pressure, WALL STREET JOURNAL, B1, Sept. 14, 1995.

Kaliner M, et al, Autonomic nervous system abnormalities and allergy, ANN INTERN MED, 96:349-357, 1982.

*****

It should never again come as a surprise that depression is not healthy for the immune system (Depression, Distress and Immunity: Risk Factors For Infectious Disease. STRESS MACHINE, 7:45-51, 1991). Refer back to Volume II if you need to recall just how bad thoughts steal from the chemistry of the brain's happy hormones.

THE BEST PSYCHIATRY/PSYCHOTHERAPY

Obviously, the psychotherapy of psychiatry and psychology have helped many people immensely. It would not have persisted as an integral part of these specialties if there were not some usefulness. But psychotherapy serves as only part of the answer, unless it gets to a level of a person's spirituality. Sure it is great to find out, for example, that you were abused as a child and that is why you have depression, anger, guilt and phobias. But until you reach the stage of **forgiveness** and allow **love to permeate** your being, you will not be able to maximally energize your happy hormones. And you could play out your anger, beating pillows in Gestalt fashion, to the point of exhaustion. But where is the forgiveness and love that must replace these emotions in order for real **emotional** and physical **healing** to take place?

For numerous studies in psycho-neuro immunology show us that **peace of mind and love and forgiveness are multiply therapeutic.** They foster the synthesis of hormones and neurotransmitters in the body that actually stimulate the **parasympathetic nervous system.** In this mode, peace of mind, love and forgiveness improve digestion, the function of glands and improve the flow and the production of healing enzymes and neurotransmitters. And you just read how harmful or negative emotions can deplete nutrients, damage the immune system, and can turn on the chemistry of depression. But a spirituality with genuine forgiveness and love is the fastest way I know of to reverse this.

You know yourself, if you are angry and uptight, or running away from a charging tiger, your body is in the **flight or fight mode.** All of your energy is used for empowering your muscles. It is being shunted away from the happy hormones of the brain and all of the healing functions of the body. These include digestive glands, hormones, and neurotransmitters of happy and satiated feelings. That is why at the end of the day when you have had a lot of anger, interruptions and problems, you feel tension in your neck and back muscles. They have been in the fight or flight mode probably all day since you blew your top. They are ready for the charging tiger to use.

Instead, if you were able to learn to humbly accept the failings of your colleagues and extend forgiveness and love in an effort to help them grow and improve, you would also simultaneously be nurturing your own body physiology. Sure, it is extremely difficult to do. But imagine the benefits to your own body and psyche, as well as your changed relationships with everyone else. It certainly is something to strive for.

TIME OUT: In the following sections, you will see much reference to God, Christianity, Jesus Christ and the BIBLE. These are teachings that guide me toward the spiritual and help my faith to grow. These are examples I will use because they are the ones I am most familiar with. It is not intended to exclude other religions, but merely to compensate for my lack of knowledge about them. The point here is that faith is a factor proven to help people heal. My mission is not to challenge or change your religious views but rather to increase your ability to lead a happy and healthy life. So please feel free to substitute the word BIBLE for KORAN (QUR'AN), TORAH, GITA, TRIPITAKA or what-ever word means for you a book of teachings from your chosen God that help your faith to grow. Now back to our message:

495

Because we can internalize so much tension by the end of a day, we need methods to help unwind: yoga (Iyengar type), meditation, reading THE HOLY BIBLE, massage, exercise and other forms of relaxing body and mind work are important for helping discharge these tensions. But instead, we often do just the opposite.

First we consume enough calories to prepare us for a battle. Then we rage a mental battle as we vicariously live through more horrors in one evening of T.V. than the average person experiences in a lifetime. And by now you ought to realize that this stress can lower and deplete minerals even further. The stress from watching an action/adventure film on T.V. can use up nutrients that are needed in the detox pathways to metabolize our daily chemicals, not to mention our happy hormones. Plus it shuts down the digestive enzymes. The result is you do not get the rest and healing you need during sleep. You have to make up for the digestion that was put off while you watched that thriller on T.V. that had you in the fight or flight mode.

One of the first things you might do is stop watching television. Your first reaction is that that is the only relaxation, reward, diversion, fun, therapy, or entertainment that you get all day. But you can use up enough adrenalin to keep you exhausted and depressed for the next day. There seems to be a competition among the thriller-diller shows on T.V. to be more intensely exciting and unbelievably thrilling than the next one.

As Phillip Keller said in GOD AS MY DELIGHT, is it any wonder that children find it so difficult to get in touch with God. For children vicariously experience more sensuality, corruption, murder and horror in one evening of television than a person might experience in a lifetime. This tends to rob them of the awes of the natural world. When you have been so overwhelmed with adrenalin-depleting horrors or video games, it strips you of the wonders, the curiosity and inspiration, and the serenity that is present in nature.

How can a child be expected to see the beauty of a spring bud when he expects to have his adrenalin pumping wildly at all times to feel "normal"? How can we blame him for turning to fast-paced rock music and video games, mind-altering drugs, alcohol and cigarettes as well as junk foods loaded with sugars, aspartame, MSG, and other excitatory additives to pump him up to that same artificial high he has become accustomed to?

And once you have a mind altered with drugs and stimulating foods like sugars and other chemicals, how can you feel the spirit of God touching you? Do you think it is any coincidence that highly religious people fast when they pray? Of course not. They want their minds as clear as possible so they can perceive the subtle energies of God. I am not saying "Don't let them ever watch T.V. again", but why not ration it to 1-3 nights a week?

That is what entertainment is supposed to be about. A vicarious change from the ordinary, from our steady diet, from our everyday pace. It is not supposed to be the steady diet, just as sweets and desserts are not intended for a steady diet. Sweets were meant to be a little treat at the end of the weekly big meal. But they, unfortunately, have become the steady diet for many people. Look around you as you drive to work and see how many people are sucking down sodas, coffee, gooey frosted donuts and other stimulants to get themselves ready for the day. And see how many candy bars appear for that afternoon "pick-me-up". Dessert is not even limited to one meal. For some, it is their whole diet. The point is, a heavy schedule of action entertainment is also not conducive to good mental health.

When I was starting out in my practice a quarter of a century ago, I realized I had to learn a great deal about psychiatry because depression and other mental diseases were rampant among loving, wonderful and normal people. I realized my failings as a doctor to help them address these, and I couldn't even control it in myself. Sure, I had a bag of pills that I could prescribe, but I thought there was something missing. So I took myself off to courses through the years. I would learn traditional psychotherapy, Gestalt psycho-therapy, Rational Emotive Therapy, TM, anything that was in vogue or hyped up or promoted to be of use.

What I finally found decades later was **the best psychotherapy is one's own spirituality which instills in them a foundation of faith.** Only then can a person get in touch with what is really important to him, set his priorities and get on with his goals. Plus it provides him with a constant set of guidelines with which he can perpetually monitor himself and his progress. It is only through spirituality that I have seen people truly unload anger, guilt, resentment, hate, jealousy and all the nasty emotions that robbed them of their health. They move far beyond their health-robbing petty emotions.

"The prayer of faith shall save the sick, and the Lord shall raise him up; and if he have committed sins, they shall be forgiven him. Confess your faults one to another, and pray one for another, that ye may be healed" (JAMES 5). My gosh, isn't this the basis of psychoanalysis? Be up front about what it is you are hiding, or what is eating at you that you cannot face. And isn't the number one reason people find it difficult to deal with many emotions is because of their fear of rejection by those who mean the most to them once these failings are found out?

How many times after a suicide have we heard loved ones lament that they wished they had known how much emotional pain the person was in; that they would have liked to share it with them and help them see that in the overall scheme of things, they were much more important than some silly short-comings. That is why it says, "confess your faults to one another". Get it out and over with. Don't let it fester and become magnified. And don't let it embarrass or shame or overwhelm or depress you as it did suicide victims.

Not a one of us was ever put here perfect. So why should you be an exception? "For all have sinned and fallen short of the glory of God" (ROM 3). So since we are all in the same boat, it should hardly be a reason for suicide or depression.

For "from the beginning God chose you" (2TH2). And "each man has his own gift from God" (1CO7). Hence he "should use whatever gift he has "(1PE4), "to accept his lot and be happy" (ECC5). How much simpler can it be? As Gary Player the famous golfer said, "Each day when I wake up I have the choice to be negative or positive."

What are your gifts? If you don't know, get some professional help (clergy, psychologist, psychiatrist, or some gifted loved ones, etc.) in finding them. For they are there. Find out what your role is supposed to be. For "do not neglect your gift that has been given you" (1TI4), but "Be diligent in these matters; give yourself wholly to them"(1TI4). In other words, get your passion energized.

And that passion cannot come about if your emotions are numbed by anti-depressants. It cannot materialize without freeing ourselves from some of the false impediments and restrictions, inhibitions and restraints that we allow others to impose upon us. How many therapies counsel us to free the child within, let it fly again, and become all that it is capable of being? To let its creativity and unconditional love and trust surface, to let it explore the majesty and wonder of the world, as seen through the eyes of a child? For "unless we become like little children" (MT18), where do we get the spark for enthusiasm, passion, fun, laughter, creativity, learning, growth, direction?

It is not easy for many to get in touch with their spirituality. In spite of many gifts from God, it took me a great deal of studying and reading. And I'm by no means where I intend to eventually be. When I couldn't find the time to go to BIBLE study classes, I bought ministers' handbooks and books for people who were teaching BIBLE study classes and taught myself. There are many wonderful ways to learn out there. There are people who are willing to help you. There are BIBLE study classes, student Bibles with explanations, and there is a phenomenal wealth of help in many books. Some of them are listed at the end of this section.

EMPOWERMENT

By now you may realize that all of this has to do with empowerment. Yes, why you got sick and what you have to do in order to heal yourself, all comes down to empowerment. In the last century, we have given power to the food industry to drop the nutrient content of our foods by 25-80%. We've allowed the food industry to saturate our diets with damaging trans fatty acids that have been known for over 40 years to be able to promote every type of illness. We've allowed the pharmaceutical industry to take over medicine with the notion of drugs for everything. We've allowed nutritional assessments to take a back seat in medicine, and insurance companies tell us what diseases we can have, how long we can have them and what treatments we can have.

I just learned that a valedictorian is not allowed to mention the word "God" in her graduation address. Are they that afraid of people becoming empowered by their faith in God that they have to outlaw him? Talk about history repeating itself! Before you know it you will have to hand in all your money so "In God we trust" can be scrapped off. In its place they will stamp "In man we trust". And you know what? I don't think there will be many who will protest. And if they do, they will be made out as Bible-toting weirdo's. How much more absurd does the world have to get before more than just a handful notices that there is something very very wrong. But then it is all written: "In the last times there will be scoffers who will follow their own ungodly drives." "These men will divide you "(JUD).

We've handed over the power of our health to our overweight physicians, who have as many health problems as we do. And we have allowed mental health to take a back seat in medicine: Mental health still has a stigma associated with it; it is used as a scapegoat when medicine is stumped and can't figure out your diagnosis. It saves face and provides another fancy label. And as many studies have shown, when depression is real, physicians have such poor recognition of it that well over half the cases remain unrecognized and undiagnosed. As a result, since many are diagnosed as depressed, when in fact we just do not know what they have, depression has also taken on a secondary connotation of hypochondriasis. This has allowed medicine to save face. For then it is not a lack of knowledge or diagnostic acumen on our part. It's all your fault and you're just making it up.

Furthermore, we are trained to almost virtually ignore or at least downplay the importance of the mind in healing. And on the other hand, we are led to deify and accentuate the role of the physician instead. But you can have the most wonderful physician in the world, and it means nothing. He can be the most skilled surgeon, diagnostician, technician, the most artful prescriber and balancer of medication. But if the mind does not want the body to heal, it won't.

Every so often I'll see a new patient in my office who has the usual parade of symptoms: depression, recurrent sinusitis, asthma, chronic fatigue, arthritis or fibromyalgia, cystitis, vaginitis or prostatitis, colitis, brain fog, migraine, chronic back pain, etc. But when we have completed the interview, I have to regrettably announce: "I've been able to help hundreds of people with your symptoms and worse. But I'm afraid I will not be able to treat you. You see, it would be a waste of your time and money. You have so much anger

502

locked up inside of you that it is a major detriment to your getting yourself well. So until you can get rid of that **anger,** I'm afraid it would be futile for us to precede. I suspect that is why there has been no physician who could help you get well." Often that has been the breakthrough they needed in order to face a major part of their total load honestly and realistically. Now they are ready to get on with the work of unloading and healing.

And as people lose power, it fuels the power of the powerful. The FDA just passed Olestra, a fat substitute. The commercials were on TV the next night promoting pretty young women who were garfing down chips like vultures, because they were low in fat. But the studies all clearly show that Olestra inhibits the absorption of cancer and arteriosclerosis- sparing vitamins A, D, E, K, and beta carotene. Have they gone mad with power? These are the same folks who want to remove vitamins from the market, and who have already taken some nutrients off the shelves that are essential to life. These are the same folks who took all sorts of drugs with a long list of side effects, some of which are potentially lethal, off prescription. The manufacturers couldn't sell enough if people had to go to their doctors to get them (Pepcid, Nicorette, Motrin, Naprosyn, Tagamet, Rogaine, etc.). And if you need further convincing, these are the same folks who allow, for example, the Pepcid T.V. commercials to blatantly prescribe its prophylactic use so you can go out and eat anything that you know tears up your stomach (Mexican was their example). So here you have turned off the normal function of the stomach secretions and then filled it with hot spicy unusual foods. It's a medical disaster waiting to happen, and apparently condoned by the FDA or FTC.

Furthermore, the NEW ENGLAND JOURNAL OF MEDICINE (Stampfer, 1993) article showed you cut your cardiovascular risk in half with only 100 I.U. of vitamin E a day. Hundreds of other articles affirm its efficacy and safety. Yet they felt they could not recommend it to the common man! But a chemical is added (Olestra) to foods that intentionally inhibits some of your vitamin E absorption. It doesn't compute.

The government has allowed the food industry to strip vitamin E from grains (flour products) and cooking oils. As a consequence we do coronary by-pass surgery like they were tonsillectomies. The only problem is they are $48,000. Then you are locked into a lifetime of drugs and doctors and many patients do not return to work. But they do, on the average, restenose or reclot those arteries. Vitamin E has been found to dramatically reduce this reclotting of the arteries. But the FDA has OK'd Olestra, the fat substitute, that inhibits absorption of vitamin E. Are they working for your health or the chemical/pharmaceutical/food manufacturing lobbyists?!? (Hodis HN, Mach WJ, Labree MS, et al, Serial Coronary Aniographic Evidence That Antioxidant Vitamin Intake Reduces Progression of Coronary Artery Arteriosclerosis, J AMER MED ASSOC, 273:1849-1854, 1995).

And you know that when you try to prove anything in medicine or science, you do double blind studies. You give both groups everything the same, except for one variable, the thing you are testing. Well, in the studies on Olestra, the majority were done by Proctor & Gamble (the fox was left to guard the hen house?), the people who make it. Furthermore, because they know it reduces 5 vitamins, they gave these vitamins to the rats who got Olestra. Then the conclusion was Olestra was non-toxic and caused no problems!

Some even suggest they may add vitamin E back to some foods. There are many problems with this. First, the government RDA for vitamin E in ridiculously less then 12 I.U. a day! Second, they will most likely use the d,l-tocophenols since they can be made synthetically and are cheaper. The trouble is, like trans-fatty acids, they are foreign to the body and can create more problems than they solve.

Folks, the bottom line is the more power you give away, the sicker you will get. Are you willing to do that?

Many have allowed society to intimidate them into not standing for their beliefs. You see it all the time. If you mention Nature, you are on safe ground. Say the word God, however, and you begin to tread on shaky ground. But say the words Jesus Christ, and you have somehow crossed over the line. You have stepped into the world of the wacky. Your credibility has taken a nose-dive.

But **it takes empowerment to get well.** No one is going to change your diet for you, detox your bedroom, make sure you check your nutrient levels, fight your insurance company or HMO to be able to get these tests, or read the rest of this book to you. No one is going to make sure you get the most from your brief stay on earth. Only you can provide the kick in the butt. **Only you can empower yourself----it's a magical thing.**

But **along with empowerment comes** the ability to take charge and **responsibility for your health.** And only you can say that unutterable word, "NO". For when you are overwhelmed, you must draw the line in order for your mental and physical energies to regenerate. And as you rise to new levels of energy it is only then that you can begin to realize that the sky is the limit in terms of how well you can get. It just depends on how much energy you want to give it.

But as you might guess, there are many who will not be happy with your new empowerment: the grocer when you ask for organic foods and glass-bottled spring water to be sold, the waiter when you want no trans-fatty acids, your boss when you ask for the pesticide ingredients, your doctor when you tell him of your plan to be drug-free, your dentist when you want your mercury out. What happened to that mindless automaton who depended on Prozac? He was so controllable, so predictable.

The most important reason for you to become empowered at this time is that medicine is fast becoming a cookbook specialty. This is so that doctors as well as patients lose their power. Right now PRACTICE GUIDELINES are being drawn up for all medical problems. What it amounts to is a giant cookbook set of guidelines so anyone can follow the recipe for each disease. It is fostered on medicine under the guise of ensuring the same quality of care across the U.S.

But what **cookie-cutter medicine** really does is say that for such and such disease, you can only use these drugs and this surgery, and that is it. **Assembly line medicine is mediocre medicine at best.** You will never get the top-of-the-line diagnostic work that is in these 4 volumes. Anything else not in the practice guidelines is either not covered by insurance, or a reason to drag your doctor in for not complying with standard treatment. And guess what? Over 98% of what is in this book is not considered by the drug industry medical moguls to be standard treatment. So you are out of luck. Unless you empower yourself to show the evidence to a caring physician who can see past the drugs-for-everything mentality that has taken over medicine, you are in danger of being ignored, and enduring depression indefinitely.

And do not doubt for a moment the power and influence that the drug industry holds over medicine. As one more tiny example, the Sunday NEW YORK TIMES can have a full page add telling arthritis suffers to ask their docs to prescribe Relafen for their arthritis. Or they can turn on T.V. and find out they can now get prescription Naprosyn as over-the-counter Aleve and treat themselves. Or they can just open their mailboxes and find a free sample. But no where in the package insert does it say that they could go on to develop the leaky gut syndrome with these non-steroidal anti-inflammatory drugs. Does it say that they promote deterioration of the arthritic joints and do nothing to repair them? Does it say that the leaky gut then can cause auto-immune diseases like lupus, multiple sclerosis, rheumatoid arthritis, thyroiditis, Alzheimer's, etc.?

And these drugs that are over-the-counter have the ability to cause gastrointestinal hemorrhage that can be fatal. You can die from the side effects! Yet have you heard of inexpensive non-prescription, safe, alternatives like **glucosamine sulfate** that has as much anti-inflammatory action, but can actually go on to regenerate new bone and articular cartilage after several months' use? (HEALTH LETTER, 1995).

Does it appear that the FDA has double standards and double agendas? For at the same time, your health food store and supplement manufacturers are prohibited from teaching you and even are prohibited from showing physicians research from the scientific literature that pertains to the biochemistry of their products. What happened to the first amendment? And efforts are underway to get more supplements off the market or under prescription control. It has already happened in some European countries and a simple mineral like zinc that used to be a few dollars is now nearly $50 on prescription. The only hope I see is in **PEOPLE POWER.** If and when there are enough educated and drug-free people to make a difference, they will make their voices heard.

People power can and does make a difference. It can rescue America and bring her to new heights. But **only real people,** offer any hope of recovery for America, **not Prozac people.** Only people emblazoned with enthusiasm, who are sure of their spirituality and goals, who have first made themselves well, can hope to regenerate the American spirit that originally founded this nation.

So when will we be free enough from our anguish, guilt, anger, jealousies, and hatred to see the beauty around us? To feel the loving spirit waiting to be unleashed. That sees not the failures and faux pas of our colleagues, but instead appreciates that they are doing all they are capable of at this moment, given their cumulative life experiences. For only when we are permeated with real emotion, not one cloaked in drugs, can we emanate the forgiveness and love that this world is all about. Only then can we hear the voice within that tells us what our purpose is. And it is not to be wallowing in self-pity and the paralysis of depression. To be sure it is a loftier intention.

REFERENCES:

Reavis DJ, THE ASHES OF WACO, Simon & Schuster NY, 1995.

Tabor JD, Gallagher EV, WHY WACO?, University of California Press, Berkeley, 1995.

Howard PK, THE DEATH OF COMMON SENSE, Random House, NY, 1995.

Tipler FJ, PHYSICS AND IMMORTALITY, Anchor Books, NY 1995.

ESCAPISM

Escapism or diversion is good for us: all work and no play.....we need rest and relaxation, entertainment, socialization, laughter, and more. But in our affluent, distorted values world, many are in a constant state of escapism. They never are in touch with their real emotions.

Some start the day with mind/emotion/happy hormone—altering coffee, cigarettes, sugars. Then proceed to their tranquilizer or anti-depressant. At night the television is their sole communication with the world, as they "relax" with alcohol and more mind-altering food choices. They are in a constant state of gratification, escapism.

In other words, they have carefully escaped from even having to face their real emotions and life's questions. What makes them worthwhile? Why are they here? What is their purpose in life? What happens after they die?

And this is the most dangerous of all things for not only the individual, but all of society. For in a state of escapism, you cannot grow emotionally or spiritually. And all empowerment vanishes as others take over progressively more aspects of your life for you. More rules to live by, more decisions made for you, until you are a mere pawn, puppet, robot, zombie of a world government. If you think it sounds like sci-fi, you're already partly there.

Then you have missed the decisions that have come down every year that should make you ask, "Are they nuts?", Have they lost all common sense?", "Do they think we're completely stupid?" Do they think we have lost our souls?"

RESPONSIBILITY

You've got it. It all boils down to responsibility. For with responsibility you have empowerment. Without responsibility you have servitude, slavery, controlled robots or zombies. We are on the way.

And there is only one thing that can save us. A force that has overthrown governments for centuries, that can unexpectedly let governments know, enough is enough. **People power** can change all this. But only if people take charge of their education and learn about health. For one of the roles of government is to look after and protect people who are incapable of doing it for themselves. But by learning how to restore your mental and physical health, you can then empower yourself to become all you are capable of being. For once the power has been transferred to someone else, they can never be as vested in your health as you are. You become an easy mark for lobbyists of billion-dollar pharmaceutical and food manufacturers. The rest is every day history.

As this goes to press, the evidence mounts. Redux, just passed the FDA as a diet pill, is a biochemical cousin to Prozac. Oddly, it has been OK'd for merely a one year prescription. But how many docs will remember to take someone off after a year? Worse yet, they just found that it causes an 18-fold increase in potentially fatal pulmonary hypertension. Hence they reduced its use to 3 months, maintaining the need to treat obesity outweighs the risk. (WSJ,B9, 8/23/96) But, would 3 months weight loss make enough of an impact on your life to be worth dying for? It just does not compute.

REFERENCES: (Must Reading)

Rand, Ayn, ATLAS SHRUGGED, 1943

Robertson, Pat, A NEW WORLD ORDER, World Publ., Dallas, 1991

White, EG, THE GREAT CONTROVERSY, Harvestime Books, Altamont TN 37301, 1988 (reprinted from 1884)

Wardner JW, THE PLANNED DESTRUCTION OF AMERICA, Longwood Communications, 397 Kingslake Dr, De Bary, FL 32713 or 1-800-TYRANNY, 1994

Tanouye E, Five drug makers post healthy profit, as managed care spurs prescriptions, WALL STREET JOURNAL, A2, Oct 23, 1996

BLOWING OFF THE UNFATHOMABLE

Allow me to present thoughts on my faith as an example of why I think a spirituality is far preferable to transient and expensive psychotherapy. Remember to substitute your own beliefs if this is not compatible with yours. For I do not know enough about other faiths to use them as examples. But science has shown that the physiologic benefits from one's faith extends through many religions.

In the 50's when women had lupus, because doctors did not know what it was, they blew off or dismissed the women as neurotic. To this day, whenever something is not understood or unexplainable, often to save face, people blow it off.

The same was done (and still is) with chemical sensitivity. I never met a doctor knowledgeable in xenobiotic detoxication chemistry who didn't acknowledge chemical sensitivity. Only those unknowledgeable will blow off the patients as psyche cases. So I guess it should come as no surprise that people who have no knowledge of the BIBLE and its history also blow it off as hogwash.

And just as improperly diagnosed medical problems make one get sicker, quicker, so does ignorance about faith also snowball. The less someone comprehends about the history of the BIBLE, the easier it is to blow the whole thing off as a fairy tale. And logically the opposite is true. The more one knows about finding the causes of medical conditions, the more he is able to get rid of every complaint he ever had and reach undreamed of heights of wellness. And likewise, faith snowballs as well. For as one has faith, he reads. As he reads and studies, he gets more knowledge and understanding and develops more faith. Just as the sick get sicker, the faithful become more faithful. The grand thing is, **you have a choice.**

Look at the history of the world. Whenever man has lacked the knowledge to understand something, he has staunchly refused to believe it and blown it off as implausible. Because man did not understand, Copernicus was ridiculed, arrested, blasphemed; blown off for suggesting that the sun and not the earth was the center of the universe. Semmelweiss was blown off for suggesting that doctors coming from the autopsy room could stop killing maternity patients by washing "invisible" germs from their hands before delivering babies. For that thought (that saved countless lives), he was ostracized and died a pauper.

Most of us were blown off for suggesting that foods, chemicals and molds can cause symptoms in people. Then as knowledge intervened, the unfathomable and unbelievable became fact. For in the end, **truth rules out,** however late it might be for some. Look at the field of environmental medicine as an example. We have been ridiculed, bad-mouthed, and blown off to the hilt. Yet, guess what? Gradually everything we **ever** stood for and taught is being proven. And not one notion has ever been disproven or shown to be wrong. I wish I had a nickel for every time a patient showed me a newspaper report about some new proven finding and gleefully noted that we had told him that 10 years ago.

And God is the most unfathomable entity of all. But He should be. We are mere mortals. We don't know squat. So what makes us so cocky that we can insist on understanding all about God before we will do him a big favor and believe? There is a wonderful series of novels by a retired priest,

Joseph Girzone. He raises our spiritual consciousness with stories about how it would be if Christ came back to earth in different times. Of course if he came today, very few would notice unless he booked Himself on Larry King or submitted to one of the "scream and shout" political commentary programs. For if someone does not conform to our artificial, self-appointed, arbitrary and capricious rules of proof, we blow them off.

Yes, god is unfathomable. So "Be still, and know that I am God." (PS 46)

"My kingdom is not of this world." (JN 18)

Truly, "His greatness no one can fathom" (PS 145)

And because God is unfathomable, we cannot use our petty, self-styled logic to prove his non-existence. How often have we heard that someone no longer believed in God, or refused to in the first place because, for example, his prayers were not answered or something "bad" happened to him? This is far from a test, since we don't know enough to test God. But in our arrogance, when God does not play by man's rules, man blows him off as a fairy tale.

"But you have no idea where I come from or where I am going. You judge by human standards." (JOHN 8:14)

It is also written: "Do not put the Lord your God to the test." (MT 4)

"Ye know not what ye ask." (MT 20)

How many times we have asked for something only to find years later that it was fortuitous that God in His infinite wisdom did not grant this. For we were far better off for having suffered and grown. Heck, if I had my health fully restored when I had asked for it years ago, it would have been the worst thing. If my health had been restored when I was a charter member of the disease-of-the-month club, what would I have been forced to learn? Nothing. For it would have made it impossible for me to learn all of this. There would not have been the motivation to drive me to all corners of the earth. There would have been no motivation to research into the wee hours of the night, nor for writing on vacations and weekends, to share the knowledge.

Yet when we begin to listen to God, study what he has caused to be written, and then see what he has done in our lives, it becomes hard to believe that we were that blocked and blind for so long.

"Have I been so long time with you, and yet hast thou not known me," (JN 14)

"The Lord seeth not as a man seeth: for man looketh on the outward appearance, but the Lord looketh on the heart" (1 SAM 16:7, KJV)

"Seek, and ye shall find." (LUKE 11)

"If any man be in Christ, he is a new creature: old things are passed away." (2CO 5)

Definitely, God's being unfathomable has held many back from accepting. But why? If he were not unfathomable, he wouldn't be God. Besides man uses that excuse only when it's convenient for him. The intricacies of how a car works is really unfathomable for many. But they trust it enough to put their lives at stake and get in the thing at 60 m.p.h. Most people haven't the faintest idea of how a plane works. But they trust it to carry them to 30,000 feet at 500 mph.

If you think about it, even if the whole "God-thing" is wrong and there is no heaven and life everlasting, it still boils down to the best philosophy by which to lead your life and direct your thoughts. And the result, a strong belief, far exceeds any form of psychotherapy that I have ever seen in over a quarter century in medicine. So there is nothing lost.

It is a win-win situation. For when you feel the Spirit of God within you, the serenity promotes the parasympathetic chemistry that promotes body functions of healing and promotes the synthesis of happy hormones. Whereas in a constant state of grief, hate, worry or anger, jealousy or other harmful emotions, we do the opposite as you have learned. We shut down digestion and healing as examples. Furthermore the rules for getting along with others (Do unto others....) fosters the optimum in personal, social, business, and international relationships.

Yes, God is unfathomable. But he has provided instruction. He has a book that answers every question. Questions that are not answered anywhere else. In fact, the 2 most important decisions of your life are not provided for anywhere else. For we have absolutely no training in what the purpose of our lives are here and after , nor in choosing a lifelong spouse. The answers are in that book. But if He were not unfathomable, there would be no drive to read, study, and learn more. No growth, no continuum, no evaluation, no excitement, no evolution.

"The Lord will guide you always" (ISA 58).

"I tell you the truth, unless you change and become like little children, you will never enter the kingdom of heaven." (MT 18)

Yes, a childlike, student nature is beneficial to restore your enthusiasm, creativity, love and wonderment. And it is an easier path to faith. Children seem to have a wholesome uncluttered way of viewing the world. It is easier for them to have faith as well as happiness. What has made you so cynical, untrusting, afraid of faith? What damaged your innocence? Was it because your faith was in things of man rather than in God?

"I have to lead my life in faith, without seeing Him." (2CO 5)

"You are all sons of God through faith" (GAL 3)

And **with faith comes responsibility.** And responsibility you recall, is a hallmark of this type of medicine, too. It is the first time in the history of medicine that the patient has been perceived as educable, intelligent, motivated, and responsible for his health. For it is not a form of medicine where the physician says, "Don't worry your pretty little head about this. Take these pills and everything will be all right." For in environmental medicine as well as in the BIBLE, you are responsible for your body and your soul, its functions and its health.

"Don't you know that you yourselves are God's temple and that God's Spirit lives in you? If anyone destroys that temple, God will destroy him; for God's temple is sacred and you are that temple (1 COR 3:16)

The evidence is clear. But people who choose not to face up to the responsibility and moral implications that acknowledging these facts entails, choose to remain ignorant of the facts. It is easier. It is similar to the people I see every day who are incredulous that their friends who are dying of cancer do not want to do some of the safe, inexpensive procedures that have proven to heal people who have been given up on by medicine. The reason is there are many who want the doctor to be responsible for their health. And if he does not recommend these things (because he is not aware of the evidence and is a puppet of drug-oriented medicine), then they will die on schedule as they have been told they should. Probably this same type wants their clergy to pray for them. They like an uncluttered life, unfettered by responsibility.

But for those who accept responsibility for their body and spiritual health, they know that:

"We are the temple of the living God." (2CO 6)

Therefore, "honor God with your body." (1CO 6)

"Whether therefore ye eat, or drink, or whatsoever ye do, do all to the glory of God." (1CO 10) That would preclude filling it with junk food that can trigger depression by a variety of mechanisms.

It goes without saying we must nourish our bodies, or we die. But we also need to nourish our minds and our souls. "Give us this day our daily bread" goes far beyond food for the gut. It is a plea to help us nourish our minds and nourish our souls. Why is it that people are willing to spend much money on a good meal when they won't spend $10-$15 on a

519

nourishing spiritual book or to share with someone more needy? The meal is over within a few hours at most. While the spiritual lesson lasts and can become magnified as we mature. Is it the Mormons and Hindus who fast one day a week and give the money to the church and temple? What a great idea since most of us are not lean and could benefit from a fast. It could help your spiritual growth while inhibiting your waist line growth!

As far as spirituality being the best form of psychotherapy, others I found share this view. For example, as psychiatrist J.T. Fisher states, "If you were to take the sum total of all authoritative articles ever written by the most qualified of psychologists and psychiatrists on the subject of mental hygiene -- if you were to combine them and refine them and cleave out the excess verbiage -- if you were to take the whole of the meat and none of the parsley, and if you were to have these unadulterated bits of pure scientific knowledge concisely expressed by the most capable of living poets, you would have an awkward and incomplete summation of the Sermon on the Mount. And it would suffer immeasurably through comparison. For nearly two thousand years the Christian world has been holding in its hands the complete answer to its restless and fruitless yearnings. Here ... rests the blueprint for successful human life with optimism, mental health, and contentment". (Wilson B, ed., THE BEST OF JOSH MCDOWELL: A READY DEFENSE, P 244, 1993, Thomas Nelson, Inc., Nashville.)

For preventing and healing wounds of the psyche, what better advise is there than "A gentle answer turns away wrath, but a harsh word stirs up anger." (PR15)

Look at all the nasty deeds that could have been averted with a few kind words.

"The tongue that brings healing is a tree of life, but a deceitful tongue crushes the spirit." (PR 15)

"A cheerful heart is good medicine" (PR 17)

"Do not let any unwholesome talk come out of your mouths, but only what is helpful for building others up according to their needs." (EPH 4:29)

For how often have we heard, what goes around comes around. Is that not what is meant by "A man reaps what he sows" (GAL 6). And the meaning can be extended further to remind us that worry and bad thoughts are counter productive. For "perfect love drives out fear" (1 JOHN 4)

Or how many lawsuits and accidents could have been avoided with:

"So in everything, do to others what you would have them do to you" (MT7)

In spite of all the legal logic, archeological and historical data, it still hinges on faith. For, "Without faith it is impossible to please Him." (HEB 11) For that is all we have to offer an unfathomable being. As mere mortals, whose only asset is freedom of choice, there is nothing more valuable that we have to offer an unfathomable Creator. What else can you do to show your love to an entity as unfathomable as God? You can't give presents or take him out to dinner. There is nothing that money could buy, for it is all meaningless, made by man.

Faith is the only thing that has meaning to God. It is so simple, we either have it or we don't.

"According to your faith it will be done to you" (MAT 9)

Then from there, we learn to exercise our faith and nurture its growth and development. For "faith without deeds is dead." (JAS 2)

HEALING HUMOR

As we discussed in TIRED OR TOXIC?, one of the most important vitamins is vitamin L: love and laughter. If you don't have a healthy dose of these in your life every day, you risk getting depressed, and ultimately sicker. And **one of the best ways of getting love is giving love.** It is a very simple formula. Yet for some reason we all seem to think we deserve it without giving it out.

As for laughter, God has a miraculous sense of humor. That's why we marry people who are totally different from us. That's why opposites attract. It would be boring if we were all the same. In fact, the yin and yang are crucial, because it improves our functionality as a unit. Our strengths compliment the deficiencies of our mates and vice versa.

Humor is therapeutic in its own right, because it forces us to look at an opposite perception and that is one of the exercises that a person recovering from depression must do. The mental exercise of seeing the humor or the opposite side of every situation is crucial to recovery, just as seeing the opposite side is crucial for management problem solving. Instead of seeing the accident as a tragedy, try to find all of the good things that came out of it, all of the positives. And believe me, there are always good things. Sometimes it takes us years however, to find. But they are there. We can always learn something as well, from every one of our failures.

I for one would have to be an idiot to not see the many times I have been rescued by the scruff of my neck. When I had severe chemical sensitivities with intermittent brain fog, I totaled 5 cars, yet walked away from each (including rolling a truck upside down a gully, and tearing its top off) unscathed. I never even went to an emergency room. But I was so ignorant, that it took many more years before I could grasp that there must have been a reason for it.

You might even want to read some books on how to be a humorist, for some of the best humorists do not poke fun and tear apart people maliciously. Instead, they see the opposite side. They see the avenue that no one thought of. And they help to increase our perception, create alternatives, and allow us to laugh at ourselves.

Humor also helps us not take ourselves so seriously. For people who have overwhelming depression often take the demands of life too seriously and place much more importance on them than they deserve. It never ceases to amaze me when I see someone who is attractive, intelligent, successful, well to do, loved, busy and depressed. Then I see someone who has had 4 catastrophes dumped on them in the last few months. One of which would be enough to depress anyone. Yet they are still smiling, still chipper and still in love with life, empathetic with others, and in touch with their Maker. It is this perception that is so intangible, yet so crucial to our mental and physical well-being.

So I'm not saying don't have psychotherapy. There are many wonderful psychotherapists and many useful forms of psychotherapy. But I am saying it is not the end of the road. Don't make it your final stop on the road to recovery. More important is to find your spiritual side and your reason for being. **For it does no good to find out why you are angry if you can't learn how to replace that damaging anger with healing love and laughter.**

RESOURCES:

Siegel B, PEACE, LOVE & HEALING', Harper & Row, NY, 1989

Siegel B, LOVE, MEDICINE & MIRACLES

Cousins N, ANATOMY OF AN ILLNESS

Cousins N, THE HEALING HEART, Avon Books, NY, 1984

Malkmus G, WHY CHRISTIANS GET SICK, Ph (423) 272-1800.

REACH OUT AND HUG SOMEONE

Physical contact is crucial to recovery from depression. In fact it is crucial to mere everyday thriving. Look at all the studies of animals and children who failed to grow and thrive just because they were in the group that did not get physical contact. Hugging, holding, embracing, and cuddling, nurture the mental as well as the physical. Unfortunately, the older people get, the less they tend to be sincerely hugged or kindly touched. But man needs touch to thrive. This includes the physical contact of pets.

And do not neglect the importance of music. For many, this can be very therapeutic.

Cochrane N, Physical Contact Experience and Depression, ACTA PSYCHIATRICA SCAND, 1990;357(82):66-73

WHERE ARE YOUR PRIORITIES?

In an era where people have unprecedented stress and pressures, a common part of the total load that creates depression is just plain being on overload. We try to do more, have more, be more, and there are only 24 hours in a day. We need to get our priorities straight. Is it more important to have the best looking lawn on the street, than to avoid depression from the lawn pesticide, or having your dog die and your toddler get cancer? We are just too plastic and admittedly we are all guilty to various extents. There are no perfect people. But when 21st century priorities endanger your physical and mental health, it may be a time to rethink just what is important.

A time that forces this realization on us is when someone close to us dies. Suddenly the needs of the world that continues to go on about us seem so trivial and meaningless. Often this is a time when we are forced to reprioritize. Suddenly only a few things matter. And they are usually the love of a select few, like spouses, friends, or children. The same happens often when someone has a fatal illness, or recovers from a near-fatal illness.

There is a book in the BIBLE, ECCLESIASTES, that is great for reprioritizing. I read it whenever I become too overwhelmed with projects and deadlines. For this overload is merely one more part man's total load that could precipitate massive depression if the rest of the total load is ripe.

For ECCLESIASTES points out that everything in life is meaningless. Compared with the overall scheme of things, everything is pure vanity, meaningless. So how seriously are we to take it all? Is it worth being depressed over. Is it worth suicide? Is it worth working ourselves to death?

For "all is vanity. What profit hath a man of all his labour which he taketh under the sun? One generation passeth away, and another generation cometh: but the earth abideth for ever."

"And whatsoever mine eyes desired I kept not from them, I withheld not my heart from any joy: for my heart rejoiced in all my labour: and this was my portion of all my labour. Then I looked on all the works that my hands had wrought, and on the labour that I had laboured to do: and, behold, all was vanity and vexation of spirit, and there was no profit under the sun."

For "To every thing there is a season, and a time to every purpose under the heaven: A time to be born, and a time to die; a time to kill, and a time to heal; a time to break down and a time to build up; A time to weep, and a time to laugh; a time to mourn, and a time to dance;"

And "As he came forth of his mother's womb, naked shall he return to go as he came, and shall take nothing of his labour, which he may carry away in his hand."

"Then shall the dust return to the earth as it was: and the spirit shall return unto God who gave it."

"Let us hear the conclusion of the whole matter: Fear God, and keep his commandments: for this is the whole duty of man." (KJV)

"Let us hear the conclusion of the whole matter: Fear God, and keep his commandments: for this is the whole duty of man." (KJV)

"For there is no difference between Jew and Gentile -- the same Lord is Lord of all and richly blesses all who call on him," (RO 10)

And remember, **meekness is not weakness.** It is strength under control, in awe, humble, in the face of the unfathomable.

"Cast thy bread upon the water: for thou shalt find it after many days."

VITAMIN L

As many psychotherapists, like Leo Buscagglia, and physicians, like surgeon Bernie Siegel have shown us, **love is one of the most fundamental ingredients for healing.** And it is not original with them, but thousands of years old.

"but have not love, I gain nothing."
"Love is patient, love is kind."
"Love never delights in evil"
"Love never fails" (1CO)

"Do everything in love"
"rather, serve one another in love" (GAL 5)

"but love covers over all wrongs" (PR 10)
"so you must love one another" (JN 13)

Become an extension of God as you do some random acts of kindness (RAKs) each day. You will begin to find many delights. **Rack up some RAKs!**

"Love your neighbor as yourself"
"Love the Lord your God" (MT22)

"Whoever lives in love lives in God"
"God is love" (1JN4)

What could be simpler? Is there a better plan? I'd love to hear it. It sure beats the "Me Generation" with its divorce rate of one in three!

You say you would like to believe that it was easy, but you haven't a clue how it could happen? Well it won't if you never open your BIBLE. Chances are nothing will happen if you never start to learn about God and his strength and compassion. It very well could remain a total mystery for you, forever, if you choose to do nothing. It could all remain mere meaningless confusing words. You can stay just as you are and never grow, if you choose not to take the initiative to find out what these things mean and that they can become a very real power in your life. What do you think makes so many people so happy in the face of life's adversities? What is their secret? They are very eager to share it.

As for the other part of vitamin L (love and laughter), the BIBLE is not without much humor. As example: "Like a gold ring in a pig's snout is a beautiful woman who shows no discretion (PROV 11:22).

So formulate your plan of action, find your chosen spiritual path. Then pick yourself up, and get on with it. Is your spiritual nature not worth even 15-30 nurturing minutes a day of reading, listening, thinking, or talking to God? And "Whatsoever thy hand findeth to do, do it with thy might;".

THE SCIENCE OF SPIRITUALITY

In over a quarter of a century in medical practice, I have seen and heard of many miraculous recoveries, for which the only explanation the patient or I could give, was the miraculous healing of God. I cannot believe there is a physician who has not experienced this wonder. I only wish I had kept a journal of all of these through the years. They make wonderful stories. But others have, and there are monthly publications (like "Guideposts"), magazines and books galore that serve as chronicles of God's ever-present healing.

One of my favorite books is by Faid, a scientist who had an inoperable cancer and was given months to live. He was agnostic, but his wife was a devout Christian. She left to pray for a weekend with friends. Meanwhile, back at the hospital, Faid's doctor sheepishly explained one morning that he could not explain it, but his cancer was gone from his most recent x-rays. They were sure there was no mix-up in films, and there frankly was just no explanation, for he had had no treatment. He was free to go home.

This obviously got Faid's attention. He rationalized that if this was a miracle, then there must be a miracle-maker. And since he was a scientist, if this was fact, he ought to be able to prove it. He set out on a journey of research and ended up writing the book, THE SCIENTIFIC APPROACH TO CHRISTIANITY. He, of course, was not the first, nor the last. There are scores of attorneys, scientists, physicians, physicists, archeologists, historians, comparative religion experts, physicians and more who have written all sorts of accounts and have gathered evidence that supports THE HOLY BIBLE.

531

But as has been true throughout all of history, man's quest for power has led him, whether he be a Pharisee or a modern man working in the name of government, science, medicine, or what-have-you, to down-play and **denigrate anything that detracts from man's self-presumed greatness.** So many have ignored creation and chalked all the wonders of the world up to the "big bang theory".

Can you imagine! The intricacies of the genetic code and the DNA helix, the fact that we have complicated cytochrome P-450 enzymes in our bodies to detoxify chemicals that were just invented yesterday, the complex interactive intricacies of nature, are all a result of some inane spontaneous "big bang theory"? (If you buy that I have a bridge to sell you.) Heaven forbid there should be an architect superior to man who knew we were going to poison ourselves in this century, and so provided us with the chemistry and knowledge (if we only use it) with which to heal.

Regardless of personal spirituality or lack thereof, all through history there is only confirmation that indeed a man called **Jesus Christ lived on earth.** There is no historical authority who denies that. It is historical fact, regardless of one's religious beliefs. The fact that a man named Jesus Christ lived on planet Earth is just as much fact as it is universally agreed upon historical fact that George Washington, Christopher Columbus, Benjamin Franklin, Julius Caesar, or Thomas Jefferson were once on this earth.

And, interestingly, over **680 years before that fact, the details were prophesied.** "For to us a child is born...." (ISA 9). And the details were all there: "He had no beauty or majesty to attract us to him, nothing in his appearance that we should desire him, He was despised and rejected by men, a man of

532

sorrow, and familiar with suffering." "By oppression and judgment he was taken away." "He was assigned a grave with the wicked, and with the rich in his death, though he had done no violence, nor was any deceit in his mouth."(ISA 53) How fascinating that the OLD TESTAMENT contains many prophecies that hundreds of years later came true. Was there any other person on earth whose coming was written about in such detail over 500 years prior?

And when we explore further about prophecy, that in itself should convince anyone of the validity of the BIBLE. Scholars show us how 60 major prophecies and 270 ramifications, all in the OLD TESTAMENT have come true. In looking at just the probability of 8 of them coming true would be 1 in 10 to the 17th power. This chance would be analogous to covering the state of Texas with quarters 2 feet deep, and turning a blind man loose to find the one quarter for which you are looking.

The more you study the BIBLE, the more you realize how easy it is to object to it all only out of total ignorance. For when you have an adequate knowledge of the facts, it becomes impossible to refute (THE BEST OF JOSH MCDOWELL: A READY DEFENSE, Thomas Nelson Publ., Nashville, 1993, p209-214). Man's denial of Christ is strikingly similar to his denial of chemical sensitivity and environmental medicine. Only those most ignorant of the details persist in denial.

In ZECHARIAH 9:9 in the OLD TESTAMENT, it predicts hundreds of years in advance that the Messiah would come humbly, "mounted on a donkey, even on a colt, the foal of a donkey" (ibid, p 252). And in PSALM 22 there is a graphic description of a crucifixion, something that was unknown to the psalmist.

And although pollution was not an issue 2,000 years ago, the OLD as well as the NEW TESTAMENTS warn against it, "Do not pollute the land", "Do not defile the land where you live and where I dwell, " (NU 35). And "The time has come for judging the dead............and for destroying those who destroy the earth" (REV 11).

And lest we take ourselves too seriously, we need only be reminded that each day is a gift from God, that is why it is called **the present;** and that eventually "all come from dust, and to dust all return" (ECC 3). We are here such a short time that it behooves us to make the best of it. "Naked a man comes from his mother's womb, and as he comes, so he departs" (ECC5). "Moreover, no man knows when his hour will come:" (NU 9). Until then, "Follow the ways of your heart: (NU 11), "For God will bring every deed into judgment" (Nu 12).

In contrast, a great deal of modern psychotherapy can be distilled down to the "Me Generation" where the individual becomes the focus. His goal seems to "be in touch" with his needs and desires and to act on them, to be his own person. He is encouraged to "go for the gusto" and grab as much for himself as he can. Yet at the same time, a big part of much depression for many is actual loneliness and lack of purpose in life. He can only adorn his body, amass material possessions, hoard money, accumulate power over others, get hooked on his own adrenalin through sky-diving or car racing, etc. And when it is all over, what does he have? None of those can permanently fill the void. Man can only worship himself so long before he becomes lonely, purposeless, and depressed. His emotional needs can be better met through a more "others-oriented" approach. And that is what God teaches us. Life is infinitely fuller when we switch from the "Me-Generation" to the "He Generation". "Stand firm in the Lord". (PHI 4:1)

In my limited opinion, there is no form of psychotherapy to surpass a strong faith. It can provide a promise, a life plan, precise directions for daily conduct, a blueprint for times of tough decision, frequent feedback, and a destiny beyond this world.

On the flip side, the man-oriented, and me-oriented psychotherapy philosophies can actually generate loneliness, one of the causes of depression. And lest we underestimate the power of loneliness in the body, there are many studies that show it has adverse biochemical effects on body physiology. As one example, rats exposed to isolation stress actually inhibited the rate-limiting (most crucial) step in conversion of essential fatty acids. And the essential fatty acids, of course, go on to play a major part in brain function. So in other words, **the brain chemistry of loneliness stopped the metabolism of fatty acids** that are essential for making the happy hormones work optimally.

Mills DE, Huang YS, Narce M, Poisson JP, Psychosocial stress, catecholamines, and essential fatty acid metabolism in rats, PROC SOC EXP BIOL MED 1994 Jan;201(1):56-61

And loneliness is in part generated by our need to accumulate. It is merely one more example of our upside down priorities. As we are driven to accumulate, we need to work like crazy to pay for it. This is done at the expense of socialization, and time to cultivate deep meaningful friendships.   Most people are too busy to maintain old friendships, much less make new ones. By the time they have worked 1-2 jobs, sculpted their bodies at a gym, and fulfilled their self-imposed duties, there is no time for nurturing new relationships. And it is surprising how little many actually know about the people they supposedly love. Look what they give them for Christmas presents as an example!

And much depression, as another example, stems from divorce. And in the current "Me Generation" we have the highest divorce rate ever. Well it doesn't take a rocket scientist to figure out you increase your chances of getting along with someone and loving them being guided by Biblical principles a lot more than by being guided by the philosophy of the "Me Generation". Much preferable to be part of the **He Generation.**

Bower B, Depression: Rates in women, men......and stress effects across sexes, SCI NEWS,147:346, June 3,1995

Just think how much improved the world would be if we were to follow but a few phrases of advise from this most unfathomable work: how many broken marriages, how many wars, how many destroyed businesses, how many wasted lives, how many lawsuits, how many personal unhappinesses could have been spared:

"Do not let the sun go down while you are still angry" (EPH 4).

"Each of you should not look at your own interests, but also to the interests of others" (PHI 2).

"Be not hasty in they spirit to be angry: for anger resteth in the bosom of fools." (ECC 7:9

And God is not without a wonderful sense of humor: "Better to live on a corner of the roof than share a house with a quarrelsome wife." (PRO 21:9)

So, "Be kind and compassionate to one another, forgiving each other,"(EPH 4)

And one of the best ones yet, "Physician heal thyself" (LU 4). Just imagine if every physician was from this day forward denied any drugs or stricken with recalcitrant drug-resistant depression, chronic fatigue, heart failure, cardiomyopathy, arthritis, chemical sensitivity, migraines, asthma, prostatitis, colitis or fibromyalgia. They would be forced to learn this type of medicine in order to heal and survive. Then look at all the people they would help hence forth.

In over 25 years of medicine, I have seen many people who were miserable, and many who were happy. And the individual circumstances in their lives had little bearing. Some of the happiest had the least reason (by non-spiritual standards) to be happy, and some of the most miserable, no reason. Yet it is perception, again. And as far as being advocates for how they got happy? Very rarely was someone consistently happy, exuberant, and a joy to be around who credited psychotherapy as the cause. But I certainly have seen many joyful people who credited their outlook on life to their spirituality and strong faith. These people are living examples.

"For what a man desires is unfailing love" (PR19). Why do you think people lavish emotions on pets? **Pets** provide unfailing, unquestioning, unconditional love. They are non-judgmental, don't harbor a grudge, are joyful to see you regardless of how their day went. They don't talk back, grumble, find fault, cast blame. They just love you. Why do you think there is a plethora of papers showing the improvement in mental and physical health of people who have pets? And why is there a push to have pets in nursing homes? It is so simple --- they provide what we perceive of as unfailing love. And with God, "We love because he first loved us" (1 JOHN 4:19)

With faith, life is simpler and more logical. As Faid's research showed him, it is historical fact that a man called Jesus Christ roamed this earth. No scholars disagree, whether they be Jewish, Muslim, Buddhist or any other religion. The only debate is whether or not he was the actual son of God. And for the answer to that question, there are only two possibilities. Either he was the son of God, or he was not the son of God.

If he was not the son of God, yet roamed the Earth for 33 years (performing miracles that multiple people wrote about) claiming to be the son of God, he would have had to be schizophrenic as hell. But there was never a single documented sign of schizophrenia, Res ipse loquitor. Since he must have been the son of God, it changes everything. It makes our spirituality and communication with God, our number one commitment. What else could possibly supersede this? In my opinion, the best way to understand how we are to behave is to read the word of God and his instructions. And it sure is less expensive than psychotherapy. And it deals with all the nasty feelings that hold people back from getting well: suppressed anger, resentment, guilt, inadequacy or inferiority, jealousy, hate, unforgiveness, and feeling a failure or unworthy or unloved.

I'm certainly no authority on any aspect of religion. I merely report that the strongest healing of the body and mind that I have observed during more than a quarter of a century in clinical medicine seems to be among people who have a strong spirituality or faith. I have observed infinitely more people attribute their improvement in mental and physical health to their faith than I have to psychotherapy.

In my mind's ear I can hear all sorts of rebuttals and objections, and I'm not qualified to refute them. But for the serious student, there is a plethora of reference material. And as many have reminded me, some people are too cerebral and analytical for their own good. But look at the people who have a strong faith and a plethora of happy hormones who cannot read, who cannot study, who do not need volumes of "scientific proof". They merely believe. You have only to receive the gift.

"it is the gift of God ---not by works" (EPH2)

PROOF FOR THE HEALING POWER OF PRAYER

Once you have begun to explore the vastness of your spirituality, you will begin to see why there is even much documented proof in the medical literature for the power of prayer. For example, one group of 192 patients was prayed for, while another group of 201 patients was not prayed for. Neither the patients, doctors, nurses nor the families of the patients knew who was in which group and none of the people praying for the patients knew any of the patients.

The result of this double blind, scientific study showed that the prayer recipients required 5 times fewer antibiotics, had 3 times fewer complications and none of them required life support systems (Randolph C. Byrd, Positive Therapeutic Effects of Intercessory Prayer in a Coronary Care Unit Population, SOUTHERN MEDICAL JOURNAL, 81:7, 826-829, 1988.)

There are many other references in the medical literature attesting to the power of prayer and the power of spirituality for improving healing from all sorts of medical conditions. These have been detailed in a book entitled THE FAITH FACTOR: AN ANNOTATED BIBLIOGRAPHY OF CLINICAL RESEARCH ON SPIRITUAL SUBJECTS (DA Matthews, DB Larson, CP Barry, published through The National Institute For Healthcare Research, July 1993, phone 703-527-NIHR).

When you look at what is wrong with the world on a macrocosm level, and proceed down to a microcosm to what is wrong with the depressed individual, the same guiding principles apply. How can you go wrong with such advice as **"Love drives out fear"** (1 J 4), or **"Who by worrying can add a single hour to his life"** (MATT 6), or **"A gentle word turneth away wrath"** (PROV 15)?

Or remember that in this high tech world, when someone is riddled with a relentless cancer, and all that medicine has to offer has failed --- chemotherapy, surgery, hormones, radiation --- how have many totally healed themselves? Many have totally healed end-stage metastatic cancers with nothing more than God-given natural food (protocol described in WELLNESS AGAINST ALL ODDS and THE

CURE IS IN THE KITCHEN, and medical proof in Carter, et al, J AMER COLL NUTR 12:3, 205, 1993).

For **"the Lord will provide"** (GEN 22) and "And the LORD GOD made all kinds of trees grow out of the ground--trees that were pleasing to the eye and good for food. In the middle of the garden were the tree of life... " (GEN 2).

"The Lord will guide you always" (ISA 58)

"For nothing is impossible with God (LUK 1:37)

"And God shall wipe away every tear from their eyes" (REV 7:17)

The beauty of the spirituality or faith approach versus the psychotherapy approach is that it stresses the importance of doing unto others as we would have them do unto us. It is more concerned with the practicality of maximizing our relationships in the here and now. It makes it a nicer world for everyone all the way around. It doesn't just help the patient himself as psychotherapy might. It doesn't just help him cope with his angers and fears and realize he is justified in having them. It goes far beyond that to diminish the bad that has happened to him compared with how great his potential is for fulfilling God's purpose for him during the rest of his life. It allows him to **forgive and forget,** which are infinitely more healing than blaming and being angry victims and martyrs.

"Let us purify ourselves from everything that contaminates body and spirit, perfecting holiness out of reverence for God" (2 COR).

And like environmental medicine, it places the responsibility for each person's health where it belongs: with the individual. I have watched people heal the impossible. I have seen them joyfully rally when 20 specialists in renowned medical schools have been stumped and given up. And the lessons they learned about how to get themselves well, have served them on a continuum. They rarely get sick anymore, and they start using these principals on their family and friends. **Just as we shouldn't go to our pastor and ask him to make us spiritual, we shouldn't rely on the physician to heal us.** Physicians don't heal. Like pastors, they merely guide and facilitate.

Each person has the gift of the responsibility for his body, mind, and soul. How he uses it is up to him. If he chooses to say, "I don't have enough time for that", then so be it. Junk foods, environmental chemicals, medications can hasten the deterioration of all three. "Don't you know that **you yourselves are God's temple** and that God's Spirit lives in you? If anyone destroys God's temple, God will destroy him: for God's temple is sacred, and you are that temple." (1 COR 3).

A minister developed colon cancer in his 40's and had already watched his mother die despite the best medical care. He opted against surgery, chemotherapy and radiation. Instead he turned to his BIBLE and to whole organic natural unprocessed God-given foods, in the manner of one of the programs described in WELLNESS AGAINST ALL ODDS. He healed himself and went on to write WHY CHRISTIANS GET SICK (Rev. George Malkmus, ph 423-272-1800).

Don't you owe it to yourself to clean up your diet and lifestyle and get rid of your depression and other ailments? "For we are the temple of the living God." (2 COR 6)

"Faith is being sure of what we hope for and certain of what we do not see....And **without faith it is impossible to please God,** because anyone who comes to him must believe that he exists and that he rewards those who earnestly seek him." (HEB 11)

And why is faith so important? Because we have nothing else to give. What do you give God? Can you give him money, a gift, take him out to dinner? No. The **only thing you can give the Unfathomable is faith.** And real faith in the Divine will lead you automatically to study the word of God and attempt to lead the life that pleases God. "Look unto Me, and be ye saved." "But seek ye first the Kingdom of God, and His righteousness; and all things shall be added unto you (MAT 6;33).

You have been learning how important the total load is to healing depression. The same might be said of your spirituality. Addressing the total load means you cannot just be spiritual by believing. That is merely the first step. It takes study and practice of the principles. For faith without deeds is dead.

"For by grace you have been saved through faith; and not of yourselves, it is the gift of God; not as a result of works, that no one should boast" (EPH 2:8)

Seek and ye shall find.

For "He heals the brokenhearted and binds up their wounds."
(PSA 147)

"Therefore if anyone is in Christ, he is a new creation: the old
has gone, the new has come ! All this is from God" (2CO)

FACT: God is unfathomable. So don't let that bog you down.
So often this becomes the stopping point for someone who
has no spirituality. He insists that if there were some proof,
or if God would only reach down His hand and give him a
sign, that then he could begin to believe.   God is
unfathomable. He is supposed to be.

But in terms of giving you a sign, he does this constantly. We
are just too spiritually naive or blind to recognize them. But
many people attest to the fact that once you awaken, you will
see a constant barrage of signs. And as has happened with
most of us, we also then were able to see the signs that we
were too blind to see. Yet they were there all along, in the
days prior to our enlightenment. Things that had looked like
the worst piece of luck we could now see as having really
been a blessing. We just could not possibly fathom it at that
point in time at the level of understanding that we were
floundering in, ignorant of His word. We are not supposed
to know the whole picture. It is unfathomable, and that is
why faith is the first step toward understanding. For "his
understanding no one can fathom." (ISA 40)

"Can you fathom the mysteries of God?" (JOB11)

Truly, "His greatness no one can fathom" (PS145)

As C. S. Lewis said in MERE CHRISTIANITY, "A man who
was merely a man and said the sort of things Jesus said

would not be a great moral teacher." "He would either be a lunatic - - on a level with the man who says he is a poached egg - - or else he would be the Devil of Hell. **You must make your choice.** Either this man was, and is, the Son of God: or else a madman or something worse. You can shut Him up for a fool, you can spit at Him and kill Him as a demon; or you can fall at his feet and call Him Lord and God. But let us not come with any patronizing nonsense about His being a great human teacher. He has not left that open to us."

"What does the worker gain from his toil? I have seen the burden God has laid on men. He has made everything beautiful in its time. He has also set eternity in the hearts of men; yet they cannot fathom what God has done from beginning to end. I know that there is nothing better for men than to **be happy and do good** while they live. That everyone may eat and drink, and find satisfaction in all his toil -- this is the gift of God. " (ECC 3)

"Behold, I stand at the door and knock; if any one hears My voice and opens the door, I will come in ..." (REV 3:20)

"A fear of the Lord is the beginning of knowledge" (PRO 1:7)

So let's get on with it. **God is unfathomable.** So there are only two choices: blind faith or start studying to learn of the overwhelming evidence. A good place to start would be to buy a student BIBLE that explains to you as you read. For without instructions and help of some sort, it is even more difficult. It was written 2,000 years ago. So don't expect the literary style of a 21st century novel. (Also the BIBLE has been recorded on cassette tapes.) The bottom line is that the word of God is the most healing form of psychotherapy I have ever witnessed. And it has produced the most truly joyful people. Is the missing part of the puzzle of your depression a lack of purpose in life? Does your lack of enthusiasm stem from a deficiency of a connectedness with God? Why not sincerely pray right this moment for guidance?

RESOURCES:

Any and all books in this section can be obtained from Sacred Melody Bookstore, Syracuse, NY phone 1-800-234-2211 or (315)437-1095

Quotations in this section were taken from many different BIBLES, but mostly THE HOLY BIBLE, New International Version, International BIBLE Society, The Zondervan Corp, Grand Rapids MI 49506, (1986) and Chambers' "MY UTMOST FOR HIS HIGHEST", Barbour & Co, POB 719, Uhrichsville OH 44683, 1935, renewed 1963

THE HOLY BIBLE. NIV, Zondervan Corp, Grand Rapids MI, 49506

Faid RW, A SCIENTIFIC APPROACH TO CHRISTIANITY, New leaf Press, P.O. Box 311, Green Forest AR 72638, 1982

McDowell J, EVIDENCE THAT DEMANDS A VERDICT, Here's Life Publ, San Bernandino, CA, 92402, 1989

Keller W, THE BIBLE AS HISTORY, Wm Morrow & Co., NY, 1964

Anderson JND, THE EVIDENCE FOR THE RESURRECTION, InterVarsity Press, POB 1400, Downers Grove, IL 60515, 1966

Giesler N, Howe T, WHEN CRITICS ASK, Victor Books 1825 College Ave, Wheaton IL 60187, 1992

McDowell J, THE BEST OF JOSH MCDOWELL: A READY DEFENSE, compiled by Bill Wilson, Sears Life Publ, San Bernadino CA, 1990.

Stoner PW, SCIENCE SPEAKS: AN EVALUATION OF CERTAIN CHRISTIAN EVIDENCES, Chicago, Moody Press, 1963

Davis GTB, FULFILLED PROPHECIES THAT PROVE THE BIBLE, The Million Testaments Campaign, Inc., 1931 and 1955

Keller WP, STRENGTH OF SOUL, Kregel Pub, Grand Rapids MI 19501, 1993

Graf JL, ed., HEALING. THE THREE GREAT CLASSICS ON DIVINE HEALING, Christian Publ, 3825 Hartzdale Dr., Camp Hill PA 17011, 1992

Eadie Betty J, EMBRACED BY THE LIGHT, 1-800-748-4900

Groothuis D, DECEIVED BY THE LIGHT, Harvest House Publ, Eugene OR 97402, 1995

Kohlenberger JR, THE ONE MINUTE BIBLE, Gaborg's, Bloomington, MN 55422, 1992

Pearsell P, MAKING MIRACLES, Avon Books, Dept FP, 1350 Avenue of the Americas, New York, NY 10019, 1-800-238-0658

Sheldon, CM, IN HIS STEPS, Fleming Revell, Baker Book House, Grand Rapids, MI 49506, 1984

Martin W, THE KINGDOM OF THE CULTS, Bethany House Publ, Minn, MN, 55438, 1965

Colson C, LOVING GOD, Harper Paperbacks, 10 East 53rd St. NY, NY 10022, 1987

Colson C, THE BODY, Word Publishing, Dallas 1992

Keller WP, A SHEPHARD LOOKS AT PSALM 23, 1970, Daybreak Books, Zonervan Publ, 1415 Lake Drive, S.E., Grand Rapids, MI 49506

Williamson M, A LAYMAN LOOKS AT THE LORD'S PRAYER, Moody Press Press, Chicago, 1976

Chapin A, 365 BIBLE PROMISES FOR BUSY PEOPLE, Tyndale House Publ, 351 Executive Dr., Box 80, Wheaton, IL 60189-0080

Colson C, AGAINST THE NIGHT, Servant Publ, Box 8617, Ann Arbor, MI 48107, 1989

Robertson P, THE NEW WORLD ORDER, World Publ, Dallas, 1991

Colson C, KINGDOMS IN CONFLICT, Harper & Row, 10E 53rd St., NY, NY 10022, 1987

Kushi M, Jack A, THE GOSPEL OF PEACE. JESUS' TEACHINGS OF ETERNAL TRUTH, Japan Publ., Kodansha, 19 Union Sq W, NY NY 10003, 1992

Colson C, THE GOD OF STONES AND SPIDERS, Good News Publ, Wheaton IL 60187, 1990

Limbaugh R, THE WAY THINGS OUGHT TO BE, Pocket Books, Simon & Schuster, 1230 Avenue of the Americas, NY NY 10020, 1992

Choate P, AGENTS OF INFLUENCE, Touchstone, Simon & Schuster, NY 1990

Lewis, CS, MIRACLES, Collier Books of Macmillan Publ. Co., 1947

Lewis, CS, THE SCREWTAPE LETTERS, IBID, 1961

Lewis, CS, THE CASE FOR CHRISTIANITY, The Macmillan Co., NY, 1952

Macartney CE, TWELVE GREAT QUESTIONS ABOUT CHRIST, Kregel Publ, Grand Rapids MI 49501, 1993

Cox JW, ed, THE MINISTERS MANUAL, Harper Collins Publ, 10 E.53rd St., NY, NY 10022, 1993

Lewis CS, MERE CHRISTIANITY, IBID, 1943

Lewis CS, SURPRISED BY JOY, Harvest Books or Harcourt Brace Jovanich, Publ, NY 1956

Swindoll CR, LAUGH AGAIN, World Publ., Dallas, 1992

Graham B, HOW TO BE BORN AGAIN, ibid, 1977

Girzone JF, THE SHEPHARD, Macmillan Publ Co, 866 Third Ave., NY 10022, 1990 (1-800-323-7445)

Girzone JF, JOSHUA, ibid, 1987

Girzone JF, JOSHUA IN THE HOLY LAND, ibid

Colson C, Eckerd J, WHY AMERICA DOESN'T WORK, Word Publ, Dallas, 1991

Colson, C, WHO SPEAKS FOR GOD?, Good News Publ, 1300 Crescent St, Wheaton, IL 60187, 1985

Stanley C, HOW TO LISTEN TO GOD, Thomas Nelson Publ, Nashville, 1985

Strauss RL, THE JOY OF KNOWING GOD, Loizeaux Bro Inc, Neptune NJ, 1986

Henry M, GREAT THEMES OF THE BIBLE, Kregel Publ, PO Box 2607 Grand Rapids MI 49501, 1993

Krieger D, ACCEPTING YOUR POWER TO HEAL, Bear & Co., (1993) Santa Fe, NM 87504-2860

Campbell, W., THE QUR'AN AND THE BIBLE IN THE LIGHT OF HISTORY AND SCIENCE, Mer, ISBN 1-881085-00-7 (no title pg)

If you need BIBLE study and cannot go to church, there is an excellent set of 4 tiny booklets (MILK, MEAT, BREAD, FISH) from:
PROSACT
P.O. BOX 1948
ROCKY MOUNT, NC 27802-1948

Benson H, BEYOND THE RELAXATION RESPONSE, Times Books, NY 1985

GUIDEPOSTS, P.O.B. 1425, Carmel, NY 10512-9824, a spiritually uplifting monthly magazine

Rubin TI, COMPASSION AND SELF HATE. AN ALTERNATIVE TO DESPAIR, David McKay Company, NY 1975

Dossey L, HEALING WORDS: THE POWER OF PRAYER AND THE PRACTICE OF MEDICINE, Harper, San Francisco and NY, 1993

Spence G, HOW TO ARGUE AND WIN EVERY TIME, St Martins Press, NY, 1995

REFERENCES:

Adar R, ed, PSYCHONEUROIMMUNOLOGY, Acad Press, 1981

Kiecolt-Glaseer JK, Glaser R. Psychoneuro-immunology: can psychological interventions modulate immunity? J CONSULT CLIN PSYCHOL 1992; 60: 569-75.

Stein M, Keller SE, Schliefer SJ. Stress and immunomodulation: the role of depression and neuroendocrine function. J IMMUNOL 1985; 827-33.

Henrotte JG, Type A behavior and magnesium metabolism, MAGNESIUM, 5:201-210,1986

McGuire R, Type A stress a drain on magnesium, MED TRIBUNE, May 15, 1984, p1

Barthrop RW, Depressed lymphocyte function after bereavement. LANCET. 2:834-836,1977

Kabat-Zinn, JOM, Ph.D., et al. Effectiveness of a meditation-based stress reduction program in the treatment of anxiety disorders. AMER PSYCHIAT July 149 (7): 943-946, 1992

Morse DR, et al, Stress induced sudden cardiac death: Can it be prevented? STRESS MEDICINE, 1992;8:35-46.

Lloyd A, et al, Cell mediated immunity in patients with chronic fatigue syndrome, Health control subjects in patients with major depression. CLINICAL EXPERIMENTAL IMMUNOLOGY, 1992;87:76-79

Then Jesus said to his disciples: "Therefore I tell you, do not worry about your life, what you will eat; or about your body, what you will wear. Life is more than food, and the body more than clothes. Consider the ravens: They do not sow or reap, they have no storeroom or barn; yet God feeds them. And how much more valuable you are than birds! **Who of you by worrying can add a single hour to his life?** Since you cannot do this very little thing, why do you worry about the rest?" *

And don't confuse worry with planning. Planning is essential, worry is worthless. And, for those of you who need a reason for everything, I might add: for worry only depletes nutrients that could have been used to make your happy hormones.

*****

* FROM:
THE STUDENT BIBLE, 1986 Zondervan Corporation, Grand Rapids, Michigan 49506

Some of you might want to start with a student BIBLE and a little paper back book, CONCORDANCE (there are many types in the bookstores). It is like a giant index to themes in the BIBLE. For example, if you want to look up healing, it gives you every reference in the BIBLE regarding that word. Some BIBLES have a limited concordance in the back. Since the BIBLE is a compilation of many books written by many people, inspired by God, this tool enables you to study a particular theme through the perspective of many writers and periods of Biblical history.

*****

You might start today by opening your eyes and seeing all the miracles you have missed.

"Know also that wisdom is sweet to your soul; if you find it, there is a future hope for you, and your hope will not be cut off" (PRO 24:14)

Now you have learned about the many major categories of causes for depression: environmental (food, chemical, and mold allergies, including Candida, pesticides and heavy metals) triggers (Volume I); then the nutrient (vitamins, minerals, essential fatty acids, amino acids and orphan nutrients, as well as some helpful herbs) deficiencies (Volume II); then the metabolic abnormalities (hormone deficiencies, intestinal abnormalities, and problems of mind and soul), that all can singularly or in any combination cause depression. (Volume III).

So now turn to Volume IV for other causes of depression, like SAD, and the total load; and finally the plan to organize the diagnosis, then treatment of the many causes of depression. Last but never least, we will explore the current state of medicine.

VOLUME IV

(CHAPTERS 10-12)

TREATMENTS

THE TOTAL LOAD, TESTS AND TREATMENTS, AND THE CURRENT STATE OF MEDICINE

CHAPTER 10

THE TOTAL LOAD

The concept of total load is crucial for the healing of all diseases; whether they be thought of as originating as disturbances in the immune system, the xenobiotic (foreign chemical) detoxication system or anywhere else.   And depression is no exception. Not only is the total load on our systems the cause of our downfalls, but understanding the concept is basic to our wellness.   Non-ecology-trained physicians should also be taught about the total load concept so that our treatments will be less mystifying to them.

I like to think of the total load as being analogous to a boat filled with twelve marked boxes. All of us are set adrift in the sea of life in the same type of boat with the same twelve boxes of cargo. The only differences are the locations of our leaks and the relative weights of our cargo boxes. Some of us have a leak up near the gunwales so that we only have to throw one or two heavy boxes overboard in order for the boat to stop taking on water. For example, we get off our junk food diets, get injections for pollens, dust and mold allergies, do the yeast program, and are no longer depressed. Others are not so lucky. They have their leak further down toward the keel and have to throw many boxes overboard before they stop taking on water (analogous to having symptoms).

Only the very worst case people have their leak located along the keel. Even if they throw overboard all twelve boxes and get rid of their entire total load, they will still continue to take on water and proceed to sink unless they are taken to dry dock for a repair job. This dry dock is analogous to the environmental control unit.

554

And not only do we vary in the location of our leaks, but in the weight of our boxes. For some, eating sugar contributes to 90% of their depression. So they are very lucky. A simple, healthful change in diet can practically cure their depression. But for another person, it may only be 2% of the problem. So when they clean up their diet, there is no noticeable improvement in their depression.

What is in the **twelve mysterious boxes?** You guessed it. The total environmental overload.

In **Box #1** are the **inhalants**; allergies to inhaled pollens, dust mites, molds, animal danders and the like. Once a person institutes environmental controls and receives immunotherapy for the inhalant hypersensitivities that he has, this box is no longer a burden: analogous to having thrown it overboard, as it no longer contributes to the symptom overload. We described how to diagnose and treat your inhalant allergies in THE E.I. SYNDROME, REVISED.

Box #2 contains **food allergies**. David was a 39 year old man who had seen several psychiatrists for 20 years of depression. He had been on many antidepressants. Within two weeks of food injections and the rotation diet, he was able to discard his anti-depressants. He was very happy and was thinking clearly for the first time in years. Food allergy was one of the major heavy boxes that he was carrying around in his boat, causing him to sink. Some victims are so damaged that they require very special healing diets like macrobiotic or the live food diet or carnivore diet in order to heal.

THE E.I. SYNDROME, REVISED describes the diagnostic diets and the Candida diets. YOU ARE WHAT YOU ATE describes how to begin the macrobiotic diet. THE CURE IS

IN THE KITCHEN describes the strict phase macrobiotics with which so many have healed the impossible. MACRO MELLOW gives recipes and menus for both stages as well as for people who merely want to begin to eat more healthfully. And WELLNESS AGAINST ALL ODDS provides other diets like the carnivore with which people have also healed the impossible.

Box #3 is chemical hypersensitivity. Betty was getting progressively more depressed, but would get a little better in summer, and thought that it was just because she was on teacher's vacation. It wasn't until she was tested to natural gas that she discovered it was a major cause of her depression. In the winter her load was increased because the heating system was turned up so high. In summer, with more time spent outdoors, she was better depending upon how much time she spent cooking with the gas stove and how often she fired up the gas clothes dryer.

Others have been depressed by formaldehyde, and used the formaldehyde spot test to help them determine which house and office products contained too much formaldehyde and were contributing to symptoms. TIRED OR TOXIC? goes into the diagnosis and treatment for this aspect, and WELLNESS AGAINST ALL ODDS provides even further help.

Box #4 contains the newer molds that have been identified as the result of our research published in the ANNALS OF ALLERGY (July, 1982; January, 1983; and May, 1984). Bill was the chairman of a college theology department and had experienced two years of extreme depression, tiredness and weakness. An evaluation at the medical center, complete with lumbar puncture and cat scan, could not elicit a cause. Within two weeks of neutralizing injections to the newer molds, his symptoms were totally clear. Whenever his injections are late, his symptoms recur. They disappear again within ten minutes after he has had his injections. Petri dishes or mold culture plates are available through the office to anyone. They should be exposed in the bedroom, at least, for anyone suspecting mold sensitivity. Once you know your enemy, it is much easier to conquer it (see Box #1).

Box #5 is labeled **phenol.** Some people never stop sinking until they are on phenol-free injections. They're just plain too chemically overloaded and sensitive to be able to improve without phenol-free injections. Phenol is the chemical preservative in all allergists' injections. The trouble is that some people are highly allergic to this.

Lynn was a 27 year old television engineer. He told me that all allergists' injections made him worse. In fact in spite of many allergies, injections made him even more depressed and even crazy. I presumed that our injections would be different because of the individualized serial dilution testing method. I was right, but for the totally wrong reason. During testing to phenol, he developed a severe psychosis, was rocking in his chair and talking to imaginary people in the ceiling. Then giving him the neutralizing injection turned off the reaction. I knew instantly why shots made him worse.

Tamara had one year of severe rheumatoid arthritis and depression with elevated rheumatoid factors and sedimentation rates. When we neutralized her to phenol we eliminated her pain and stiffness. This event was filmed double-blind to teach other physicians. It also served to prove to her that a chemical hypersensitivity was at the root of her symptoms and led us to know what chemicals she had to remove from her home in order to become symptom-free. (see boxes #1 and #3).

Box #6 contains **Candida.** David was a 42 year old attorney from New York City. He had extreme lethargy, depression, weakness and headaches for two years following surgery for which antibiotics were prescribed. Treatment of his Candidiasis markedly improved his well-being. But a major misunderstanding by many who have Candida problems is that if they just address the Candida, they will be well. But nothing could be further from the truth.

For many of these people will never permanently get rid of Candida, or any other intestinal dysbiosis, until they unload enough. They may need to correct nutrient deficiencies, heal a leaky gut, or reduce ambient home chemicals, for example, so that the body is no longer vulnerable to this normally harmless yeast. It must be remembered that Candida hypersensitivity syndrome is only a problem for people who are not playing with a full deck of protective nutrients and whose load is too high (see boxes #1 and #3).

Box #7 is labeled **nutrition.** Suzanne had depression and other symptoms for thirteen years. John had psoriasis for fifteen years. Correcting both of their deficiencies of essential fatty acids with supplements cleared both of their problems. They each had an essential fatty acid deficiency that caused completely different symptoms. The bottom line is that until you find the vitamin, mineral, essential fatty acid, amino acid and other deficiencies, you cannot help someone get completely free of symptoms. (see box #3).

Box #8 is **hormone** hypersensitivity or dysfunction. Paula had severe PMS (pre-menstrual syndrome). She was psychotic and extremely depressed for four days before her period. A minute titrated injection of the correct dose of progesterone brought her out of this within 3 minutes and helped her to remain asymptomatic as long as she received them monthly. All hormones have a delicate balance in our systems, just as do the nutrients. Some people have sub-clinical deficiencies of hormones that are often overlooked by conventional testing, as in a DHEA deficiency. This can be the cause of chronic depression and fatigue and multiple other difficult to treat symptoms (boxes #1 and #3).

Box #9 is labeled **toxic.** It signifies people who are overloaded with heavy metal poisoning such as cadmium from auto exhaust, or aluminum from years of antacids, or any of the many other chemicals, like pesticides, volatile hydrocarbons, solvents and metals that the body stores when it is not able to get rid of them. Some people do not recover, for example, until their mercury amalgam dental fillings are all replaced. There are many ways to unload the body of toxic chemicals and heavy metals. Sauna programs, the macrobiotic diet, chelation (oral or I.V.) are but a few (boxes #1 and #3).

Box #10 contains **stress.** Many people never had environmental illness until after the death of a spouse, a divorce, or an extremely stressful time. We know the immune system is extremely vulnerable to stress. We have seen men whose wives were dying of breast cancer who had very low levels of T-suppressor cells during the last month of their wives' lives. These cells are crucial in restricting the amount of harmful antigens that are produced. There are many psychological problems that have environmental triggers and nutritional deficiencies at their root. And the opposite is also true: that the healing progress of some is stone-walled until they can get over certain psychological hurdles. And we know that the longer psychological stresses are ignored, the more damage (like nutrient depletion that then goes on to create new symptoms) that occurs. (boxes #1, #2, and #3).

Box #11 is labeled **"miscellaneous"**. It contains various mediators such as histamine, serotonin and heparin, as well as bacterial and viral vaccine neutralizations that help some people's symptoms. It can include sensitivity to electro-magnetic fields and the myriad of environmental stressors that we probably have not even recognized yet. It is the largest and most rapidly growing box, for it contains all the new things discovered. (For example, intestinal dysbiosis can cause the hyperpermeable leaky gut which can be the hidden cause of rapidly escalating and seemingly incurable food allergies, which can cause depression. (boxes #1, #2, and #3).

The last **Box #12**, is called the **mystery box**, because indeed the twelfth box was a mystery to me for a long time. I knew this box contained something extremely important. Now I see that it is not nearly as elusive as we all would like to think. It is the patient's willingness or unwillingness to take **responsibility** for his own health, to constantly educate himself, and to deal with his total load.

Whenever I see someone who is not improving as much as he might, I find that he usually still has a gas-heated house or some other tremendously potent overload that continues to sink his boat. He frequently has to go outside because he does not have a safe oasis to which he can escape. He often has to fast to reduce his total load because he is often cheating and not rotating his diet. He needs frequent quick fixes to keep him out of deep trouble. Or worst of all, he has a spouse who is not willing to read and learn about environmental illness and become a much-needed partner in his healing.

Some people are just not sick enough to dig in and get themselves well. Unfortunately for others, they are too sick, and their inertia is part of their symptoms. This presents a real problem, because this specialty requires marked patient and spouse education and participation. The optimistic part is that by following some simple suggestions, as for a healthier diet and then by getting some nutrient deficiencies identified and corrected, many can start crawling far enough out of the hole of depression to then start helping themselves even further. Reading and learning are the key.

By periodically reminding ourselves of the concept of the total load and of the contents of each hypothetical box, you should be able to progress toward total wellness. For it is only when the total load is sufficiently reduced that the body is able to heal itself. The priorities of the body are first to keep all vital systems working, such as heart and respiration. Having accomplished that, other functions can be allowed that maintain life, like digestion.

But it is only when the total body burden of mental and physical stressors has been sufficiently reduced that the body is able to reverse damages from years of overload, and heal whatever was damaged or overloaded, including the chemical detoxification system. For each day the total cumulative effect is that we regress, stay the same, or heal new areas. What was the result of your total effort today? The status of the total load determines which of these occurs. What is still contributing to your total load and inhibiting healing?

For details of all these parts of the total load, see Volumes I, II, and III. For ease in conceptualization your total load, it has 3 basic categories: environmental, nutritional and metabolic causes. The environmental cause (Vol. 1) include boxes 1,2,3,4,5, and 9. The nutritional causes (Vol. II) are box 7 and the rest, metabolic causes (Vol. III) are boxes 6,8,10,11 and 12.

CANDIDA RAISES CHEMICAL VULNERABILITY AND THE TOTAL LOAD

As you've learned (in Volumes I and III), Candida is a yeast that grows in the intestines if too many antibiotics are taken, with too much sugar in the diet, or if the individual is particularly vulnerable, such as having undiagnosed nutrient deficiencies or other diseases. The problem is that is raises the vulnerability or susceptibility to chemical sensitivity, the leaky gut, auto-immune diseases and depression by adding to the total load.

And of course, there is always the fact that you had to be low in something, or "not playing with a full deck of nutrients" in order to get Candida is the first place. So it is the old sick get sicker when you do not deal with symptoms as soon as they appear.

REFERENCE:

Kitabatake M, et al, Effects of exposure to NO2 or SO2 on bronchopulmonary reaction induced by Candida albicans in guinea pigs, J TOXICOL ENVIRONM HEALTH 45:75-82, 1995

FATIGUE VERSUS DEPRESSION:
WHAT COMES FIRST, THE CHICKEN OR THE EGG?

It is sometimes impossible to separate fatigue and depression, and they often accompany one another.   In fact, Prozac has been used to treat fatigue since depression is one of the accompanying symptoms of the chronic fatigue syndrome. (Mehta VK, Blume GB, A randomized trial of fluoxetine in a patient with persistent fatigue, J AMER BOARD FAM PRACT 8:3, 230-232, May-June 1995).

The problem is that all the term **"chronic fatigue syndrome"** means is "We don't know why you are so tired all the time." It is no different than the **fibromyalgia syndrome**, which merely means, "We don't have a clue as to why you ache and hurt all over", or **irritable bowel syndrome**, which means "We don't know why your gut is all messed up". And the other thing that all of these "new" syndromes have in common is that these nebulous names also mean that the patient has not consulted a doctor trained in finding the causes.   For looking for the environmental triggers and the nutritional deficits is not standard.   In fact by ignoring this causal approach to chronic fatigue and depression, they have a pretty dismal treatment record (Gorensek MJ, Chronic fatigue and depression in the ambulatory patient, PRIMARY CARE 18:397-419, 1991).

AN EXAMPLE OF THE INTER-RELATEDNESS OF DISEASES AND DEFICIENCY SYMPTOMS

By now you have the correct idea that **if you have even one symptom, you are a set-up for the downhill spiral of disease,** which can eventually involve the brain as a target organ, and depression as your label. And if you already have depression as a symptom, you had better concentrate on getting your body so healthy that it gets rid of all symptoms, not just the depression. For if you target only one symptom, you'll ignore finding the causes for the rest of the problems, which can perpetuate the **downhill descent** into the world of chronic illness. You can worsen or initiate emerging depression by this route.

By now you also realize that we could have written a whole book on the influence of any single nutrient on depression: for any one deficiency of a vitamin, mineral, amino acid, essential fatty acid, or accessory nutrient can precipitate or continue depression. Likewise, any single food, chemical or mold sensitivity, or any hormone deficiency, or other condition like the leaky gut, or hypoglycemia, etc. can cause depression.

And the majority of victims, do not have one single isolated cause, for the rule is the causes are **multi-factorial.** The beauty of it is, that once you identify the triggers, you will most likely arrive at a state of wellness far beyond anything you ever knew existed. For when you actually find the causes of a symptom and correct them, as opposed to merely masking them with a drug, you bring the body up another notch or two on the overall health scale.

You now know how and why we get so deficient in this era. And if the processed foods diet which then creates further cravings were not enough, stress, prescription and non-prescription drugs, and ambient chemicals actually use up or deplete nutrients even further. And as specific nutrients become depleted, then the body is vulnerable for environmental heavy metals and chemicals to damage enzymes even further. Thus the old sick get sicker, quicker scenario.

Magnesium is a great example of how crucial the total load is. U.S. government studies tell us the average U.S. diet only provides 40% or less than half of what we need in a day. Then stress can lower it even further (Henrotte JG, Type A behavior and magnesium metabolism, MAGNESIUM, 5:201-210,1986). Then magnesium deficiency can go on to cause or contribute to a variety of common problems which are rarely considered as having any bearing on depression.

High cholesterol, arteriosclerosis, high blood pressure, and cardiac arrhythmia are common magnesium deficiency symptoms which are in the category of cardiovascular disease, the number one cause of death and illness in the U.S. Yet they are treated as drug deficiencies (deficiencies of cholesterol-lowering drugs, deficiencies of anti-hypertensive drugs, anti-arrhythmia drugs or calcium channel blockers, etc.). Rarely is the cause sought, such as a simple magnesium deficiency. To neglect the deficiency part of the total load is a grave mistake in any disease.

Again, to point out the importance of the total load, patients for example with celiac disease, often have depression. But in one study when they were on a gluten free diet for years and their depression did not improve, it was found that once their B6 deficiency was corrected, then their mental disease improved (Hallert C, et al, Reversal of psycho-pathology in adult celiac disease with the aid of pyridoxine (vitamin B6), SCAND J GASTROENTEROL, 18(2):299-304, 1993.

For remember, nearly **all diseases have deficiencies** associated with them to begin with and many diseases are caused totally by deficiencies. Then when medications are used to mask symptoms, they create further deficiencies. For example, a child who was treated with ACTH developed depression. It improved with intravenous vitamin C, but what if the pediatrician had never thought of the nutrient connection? (Cocchi P, et al, Anti-depressant effect of vitamin C, PEDIATRICS 65:862-863, 1980.) So never lose sight of the inter-relatedness of all symptoms, and learn to cover the total load.

REFERENCES:

Vitale JJ, White PL, Nakamura M, Hegsted DM, Zamchick N, et al, Interrelationships between experimental hypercholesterolemia, magnesium requirement and experimental arteriosclerosis, EXP MED 106:757-767,1957

Ouchi Y, Tabata RE, Stergiopoulos K, Sato F, Hattori A, et al, Effect of dietary magnesium on development of arteriosclerosis in cholesterol-fed rabbits, ARTERIO-SCLEROSIS, 10:732-737,1990

Davis WH, Leary WP, Reyes AJ, Olhaberry JV, Monotherapy with magnesium increases abnormally low high density lipoprotein cholesterol: a clinical assay, CURR THER RES 36:341-346, 1984

Dyckner T, Wester PO, Effect of magnesium on blood pressure, BR MED J 286:1847-1849,1983

Iseri LT, French JH, Magnesium: nature's physiologic calcium channel blocker. AM HEART J, 108:188-193,1984

MAGNESIUM AND MIGRAINES

And of course, arteriosclerosis is a direct cause of one of the most common forms of depression, the **senile brain**. For as you have learned, once you choose to go the medication route, as an example, for hypertension, you set yourself up for a worsening of magnesium and other deficiencies. Plus you guarantee that you will get other symptoms and speed up the process of aging. And if you go on cholesterol-lowering drugs, you even deny the brain and neurotransmitters the lipids they require and set yourself up for suicidal depression. And this does not even address the nutrients that are further depleted in the work of detoxifying the drugs. This leads to further depression via other biochemical routes.

For even when the brain is the target organ itself, as in migraine, the cause is rarely sought. This is again in spite of voluminous research data. Instead migraine medications, as an example are prescribed. Thus we allow the undiscovered deficiencies like magnesium to go on to cause depression or sudden cardiac death, as you have learned. And just as magnesium is one of many potential causes of migraine, it is one of many for the causes of depression.

In spite of overwhelming evidence for magnesium deficiency being one of the causes of migraine, we only see expensive medications as the prescribed and sanctioned treatment. Yes, with all the migraine patients I see, with all of their million dollar neurology work-ups, I have never seen one who was given the benefit of the doubt that maybe an inexpensive trial of magnesium might be the answer. And sometimes you can even stop a migraine in progress with a simple 2 cc I.M. injection of 50% magnesium sulfate.

REFERENCES:

Altura BM, Calcium antagonist properties of magnesium: implications for anti-migraine actions, MAGNESIUM 4:169- 175,1985

Baker B, New research approach helps clarify magnesium/migraine link, FAM PRACT NEWS, p16 Aug 15, 1993

Ramadan NM, Halvorson H, Vande-Linde A, Levine SR, Helpern JA, et al, Low brain magnesium in migraine, HEADACHE 29:590- 593,1989

Faccinetti F, Sances G, Borella P, Gonazzani AR, Nappi G, Magnesium prophylaxis of menstrual migraine: effects of intracellular magnesium, HEADACHE, 31:98-304,1991

Weaver K, Magnesium and migraine, HEADACHE, 30:168, 1990

Swanson DR, Migraine and magnesium: eleven neglected connections, PERSPECT BIL MED, 31:526-557,1988

DEPRESSION ACCOMPANIES
MANY OTHER DISEASES

With that in mind, it is no wonder that other diseases like renal stones or fibromyalgia or premenstrual tension and pain are not thought of as related or having any bearing on depression. Even when a person has fatigue, a symptom that is often linked with depression, and even though there are many papers showing that a magnesium deficiency could be the cause of either symptom, it is usually not sought as a cause for either.

And don't forget that many of the **paradigm protectors** are on the committees that make the **practice guidelines**. This is the giant cookbook that dictates to doctors and insurance companies what treatments are "O.K." for each disease. The problem is that most of the recipes only involve, drugs and surgery. **Cause is not a consideration.** And I'll spare you the details of how these decision makers are affiliated with the industries that profit from this control, as many other books on medical politics give the intimate details.

As a simple example, even though the control of blood sugar has a marked bearing on brain function and chemistry, and even though magnesium is in part responsible for blood sugar control, still it is not checked. Now you see the urgency for a book like this. For even though depression itself can be the only symptom of a magnesium deficiency, it is rarely looked for even though it might be accompanied by other classic magnesium-deficiency symptoms like fatigue or hypoglycemia. And it is so inexpensive to treat. And if that is the only cause, it can actually be cured!

Depression is an expected accompaniment to many syndromes, like chronic fatigue, lupus, chemical sensitivities, fibromyalgia, cancer, ankylosing spondylitis, etc. And in some cases, it is nigh impossible to separate some of the symptoms or which came first. And since most symptoms have to have underlying deficiencies, it is no wonder that depression eventually tags along as well. Then we compound the problem with a case of low stomach acid as in hypochlorhydria, or as is more commonly done by using drugs, like antacids to sop up the acid, or like Tagamet or Zantac to suppress acid formation in the stomach. The lowered acid can so drastically reduce mineral absorption, for example, as to lead to any number of new symptoms, one of which is commonly depression.

It makes me shudder when I read common current articles like this from a respected journal: Ginsburg KA, Some practical approaches to treating PMS, INTERN MED 71-82, July 1995. The approaches stressed are drugs which include the gamut from diuretics (fluid pills), to anti-depressants like Prozac and others, strong beta-blockers, tranquilizers, analgesics to include NSAIDs, and of course, a D & C or even hysterectomy if hormones and non-steroidal anti-inflammatory drugs fail. The author even mentioned naloxone which is really for the withdrawal from opioids. This author at least did mention a little about nutrition and diet, but excluded the "how-to", as the focus was drugs. He conveys the universal message that the condition, PMS, must be a deficiency of drugs and surgery. Yet PMS is merely a constellation of deficiency and/or sensitivity symptoms, one of which is depression.

Whenever there is more than one symptom, as there is with most "syndromes", that would make me highly suspicious of multiple triggers as well. And that is exactly what has been found. (The worse the symptoms, usually, the more factors that need to be addressed) (Indeed, the more symptoms, the more nutrient deficiencies we find, and the more dietary and environmental triggers.)

You are beginning to see the vast **inter-relatedness** of the body and the importance of the total environmental and nutritional influences, and how ludicrous and dangerous it is to overlook all this by giving medications to merely suppress or turn off symptoms.

REFERENCES:

Johansson G, et al, Effects of magnesium hydroxide in renal stone disease, J AM COLL NUTR 1:179-185,1982

Prien EL, Gershoff SN, Magnesium oxide-pyridoxine therapy for recurrent calcium oxalate calculi, J UROL 112:507-512,1974

Abraham GE, Flechas JD, Management of fibromyalgia: rationale of the use of magnesium and malic acid, J NUTR MED 3:49-59, 1991

Abraham GE, Lubran MM, Serum and red cell magnesium levels, in patients with premenstrual tension, AM J CLIN NUTR 34:2364-2366,1981

Sherwood RA, Rocks BF, Stewart A, Saxton RS, Magnesium and the premenstrual syndrome, ANN CLIN BIOCHEM 23:667-670, 1986

Facchinetti F, Borella P, Sances Gm Fioroni L, Nappi RE, et al, Oral magnesium successfully relieves premenstrual mood changes, OBSTET GYNECOL 78:177-181, 1991

Gaby AR, Wright JV, Nutritional regulation of blood glucose, J ADVANCEMENT MED 4:57-71,1991

Ewald U, Gebbre-Medhin M, Tuvemo T, Hypomagnesemia in diabetic children, ACTA PAEDIATR SCAND 72:367-371, 1983

Yajnik CS, Smith RF, Hockaday TDR, Ward NI, Fasting plasma magnesium concentrations and glucose disposal in diabetes, BR J MED 228:1027-1028, 1984

Paolisso G, Sgambato S, Gambardella A, Pizza G, Tesauro P, et al, Daily magnesium supplements improve glucose handling in elderly subjects, AM J CLIN NUTR 55:1161-1167, 1992

Brilla LR, Wenos DL, Perceived endurance to exercise following magnesium supplementation, MAG TR ELEM 9:319- 320, 1991

Deulofeu R, Gascon J, Gimenez N, Corachan M, Magnesium and chronic fatigue syndrome, LANCET 338:641, 1991

Clague JE, Edwards RHT, Jackson MJ, Intravenous magnesium loading in chronic fatigue syndrome, LANCET 340:124-125, 1992

Cox IM, Campbell MJ, Dowson D, Red blood cell magnesium and chronic fatigue syndrome, LANCET 37:757-760, 1991

Shealy CN, Cady RK, Veehoff D, Burnetti M, Houston R, et al, Magnesium deficiency in depression and chronic pain, M MAG TR ELEM 9:333, 1990

Bland JS, A functional approach to mental illness. A new paradigm for managing brain biochemical disturbances, TOWNSEND LETTER FOR DOCTORS, 1335-1341, Dec 1994

Null G, Feldman M, Nutrition and mental illness: Sampling of the current scientific literature, ibid, 40-48, Oct 1995

GENETICS ARE NOT CAST IN STONE

Gene therapy is the wave of the future in medicine. I just picked up a new biochemistry textbook in the medical school book store and much to my amazement, the small sections that used to be allotted to the chemistry of nutrients like vitamins and minerals, has become even smaller. This is in spite of the fact that we have volumes of more studies on nutrients. Instead there is a huge addition of sections on gene therapy. So it looks like the future thrust of medicine is going to be in genetic alteration and we will continue to ignore the environmental and nutritional approach to cause. The motto of medicine will remain the same: ignore the cause, and stick with expensive and high-tech procedures that make the most money. And daily perusal of such publications as the WALL STREET JOURNAL supports this.

But even though you may have been dealt a crummy hand in terms of genetics, there are lots of ways to over-ride these defects without gene therapy. And again a cause-oriented environmental approach is far less expensive. A simple example is the diabetic who learns that by a healthful lifestyle and orphan nutrients like vanadium and lipoic acid, for example, he can thwart his genetic determinations. For it still takes multiple parts of the total load to produce disease. Examples are rampant of how genetic disease can be attenuated, such as the use of urea and vitamin E for sickle cell disease. And the reverse is true, that with enough of the wrong lifestyle and medication, you can accentuate bad genetics, and even override good genetics.

Another example is the group of people who get severe migraines from tyramine containing foods, like certain wines, cheeses, chocolate, etc. These people lack a gene to give them sufficient amounts of an enzyme, monoamine oxidase (MAO). But you can turn anyone into a tyramine victim by just giving him a class of anti-depressants called the MAO inhibitors. Both groups will get such wicked headaches and hypertension from tyramine containing foods that you won't be able to tell who has the bad genetics and who has the drug.

There are still foolish denigrators who insist that everyday chemicals cannot cause auto-immune disease states like lupus. But we need merely remind them that hydrazine, for example, is but one of several chemicals in the environment. It is in some mushrooms. It is also related to the chemistry of some prescription drugs for TB (INH). And it can cause cancers. It's used in the manufacturing of plastics, pesticides, rubber, dyes, medicines, anti-corrosives and much more. In the 52% of **the population who are slow acetylators** genetically, they do not have as much of specific detoxification enzymes as others. So they are susceptible to induction of lupus with the appropriate total load. They don't have to even have a leaky gut to get lupus. They merely need exposure to the chemical and their genetics that makes them slow acetylators. In other words, half the population has the genetics whereby they do not metabolize foreign chemicals as well as the other half. Thus a subset of the population is vulnerable for getting lupus from such prescribed medications like hydralazine for hypertension (minoxidil) and procainamide for cardiac arrhythmias (Reidenberg, MM, et al, Lupus erythematosus - like disease due to hydrazine, AM J MED, 75:365-369, Aug 1983).

Unfortunately, we are the first generation of man exposed to many of these chemicals every day. And they are the cause of many diseases and symptoms that medicine continues to label as having no known cause or treatment. When physicians have no mechanism to explain a symptom, they often use "It's a virus", as cancer was for years, or "It's auto-immune" (but they never test for leaky gut), or "It's genetic," or the one most of you readers have so often heard, "It's all in your head."

As another example, Parkinson's disease is the result of environmental factors acting on genetically susceptible individuals against a background of normal aging. For significantly more Parkinsonian than control subjects (who are partially or totally defective in an enzyme system which causes a metabolic step called 4-hydroxylation of debrisoquine) have earlier onset of disease. In other words, again, there are volumes of data to now show that Parkinson's disease, like most others, has multiple environmental triggers which play on the backdrop of the biochemical individuality of people. Whether you are susceptible depends only in part on your genetics. The good news is that **there is a tremendous amount of control that you have over your health in spite of your genetics.** (Barbeau A, et al, Ecogenetics of Parkinson's disease: 4-hydroxylation of debrisoquine, LANCET, Nov 30, 1985, 1213).

Furthermore, numerous studies now show that with various nutrients and phytochemicals and other nutrients in the diet, you can change your genetic expression (editorial, Metabolic control of gluconeogenesis in transgenic mice: Regulation of the phosphoenolpyruvate carboxykinase gene, NUTR REV 52;8:275- 282, Aug 1994).

Many of us had family histories full of depression, suicides, alcoholism and allergies. But that does not mean that we have to chose to be saddled with these. I hope you now understand why, and how to avoid it.

CANCER: THE LAST WAKE-UP CALL,
BUT HARDLY AN EXCUSE FOR DEPRESSION

Do not forget that there are numerous potential causes for depression, not the least of which is cancer. **Often long before a person knows he has a cancer, he is just plain fatigued, or depressed.** You might think that would be a reason to be depressed if you knew you had cancer. But actually, it is a reason to be happy. You see we all have cancer cells in us. But we take care of them on a daily basis. When finally the cancer is further ahead than the body, it becomes diagnosable. But it is a disease of optimism, for it gives you one last wake-up call.

You see, **the body is trying to get our attention to repent or mend our ways every time we have a symptom.** If you have a little ache, depression, fatigue, colitis, or whatever, **every symptom is a God-given alarm** that says you had better look for the environmental trigger and the biochemical glitches before you get something worse. But we often ignore the wake-up call, stuff a medication down our gullets, and move on to the inevitable next symptom in time. **Whenever we get the wake-up call, we have a choice** of finding the cause, or stifling the alarm with a drug. And so on it goes until we get the final call, a stroke, heart attack, etc.

But **cancer is curable,** even when you have been given up on by medicine. And if not curable, you can measurably increase your survival and well-being. But it is all under your control. Don't expect to find a doctor to take this over. For there is no money in it and it does not feed the drug industry. Subsequently, if a therapy does not support the drug and medical industries, it is discredited as having any value (call the cancer hotline 800 number and hear for yourself).

So let's look at some of the evidence. In one study, cancer specialists (oncologists) in Finland gave high doses of nutrients to one group of patients in addition to the chemotherapy and radiation. These were lung cancer patients with an expected 1% survival at 2 1/2 years. In other words, of 100 patients with lung cancer, only one was expected to be alive in 2 1/2 years if everything that medicine has to offer had been done. But for the group who also got the nutrients, in 6 years, 44% were still alive when the study ended. So that's **44 out of 100 alive at 6 years versus one, just with some unsophisticated and inexpensive nutrients!** Just imagine their results if they had actually measured levels and corrected each accordingly and put them on the macro diet? But show me oncologists who do this.

In another study at the West Virginia Medical School, they looked at patients with cancer of the bladder. Again they blindly gave only 4 vitamins; no levels were measured, no amino acids, no minerals, no essential fatty acids, and no specific healing diet. Yet they dropped the recurrence rate in half. In other words, in 2 years, over 80% of the patients get their cancer back, when you do everything known to science. But **for the vitamin group, the recurrence rate was only 40% versus 80%.** With 4 simple nutrients they cut the cancer recurrence rate in half! (Lamm, J UROL, Jan 1994)

Or look at another study of cancer patients where one group ate a healthier diet and had some supplements. The average life-span was 6 months. In the test group, 47% lived 6 years, not 6 months! And 32% were still alive at 10 years when the study ended (had to publish it before the researchers died).

In yet another study at the University of Hawaii, 675 lung cancer patients were studied for 6 years. The more vegetables they ate, the longer they lived. In another study at the University of British Columbia, patients were studied who had had remarkable "spontaneous regressions" of their cancers. Eighty-seven percent had made a vegetarian diet change, 55% used detoxification procedures (like coffee enemas, etc.), and 65% took supplements (Directions are in WELLNESS AGAINST ALL ODDS). Yet patients continually tell me their oncologists advise them to eat whatever they want. They tell them diet has no bearing on their cancer.

And in one more study at Tulane University, they studied cancer of the pancreas. In one year if everything that medicine has to offer is done, 90% of the patients are dead. But for patients doing the macrobiotic diet, only 48% were dead. **So survival at one year was up to 52% versus 10% with diet alone.** And also it represented a vast savings, for many of these people only did the diet and did not do surgery, chemotherapy or radiation. That means that by avoiding the nutrient-depleting procedures, they simultaneously protected themselves from further lowering their nutrient status.

In another part of the same study they looked at cancer of the prostate. If you did everything that medicine has to offer, **median survival was 3.7 years, versus 12.3 for the macro group.** So **a diet** which the specialists are loathe to recommend **more than tripled survival,** and with minimal cost and horrendous cost savings. And look at the savings in sickness from side effects and further nutrient losses.

Then there is Carter's study (JACN 12:3,1993). If you do everything medicine has to offer for cancer of the prostate (chemo, radiation, surgery, hormones), the median survival for these patients was 6 years. But if the macrobiotic diet was done (as described in THE CURE IS IN THE KITCHEN), the **survival more than tripled** to 19 years, and many are still alive. They just had to stop the study somewhere so they could publish before the researchers died.

In spite of all the evidence for a sound nutritional assessment in cancer, it is not standard. It is not part of the treatment guidelines, and not covered by insurances. This is in spite of the fact that not only did you have to have nutrient deficiencies to get cancer, depression, or any disease, but the treatments (drugs, radiation) have all been known for decades to further lower the nutrient status.

So if you have a cancer, start with WELLNESS AGAINST ALL ODDS. Then proceed to YOU ARE WHAT YOU ATE, then THE CURE IS IN THE KITCHEN. The combination contains information that the successful cancer survivor needs to know, regardless of what diet type he eventually chooses. (Call 1-800-846-6687 for the subscription newsletter and/or a scheduled private consultation for more information and guidance).

REFERENCES:

Jaakkola K, Lahteenmaki P, Treatment with antioxidant and other nutrients in combination with chemotherapy and irradiation in patients with small-cell lung cancer, ANTICANCER RES, 12:599-606, 1992

Lamm DL, Riggs DR, Shriver JS, van Gilder PF, Megadose vitamin in bladder cancer: a double-blind clinical trial, J UROL, 151:21-26, 1994

Hoffer A, Pauling L, Hardin Jones biostatistical analysis of mortality data of cancer patients, J ORTHOMOLECULAR MED, 5;3:143-154, 1990

Goodman MT, Vegetable consumption in lung cancer longevity, EUR J CA, 28;2:495-499, 1992

Foster HD, Lifestyle influences on spontaneous cancer regression, INT J BIOSOC RES, 10;1:17-20, 1988

Carter JP, et al, Macrobiotic diet and cancer survival, J AMER COLL NUTR, 12;3:209-215, 1993

Schreurs WHP, et al, The influence of radiotherapy and chemotherapy on the vitamin status of cancer patients, INTERNAT J VIT NUTR RES, 55 (1985) 425-432

SLEEP

Your grandmother can tell you that if you don't get a good night's sleep, that can be part or all of the cause of your depression. And researchers tell us that over 29% of the general population has sleep problems (Anonymous, Single question identifies sleep disorders in a working population, INTERN MED WORLD REP, 10:9;34, May 1-14, 1995, and Kupperman et al, J GEN INTERN MED 10:25-32, 1995).

For many, their insomnia is related to what they ate. A simple way to solve the problem for a large number is to have a darkened room, a quiet room or one with a steady noise to blot out intrusive noises, and an air cleaner (which cleans the air and can provide a background noise to block street noises). Stop all sugar, alcohol, tobacco, do not eat after 6 p.m., chew each mouthful 50-100 times, and watch no TV. If that does not solve the problem, get a magnesium loading test (in TIRED OR TOXIC?). If a good sleep still eludes you, then a full work-up is in order. It could still be something simple like the side effect of a medication, or something more difficult like thyroiditis.

Of course there will probably be more insomnia after viewers follow the directive for the T.V. commercial to go and pig out on Mexican food (even though you know it "kills" you) and take the H-2 blocker. This in effect shuts off the stomach digestive acids. It should be a fun filled 2 days while all that undigested Mexican food tries to pass through the gut.

Two over-the-counter safe and effective remedies to start with would be Valarian and melatonin (see discussion on each in Volume II).

REFERENCES:

Moldofsky H, Rheumatic pain modulation syndrome: The interrelationship between sleep, central nervous system serotonin, and pain, ADVANC IN NEUROL, 33:51-57, 1982

Morriss, Richard, et al, Abnormalities of sleep in patients with chronic fatigue syndrome, BRIT MED, 306:1161-4, 1993

Wehr, Thomas A., M.D., Improvement of depression and triggering of mania by sleep deprivation, JAMA, January 22/29; 267(4):548-551, 1992

Carney, Robert M., et al, Insomnia and depression prior to myocardial infarction, PSYCHOSOMATIC MEDICINE, 52:603-609, 1990

Anonymous, Hormone helps elderly sleep, SCIENCE NEWS, 148:175, 1995

EMF OR ELECTROMAGNETIC FIELDS

If you have followed the other books, you know there are electromagnetic fields all about us. They are the waves of energy that radiate from electric wires that carry electricity. They are wrapped around the walls of every room. And the field of invisible waves is stronger, obviously when you are near very powerful electrical sources. Robert Becker, M.D., Cyril Smith, Ph.D., and other brilliant people in the field have written volumes explaining and documenting the effects of these fields on the human body, including the mind.

People who slept in beds near an outside transformer, or whose homes were near high voltage power lines, or who worked in submarines had higher rates of various cancers. Even cows grazing under high voltage lines had more abortions, cancers, other diseases, and erratic behavior. Some people are so sensitive to electromagnetic fields that they get the same effects they would if they were exposed to a nasty chemical to which they are sensitive.

If you awaken irritable, edgy, or depressed, you owe it to yourself to determine whether EMF might be a factor. Merely sleep outdoors for a night. Or turn off the circuit breaker to your room during the night. And at least, get all electrical devices at least 5 feet away from your head where you sleep. This will also entail moving your head away from the wall where the wires are housed. Sleep with your head at the foot of the bed, preferably pointing north.

And don't forget that the TV is always "on", unless unplugged. For there is a warming devise inside that keeps the cathode ray tube in a constant state of readiness. That is why you don't have to wait 5 minutes for the picture tube to "warm up" before you can see an image on it, as in the early days of television in the 50's. There are other atmospheric effects that can change brain function, like negative ions, and the reader is referred to our other books and those below.

REFERENCES:

Wilson B, Chronic exposure to ELF fields may induce depression, BIOELECTROMAGNETICS, 9:195-205, 1988

Becker RO, Selden G, THE BODY ELECTRIC, Wm Morrow & Co, NY, 1985

Rea WJ, CHEMICAL SENSITIVTY, VOL II, Lewis Publ, Boca Raton, 1992

Smith CW, Best S, ELECTROMAGNETIC MAN: HEALTH AND HAZARD IN THE ELECTRICAL ENVIRONMENT, London, J.M. Dent, 1989

Rea WJ, Electromagnetic field sensitivity, J BIOELECTRICITY 10; 1&2:241-256, 1991

Persinger M, Ludwig H, et al, Psychophysiological effects of extremely low frequency electromagnetic fields: A review, PERCEPTUAL & MOTOR SKILLS, 96:1131-1159, 1973

ELECTRICAL SENSITIVITY NEWS (Newsletter), Weldon Publ, PO Box 4146, Prescott AZ 86302

LIGHT:
SEASONAL AFFECTIVE DISORDER OR SAD

John Ott demonstrated decades ago how important the amount of light that falls on the retina is for our moods. Through even further investigations by others, it has been discovered that there is a subset of people whose depression is definitely worse in proportion to their lack of sunlight. The use of full spectrum (more like sunlight) reading and working lights has been a boon for many.

As with any of these abnormalities, however, it usually does not occur as an isolated occurrence or cause. For example, many of the SAD victims also have food cravings, nutritional deficiencies, and food allergies. In fact, carbohydrate craving is one of the earliest symptoms of winter depression.

Green light has been found more therapeutic than red but white is beneficial too. And do not overlook the fact that real sunlight can't be beat. If you have healthy levels of B-carotene, vitamins A and E, phosphatidyl choline, and other nutrients, it is not harmful in discretionary amounts, and in fact is very essential.

REFERENCES:

Oren, DA et al, Treatment of seasonal affective disorder with green light and red light, AMER PSYCHIA, 148:4:509-511, April 1991

Bielski, Robert J., et al, Phototherapy with spectrum white fluorescent light: A comparative study, PSYCHIA RESEARCH, 43:167-175,1992

Rosenthal NE, et al, Antidepressant effects of light in seasonal affective disorder, AM J PSYCHIATRY, 142(2):163- 170,1985

Rosenthal NE, et al, Seasonal affective disorder and phototherapy. Presented at the New York Academy of Sciences, Nov, 1984

Ott J, Influence of fluorescent lights on hyperactivity and learning disabilities, J LEARN DIS, 9:417-422, 1976.

Ott J, HEALTH AND LIGHT (THE EFFECTS OF NATURAL AND ARTIFICIAL LIGHT ON MAN AND OTHER LIVING THINGS), Pocketbooks, NY, 1976

Eastman, Charmane, I., et al, A placebo-controlled trial of light treatment for winter depression, AFFECT DISORDERS, 26:211-222, 1992

Sack, Robert L., M.D. et al, Morning vs. evening light treatment for winter depression: Evidence that the therapeutic effects of light are mediated by circadian phase shifts, ARCHIVES OF GENERAL PSYCHIATRY, 47:343-351, Apr 1990

Steward, Karen T., et al, Treatment of winter depression with a portable, head-mounted phototherapy device, NEURO-PSYCHOPHARMACOL BIOLOGIC PSYCHIATRY, 14:569-578, 1990

Anonymous, Therapy with light found effective in treating insomnia, INTERN MED WORLD REP, 10:13, 46, July 1995

EXERCISE

Many papers stress the importance of exercise in treating depression, for a variety of reasons. For one, exercise can promote the release of brain neurotransmitters that make happy hormones. But an important one is often omitted. When you exercise, you sweat. And sweat is one of the ways that the body can accelerate its loss of accumulated chemicals that can damage brain chemistry and lead to depression.

REFERENCES:

Johnson HL, Maibach HI, Drug excretion in human eccrine sweat, J INVESTIG DERMATOL, 56;3:182-188, 1970

Weyerer, S., Physical inactivity and depression in community: Evidence from the Upper Bavarian Field Study, INTERNAT SPORTS MED, 13(6):492-496, 1992

Martinsen, Egil, W., Benefits of exercise for the treatment of depression, SPORTS MED; 9(6):380-389,1992.

And just as every phenomenon is subject to the bell curve, so is exercise. In other words, every thing that can be harmful if there is not enough, can also be harmful if there is too much. **Life is a delicate balance.** And so it is with exercise, as there is a depression that comes from over-training. For example, several studies now show that training lowers the levels, or increases the need for anti-oxidant nutrients like vitamin E (references in newsletter, 1995).

Budgett, R., MB., BS, et al, Over-training syndrome, BRIT SPORTS MED; 24(4):231-235,1991

SMOKING

Smoking can lead to depression in several ways: it is an excuse to cover up or ignore what is really eating at you as you divert your attentions to the calming effect of the nicotine. It also leads to insomnia for many. They have withdrawal in the night or a rebound phenomenon when their nicotine level takes a dive. That's why they don't feel good again until they tank up with nicotine in the morning and get their levels back up.

More importantly, the work of detoxifying the tobacco uses up nutrients that could have used to make happy hormones. And some of the nastiest stuff is in cigarettes. Since tobacco leaves are not a food, some of the most carcinogenic pesticides can be used that were banned from use in foods. But manufacturers are covered since there is already a warning on the side that it may cause cancer.

Smoking also decreases one of the control enzymes (MAO or monamine oxidase) for the brain's happy hormones (Fowler, JS, NATURE, 379: 733, 1996) thus releasing dopamine, a neurotransmitter, that contributes to addiction.

Withdrawal symptoms, obviously, can be more severe in people who are prone to or are depressed. Before you take anything away that brings you pleasure, you must find a replacement that gives you equal, or preferably more pleasure. So what gives you more pleasure than smoking? If there is nothing at present, do not give it up just yet. It may worsen your depression.

Breslau, Naomi, Ph.D., et al, Nicotine withdrawal symptoms and psychiatric disorders: Findings from an epidemiologic study of young adults, AMER PSYCHIA;149:4:464-469, Apr 1992

VISUAL DISTURBANCES

Of note, there is a remedy for schizophrenia that includes correction of visual spatial disturbances. Because the results were so wonderful when all else had failed, I urge anyone with recalcitrant problems to read RICKIE, by Fred Flack, M.D., 420 E. 51st Street, New York NY, 10022 (212 355-0882), and also published by Ballantine Books, NY.

ARTERIOSCLEROSIS IS REVERSIBLE

One delightful gentleman was so depressed for years that he took early retirement to look at every aspect that he could think of that might be a cause of his depression. Then one day he developed severe chest pain, and an emergency angiogram revealed that he had serious occlusion of four major cardiac (heart) blood vessels. Certainly an angioplasty (much like a plumber's rooter) can clean out some of the vessels. And through by-pass surgery new vessels can even be grafted onto the heart. But if someone has this serious a case of arteriosclerosis in the heart, shouldn't it also be in other vessels, and most likely the cause of his recalcitrant depression? And won't the new cardiac vessels eventually clog up again?

We can repair cardiac vessels, but brain vessels can only be cleaned out through chelation or major diet change. And this process takes a year or more with a strict macrobiotic diet. But recall the studies of Dr. Dean Ornish (LANCET, 1990) where end-of-the-road cardiac cases reversed their arteriosclerosis of cardiac vessels. And the proof of the pudding was that their symptoms were cleared and the PET scans showed corresponding improvement. Certainly compromised blood flow in the brain can result in depression. Hence, one more reason for a strict macrobiotic diet if all else fails. For this is one proven way to reverse arteriosclerosis in inoperable vessels.

The sad fact is that it has been known in medicine for years that much of arteriosclerosis can be prevented with good nutritional medicine. For example, many people with elevated homocysteine (an amino acid) levels, will go on to get arteriosclerosis. But **homocysteine,** like many other "bad" things is only elevated if the pathway for its metabolism is deficient in one or more of some inexpensive nutrients. Most commonly these include vitamins B6, B12, B1, B2, betaine, choline or folic acid. And when these deficiencies are located and corrected, alas, not only does the homocysteine level normalize, but so does the cholesterol, triglycerides, and LDL ("bad") cholesterol (ARTERIOSCLEROSIS, 75:1-6, 1989).

But when homocysteine is allowed to go undetected, the result is coagulation abnormalities (strokes, heart attacks, blood clots) and arteriosclerosis (ANN REV NUTR, 12:279-298, 1992). Even the JOURNAL OF THE AMERICAN MEDICAL ASSOCIATION (268:877-881, 1992) calls this a **modifiable risk factor.** In other words, it is something that can kill you and is easily prevented. But it does not sell drugs. And it should come as no surprise that these deficiencies and the increased tendency toward arteriosclerosis both accentuate the risk of neurological and psychiatric disorders (NEW ENGL J MED, June 30, 1988). But if we ignore cause, prescribe a lot of drugs and surgery to fix the problem after symptoms have progressed, this keeps medicine in business and the insurance companies happy, many of which are cloaked spin-offs of chemical/pharmaceutical concerns.

And remember all biological phenomena act like a bell-shaped curve. In other words, too little as well as too much of a substance can cause symptoms. So likewise, depression has been caused by too low a blood pressure (Barrett-Connor E, Palinkas LA, Low blood pressure and depression in older men: A population based study, BRIT MED J, 308:446-449, 1994). Why not buy a blood pressure cuff and check your own weekly, rather than waiting for a yearly exam? Besides you can experiment and learn what changes will lower it.

It should not come as a surprise to you now that people with high cholesterol, as an example of one facet of arteriosclerosis, more often have depression. For you now know that in order to have abnormal cholesterol chemistry, you need to have deficiencies of nutrients that can simultaneously cause depression (Morgan R, Barrett-Connor E, et al, Plasma cholesterol and depressive symptoms in older men, LANCET 341:75-79, 1993).

And by now you also know that you want to do your utmost to avoid taking a drug for any such foolishness. For the metabolism of the drug by your body will create further deficiencies which can cause or deepen existing depression (Duits N, Bos FM, Depressive symptoms and cholesterol lowering drugs, LANCET 341:114, Jan 9, 1993).

There are many other ways of improving cardiovascular and neurovascular disease. These include chelation and oxidative therapies like ozone and peroxide. But they are beyond the scope of this work.

ENVIRONMENTAL CONTROL
UNIT & DETOXIFICATION

For people who have depression from a detoxication system severely damaged by 21st century chemicals, there is sometimes far too much damage for them to heal in this polluted world. For these individuals, there is a special environmentally safer and controlled unit where they can have all of these tests done, and where the body can begin to heal, once part of its daily total load or burden of accumulated chemicals is lessened. Information is available by writing Dr. Wm. J. Rea, 8345 Walnut Hill Lane, Ste 205, Dallas TX, 75231 (ph 214/368-4132).

There is a sauna program, useful for sweating out pesticides and other damaging xenobiotics. For many it is imperative that they depurate or get rid of stored pesticides and other chemicals that are causing their cardiovascular or neurovascular disease. The program also includes special hyperalimentation for people with severe wasting from bowel involvement, as well as many other treatment modalities unavailable anywhere else in the world. They are truly on the cutting edge and adding new techniques constantly.

REFERENCES:

Rea WJ, CHEMICAL SENSITIVITY, VOL I, II, III, IV, 1-800-428-2343

Kilburn K, et al, Neurobehavioral dysfunction in firemen exposed to polychlorinated biphenyls (PCBs): Possible improvement after detoxification, ARCH ENVIRON HEALTH, 1989;44(6):345-350, Nov/Dec 1989

Abuelo JG, Renal failure caused by chemicals, foods, plants, animal venoms, and misuse of drugs, ARCH INTERN MED 150:505- 510, 1990

Rea WJ, Brown OD, Mechanisms of vascular triggering, CLIN ECOL 3(3):122-128, 1985

Rea WJ, Environmentally triggered cardiac disease, ANN ALLERGY, 40:243, 1978

Rea WJ, Suits CW, Cardiovascular disease triggered by foods and chemicals, in FOOD ALLERGY: NEW PERSPECTIVES, TW Gerrard, Ed., Charles C. Thomas, Springfield IL, p 99-143, 1980

593

AD INFINITUM

There will never be an end to the total load, because man is constantly knocking himself out to find new ways to harm the body and the earth. Fortunately, there will probably also never be an end to entities that can heal depression. Some of them are so logical that our grandmothers would recommend them such as **music therapy** for elderly depressed individuals (Hanser SB, Thompson LW, Effects of a music therapy strategy on depressed older adults, J GERONTOL,49:265-269, 1994). And we partly worship God through singing.

As an example, we know that irradiated foods silently being introduced steadily into our diets are lower in nutrients. But did you know that your microwave also destroys nutrients faster? Vitamin E is one that is lowered, which is a shame since it has already been significantly stripped from our grains and oils. Vitamin E has a uniquely protective effect on the brain and its happy hormones and even protects the brain after stroke. So in spite of processing it out of many of our grains and oils, we further reduce it with radiation and microwaving.

Likewise, the new "fat substitutes", like Olestra inhibit the absorption of crucial vitamins like A, D, E, K, and beta carotene. So by eating the processed foods that contain it, you have lowered your nutrient status by ingesting processed versus whole foods. You have inhibited your absorption of nutrients from the gut (that you might have gotten from other food choices) via the Olestra. See the 1996 HEALTH LETTER for references regarding the crooked science behind the tests that led to the FDA passing this chemical as safe for our ingestion. And beware of foods labeled "fat free".

And periodically you will read of breakthroughs in drugs that will help the brain, but you must learn to read through to find the real meaning. For example, a new anti-depressant has been found to suppress auto-immune encephalomyelitis and multiple sclerosis (Sommer N, et al, The antidepressant rolipram suppresses cytokine production and prevents auto-immune encephalomyelitis (NATURE MEDICINE, 244, 1995).

The problems with this is that this type of excitement appears routinely, and within a few months is found to be no good or of minimal significance. For researchers are still not attacking the underlying cause. Hence, the benefit is short-lived. **The cause will never be a drug deficiency.** And why are clinicians not questioning why an anti-depressant drug is working in auto-immune diseases? Clearly, suppression of cytokine production down-regulates the inflammatory response. But in auto-immune diseases, inflammation is a response to something one is reacting to (allergy is a basic causes of inflammation). Wouldn't it be better to find the cause of the inflammation and get rid of it rather than turn off the body's coping mechanism? Diagnose and heal the leaky gut, find the antigenic triggers, and correct nutrient deficiencies to strengthen the body's defenses and healing.

But then if they were that questioning they would have realized years ago that most **anti-psychotic and anti-depressant drugs also have anti-histaminic (anti-allergy) properties.** It has been known that drugs for depression and other brain dysfunctions are pharmacologically such strong anti-histamines that the patient should be taken off them before allergy testing, if possible, as they may lessen his reactivity. So why not look for the **hidden allergic causes of depression** in the first place (Volume I)? As you see, it is a long way off. That is why we've found it necessary to show you how. Clearly **the brain is an allergic target organ** subject to the same rules of total load as any other target organ is.

Then there is the Wall Street wizard, multi-millionaire Jack Dreyfus' book. As a person for whom money was no object, he could not get out of his depression. When he stumbled onto Dilantin, a medication for epilepsy or seizures, it relieved his depression. He wanted the medical world to know about it. So with his own funds, he created a medical foundation to educate physicians. He wrote the story of his suffering, endless exams and medication trials, and ultimate success with Dilantin. Then he sent a free copy to every physician in the country. Now that is laudable, I must say. He even quit Wall Street and devoted 8 years to attempting to awaken the federal government and physicians, again to no avail. So he wrote a next book for the lay person. Still it has made little impact, although the intent was praise-worthy (Dreyfus J, A REMARKABLE MEDICINE HAS BEEN OVERLOOKED, Simun & Schuster and Dreyfus Medical Foundation, NY, 1981)

What he is not aware of is that Dilantin merely "normalizes" some of the brain circuitry; a problem that is solved better by identifying the mineral and other deficiencies that caused that abnormality in the first place. Case in fact: Larry was 7 years old when referred to our clinic with seizures that resisted all anti-seizure medication.   But by identifying the mineral deficiencies that led to abnormal electrical activity in the brain, he no longer needed any medications, for he no longer had any seizures. It was the first time the medical school neurologists had seen an EEG (brain wave) revert to normal, they said. And it is easy to see why. It is the first time they

596

saw a drugless cure and what happens when you fix what is broken.

Obviously, there will be an unending list of new items discovered, as many of us are in constant search for the total load. It is a fascinating field, as every few months there has never failed to be more to enlighten and enthuse us. For over 25 years, I have never ceased to be amazed by the discovery of something new and excitingly useful every few months. For after all, we are the first generation of all this; the infants, if you will, in an historical perspective. Exploring the magic of science has been one of God's gifts to those of us who are amused and excited by the wonders of Nature.

REFERENCES:

Yoshida H, et al, Effects of microwave energy on the relative stability of vitamin E in animal fats, J SCI FOOD AGRIC 1992; 58:531-534

Castano A, et al, Changes in the turnover of monoamines in prefrontal cortex of rats fed on vitamin E-deficient diet. J NEUROCHEM, 58:1889-1895, 1992

Trojan S, Protective effect of vitamin E in stagnant hypoxia of the brain, PHYSIOL RES (Prague) 40:595-597, 1991

Anonymous, FDA panel probes safety of fat substitutes, CHEM & ENGINEER NEWS, 11, Nov. 20, 1995

CHAPTER 11
FIXING WHAT'S BROKEN:

ENVIRONMENTAL OVERLOAD
AND NUTRITIONAL UNDERLOAD

It is quite apparent by now what the causes of depression are. So let's get busy correcting them. But before we do, let's address some other issues. Foremost is that along with cure comes empowerment. For this is the first specialty in medicine that relies on the patient being optimally empowered with the knowledge to get himself well. And for some this is strange, even scary. They never thought of having responsibility for their health, mental or physical. They always thought of it as something beyond their grasp that only a revered doctor could fix. To suddenly realize that only they possess the power to really get themselves well is a little frightening. Then when you throw in all this other information about the world of pollution, malnutrition, and corruption, it can seem overwhelming.

IF I WASN'T DEPRESSED BEFORE,
I SURE AM NOW!
OR
FROM THE DEPTHS OF DESPAIR
TO SWINGING ON A STAR

Having dealt with well over 15,000 people for over a quarter of a century, I can hear in my mind's ear some saying, "Gee, if I wasn't depressed before, I sure am now!" Where do I begin? There are hundreds of possible causes. It's easier to just take a pill!"

598

"Furthermore, the world is in a mess, from our food, water and air, right down to the politics of medicine. Moral decline is rampant. In an attempt to cope with the world, before I knew of all these solutions, I was put on a drug for over $200 a month. Now I learn it could lead to addiction or suicide. And now I know there are hundreds of causes. And if I don't correct them something worse will happen to me. And you want me to rejoice?"

But remember the basis of all humor, problem solving and life itself: **you must be able to see the alternatives**. Would you rather not know the side effects of the drugs you are taking? Would you rather not know that by not fixing what is broken in your system, you will inevitably go on to develop further, yet seemingly unrelated mental and medical problems? Would you rather not know about the multitude of possibilities that may be causing your depression? Most of the causes are not only diagnosable, but many of them are very inexpensive and easily done at home. And most of them are correctable, not only for the moment, but permanently, once you understand how you got in this predicament. Would you rather not have the power to get yourself healthier and happier than you've ever been before?

On the contrary, you should be ecstatic, just knowing there is a light at the end of the tunnel. "But it is all so overwhelming. I don't have the energy. I don't have the time. I don't have the motivation. And I haven't a clue as to how to begin", you moan. So start with something simple. Many will start to feel a high just on fasting. That tells you that you have hidden food allergies or possibly Candida overgrowth. Just do not eat for a few days. Or if you must, live on carrot juice or do a watermelon fast or the sweet vegetable drink (WELLNESS AGAINST ALL ODDS) for 2-6 days. And whether or not you are improving, do not go back to your old eating habits. The odds are in your favor that just with a water fast or carrot juice fast, you will notice some improvement. (In that case you know you had better evaluate your diet, or gut, or both.)

WHAT YOU CAN DO TODAY?

Once you start to feel even a glimmer of hope, you may still be groaning, "You think I was depressed before, you ought to see me now! How do I ever sift through all these possibilities to find the solutions relevant to me?" (Actually that's a good sign, for it shows you see that there is hope, you are getting a little of your humor back, and you are actually entertaining the possibility of healing yourself.)

But the truth is that regardless of what type of medical or mental problem you have, this frustration is a normal part of getting well.   It shows you are thinking about doing something about your symptoms, but don't quite know how or where to start. So when in doubt, we go back to the old 80-20 rule. We know from experience that 80% of the people will improve by doing just 20% of what we have to offer. So let's go for it.

Start a diet with which you can heal:

1. DO NOT EAT ANY sugar, white flour products, alcohol, tea, coffee, soda, chocolate, processed foods, or smoke.

If at first you are not successful, recall that no one was ever put here perfect. It takes time and hard work and dedication to a dream to stop years of bad habits. So something

600

pleasurable must replace them: you need a reward, you need nurturing to not only take up the slack that these deprivations leave, but to make up for all the nurturing you have missed out on.

And if you fail, do not be too rough on yourself. You may have relentless cravings because of yet undiscovered nutrient deficiencies, diabetes, hypothyroidism, chemical sensitivities or a gut full of Candida, as examples. And if you cannot stop cigarettes, as an example, maybe you should not. Many times I've seen someone who is a veteran smoker who presents with asthma. But when I find out she recovered from alcoholism on her own, supports a disabled husband and has a retarded child, I'd be a fool to ask her to relinquish one of her main props until we are much further into wellness. And inevitably, there comes a time when she can get so healthy that she realizes she no longer needs the crutch. For she is **high on health**, high on living. But for now, it may be necessary to continue smoking.

On the flip side, if you cannot get rid of any of these, you had better back up and ask yourself **how you were so severely emotionally damaged** that you do not want to help yourself. Where is the pain? Then start addressing that. There are many terrific resources for this (Siegel, LeShan), and most likely professional counseling is indicated. Or perhaps you need a temporary crutch. There is nothing wrong with a temporary prescription of a anti-depressant to help you keep your job while getting into a healing program.

2. Eat as organic as possible. Most health food stores have organic whole grains, beans, sea vegetables, sunflower and other seeds, almonds and other nuts. The above and below ground vegetables, if not organic, should be purchased as

fresh as possible, usually from the local Saturday morning farmers' market.

3. Do not drink city chlorinated, fluorinated water. Drink only clean non-chlorinated water in glass bottles, or from a reverse osmosis unit, distiller, inexpensive tap filter, or nearby spring or well. Check the source of water, as there can be a problem with all of the above. Better yet, start carrot juicing for high density nutrients as well (WELLNESS AGAINST ALL ODDS has instructions).

4. Read YOU ARE WHAT YOU ATE, MACRO MELLOW, then THE CURE IS IN THE KITCHEN, even if your diet prescription is not macrobiotic or vegetarian, to learn about whole foods. For the food you eat and how you nourish the brain has a major bearing on the brain's function. **I believe that who prepares your food is as important if not more, than who you chose for your doctor.**

5. Try not to eat more than 3 meals a day, especially if you are overweight. If you need a snack, try rice cakes, unsalted organic almonds or more preferably carrot, cucumber and celery sticks. When in doubt, eat a vegetable.

Create a bedroom in which you can heal:

1. Get all cotton bedding, sheets, pillow cases, and mattress pad. If new, wash several times in baking soda to remove the formaldehyde (new smell). Why overwork your detox system all night so that you awake exhausted?

2. Put several layers of old cotton blankets (from attic sales) over the mattress; be sure they are washed in baking soda. If unable to do this, go to a restaurant supply and get a large

roll of heavy duty aluminum foil, and put 6 layers over the mattress (under the sheets and cotton mattress pad), shiny side up. Special hypoallergenic barrier foil called Dennyfoil, is available from E.L. Foust Co., Elmhurst IL, 1-800-225-9549, and further directions in THE E.I. SYNDROME.

3. Get a room air cleaner and put a molecular absorber in the room, but not near the bed, but across the room (to minimize EMF).

4. Remove as much from the bedroom as possible, especially dry cleaned clothes, polished or new shoes, belts, and other leather or plastic items, cosmetics, dust catchers.

5. Open windows in the late evening or early dawn to allow fresh air in, free of traffic pollutants. If the air quality is not good, build a filter (a simple wood frame the size of the opened window with screening on both sides, and fill the middle with purafil (available from the E.L. Foust Co. or from N.E.E.D.S.).

6. Reorganize the room to minimize your head being near electromagnetic fields of wall wiring, and the particle board head board, electric clocks, radios, air conditioners, fans, heaters, air cleaners, and TVs.

7. This is the hardest for most, but often the most therapeutic: get rid of smelly drapes and carpet (most had no idea how much they reeked of formaldehyde and other chemicals until they got rid of them and got clear enough to be able to smell things properly again).

8. Read THE E.I. SYNDROME, REVISED then TIRED OR TOXIC? for further environmental controls and a multitude

of important details (assuming you have already read Volume I). I would suggest the HEALTH LETTER (subscription from the same publisher) as well. As I have said, I am not into selling books, but it is the cheapest way I can think of for sending the intelligent consumer to medical school for an education in 21st century medicine. It is the least expensive way I know of to enable him to claw his way out of the drugs and surgery-oriented machine and start healing the impossible. If you cannot awaken feeling perky, the bedroom environment may be the problem. The work of detoxifying the toluene from the carpet all night can lead to awakening with depression.

9. Send for three mold plates (this publisher) and culture your bedroom, office, and the family room or kitchen (wherever you spend the most time, see Volume I). Directions for exposure and a mailer will be included. Then the results of what types and amounts of molds are present will be mailed back to you. Then you will have an idea about how much mold is in your environments that can contribute to depression, but that also can be easily remedied. Generally you pick the 3 environments where you spend your life - - - work, leisure, and sleep (office, family room or kitchen, and bedroom).

10. Send for the Formaldehyde Spot Test and test items in the bedroom to determine if the formaldehyde level is too high. Then you can proceed to test other areas.

11. You may need a **liver detoxification panel** that will tell whether the liver is overloaded by chemical exposures. It tells you which path is overloaded, phase I or phase II. Then we know which nutrients need correcting. The **lipid peroxides** test shows if your system is over-burdened enough

to be destroying membranes and accelerating aging and disease process. You can perform one at the end of a work week and another after a weekend at home to determine which environment is the culprit. For if you cannot awaken feeling well, you might as well start with the bedroom, as it is the one room environment that is the easiest to alter. It matters little what it looks like, as you will be asleep. But it is a good opportunity to help you discover if a reduced chemical load is what you need in order to start healing.

There are other useful tests to assess if you are chemically overloaded: **urinary D-glucaric acid** and **mercapturic acid** are urinary determinations of phase I and phase II detox overload or depletion as well. For these 4 indispensable tests, the liver detox and lipid peroxides are available from Great Smokies Lab, 1- 800-522-4762 and the second two above from Doctors' Data, 1-708-231-3649. They are essential for proving chemical sensitivity and overload from specific environments.

Start with a body chemistry that can heal:

1. GET A BIOCHEMICAL WORK-UP :
A good start (after a regular history and physical, chest x-ray, EKG, urinalysis, chemical profile, cbc with differential, thyroid study, etc.) would be to do the **magnesium loading test.** Magnesium deficiency is one of the leading and simultaneously unrecognized deficiencies and can be a major cause of depression and fatigue. (Complete directions in TIRED OR TOXIC?)

Then proceed with rbc (red blood cell) levels to assay the following minerals: rbc zinc, rbc copper, rbc chromium, rbc molybdenum, rbc manganese, rbc potassium, rbc calcium, rbc selenium and rbc folate. Be absolutely certain that "rbc" precedes each test name, or you'll get the worthless serum values. Next vitamins B1, B12, B6, A, C, E, and 1,25-OH D3, plus a DHEA unconjugated can be assayed (not the sulfated DHEA). Bear in mind all this is usually not necessary. In many cases we can order just the minerals, for example. But for many people, assay of vitamin levels shows many serious deficiencies. The proof of the pudding comes when they joyfully begin to rally once we write a prescribed regimen to correct the deficiencies. Much more can be assessed but so many do well with only this, that they need not go further.

Even though amino acid deficiencies can trigger depression, they are usually not necessary to obtain. You see, in order to work properly, the amino acids require enzymes. It is the deficiencies of minerals in these enzymes that run the aminos (that then go on to make the happy hormones like serotonin). So once you fix the mineral deficiencies, you often are done. The most common mineral and vitamin deficiencies that compromise amino acid metabolism are magnesium and B6. So play the odds. It's very inexpensive to do a trial for one week of 50 mg B6 and 200 mg magnesium. If you feel worse, stop it. If you feel better, you know you found some of your deficiencies, but here is where caution is needed. After a few weeks or months you may go downhill. That is because it is unlikely you have only 1-2 deficiencies. Since you did not find the others, they eventually rear their ugly heads, screaming to be discovered.

The solution is to get on a balanced prescribed program to correct the deficiencies, check to see what corrected in a few months, and proceed to other assessments if wellness is still elusive. Just whittle through the total load, depending on what seems likely, whether it be amino acids, or burdens of heavy metals, pesticides and other toxicities.

2. Or if cost prohibits, a trial of some commonly helpful nutrients may be useful. To build the body, you and your doctor may decide to start you with the primary anti-oxidants, vitamins A, C, and E at total daily levels of 5,000 to 10,000 for A, 500-8,000 for ascorbic acid or C and 400-800 for E. The vitamin E should be explicitly d-alpha tocopherol (preferably with mixed tocopherols), and **not d,l-alpha** tocopherol or **unspecified**. Unique E is the best form I have found. And I find most get better response from Klaire's (Vital Life) ultra-refined pure ascorbic acid power or ARG's buffered powdered vitamin C than capsules or tablets. The multi-mineral should contain selenium, chromium, zinc, manganese, calcium, magnesium, molybdenum, copper, and vanadium at least. Of course, there are many other nutrients needed. A multiple B vitamin could be added with B6 (pyridoxine), 50-500 mg, because B6 directs so much of the amino acid chemistry and most diets are low in it.

As part of the magnesium loading test you'll be doing a trial of 200-400 mg of magnesium a day, and that is often therapeutic as well as diagnostic.

You may want to evaluate even more complementary nutrients with these, like N-acetyl or L-carnitine (250-500 mg, twice a day), Phos Chol Concentrate (1 tsp a day), L-glutamine (one tsp. twice a day in water, between meals), 100-300 mg lipoic or thioctic acid (2-3 times a day), CoQ10 (30-60 mg 2-3 times a day), HC-MET (one a day), and/or Detoxification Factors (1-2, 2-3 times a day). Recancostat (1-4, 2-3 times a day), helps improve all symptoms by improving detoxification. The powder form is even more potent, as it is a less expensive way to get a much larger dose.) And don't forget to do a trial of an oil change with cold-pressed flax oil (one tsp. per day). Always start with the lowest doses, then

607

slowly build. Do not go to maximum doses until you have consulted your healthcare professional. In the beginning, spread this daily allotment out over 2-3 days at first, rather than trying to spread it out over one day.

A specialized comprehensive detoxification panel will show whether you need correction with such specialized items as calcium-D-glucarate, glycine, glucosamine sulfate, pips anthocyanidins and other bioflavenoids and more.

Or you may want to do a trial of herbs like St. John's wort and/or ginkgo biloba, plus grape pips pycnogenol (100mg, 2-3 capsules 2-3 times a day). There is constant new info.

If at any point something makes you worse, stop immediately and see your guiding physician. Usually an adverse reaction (every down side has an up) is wonderful news. For it gives indispensable clues to your chemistry and to the causes of your depression. For example, if you got severe headache or more depressed stopping coffee, more than likely that is a withdrawal reaction and shows that it is indeed one of the factors contributing to your symptoms. You can learn how to overcome and shorten the withdrawal with special detoxification procedures in WELLNESS AGAINST ALL ODDS.

Or if magnesium made you worse, in spite of the fact that the loading test showed you were deficient, it means that taking the magnesium is lowering something else that was deficient also, like calcium. So it can mean that you need to correct that first before your body will allow a correction of the magnesium.) For never lose sight of the fact that these nutrients all work in harmony. They are not solo drugs.

608

Often people worry right away about their calcium status, but we see people getting depressed by calcium, probably because it can lower magnesium and potentiate a magnesium-deficiency-induced depression. Obviously there are people who also need calcium for depression. Once all your deficiencies are figured out, then a balanced regimen can be prescribed that would take into account your calcium needs. But recall that even a low rbc calcium may not indicate a need for calcium as much as it indicates a damaged calcium pump in the cell membrane. (Phosphatidyl choline, flax oil, choline citrate 650 mg, vitamin E as d-alpha tocopherol with mixed tocopherols, etc., are needed to repair the membrane and it takes months. Also strict avoidance of trans-fatty acids is necessary. Symptom evaluation, nutrient re-assessment, and restructuring of your supplement program is crucial every 3 months until everything is corrected, you feel great, and all has remained stable for a year or two.

Start with a body with which you can heal:

1. Do not use any fragrant soaps, cosmetics, shampoos, after shave, deodorants, fabric softeners. In other words, why use up detox nutrients that could have been used for making happy hormones? A 1996 summer WALL STREET JOURNAL told how Downey fabric softener is sprayed on carpets in computer offices now to reduce static electricity. We never seem to run out of ways to challenge and overload our detox pathways!

2. Do body scrubs daily, or yoga, massage, chiropractic, Tai Chi, or other body work. It opens lymphatics, acupuncture meridians, restores circulation to stagnant areas.

3. Get some exercise in fresh air, even if it is raining or snowing; if you are too sick, do mild stretching, Iyengar yoga or get a loving massage.

4. Get in the sun at least 1/2 hour a day, with no glasses, sun or otherwise, and no lotions.

5. Nurture yourself physically as well as mentally. After you have started correcting the many environmental, biochemical, medical, and psychiatric causes for depression, you want to learn how to nurture yourself. One good way to start is with Iyengar Yoga. It is therapeutic physically as well as giving you time to meditate and relax your mind as well as your body.

Often people have a distorted view of yoga. They think it is some passive form of sitting and contemplating your navel, or that it does not do anything to help tone and strengthen the body. Or they think it is limited to turning yourself into a pretzel and has nothing to do with retarding the physical and emotional aging of the body. But if you explore it, you will find it may be another turning point in your life.

You may also be under the illusion, as I was, that it would take hours a day and only interfere with an already over-crammed schedule. But you can learn to fit your toning stretches and workouts into times that are otherwise wasted, as standing in lines, doing dishes, etc. Others erroneously think that in order to do it they have to become proficient in Sanskrit. Or you may think that the exercises look too simple and could not possibly be something that would benefit a jock.

Often a chronic back problem is the reason someone is depressed. It severely limits their pleasures and the chronic pain is draining. If you have any back problems, as the vast majority of Americans do, a great yoga book to start with would be Schatz MP, BACK CARE BASICS. A DOCTOR'S GENTLE YOGA PROGRAM FOR BACK AND NECK PAIN RELIEF, Rodmell Press, 2550 Shattuck Ave, Ste 18, Berkeley CA 94704, ph 510-841-3123. This book was written by a medical doctor with a chronic bad back who had failed at everything that medicine had to offer, then got relief from this form of yoga, which is simply and perfectly taught. I've seen it help many. That combined with WELLNESS AGAINST ALL ODDS has enabled many with chronic pain, fibromyalgia, sciatica and more, to become pain-free.

Start with a mind that is ready to heal:

1. Get rid of old guilt, anger, jealousy, hate, and fear. Learn how to forgive and love. Give thanks and **gratitude** for as much as you can. It is more difficult to feel unhappy when you feel grateful. And it is easier to give love, which usually comes back, multiplied.

2. **Practice seeing the bright side of everything**. Mentally see through someone else's eyes if you must, but find a view opposite to your negative or depressive view. If you get stuck, ask a more uplifting person how he views the alternatives and sees the good that can come from your predicaments.

3. **Sing happy songs** each day. Learn the tune and words to old standards like "Look for the silver lining", "When you wish upon a star", "Zippity Doo Da", " Oh what a beautiful morning", "It's a grand night for singing", "It's a most

unusual day", "I've got the world on a string", "Almost like being in love", etc., or get tapes or CDs. Smile much.

4. **Get some laughter each day.** Find some humor or delight in every circumstance you can.

5. Get and give some **physical hugging** each day.

6. Do something unexpectedly nice for someone else each day that brings them joy. **Random acts of kindness (RAKs) are a must.** So rack up some RAKs!

7. Read about getting well each day so that you are continually growing. **Keep growing in your knowledge of health.** Periodically review this book for new ideas.

8. Find out what your **passion** is....what fills you with a zest for living and DO IT.

If you don't have a passion at the moment, **make your passion getting well.** Read like crazy and learn all the possible things you can do to get well. Who knows, it may lead to a new career or hobby, or lead you to help someone in need. And invariably when you get more energy, the passion and ideas will flow. Don't expect too much yet from a sick body. Give yourself a break. After all, remember, it's often the unrealistic expectations that fueled depression in the first place.

So **go easy on yourself.** It is much easier to heal any other target organ than the brain. Because no matter how bad your lungs, your back or your gut is, you still have your brain and you still have hope. But when the brain is sick, it multiplies the difficulty, because depression by definition is loss of hope. And it is **hope that fuels and motivates** one toward wellness. **Hope can be found in your spirituality and faith.** But if you have none, then follow the guidelines to start lifting out of depression enough to get in touch with your passion.

9. **Pull back** from overwhelming commitments. Remember, if we died tomorrow, the world wouldn't even miss a beat. Learn to say, "No".

10. **Renew your spirituality** as you have never done before. For example, if it harmonious with your beliefs, read your BIBLE each day, and if it is meaningless, start with THE STUDENT'S BIBLE or some fellowship study groups through your church, temple or synagogue, or read some of the books suggested here.

11. **Spend time with God each day.** Let him hold you in his arms. Learn to pray, learn to listen to Him and hear His messages, and then do it daily. **Meditation is being quiet and listening to God.** Praying is speaking to God. You need both. There is no effective relationship where only one person does all the talking. Meditation is a discipline that forces you to tune out all the mental confusion from the world and focus on what is of the utmost importance. It is a technique to control your random thoughts and focus your energies on receiving one important message. Many books will guide you.

Once you reduce the stress to your system with detoxifying your body, bedroom, home, office, and mind, you are ready to get a work-up for the causes of depression. There is a fortunate group who will need to go no further. Just with the above they are on the road to healing.

GETTING OFF DRUGS

CAUTION. CAUTION. CAUTION. As much as I would like to enable everyone to be medication-free, the fact of the matter is that drugs do many wonderful things that we have not figured out how to do in any other way. We do not have the answer for everyone's chemistry. Some individuals may never be drug-free. And that is O.K.

If you can gain some mental and physical health benefits with the suggestions in here, but still need your drug, **don't knock yourself out trying to get off the drugs. Some progress is better than no progress.** For some people it is not possible, or it is not the right time. Or the stresses in your life are yet too great, or your chemistry, diet or environment are not yet optimal enough to support you without drugs. Or perhaps the answer to your biochemical glitches won't be discovered for 40 more years. Who knows? The goal here is to help you get as well as possible. No one ever wants you to get worse. So exercise great caution, even with the help of your doctor.

It makes no sense if you have been better on a medication to stop it cold and go on this program. Instead, it makes much more sense to continue the medication, find as many triggers as possible, and start to feel what wellness is about. Then discuss with your doctor how you are going to do a trial of slowly weaning from the drugs.

If you are on medications, most likely you have nutrient deficiencies. This is because :

(1) medications only cover up or hide the symptoms which must be at least partially the result of deficiencies. You want to find the causes, if possible, and get rid of them once and

for all. For example, is your high blood pressure due to a magnesium, calcium, or potassium deficiency (for which there are numerous references in the literature)? Or do you have high cholesterol because you are deficient in chromium, manganese, magnesium, etc.?

(2) The second reason for trying to get off as many medications as possible, is that they are a foreign chemical and use up or deplete nutrients in the body's work of metabolizing or detoxifying them. In other words, **drugs invariably worsen existing deficiencies**. These nutrients could have been put to better use in making extra happy hormones in the brain.

Your goal is to replace everything that is damaging, with things that are beneficial so that you may unload the body and allow it to heal. Only when you feel improvement should you consider weaning off drugs. Most medicines do not cure, except antibiotics by killing bugs. Instead, most medications merely mask symptoms. The only thing that heals or cures a body is the body chemistry itself. But you must make the body healthy enough to do so. And the energy to do so comes from food. If you have not made very positive steps in changing to a healthier diet, then I would not recommend even thinking of getting off any medications for depression.

In the course of getting off medications and finding why you needed them in the first place, you will discover deficiencies. You have to. If nothing is found, check to see that the correct RBC levels were done and extend into the total load to find what else is awry in your system to have created your symptoms. In 26 years I have NEVER seen a depressed person whose nutrient levels were all normal (Volume II).

Consult someone who is trained and knowledgeable in the elusive other 80% of factors that can contribute to the particularly difficult causes of depression.

Then remember to wean slowly with the help of your physician. Changes in anti-depressant drug doses should be done slowly, because it may take weeks to get a recurrence of symptoms after you discontinue and actually clear the drug from your system. Also abrupt stopping of a drug can precipitate a worsening of symptoms. You don't need to go through anything like that. Remember, you are working at decreasing the stress in your life, not increasing it.

So if you're on a drug 3 times a day, try reducing it to 2 a day for a month. Then 1 a day for a month, then every other day for a month, then take it every 3rd day for a month. Then off. At any time if you are worse, go back to the previous dose and stay there for 6 months while you work through other parts of the total load.

Start with a gut that is ready to heal:

1. Get on a good diet (see diet section).

2. Get a 7 day Candida culture or have an empirical trial of the yeast program (saves money, especially if you have had many antibiotics and it's fairly likely that Candida (Volumes I and III) is part of your load). THE E.I. SYNDROME, REVISED describes the Candida treatment.

3. Get a CDSA to assess digestion and abnormal organisms (bacteria). If money is an obstacle, a colon cleanse may suggest bacterial or protozoal overload, if you feel happier

616

after unloading the gut (details in WELLNESS AGAINST ALL ODDS).

4. Intestinal permeability test to rule out leaky gut syndrome or malabsorption. Get a blood test for anti-gliaden and anti-gluten antibodies if malabsorption is present (see Volume III for treatments).

5. Purged parasites test if infection is suspected or the gut is a definite target organ.

6. Secretory IgA test if recurrent infection is suspected (is included in CDSA in some labs).

7. Conventional work-up (x-rays, scopes) if bowel a problem and cause not found. Review old records to see how thorough the work-ups were.

8. Food allergy tests or the Rare-food Diagnostic Diet.

9. Remember the gut can be a target organ for chemical sensitivity (like pesticides) or heavy metal toxicity (Volume I and TIRED OR TOXIC? and WELLNESS AGAINST ALL ODDS).

10. Consider hyperalimentation. When a part of the body is sick, we rest it; we don't go dancing if we have a broken leg, we don't sing with a sore throat. But constant gut problems rarely stop us from eating. Sometimes the gut needs to be put to rest while nourishment is taken by vein. Before this is entertained, hypoallergenic nutrient sustaining and reparative substances like Ultra Clear can be the answer.

11.   There is much more; these are merely starters that frequently solve the problem. A brain tumor, for example, can cause recalcitrant nausea and depression. So could a sub-dural hematoma (brain clot) from head trauma months prior. See your doc for a physical.

There are a number of over-the-counter remedies that may give you a head start. In general they are not sufficient for tough cases. But they could help to speed up your healing until you can get the prescriptions you need.

A good all-purpose phase I gut treatment might include an herbal product to eradicate harmful yeasts, protozoa and bacteria. **Paragard** (2 caps 2-3 times a day) contains many time-honored anti-fungals, for example, like wormwood and walnut hull extract. **Permeability factors** (1-2 three times a day, between meals) contain the glutamine needed to begin to heal the gut, plus other nutrients. And **Enterogenic concentrate** contains the probiotics or beneficial flora to recolonize the gut as well as FOS (fructo-oligosaccharides) to encourage intestinal wall healing. There are many fine companies. I merely gave an example of some combination products that I am most familiar with that can simplify the scheme for you. There is not room to make this a comprehensive book on treatment, as its thrust was for diagnosis and concept. Our other books, future books, subscription newsletter and phone consultations explore difficult treatments in detail.

12.   Between the rare-food diagnostic diet (in THE E.I. SYNDROME REVISED), the macrobiotic diet (begins in YOU ARE WHAT YOU ATE and progresses to THE CURE IS IN THE KITCHEN) or the carnivore diet (WELLNESS AGAINST ALL ODDS) you will find your best healing plan.

WHERE DO I GET THE TIME FOR HEALING?

Start with a lifestyle which makes time for healing:

1. Last of all, assess your life and decide what you are going to trade so that you have time to begin some HUMBLE HEALING. For the start of this program involves simple, humble, changes in your diet and lifestyle. Many are lucky and this is as far as they need to go in order to get well. But you must make time for reading and doing your program. It's your choice; it is your life.

Decide right now what you are going to put on the shelf for a while in order to make more time for reading and healing. If you cannot postpone anything, does that mean that you are not worth it? Nothing is more important than your mental health. If it cannot take top priority, perhaps it could take second or third place in priorities. For if you can't, you are not in nearly as deep a predicament now as you will be when your condition snowballs. Remember a stitch in time saves nine. Are you going to wait until your first heart attack? Or maybe you won't be lucky enough to get a warning that you survive.

As you have seen, it does not matter what we call anything. **The label is of no consequence.** It can be depression, chronic fatigue, fibromyalgia, lupus, multiple sclerosis, sarcoidosis, asthma, cancer; the name or label is inconsequential. The bottom line is how much do you have to do to get your body healthy enough to win, healthy enough to heal itself. Healthy enough to experience wellness, against all odds.

Obviously, this will also entail changes in your lifestyle and probably even your friends. You may want to join some local

619

support groups of people who are into nutrition and health or spirituality. Surround yourself with stimulating friends and ideas to help you get well and stay well. The amount of work and dedication you will need will depend upon your genetics, the severity of your disease and your will to live and be healthy. And watch out for people who do not want you to get well. In some relationships, depression with dependency **feeds the needs** of the other person. They may be displeased by your loss of dependence, or threatened by your new independence, as your predictability with control over you vanish. Or intensive looking after you may fulfill a need for them.

So an oversimplified start for the 7 trade-offs would be:

Trade:	**For:**
1. Sugar	Fresh vegetable juices
2. Processed foods	Organic whole foods
3. Coffee, alcohol, sodas	Filtered spring water
4. Chemical overload	Environmental controls air cleaner
5. TV	Spirituality, reading, socializing, sports
6. Medications	Nutrient levels (physician assisted) and
7. Your choice	HUMBLE HEALING

Empower yourself to make time to heal:

In other words, CUT the CRAP out of your life!

C= coffee, cigarettes and chemicals
R= refined sugar & flour products
A= alcohol
P= processed foods as in anything that has passed through a factory and comes in a bag, jar, wrapper or box with a list of chemicals on the label. And once you do all this and start working on the rest of your total load, you should also get to a point where, with the guidance of your doctor, you can shrug any of your prescription drugs.

Instead, eat only whole preferably organic foods, like whole grains, greens, and beans, seeds, and weeds, roots, and fruits.

Start with a work environment in which you can heal:

1. Once you make sure you can feel well at home, you'll need to be sure you don't feel worse at work. If you think the work environment makes you worse, do the **comprehensive liver detox panel** and **lipid peroxides,** and possibly D-glucaric acid and mercapturic acid after 4 days at home. Then repeat them after 4 days at work. It will be real easy to prove then which environment is causing your detox overload.

2. See if other workers are bothered and have adverse health effects, mental or physical at work. Make a study of them. Often others are not as knowledgeable as you and won't comprehend the correlation. But you can have them read this book (start with Volume I).

3. Expose mold plates at work (1-800-846-6687) and see if the problem is easily remedied by increasing air circulation and filtration and with some simple cleaning.

4. Consult an environmental physician (board certified by the American Academy of Environmental Medicine) who can help you identify other problems in the work environment. You will need a list of chemicals used at work, plus what is used for cleaning and pesticiding for starters.

5. **The solution to pollution is dilution.** It is very logical that if a chemical is bothering you, you should increase the flow of good air to dilute the level of the chemical. Sometimes the solution to pollution can be as simple as creating a **reading box** or **computer box** at home or at work for paper materials and computers out-gas many chemicals (formaldehyde, toluene, pthalates, TCE etc.) that can precipitate brain fog or depression.

For a reading box, a sheet of glass is mounted on brick corners. A skirting of cotton allows you to put your hands underneath to write and turn pages. A tiny fan inside the "box" can blow the fumes from printed material out a wind-sock type of sleeve at the back of the box and out a window. Some people are fine if they merely have their desk facing a window and a fan behind them to blow the fumes out the window.

Start to identify your hidden food allergies:

1. Once you have gotten yourself this far, you are on your way to wellness. Using THE E.I. SYNDROME REVISED, do the Rare Food Diagnostic Diet (or the Lazy-Bones Diet) to identify your "downer" foods.

ACTUAL TESTS AND NUTRIENTS

So let's say you are plowing through the other books to do what you can do to get yourself well. A good start would be to read THE E.I. SYNDROME REVISED, then TIRED OR TOXIC?, then WELLNESS AGAINST ALL ODDS for starters, to learn what you can do yourself. For many, it was all they needed.

If you need testing, you may want to have your doctor start by ordering any of the following:

1. Magnesium loading test (directions in TIRED OR TOXIC?)

2. RBC levels for any or all of the following: zinc, copper, manganese, chromium, calcium, potassium, selenium, molybdenum, folate, and iron.

3. Vitamins: B1, B12, B6, A, or 1, 25-OH D3 for starters. The more sensitive functional assays are in TIRED OR TOXIC?

4. Hormones: unconjugated DHEA, a 6 hour glucose tolerance test (interpretation in Volume III).

5. Intestinal permeability test (for leaky gut; can be done at home).

6. CDSA (comprehensive digestive and stool analysis); can also be done at home and assays digestion, secretory immunoglobulin A (s IgA), some detoxification paths, and abnormal bugs that can cause leaky gut.

7. Comprehensive detox panel (to see where and how extensively the many detox pathways are damaged).

Specific nutrients can then artfully be prescribed to repair or heal this.

Obviously, all of these are not needed for everyone. And for the severely affected individual they may not be anywhere near enough. There are many more tests. However this is a great start for many, as it spells out the **most common areas of trouble** quickly. When people come to the office with these test results in hand, for example, it can speed up their work-up by many weeks.

Or if the cost of nutrient tests is prohibitive, here are some average nutrients and their doses. Obviously, **there is not one blanket prescription for everyone.** And none of us could take all the nutrients we would like in a day, which makes selection even trickier. Special sources, doses, and tips are in the nutrient section (Volume II) under the specific nutrients. And there are many fine sources not mentioned for the sake of brevity. I merely give the first that came to mind and this in no way negates others. Some do have special or unique advantages, while others do not, as many companies use the same sources for raw products.

NUTRIENT	MY PREFERRED SOURCE	AVERAGE STARTING DOSE
A	A-Emulsion forte, 12,500 u/drop	1 drop/daily
B-carotene	25,000 u (or carrot juice)	1/daily
C	ascorbic acid powder, 2.2 gm/tsp	1-3 tsp, 1-3 x/d
D	D3 100 IU	1-4/daily

E	Unique E, 400 IU/cap	1-5/daily
Multiple	Multiplex-1 w/o FE	1-4/daily
Magnesium	Magnasorb 100 mg or 18% magnesium chloride solution, 100 mg/tsp	1-4/daily 1-4 tsp/daily
Extra B6, folate, B12	HC-MET	1/daily
Multiple mineral	Mineral complex w/o FE	1-3/daily
Phosphatidyl choline	Phos Chol concentrate	1 tsp/daily
Flax oil	Organic, dated, pure	1 tsp/daily (can use on food, but do not cook)
Glutathione	Recancostat	1-4, 2-3 x daily
Lipoic acid	Thioctic acid 100 mg caps	1-3, 2-3 x daily
L-carnitine	ARG acetyl-L-carnitine 500 mg cap	1 cap 2-3 x daily
CoQ10	Biotics CoQ10 30 mg or Vitaline CoQ10 60 mg or Physiologics CoQ10 30 mg	1-3 x daily
Bioflavonoid	pips pycnogenol 100 mg or acanthocyanidins	1-4,2-3xdaily
Digestive	Similase or Biogest	2-4 with meals

And remember to listen to your body. Some need to spread a day's worth of nutrients over 2 or 3 days. And remember there are only so many carrier proteins, so spread the day's worth out over as many meals as possible. Don't make all those minerals battle for the same carriers all at once. It makes sense that you'll get better absorption by spreading them as far out through the day as possible. In fact, a **"pocket full of pills"** works great. Pop a few throughout the day. And when your body tells you it's time for a few days or weeks off, listen to it. To make organization easier, use the sausage method in WELLNESS AGAINST ALL ODDS.

WHY SOME PEOPLE NEVER GET BETTER

The age old question is always there: why can some never get better? Obviously, no plan will diagnose and treat everyone. We are mere infants in the scheme of things. But after 26 years I have seen some fairly recurrent themes and I'll run them by you in case they may jog a nerve that helps you overcome a hurdle. When I've explored them with others, they have often worked for them.

1. I feel some individuals are really waiting for someone to come along and get them well.
2. I think some have such an abnormal gut that until they heal that, nothing else works optimally.
3. Many are just too chemically and/or food overloaded. They cannot expend the effort needed to do what they need to do to reduce these major parts of the **total load**. Often they are not sick enough to be motivated.
4. Some have a detox chemistry that is severely damaged. They lack phosphatidyl choline, tocopherols, glutathione, anti-oxidants, and serious nutrient corrections. They have grossly abnormal detox panels and multiple symptoms.
5. They lack the committed support of a spouse who is willing to read all the materials and work through the total load with them.

There is more but these are the major ones I have seen make a big turn-around. And like I say, no one has all the answers.

FINDING A DOCTOR

How do you find a doctor who does all of these things? How do you know if he is familiar enough with all these potential causes and more? You can test him during your first interview. Ask him what his intended work-up will entail. If that fails to uncover the cause of your depression, what is his next plan? If you meet with resentment or indignation or a negative attitude for even having asked such a question, you may choose to make this your last visit with him. Move on to a more enlightened approach to the pursuit of health for your brain.

Or you may just luck out and find someone who is untrained in all of this, but is eager to read and learn with you. He may even eventually come to our physicians' courses as he sees how powerful his new knowledge is in healing the impossible. If you have a physician whom you want to entice to learn this, lend him a copy of THE SCIENTIFIC BASIS OF SELECTED ENVIRONMENTAL MEDICINE TECHNIQUES. Then TIRED OR TOXIC?, followed by WELLNESS AGAINST ALL ODDS, then CHEMICAL SENSITIVITY, in that order. Then you could give him a copy of this book.

For those who would like to brain-storm about their symptoms, we have scheduled telephone consultations. You can schedule to speak with me personally, and send your records and lab tests if you like. We can explore the diagnostic and therapeutic alternatives that appear to be most likely to help you. After learning your particular story, we can help you map out what tests would likely be the most

627

beneficial for your doctor to order. And we can assist in the interpretation of them and implementation of a program with him if desired. Do not send any material, however, until you have scheduled a telephone consultation. For materials without a file are discarded.

I have not listed all the things you can do, but these are a good start, and they are the foundation for whatever else it may take to improve your chances of reaching your **maximum mental well-being**. Besides that , if you remember the old 80-20 rule, 80% of the people will be better on the core of 20% of the therapy. The odds are with you that you will not have to explore some of the more esoteric possibilities. A subscription to our bimonthly newsletter, HEALTH LETTER, will keep you abreast of new findings and publications.

SO LET'S GET HIGH ON HEALTH!

All nutrients can be found at your local health food store or N.E.E.D.S. 1-800-634-1380.

CHAPTER 12

THE CURRENT STATE OF MEDICINE

THE POLITICS AND PROFITS OF DEPRESSION

Depression is epidemic. Major depression is estimated to be 9% of the primary care practice with over 50% of the people yet undiagnosed. And that is only for major depression (ANN INTERN MED, 122:913, June 15, 1995). It says nothing of lesser types, which are far more prevalent. If mental illness diagnoses did not have such a stigma associated with them, it would help with some of the undiagnosed being recognized. And if there were known definitive treatments rather than a lifetime of anti-depressant drugs for $100-$200 a month, that might spur physicians to diagnose it more readily, too. In essence, if physicians thought there was something they could do that would actually cure it and that would not incur enormous expense, they might be more likely to properly diagnose depression. Well now you know that all of that is possible. Any doctor can learn how to **manipulate the molecules of emotion.**

PENNY-WISE AND POUND FOOLISH
HOW COST EFFECTIVE IS ENVIRONMENTAL MEDICINE?

As we have seen, tight buildings and processed diets have accounted for many of the symptoms characterized as chemical sensitivity [1], depression, and many other diagnostic labels. And once indoor air problems are diagnosed, there is then the total load to address in order to bring about wellness [2]. But one major part of that total load has far reaching financial, legal, and political ramifications: change in the work environment. Because treating the **sick building syndrome** involves many changes in how we view disease and treatment in medicine, **a whole new generation of physicians must be trained;** trained in patient education, patient responsibility, and diet selection. And they need to be conversant in how manufacturers and food processors make their products, the pharmaceutical control over medicine, the fate of pending legislation attempting to take nutrients off the market, and many other facets, not the least of which is the **employer's modification of the work environment.**

But no part of the total load that leads to chemical sensitivity and its resultant symptoms, brain fog (toxic encephalopathy), fatigue, and depression, stands alone. "Getting" chemical sensitivity involves many factors beyond the work environment. Chief among them are the individual's own genetics and biochemistry, as well as his diet, nutrient status, home environment, and psyche. There is no protection for the employer against the worker who abuses his detoxication system with smoking, alcohol, fast foods, and/or a toxic home environment. Hence, it may appear that an unfair burden is levied upon him to have to change the work environment against such odds.

Unfortunately, there are increasing numbers of people seeking disability for chemical sensitivity. This suggests that until the impact that the work environment has on mental health is fully understood by all involved, we may all end up paying more in the long run. Fortunately, many are able to solve their problems without employer intervention. Some of the more common solutions may spark ideas for those still seeking solutions:

* One chemical engineer had the classic toxic brain symptoms or brain fog (inability to concentrate, unwarranted depression, dizziness, feeling dopey and spacey), and headaches. All of his symptoms were worse at work. He also had arthralgia, post nasal drip and gastric irritability and nausea.

In the course of the work-up, he was found to be deficient in intracellular selenium, magnesium and zinc. Years of antibiotics for periodic sinusitis from untreated allergies resulted in overgrowth of yeast in the esophagus. This in turn propelled him to the gastroenterologist for an H2 blocker. Subsequently, this not only decreased acid secretion which is so necessary for mineral assimilation, but competed for his xenobiotic detoxication cytochrome P-450 pathways. Upon correcting his allergy, nutrient deficiencies, yeast overgrowth and instructing him in a better diet and environmental controls, he has been able to continue at work.

* Others with similar circumstances, have had to go to further extremes in order to remain at work. Some use oxygen at their desks delivered via ceramic mask and stainless steel tubing. Others change offices to ones that have not been recently renovated. Still others remove as many 20th century products such as carpet and drapes, bring air depollution devices from home, and seal themselves off from the office ventilation system that mainly circulated old air.

* An elementary teacher began having episodes of unconsciousness. On seven occasions, she was unable to be revived for 2 hours at a time in the emergency room. Work-up revealed that she had precipitously become hypersensitive to atomized toiletries as well as many other incitants. Her co-workers and students merely asked what they could do to

help her. By their voluntarily abstaining from using scented aerosol toiletries, she has been free of attacks except when inadvertently exposed on 2 occasions. One attack was while in the doctor's office, and once in the grocery. With continued treatment of her total load, and being given a work environment in which she could heal, she no longer reacts in these situations; her chemical tolerance due to enhanced detoxication is improved.

* For children with asthma and learning disability triggered by xenobiotics, entire classrooms have discontinued smelly fabric softeners, hairsprays, perfumes, cosmetics, deodorants. And schools have ceased pesticiding and cleaning and waxing floors with smelly solvents, all in the goal of helping those with xenobiotic overload.

It is interesting that often adults cannot show the same courtesy and common sense. Employers allow smoking, for example, in small offices where the heating/air conditioning system was designed for non-smoking. This is in spite of voluminous papers demonstrating the enhanced dangers of side-stream smoke (recipients do not get the benefit of the filter). And it is in spite of research detailing the smoke-induced increased local irritation of the respiratory tract and increased respiratory illnesses and absenteeism. And in some, side-stream smoke triggers headache, brain fog, and/or depression. It is a testimony to the fact that recalcitrant addiction over-rules all medical evidence when you realize that smoking was not banned on airlines until 1988 or in my hospital until 1990, as examples.

* One accountant set up his own business in his home, after having left a huge corporation on disability. He has a separate room for the papers from clients. This is necessary

because they often reek of cigarette smoke and other fumes, like wood smoke, from clients' homes. Many cottage industries have of necessity sprung up for the chemically sensitive. Computer work is particularly suited to working at home, once you make a reading or computer box for the computer (as described in the previous section).

* One physician removed all the carpet and installed quarry tile floors, air cleaners, vented the copy machine and changed to a clinical laboratory whose reports did not arrive on carbonless copy paper, a major source of headaches for several of the staff.

OFFICE POLLUTION
A REMEDIAL SOURCE OF DISABILITY

Obviously, the manufacturing industry has unique problems in terms of chemical exposure of workers. But a vast majority of chemically sensitive individuals come not from a factory environment, but from the office environment. In fact, a large number of people seek disability from the office environment each year on the basis of chemical sensitivity or intolerance.

Luckily, there are some fairly common recurring themes which lend themselves to common sense. Many can be inexpensively remedied, and many more can be countered prophylactically. For example, pesticiding is a common initiator of chemical sensitivity. But may offices, schools, and institutions spray not when pests are observed, but on a contract basis, regardless of need. Furthermore, there are many non-toxic pesticide alternatives.

For obvious business reasons, renovations are frequently done. But there is still lack of awareness about selecting the best time of year when windows might be opened. Employers need help in selecting less chemically contaminated products, or at least testing them by evaluating small aliquots of the materials proposed for use. A host of sins could be ameliorated with the installation of an exhaust fan (as one would have for a stove) over copy machines and other machines that have been notorious in initiating chemical sensitivity. Since adhesives are a major source of IAQ problems, the avoidance of glued (versus nailed) moldings, mop boards and carpets have prevented many cases of chemical sensitivity [3]. Often productivity reaches its nadir as mood swings peak in offices in the summer. Such mood changes can result merely from the fresh air intake being located on the tarred roof where the outgassing of hydrocarbons is accelerated by the afternoon sun. Or the intake pipe is adjacent to loading docks or incinerators.

And when it comes down to employers making changes, it seems that resistance is penny-wise but pound foolish. Dr. Hal Levin, editor of INDOOR AIR BULLETIN gives us a crash course:

"Typically, energy costs for operating office buildings run around $1 to $2 per sq. ft. per year. Assuming an average employee cost (salary, insurance, and benefits) of $40,000 per year and an average 200 sq. ft. per employee, energy cost is between 0.5 and 1% of employee cost. Reducing ventilation rates to save money can raise contaminant levels; if impaired IAQ (indoor air quality) lowers productivity, it's a false economy. In fact, doubling energy expenditures ($200-400) would be cost-effective if it could provide a mere 1% improvement in productivity (adding $400 value).

Now we'll factor in other operating and capital costs. Total operating cost is about $7 per square foot per year, and the annualized capital cost is in the neighborhood of $10 to $15 per square foot; total building costs are thus in the range of $17-22 per year. Rounding off to $20 a sq. ft., an employee's work-space costs $4,000 per year. A 1% improvement in an employee's productivity would justify a 10% investment in improving work space.

We don't advocate using more energy; you can reduce consumption by improving efficiency. For example, minimizing waste heat from lighting reduces cooling requirements. Also capital investments in energy efficiency pay for themselves very quickly [4].

In any case, far more is spent on employees than on buildings. There appears to be a resistance to factor the building into the equation for wellness. Improvement in employee productivity will easily pay for the small increments in building costs. For example, he calculated the amortized additional cost of installing 200 sq. ft. of polyurethane-backed (rather than SGR-latex-backed) carpet that would not emit 4-PC as equivalent to the salary cost for about one employee's coffee break. Increasing the quality of the ventilation system or spending slightly more to operate or maintain it, can easily be paid for if employees are healthier, absent less and therefore more productive.

Much of office indoor air pollution stems from simple, yet overlooked and easily remedied factors. For example, offices whose heating and air-conditioning systems were designed for an open space have been partitioned with (formaldehyde-emitting) dividers. These "after-thought" divisions significantly compromise fresh air flow. But due to efforts to conserve energy, the fresh air admixture has often been decreased rather than increased. Add to this the Madison Avenue hype for more scented toiletries, the addition of more computers and other machines that perpetually outgas xenobiotics (foreign chemicals), and we have some of the necessary ingredients for initiating chemical sensitivity.

Enough of a problem has been generated from the increasing numbers of people who have developed chemical sensitivity and seek disability. Yet increasingly more evidence points to correctable environmental triggers as the unsuspected causes for many common symptoms [5]. By generating awareness, we are in a unique position to encourage employers to make meaningful and cost effective changes in office environments. At the same time we encourage victims to read [6, 7, 8, 9, 10] so that they might realize that responsibility for chemical sensitivity is shared by employer and employee. For we now have the information with which to instruct people, in order that they may make changes in their environments and diets that will lead to significant improvements in their health.

REFERENCES:

[1]   Rogers SA, Chemical sensitivity, Part I, INTERNAL MEDICINE WORLD REPORT, 7:3, 1,15-17, Feb 1-15, 1992

[2]   Rogers SA, Chemical sensitivity, Part II, INTERNAL MEDICINE WORLD REPORT, 7:6, 8,21-31, Mar 15-31,1992

[3]   Arlien-Soborg P, SOLVENT NEUROTOXICITY, CRC Press, Boca Raton, FL, 1992

[4]   Levin H, ed., INDOOR AIR BULLETIN, 1:7, 1, Dec, 1991. P.O. Box 8446, Santa Cruz, CA 95061-8446

[5] Rogers SA, Chemical sensitivity, Part III, INTERNAL MEDICINE WORLD REPORT, 7:8, 13-16,32-33,40, Apr 15-30, 1992

[6] Rousseau D, Rea WJ, Enwright J, YOUR HOME AND YOUR HEALTH, Hartley & Marks Publ., Vancouver, BC, 1987

[7] Rapp DJ, IS THIS YOUR CHILD ?, Wm Morrow Co., NY, 1991

[8] Rogers SA, The E.I. SYNDROME, REVISED, Prestige Publ., Syracuse, NY, 1986 and 1995

[9] Randolph TG, Moss RW, AN ALTERNATIVE APPROACH TO ALLERGIES, Bantam Books, NY, 1987

[10] Rogers SA, TIRED OR TOXIC ?, Prestige Publ., Syracuse, NY, 1990

WHEN STUMPED,
THINK ENVIRONMENTAL MEDICINE

In various publications, I have presented the environmental medicine approach to a patient. So let's approach an actual office case. This case is simple and uncomplicated, and an example of how every physician can begin to make cost effective changes in how he treats a patient. Any physician can start to incorporate the principles of environmental medicine into his practice, at any time, saving the patient much money and grief.

The patient was a 39 year old female who complained of depression and headaches for two years. The depression had sneaked up on her and was ruining her life. The head pains were throughout her head, and would come and go daily. They were getting progressively more frequent and severe. They could occur anywhere, but were predictably more troublesome at work.

She also experienced frequent unexplained nausea without other associated gastrointestinal symptoms. And she had dizziness, spaciness, chronic fatigue and inability to concentrate or think well at times. All symptoms were present nearly every day, but would wax and wane unpredictably. But the constant headaches were definitely worse at work. Her internist did the standard complete work-up with history, physical, chemical profile, EKG, chest x-ray, CT scan, upper GI, stool for occult blood, tetanus booster, and urinalysis. He then sent her for consultation with the neurologist who ordered an MRI. He could find no cause for her headaches and offered a trial of medications.

She was referred to ENT for her dizziness. But tests revealed a normal vestibular system. She also consulted a gastroenterologist for the nausea which was getting worse. When his work-up of x-rays and scoping yielded no explanation for her symptoms, he diagnosed her in his referral letter as neurotic. He rationalized she was neurotic because she had **"too many complaints in different target organs without any pathology being found in any one of them"**. This is a classic comment revealing glaring ignorance of environmental medicine principles. Nothing frustrates a doctor more than numerous symptoms in many different target organs, none of which even vaguely resemble any disease he ever studied. But this is the **hallmark of chemical, food, and mold sensitivities with nutrient deficiencies.** Meanwhile, there was nothing more that her four specialists could offer, so to save face, they were beginning to doubt her sanity. Thus, she reasoned she should look elsewhere for a cause for her symptoms.

GATHERING CLUES

Clue #1. One of the pertinent clues is to ask the patient how long each of the symptoms has been present, and then to see what other life events were going on 0-3 years before. It turned out that a year prior to the onset off headaches, she purchased new carpets for the living room and bedroom, and started her present job.

Clue #2. Her job was that of parking booth attendant for the new physicians' office building that was recently added on to the hospital.

Clue #3. In review of systems, she had years of nasal congestion, but had become so used to it that she never mentioned it any more. Besides, nowadays her current symptoms were much more bothersome.

Clue #4. Her diet was predominantly juice, coffee, and toast for breakfast, fast foods (fries, burger, soda) for lunch, with a standard meat, potatoes, salad and vegetable dinner.

The laboratory investigation for her consisted of 4 parts:

1. We looked at a few of the most commonly low nutrients. The goal was to identify a few that were low to impress upon her that her diet was part of the cause of her fatigue. Indeed, she had a thiamine deficiency (vitamin B1), pyridoxine deficiency (vitamin B6), and an rbc zinc deficiency. A carbon monoxide level after a day at work was drawn and one after a weekend at home. The one after a day at work was 6 times higher than normal.

2. Inhalant testing by serial dilution titration revealed sensitivities to dust, mites and many airborne molds.

3. Mold plates exposed at home and at work, revealed excessive levels of fungi to which she was sensitive in both environments.

4. When she did the elimination diet, she found eliminating sweets and ferments reduced, but did not eliminate, her headache and nasal congestion.

The treatment consisted of 5 parts:

1. She began receiving weekly injections to her fixed titrated dose of inhalant antigens, and

640

2. a prescription was written to correct the nutrient deficiencies.

3. She was instructed in environmental controls to minimize her dust/mold exposures at home. She also used the formaldehyde spot test at home to help her identify and remove heavily outgassing materials, since chemical sensitivity is a common concomitant problem.

4. She was instructed in a healthier diet.

5. She was given a note along with a copy of her before and after blood tests showing exposure to carbon monoxide. The note suggested to her boss that the carbon monoxide poisoning would be lessened by ventilating the booth with fresh air taken from the rooftop of the building as a first measure.

The result was that in 3 months she described herself as 95% better in all of her symptoms. Each step of the program brought gradual improvement. At a 4 year follow-up, she had the same improvement and had continued to work at the same place. She did know that she was sensitive to other chemicals now, but was able to avoid them easily before they produced symptoms. She was only able to extend the interval between injections to 2 weeks, which suggested her immunologic memory was not optimal, nor was her diet. On questioning she admitted the diet was not as good as she knew it needed to be for her to feel maximally well. In fact, it majored in junk food and soda, and she was smoking. But she was content with her status and did not want to put more energy into a healthier diet and lifestyle at that time.

She did admit she had been a little tired, again, but nothing like she was when she was first diagnosed. So she had, on her own, resumed the prescribed nutrients of 4 years earlier. This quickly brought to mind the following summation: (1) Taking a regimen that was formerly prescribed to correct a specific zinc deficiency could induce a copper deficiency. (2) Her continued chemical sensitivity, even though it was mild, also suggested she was copper deficient. (3) So an rbc copper was drawn and found to be predictably low.

The lessons to be learned from this **typical case** (as typical as they can be when everyone is so unique) are 10-fold:

1. Addressing the **total load is crucial to success.** Indeed she found step-wise improvement as attention was paid to the inhalant allergies, food intolerances, nutrient deficiencies and chemical toxicities.

2. Depression, fatigue, headaches, and nausea are common CNS symptoms of chemical sensitivity, especially carbon monoxide poisoning. And a carbon monoxide level is an easily obtained indicator of poor ventilation [4].

3. Nutrient corrections must be followed up in 3 months. Thereafter, they should be followed at least yearly until the person is on a predictably good diet, and has read about their condition and understands the importance of diet and home environmental controls. Also it is important to remind the patient that the prescribed nutrients were intended to correct a particular imbalance in the chemistry. As a result, an intentionally unbalanced amount of nutrients is prescribed to correct this. However, once this is corrected within a few months, then a balanced maintenance program could be prescribed that

could be taken long-term. This is especially important if the individual has no intention of improving her diet in the near future.

4. There should eventually be sufficient incentive for the patient to change the diet so that nutrients are not needed.

5. The cost of the work-up was far less than the other work-ups she had and the only one to clear the symptoms.

6. Most environmental medicine cases are diagnosed as psychological problems. If you think about it, this is pretty egocentric of medicine, and analogous to saying "We're so smart that if we don't know what you have, then you don't have anything very serious". It was also interesting that all four of these doctors she consulted who were stumped, passed by her booth each morning when they parked their cars in the garage. And they even recognized her as a patient. They saw their patient sitting in this little open booth surrounded by idling cars on 3 sides. In addition, only the booth side wall separated her from the street on the third side. Being sandwiched between the 3 major hospitals, this street had a heavy traffic flow. Yet none ever questioned whether the air she was breathing could have a bearing on her recalcitrant symptoms, even though they were classic for the **"sick building blues"**.

7. Often a patient feels quite well by correcting food, mold and chemical problems as well as nutrient deficiencies. This decreases their motivation for addressing the rest of the total load. For by doing so they could acquire even better health and eventually free themselves from

643

injections and supplements. We make them aware that this is their choice and O.K.

8. She did not have the typical cherry red lips that we associate with carbon monoxide poisoning, nor were her co-workers affected with identical symptoms.

9. A person's smoking history, the integrity of his auto exhaust system and the functioning and exhaust system for the home heating system would be other important sources of the carbon monoxide.

10. Even though an internist just learning about environmental medicine may not be able to do all these things, he certainly could have taken a better environmental history. And he could have ordered the before and after carbon monoxide levels. For CO poisoning symptoms are classically headache, dizziness, fatigue, and inability to concentrate. Or he could have referred her to a specialist in environmental medicine if he chose not to do the work-up himself. As well, he could have looked at some commonly low nutrients after obtaining a dietary history. Furthermore, he could have recommended any number of books to the patient so that she could have figured out some of her problem on her own [5, 6, 7, 8].

Some or partial improvement is always better than no improvement. For that in itself can unload and motivate the patient to go further, even if the physician is unable to.

The moral of the story is when you have exhausted all that current medicine has to offer, think of environmental medicine. When more than 3 specialists have been stumped, you can be pretty sure you need the medicine of the future, environmental medicine.

REFERENCES:

[1] Rogers SA, INTERN MED WORLD REP, Chemical sensitivity, part I, Feb 1-15, 1992

[2] Rogers SA, INTERN MED WORLD REP, Chemical sensitivity, PART II, Mar 15-31, 1992

[3] Rogers SA, INTERN MED WORLD REP, Chemical Sensitivity, Part III, Apr 15-30, 1992

[4] Kindwall EP, Carbon Monoxide, in Zenz C, OCCUPATIONAL MEDICINE, 2nd Ed, 503-508, Year Book Medical Publ., 1988

[5] Randolf TJ, Moss RW, AN ALTERNATIVE APPROACH TO ALLERGIES, Bantam Books, NY, 1987

[6] Rogers SA, TIRED OR TOXIC?, Prestige Publishing, Box 3161, Syracuse, NY 13220, 1990

[7] Rogers SA, THE E.I. SYNDROME REVISED, ibid, 1995

[8] Rogers SA, CHEMICAL SENSITIVITY, Keats Publ, New Canaan Ct, 1995

MEDICINE:
THE ONLY PROFESSION WHERE
YOU ARE PAID REGARDLESS OF FAILURE

W.S. was a 48 year old landscape architect who four years prior started to lose his vision. Four ophthalmologists and 3 years later, no cause could be found for swelling of his retina. His vision had deteriorated to the point where he was no longer able to even drive his car.

Because of a concomitant atopic dermatitis of his legs, periodic abdominal gas, bloating and diarrhea, headaches, chronic nasal congestion, worse in spring and fall, inability to concentrate, and depression, he also consulted an internist, dermatologist, allergist, gastroenterologist, infectious disease consultant, and neurologist. He was either intolerant of the recommended drugs or they were ineffective. The allergist told him he was not allergic.

An environmental medicine work-up revealed he had extensively renovated his home 1 year prior to the onset of his ophthalmologic symptoms. Further work-up revealed sensitivity to a variety of inhalant antigens (pollens, dusts, and molds), chemicals (phenol, toluene, trichloroethylene), foods, and deficiencies in intracellular magnesium, chromium, copper, zinc, and selenium.

Correction of these plus the usual program of environmental controls and the healing phase diet restored his vision to normal. All the other symptoms improved or left. However, he must be careful to maintain his program. If he so much as opens a scented bill, he cannot see for three days. If he has a pizza, he cannot see for three weeks. Out of doors or in a clean environment, his vision is good. Unfortunately, his employer recently renovated his office, so he no longer tolerates that job environment.

******

A.R. was a 53 year old with 11 years of headaches, depression, and fatigue, plus multiple other symptoms. Work-ups included family doctor, internist, neurologist, allergist, and ENT (ear, nose, and throat specialist). She was eventually told she must be neurotic since no cause could be found, and that she would just have to learn to live with her symptoms.

Environmental medicine work-up revealed that she had worked in the same plastics factory for 15 years. Blood level of **trichloroethylene** (TCE) after a day at work was 26.1. After 2 weeks out of work, it was 18. Normal is none. Testing to inhalants revealed multiple sensitivities. Environmental controls, injections, and healing phase diet were begun. After 8 months out of work she was 50% better by her estimate, but she still had her headaches. They were definitely worse if she entered the factory, and increased in severity with duration of exposure there.

The chemical used in plastics that was so high in her blood was TCE. She clearly had trouble detoxifying it. TCE is metabolized first in phase I of xenobiotic detoxication by the enzyme, alcohol dehydrogenase. Since zinc is the mineral important in the enzyme's function, an rbc (red blood cell) zinc was drawn and found to be low. Upon correction of the deficiency with $8 worth of zinc, 11 years of headaches were gone within one month. The reason is easy; she was now able to efficiently metabolize backlogged xenobiotics (chemicals), and indeed her blood level of TCE precipitously dropped. Her depression vanished.

Basically, that's what environmental medicine is all about. We look for any foods, chemicals or molds that are triggering symptoms. We implement environmental controls to reduce overload to the system and initiate a healing phase diet to promote repair. Then we give special titrated injections when needed and identify any nutrient deficiencies that are hampering normal detoxication. The formula is logical.

Environmentally-triggered illness can present as any symptom, any disease. We are merely looking for a cause. This is in marked contrast to the current medical system where a diagnostic label is the ticket to drugs and surgery, which stifle or mask symptoms.

But environmental medicine is **not** toxicology as the American Academy of Family Practice promotes. It is **not** limited to occupational exposures as the new addition to the American College of Occupational and Environmental Medicine's name might have us believe. And it is **not** solely an immunological disease as the American Academy of Allergy suggests. And it is **not** new, even though the above organizations are just beginning to offer courses in it.

It has been around since first described in 1951, but is only now being recognized. Let's not take another 40 years to argue about what it is. It has already been defined and practiced for over 4 decades. Instead, let's get on with learning the techniques (for those interested in incorporating it into their practices) and helping those with "undiagnosable" and "incurable" conditions. It is well-known even in general medicine that at least 2/3 of patients presenting to the emergency room have medical causes for their psychiatric symptoms. This is great news. It means that some physicians have found that there are medical causes behind mental illness. Who knows how long it will be before it is imperative for the practice of conscientious medicine to look for a cause.

REFERENCES:

Rodnick JE, 'Environmental medicine' series, AMER FAM PHYS 46:4, 1059, Oct 1992

Rogers SA, Is it senility or chemical sensitivity? INTERNAL MEDICINE WORLD REPORT, July 1992

Henneman PL, et al, Organic etiology found in most alert adults presenting to ED with new psychiatric symptoms, ANN EMERG MED 24:672-676, 1994.

THE COST-EFFECTIVENESS OF THE
CAUSAL APPROACH TO DISEASE

We've cited the paper (LANCET) where the **post-operative hospital stay was chopped in half** from 44 to 22 days in hip fracture patients (median patient age was 82) by the mere use of a multi-vitamin-mineral preparation. We've cited Lamm's paper (J UROL, Jan 1994) where the **cancer recurrence rate was chopped in half** with the mere use of again a few simple vitamins.

We've cited papers (Carter, JACN 12:3;205, 1993) where they have **more than tripled the survival from end-stage cancers** for which nothing more could be done with the macrobiotic diet. Levin has shown the cost effectiveness of environmental control measures for treatment of sick building syndrome symptoms. And we have presented hundreds of references documenting the many correctable causes of depression. There is no question of the long range health, quality of life, social, work, economic and other benefits from the causal approach to depression. This should be sufficient evidence to outlaw the mere masking of symptoms with drugs that have a host of adverse effects, including addiction and death, not to mention the inevitable worsening and development of new symptoms.

In one study of 18 patients hospitalized for depression, the 10 patients who were treated with folic acid had marked savings. Folic acid was added to their treatments. As a result, a nutrient that costs pennies cut the hospital stay by 1/3. The folate-treated group spent 23.3 days in the hospital, while the control group averaged 32.9 days.

Carney MWP, Psychiatric aspects of folate deficiency, in Botez MI, Reynolds EH, Eds., FOLIC ACID IN NEUROLOGY, PSYCHIATRY, AND INTERNAL MEDICINE, Raven Press, NY 1979

This and scores of other studies on folate (Volume I) suggest we cannot rely on a macrocytosis and should check folate in everyone. Yet this simple blood test is not routine before sentencing anyone to a lifetime of Prozac which is over $2 a day, and could lead to suicide or addiction (Abou-Saleh MT, Coppen A, The biology of folate in depression: Implications for a nutritional hypothesis of the psychoses, PSYCHIATRI RES 20(2):91-101,1986).

As well, studies have shown that psychoactive drugs are responsible for more motor vehicle accidents than in people who are not taking them. Of course, the elderly are even more at risk because they have had a lifetime to accumulate nutrient deficiencies. Furthermore, they often have many other drugs vying for the same nutrients that could keep them alert.

Ray WA, Psycho active drugs and the list of injurious motor vehicle crashes in elderly drivers, AMER J EPIDEMIOL, 1992; 136 (7):873-883.

THIS IS BIGGER THAN DEPRESSION: IT ENCOMPASSES ALL OF MEDICINE

You can take any disease and build a case for an environmental medicine work-up. We've presented the evidence for the fact that a magnesium deficiency is very prevalent, usually goes undiagnosed, and may be a cause of sudden cardiac death. But do you know how many sudden cardiac deaths there are a year? 400,000! This is one at least every 2 minutes. And yet how many patients that trudge through the cardiologists' offices get a magnesium loading test? I've never met one yet.

The examples are endless as you look at the warnings now about increased risk of death while on calcium channel blockers, or other arrhythmia drugs (Wehrmacher WH, Cardiologists respond to "Deadly Medicine": Issue joint statement, INTERN MED WORLD REP, 10:10, 26, May 15-31, 1995).

We're talking repeated travesties! For example, the Cardiac Arrhythmia Suppression Trial was halted in 1989 because more patients died on the drugs than on nothing. Of course they would. For the most irresponsible and dangerous thing you can do for a cardiac arrhythmia is to mask the symptoms with a drug in place of finding a biochemical cause of the electrical glitch. Furthermore, the detoxification of the drug further lowers remaining nutrients faster. And now you know more than all those cardiologists, because you know why. They not only failed to find the nutrient deficiencies and environmental triggers to the disease, but they gave chemical drugs that further used up or depleted the already dwindling nutrient reserve. (Moore TJ, DEADLY MEDICINE: WHY TENS OF THOUSANDS OF HEART

PATIENTS DIED AFTER AMERICA'S WORST DRUG DISASTER, Simon & Schuster NY, 1995) In fact, the death toll from this drug experiment was larger than American combat losses in Korea AND Vietnam! Over 55,000 people died from this arrhythmia drug that was prescribed by their cardiologists. Yet, the practice of cardiology continues to rely on drugs and surgery.

Or remember the NEW ENGLAND JOURNAL OF MEDICINE paper that showed that a lousy 100 I.U. of vitamin E tested in 85,000 people cut the cardiovascular disease rate in half? (Stampfer MJ, et al, N ENG J MED, 328:1444-1449, 1993; Rimm EB, et al, ibid 1450-1456). Well it has been calculated that if this were recommended for primary prevention, the cost effectiveness would amount to **$33,500 per year saved per person and only cost them $56.07 per year for the vitamin.** (Prescott LM, Vitamin E worthwhile for secondary prevention in CHD, INTERN MED WORLD REP, 10:9;11-12, May 1-14, 1995).

But the conclusion was that physicians had better not tell people to take vitamin E yet. This is in spite of literally thousands of papers on its benefits and safety. Yet the FDA continually O.K.'s foods like Olestra that intentionally inhibit the absorption of E, O.K.'s microwaves and irradiation of foods that destroy vitamin E, and ignores the food manufacturers stripping vitamin E from oils and grains. And heart attacks continue to increase.

Just look at how many prescription drugs have gone non-prescription. Naprosyn, Tagamet, Motrin, Pepcid, Rogaine, and now even the nicotine patch. It was prescription for 12 years. But surveys showed people refused to go to the doctor to get it, so they just made it non-prescription. It still has the same dangers and side effects.   But suddenly and miraculously it no longer requires physician supervision. (Prescription rule removed for Smith Kline's Nicorette, WALL STREET JOURNAL. B10, Feb 12, 1996).

And **Rogaine** for hair regrowth only works in 30% of the cases, costs over $30/month, and must be continued for its effect. The unbelievable part is that this formerly prescription drug has a side effect of **papillary muscle necrosis.** Translation: the cords that hold down the heart valves (so they don't flop in the breeze, turn inside out and cause sudden death) actually rot and drop off!

And now you are almost becoming clairvoyant as you read of other medical mistakes because medicine is the puppet of the drug industry. For example, several studies revealed that the patients treated with **calcium channel blockers** for their hypertension had an increased risk by 60% of heart attack. Well you don't have to be Einstein to figure out why, or to predict it. For the need for calcium channel blockers means the lipid membrane is defective from too many trans fatty acids, insufficient eicosapentaenoic acid, vitamin E, phosphatidyl choline, and most probably an undiagnosed magnesium deficiency, bare minimum.

And if you don't treat it, the patient will go on to have a heart attack. And that's what some patients did! And if you want to kill the patient faster, add to the calcium channel blocker, a diuretic. And of course, that was done, since the study had to follow the national guidelines for treatment of hypertension. You recall, however that a **diuretic accelerates the loss of magnesium and potassium.** So of course, the sick get sicker, quicker. How dumb can we get? It seems there is no end. For medicine continually ignores biochemistry in favor of blindly prescribing drugs.   (Psaty, et al, ARCH INTERN MED, 153:154, 1993;De Koven D, Calcium-channel blockers indictment in lay press dispelled by cardiology community, INTERN MED WORLD REP 10:9;17, May 1-14, 1993).

They just don't read. We've cited the literature, and a lot of it goes back 1-2 decades, so it is not new.   There is lots more, but I don't want to make this a book on cardiology.   Yet studies keep appearing that suggest they think they have stumbled onto something new when they reprove some of this old knowledge. For example, they just reported on 194 hospitalized patients with a heart attack. And guess what!!! The ones who were lucky enough to be in the group that got an **I.V. of magnesium had a walloping 74% lower death rate**. Now if they had only had their magnesium checked a few years ago when they first got tired, or got muscle spasm or hypertension, or angina, or depressed, they may not have even had the heart attack. And the research supporting this simple, inexpensive test has been around for over a decade.

But is it criminal that they denied one group magnesium in order to do the study. What if you were in the group that did not get the shot of magnesium when you entered the hospital with a heart attack? Folks this study is after a decade of studies to show that magnesium more than doubles your chance of survival (Schecter M, et al, Magnesium therapy in acute myocardial infarction for thrombolytic therapy, AM J CARDIOL 1995; 75:321-323). And if you run across a doc who says the studies were not that conclusive, remind him that a shot of magnesium is not a cure-all and the sole cause and treatment of a heart attack. It is one of many causes.   It took an accumulation of the total load to produce such a massive revolt of the body. So when something so simple, relatively harmless, and very inexpensive as a shot of magnesium has such a dramatic benefit for so many (like more than doubling survival), it seems that it should be tattooed on the forearms of every cardiologist and emergency room physician.

Another study showed that 40% of **migraine** patients had a magnesium deficiency. Yet most are led to suffer and then be given the current expensive new migraine injection to "save the day". (Kunkel RS, Magnesium for migraine?, CONSULTANT, June 1994;827) Or look at another study of migraine patients who were given cheap vitamin B2, riboflavin. It produced 68% improvement in headaches, and it cost next to nothing and had no side effects. (Schoenen J, et al, High dose riboflavin as a prophylactic treatment of migraine: Results of an open pilot study, CEPHALGIA, 1994;14:328-329). There is no end to the evidence for the cost effectiveness of doing medicine correctly in the first place.

And some might argue that it costs less to ignore cause and use drugs. But on the contrary. Why even educational suggestions save money as well as lives. Take the study that showed that you cut the cancer mortality by 40% and overall mortality from other diseases by 20% just by excluding meat from your diet. (Thorogood M, et al, Risk of death from cancer and ischemic heart disease in meat and non-meat eaters, BRIT MED J, June 25, 1994;308:1667-171). And this could be intelligently modified for the carnivores who might be properly scared off by this proposition (directions in WELLNESS AGAINST ALL ODDS).

Or recall the benefits of **glutamine** for depression? Well they studied its use with bone marrow recipients to improve healing. It significantly cut the hospital stay, saving each patient over $10,000, each. This is a considerable amount, especially when multiplied times the number of people that will have a transplant each year. Yet how many physicians have ever even heard of it, much less its use in depression, promoting healing after a bone marrow transplant for cancer, etc.? (MacBurney M, et al, A cost-evaluation of glutamine-supplemented parenteral nutrition in adult bone marrow transplant patients, J AMER DIET ASSOC, Nov 1998;94(11):1263-1266). Also see Volumes II and III.

When general medicine can ignore the welfare of the patient this badly, guess what kind of treatment the depressed or mental patient gets. Worse! Hell, he's even prescribed electrocution of the brain in 1995, as you will learn. Folks, we could write volumes on this, but you get the picture. **It is criminal to carry on in medicine as though every disease were a drug deficiency.** The era of molecular medicine arrived years ago. With all the data presented here and the over 1700 deaths on Prozac alone, how much more data, and how many more lives will it take before we do conscientious, intelligent, cause oriented medicine?

CURRENT CHOLESTEROL TREATMENT CAN KILL YOU

You have just learned some very important facts that I would like to collate for you in a different way so that you can now see how the **current practice guidelines** (the only accepted way of treating) for high cholesterol is the worst thing that could happen. For it **could kill you**.

High cholesterol can accentuate arteriosclerosis and depression through a variety of mechanisms.

For starters, high cholesterol can come from a magnesium deficiency. This can only properly be diagnosed by a magnesium loading test, but is rarely done. It can also come from calcium, potassium, chromium, or copper deficiencies. In fact, elevated cholesterol can stem from any number and combinations of deficiencies that impair the ability of the body to properly metabolize cholesterol.

High cholesterol can also come from disruption of some of the cholesterol pathways by exposure to various everyday hydrocarbons like toluene (from paint or carpets), or pesticides like dioxin, or heavy metals like cadmium. Furthermore, diet plays a role in some cases. So foods, chemicals and nutrient deficiencies play a role, and so do fungi (Constantini).

But the accepted treatment consists of prescribing margarines, plastic eggs, and other processed foods that have (trans-fatty acids) hydrogenated oils that worsen arteriosclerosis more than cholesterol does. In addition, medications prescribed to lower cholesterol have caused suicide and accident rates to go up, as they should. For the body cannot live without cholesterol. For one, without sufficient cholesterol, you cannot make the happy hormones, much less sex hormones, stress hormones, and much more that is necessary for the proper function of the body.

Even such simple measures as cabbage or sauerkraut each day can have an effect on improving cholesterol metabolism. And eggs have been found safe, and in fact beneficial as they provide phosphatidyl choline and other nutrients crucial in not only cholesterol metabolism, but in brain metabolism and in synthesizing the happy hormones. And nutrients like vitamin C have not only a strong role in cholesterol metabolism, but are important in keeping the chemistry of the brain normal.

The body is all connected. It is an interactive whole. You can't shut down cholesterol absorption without creating serious biochemical repercussions. And depression with resultant suicide has already been proven. Drugs work by effectively isolating biochemical events in the body. They usually annihilate one pathway. That is basically how a drug stops you from sensing a particular symptom. The point of this is that regardless of your disease, find the total load of triggers. For if you merely cover symptoms with a drug, eventually other diseases, including depression, will inevitably occur.

In one study, they found that major predictors of recovery or survival after expensive heart surgery were sleep, low anxiety and social support. But remember, that it is always a 2-way street. For example, magnesium deficiency can cause insomnia, anxiety, and heart attack. So probably the reason the ones who were less anxious and able to sleep survived was because of their nutrient status. For the nutrient status directly relates to the symptoms that promote recovery plus the cause of the heart attack in the first place.

You can begin to see how ridiculous much of the research is when viewed through the eyes that all "cures" must come from only drugs that either axe or poison a pathway, or from surgery which removes the organ. You might think that only chemotherapy poisons the body. But remember the basic **action of most drugs is to poison specific pathways.** If you have angina, hypertension or arrhythmia's, then calcium channel blockers or beta blockers or ACE inhibitors are used. **When you don't look for cause, you can only poison a**

pathway to relieve symptoms. Even a drug as simple as aspirin is a blocker. It blocks the cyclo-oxygenase pathway in the prostaglandin scheme.

In terms of drug withdrawal symptoms, it has been proven that one of the determinants of nervous system recovery is if there are sufficient nutrients on board with which to heal. In the face of undiagnosed nutrient deficiencies, drugs often go on to cause the side effect of tardive dyskinesia as well as overt withdrawal symptoms once weaning is attempted. And you learned of the many nutrients that have cured tardive dyskinesia.

And cholesterol is one of the factors necessary for the recovering brain, as there must be sufficient cholesterol to restore the damaged brain chemistry. For **cholesterol is also an anti-oxidant,** and one of its functions is to sacrifice itself in the face of free radicals triggered by a damaging chemical that is forced upon the brain, like a drug for depression.

We cannot live without cholesterol. It functions in the arteries to patch up holes made by free radicals. And so it is actually performing a service. But because it is associated with disease, it is viewed as the cause. Actually it only becomes damaging when it is oxidized. When we eat plastic foods (processed foods like artificial eggs, corn oil margarines, and other cardiologist-recommended foods that are known to potentiate illness), these generate free radicals or wild electrons that damage tissues and accelerate disease and aging. It's the free radicals that eat holes in cell membranes and blood vessels. Cholesterol merely provides the patch.

When free radicals from bad foods and chemicals eat holes in cell membranes, they cause lipid peroxidation (which we can measure) and damage the calcium pumps that sit in the membrane. Hence, the most heavily prescribed cardiology drug is, you guessed it, a calcium channel blocker. When the holes are in the blood vessel, the body calls for mobilization of cholesterol to patch it up. But we prescribe cholesterol inhibitors!

In the January 3, 1996 JOURNAL OF THE AMERICAN MEDICAL ASSOCIATION, Newman and Hulley reported how taking cholesterol-lowering drugs raises your risk of cancer. Of course it should. You are (1) not fixing what was broken in the cholesterol metabolism, (2) you are depleting nutrients further in the work of detoxing the drug, and (3) you are inhibiting the absorption of cholesterol needed for many cancer-protective mechanisms. It does not take a rocket scientist to appreciate this.

Cholesterol is merely the innocent patch sent in to remedy the problem so we don't bleed to death. But we're shooting the messenger! And studies show that eating eggs is safe, as long as you have adequate nutrient levels. (Schnohr P, et al, Egg consumption and high-density-lipoprotein cholesterol, J INT MED 235(3):249-251, 1994). There are many other more important culprits, like homocysteine, that have a direct bearing on arteriosclerosis. And homocysteine only forms when you do not have sufficient vitamins B12, B6, folate, betaine, etc.

So it should come as no surprise, although it went practically unnoticed, that in huge studies of arteriosclerosis, over 40 % of the population was deficient in B12 (Lindenbaum J, et al, Prevalence of cobalamin deficiency in the Framingham

661

elderly population, AMER J CLIN NUTR, 60(1):2-11, 1994). And you just learned that a B12 deficiency promotes arteriosclerosis. But instead, researchers focus on cholesterol-lowering drugs rather than fixing what is broken. By addressing the nutrient deficiencies, cholesterol metabolism could be normalized. Then the suicides and depressions that resulted from cholesterol-lowering drugs could have been avoided.

And even though it is known that **trans fatty acids** also **potentiate arteriosclerosis**, they are blatantly recommended by the AMA, hospital nutritionists, and cardiologists. In addition they even potentiate EFA (essential fatty acids) deficiencies which is another cause of arteriosclerosis. And they raise cholesterol, LDL's, and promote depression. Yet cardiologists and hospital nutritionists continue to recommend processed foods containing hydrogenated soy and other vegetable oils, corn oil, and other polyunsaturated hydrogenated grocery store oils, margarines, and egg replacers. All of these are loaded with trans fatty acids.

The FDA even lets food manufacturers put the misleading picture of a heart on your margarine. Yet they make it a criminal offense for vitamin manufacturers to give you scientific references pertaining to the ingredients in their non-prescription products. Does that sound like freedom of the press, speech and a few other things have been selectively lost along the way?

Fish oil is protective to the coronaries, so what do they do? Farm the fish and screw up its chemistry. For real fish eat other fish and sea vegetables, all high in omega-3 oils. But farmed fish are fed omega-6 oils from soybean products that are purchased at the local feed store (and are actually leftovers of the food processing industry). Hence, the chemistry of farmed fish is high in omega-6 oils. You might as well have a steak and enjoy it!

The cost effectiveness of this causal approach to medicine is astronomical, not only in terms of money saved, but in lives. The cost of many of these measures if negligible, compared with a life-time of $120/month of a cholesterol-lowering drug which simultaneously hurries the time during which a heart attack, or other illness, not to exclude depression will occur. Then these, too, are merely masked with drugs. And no one is the wiser that they had the potential to live a healthier and happier life, drug-free, and longer! And if suicide results, as has already been documented, the chance has been permanently missed.

REFERENCES:

Oliver MF, Reducing cholesterol does not reduce mortality, J AM COLL CARD, 12;3:, 814-817, 1988

Takahashi S, Tanabe K, Increased plasma free fatty acid and triglyceride levels, after single administration of toluene in rabbits, J TOX ENVIRON HEALTH, 1:87-95, 1988

Brewster D, Bombick D, Matsumara F, Rabbit serum hypertriglyceridemia after administration of 2,3,7,8- tetracholorodibenzo-p-Dioxin (TCDD), J TOX ENVIRON HEALTH, 25:495-507, 1986

Newman TB, Hulley SB, Carcinogenicity of lipid-lowering drugs, J AMER MED ASSOC, 275 (1): 55-60, 1996

Rath M, Pauling L, Hypothesis: Lipoprotein(a) is a surrogate for ascorbate, PROC NATL ACAD SCI USA, 87:6204-6207, Aug 1990

Muldoon MF, Herbert TB, Patterson SM, Kameneva M, Raible R, Manuck SB, Effects of acute psychological stress on serum lipid levels, hemoconcentration, and blood viscosity, ARCH INT MED, 155:615-620, 1995

LeBlanc GA, et al, Effect of the plant compound indole-3-carbinol on hepatic cholesterol homeostasis, FD CHEM TOXIC 32;7:633-639, 1994

DeGroen PC, et al, Central nervous system toxicity after liver transplantation: the role of cyclosporine and cholesterol, N ENG J MED, 317(14):861-866, 1987

Roo C, et al, Obligatory role of cholesterol and apolipoprotein in the formation of large cholesterol-enriched and receptor-active HDL, J BIO CHEM, 260(22):11934-11943, 1985

Morgan R, et al, Plasma cholesterol and depressive symptoms in older men, LANCET 341:75-79, 1993

Duits N, Bos FM, Depressive symptoms and cholesterol lowering drugs, LANCET, 341:114, 1993

Ascherio a, et al, Trans-fatty acids intake and risk of myocardial infarction, CIRCULATION,98(1):94-101, Jan 1994

Oliver MF, Opie LH, Myocardial ischemia and arrhythmias, LANCET,343:155-158, Jan 1994

Judd JT, et al, Dietary trans fatty acids: Effects on plasma lipids and lipoproteins of healthy men and women, AMER J CLIN NUTRIT, 59:861-868, 1994

Wahle KWJ, James WPT, Isomeric fatty acids and human health, EUR J CLIN NUTR 47:828-839,1993

Litin L, Sacks F, Trans-fatty-acid content of common foods, NEW ENGL J MED, 329:1969-1970, 1993

Enig MG, Atal S, Kenney M, et al, Isomeric trans fatty acids in the U.S.diet. J AMER COLL NUTR 9:471-486, 1990

Jonnalagadda SS, Mustad VA, Champagne C, Kris-Etherton PM, Margarine and plasma cholesterol--a perspective for dietitians on trans fatty acids in the diet, PERSPECT APPL NUTR 2:3, 9-16, 1995

Schnohr P, et al, Egg consumption and high-density-lipoprotein cholesterol, J INTERN MED, 235:249-251, 1994

Mertz W, Chromium in human nutrition: A review, J NUTRIT, 123:626-633, 1993

Jacques PF, Ascorbic acid and plasma lipids, EPIDEM, 5(1):19-26, Jan 1994

Constantini has a bibliography and explanation of the role of fungi in causing arteriosclerosis. Presented at Man and His Environment in Health and Disease, Dallas, Feb 1994 (Dr. William Rea, Director, 8345 Walnut Hill Ln, Ste 205, Dallas TX 75231). Also available on cassette tape from Insta-Tape, Monrovia CA., 1-800-NOW-TAPE.

Heron DS, Alleviation of drug withdrawal symptoms by treatment with a potent mixture of natural lipids, EUROP J PHARMACOL 83(1982)253-261

Mesnink RP, Effect of dietary trans fatty acids on high-density and low density lipoprotein cholesterol levels in healthy subjects, N ENG J MED 323;7:439-445, 1990

Hill EG, et al, Intensification of essential fatty acid deficiency in the rat by dietary trans fatty acids, J NUTR 109:1759-1766, 1979

Editorial, Trans-fatty acids and serum cholesterol levels, NUTR REV, 49;2:57-59, Feb 1991

Kromhout D, et al, The inverse relation between fish consumption and 20-year mortality from coronary heart disease, N ENG J MED, 312:1205-1209, 1985

Ballard-Barbash R, et al, Marine fish oils: Role in prevention of coronary artery disease, MAYO CLIN PROC 62:113-118, 1987

Mc Cully KS, Vascular pathology of homocysteinemia: Implications for the pathogenesis of arteriosclerosis, AMER J PATHOL, 56:111-128, 1969

Gruberg ER,, Raymoond SA, Beyond cholesterol: A new explanation for arteriosclerosis, ATL MONTHLY, 59-65, May 1979

Morin RJ, Peng SK, The role of cholesterol oxidation products in the pathogenesis of arteriosclerosis, ANN CLIN & LAB SCI, 1:19;225-237, 1991

McCully KS, Chemical pathology of homocysteine. IOI. Carcinogenesis and homocysteine thiolactone metabolism, ANN CLIN LAB SCI, 24:27-59, 1994

Harker LA, Homocysteinemia: Vascular injury and arterial thrombosis, NEW ENGL J MED, 291:537-543, 1974

McCully KS, Ragsdale BD, Production of arteriosclerosis by homocysteinemia, AM J PATHOL 61:1-11, 1970

Stampfer M, et al, A prospective study of plasma homocyst(e)ine and risk of myocardial infarction in US physicians, JAMA 269:877-881, 1992

Leaf A, Weber PC, Cardiovascular effects of n-3 fatty acids, NEW ENGL J MED, 318:549-557, 1988

Olszewski AJ, McCully KS, Fish oil decreases serum homocysteine in hyperlipidemic men. CORONARY ARTERY DIS, 4:53-60, 1993

Hubbard HW, et al, Atherogenic effect of oxidized products of cholesterol, PROG FOOD NUTR SCI 32:40-57, 1979

Gey KF, et al, Plasma levels of antioxidant vitamins in relation to ischemic heart disease and cancer, AM J CLIN NUTR 45:1368-1377, 1987

Mc Cully KS, Chemical pathology of homocysteine. I. Atherogenesis, ANN CLIN LAB SCI, 23:477-493, 1993

Smith LL, Another cholesterol hypothesis: Cholesterol as antioxidant, FREE RAD BIOL MED, 11:47-61, 1991

Bell IR, Edman JS, Selhub J, Morrow FD, Marby DW, Kayne HL, Cole JO, Plasma homocysteine in vascular disease and in nonvascular dementia of depressed elderly people, ACTA PSYCHIATRICA SCANDINAVICA, 86(5): 386-90, Nov 1992.

Abstract: Twenty seven depressed elderly acute inpatients by DSM III R criteria had significantly higher plasma homocysteine (HC) levels and lower cognitive screening test scores than did 15 depressed young adult inpatients. HC was highest in the older patients who had concomitant vascular diseases. HC was lowered in the older depressives who had neither vascular illness nor dementia comparable to the young adult depressives. Higher HC correlated significantly with poorer cognition only in the nonvascular geriatric patients (rs=0.53).

Newman TB, Hulley SB, Carcinogenicity of lipid lowering drugs, J AMER MED ASSOC, 275:55-60, 1996

Folkers K, Lansjven P, et al, Lovastatin (a cholesterol-lowering drug) decreases coenzyme Q10 levels in humans, PROC NAT ACAD SCI USA, 87:8931-8934, 1996

Lockwood K, Moesgaard S, Folkers K, Partial and complete regression of breast cancer in patients in relation to dosage of coenzyme Q10, BIOCHEM BIOPHYS RES COMMUN (US), 199;34:1504-1508, 1995

The bottom line: When you have one medical problem (in these examples, a common risk factor for arteriosclerosis), you are more likely to have depression, and vice versa. So what's new? The scary part is prescription drugs also depress levels of nutrients needed to prevent and even cure many conditions from depression or arteriosclerosis to chemical sensitivity or cancer. As an example, cholesterol-lowering drugs actually lower CoQ10, a nutrient needed to maintain normal cardiac function. So taking the drug raises your risk of depression, suicide, cancer, and heart disease. What a deal.

PARADIGM PIONEERS MUST BREAK PARADIGM PARALYSIS

A paradigm is merely a model, or a way of conceptualizing something so that you can better deal with it. The problem is that with the growth of knowledge, often paradigms are shown to no longer be applicable and actually block further growth of knowledge until the paradigm is corrected. Unfortunately paradigms, being etched in our subconscious, are slow to die. Sometimes change is resisted because of financial investment in the status quo. We have many examples in the history of science.

Copernicus was denigrated for daring to think that the sun and not the earth was the center of the universe. Semmelweiss was ostracized for thinking that invisible germs could be carried on surgeons' hands. Pasteur for believing again in invisible germs. And now we are saddled with changing the current medical paradigm that is paralyzing progress into the era of molecular and environmental medicine. For invisible chemicals, foods, molds, inhalants, EMF (electromagnetic fields), intestinal dysbiosis, and leaky gut, as well as hormonal and nutrient deficiencies are some of the many causes of mysterious symptoms. Yet as you will see in some of the examples that follow, evidence and proof mean nothing. People are always astounded when they learn this information and wonder why medicine does not immediately embrace it whole-heartedly. But as you see from these examples, to those with opposite agendas, even evidence in their own journals for over 20 years is conveniently ignored.

One paradigm in medicine is that you cannot treat food allergy symptoms with allergy injections. This notion is staunchly upheld by medicine today in spite of the fact that the technique has been successful for thousands of patients for over 3 decades. It has been staunchly denied even though no studies by the opponents have been properly done to disprove it. It has been staunchly denied even though we use the very same injections to protect us against tetanus, polio, hepatitis, and measles. And it is the very same principle behind allergy injections to lesson the misery of hayfever.

I had 6 years of horrible red cysts and scales on my face and my husband and I scoured the globe looking for a cause and treatment. It wasn't until he suggested I consult one of the pioneers in food allergy injection, Dr. J.B. Miller of Mobile Alabama, that within 2 weeks my 6 years of eczema was better than it had been in 6 years. And as a bonus, I was able to eat over 50 foods that prior had triggered it. And there is no lack of data. It is just that there are certain controlling factions, self-appointed authorities, if you will, in every field who prefer to remain in control, and refuse to acknowledge paradigm shifts. Some, for example, hold medical school positions and the majority of their research grant money comes from the pharmaceutical industry. So they are forced to seek in that direction. It is a story as old as history itself.

Dr. Miller started reporting these results in the official journal of the American College of Allergy and Immunology back in 1977 (Miller JB, A double-blind study of food extract injection therapy: A preliminary report, ANN ALLERGY 38:185,1977). Yet conventional allergists vehemently deny to this day the benefit of allergy injections for food allergy. But through the years numerous other papers appeared, even in this journal, substantiating it. Look at this one in 1990: Bakers and pastry chefs with wheat allergy were treated to 20 months of immunotherapy to wheat, and not only did they have subjective symptom improvement, but a significant decrease in hyper-responsiveness to methacholine, skin sensitivity and specific IgE.

In other words, by giving injections to these chefs who were allergic to wheat in the air and in the diet, they made sufficient blocking antibody to improve their symptoms (Baker's asthma: prevalence and evaluation of immunotherapy with a wheat flour extract (Armentia, A., et al, ANN ALLERGY, 65:4, 265-272, Oct 1990). Who said you can't treat with food antigens? (For scores of other references, see THE SCIENTIFIC BASIS OF SELECTED ENVIRONMENTAL MEDICINE TECHNIQUES). Yet most allergists still maintain that you cannot treat food allergies with injections. And those who sit on insurance boards in an advisory capacity recommend that it not be covered.

Likewise, the same staunch protectors of the current paradigm promote the idea that assessments of vitamins has little if any role to play in the treatment of asthma. But in another study, again in their own journals, vitamin C significantly increased the FEV1 (the amount of air that an asthmatic can blow out in one second) only one hour after treatment. In other words, by correcting a vitamin C deficiency, asthmatics improved their breathing capacity (Effect of vitamin C on histamine bronchial responsiveness of patients with allergic rhinitis. Bucca C, ANN ALLERGY, 65;4, 311-314, Oct 1990). Who says there is no place for nutritional medicine in allergy? Yet coverage is often denied while liberally given for drugs, many of which do not have high enough efficacies to warrant taking them.

The problem you might think is a small one, because patients could just go to the best physician. But unfortunately for them, some of these paradigm protectors sit on the governing boards of insurance companies, so you have no choice. That is unless you want to pay for it yourself, while everyone else is getting reimbursed for techniques that the paradigm protectors have O.K.'d yet often have inferior merit. Does it have anything to do with the fact that these physicians are often directors of allergy departments in medical schools and derive part of their income from research subsidized by the pharmaceutical companies? Or that they also consult part time for insurance companies that are wholey-owned subsidiaries of the chemical industry (which spins off pharmaceutical companies)? And the problem is multiplied for people in HMO's. For they dictate what doctors, diagnostic tests, and treatments you can have. And the decisions are based on immediate cost and control of participating physicians. Long term health effects are practically a non-existent priority, as it is of no consequence that these treatments have turned off symptoms.

As another example, the preservative in nebulized bronchodilators caused bronchoconstriction in susceptible individuals. In other words, asthmatic patients were actually allergic to the preservative in their inhaled medicines that were prescribed to help them during a severe attack. But because the paradigm protectors denigrate the notion of chemical sensitivity (until recently when they (re-) "discovered" latex allergy) manufacturers put the same preservatives in all brands. So the patient is left with no alternatives or options. Consequently, there is a subset of asthmatics who can die from the preservatives in the very medications they are prescribed for control of life-threatening asthma. For the lucky ones, it merely made them worse (Zhang YG, Wright WJ, Tam WK, et al. Effect of inhaled preservatives on asthmatic subjects. II. Benzalkonium chloride. AM REV RESP DIS, 141:1405-1408, 1990). Who said patients can't react to trace amounts of preservatives?

Bear in mind that all of these simple examples represent issues that many doctors still tell us are not possible; conventional allergists maintain you cannot get injections to help food allergy, that vitamins have no part in the work-up of asthmatic patients, and rarely is sensitivity to a component of an asthmatic's medication thought of as the very thing that causes his asthma, much less his death. And when pressed for an explanation, hypochondriasis is often the scapegoat.

I only pick on the allergists because that is the field I know best. But the resistance to paradigm shifts is pervasive. For example, you just read of over a thousand reasons why you should not be sentenced to a lifetime of anti-depressant medication without benefit of an environmental and nutritional assessment. But now see how difficult it is to find any physician, including a psychiatrist whose very specialty it is, be well-versed in all this. And then see how much fun it is to fight your insurance company for reimbursement, in spite of all the evidence. (For a list of physicians, including psychiatrists who do use these techniques, write the American Academy of Environmental Medicine, 4510 W. 89th St., Prairie Village KS 66207; but relocating as this goes to press.)

And the biggest paradigms you fight by far in medicine today are the ones that say " Arthritis is a Darvon deficiency". Is a headache a Motrin deficiency, is Depression a Prozac deficiency?

"Why would there be such resistance to helping so many people lead happier and more productive lives?" you ask.

There are many reasons and they all filter down to two motivating forces, **power and money.** And for your best health, mental and physical, you need to understand some of the dishonesty in medicine. And you need to know how to assert yourself when a paradigm protector tries to belittle or intimidate you. I could proceed with the documentation and evidence, but that is not the motive of this work. Our job, and a much too big one for one book, is to get you happier and healthier.

The examples and references are endless. Now we have to communicate and teach. So when all looks bleak and incurable, it may just be that it is time to change your paradigm. In other words, if you merely shift gears into the 21st century medicine, and start to look for environmental triggers and nutritional biochemical defects that underlie most symptoms, it is amazing what "incurable" conditions can suddenly vanish.

Well, you will never be the same again. Because like it or not, you have just brought your mind into the 21st century. If you have read this far, you are irreversibly the wiser. There is no going back. Granted, it may be rough sailing as you encounter people who do not believe you. Because what you are saying is **unfathomable.** They do not comprehend all the data that you do. They have never even heard it. But never again will any physician be able to pull the wool over your eyes by making you think that your problem is a drug deficiency. Never again will you tremble when told that there is no known cause, no known cure for what you have. We've started this series with the disease, depression, because it is the only disease whose definition includes hopelessness. I trust this has shown you that depression is anything but hopeless.

LABELITIS:
THE NUMBER ONE CAUSE OF DEATH

So, the label really does not matter. Depression is merely one label, but most people with chronic fatigue, fibromyalgia, PMS, and multiple chemical sensitivities have depression as well. And they all have multiple causes which include environmental triggers and/or nutritional deficiencies (Buchwald D, et al, Comparison of patients with chronic fatigue syndrome, fibromyalgia, and multiple chemical sensitivities, ARCH INT MED 1994; 154:2049-2053). And in contrast to the authors of this study, you know the reasons why! How can you ever again let any physician intimidate you with some meaningless label when you are light years ahead of him in understanding the actual causes and actual cure of disease?

NEVER UNDERESTIMATE
THE POWER OF MEDICAL ADVERTISING

In the first 2 years that Prozac was on the market, it grossed more money than all of the other antidepressants together in the previous 2 years. But it was in large part due to advertising. For you see, a double blind placebo controlled study was recently done right here at home at the Upstate Medical Center (now renamed State University of New York, Health Sciences Center at Syracuse). The study showed that even though Prozac has been called the "wonder drug" by a popular weekly news magazine, it has no greater long lasting anti-depressant effect than other anti-depressants.

What they did show was that the skillful marketing to physicians and lay people was the main impetus for popularizing Prozac, not its clinical merit based on studies. In fact, they found that in time, the benefits of Prozac dwindle. Of course, you and I would expect that since physicians had done nothing to correct the environmental triggers and biochemical defects that were causing the depression. And the metabolism of Prozac depletes further nutrients. Once this happens, it changes how the drug is metabolized, eventually diminishing its effectiveness.

Therefore, since nutrients are used up in the actual work of detoxifying the drug, there is only one way to go; and that is downhill. **The sick get sicker quicker**, because the physician has failed to fix what is broken and has even added another stressor to the detox system (Greenberg RP, A Meta-Analysis of Fluoxetine Outcome in the Treatment of Depression, NERV MENT DIS, 182:547-51, 1994).

The researchers further showed that Prozac is being marketed as having "benign" side effects, because manufacturers rationalize that the **side effects** are not undesirable. They **serve as a distracter** for the person. In other words, the victim is so concerned about the nausea, numbness, nervousness, insomnia or whatever other side effect he has, that he tends to forget about his depression. And over half the patients treated with anti-depressants have side effects from the drug.

It never ceases to amaze me how so much good data can be selectively ignored and replaced by the mentality that drug deficiencies are at the root of all diseases. Many sufferers of chronic fatigue syndrome, for example, are prescribed Prozac. This is in spite of studies that show it has no beneficial effect (Vercoulen H, et al, Randomized, double-blind, placebo-controlled study of fluoxetine in chronic fatigue syndrome, LANCET 347: 856-861, 1996). And insurance companies pay for it!

But chronic fatigue is a classic example of a disease that requires the environmental medicine approach. Victims invariably have allergies, hormone deficiencies, nutrient deficiencies, intestinal dysfunction, and/or membrane pathologies. The mitochondrial (energy synthesis) membranes are damaged. In fact in the few cases where Prozac does help, that's why it works, at least for a while. For Prozac enhances serotonin's effectiveness by keeping it outside of cells and working longer. One reason it needs to be kept out of cells is because the cell membranes are damaged or leaky! They lack the integrity produced by adequate levels of phosphatidyl choline, d-alpha tocopherol, eicosapentaenoic acid, magnesium, etc. (I just realized how smart you have become. Many physicians would have trouble comprehending that, but now after your crash course in environmental medicine, you are right on top of it all.) And as you saw earlier, antidepressants suppress cytokines and have antihistaminic properties as well.

A scary part is the increasing and sometimes mandatory, use of Prozac in children. This is in spite of studies that show it can dangerously cause toxic reactions in the heart. (Hazell, et al, BRIT MED J, 310: 897, Apr 8, 1995). This study also showed that Prozac in children and adults can cause rapidly **cyclic bipolar disorder**. This is characterized by severe fluctuations between normal moods and disabling depression and is resistant to medications.

Of course, you experts in environmental medicine know why this serious form of depression can be triggered by Prozac (or any medicine) and is resistant to medication: the nutrient depletion has reached such a low that there is not sufficient reserve for the metabolism of the drug to lead to its desirable effect. These people are in serious biochemical trouble and are in urgent need of a proper biochemical/nutritional workup (Sansone RA, Sansone LA, Dysthymic disorder: the chronic depression, AMER FAM PHYS, 53; 8: 2588-2596, June 1996).

It is not a surprise that kids on Prozac will exhibit bizarre and criminal behaviors. One 10 year old boy grabbed his 3 year old niece as a shield as he aimed a 12-gauge shotgun at a sheriff's deputy who accompanied a truant officer to his home (Assoc. Press, Boy, 10, to use Prozac defense in court, A8, SYRACUSE HERALD-JOURNAL, May 8, 1996). Folks these are mere samplings.

Meanwhile, medicine continues to ignore the fact that a vast number of people have treatable and permanently correctable causes for their depression. It can be as simple as eliminating sugar or other allergens such as wheat from the diet, isolating chemical sensitivities such as formaldehyde and natural gas, which are very common, identifying mold sensitivities and hidden hormonal deficiencies, the leaky gut, intestinal dysbiosis and last but probably most important, nutritional deficiencies.

A simple magnesium deficiency can cause depression. And government studies show that the average American diet only provides 40% or less than half the magnesium you need in a day. As well, many other vitamins, minerals, essential fatty acids and amino acids as well as accessory nutrients have a tremendous bearing on depression and are equally deficient in this era.

So for all of my friends out there, please don't ever think that depression is a Prozac deficiency. But get yourself some place where you can have the cause identified. A good start would be with TIRED OR TOXIC? followed by WELLNESS AGAINST ALL ODDS.

HOW THE SICK WILL GET SICKER,
AND YOU WILL PAY FOR IT

With the amount you have learned now, let's look at **the top 10 prescribed drugs** in the U.S. for 1991 and see how they make the sick get sicker and guarantee the perpetuation of the drug industry as the number one, for profit, industry in the U.S.

The number one drug is **Amoxil,** an antibiotic, which has enjoyed over 23 million prescriptions. This will foster Candida overgrowth in the gut which in some vulnerable individuals will go on to cause the leaky gut and depression.

The next most commonly prescribed drug is **Premarin** with 22 million scripts, which actually does help much post-menopausal depression. However, if you look for the other causes presented in this book, or use a natural plant-based hormone (see Volume III and WELLNESS AGAINST ALL ODDS), many will not need it. Don't overlook the fact that it can trigger cancer, since it is unnatural. I doubt God wants me dependent on pharmaceutical companies for good health for the rest of my post-menopausal life.

Number 3 on the "most commonly prescribed drugs" list is **Zantac,** for turning off acid secretion in the stomach. It will promote mineral deficiencies and subsequent diseases like arteriosclerosis, cancer, auto-immune disease and depression through impaired digestion.

Number 4 is **Lanoxin,** for the heart. It is used by docs who have failed to look at the magnesium loading test, rbc levels of manganese, copper, zinc, selenium, potassium, and calcium, and who do not correct carnitine, essential fatty acid, CoQ10, taurine, phosphatidyl choline and many other deficiencies. These have enabled many people to no longer require Lanoxin.

Next is **Xanax,** a tranquilizer which is potentially addicting, can cause brain deterioration, accelerate brain aging, and cause depression and poor memory. But a simple magnesium deficiency or food or chemical sensitivity is often the cause. You get the picture with the first 5 drugs on this top 10 list.

Or look at the introduction of the chickenpox vaccine this year. It took the market by surprise, and got full FDA approval. It costs $56 average, not including the pediatrician's office visit. And they are not even sure how long the vaccine will last, or if there is a possibility of any delayed auto-immune phenomenon. But they are sure that Merck will generate $210 million in annual revenue just from Varivax in 1996 (Winslow R, Chickenpox vaccines are here, but some are wondering why, WALL STREET JOURNAL, May 5, 1995, B1 and B6). Does that confirm any notion of how the process works?

If you still have any doubts, remember the new antihistamine, Claritin, that made front page of USA TODAY and CNN? Of course, we were not exactly breathless for another antihistamine, since there are over 35 already. And this one was a real bargain, as the side effects listed infertility and cancer of the liver. Plus it was only $186 a bottle of 100 when I checked our local pharmacy. But most people have co-pay insurance, and are oblivious to the cost of drugs. They pay their $1-$5 co-pay and never know that we are all paying for the remaining $181. Yet this same FDA wants to take nutrients off the market, that can cut healing time, cardiovascular disease, and cancer recurrence by more than 50%, and have no side effects. And many nutrients like magnesium, vitamin C and various bioflavonoids have anti-histaminic properties. They are Natures' antihistamine. And don't forget how common a deficiency copper is. It is essential in the enzyme histaminase, to enable you to break down or metabolize histamine.

And some insurance companies push patients to get off allergy injections and on to antihistamines. Now an allergy injection twice a month, for example, costs 1/5th price of a month's prescription for Claritin. And Canadian studies showed there is **increased risk of cancer with antihistamines**, plus the other side effects. But injections build blocking antibodies to turn off the allergy, and serve to decrease all the other associated symptoms like fatigue and depression. They foster antibody production just as other immunizations for polio and measles do. Rather than poison a pathway like that of histamine release, allergy injections are designed to build up the body resistance through the synthesis of blocking antibodies, as do protective immunizations. Of course, when people eat right, etc., they then reach a higher level of wellness where they no longer require injections. This is even cheaper and safer and more beneficial to the reduction of symptoms. It seems the closer we get to nature, the better off we are all the way around.

Anyway, the drug Claritin had full FDA endorsement, and was tested on 12,800 people. But when they did the study on not 12,800 but 85,000 medical personnel and found that 100 mg of vitamin E cut the cardiovascular risk in half, and that it cost next to nothing, and that it had no side effects, it was not recommended (NEJM, 1993). Instead the comment was that it needed more study. Folks, something is rotten, and it is not in the state of Denmark.

In terms of arteriosclerosis, a major risk factor, probably more important than your cholesterol status is the homocysteine level. But it is not routinely checked because the correction requires vitamins B6, B12, folic acid, betaine, etc. and they would rather prescribe drugs. For supplements cannot be patented, hence, there are no huge profits to be made.

There have been efforts over the last few years by the government to get vitamins and other supplements off the market. The scientific data carries no weight. And you just saw evidence of how even when the data is accepted for publication in their very journals, the self-appointed authorities can refuse to ignore it indefinitely. For money (and lobbyists) talk. Those in control are already aware of many of these facts, but could care less. For it simply does not meet their agendas. That is why a book like this is for you.

Recently shock waves riveted through the scientific community as the California EPA ordered state scientists to destroy records and research data. This pertained to research on chemicals, industrial emissions and hazardous wastes whose results differed from their administrator's final decision (Lifsher M, California EPA stirs anger by ordering disposal of data disputing its findings, WALL STREET JOURNAL, Oct 1, 1996, Pg B5). This is unbelievably unreal and scary.

We could go on all day with the **double standard that exists in medicine,** when benefits to industry (food, chemical, manufacturing) are at stake. For example hydrogenated corn oil and soybean oil products which contain trans fatty acids, known to be deleterious to cardiac tissues, can sport a picture of a heart on their package to induce people with heart problems to buy them with the implied belief that they are healthful for the heart. And they can blatantly advertise this misconception on T.V.

But the manufacturers of vitamins and minerals and other supplements have strict and irrational rules which restrict the marriage of scientific publications with their product advertisements. Drug manufacturers can huckster you on television, in newspapers, magazines, and via the mail for drugs for which the mechanism of action is unknown; for drugs that last year required a prescription and magically this year do not; for drugs that can have fatal consequences; for drugs that delay making the proper life-saving diagnosis.

And in terms of side effects, you won't believe this, but we pay more for that than we do for the drugs! "Estimates for prescription medication in 1994 have exceeded $73 billion.

Recent literature has indicated that the substantial costs associated with inappropriate drug use behavior may even exceed these initial expenditures for drug therapy. To date, research has primarily documented increased rates of hospitalization secondary to medication non-compliance and/or adverse drug effects." (Johnson JA, Bootman JL, Drug-related morbidity and mortality. A cost-of-illness model, ARCH INTERN MED, 155:1949-1956, 1995).

Folks, a cardiac catheterization in the U.S. averages $12,000. An angioplasty is $23,000, and by-pass surgery averages $48,731 (Clark JB, How to survive a heart attack, KIPLINGER PERSONAL FINANCE MAGAZINE, 49, Feb 1996). This does not include the lifetime of drugs, blood tests, and doctor visits afterwards. This is big business. No wonder Dr. Dean Ornish's program to reverse coronary deposits with diet was not embraced enthusiastically. Many cancer victims spend close to a third of a million dollars and die within months or at best within a few years of diagnosis. But the macrobiotic diet (described in THE CURE IS IN THE KITCHEN) has enabled people to totally heal, including metastases. This is not a battle of science. It is **a battle of money and politics.**

Without people being educated, they will suffer further disempowerment and atrocities. Right now there is a "growing concentration of power by insurance carriers. The 8 largest insurance companies now own 45% of the country's almost 600 HMOs". And **"patients have a lot less to say about the medical services they receive."** (Orsher SI, Business? It's quite simple. It's other people's money, MSSNY'S NEWS OF NEW YORK, 4, Oct 1995). This is the first time ever that people's insurance plans have so totally dominated and restricted their choices in medicine. As we tried to show in the empowerment section, **your health is on the line** in multiple ways.

FROM SAD TO GLAD

So I trust you now have the big picture. Not only does it border on malpractice to mask the symptoms of depression with drugs without looking for the myriads of curable causes, but it goes far beyond that. For example, **serotonin inhibits tumor necrosis factor.** This means that an anti-depressant drug can **promote cancer** not only in its consumption of detox nutrients. It can promote cancer not only in helping ignore the underlying biochemical defect that caused the depression. But it also can help promote cancer, not only in the myriad of ways that we described, but by directly inhibiting one of the substances that the body makes to fight off cancer. There is no question that our vulnerability to cancer and every other disease is tied into the biochemistry of the brain. To artificially change it with a drug is against nature; and it is cancer-promoting (Schook).

Fortunately, from all areas of medicine, physicians are discovering this **paradigm shift in medicine.** One lovely example is Dr. Lorraine Day, an orthopedic surgeon who was head of the trauma unit at San Francisco General Hospital. That in itself is a unique accomplishment. But it wasn't until she got breast cancer herself that she was forced to investigate these principles in order to get herself well without surgery, radiation or chemotherapy. And she is now doing a great job in educating the public.

REFERENCES:

Schook LB, Laskin DL, XENOBIOTICS AND INFLAMMATION, p 124, Academic Press, NY, 1994

Day, L, CANCER DOESN'T SCARE ME ANYMORE, Rockford Press, POB 952, Rancho Mirage CA, 92270, 1-800-574-2437

THE HYPERTENSION HOAX

Just look at how we approach one of the most common diseases, hypertension or high blood pressure. You know by now that it has many causes, from nutrient deficiencies to food and chemical sensitivities. Yet in spite of deaths due to drug treatments that fail to correct the underlying cause, we persist in treating hypertension as though it was solely a deficiency of drugs. And so the sick get sicker until they have the ultimate symptom, sudden cardiac arrest.

Other blatant tragedies that have been swept under the carpet include the use of a drug, Tambocor (flucainide acetate) for control of life-threatening cardiac arrhythmia. Well any fool knows that an underlying problem in a cardiac arrhythmia is mineral deficiencies that predispose to electrical misconduct. So by selling these poor unsuspecting people a drug that was supposed to stop the life-threatening arrhythmia, they precluded any chance of investigating the biochemical cause. Furthermore for some folks, an arrhythmia is the only compensation the body has of keeping them alive as improperly functioning electrical pathways shunt to other (abnormal) paths in order to keep the heart going. To stifle or suppress this compensatory route is to invite death. As a result, over 50,000 people died from cardiac arrest because of taking a drug that was supposed to stop cardiac arrest.

This single medical catastrophe of the drug industries and FDA produced more deaths than the combined combat losses for the U.S. in Korea and Vietnam. And the fact that you never heard of it shows you how powerful this sector is. You don't know what power and control are until you understand this type of inhumane deceit (Moore, 1995).

REFERENCES:

Moore TJ. DEADLY MEDICINE, Simon & Schuster, NY, 1995

Kobayishi H, Hobara T, Kawamoto T, Higashishara E, Shimazu W, Sakai Tm, Effect of sceral organic solvents inhalation on systemic blood pressure, YAMAGUCHI MED J 32:211-216, 1983

Psaty BM, et al, The risk of incident myocardial infarction associated with antihypertensive drug therapies, CIRCULATION, 91(3):925, abs #18, Feb 1, 1994

Anonymous, Calcium-channel blocker study raises patients' concerns, INTERN MED WORLD REP, 10:7, 1, 25, Apr 1-14, 1995

Kang SS, Wong PWK, Malinow MR, Hyperhomo-cyst(e)inemia as a risk factor for occulusive vascular disease, ANN REV NUTR 12:279-298, 1992

Olszewski AJ, Szostak WB, et al, Reduction of plasma lipid and homocysteine levels by pyridoxine, folate, cobalamin, choline, riboflavin, and troxerutin in arteriosclerosis, arteriosclerosis, 75:1-6, 1989

Bell IR, Edman JS, Sclhub J, Morrow FD, Marby DW, Kayne HL, Cole JO, Plasma homocysteine in vascular disease and in nonvascular dementia of depressed elderly people, ACTA PSYCHIATR SCAND 86:386-390, 1992

Kesteloot H, Lesaffre E, Joossens JV, Dairy fat, saturated animal fat, and cancer risk, PREV MED, 20:226-236, 1991

HOW COMMON HEART
DRUGS CAUSE CANCER

Among the top ten drugs prescribed in the U.S. is a category called **calcium channel blockers**. There are scores of types and here are just some of the common names: Adalat, Calan, Cardene, Cardizem, Dilacor, Dynacirc, Isoptin, Nimotop, Norvasc, Plendil, Procardia, Vascor, Verelan, Nifidipene.

Calcium channel blockers are very popular for treating cardiac arrhythmias, hypertension, and angina. Most doctors do not know enough about them to know that they potentiate cancer. If you find it hard to believe, ask the doc who prescribes it what a **gap junctional protein** is.

I'll explain this difficult concept to you now because you know enough medicine to be able to understand the problem. Then you will get the shock of your life: that the drug manufacturers have to know all this chemistry and more in order to develop the drug. In other words, they knowingly bypass inexpensive nutrient corrections that could save your life and actually cure your condition. Instead, they go to elaborate extremes to manufacture an expensive drug that allows not only the sick to get sicker, quicker, but to get cancer quicker.

Here's how it works: The cell membrane is a sandwich of fats called lipids. You learned that the essential fatty acid, eicosapentaenoic acid (EPA) is part of one of the layers in that sandwich. And so is phosphatidyl choline, vitamin E, and a host of other nutrients. Now this envelope around the cell has to have a way for nutrients to get inside the cell. So the membrane is studded with pores called calcium channels. They are called this because through these pores calcium is pumped back into the cell. There are many other pores. Some pump potassium, some pump sodium, etc.

When the cell does its daily work, calcium crosses this membrane. In order to restore the cell to perpetuate its ability to do its daily work, it needs to actively pump the calcium back out of the cell. For it is needed in the mitochondria (where energy is made) and in the endoplasmic reticulum (where chemicals, drugs, hormones, neuro-transmitters and more are detoxified).

This process of pumping calcium through the calcium channel is not easy. It requires energy. It also depends upon the cell sandwich for having the exact correct types of layers in the membrane. For the pore or channel partly runs on an electric current that is generated by the polar side arms that stick out from the molecules in the lipid sandwich. In essence, if you do not have the right layers in the sandwich, you do not have the correct electrons in the pore lining. Hence the calcium pump is broken, or does not function correctly.

Normally, the synchronized contraction of the heart muscle is brought about by the flow of ions through these pores. And through these pores, also flows or is pumped substances to feed and nourish the cell. But when a cell is metabolically damaged or depressed because it lacks phosphatidyl choline, as one example, the calcium pump does not work. So massive amounts of calcium leak back into the cell, and cannot be pumped out. When the membrane pore calcium pump is damaged by lack of nutrients, too much calcium floods the cell interior and causes the cell to first malfunction, then die. So calcium channel blockers were synthesized in order to poison the area where the calcium is leaking in. Calcium channel blockers actually close off or shut down or poison these important regulatory channels, so there is now essentially no channel at all.

Now since the person's angina, hypertension, or arrhythmia is better, you think, what's so bad about that? The problem is that closely related to the calcium channels are structures called **gap junctional proteins**. And researchers have learned some additional interesting things about these gap junctional proteins.

Gap junctions can also act somewhat like channels or pores. They are actually more like little protein tubules that connect cells one to another. And it is through these protein tubules that **cells talk to one another**. No man is an island, and no cell is autonomous unto itself. Cells, like nutrients and like people, work best in concert or symphony. For example, signals that run from cell to cell, tell a cell when to stop growing, that it is crowding its neighbor. I can hear the cells yelling down the picket fence now: "Hey, you down there. Yes, you, third cell from the right. You're crowding me. Stop growing".

Many environmental chemicals, like pesticides, can damage these gap junctions. And specific nutrients, like vitamin A can help regenerate them. Well guess what makes the difference between a normal cell and a cancer cell? **No gap junctional proteins on the cancer cell**. So no wonder cancers grow wildly out of control and even spread throughout the body. They have lost their cell-to-cell communication link.

And you recall that the job of calcium channel blockers is to intentionally poison the calcium channel, since after a lifetime of trans fatty acids, etc., it not longer works. But intentionally poisoning the cell membrane calcium channels affects the closely allied gap junctional proteins as well; thus they can speed the way toward cancer. Plus by taking the calcium channel blockers, you ignore repairing the cell membrane. You don't look for the deficiencies in the lipid sandwich and channel.

The interesting thing is that I had to spend thousands of dollars on medical searches and thousands of hours to learn that this has been known for decades. In fact the designers of drugs have to know it in order to figure out how they are going to make money on a biochemical glitch in your body.

From that point on, it's really easy pulling the wool over doctors' eyes. Just overwork them, and constantly flood the market with new drugs so they feel intimidated for not using the latest one. And never teach them the biochemistry. Give them just enough facts so they feel important telling everyone it is a calcium channel blocker. That is meant to stop anyone from wanting to know more. For if you tell docs too much, they might figure out that there is a cheaper, more definitively healing, and more ethical way to fix the problem.

The WALL STREET JOURNAL in the winter of 1996 sported articles on the fact that **patients who took calcium channel blockers had 60% more chance of dying of a heart attack.** But, of course, they never knew why. But you do. You are taking a system that is broken and damaging it more. You are taking a fellow who is down and kicking him in the teeth. How long he rallies with the plastic Band-Aid is dependent on his total load of stressors.

So I'm sorry to have to be the one to tell you what goes on in medicine, but I don't know who else will. But once you know the score, you can make infinitely more intelligent, and empowered choices about your health. And that's all that counts.

REFERENCES:

Voet D, Voet J, BIOCHEMISTRY, 304-305, John Wiley & Sons, Inc, NY, 1995

Ruch RJ, The role of gap junctional intercellular communication in neoplasia (review), ANN CLIN LAB SCI, 24(3):216-231, May-Jun 1994

Trosko JE, Chang CC, Madhukar BV, The role of modulated gap junctional intercellular communication in epigenetic toxicology (review), RISK ANALYSIS, 14(3):303-312, Jun 1994

Rogers M, Berestecky JM, et al, Retinoid-enhanced gap junctional communication is achieved by increased levels of connexin 43 mRNA and protein, MOLECULAR CARCINOGENESIS 3:335-343, 1990

Zhang LX, Cooney RV, Bertram JS, Carotenoids up-regulate connexin43 gene expression independent of their provitamin A or antioxidant properties, CANCER RESEARCH 52:5707-5712, 1992

Ruch RJ, Klaunig JE, Effects of tumor promoters, genotoxic carcinogens and hepatocytotoxins on mouse hepatocyte intercellular communication, CELL BIOL TOXICOL 2:4, 469-483, 1986 (**How prescription drugs, pesticides, food additives, like saccharin damage gap junctions and promote cancers.**)

JUST THE BEGINNING:
DANGER LURKS HEAD FOR THE
UNKNOWLEDGEABLE

As this book draws to a close, I revel in the thought that many now share the enthusiasm I have for a paradigm shift. I thank you for suffering through my amateurish writing. But I am glad to have had the privilege of bringing you to a **point of no return.** Never again will you be intimidated by medicine. And you will forever be more questioning and a real thinker, **IN CONTROL** of your health.

And it is not for naught that you now know more **real medicine** than the majority of all the physicians you will encounter in the future. For you will need every ounce of data I have been able to provide and more. Old fashioned medicine is not going to die gracefully. It just has too much invested. And if you for one moment think that all you have learned is going to be eagerly embraced and that medicine is going to change, just look at what I found in the last few months:

- The high rate of depression is one of the major public health concerns in the United States, reports PSYCHIATRIC NEWS (AMER FAM PHYS, 1639, Nov 1, 1995).
- Depressed persons use health care more extensively than persons without depression, and still
- 50% of patients with major depression are not even diagnosed. This is major depression and does not even begin to relate to those with less severe depression (AMER FAM PHYS, 1559, Oct 1995).
- The leading publication from which family doctors learn recommends that if a patient's depression is resistant to

medication, then electro-convulsive therapy (ECT) (as in ONE FLEW OVER THE CUCKOO'S NEST), should be used. But they never yet have taught the comprehensive workup to find the causes and get rid of the depression, as you have learned here (Banazak DA, Electroconvulsive therapy: A guide for family physicians, AMER FAM PHYS, 53:1:273-278, Jan 1996). You read right, Folks. In spite of the fact that you learned that it is only good for about a month of improvement (reference in Volume I), they recommend (in 1996!) electrocuting the already damaged brain 3 times a week for 12 treatments. And you can bet that if your insurance pays for it, that it will be recommended over any treatment that it does not pay for. Killing brain cells is not the answer, as you know. Are we in danger of having a nation of robots?

- And remember, that Prozac (or any other drug) is capable of causing a worse depression that becomes dangerous to society and resists all medicines. Are we going to see ECT recommended for these adults and children? It may not be that far away.

- And guess what? Prozac has just become the world's first prescription mental-health drug to have surpassed $2 billion in annual receipts. Sales grew a walloping 24% last year, and 37% the year prior. Because they are nervous about the 13% drop, it is now recommended for obsessive-compulsive disorders, attention deficit disorder, attention deficit hyperactivity disorder, learning disability, panic attacks, shyness, boredom, and premenstrual syndrome. Yes, you read correctly. Increased use of Prozac is recommended for children with ADD, ADHD, and LD. While what these precious children really deserve is an environmental medicine workup as described.

694

- And did you know that it "makes good economic sense" that "managed-care groups have shown a tendency to encourage drug prescriptions instead of potentially more expensive psychiatric counseling". In other words, it is cheaper to drug you, so let's do it. Needless-to-say, they do not even consider the differential causes listed here in this book (Burton TM, Lilly sales rise as use of Prozac keeps growing, WALL STREET JOURNAL, B1, 1/31/96 and Castellano M, The secret deal that won the Prozac case, JERSEY LAW JOURNAL, May 1, 1995). We are in deep trouble. **For a drugged person is not in complete control of his feelings and emotions, and more important, his spirituality.**

- To compound matters, the large insurance companies are planning on merging. In essence, the day may not be far off when there is a monopoly and you simply will have no choices. You will receive the type of medicine that they consider best for the business of making money, not healing people. In fact, physicians in some plans are now prohibited from disclosing all the options for treatment. Doctors can lose their jobs if they tell you about options that their HMO does not offer in order to increase profits. (Tomsho R, Blue Cross in Texas, Illinois plan to merge, WALL STREET JOURNAL, 1/31/96, and Coleman B, AMA rebels against HMO gag clauses, SARASOTA HERALD-TRIBUNE, D1, June 28, 1996).

- Or look at the calcium channel blockers that you learned about. They do not fix the underlying problem, can promote further illness, including depression, senile dementia, and **cancers**. And it is common knowledge already that one of them, "nifedipine didn't do any good and may increase the risk of heart attack" (McGinley L, FDA is advised against the use of certain drugs, WALL STREET JOURNAL, B3, 1/26/96). But they are not off the market. This is in spite of the fact that "patients treated for high blood pressure with **fast-acting calcium channel blockers had a 60% higher risk of heart attacks** than those on other types of pressure-lowering drugs." Could it have anything remotely to do with the fact that they are "the biggest-selling classes of pharmaceuticals in the world, have estimated annual sales of $8 billion" and "are taken by 6 million Americans"? (McGinley L, FDA to assess drugs to treat hypertension, WALL STREET JOURNAL, B1, 1/25/96, and Tanouge E, Hypertension drugs linked to cancer, WALL STREET JOURNAL, B6, June 26, 1996).

- The cholesterol lowering drugs cause depression, suicide, and **cancer**. The subsequent use of anti-depressants must lead to the sick getting sicker, quicker. But that's only if they don't cause suicide first, as you have learned (Newman TB, Hulley SB, Carcinogenicity of lipid-lowering drugs, J AMER MED ASSOC, 275:55-60, 1996). Clearly, using drugs to cover-up symptoms and poison ailing pathways uses nutrients even faster, accelerating all diseases, especially cancer. Finding the causes as outlined here is the only logical and humane solution.

- Folks, it just doesn't end and you are the only ones who know enough to protect yourselves. Where else have all these facts been collated? (Our subscription HEALTH LETTER will keep you updated.)

- And now there is a new pill to help lose weight. And you guessed it, Redux (dexfenfluramine) is a **close bio-chemical "cousin"of Prozac**, the blockbuster drug used to treat depression in millions of Americans." Of course there is no mention of the deaths, cardiotoxicity, and worsening of depression, nerve damage, etc., nor finding out what nutrients are desperately needed by the body in order to stop its merciless food cravings (Langreth R,

Obesity drug appears close to approval, WALL STREET JOURNAL, B1, 1/29/96). And they just released in the WSJ that it causes at least an 18-fold increase in fatal pulmonary hypertension. To prey on children, the obese, the depressed, the undiagnosable or chronic pain patient is unconscionable when an environmental workup holds the potential for total cure.

- And the HMO's (health maintenance organizations or more properly, drugs and disease maintenance organizations) are now giving people antidepressants to save money. Rather than look for treatable causes or even prescribe psychotherapy, doctors instead cover up the symptom with anti-depressants because it's quicker and cheaper. In fact, they don't even get a large selection of drugs from which to chose, because of bulk buying and quantity discounts that the HMO's get. So with the actual drug or medicine as well, you get the cheapest, not the best (Pollack EJ, Managed care's focus on psychiatric drugs alarms many doctors, WALL ST J, 1996).

- There is no question, medicine is **in deep trouble**, or rather **the unwary patient is.** For a mind controlled by mind-altering drugs is not in total control of its own chemistry. Such a person is more easily intimidated, manipulated, and overwhelmed. He is zombie-like, robot-like, stripped of the biochemical freedom needed to nurture the **soul.**

One might say that all this is enough to depress even the happiest person. But on the contrary, it is far better to know the problem. There has never been a better time in which to be sick. Not only do we have the greatest medications and surgical techniques, but also, we are on the cutting edge of Environmental Medicine and Nutritional Biochemistry.

And now you comprehend why the total load as well as the politics of medicine are in the TREATMENT VOLUME. For the total load is indeed the treatment. And once you get well and have the fortitude to empower yourself and others, it is only people power which can bring about this type of medicine as the norm. Correct the cause once and for all versus a sentence of a lifetime of drugs which must eventually make the sick get sicker.

Congratulations! You are fantastic. You have just brought yourself into the era of molecular medicine. Hence, you have a multitude of tools with which to identify the causes of symptoms and heal the impossible. There have never before been so many reasons to be fueled with hope.

The ball is now in your court. You have all the evidence. Can you afford to become such a zombie, puppet, robot of drug-oriented medicine? Are you going to ignore all this and see what happens? I doubt it. You have come too far, and you know too much.

Do you honestly believe that depression is a Prozac deficiency? You are much too smart now. There is no turning back once you are this knowledgeable. You are one of the elite few who have the knowledge to see to it that your soul is nurtured and that your **DEPRESSION IS CURED AT LAST!**

JUST THE BEGINNING

4-PC, 118, 635

A

acetylcholine, 101, 103, 105, 107, 249, 250, 347, 348, 350, 351, 352, 353, 355, 360, 361, 362, 363, 371, 378, 380, 384, 385, 386, 454, 462

addiction, 15, 28, 29, 43, 64, 70, 74, 125, 166, 313, 365, 393, 421, 468, 588, 599, 632, 650, 651

addictions, 15, 421

additives, 55, 56, 57, 58, 59, 70, 73, 158, 311, 399, 422, 429, 445, 497, 692

ADHD, 84, 694

aging, 17, 18, 27, 29, 57, 68, 94, 95, 97, 111, 114, 116, 120, 138, 196, 210, 231, 238, 251, 252, 255, 275, 282, 327, 355, 363, 367, 368, 371, 378, 380, 382, 392, 405, 408, 414, 439, 501, 524, 567, 572, 575, 592, 605, 610, 615, 660, 679, 691

alcohol, 5, 17, 39, 54, 64, 65, 70, 79, 89, 120, 140, 141, 166, 168, 172, 177, 181, 226, 233, 243, 252, 255, 257, 266, 268, 283, 293, 294, 299, 312, 319, 332, 333, 365, 366, 369, 397, 422, 429, 430, 438, 440, 451, 460, 465, 468, 481, 485, 497, 510, 575, 581, 600, 601, 620, 621, 630, 647

aluminum, 94, 129, 132, 133, 139, 143

Alzheimer's, 15, 94, 131, 132, 133, 139, 143, 153, 209, 252, 253, 255, 263, 268, 274, 280, 291, 347, 360, 362, 377, 379, 381, 395, 424, 461, 476, 479, 507

amalgam, 129, 136, 137, 559

amino acids, 57, 64, 73, 76, 119, 122, 184, 209, 231, 246, 254, 296, 299, 305, 306, 307, 308, 315, 317, 318, 319, 323, 324, 325, 345, 346, 360, 372, 399, 429, 552, 577, 606, 677

amyloid, 252, 255

anorexia, 6, 15, 288, 321

antacid, 129, 131, 132, 139, 140, 175, 237, 559, 570

anti-oxidants, 208, 382, 383, 450, 452, 626

arrhythmia, 23, 191, 205, 206, 256, 258, 259, 260, 266, 315, 330, 363, 364, 396, 565, 574, 652, 659, 664, 686, 688, 690

arteriosclerosis, 66, 175, 190, 191, 192, 196, 198, 201, 202, 203, 205, 212, 222, 223, 231, 232, 238, 248, 249, 256, 260, 261, 273, 274, 286, 328, 330, 355, 363, 368, 375, 384, 404, 405, 419, 503, 565, 566, 567, 589, 590, 591, 657, 658, 661, 662, 665, 666, 667, 679, 681, 687

arthritis, 1, 15, 26, 43, 46, 82, 88, 110, 115, 124, 145, 178, 200, 249, 280, 342, 374, 375, 396, 428, 430, 431, 432, 433, 434, 435, 455, 465, 474, 476, 478, 502, 507, 537, 557

ascorbic acid, 132, 174, 248, 249, 250, 251, 607, 624

Aspartame, 56, 58, 59

asthma, 46, 51, 61, 88, 124, 163, 164, 165, 169, 178, 180, 263, 266, 339, 340, 341, 428, 433, 434, 436, 502, 537, 601, 619, 632, 670, 671, 672

attention deficit, 15, 24, 34, 57, 81, 84, 112, 434, 694

autism, 15, 34, 39, 168
auto exhaust, 92, 94, 116, 129, 130, 134, 142, 279, 425, 559, 644

B

B1, 140, 167, 175, 225, 226, 235, 236, 237, 238, 240, 241, 242, 243, 245, 246, 272, 282, 401, 486, 493, 544, 590, 606, 623, 625, 640, 654, 661, 679, 681, 695, 696, 697
B1 deficiency, 167, 225, 226
back pain, 32, 205, 256, 502
Basidiomycete, 169
bell-shaped, 71, 175, 212, 308
benzene, 94
beta blockers, 144
biochemical, 7, 13, 15, 29, 37, 45, 58, 65, 71, 73, 87, 97, 106, 123, 124, 190, 193, 196, 206, 226, 231, 232, 238, 247, 249, 250, 251, 265, 299, 300, 307, 308, 316, 320, 328, 336, 347, 350, 368, 377, 387, 413, 423, 434, 444, 511, 535, 567, 572, 575, 576, 610, 614, 652, 659, 673, 675, 677, 684, 686, 691, 696, 697
blood sugar, 48, 49, 291, 415, 416, 422, 569
Brain fog, 93, 432
bulimia, 6, 15, 285

C

cadmium, 130
caffeine, 50, 61, 62, 63, 76, 430, 438, 486
calcium, 140, 189, 195, 196, 197, 199, 200, 201, 208, 216, 219, 258, 259, 261, 267, 268, 269, 295, 296, 307, 356, 363, 405, 565, 566, 571, 605, 607, 608, 609, 615, 623, 652, 654, 658, 659, 661, 679, 688, 689, 690, 691, 695
calcium channel blocker, 259, 364, 654, 661, 689, 691, 696
cancer, 1, 7, 8, 9, 15, 26, 36, 66, 67, 68, 103, 108, 125, 136, 140, 141, 142, 145, 155, 163, 175, 177, 187, 188, 191, 192, 203, 207, 210, 212, 213, 214, 215, 223, 242, 248, 249, 317, 322, 328, 330, 337, 338, 351, 354, 355, 359, 364, 365, 367, 374, 375, 382, 397, 403, 404, 406, 408, 423, 443, 444, 448, 450, 456, 457, 458, 460, 472, 473, 474, 475, 476, 477, 478, 479, 483, 490, 491, 492, 503, 519, 526, 531, 540, 542, 559, 570, 574, 575, 576, 577, 578, 579, 580, 583, 588, 619, 650, 656, 657, 661, 666, 667, 678, 679, 680, 683, 684, 687, 688, 690, 691, 692, 695, 696
Candida, 26, 48, 49, 50, 141, 142, 165, 166, 167, 168, 170, 171, 172, 173, 174, 175, 180, 181, 182, 184, 225, 231, 317, 397, 399, 410, 412, 422, 429, 431, 432, 438, 442, 446, 458, 465, 466, 467, 468, 469, 477, 552, 555, 558, 562, 599, 601, 616, 678
cardiac arrest, 125, 198, 260, 376, 686
carnitine, 333, 354, 371, 372, 374, 376, 377, 378, 379, 380, 381, 387, 607, 625, 679
carnivores, 72, 656
carpet, 89, 90, 91, 115, 116, 118, 121, 122, 124, 142, 149, 176, 311, 349, 351, 425, 603, 604, 609, 631, 633, 634, 635, 639, 658, 686

CDSA, 438, 439, 442, 449, 616, 617, 623

celiac disease, 51, 429, 430, 438, 441, 444, 445, 451, 463, 474, 565

chemical exposures, 33, 105, 273, 287, 371, 604

chemical sensitivity, 1, 14, 18, 46, 66, 88, 90, 92, 94, 99, 102, 105, 123, 124, 126, 129, 148, 149, 151, 158, 160, 162, 163, 202, 205, 208, 210, 212, 223, 256, 260, 264, 282, 283, 315, 328, 330, 336, 337, 339, 340, 341, 348, 363, 375, 382, 410, 425, 431, 438, 442, 465, 474, 513, 533, 537, 562, 605, 617, 629, 630, 633, 634, 636, 641, 642, 649, 667, 671, 679

chloral hydrate, 91, 113

chlorine, 66

chlorpyrifos, 101, 102, 106, 107

chocoholics, 231, 313

cholesterol, 1, 15, 48, 72, 101, 125, 139, 143, 144, 146, 175, 190, 201, 206, 207, 222, 228, 259, 273, 274, 275, 276, 277, 285, 286, 290, 297, 330, 331, 338, 351, 356, 375, 376, 377, 387, 388, 419, 420, 423, 431, 492, 565, 566, 567, 590, 591, 615, 657, 658, 659, 660, 661, 662, 663, 664, 665, 666, 667, 681, 696

cholesterol lowering drugs, 190

chromium, 48, 50, 190, 199, 201, 203, 206, 285, 286, 287, 291, 376, 406, 415, 416, 419, 420, 423, 605, 607, 615, 623, 646, 658

chronic fatigue, 1, 6, 11, 15, 38, 39, 42, 101, 146, 148, 198, 205, 256, 263, 268, 269, 275, 330, 337, 410, 414, 433, 434, 469, 502, 537, 550, 563, 570, 572, 582, 619, 638, 674, 675, 676

Cladosporium, 169, 180

copper, 174, 185, 189, 195, 196, 206, 210, 216, 221, 222, 223, 224, 273, 274, 275, 276, 277, 278, 279, 280, 291, 293, 297, 298, 376, 406, 423, 431, 605, 607, 623, 642, 646, 658, 679, 680

copper,, 174, 185, 189, 195, 196, 210, 224, 273, 277, 279, 291, 297, 376, 406, 605, 607, 623, 646, 679

crime, 76, 84, 85, 86

cystitis, 1, 46, 169, 433, 476, 502

D

d-alpha tocopherol, 253, 607, 609, 676

deanol, 384, 385, 386

deficiencies, 2, 3, 5, 18, 33, 35, 50, 51, 66, 84, 90, 104, 120, 121, 125, 140, 141, 142, 158, 167, 174, 175, 184, 188, 189, 190, 191, 193, 196, 203, 205, 206, 208, 215, 216, 217, 219, 220, 221, 222, 223, 231, 235, 237, 248, 256, 257, 262, 264, 265, 273, 275, 276, 280, 283, 286, 287, 288, 296, 297, 298, 305, 306, 313, 317, 318, 324, 328, 332, 336, 339, 346, 368, 375, 376, 397, 399, 404, 405, 413, 416, 423, 424, 429, 431, 432, 437, 439, 440, 442, 451, 452, 458, 467, 475, 490, 491, 522, 552, 558, 559, 561, 562, 565, 567, 570, 571, 579, 585, 590, 591, 595, 596, 601, 605, 606, 609, 614, 615, 631, 639, 641, 642, 643, 646, 648, 651, 652, 658, 660, 662, 668, 674, 675, 676, 677, 679, 686, 691

delinquency, 76, 84, 85, 86, 87

delirium, 6, 7

E

F

G

gluten enteropathy, 51, 444, 451

H

happy hormones, 6, 39, 47, 56, 57, 64, 71, 72, 94, 102, 104, 134, 150, 157, 159, 166, 220, 231, 249, 253, 254, 260, 276, 280, 299, 306, 307, 311, 315, 317, 319, 322, 326, 328, 347, 351, 352, 353, 354, 365, 368, 372, 373, 374, 389, 445, 491, 493, 494, 496, 517, 535, 539, 551, 587, 588, 594, 606, 609, 615, 658
heavy metal, 129
high blood pressure, 15, 139, 144, 163, 259, 274, 311, 396, 565, 615, 686, 696
histamine, 51, 61, 155, 227, 228, 229, 249, 251, 307, 311, 348, 363, 373, 374, 389, 560, 595, 670, 680
homeostasis, 208, 291, 295, 664
Hormondendrum, 169
hormones, 6, 39, 47, 55, 56, 57, 64, 71, 72, 94, 102, 104, 134, 150, 157, 159, 165, 166, 220, 225, 231, 249, 253, 254, 260, 265, 270, 271, 276, 280, 299, 306, 307, 311, 314, 315, 317, 319, 321, 322, 324, 326, 328, 347, 349, 350, 351, 352, 353, 354, 363, 365, 368, 372, 373, 374, 376, 387, 389, 404, 405, 406, 407, 410, 445, 491, 493, 494, 496, 517, 535, 539, 540, 551, 559, 570, 579, 587, 588, 594, 606, 609, 615, 658, 689
host, 6, 85, 103, 115, 138, 148, 150, 172, 173, 182, 264, 285, 290, 299, 300, 362, 367, 415, 449, 458, 634, 650, 688
hydrocarbon, 90, 97, 124, 152, 154, 425, 559, 634, 658
hydrocephalus, 213
hydrogenated oils, 197, 326, 329, 330, 331, 658
hyperactivity, 6, 15, 39, 55, 56, 57, 58, 84, 86, 134, 332, 334, 586, 694
hypochondriac, 41, 158, 395
hypoglycemia, 34, 46, 48, 49, 62, 190, 197, 285, 286, 287, 291, 377, 382, 415, 416, 417, 418, 419, 422, 423, 424, 425, 564, 569

I

immunizations, 148, 680
inert ingredients, 109
insomnia, 23, 39, 55, 125, 145, 189, 256, 266, 285, 377, 413, 581, 586, 588, 659, 675
irradiated foods, 67, 68, 163, 164, 177, 460, 594
irritability, 17, 50, 61, 80, 103, 256, 259, 264, 265, 486, 631

L

labels, 6, 41, 84, 93, 271, 419, 460, 629
laboratories, 320
LD, 17, 18, 29, 33, 38, 39, 54, 59, 74, 76, 77, 81, 84, 86, 87, 96, 123, 145, 146, 156, 162, 164, 169, 179, 198, 202, 221, 270, 305, 333, 384, 389, 394, 412, 418, 459, 512, 533, 534, 548, 581, 583, 586, 590, 636, 637, 645, 649, 652, 653, 655, 662,

677, 687, 694, 695

lead, 129, 134

leaky gut, 2, 167, 324, 355, 367, 375, 400, 423, 427, 429, 430, 432, 433, 434, 436, 437, 440, 441, 442, 443, 444, 445, 446, 447, 449, 450, 451, 457, 458, 460, 461, 462, 463, 465, 473, 477, 507, 558, 560, 562, 564, 574, 575, 595, 617, 623, 668, 677, 678

L-Glutamine, 365

lipid peroxide, 120, 150, 604, 605, 621

Lipoic acid, 382, 625

lithium, 246, 268, 293, 295, 402

lobotomy, 28, 29

lupus, 1, 46, 330, 395, 434, 473, 476, 507, 513, 570, 574, 619

M

macrocytosis, 235, 236, 240, 651

magnesium, 5, 48, 130, 134, 135, 139, 142, 143, 175, 185, 188, 189, 190, 191, 194, 195, 196, 197, 198, 199, 200, 201, 202, 203, 205, 206, 207, 208, 209, 210, 219, 220, 232, 256, 257, 258, 259, 260, 261, 262, 263, 264, 265, 266, 267, 268, 269, 270, 271, 278, 291, 293, 294, 297, 298, 300, 376, 406, 423, 426, 431, 492, 493, 550, 565, 566, 567, 568, 569, 571, 572, 581, 605, 606, 607, 608, 609, 615, 625, 631, 646, 652, 654, 655, 656, 658, 659, 676, 677, 679, 680

malabsorption, 51, 254, 255, 418, 429, 430, 431, 432, 438, 441, 443, 444, 445, 449, 617

malnutrition, 75, 78, 80, 85, 213, 216, 221, 454, 598

manic-depression, 6, 170

MAO inhibitors, 311, 312, 574

McDonald's Massacre, 150

melatonin, 413

memory loss, 102

mercury, 129, 130, 136, 137, 148, 382, 506, 559

methionine, 322, 323, 354, 372, 374

migraines, 34, 46, 78, 162, 165, 263, 396, 465, 537, 573

milk allergy, 33, 61

mineral, 26, 40, 130, 140, 209, 210, 248, 253, 257, 275, 293, 296, 297, 317, 405, 423, 429, 596, 606

mold, 2, 34, 49, 54, 67, 68, 119, 121, 141, 142, 156, 157, 158, 162, 163, 164, 165, 167, 169, 170, 171, 176, 177, 178, 179, 180, 184, 249, 306, 324, 341, 346, 348, 351, 397, 399, 416, 417, 424, 430, 436, 446, 460, 470, 475, 492, 514, 552, 554, 555, 556, 564, 604, 622, 634, 639, 640, 641, 643, 646, 648, 668, 677

mold allergy, 54, 162, 170, 176, 180

monoamine oxidase, 108, 127, 166, 168, 271, 311, 312, 325, 389, 390, 392, 411, 574

mood swings, 15, 34, 39, 48, 62, 89, 111, 112, 115, 124, 125, 190, 256, 285, 286, 359, 415, 417, 422, 634

MSG, 56, 59, 60, 422, 497

muscle spasm, 139, 256, 376, 655
mycotoxins, 67, 68, 163, 177, 460
Mylanta, 139, 140, 237

N

natural gas, 110, 149, 163, 556, 677
neurotransmitters, 47, 76, 77, 94, 157, 166, 252, 254, 264, 276, 299, 308, 311, 319, 325, 347, 365, 366, 373, 387, 494, 495, 567, 587
niacin, 227, 229, 230
norepinephrine, 104, 168, 231, 308, 310, 321, 324, 373
nutrient deficiency, 22, 208, 209, 236, 286, 425

O

obsessive compulsive disorder, 15, 24
off-gassing, 117
omega-6, 326, 328, 330, 332, 334, 336, 342, 662
osteoporosis, 138, 195, 197, 205, 208, 256, 296, 297, 375, 404, 405
over-eating, 39, 287

P

pancreas, 33, 34, 370, 395, 415, 416, 418, 422, 424, 425, 451, 474, 578
panic attacks, 6, 15, 34, 162, 264, 266, 408, 694
pantethine, 387, 388, 397
Pepcid, 26, 140, 144, 237, 467, 477, 503, 653
perfumes, 113, 116, 632
pesticides, 33, 99, 101, 102, 103, 104, 105, 108, 109, 111, 115, 119, 149, 150, 184, 228, 276, 348, 350, 353, 406, 425, 451, 475, 552, 559, 574, 588, 592, 606, 617, 658, 690, 692
phenylalanine, 56, 231, 313, 314, 321
phosphates, 195, 257, 296, 405
phosphatidyl choline, 346
PMS, 6, 15, 259, 266, 270, 271, 272, 289, 332, 407, 410, 416, 465, 558, 570, 674
prostatitis, 1, 46, 169, 433, 476, 502, 537
provocation-neutralization, 95, 156
Prozac, 2, 5, 6, 9, 15, 20, 21, 22, 24, 25, 29, 33, 39, 43, 47, 84, 94, 104, 112, 138, 232, 237, 249, 253, 270, 271, 272, 299, 300, 301, 306, 363, 413, 481, 506, 508, 511, 563, 570, 651, 657, 672, 674, 675, 676, 677, 678, 694, 695, 696, 698
Pullularia, 163, 177, 470
pyridoxal kinase, 232, 283

R

Redux, 24, 511, 696

rhinitis, 46, 163, 340, 341, 670

S

SAM, 322, 516

schizophrenia, 6, 15, 34, 39, 46, 52, 89, 92, 103, 125, 162, 169, 170, 217, 227, 229, 230, 243, 250, 251, 265, 268, 269, 277, 291, 309, 321, 324, 332, 333, 334, 338, 445, 538, 589

sea vegetables, 197, 237, 242, 336, 601, 662

seizures, 15, 34, 39, 46, 55, 77, 145, 295, 315, 596

Selenium, 296

serotonin, 23, 24, 39, 47, 72, 73, 104, 107, 166, 168, 231, 246, 252, 271, 272, 289, 291, 292, 300, 301, 302, 304, 305, 306, 307, 308, 321, 325, 328, 333, 346, 347, 363, 373, 413, 414, 560, 582, 606, 676, 684

serum, 73, 173, 199, 200, 201, 202, 203, 206, 207, 208, 210, 211, 219, 237, 241, 243, 244, 245, 256, 257, 259, 260, 265, 268, 277, 282, 331, 356, 360, 388, 408, 413, 493, 606, 663, 664, 665, 666

sick building, 118, 630, 643, 650

sinusitis, 46, 163, 436, 502, 631

spacey, 91, 93, 111, 115, 124, 631

spiral, 48, 191, 212, 259, 265, 287, 563

spreading phenomenon, 117, 121, 260

St. John's Wort, 389

stress, 6, 18, 20, 42, 102, 104, 111, 118, 119, 127, 136, 140, 141, 150, 159, 228, 252, 255, 257, 264, 265, 266, 269, 288, 290, 308, 309, 324, 332, 334, 371, 373, 374, 383, 405, 412, 425, 444, 469, 474, 485, 486, 490, 491, 492, 493, 496, 526, 535, 536, 541, 550, 559, 560, 561, 564, 565, 570, 587, 613, 614, 616, 658, 664, 675, 692

sudden death,, 205, 266

sugar, 48, 49, 50, 52, 54, 55, 56, 61, 78, 116, 119, 141, 166, 170, 173, 174, 177, 254, 257, 266, 285, 286, 291, 294, 332, 415, 416, 417, 419, 421, 422, 424, 439, 441, 474, 497, 510, 555, 562, 569, 581, 600, 621, 677

suicide, 3, 11, 17, 19, 21, 22, 23, 25, 28, 32, 37, 101, 144, 190, 207, 249, 250, 268, 276, 302, 387, 424, 481, 482, 499, 527, 575, 599, 651, 658, 659, 662, 663, 696

superoxide dismutase, 210

T

Tagamet, 26, 140, 144, 237, 451, 467, 477, 503, 570, 653

target organ, 33, 34, 49, 51, 66, 70, 71, 89, 99, 103, 111, 124, 162, 163, 165, 169, 170, 178, 191, 258, 339, 395, 415, 416, 418, 424, 434, 442, 487, 564, 567, 596, 612, 617, 639

target organs, 99, 103, 339, 639

tartrazine, 56, 59

taurine, 315

thiaminase, 167, 225

thiamine, 167
thyroid deficiency, 400
TIA's, 47
tight building syndrome, 118, 123, 179
toluene, 91, 109, 113, 117, 118, 120, 124, 125, 126, 127, 128, 153, 163, 311, 349, 351, 352, 375, 425, 604, 622, 646, 658, 663
total load, 3, 6, 33, 51, 56, 157, 172, 173, 178, 191, 192, 195, 205, 256, 294, 307, 318, 378, 412, 438, 447, 452, 489, 503, 526, 543, 552, 554, 560, 561, 562, 565, 566, 573, 574, 592, 594, 596, 597, 606, 615, 616, 621, 626, 629, 630, 632, 642, 643, 655, 659, 692, 698
toxic encephalopathy, 2, 18, 93, 94, 111, 112, 113, 114, 127, 153, 432, 630
toxic teachers, 116
trans-fatty acids, 326, 327, 328, 329, 330, 331, 332, 355, 458, 505, 506, 609, 658
trichloroethylene, 89, 90, 91, 109, 646, 647

V

Valerian, 393
ventricles, 212
vitamin A, 174, 187, 192, 212
vitamin B6, 240, 640
vitamin C, 192, 193, 248, 249, 382, 566, 607, 670
vitamin E, 25, 191, 192, 193, 222, 248, 252, 253, 382, 504, 505, 607, 653

W

water, 66, 78, 94, 95, 109, 110, 113, 122, 125, 129, 131, 132, 133, 138, 139, 175, 176, 261, 273, 276, 280, 286, 354, 368, 374, 430, 446, 448, 506, 528, 554, 599, 602, 607, 620
wheat, 51, 52, 78, 81, 116, 185, 257, 416, 423, 424, 430, 436, 444, 669, 670, 677
withdrawal, 24

X

xenobiotic, 124, 184, 186, 191, 438, 513, 554, 592, 631, 632, 636, 647

Z

Zantac, 5, 140, 144, 237, 467, 477, 570, 679
zinc, 56, 59, 89, 120, 121, 123, 130, 140, 185, 189, 195, 196, 205, 210, 216, 221, 222, 223, 224, 232, 276, 282, 283, 284, 291, 297, 303, 323, 406, 415, 475, 508, 605, 607, 623, 631, 640, 642, 646, 647, 679

The address to our office is:

Northeast Center for Environmental Medicine
Sherry A. Rogers, M.D., Medical Director
2800 W. Genesee Street
Syracuse, NY 13219
(315) 488-2856

Address correspondence to:

Box 2716
Syracuse, NY 13220-2716

RESOURCES

For courses for physicians in nutritional biochemistry and for names of physicians (**in various stages of learning**) near you who may practice this form of medicine, write to:

The American Academy of Environmental Medicine
4510 W. 89th Street
Prairie Village, KS 66207
(currently relocating office)

Articles from Environmental Medicine column, edited and written by Sherry A. Rogers, M.D.   Available from INTERNAL   MEDICINE   WORLD   REPORT,   322-D Englishtown Rd., Old Bridge, NJ 08857

1. Rogers SA, Chemical sensitivity: Breaking the paralyzing paradigm, Part I, INT MED WORLD REP, 7:4, pp 1, 15-17, Feb 1-15, 1992

2. Rogers SA, Chemical sensitivity: Breaking the paralyzing paradigm, Diagnosis and treatment. Part II, INT MED WORLD REP, 7:6, pp 2, 21-31, Mar 1-15, 1992

3. Rogers SA, Chemical sensitivity: Breaking the paralyzing paradigm. How knowledge of chemical sensitivity enhances the treatment of chronic diseases. Part III, ibid, 7:8, p 13-16, 32-33, 40-41, Apr 15-30, 1992

4. Letters to the editor, May 1-15, 1992

5. Rogers SA, When stumped, think environmental medicine, INT MED WORLD REP, 7:10, p 24-25, May 15-31, 1992

6. Rogers SA, Is it senility or chemical sensitivity?, INT MED WORLD REP, 7:13, p 3, July 1992

7. Rogers SA, How cost effective is improving the work environment?, INT MED WORLD REP, 7:14, p 48, Aug 1992

8. Rogers SA, Is it recalcitrant arrhythmia or environmental illness?, INT MED WORLD REP, 7:19, p 28, Nov 1-14, 1992

9. Rogers SA, (ed.) Chester AC, Sick building syndrome and the nose, INT MED WORLD REP, 8:4, p 25-27, Feb 1993

SCIENTIFIC PUBLICATIONS
BY SHERRY A ROGERS M.D.
IN PEER REVIEWED MEDICAL JOURNALS

1. Indoor fungi as part of the cause of recalcitrant symptoms of the Tight Building Syndrome, ENVIRONMENT INTERNATIONAL, 17:4, 271-276, 1991

2. Unrecognized magnesium deficiency masquerades as diverse symptoms, evaluation of an oral magnesium challenge test, INTERNATIONAL CLINICAL NUTRITION REVIEWS, 11:3, 117-125, July 1991

3. A practical approach to the person with suspected indoor air quality problems, INTERNATIONAL CLINICAL NUTRITION REVIEWS 11:3, 1265-130, July 1991

4. Zinc deficiency as a model for developing chemical sensitivity, INTERNATIONAL CLINICAL NUTRITION REVIEWS, 10:1, 253-259, January, 1990

5. Diagnosing the Tight Building Syndrome or diagnosing Chemical Hypersensitivity, ENVIRONMENT INTERNATIONAL, 15, 75-79, 1989

6. Diagnosing Chemical Hypersensitivity: case examples, CLINICAL ECOLOGY 6:4, 129-134, 1989

7. Provocation-neutralization of cough and wheezing in a horse, CLINICAL ECOLOGY, 5:4, 185-187, 1987/1988

8. Resistant cases, response to mold immunotherapy and environmental and dietary controls, CLINICAL

ECOLOGY, ARCHIVES FOR HUMAN ECOLOGY IN HEALTH AND DISEASE, 5:3, 115-120, 1987/1988

9. Diagnosing the Tight Building Syndrome, ENVIRONMENTAL HEALTH PERSPECTIVES, 76, 195-198, 1987

10. A thirteen month work, leisure, sleep environmental fungal survey, ANNALS OF ALLERGY, 52, 338-341, May 1984

11. A comparison of commercially available mold survey services, ANNALS OF ALLERGY, 50, 37-40, January, 1983

12. In-home fungal studies, methods to increase the yield, ANNALS OF ALLERGY, 49, 35-37, July, 1982

13. A case of atopy with inability to form IgG, ANNALS OF ALLERGY, 43:3, 165-166, September, 1979

14. Is your cardiologist killing you?, JOURNAL OF ORTHOMOLECULAR MEDICINE, 8:2, 89-97, 1993

15. Is it chronic back pain or environmental illness, JOURNAL OF APPLIED NUTRITION 48:4, 106-109, 1994

16. How the sick get sicker by following current medical protocol: the example of undiagnosed magnesium deficiency, J ORTHOMOLECULAR MED, 11;2: 63-68, 1996

SCIENTIFIC ARTICLES
BY SHERRY A ROGERS, M.D.
IN PROCEEDINGS OF INTERNATIONAL SYMPOSIA

1. A Practical approach to the person with suspected indoor air quality problems, The 5th International Conference on Indoor Air Quality and Climate, Toronto, Canada, Canada Mortgage and Housing Corporation, Ottawa, Ontario, volume 5, 345-349.

2. Diagnosing the Tight Building Syndrome, an intradermal method to provoke chemically induced symptoms, man and his ecosystem, proceedings of the 8th World Clean Air Congress 1989, Brasser LJ, Mulder WC, editors. The Hague Netherlands Society for Clean Air in the Netherlands, PO Box 186, 2600 AD Delft, Netherlands, 199-204, volume 1.

3. Case studies of indoor air fungi used to clear recalcitrant conditions, Healthy Buildings, '88, CIB Conference in Stockholm, Sweden, September 1988, Swedish Council for Building Research, Stockholm Sweden, Berglund, B, Lindvall T, Mansson L-G, editors, 127, 1988.

4. Diagnosing the Tight Building Syndrome, an intradermal method to provoke chemically induced symptoms, IBID, 371.

5. Diagnosing the Tight Building Syndrome, Indoor Air '87, proceedings of the 4th International Conference on Indoor Air Quality and Climate, West Berlin, Seifert B, Esdorn H, Fischer M, Ruden H, Wegner J, editors, Institute for Water, Soil and Air Hygiene, D 1000 Berlin 33, Volume 2, 772-776.

6. Indoor air quality and Environmentally induced illness, a technique to revoke chemically induced symptoms in patients. Proceedings of the ASHREA conference, IAQ 86, Managing indoor air for health and energy conservation, 71-77, ASHRAE, 1791 Tullie Circle, NE, Atlanta, GA 30329.

Also listed in Indoor Air Reference Bibliography, United States Environmental Protection Agency, Office of Health and Environmental Assessment, Washington, D.C., July, 1990, p C81 and C162.

THE
E.I.
Syndrome
An Rx
For Environmental Illness

Are You Allergic To
The 21st Century?

by SHERRY A. ROGERS, MD

THE E.I. SYNDROME, REVISED is a 635 page book that is necessary for people with environmental illness. It explains chemical, food, mold, and Candida sensitivities, nutritional deficiencies, testing methods and how to do the various environmental controls and diets in order to get well.

Many docs buy these by the hundreds and make them mandatory reading for patients, as it contains many pearls about getting well that are not found anywhere else. In this way it increases the fun of practicing medicine because patients are on a higher educational level and office time is more productive for more sophisticated levels of wellness. It covers hundreds of facts that make a difference between E.I. victims versus E.I. conquerors. It helps patients become active partners in their care while avoiding doctor burnout. It covers the gamut of the diagnosis and treatment of environmentally induced symptoms.

Because the physician author was a severe universal reactor who has recovered, this book contains mountains of clues to wellness. As a result many have written that they healed themselves by reading this book. This is in spite of the fact, that no consulted physicians were able to diagnose or effectively treat them. If you are not sure what causes your symptoms, this is a great starter.

Many veteran sufferers have written that they had read many books on aspects of allergy, chronic Candidiasis and chemical sensitivity and thought that they knew it all. Yet they wrote that what they learned in **THE E.I. SYNDROME REVISED** enabled them to reach that last pinnacle of wellness.

You Are What You Are

A MACROBIOTIC WAY

An Rx
For The Resistant Diseases
Of The 21st Century

by SHERRY A. ROGERS, MD

YOU ARE WHAT YOU ATE. This book is indispensable as a primer and introduction to the macrobiotic diet. The macrobiotic diet is the specialized diet with which many have healed the impossible, including end stage metastatic cancers. This is after medicine has given up on them and they have been given only months or weeks to live. Yes, they have rallied after surgery, chemotherapy and radiation had failed. Life was seemingly, hopelessly over.

Understandably, this diet has also enabled many chemically sensitive universal reactors, and highly allergic and even "undiagnosable people" to heal. It has also enabled those to heal that have "wastebasket" diagnostic labels such as chronic fatigue, fibromyalgia, MS, rheumatoid arthritis, depression, chronic infections, colitis, asthma, migraines, lupus, chronic Candidiasis, and much more.

Although there are many books on macrobiotics, this is one that takes the special needs of the allergic person and those with multiple food and chemical sensitivities as well as chronic Candidiasis into account. It provides details and case histories that the person new to macrobiotics needs before he embarks on the strict healing phase as described in **THE CURE IS IN THE KITCHEN.**

Even people who have done the macrobiotic diet for a while will find reasons why they have failed and tips to improve their success. When a diet such as this has allowed many to heal their cancers, any other condition "should be a piece of cake".

TIRED OR TOXIC? is a 400 page book, and the first book that describes the mechanism, diagnosis and treatment of chemical sensitivity, complete with scientific references. It is written for the layman and physician alike and explains the many vitamin, mineral, essential fatty acid and amino acid analyses that may help people detoxify everyday chemicals more efficiently and hence get rid of baffling symptoms.

It is the first book written for laymen and physicians to describe xenobiotic detoxication, the process that allows all healing to occur.   You have heard of the cardiovascular system, you have heard of the respiratory system, the gastrointestinal system, and the immune system. But most have never heard of the chemical detoxification system that is the determinant of whether we have chemical sensitivity, cancer, and in fact every disease.

This program shows how to diagnose and treat many resistant everyday symptoms and use molecular medicine techniques. It also gives the biochemical mechanisms in easily understood form, of how Candida creates such a diversity of symptoms and how the macrobiotic diet heals "incurable" end stage metastatic cancers. It is a great book for the physician you are trying to win over, and will show you how chemical sensitivity masquerades as common symptoms. It then explores the many causes and cures of chemical sensitivity, chronic Candidiasis, and other "impossible to heal" medical labels.

Macro
Mellow

Recipes For
Macrobiotic Cooking

by Shirley Gallinger
& Sherry A. Rogers, M.D.

MACRO MELLOW is a book designed for 4 types of people: (1) For the person who doesn't know a thing about macrobiotics, but just plain wants to feel better, in spite of the 21st century. (2) It solves the high cholesterol/triglycerides problem without drugs and is the preferred diet for heart disease patients. (3) It is the perfect transition diet for those not ready for macro, but needing to get out of the chronic illness rut. (4) It spells out how to feed the rest of the family who hates macro, while another family member must eat it in order to clear their "incurable" symptoms.

It shows how to convert the "grains, greens, and beans" strict macro food into delicious "American-looking" food that the kids will eat. This saves the cook from making double meals while one person heals.

The delicious low-fat whole food meals designed by Shirley Gallinger, a veteran nurse who has worked with Dr. Rogers for nearly two decades, use macro ingredients without the rest of the family even knowing. It is the first book to dovetail creative meal planning, menus, recipes and even gardening so the cook isn't driven crazy.

Most likely your kitchen contains a plethora of cookbooks. But you owe it to yourself and your family to learn how to incorporate healing whole foods, low in fat and high in phyto-nutrients into their diets. For who you have planning and cooking your meals is proven to be as important if not more important than who you have chosen for your doctor. For medical research has proven the power of whole food diets to heal where high tech medicines and surgery have failed.

The Cure
Is In
The Kitchen

A Guide To Healthy Eating

Foreward by Michio Kushi

by Sherry A. Rogers, M.D.

THE CURE IS IN THE KITCHEN is the first book to ever spell out in detail what all those people ate day to day who cleared their incurable diseases, MS, rheumatoid arthritis, fibromyalgia, lupus, chronic fatigue, colitis, asthma, migraines, depression, hypertension, heart disease, angina, undiagnosable symptoms, and relentless chemical, food, Candida, and electromagnetic sensitivities, as well as terminal cancers.

Dr. Rogers flew to Boston each month to work side by side with Mr. Michio Kushi, as he counseled people at the end of their medical ropes. As their remarkable case histories will show you, nothing is hopeless. Many of these people had failed to improve with surgery, chemotherapy and radiation. Instead their metastases continued to spread. It was only when they were sent home to die in a few weeks, that they turned to the diet.

Medical studies confirmed that this diet has more than tripled the survival from cancers. And the beauty of this diet is that you use God-given whole foods to coax the body into the healing mode. It does not rely on prescription drugs, but allows the individual to heal himself at home.

If you cannot afford a $500 consultation, and you choose not to accept your death sentence or medication sentence, why not learn first hand what these people did and how you, too, may improve your health and heal the impossible.

WELLNESS AGAINST ALL ODDS is the 6th and most revolutionary book by Sherry A. Rogers, M.D. It contains the ultimate healing plan that people have successfully used to beat cancer when they were given 2 weeks, some even 2 days to live by some of the top medical centers. These people had exhausted all that medicine has to offer, including surgery, chemotherapy, radiation and bone marrow transplants. Some had even been macrobiotic failures. And one of the most unbelievable things is that the plan costs practically nothing to implement and most of it can be done at home with non-prescription items.

Of course, in keeping with the other works and going far beyond, this contains the mechanisms of how these principles heal and is complete with all the scientific references for physicians.

Did you know, for example, that there are vitamins that actually cure cancer, and over 50 papers in the best medical journals to prove it? Likewise, did you know that there are non-prescription enzymes that dissolve cancer, arteriosclerotic plaque, and auto-antibodies like lupus and rheumatoid? Did you know that there is a simple inexpensive, but highly effective way, to detoxify the body at home to stop the toxic side effects of chemotherapy within minutes? Did you know that this procedure can also reduce chemical sensitivity reactions (from accidental chemical exposures) from 4 days to 20 minutes? Did you know that there are many hidden causes for "undiagnosable" symptoms that are never looked for, because it is easier and quicker to prescribe a pill than find (and fix) the causes?

The fact is that when you get the body healthy enough, it can heal anything. You do not have to die from labelitis. It no longer matters what your label is, from chronic Candida, fatigue, or MS to chemical sensitivity, an undiagnosable condition, or the worst cancer with only days to survive. If you have been told there is nothing more that can be done for you, you have the option of kicking death in the teeth and healing the impossible. Are you game?

The
Scientific Basis
for
Selected
Environmental
Medicine
Techniques

by

Sherry A. Rogers, M.D.

THE SCIENTIFIC BASIS FOR SE-LECTED ENVIRONMENTAL MEDI-CINE TECHNIQUES contains the scientific evidence and references for the techniques of environmental medicine. It is designed with the patient in mind who is being denied medical payments by insurance companies that refuse to acknowledge environmental medicine.

With this guide a patient may choose to represent himself in small claims court and quote from the book showing, for example, that the **JOURNAL OF THE AMERICAN MEDICAL ASSOCIATION** states that "titration provides a useful and effective measure of patient sensitivity", and that a U.S. Government agency states that "an exposure history should be taken for every patient". Failure to do so can lead to an inappropriate diagnosis and treatment.

It has sections showing medical references of how finding hidden vitamin deficiencies have, for example, enabled people to heal carpel tunnel syndrome without surgery, or heal life threatening steroid-resistant vasculitis, or stop seizures, or migraines, or learning disabilities.

This book is designed for patients who choose to find the causes of their illnesses rather than merely mask their symptoms with drugs for the rest of their lives. It is also for those who have been unfairly denied insurance coverage. And it is the ideal book with which to educate your PTA, attorney, insurance company, or physicians who still doubt your sanity.

CHEMICAL SENSITIVITIES. This 48 page booklet is the most concise referenced booklet on chemical sensitivity. It is for the person wanting to learn about it but who is leery of tackling a big book. It is ideal for teaching your physician or convincing your insurance company, as it is fully referenced. And it is a good reference for the veteran who wants a quick concise review.

Most people have difficulty envisioning chemical sensitivity as a potential cause of everyday maladies. But the fact is that a lack of knowledge of the mechanism of chemical sensitivity can be the solo reason that holds many back from ever healing completely. Some will never get truly well simply because they do not comprehend the tremendous role chemical sensitivity plays. For failure to address the role that chemical sensitivity plays in every disease has been pivotal in failure to get well. The principles of environmental controls are of especially vital importance for cancer victims.

If you are not completely well, you need to read this book. If you have been sentenced to a life-time of drugs, whether it be for high blood pressure, high cholesterol, angina, arrhythmia, asthma, eczema, sinusitis, colitis, learning disabilities, or cancer, you need this book. It matters not what your label is. What matters is whether chemical sensitivity is a factor that no one has explored that is keeping you from getting well. Most probably it is, and this is an inexpensive way to find out.

ENVIRONMENTAL MEDICINE VIDEO

On this 16 minute VHS video, Dr. Sherry Rogers teaches the basic principles of environmental medicine and chemical sensitivity. As you begin to learn how to diagnose and treat using environmental medicine techniques, it opens up a whole new world of options for getting well, regardless of diagnosis.

Also there are actual case presentations who will explain aspects of their emergence from E.I. (environmental illness) victims to E.I. conquerors. Each of them as well as Dr. Rogers herself were highly chemically sensitive and learned how to heal. This shows newly diagnosed people that there is hope.

This is a great video for the PTA, church groups, work groups, and special disease support groups to whom you want to introduce the concept of chemical sensitivity.

HEALTH LETTER

This referenced monthly newsletter will keep you up to date on new findings. Since we are constantly researching, lecturing around the globe, maintaining a private practice, doing television and radio shows, writing for health magazines and physicians, and have published 17 scientific papers and 9 books in 10 years, we are peddling as fast as we can. Increasingly, we cannot get the information out fast enough, so we use the newsletter as our communication link. It will teach you useful facts years before they will be presented elsewhere. And it is practical and action-oriented. You really cannot afford to be without it.

MOLD PLATES

Since mold is a common, yet remedial cause of symptoms, you first need to know if you have too much. By exposing special petri dishes (or mold plates) in your bedroom, family room, and office, you have effectively assessed your 24 hour mold environment. Each plate comes with directions for exposure and a return mailer. In 3-9 weeks after the slow-growing fungi have appeared for identification, the report will be mailed to you detailing all of the specific molds and how many molds are present. We purposely take as long as we need, since we wait for the last molds to grow out before completing the report. We do not want to neglect the "slow growing" molds like other labs do. You will need to order one plate for each room you want to assess at home or work. If you do not know how moldy your environment is, you may erroneously be attributing symptoms to chemical or food sensitivities. It is always best to meet the enemy head on in order to identify the problem and solve it.

PHYSICIAN SLIDE SHOW

This 35mm presentation contains 56 slides plus the script, which the physician can read or easily memorize. It is a great way for him to introduce to colleagues his incorporation of environmental medicine techniques into his practice. He can present this lecture as "The Biochemistry of Chemical Sensitivity" to other physicians at the hospital to further substantiate his rapidly expanding and firm foundation of knowledge in the field of environmental medicine.

Instructions then tell how with minor reorganization, he can use the same lecture retitled "Are You Tired or Toxic?" to present to lay groups like church groups, the PTA, and other special interest support groups to advertise his expertise in this area. As time rolls on he can add slides of his own such as case examples and new information as his audiences grow in sophistication.

It is meant to simultaneously instruct as well as build his credibility and practice. And you actually learn yourself as you rehearse it. He can also deflect the cost of renting an auditorium by selling the companion book (TIRED OR TOXIC?) after the talk (available at 40% discount in quantities of 40 or more). Subsequently, as people learn more about the environmental medicine approach to solve their medical problems, they progressively appreciate the limitations of the drug-oriented approach and find less use for it.

Remember, you can be a terrific physician, but if no one knows of your expertise or the rationale for referring recalcitrant patients to you, your talent may lay dormant and wasted. Happily, you will find that every time you present your lecture, many in the audience will benefit from being introduced to these revolutionary diagnostic and therapeutic concepts. And as they begin to heal they become your best advertisers.

PHONE CONSULTATIONS

Many people are stuck. They have an undiagnosable condition. Or they have a label but have been unable to get well. Or they have a "dead-end" label which means nothing more can be done. And many are not able to find a physician who is trained in what our 9 books explore.

These people could benefit from a personal consultation with Dr. Sherry Rogers to explore what diagnostic and treatment options may exist that they or their physicians are not aware of. For this reason we offer prepaid, scheduled phone consultations with the doctor. These can be scheduled through the office by calling (315) 488-2856.

If you wish to send copies of your medical reports and/or also have your doctor on the line, this can be helpful as well. Reports must be received at least 3 weeks prior to the consult and not be on fax paper. They should be copies and not originals as they are not returnable. Do not send records without first having secured a scheduled appointment time, for records without an appointment are discarded.

Because you have not come to the office and been examined, you are not considered a patient (although you could elect to become one). In spite of that, you can learn what tests your physician could order and what plans you could follow. If he needs help in interpreting the tests, a scheduled follow-up consultation can allow you to explore treatment options with specific nutrient and other treatment suggestions. The point is, you do not have to be alone without guidance in your quest for wellness.

PRESTIGE PUBLISHING
P.O. BOX 3068
Syracuse, NY 13220
(800) 846-ONUS (6687) ◊ (315) 455-7862

HARD-COVER BOOKS

Depression Cured at Last!...	$24.95

SOFT-COVER BOOKS

The E.I. Syndrome Revised..	$17.95
You Are What You Ate..	$12.95
Tired or Toxic?..	$17.95
Macro Mellow...	$12.95
The Cure Is In The Kitchen...	$14.95
Wellness Against All Odds..	$17.95
Scientific Basis	$17.95
Chemical Sensitivity..	$ 3.95
The Cure Is In the Kitchen (Spanish version)............	$30.00
Tired or Toxic?..	$30.00
Environmental Video 16 minute VHS........................	$12.95
Dr. Rogers Health Letter published monthly on	
current wellness and healing information............1 yr	$39.95
Mold Plates (one room)...	$20.00
Formaldehyde Spot Test Kit	$45.00
Slide show for physicians	$305.00

Shipping/Handling .... $4.00 per single item
$1.00 additional items

Telephone consultations available for specific problems.
Contact Dr. Rogers' office (315) 488-2856 to schedule.

Name: _____

Address:_____

City:_____ State: _____ Zip:_____